Ancient Israel
From Abraham to the Roman Destruction of the Temple
THIRD EDITION

EDITED BY HERSHEL SHANKS

Prentice Hall

Boston Columbus Indianapolis New York San Francisco Upper Saddle River
Amsterdam Cape Town Dubai London Madrid Milan Munich Paris Montreal Toronto
Delhi Mexico City Sao Paulo Sydney Hong Kong Seoul Singapore Taipei Tokyo

BIBLICAL ARCHAEOLOGY SOCIETY

WASHINGTON, DC

PEARSON

Editorial Director: Craig Campanella
Editor in Chief: Dixon Musselwhite
Publisher: Nancy Roberts
Editorial Assistant: Nart Varoqua
Managing Editor: Maureen Richardson
Operations Specialist: Christina Amato

BIBLICAL ARCHAEOLOGY SOCIETY

Publisher: Susan Laden
Assistant Editor: Joey Corbett
Administrative Editor: Bonnie Mullin
Production Manager: Heather Metzger
Maps: Dorothy Resig

Library of Congress Cataloging-in-Publication Data

Ancient Israel: from Abraham to the Roman destruction of the Temple/
edited by Hershel Shanks.—3rd ed.
p.   cm.
Includes bibliographical references and index.
ISBN 978-1-935335-41-2 (hardcover)—ISBN 978-1-935335-40-5 (paperback)
1. Jews—History—To 70 A.D. I. Shanks, Hershel.
DS121.A53 2010
933—dc22   2010027476

Design by AURAS Design
ISBN 10: 0-205-09643-3 (paperback)
ISBN 13: 978-0-205-09643-5 (paperback)

ON THE COVER: The golden Dome of the Rock and the eastern wall
of the Temple Mount as viewed from Jerusalem's Mount of Olives.
Photo by Garo Nalbandian.

Prentice Hall
is an imprint of

www.pearsonhighered.com

Table of Contents

Illustrations

Color Plates

Maps and Charts

The Authors

Joseph A. Callaway led the archaeological expedition to et-Tell (biblical Ai) from 1964 to 1976. He also excavated at Jericho, Shechem and Bethel. A professor of biblical archaeology at Southern Baptist Theological Seminary from 1967 to 1982, Callaway also served as president of the William F. Albright School of Archaeological Research in Jerusalem. He died in August of 1988.

Shaye J.D. Cohen is the Littauer Professor of Hebrew Literature and Philosophy in the department of Near Eastern Languages and Civilizations at Harvard University. Before arriving at Harvard in 2001, he was the Ungerleider Professor and Director of Judaic Studies at Brown University. A specialist in the emergence of rabbinic Judaism, he has written or edited several books and many articles, including *From the Maccabees to the Mishnah: A Profile of Judaism* (Westminster Press, 1987; second edition, 2006) and *The Beginnings of Jewishness* (University of California, 1999).

Siegfried H. Horn directed the excavation of Hesban (biblical Heshbon), Jordan, from 1968 to 1973, after having dug at Shechem for four seasons in the 1960s. From 1951 to 1976, Horn taught archaeology and the history of antiquity at Andrews University, in Berrien Springs, Michigan. He also served as dean of the university's seminary and founded the school's archaeological museum, which was renamed for him in 1978. The author of 12 books and more than 800 articles, Horn formerly directed the American Center of Oriental Research in Amman, Jordan. He died in November 1993.

André Lemaire is professor of Hebrew and Aramaic philology and epigraphy in the department of Historical and Philological Sciences at the École Pratique des Hautes Études at the Sorbonne in Paris. He has worked for more than 35 years in the fields of Northwest Semitic epigraphy, archaeology, ancient Hebrew literature and history and has published more than ten books and 400 articles on those subjects. In addition, he has participated in excavations at Lachish, Tel Keisan, Yarmouth and other sites in Israel.

Lee I. Levine holds the Lauterman Family Chair in Classical Archaeology in the department of History of the Jewish People at The Hebrew University of Jerusalem. He has directed the excavation of an ancient synagogue at Horvat 'Ammudim and codirected two seasons of excavations at Caesarea. His numerous books include *Judaism and Hellenism in Antiquity* (University of Washington, 1998), *The Ancient Synagogue* (Yale University, 2000) and *Jerusalem: Portrait of the City in the Second Temple Period* (Jewish Publication Society, 2002).

P. Kyle McCarter, Jr., is the William F. Albright Professor of Biblical and Ancient Near Eastern Studies at The Johns Hopkins University, in Baltimore, Maryland. He taught at the University of Virginia from 1974 to 1985 and has held visiting professorships at Harvard University and Dartmouth College. A former president of the American Schools of Oriental Research, McCarter wrote the commentaries on 1 Samuel and 2 Samuel in the Anchor Bible series. His many other writings include *Ancient Inscriptions: Voices from the Biblical World* (Biblical Archaeology Society, 1996). Most recently, he has written and contributed to several important articles on the paleography of the newly discovered Tel Zayit abecedary.

Eric M. Meyers, the Bernice and Morton Lerner Professor of Religion at Duke University and director of the university's Center for Jewish Studies, has directed digs in Israel (and Italy) for more than 35 years and is currently completing the publication of his most recent excavation at Sepphoris in the Galilee. Together with his wife Carol Meyers, he coauthored commentaries on Haggai and Zechariah in the Anchor Bible series, *Excavations at Gush Halav* (Eisenbrauns and ASOR, 1991) and, most recently, *Excavations at Ancient Nabratein* (Eisenbrauns and ASOR, 2009). He served as editor-in-chief of *The Oxford Encyclopedia of Archaeology in the Near East* (1997) and cowrote *The Cambridge Companion to the Bible* (1997). He also served for three terms as president of the American Schools of Oriental Research.

Nahum M. Sarna was the Dora Golding Professor of Biblical Studies at Brandeis University, in Waltham, Massachusetts. He was the author of the widely acclaimed *Understanding Genesis* (Schocken, 1970), *Exploring Exodus* (Schocken, 1986) and *Songs of the Heart—An Introduction to the Book of Psalms* (Schocken, 1993). He was also the general editor of the Jewish Publication Society's five-volume commentary on the Torah and author of the volumes on Genesis and Exodus. He died in June 2005.

Hershel Shanks is founder of the Biblical Archaeology Society and editor of *Biblical Archaeology Review*. He has written and edited numerous books on the Bible and biblical archaeology, including *The Mystery and Meaning of the Dead Sea Scrolls* (Random House, 1998), *Jerusalem's Temple Mount* (Continuum, 2007), *Jerusalem: An Archaeological Biography* (Random House, 1995) and *The City of David: A Guide to Biblical Jerusalem* (Tel Aviv: Bazak, 1973; reprinted many times). A graduate of Harvard Law School, he has also published widely on legal topics. His autobiography, *Freeing the Dead Sea Scrolls and Other Adventures of an Archaeology Outsider,* was published by Continuum in 2010.

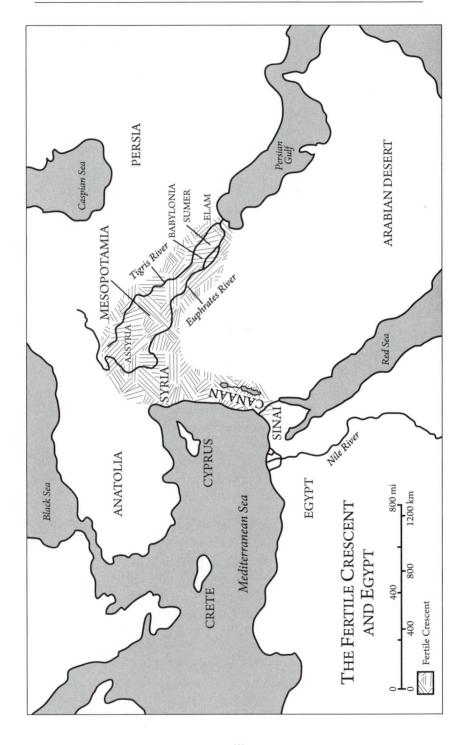

THE FERTILE CRESCENT
AND EGYPT

Fertile Crescent

0   400   800   800 mi
0   400   800   1200 km

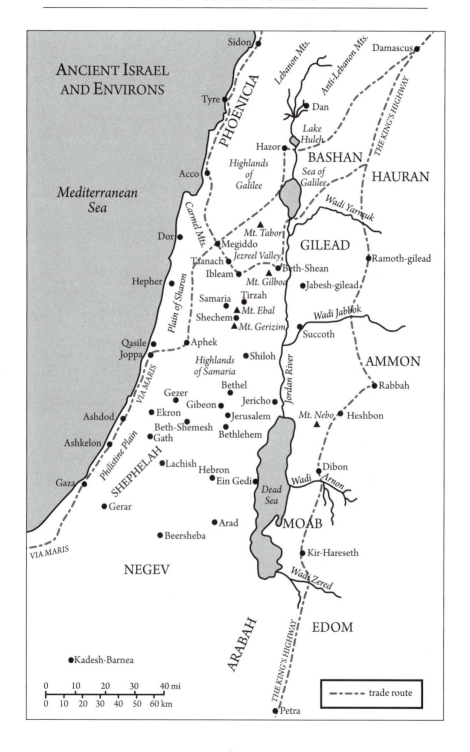

ANCIENT ISRAEL AND ENVIRONS

Mediterranean Sea

PHOENICIA

Sidon

Tyre

Lebanon Mts.

Anti-Lebanon Mts.

Damascus

THE KING'S HIGHWAY

Dan

Lake Huleh

Hazor

BASHAN

HAURAN

Acco

Highlands of Galilee

Sea of Galilee

Wadi Yarmuk

Carmel Mts.

Dor

Mt. Tabor

Megiddo

Jezreel Valley

GILEAD

Ramoth-gilead

Taanach

Ibleam

Beth-Shean

Mt. Gilboa

Jabesh-gilead

Hepher

Plain of Sharon

Samaria

Tirzah

Mt. Ebal

Shechem

Mt. Gerizim

Wadi Jabbok

Succoth

Qasile

Joppa

Aphek

Highlands of Samaria

Shiloh

Jordan River

AMMON

Rabbah

VIA MARIS

Gezer

Bethel

Gibeon

Jericho

Mt. Nebo

Heshbon

Ashdod

Ekron

Jerusalem

Beth-Shemesh

Gath

Bethlehem

Ashkelon

Philistine Plain

SHEPHELAH

Lachish

Hebron

Ein Gedi

Dead Sea

Wadi Arnon

Dibon

Gaza

Gerar

MOAB

Arad

Beersheba

NEGEV

Kir-Hareseth

Wadi Zered

ARABAH

THE KING'S HIGHWAY

EDOM

Kadesh-Barnea

0   10   20   30   40 mi
0   10   20   30   40   50   60 km

- - - - - trade route

VIA MARIS

Petra

ix

Abbreviations

AASOR	*Annual of the American Schools of Oriental Research*
ABD	*The Anchor Bible Dictionary*, 6 vols., ed. David Noel Freedman (Garden City, NY: Doubleday, 1992)
AJS	Association for Jewish Studies
ANET	*Ancient Near Eastern Texts*, ed. James B. Pritchard (Princeton, NJ: Princeton University Press, 3rd ed., 1969)
Antiquities	Josephus, *Antiquities of the Jews*
AOAT	*Alter Orient und Altes Testament*
Apion	Josephus, *Contra Apion*
ASOR	American Schools of Oriental Research
AUSS	*Andrews University Seminary Studies*
B	Bavli, Babylonian Talmud
BA	*Biblical Archaeologist*
BAR	*Biblical Archaeology Review*
BASOR	*Bulletin of the American Schools of Oriental Research*
BN	*Biblische Notizen*
BR	*Bible Review*
BS	*Bibliotheca Sacra*
BZAW	*Beihefte zur Zeitschrift für die alttestamentliche Wissenschaft*
CAH	*Cambridge Ancient History*, ed. I.E. Edwards (Cambridge: Cambridge University Press, 1981)
CBQ	*Catholic Biblical Quarterly*
CHJ	*Cambridge History of Judaism*, ed. W.D. Davies and Louis Finkelstein (Cambridge: Cambridge University Press, 1994)
COS	*The Context of Scripture*, 3 vols., ed. William W. Hallo and K. Lawson Younger, Jr. (Leiden: Brill, 1997–2002)
DSD	*Dead Sea Discoveries*
GLAJJ	*Greek and Latin Authors on Jews and Judaism*, 3 vols., ed. Menahem Stern (Jerusalem: Israel Academy of Sciences and Humanities, 1974–1984)
History	Herodotus, *The Histories*
HTR	*Harvard Theological Review*
HUCA	*Hebrew Union College Annual*
IAA	Israel Antiquities Authority
IEJ	*Israel Exploration Journal*
JAOS	*Journal of the American Oriental Society*
JBL	*Journal of Biblical Literature*
JCS	*Journal of Cuneiform Studies*
JJS	*Journal of Jewish Studies*
JNES	*Journal of Near Eastern Studies*
JNSL	*Journal of Northwest Semitic Languages*
JQR	*Jewish Quarterly Review*
JSJ	*Journal for the Study of Judaism*
JSOT	*Journal for the Study of the Old Testament*
JSQ	*Jewish Studies Quarterly*
LA	*Liber Annuus*
LCL	*Loeb Classical Library*
M	Mishnah
MDOG	*Mitteilungen der deutschen Orient-Gesellschaft*
NEA	*Near Eastern Archaeology*
NEAEHL	*The New Encyclopedia of Archaeological Excavations in the Holy Land*, 5 vols., ed. Ephraim Stern (Jerusalem: Israel Exploration Society and Carta, 1993; vol. 5, 2008)
NRSV	New Revised Standard Version
OBO	*Orbis Biblicus et Orientalis*
OEANE	*The Oxford Encyclopedia of Archaeology in the Near East*, 5 vols., ed. Eric M. Meyers (New York and Oxford: Oxford University Press, 1997)
OLA	*Orientalia Lovaniensia Analecta*
OTS	*Oudtestamentische Studiën*
PAAJR	*Proceedings of the American Academy for Jewish Research*
PEQ	*Palestine Exploration Quarterly*
RB	*Revue Biblique*
REJ	*Revue des Études Juives*
RQ	*Revue de Qumran*
SBL	Society of Biblical Literature
SEL	*Studi Epigrafici e Linguistici*
SWBA	*The Social World of Biblical Antiquity*
T	Tosefta
TB	*Tyndale Bulletin*
VT	*Vetus Testamentum*
War	Josephus, *The Jewish War*
Y	Yerushalmi, Jerusalem (Palestinian) Talmud
ZAW	*Zeitschrift für die alttestamentliche Wissenschaft*
ZDPV	*Zeitschrift des deutschen Palästina-Vereins*
ZPE	*Zeitschrift für Papyrologie und Epigraphik*

Introduction to the Third Edition

VERY FEW BOOKS, EVEN TEXTBOOKS, GO INTO A THIRD EDITION. WE
are pleased and proud to be among the few, we happy few.

We certainly had no idea when we originally produced this book in 1988
that it would be so successful. Indeed, it has become one of the most widely
used textbooks on the history of ancient Israel used throughout the world.
This gives us a special responsibility to keep it up-to-date, however.

Already in the second edition, which grew to 356 pages from 267 pages,
we had to make a slight change in the title: We eliminated the words "A Short
History" from the beginning of the subtitle, reducing it to "From Abraham
to the Roman Destruction of the Temple." Now we are again increasing the
number of pages, but not quite so substantially.

Moreover, in what became the second edition, we thought it might be
chutzpadik to call it that, as if we were somehow anticipating higher numbers,
so we simply called it a "Revised and Expanded" edition. This time, we boldly
call it the third edition. (What else could we call it?)

The "Revised and Expanded" edition came out a little more than a decade
after the original edition—in 1999. This third edition is again coming out a
little more than a decade after the second edition—in 2010. It will undoubtedly be the last by this editor, who has just celebrated his 80th birthday.

Already a number of the original scholarly contributors have died or have
otherwise been unable (or declined) to update their chapters. One of the
strengths of this text is that each chapter represents the work of a leading
scholar in the particular subfield of Israel's history. But the attribution of
authorship can get complicated when a second and now a third scholar

updates and revises a chapter. In the second edition, when another scholar updated and revised the original chapter, we simply listed the original scholar's name as author and the second scholar's name as having revised the chapter.

In the third edition, with possibly three scholars involved, that simply got too cumbersome. Besides, in some cases, there was very little, if any, left of the original author's work. In other cases, it was little, if any, of the reviser's work that survived.

Happily, in two cases, the original author has revised and updated his chapter twice. André Lemaire wrote the original Chapter IV, on the United Monarchy, and has updated it twice (and, actually, a third time during the production of this latest edition so as to include some late discoveries).

And Lee Levine has twice revised and updated Chapter VII: The Age of Hellenism.

These are the simple ones. Let me describe each of the other chapters in order:

Chapter I, The Patriarchal Age, was written by Kyle McCarter, revised for the second edition by Ronald Hendel and revised for the third edition by Kyle McCarter. It is therefore time simply to list Kyle as author and reviser. And I know Ron Hendel well enough so that I am certain he will concur in this decision.

Chapter II, The Exodus, was originally written by the late great Nahum Sarna. When he died, I substantially revised the chapter, especially in light of some of the criticism in reviews, but retaining as much of Nahum's language as I could. I did the same thing for this edition. I still have enormous respect for Nahum's scholarship (and for the man). Especially in light of the fact that a good deal of the language is still his, I have listed him and myself as authors. I also wish to acknowledge and thank Professor Gary Rendsburg and Professor Philip J. King, both good friends, for trying, not always successfully, to keep me from error in this chapter.

Chapter III, The Settlement, was originally the work of the leading archaeologist and Bible scholar, Joseph Callaway. By the time of the second edition, Joe too had died and Maxwell Miller, then of Emory University, revised it. By the time of the third edition, Max had retired from teaching and assumed a responsible museum position in an unrelated field. He nevertheless knew the scholarship, so I attempted to twist his arm to bring the chapter up-to-date again—without success. During several conversations in which I expressed my ideas as to what it needed, Max responded: "Hershel, why don't you do it?" So I did. Since some of my ideas differed from Max's, however, and I incorporated these ideas into the chapter, it would be improper to retain Max's name in the authorship of the chapter. But I would like to record my

The Student and This Text

In addition to being updated, the third edition of *Ancient Israel* has been enhanced in two respects. The text itself is of course a graciously written account by some of the world's leading scholars on the periods in which they are especially expert. This is basic. In this edition, however, we have brought the citations to especially relevant articles from *Biblical Archaeology Review* and *Bible Review* forward as footnotes, instead of citing them with the more scholarly endnotes at the back of the book. These articles are readily available to the student—and fully searchable—in the BAS On-Line Archive. In addition, each chapter in this text contains a "Learn More" sidebar describing in more detail a development or developments covered in particular articles, enticing the student to go beyond the text of the book. (Directions for accessing the BAS On-Line Archive are printed after the "Acknowledgements" page of this book.)

Finally, the voluminous scholarly endnotes at the back of the book provide the basis for more in-depth investigation by both the advanced student as well as the teacher.

We hope all this will make this text even more versatile and useful. —*Ed.*

acknowledgement of and appreciation for Max's contribution to this chapter, even though he is not listed as an author. I also acknowledge the assistance of Gary Rendsburg, as well as my distinguished long-time friend William G. Dever for their careful review of my revision of this chapter. Perhaps foolishly, I did not always listen to their advice, so any surviving errors are solely my responsibility.

Chapter V, The Divided Monarchy, is another chapter that was originally written by a great scholar and archaeologist who died before the second edition came out, Siegfried Horn. I cannot refrain from adding that Siegfried was also an extraordinary human being who lived an extraordinary life; among other things, he was interned by the Japanese in World War II. Siegfried's chapter was substantially revised and updated for the second edition by Kyle McCarter who again did so for this edition. It is therefore time to list Siegfried and Kyle as joint authors of this chapter.

Chapter VI, Exile and Return, was originally written by a fine scholar specializing in this period, James Purvis. The chapter was very substantially rewritten for the second edition by Eric Meyers. It was again substantially rewritten by Eric for this edition, but this time he did so with the assistance of an up and coming younger scholar, Sean Burt, an adjunct professor of religious studies at North Dakota State University who specializes in the Persian period and the Books of Ezra and Nehemiah. Very little, if anything, of the original material in this chapter has been retained. Therefore it seemed appropriate to list the author of this chapter as Eric Meyers with the assistance of Sean Burt.

Chapter VIII, Roman Domination, was originally written by Shaye Cohen and was updated for the second edition by Michael Satlow. For this edition it was updated by Shaye himself. In these circumstances, it seemed to me no longer necessary to include the name of Michael Satlow in the authorship of the chapter, but to acknowledge and thank him here for his contribution.

I need not expatiate on the merits of this textbook. They are described in some detail in my introduction to the original edition, which is reprinted here. As I said in the introduction to the second edition, also reprinted here, I stand by what I said of the unique characteristics of this text. This continues to be my stance.

I would also commend my introduction to the original edition for its suggestions as to how to use this book and, more specifically, the different kinds of historical problems that must be faced at different times in the sweep of this account of nearly 2,000 years of Israel's history.

Rereading my introduction to the revised edition, I seem to reflect the view that we now have a definitive history of ancient Israel that can be carved in stone, that will need no change. Of course that is not so. Our knowledge and insights continue to expand—and do so excitingly. New excavations are constantly producing new material—and the new finds need interpretation to be understood. Moreover, the broader fields of history, anthropology, sociology, to say nothing of new scientific techniques in the field of archaeology are continually bringing new light and sometimes new debates concerning the history of ancient Israel.

So, in all candor, we can only present this as a tentative reconstruction of the history of ancient Israel. Yes, the main lines seem to have been fixed, but the nuances, the details, are constantly changing and broadening our understanding. At whatever level you are coming to this text, however, you are in for a treat. You are getting on a moving train that will continue over the years to open new vistas.

Hershel Shanks
June 2010
Washington, D.C.

Introduction to the Revised Edition

I HAVE BEEN CRITICIZED FOR HEAPING TOO EXTRAVAGANT PRAISE in introductions to books I have edited. So restraint is in order. Yet, I confess, once again I am finding it difficult to contain my excitement. This new edition of *Ancient Israel* is a major advance in a text that was already excellent.

It is unnecessary to expatiate on the merits of this book, however, because the extravagant praise is already there in my introduction to the original edition—and I stand by it! The major change I would make in that introduction is to omit references to the text as "short." Indeed, we have deleted that word from the subtitle of this revised edition. Instead of calling it "A Short History from Abraham to the Roman Destruction of the Temple," it is simply "From Abraham to the Roman Destruction of the Temple."

Since its publication in 1988, this work has established itself as the leading history of ancient Israel. Yet it was clear that after a decade the text needed revision—not only because of the artifacts that have continued to emerge from the ground, but also because of new developments in scholarly perspectives. This was especially true for the earlier periods.

In a sense, however, revision is an inapt word to describe what we have done. It does not imply that we have simply eliminated errors in the original edition. For the most part, we have tried to take account of what is new since the original edition was published. Indeed, very few of our conclusions have changed. Instead, we have added new evidence, a new bibliography and, most importantly, new insights and new analysis.

Unfortunately, what is new has not clarified matters; in most cases, it has complicated the story still more. Hence, the need for expansion, rather than, as might have been hoped, a shorter text based on more definitive answers to persistent cruxes.

What has become clear is that our initial decision to enlist the expertise of a variety of scholars was the right one. It is unlikely that a single scholar will ever write a history of ancient Israel on the scholarly level of this text and covering the period from Abraham to the Roman destruction of the Temple. There is simply too much material for one person to control. The disadvantage of a multi-authored book is, of course, the bumps in style and perspective. I think we have largely eliminated these bumps, thanks to the hard work and cooperation not only of the original authors but especially of the revisers. I can only offer praise and appreciation to these revisers, all of them, in their willingness to work and rework the text in an effort to smooth out the bumps.

Only two of the chapters have been revised by the original authors—André Lemaire on the United Monarchy and Lee Levine on the Hellenistic period. Sadly, two of the original authors—Joseph Callaway and Siegfried Horn—have died. The remaining original authors chose to give other scholars a free hand to revise as needed—as needed, in the latter's judgment, I should add.

Kyle McCarter's chapter on the patriarchal period deserves special mention. It has been widely recognized as a major original contribution to the scholarship of this opaque period. I vividly remember the lunch with Kyle and his close friend Ronald Hendel at which Ron offered to revise Kyle's chapter and Kyle accepted with alacrity. At the same time, Kyle offered to revise Siegfried Horn's chapter on the Divided Monarchy, a chapter that would obviously require extensive revision and expansion, especially in light of new editions of ancient extrabiblical texts that have recently appeared, to say nothing of new archaeological finds. There is only one way to describe what I saw at that luncheon: It was beautiful. Here were two major scholars, unprepossessing and unpossessive, joyous in their scholarly endeavors. I wonder if Kyle realized then what an effort it would take to revise Siegfried Horn's chapter; the revised chapter is now a short book in itself—and a splendid one. I think Siegfried would be pleased. And Kyle's original chapter now has an added sparkle—Ron Hendel's artful new insights into such matters as the historical implications of the Genesis genealogies.

Although I substantially revised Nahum Sarna's chapter on the Exodus, I have come to appreciate even more now than when I originally edited the chapter the enormous erudition embodied in the text. It was a pleasure to build on the insights and scholarship Sarna provided. For added support, I turned to scholarly friends—Kyle McCarter, Baruch Halpern and William Hallo—who read my draft and made sage comments and necessary corrections. With the customary release, I hereby absolve them from responsibility for all remaining errors.

The emergence of Israel in Canaan at the beginning of the Iron Age is one of the most hotly debated issues in biblical history. Joseph Callaway's original chapter squarely faced the problem of balancing the biblical text against the seemingly negative archaeological evidence. Max Miller's revision is no less courageous—and equally well-balanced—bringing the latest scholarly perspectives on the issue, supported by the newest archaeological finds. We learn not only of the complexity of the archaeological evidence but also of the complexity of the biblical text. There is no sounder or more careful weaving together of the evidence than in this nuanced treatment of the issue.

André Lemaire concisely and authoritatively revised his own chapter on the United Monarchy, expanding his treatment to deal with the new attacks on the historicity of this period coming from the so-called biblical minimalists. For Lemaire (and for Lee Levine) all the credit—both for the original and the revision—goes to a single expert source.

We were unusually fortunate at being able to enlist Eric Meyers to update James Purvis's chapter on the Babylonian Exile and the return of the exiles to Israel, commonly referred to in scholarly literature as the Persian period. Meyers had excellent material to work with, and he added his own fresh insights and vast archaeological knowledge with his customary felicity of expression.

As noted, Lee Levine revised his own chapter on the age of Hellenism. Interestingly enough, it was the latest periods that needed the least revision—perhaps because so much material was already available. This is also true of Shaye Cohen's chapter on the Roman period, which was revised by Cohen's former student, now a senior scholar in his own right, Michael Satlow. Nevertheless, the chapters on Hellenism and Roman domination have been sharpened and updated so that they appear with a special new sheen.

It has been an inspiration to me—and a wonderful learning experience—to work with these great scholars. I believe that our readers will respond to this text in the same way.

Hershel Shanks
November 1998
Washington, D.C.

Introduction to the Original Edition

THIS IS A UNIQUE HISTORY OF ANCIENT ISRAEL. OBVIOUSLY, THERE are many other histories of ancient Israel, some of them recent, but none like this one. These are the features that make this book unique:

■ It is short. The text itself—from Abraham to the Roman destruction of the Temple—is only 235 pages, including pictures, charts and maps.

■ The scholarship is absolutely first-rate. This is because each of its eight chapters has been written by a world-famous scholar treating his specialty.

■ This history reflects the most recent developments and the latest archaeological discoveries. While thinking about producing this book, I asked experts in the field to name a first-rate short history of ancient Israel, and they invariably came up with something 25 or 30 years old and therefore necessarily out-of-date.

■ This book is intended for people of all faiths—and for skeptics, too. It reflects no particular religious commitments—nor is it antireligious. The authors include Protestants, Catholics and Jews. They live in Israel, France and the United States.

■ This history of ancient Israel spans the centuries from her patriarchal beginnings to 70 C.E., when the Romans burned Jerusalem and destroyed the Temple. Almost all other histories of ancient Israel either begin later (for example, with the settlement period) or end earlier (for example, with the return to Jerusalem of the Babylonian exiles). By contrast, here the reader will face the full impact of an unparalleled historical sweep.

■ This text is highly readable—written to be understood, as we say at the Biblical Archaeology Society. It has been carefully edited, so that the words of the text are an enticement, not an obstacle. All arcane academese has been purged. I must add that the eminent scholars who wrote the text have been most cooperative during the sometimes arduous editing process; their aim, like the editor's, has been maximum clarity and maximum readability consistent with accuracy.

■ Although it is short and readable, the text is fully annotated, so that the interested student has the references with which to explore in greater detail any matter of particular interest. Moreover, despite the brevity of the text, we have tried to give the evidence, or at least examples of the evidence, that lies behind the historical judgments. We hope we have avoided the unsupported assertion: "Trust me; I know the answer." There is enough evidence here to let the reader make his or her own judgment.

■ Finally, the text is festooned with beautiful pictures—many of them in full color—that enhance and illuminate the text.

■ For these reasons, I believe this is the best book available for all those who are taking their first serious look at the history of ancient Israel—religious school students, college students, seminary students, adult study groups and the intellectually curious of all ages. This book also provides a short, but comprehensive and up-to-date refresher course for those who have been here before.

There are many ways to use this book—as many ways as there are teachers, students and interested readers. But for all, I would suggest a quick initial reading. Read it like a novel from beginning to end. If you begin to bog down in too many details for this kind of reading, then skip ahead—but keep going.

It is important to get the sweep of things, the big picture. This is a remarkable story, an immensely moving passage through time—about 2,000 years of it, ending nearly 2,000 years ago. I don't mean to suggest that reading this book is like attending a Cecil B. DeMille saga. This is a serious study. But beneath the details is a panorama of historical movement that is spiritually elevating as well as intellectually stimulating. No reader should miss this scope.

Moreover, a quick reading should make the reader comfortable with the overarching structure of ancient Israel's history. The major segments in that history—the patriarchal wanderings, the Egyptian sojourn and the Exodus, the settlement of Canaan in the time of the Judges, the institution and development of the monarchy under Saul, David and Solomon, the split-up of the kingdom, the destruction of the northern kingdom by the Assyrians, the destruction of Solomon's Temple and the southern kingdom by the Babylonians, the Exile in Babylonia and Egypt, the return to the land, the rise of a new Jewish state under the Maccabees, the Hellenization of the Jewish world, the tensions of Roman domination in the Herodian period and, finally, the burning of Jerusalem and destruction of the Second Temple that effectively ended the Jewish revolt against Rome—will be firmly fixed in your mind. Then details can be filled in on a slower, more intensive second reading.

A word of clarification may be appropriate to explain why we begin and end where we do. Why we begin with Abraham is simple. According to the Bible, he was the first Hebrew. The first 11 chapters of Genesis, before the introduction of Abraham, are referred to as the Primeval History. They do not purport to cover Israelite history.

Moreover, the first 11 chapters of the Bible, in the judgment of critical scholars, are mythic, not historic. This does not diminish the power or meaning of these stories, but it does mean that from a factual viewpoint we must approach them differently. Of course, this judgment sometimes collides with the religious faith of people who are committed to the literal truth of Scripture. This issue, however, need not detain us here because even in the Bible's own terms, the history of Israel begins with Abraham, the first Hebrew.

For many scholars, the more difficult question will be why we begin so early, rather than so late—with the patriarchs rather than, say, with the Israelite settlement in Canaan. Some scholars will question whether there is any discoverable history in the Bible's stories about the patriarchs Abraham, Isaac and Jacob. There is obviously a historiographic problem here, to which we shall return. Suffice it to say at this point that the fact that the Bible recites the stories of the patriarchs as the earliest chapters of Israelite history is enough to require a consideration of the extent, if any, to which these stories reflect or contain history of one sort or another. We are not, *a priori,* committed to an answer, but we are committed to asking the question.

At the other end of the time continuum, many scholars will question our decision to end with the Roman destruction of the Temple in 70 C.E. In discussing this project with scholars, I was told several times that it would be more appropriate to continue the story to 135 C.E., when the Romans finally suppressed the Second Jewish Revolt, the so-called Bar-Kokhba Revolt.

There is substance to this contention. I nevertheless rejected it for several reasons. First, any cutoff is to some extent arbitrary. The world always goes on, or at least it has until now. And past events always influence the future. Second, the final destruction of the Jewish Temple in Jerusalem in 70 C.E. was such a cataclysmic event that it can lay claim to marking a historic termination and a new beginning. Third, the book was already long enough, especially as a short history. Fourth, and perhaps decisive, we hope to produce a subsequent volume tracing the parallel developments of Christianity and Judaism during the early centuries of the Common Era; in that book, we will cover the events both leading up to and following the Bar-Kokhba Revolt.*

I have mentioned the sweep of the story and the overarching structure of the historical development. The reader will also notice another development as the story moves along. This development relates to the nature and reliability of the sources from which this history is constructed.

Let us consider the kinds of sources on which the recovery of our history depends. From the patriarchal period through the Exile (Chapters I through VI), the primary source is the Bible. The biblical account is supplemented by what we loosely call archaeological discoveries. (They may or may not have been recovered in a scientifically controlled excavation.) These archaeological artifacts are of two kinds—the "word" kind and the "non-word" kind. The "word" kind includes inscriptions and texts. The "non-word" kind includes anything from a pollen sample to a pottery sherd to the wall of an ancient palace. In addition to the Bible and to archaeological discoveries, we occasionally have a late copy of an earlier book whose author refers to or makes use of ancient sources now lost. But this last category is relatively rare.

The reader will notice that archaeological discoveries are more helpful in uncovering the past as we move along the time line. They are least helpful and least specific in the patriarchal period. Gradually they become more helpful and more specific.

There is another kind of development—a development on the continuum of reliability. We are least sure of what happened in the patriarchal period. Gradually, we become more confident of the history we are recounting as time moves on. Where we are least sure of what happened, we are most reliant on the biblical text. This might be thought to lead to the conclusion that archaeological discoveries are what really give reliability to the biblical text. But this is not true. The biblical text is overwhelmingly more important than the archaeological discoveries. We would pretty much know what happened from the biblical text even without the archaeological discoveries. The reverse is not at all true.

Why then is the early history of ancient Israel less reliable than the later history? The answer relates not to the illumination archaeology provides but to the nature of the biblical text. The traditional, etiological stories of the patriarchal period present far different historiographic problems than the account of, for example, the Divided Kingdom, which the biblical writers took largely from royal annals.

*In 1992, we realized this hope with the publication of *Christianity and Rabbinic Judaism: A Parallel History of Their Origins and Early Development* (Washington, D.C.: Biblical Archaeology Society). A revised and updated edition will be published in 2011.—**Ed.**

As a result, the reader will notice another kind of development. In the early chapters of this book, the authors devote major attention to the reliability of the biblical account and to the ways they can penetrate the text to discover what in fact happened. In the earlier periods, we are more concerned with how to deal with the biblical text than with how to interpret the history recounted. Gradually, the emphasis shifts. By the time we reach the Divided Kingdom, we can pretty much rely on the facts given in the Bible, and the historian's task is chiefly to present and interpret those facts to create a modern history. By contrast, in the patriarchal age we confront a basic question of biblical historicity. Were the patriarchs real people who lived at a particular time in history?

In the period of the Egyptian sojourn and the Exodus, we are still at an early time when we must ask whether there was an Egyptian enslavement and an Exodus, but it seems relatively clear that something like that in fact occurred. We are more concerned with placing events in a particular period and with assessing the reliability of details.

By the time we reach the period of the settlement and the Judges, we are on firm, datable historical ground. But here we are faced with a fundamental question. Did the Israelites possess the land by military conquest or by peaceful infiltration into uninhabited areas, or was there perhaps an internal revolt of the underclass that led to Israel's emergence in Canaan? This is obviously a different kind of historiographic problem from those faced by the authors of the previous chapters.

In the period of the United Kingdom, the question of factual historicity begins to fade into the background. The major historical problem is to redress the biases reflected in the text, so that we can arrive at a more objective history of the period.

When we deal with the period of the Divided Kingdom, and with the Babylonian Exile and return, less attention is paid to historiography or the question of reliability, although these questions never disappear.

For the history recounted in the last two chapters of the book, dealing with the Hasmonean period and Roman rule, only a few late books of the Bible are relevant. Equally, if not more important, is a host of classical authors, especially the first-century C.E. Jewish historian Josephus. So-called intertestamental texts, pseudepigrapha and apocrypha, such as Maccabees, as well as later rabbinic writings and the New Testament also provide evidence. The amount of archaeological material that sheds light on this period is enormous. Pride of place, of course, goes to the famous Dead Sea Scrolls, many of which are only now becoming available to scholars. But scholars must also absorb a host of other religious and nonreligious texts, as well as archaeological artifacts ranging from buildings to coins.

Another contrast: In the earlier period described in this book the relevant evidence is sparse, and we must squeeze it in a dozen different ways to get what we reliably can from it. In the later periods, on the other hand, the amount of evidence is truly overwhelming, beyond the capacity of any human being to command. Here the task is to find meaningful strands, overarching trends in a sea of material.

The differences in the various chapters of the book reflect the differences outlined above—in the nature and reliability of the sources; in the historiographic problems; in the light archaeology sheds on the particular period; and in the sheer quantity of material that must be taken into account. The result is a fascinating variety. Reading this story will be a richer experience if these differences are kept in mind.

Ancient Israel was, in the end, defeated; but it was not destroyed. It survived. And it continued to shape the world, as the Bible says, "to this day." To understand this history is to discern why its influence endured. And only in terms of this history can we truly appreciate the scriptural treasures it left us. It is a history that is at once intellectually penetrating and spiritually uplifting. Now, in the words attributed to the great first-century sage Hillel, "Go and study!"

Hershel Shanks
June 1988
Washington, D.C.

Acknowledgments

WHILE THE UPDATED CONTENT OF THIS THIRD EDITION OF *Ancient Israel* certainly would not have been possible without the contributions of the scholars praised in the introduction, the editing and final production of this masterful volume owes much to the talents, expertise and labors of the staff of the Biblical Archaeology Society.

BAS publisher and president Susan Laden skillfully oversaw and managed, from start to finish, all of the moving parts that make an edited volume like this possible. Administrative editor Bonnie Mullin made sure the various contributors (including myself) understood their responsibilities and deadlines, and also had the thankless task of editing the countless endnotes that help make this book such a valuable resource. The book's detailed and wonderfully illustrated maps were updated by managing editor Dorothy D. Resig, while thanks for the superb indexing of the volume goes to Connie Binder. The overall consolidation and editing of the individual chapters, illustrations and notes into a single whole was brilliantly handled by assistant editor G. Joseph Corbett, while the final production of the printed copy was under the watchful eye of production manager Heather Metzger. As with the first two editions of *Ancient Israel,* design and layout of the book fell to our longtime creative designer Rob Sugar and his excellent team at AURAS Design, especially Melissa Kelly. As always, they did a wonderful job. My thanks to all for making this updated edition a stellar accomplishment.

Hershel Shanks

The BAS
On–Line Archive

THE THIRD EDITION OF *ANCIENT ISRAEL* HIGHLIGHTS countless articles from the pages of *Biblical Archaeology Review* and *Bible Review* that will allow both scholars and students to delve deeper into the discoveries, debates and personalities that continue to shape our understanding of ancient Israel These articles are easily accessible in the BAS On-Line Archive.

Specifically designed for educational institutions, an institutional license allows all members of an educational community access to the entire corpus of past and present BAS periodicals, including *Biblical Archaeology Review, Bible Review* and *Archaeology Odyssey,* as well as five monographs from the BAS-Smithsonian lecture series. The archive allows the user to search all of these publications by title, author, subject, word, issue or date. It contains over 6,000 articles and more than 18,000 pictures and maps with comprehensive captions. Most of the images are in full color.

Librarians can register for a site license or for more information go to www.basarchive.org.
Or contact:
BAS Archive
4710 41st Street NW
Washington, DC 20016
202-364-3300
e-mail: archive@bib-arch.org

*For individual use, subscribe to the members library at www.bib-arch.org/library.

ONE

The Patriarchal Age
Abraham, Isaac and Jacob

P. KYLE McCARTER, JR.

THE HISTORY OF ISRAEL BEFORE THE EXODUS FROM EGYPT IS, AS THE
Bible presents it, a family history. The story begins with the departure of Abram,
son of Terah, from Ur, his ancestral homeland in southern Mesopotamia.* He
journeys to Haran, a city in northwestern Mesopotamia, and from there to the
land of Canaan (Genesis 11:31–12:5) In Canaan, Abram's son Isaac is born, and
Isaac, in turn, becomes the father of Jacob, also called Israel (Genesis 32:29).
During a famine, Jacob and his 12 sons, the ancestors of the 12 tribes of Israel,
leave Canaan and settle in Egypt, where their descendants become slaves.

This segment of Israel's history, therefore, is the story of the patriarchs:
Abram or Abraham (as he is called in Genesis 17:5), Isaac, Jacob (Israel)
and the 12 sons of Jacob.

The biblical description of the patriarchal period is concerned largely
with private affairs, as one would expect in the story of an individual
family. There are only a few references to public events, and none of these
corresponds to a known event of general history. Genesis 14, for example,
describes a war in which the kings of the five Cities of the Plain (Sodom,
Gomorrah, Admah, Zeboiim and Bela, or Zoar) are arrayed against an
alliance of four kings led by Chedorlaomer, king of Elam, a country that lay

---

*For competing ideas about the location of biblical Ur, see Alan Millard, "Where Was
Abraham's Ur?" *BAR*, May/June 2001; Hershel Shanks, "Abraham's Ur—Is the Pope Going
to the Wrong Place?" *BAR*, March/April 2000.

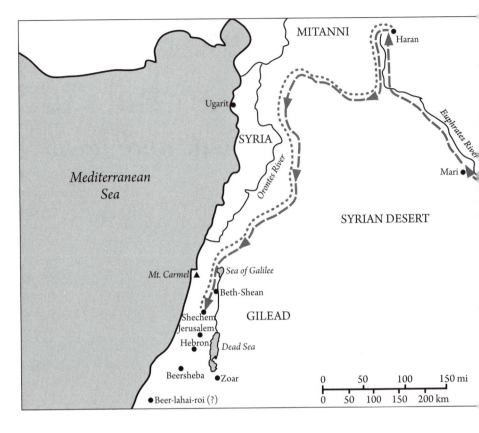

east of Mesopotamia. Chedorlaomer is said to have ruled over the Cities of the Plain before they rebelled (Genesis 14:4). There is no extrabiblical record of these events, and neither the name of Chedorlaomer nor that of his ally Amraphel, king of Shinar (Babylonia), has been found in Mesopotamian records. Despite numerous attempts, no scholar has succeeded in identifying any of the nine kings involved in the war. The same is true of the other public figures mentioned in the patriarchal history: None can be identified from extrabiblical sources. Thus we know nothing of Melchizedek, king of Salem, apart from what we read in Genesis 14, or of Abimelech, king of Gerar, apart from what is said in Genesis 20 and 26. No external source mentions the Egyptian officer Potiphar (Genesis 39) or Hamor (Genesis 34), who was apparently a ruler of Shechem, or Ephron the Hittite (Genesis 23), a prominent citizen of Hebron. The early kings of Edom listed in Genesis 36:31–39 are known only from the Bible. We might expect to be able to identify the pharaoh of Genesis 12:10–20 or the pharaoh of the Joseph story, but neither ruler is called by name in the Bible.

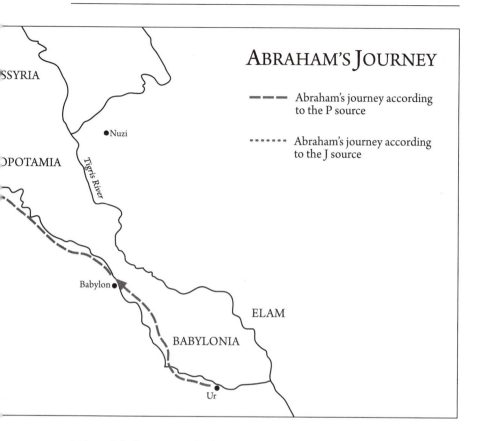

ABRAHAM'S JOURNEY

– – – – Abraham's journey according
to the P source

· · · · · · Abraham's journey according
to the J source

SSYRIA

●Nuzi

)POTAMIA

Tigris River

Babylon ●

ELAM

BABYLONIA

● Ur

When did the patriarchs live?

In the absence of references to persons or events of general history, it is very
difficult to determine the historical context of the stories in Genesis 12–50.
The initial question, then, is a simple one: When did the patriarchs live?
Or, to put it more precisely, can we correlate the biblical and the historical
evidence to arrive at the time of the patriarchs?

At first glance, an answer to this question seems to be available from chronological indications in the biblical narrative itself. We are told that Abraham was
75 years old when he set out for Canaan (Genesis 12:4) and 100 when Isaac was
born (Genesis 21:5). According to Genesis 25:26, Isaac was 60 years old when
Jacob was born. Then, if Jacob was 130 when he descended into Egypt, as we
read in Genesis 47:9, the full time the patriarchs spent in Canaan before going
to Egypt was 215 years. Subsequently, we are told that the period of slavery in
Egypt lasted 430 years (Exodus 12:40), and that the time from the Exodus from
Egypt to the beginning of the construction of the Temple in the fourth year of
Solomon's reign was 480 years (1 Kings 6:1). This brings us close to the period

where we have relatively reliable chronological information: Most scholars agree that Solomon died within a decade or so of 930 B.C.E.* According to 1 Kings 11:42, he reigned 40 years. It follows that his fourth year, the year work began on the Temple, was about 966 B.C.E. Reckoning backward from this date and using the numbers cited above, we arrive at the following scheme:

2091 B.C.E.	Abram's departure for Canaan
1876 B.C.E.	The descent of Jacob's family into Egypt
1446 B.C.E.	The Exodus from Egypt
966 B.C.E.	The beginning of the construction of Solomon's Temple

According to these calculations, the patriarchal period (the time of the sojournings of Abraham, Isaac and Jacob in Canaan) lasted from 2091 to 1876 B.C.E., and the Israelites were enslaved in Egypt between 1876 and 1446 B.C.E.

Unfortunately, there are serious problems with this scheme. First, it accepts the impossibly long life spans assigned the patriarchs. Second, it is internally inconsistent. Moses and Aaron were fourth-generation descendants of Jacob's son Levi (1 Chronicles 6:1–3, 1 Chronicles 5:27–29 in Hebrew). The 430-year period assigned the slavery in Egypt is too long for the three generations from Levi to Moses and Aaron, an average of about 143 years a generation. In any event, this is inconsistent with the notice that Joshua, a younger contemporary of Moses and Aaron, was a 12th-generation descendant of Levi's brother Joseph (1 Chronicles 7:20–27). If this were true, the 11 generations from Joseph to Joshua would average about 39 years each.

Third, the dates produced by this chronology for the Exodus and settlement do not correspond well with the evidence of history and archaeology. If the Exodus occurred in about 1446 B.C.E., then by the same chronology the conquest of Canaan must have begun 40 years later, in about 1406 B.C.E. There is, however, no archaeological evidence of a widespread destruction or change of population at the end of the 15th century. Rather, the changes in material culture that archaeologists associate with the appearance of the Israelites in Canaan may be dated, in general, to the 13th or 12th century B.C.E., and the first clear historical evidence for the presence of Israel in Canaan is the inscription on the so-called Israel Stele of the Egyptian pharaoh Merneptah, dating to about 1207 B.C.E. (see Chapter III, "The Settlement in Canaan: The Period of the Judges").

*B.C.E. (Before the Common Era) and C.E. (Common Era) are the alternative designations for B.C. and A.D. often used in scholarly literature.

Who Wrote Down the Stories of the Patriarchs and When?

The patriarchal characters and stories in Genesis are some of the most compelling in the entire Bible, yet are among the most difficult to identify historically or archaeologically. But despite the fact that no material or textual evidence of Abraham, Isaac, Jacob or Joseph has ever been found, many early-20th century archaeologists, led by William F. Albright, the pioneer of American "biblical archaeology," were convinced that material and textual discoveries proved that the patriarchs were best understood and had in fact lived during the first half of the second millennium B.C.E. Yet as historian and textual scholar Maynard Maidman makes clear in his insightful *BAR* article "Abraham, Isaac & Jacob Meet Newton, Darwin & Wellhausen" (May/June 2006), the Albrightian formulation of the patriarchal period had been undone by a kind of "archaeology" of the biblical text undertaken by German biblical scholar Julius Wellhausen over a half-century earlier.

Wellhausen's so-called "documentary hypothesis," brilliantly summarized and defended by biblical scholar Richard Elliot Friedman in his *Bible Review* article "Taking the Biblical Text Apart" (Fall 2005), proposed that the patriarchal stories in Genesis (along with the rest of the books of the Torah, or the Five Books of Moses) consisted basically of four separate textual strands, or schools of authors, writing at different times and in different contexts during the Israelite monarchy of the first half of the first millennium B.C.E., also called the Iron Age, or shortly thereafter. These four authorial strands, which may also include much earlier traditions, are identified by scholars as the J (or Jahwist) source, the E (or Elohist) source, the P (or Priestly) source and the D (or Deuteronomist) source, all of which give their own spin to the patriarchal narratives. As such, the written stories of the patriarchs—wherever and whenever the oral traditions of Israel's ancestors originated (see Kyle McCarter's discussion below)—reflect primarily the Iron Age Israelite context in which they were first compiled and edited. —*Ed.*

The Bible's own chronological scheme, therefore, does not provide intelligible evidence for the dating of the patriarchal period. This fact, combined with the absence of references to events of general history as noted above, indicates that the patriarchal narratives in Genesis cannot be used as historical resources in any simple or straightforward fashion. They must be interpreted on the basis of an understanding, first, of their distinctive literary history and the purposes for which they were composed, and, second, of the development of the traditions upon which they are based.

Scholars generally agree that the patriarchal narratives, as we now have them, are composite (see "Who Wrote Down the Stories of the Patriarchs and When?" previous page). They contain at least three written strata, or strands, the earliest of which was composed during the time of the kingdoms of Israel and Judah (tenth to sixth century B.C.E.)* and the latest after the Babylonian destruction of Jerusalem (586 B.C.E.). All of these strata were brought together and arranged in approximately their present form at some time in the Second Temple period (after 538 B.C.E.) or, at the earliest, during the Babylonian Exile (586–538 B.C.E.). On the surface, therefore, the biblical patriarchal history reflects the political and religious viewpoint of the Judahite monarchy and priesthood. Thus, for example, the promise made to Abram in Genesis 12:2 is that his descendants will be, not simply a numerous people, but a great "nation."

Are the patriarchs historical individuals or eponyms?

On this level, the men and women who appear in Genesis 12–50 are less accessible as historical individuals than as typological prefigurations of the later Israelites and their neighbors. In many cases they are eponyms, that is, persons from whom the names of the later groups were supposed to be derived. Thus Jacob is also called "Israel" (the name of the nation in later times), and his 12 sons are the eponymous ancestors of the 12 tribes of Israel. The narratives and genealogies characterize the various peoples of the writers' own times and delineate the relationships among them from an Israelite perspective. Israel's ancestors are born under auspicious circumstances, for instance, whereas the eponymous ancestors of the Moabites and Ammonites, "Moab" and "Ben-ammi," are born of incestuous unions of Lot and his daughters (Genesis 19:30–38).** Jacob (Israel) outwits his brother Esau, who is also called "Edom" (Genesis 25:30, 36:1), and wins Esau's

---

*This is the earliest period in Israel's history when written historiography could be expected to develop. See Chapter IV, "The United Monarchy: Saul, David and Solomon," on the period of the United Kingdom.

**Konstantinos Politis, "Where Lot's Daughters Seduced Their Father," BAR, January/February 2004.

birthright and blessing. Ishmael, the eponymous ancestor of the tribes that inhabited the desert region between Judah and Egypt, is the child of the Judahite patriarch Abram and Sarai's Egyptian maid Hagar (Genesis 16). This kind of material, though of great value in considering the political outlook of later Israel, is very difficult to use in a historical reconstruction of the world of Israel's ancestors.

If Genesis 12–50 in its present form reflects the time of the biblical writers (that is, the time of the monarchy or later) rather than the time of the patriarchs, is it possible to look behind the present, literary form of the biblical narrative to examine the traditions upon which this material is based? Such a procedure might shed light on the development of the traditions and, ultimately, provide information about the history of the patriarchal age. Modern scholars, therefore, have developed methods for studying the preliterary history of the stories in Genesis.

Searching for the social context of the patriarchs

One such method, which was especially popular in the middle decades of the 20th century, was based largely on archaeology. The scholars associated with this method took a generally positive view of the historical value of Genesis 12–50. They acknowledged that the patriarchal narratives in their present form were composed no earlier than the United Kingdom (tenth century B.C.E.). Nevertheless, they argued that these materials were based on historically reliable traditions deriving from earlier periods. Excavations had provided extensive new data, including a substantial amount of written material. After studying these texts, many scholars were convinced that the biblical patriarchal stories contained authentic details preserved from the time of their origin. It seemed reasonable, therefore, to suppose that there was a historical patriarchal period and to hope that it might be identified.

This point of view is associated most closely with the work of William F. Albright and his students.[1] It was also developed and promoted by other prominent scholars, especially Ephraim A. Speiser of the University of Pennsylvania.[2] In brief, the argument of this "school" was as follows: Certain details in the biblical patriarchal stories—including personal names, social customs, legal practices and aspects of lifestyle—correspond to known features of second-millennium culture in Mesopotamia, Syria and Canaan. Many of the same details, moreover, do not fit into the culture of the Israelite monarchy, the time when the stories were written down. In the judgment of Albright and those who shared his viewpoint, it seemed likely that these details preserved authentic elements of the civilization of the patriarchal period; by studying them and comparing them to surviving second-millennium materials outside the Bible, we should be able to determine the original historical context of the patriarchal traditions. As Albright put it,

> So many corroborations of detail have been discovered in recent years that most competent scholars have given up the old critical theory according to which the stories of the Patriarchs are mostly retrojections from the time of the Dual Monarchy [late tenth century B.C.E. and later].[3]

He wrote elsewhere,

> As a whole, the picture in Genesis is historical, and there is no reason to doubt the general accuracy of the biographical details and the sketches of personality which make the patriarchs come alive with a vividness unknown to a single extrabiblical character in the whole vast literature of the ancient Near East.[4]

In general, Albright's students did not express this viewpoint quite so strongly. As they acknowledged, archaeology cannot be expected to corroborate biographical details or specific references to private events. Nevertheless, they contended, archaeology might be able to shed light on the general historical context of the patriarchal stories (see "Who Wrote Down the Stories of the Patriarchs and When?" p. 5). They argued that the general cultural milieu of the patriarchal stories—as indicated by the details of social, economic and legal customs mentioned in the Bible—could best be identified with an early period and, more particularly, with the early second millennium B.C.E. As Harvard's G. Ernest Wright wrote:

> We shall probably never be able to prove that Abram really existed, that he did this or that, said thus and so, but what we can prove is that his life and times, as reflected in the stories about him, fit perfectly within the early second millennium, but imperfectly with any later period.[5]

The reconstruction of patriarchal history achieved by Albright, Speiser and others has had far-reaching consequences. Recent research, however, has cast substantial doubt on many of its arguments, and the confidence these arguments inspired in scholars a generation ago has dissipated. To understand why this change has taken place, we must look more closely at their reconstruction and the evidence upon which it was based.

An urban culture flourished in Syria and Canaan during the Early Bronze Age, which spanned much of the third millennium B.C.E. During the last quarter of the third millennium, however, this civilization collapsed and was replaced by a predominantly nonurban, pastoral culture. The factors that produced this change are not fully understood. The third dynasty of the city of Ur held sway in Mesopotamia at the time, and the records of the Ur III rulers complain of chronic trouble with nonurban peoples who were laying claim to lands previously controlled by the city. Scholars long supposed, therefore, that a chief factor in the urban collapse was an invasion—or at least a massive immigration—of nomadic peoples from the desert fringes of the region. These peoples, called *Amurru*—that is, "Westerners" or "Amorites"— in the Mesopotamian sources, gradually gained ascendancy in the settled portions of both Syria-Canaan and Mesopotamia, so that in the early second millennium they took the leadership in reestablishing urban centers.

The theory that an invasion or immigration of Amorites was responsible for the radical cultural changes that characterized the transition from the Early to Middle Bronze Age is sometimes called "the Amorite hypothesis." A corollary of this hypothesis identifies the biblical patriarchs as Amorites. Albright associated Abraham's wanderings with the Amorite movements and dated the Abraham phase of the patriarchal period to the end of the third millennium. He called this period, which he dated to 2100–1900 B.C.E., Middle Bronze I (MB I), since it represented a break from the preceding Early Bronze Age and was characterized by the arrival of the people who would assume cultural leadership later in the Middle Bronze Age.

The succeeding period, which Albright called MB IIA, was an age of unwalled villages in Syria and Canaan. The strong XIIth Dynasty kings of Egypt encouraged the gradual development of a system of city-states in Syria and Canaan. Then, as Egypt began to weaken at the end of this period, the new urban centers entered a period of independence, prosperity and high cultural attainment. Albright identified this period, which he called MB IIB, as the time of the patriarch Jacob. This was the Old Babylonian period in Mesopotamia, when Hammurabi and his successors ruled. In Syria it is sometimes called "the age of Mari," after a city on the Upper Euphrates that attained a position of ascendancy in Syria and western Mesopotamia at the time. The life and history of Mari are recorded in a major cuneiform archive found at the site, called Tell Hariri, on the Syrian side of the modern Syro-Iraqi frontier. Local leadership for the process of reurbanization came from the previously nomadic Amorite population. We know this because the new ruling dynasties in the city-states of Syria and Mesopotamia have characteristically Amorite names. There remained, however, a substantial nomadic population, which was also Amorite. The royal archives of Mari provide ample illustration of the coexistence of the two groups.

9

Many scholars—including several of Albright's own students—were reluctant to be as precise as Albright in dating the Abraham phase of the patriarchal period to MB I and the Jacob phase to MB IIB. They preferred a more general date, contending "simply that the Patriarchal stories are best understood in the setting of the early second millennium."[6] This position had the advantage of avoiding one of the problems of the Amorite hypothesis in its original form: Although MB I (to which Albright assigned the Abraham phase) was a strictly nonurban period, the Abraham narratives in the Bible do mention several cities.* None of the archaeological sites associated with these biblical cities, however, has yielded any substantial MB I remains.[7] It seemed better, therefore, to identify the patriarchal age with the subsequent period of reurbanization in MB II and, more particularly, MB IIB. Throughout Genesis, Abraham, Isaac and Jacob are depicted as living in tents in proximity to urban centers, a situation that may be compared with the coexistence of nomadic and urban peoples at Mari and other cities in MB IIB. Thus it was argued that the patriarchal way of life as depicted in the Genesis narratives was especially compatible with what we know of the civilization of the early second millennium.[8]

In addition to general observations of this kind, two arguments were developed to support the association of the patriarchs with the early second millennium. The first was based on the analysis of the personal names found in Genesis 12–50; the second, on studies of the social customs and legal practices mentioned in the patriarchal narratives.

Evidence for a second-millennium context?

Let us consider the personal names first. As indicated above, Amorite names form a distinctive group. They may be identified by a number of peculiar linguistic features. Names of this type are common in texts from the first half of the second millennium. Advocates of a similar date for the patriarchal age point out that the names in the patriarchal narratives are largely of the same type. A form of the name "Jacob," for example, occurs several times in early-second-millennium materials, and the name "Abram" is said to be attested for the same period.[9] No examples of "Isaac" or "Joseph" have survived, but both of these names are of the Amorite type. The argument, therefore, was that the biblical names from the patriarchal period fit well in the historical context of the early second millennium but could not have originated later,

---

*These include the various cities of the Jordan Valley (Genesis 14:2), the Philistine city of Gerar (Genesis 20:1) and the fortified city of Hebron (Genesis 23:2), among others. For a summary of recent excavations in the region of Hebron, see Jeffrey Chadwick, "Discovering Hebron," *BAR*, September/October 2005.

that is, at the time of the biblical writers.

Second, Albright, Speiser and others cited numerous parallels between social and legal practices mentioned in extrabiblical texts from the second millennium and social and legal practices referred to in the biblical patriarchal narratives. Cuneiform texts from Nuzi in Upper Mesopotamia were especially important to this discussion.[10] The Nuzi tablets reflect the practices and customs of the Hurrians, a people who flourished in the eastern Tigris region in the middle of the second millennium. Although no one attempted to associate the patriarchs directly with the Hurrian kingdom of Mitanni, it was well known that Hurrian influence was widespread in Syria and even Canaan in this period. Thus, numerous connections between the Hurrians and the Bible were proposed. According to the terms of a Nuzi marriage contract, for example, a barren wife is required to provide a slave woman to her husband to bear his children.[11] In Genesis 16:1–4, the barren Sarai sends her maid Hagar to Abram to bear children. The parallel is obvious. At Nuzi, if this union produces a son, the slave woman's child may not subsequently be expelled; compare Abraham's unwillingness to send away Hagar and her son, Ishmael, in Genesis 21:10–11. Further, as interpreted by Speiser,

> In Hurrian society a wife enjoyed special standing and protection when the law recognized her simultaneously as her husband's sister, regardless of actual blood ties ... This dual role conferred on the wife a superior position in society.[12]

According to Speiser, this custom lies behind those episodes in Genesis in which Abraham (12:10–20, 20:1–18) and later Isaac (26:6–11) introduce their wives as their sisters.

The story of Sarai and Hagar and the wife-sister episodes are only two of the numerous details of the patriarchal narratives that were interpreted in light of Middle Bronze Age texts (dating to about 2000–1550 B.C.E.). The general argument was that many social and legal customs referred to in Genesis have parallels in middle- or early-second-millennium practice, but that the same customs are without parallel in later times. From this it was concluded that the presence of these references in Genesis was an indication of the early-second-millennium origin of the biblical traditions.

A scholarly failure

Despite its attractions, this reconstruction has proved vulnerable to criticism of various kinds.

Doubts about the application of the Amorite hypothesis to the problems of the patriarchal period have led to a serious modification and abandonment of many of the positions cited above. It now seems unlikely that an invasion or immigration of nomads was a primary factor in the collapse of urban civilization in the last part of the third millennium.[13] The pastoral peoples so prominent in this period were present in earlier times as well, living alongside the established urban centers. Instead, overpopulation, drought, famine or a combination of such problems may have exhausted the resources necessary to the maintenance of an urban way of life. When the cities disappeared, the nomadic encampments remained. Other nomads, originally living on the fringes of the desert, probably took advantage of the new situation to infiltrate previously settled areas; but there was no widespread immigration, and most of the cultural changes detected by archaeology can best be explained as indigenous, not produced by the arrival of outsiders. The period called MB I by Albright, therefore, was really the last, posturban phase of the Early Bronze Age, and an emerging consensus of scholarship now prefers to call it Early Bronze IV (EB IV).*

If no invasion or widespread migration took place in EB IV, there is no reason to associate Abram's wanderings with the events of that period, especially in view of the difficulty, already noted, created by the absence in this period of the urban centers mentioned in Genesis 12–25.

On the other hand, the circumstances of what we now call late MB I (Albright's MB IIA) and MB II (MB IIB), during which nomads and urban dwellers lived side by side in Syria and Canaan, do provide a suitable context for the patriarchal stories.[14] Also, as we have seen, a modified version of the Amorite hypothesis located the patriarchal period more generally in the early second millennium. Yet it is becoming increasingly clear that this "dimorphic" pattern—of city dwellers and tribal peoples (including both pastoralists and villagers) living contiguously—has been typical of the Middle East from ancient until modern times.[15] This pattern prevailed even in the third millennium; after the interruption of EB IV, it resumed in the Middle Bronze Age, as the archives from Mari show.[16] Although we do not have archival evidence for later periods, as we do for the earlier period at Mari,

---

*Many scholars also now believe that Albright's dates for this period were about a century too low. Our dating and periodization of the Middle Bronze Age, in contrast to the scheme developed by Albright, are shown in the following chart. In general we follow William G. Dever:

Date	Archaeological Period	Albright's Scheme	Albright's Date
2250–2000	EB IV	MB I	2100–1900
2000–1800	MB I	MB IIA	1900–1750
1800–1630	MB II	MB IIB	1700–1600
1630–1550	MB III	MB IIC	1600–1550

there is no reason to doubt that the pattern persisted throughout the Late Bronze Age and beyond. The archaeological evidence and modern anthropological studies seem to confirm this.[17] That this dimorphic lifestyle is a fitting background for the stories about the patriarchs provides no basis for locating them in MB I and II in preference to other periods.

The other criteria urged in favor of an early second-millennium date for the patriarchal age have also been challenged. In almost every specific instance, the proposed parallels between details of the patriarchal stories and information found in surviving second-millennium documents have now been disputed.[18] Many of the parallels are no longer regarded as valid. In several other cases, the phenomena in question have been identified in texts from one or more later periods, thus diminishing the importance of the parallels for dating the patriarchal tradition. More particularly, the Nuzi evidence, which once figured so prominently in the discussion, has been vitiated by the discovery that the information it provides about private life reflects widespread Mesopotamian practices rather than distinctively Hurrian customs that might be assumed to have penetrated into Canaan.[19]

We can no longer argue, for example, that the patriarchal names fit best into the early second millennium. Names similar or identical to the names found in Genesis are attested from a number of different periods. The identification of the name "Abram" or "Abraham" in Middle Bronze materials is uncertain or dubious, whereas forms of this name ("Abram," "Abiram") occur several times in texts from the Late Bronze Age (1550–1200 B.C.E.) and later.[20] Moreover, names with the same structure are exceedingly common, attested in almost all periods.[21] Similarly, the name type to which "Isaac," "Jacob" and "Joseph" belong is widely distributed across the history of the ancient Near East. It is especially well known from Middle Bronze sources and, in fact, is the most characteristic type of Amorite name.[22] But there is no reason to believe that its use diminished significantly after the Middle Bronze Age;[23] in the Late Bronze Age, it is well attested in Ugaritic and Amarna Canaanite names;[24] and in the Iron Age it occurs in Hebrew inscriptions as well as in the Bible.[25] While it is true that the name "Jacob" is very common in the Middle Bronze Age, it is also found in Late Bronze sources,[26] and related names occur in both Elephantine (fifth century B.C.E.) and Palmyrene (first century B.C.E. through third century C.E.) Aramaic.[27]

Similar difficulties arise with the proposition that the legal practices and social customs referred to in the stories in Genesis support a Middle Bronze date for the patriarchs. Reexamination of the second-millennium parallels proposed by Albright, Speiser and others has shown that many cannot be restricted to a single, early period. The Nuzi parallel to Genesis 16:1–4, for example, in which the barren Sarai provides her husband with her bondwoman, is not unique: The responsibility of a barren wife to provide a slave woman to her husband to bear children is cited in Old Babylonian, Old Assyrian and Nuzi texts (all from the Middle Bronze Age), but also in a 12th-century Egyptian document and a marriage contract from Nimrud, dated 648 B.C.E.[28] As for the biblical "wife-sister motif," it now seems doubtful that relevant parallel material is to be found in the Nuzi archives. In the contracts cited by Speiser, the adopting "brother" is usually not the future husband of the adopted woman.[29] Although in one instance a "brother" does subsequently marry his "sister," this is a special case requiring a document of marriage to replace the earlier document of adoption. In the biblical stories, moreover, the designation of the wives of the patriarchs as sisters is a trick to protect the patriarchs from men who might lust after their wives, not a legal procedure intended to confer status. Speiser recognized this, suggesting that the "original" meaning was lost; but Speiser's assumption is highly questionable in view of the inapplicability or at least ambiguity of the Nuzi parallels.[30]

The search for the history of tradition

A second and very different attempt to trace the preliterary history of the patriarchal stories—undertaken at about the same time that Albright and the others were investigating the archaeological materials—is associated with the names of Martin Noth and his teacher Albrecht Alt. These two scholars sought to penetrate to an early stage in the patriarchal tradition through a critical analysis of the biblical literature itself.

On the basis of his study of the biblical materials pertaining to the premonarchical period, Noth was convinced that the larger entity of Israel had been formed by an amalgamation of various clans and tribes, a process that took place gradually during the period of settlement in Canaan.[31] From Noth's viewpoint, therefore, it seemed impossible that all of these clans and tribes could have known all of the traditions about the presettlement period—about the patriarchs, the captivity in Egypt and the Exodus, the wanderings in the wilderness, the revelation at Sinai and the conquest of Canaan. Instead, individual elements of these traditions must have been passed down within individual tribes or clans. As these groups were absorbed into the larger association of Israel, the various elements of tradition were combined and incorporated into a common heritage.

Drawing on the form-critical method devised by Hermann Gunkel,[32] Noth tried to reconstruct the history of discrete units of tradition from their origin within a particular tribe or clan to their integration into the larger story.[33] This method has been described as the "history of traditions."

A major clue to the origin of a particular element of a tradition is its connection with a region, place or other geographical feature. The narratives about the individual patriarchs have certain clear geographical connections. Abraham is generally associated with southern Canaan, and his principal residence is at the "oaks of Mamre" near Hebron (Genesis 13:18, 14:13, 18:1). Isaac dwells at the oases of Beersheba (Genesis 26:32–33) and Beer-lahai-roi (Genesis 24:62, 25:11). Jacob is most closely identified with Shechem (Genesis 33:18–19) and Bethel (Genesis 28:18–19, 35:1–8), though he also has important associations with the region of Gilead, east of the Jordan River (Genesis 31:43–50, 32:2–3, 32:30, 33:17). It therefore seemed likely to Noth that the traditions about Abraham came from the Judahite hills, those about Isaac from southwestern Judah and the Negev and those about Jacob from the central Ephraimite hills. Noting that the immediate ancestor of the Israelites, Jacob (whose name is also Israel), is linked with the heartland of the country, Noth concluded that the Jacob tradition was the oldest component of the patriarchal lore. As Israel expanded southward, absorbing Judah and the northern Negev, Abraham and Isaac entered the tradition and then were linked by genealogy with Jacob. The priority eventually assigned to Abraham (the first patriarch) is an indication of the southern development of the tradition as it has come down to us.

When did this blending of patriarchal traditions take place? That is, when were the stories about Abraham and Isaac combined with those about Jacob? It is obvious that this development was already completed during the time when the stories were being transmitted orally, that is, before the composition of the so-called J source,* the earliest of the literary strands in Genesis, in which Abraham, Isaac and Jacob are represented as members of the same family. The dates biblical scholars assign to J differ widely, however, ranging from the tenth to the sixth century B.C.E. A better clue to the date when the northern and southern patriarchal traditions were combined, therefore, is the priority that was assigned the southern patriarchs when the combination took place. The fact that a southern patriarch (Abraham) was regarded as the eldest suggests that the combination occurred at a time when Judah was in ascendancy over Israel. Such a political situation cannot have existed, however, before the establishment of the Davidic monarchy. Indeed, it is unlikely that Judah was incorporated into Israel before the reign of David.[34]

---

*According to the documentary hypothesis, the Pentateuch is an amalgam of at least four strands or sources: the J source (the Yahwist); the E source (the Elohist); the P source (Priestly material) and the D source (Deuteronomistic material). J and E were combined before the introduction of D and P. Many scholars now doubt that E had an independent existence apart from J.

And even if Judah was a part of Israel when David came to the throne, it had not been so for long, since the earliest tribal list makes no mention of the southern tribes (see Judges 5:14–18).

It is not likely, therefore, that patriarchal figures from the newly incorporated regions of Hebron and Beersheba, in the south, would have been accorded priority over the old Israelite patriarch Jacob before the radical realignment of power that took place when David the Judahite became king of Israel. The combination of traditions preserved in the patriarchal stories cannot have been complete before the end of the 11th century B.C.E. We must not forget, however, that this combination was one of the last phases of a lengthy and complex development that must have gone on for centuries. Noth believed that the development of the tradition was coeval with the development of Israel itself. That is, the process that shaped the patriarchal tradition was concurrent with the long series of clan and tribal alliances by which Israel grew from the earliest group that bore the name to a larger tribal association and, finally, to a kingdom.

Although Noth believed that the history of traditions allows us to trace the preliterary development of the traditions about the patriarchs, it provides only very indirect information about the patriarchs themselves. Noth did not deny that the patriarchs may have actually lived, but he believed that even if they did, they were now inaccessible as historical figures. Because the patriarchal traditions as we know them are products of the settlement period, he argued, they may not be relied upon to preserve authentic historical information about the patriarchal period itself.[35]

Another scholarly failure

Noth assumed that the patriarchal tradition grew from small, originally independent literary units into its present complex pattern. In this assumption he followed Gunkel, who believed that folk literature evolved from short, simple units into extended, discursive complexes. Thus, for Noth, a story with a complex structure was necessarily late, whereas a simple narrative unit was likely to be early. Subsequent improvement in our understanding of oral literatures, however, has exposed the error of this view.[36] We now know that in the preliterary, oral stage of transmission, long stories with complex structures were routine in most traditional literatures. Homer, for example, was almost certainly an oral poet; the Ugaritic myths and epics,* if they are

---

*See Edward Greenstein, "Texts from Ugarit Solve Biblical Puzzles," *BAR*, forthcoming. Ugarit was the name of a city on the northern coast of Syria that flourished in the 14th and 13th centuries B.C.E. A large cuneiform archive has been found at the site, modern Ras Shamra.

not actual transcriptions of oral performances, stand very close to the stage of oral composition. Both the Homeric and Ugaritic literatures are characterized by extended narratives with complex structures.

Recent analysis of the patriarchal tradition itself shows that Noth's account of its evolution from isolated units to interconnected patterns requires revision. As we noted at the outset of our discussion, the story of the biblical patriarchs is a family story. The traditional complex that underlies the narratives of Genesis expresses, among other things, an elaborate account of kinship relationships that existed (or were believed to exist) between the ancestors of Israel and their neighbors. Modern anthropological research has shown that kinship patterns are very often the central factors in the social structure and self-definition of a community. In other words, the final constellation of stories is not just a magpie's nest of individual brief stories contributed by various clans and tribes, but has its own coherence as a complex genealogical narrative through which Israel defined herself and her relationships with her neighbors.[37]

Did this genealogical pattern influence the evolution of the stories in Israelite oral traditions? To be sure, these stories are not mere "etiologies" of ethnic relationships, as some have maintained. The conflicts and personal relationships in the stories are so closely tied to the genealogical relationships that the two aspects—genealogy and story—were very likely intertwined in the oral traditions. Analogies from Arabic, Greek and other traditional literatures show this is to be expected in stories about a culture's ancestors. Therefore, it is reasonable to suggest that the genealogical structure of the stories is a feature not only of the final literary form, but also of the preliterary development of the stories.

If there is such an organizational structure inherent in the genealogical framework of the stories (though genealogies, too, are changeable over time), and if the length or complexity of a story has no intrinsic bearing on its date of origins, then the chief pillars of Noth's history-of-traditions method fall to the ground. This is not to say that all of Noth's conclusions are invalid, but a more adequate method would be needed to substantiate any of them.[38]

A kernel of history

In contrast to the confident scholars of an earlier generation, today's historians of ancient Israel approach the prehistory of Israel with extreme caution. Most remain convinced that the stories about Abraham, Isaac and Jacob contain a kernel of authentic history. Recognizing the complexity of the oral and literary development of the narratives in Genesis 12–50, however, they are reluctant to designate individual features as historically authentic. The best hope for success probably lies in the selective application of the methods used in the past (archaeology, philology and tradition history), supplemented or modified according to the results of more recent research, including studies using the methods of sociology and anthropology.

In this effort, we must always be aware that the patriarchal narratives are ideology, not history. They were cast into literary form in the first millennium B.C.E. by authors with varying political, theological and literary motivations. They cannot be approached as historiography in anything like the modern sense. If we tried to do so, we would not only arrive at a spurious prehistory of Israel but would also overlook the authentic information the patriarchal narratives do provide.

It does not follow from this that Genesis 12–50 has no value for the reconstruction of the prehistory of Israel. It is safe to assume that the Israelites, like almost all other peoples, had traditions about their own past, and it seems likely that the biblical writers were drawing upon and interpreting these traditions.

Is it possible to separate the older from the more recent traditions in the current form of the literary compositions? We saw that Noth's approach was flawed, but, by heeding a principle stressed by Hermann Gunkel, we may be able to gain some reliable insights into the history of tradition.

In one of his early works, Gunkel formulated a still-viable rule for identifying old traditions:

> Certain features, which once had a clear meaning in their earlier context, have been so transmitted in their newer setting as to have lost their meaningful context. Such ancient features, fragments of an earlier whole, are thus left without context in their newer setting and so appear hardly intelligible in the thought-world of the narrator. Such features betray to the investigator the existence of an earlier narrative.[39]

A feature in a narrative that is anomalous in its present literary context, but which is intelligible in an earlier context, may be a relic of an earlier stage of the tradition. This principle is clearly illustrated by such anomalous stories in Genesis as the account of the sexual escapades of the Sons of God and the daughters of men in Genesis 6:1–4, where the brevity and obscurity of the story points to a fuller context in the preliterary oral tradition, perhaps even in pre-Israelite Canaanite tradition where the Sons of God (literally Sons or Children of El, the high god of the Canaanite pantheon) are prominent figures.[*40]

*Ronald S. Hendel, "When the Sons of God Cavorted with the Daughters of Men," BR, Spring 1987.

By such means we are able to probe the preliterary traditions of the stories and discern aspects of their history that might otherwise be unnoticed. But to detect features that belong to an earlier historical context, we must first determine the historical context of the final form of the stories.

The patriarchal history as self-understanding

The story of the patriarchs in its final form reflects the self-understanding of the community at the end of the period of settlement, about 1000 B.C.E. (A few details suggest that the stories were first written down some generations later, perhaps in the ninth or eighth century B.C.E.)[41] Israel is represented as a 12-tribe entity with the southern tribes, and notably Judah, in full membership, something that probably did not occur until David's time. This scheme reflects considerable southern development: The eldest patriarch (Abraham) is especially associated with Hebron, the traditional capital of the Judean hill country in the southern part of the country; the second patriarch (Isaac) is at home even farther south, in the northern Negev. The patriarchal stories are not likely to have existed in this form before the institution of the Davidic monarchy in about 1000 B.C.E.[42] The priority of Abraham as the eldest patriarch suggests the intertribal relationship that existed during the reigns of David and Solomon and, in any case, reflects a Judahite point of view.

To a limited extent, the evolution of the tradition can be reconstructed from biblical and extrabiblical evidence. The 12 sons of Israel who appear in the current form of the stories about Jacob and Joseph reflect the tribal roster as it stood at the end of the process. A somewhat different list is preserved in Judges 5:14–18, part of an ancient poem describing the victory of the Israelite tribes over a Canaanite foe: Here there is no mention of the southern tribes, Judah and Simeon, suggesting that southern Canaan had not yet been incorporated into Israel. Moreover, Manasseh and Gad are also missing in this old poem, while two tribes are cited that do not appear in the later list, namely, Machir (Judges 5:14) and Gilead (Judges 5:17).[43] This list in Judges 5 provides us with a glimpse of the tribal association as it stood about the middle of the 12th century, say 1150 B.C.E.[44] Moreover, we know that a group named Israel already existed, at least in rudimentary form, by about 1207 B.C.E., when the Egyptian king Merneptah boasted, on an inscribed stela, of having defeated a people named "Israel."*[45]

It follows that tribal Israel existed in the central hills before 1150 B.C.E.

*See "The Merneptah Stela: Israel Enters History," sidebar to "Face to Face: Biblical Minimalists Meet Their Challengers," *BAR*, July/August 1997.

and probably as early as 1207 B.C.E. Though this community may have been newly formed, it already had a sense of ethnic identity: Its members were Israelite or "Hebrew" and not something else.[46] This identity found expression in and, at the same time, derived its authority from the ancestral tradition preserved in the patriarchal narratives of the Bible.

The insistence upon ethnic separateness is one of the most conspicuous features of this tradition. The stories uniformly assert that the ancestors of Israel were foreigners, not natives of Canaan. They came from "beyond the River," that is, beyond the Euphrates (see Joshua 24:2–3), in the region we call Mesopotamia (modern Iraq and eastern Syria). Whatever the ultimate origin of the term "Hebrews," this was the meaning it came to have in the tradition: The 'Ibrîm, "Hebrews," were those who came from 'ēber, "beyond," the Euphrates.

As explained in Chapter III, "The Settlement in Canaan: The Period of the Judges," the early Israelites were probably of diverse origin, and many seem to have been indigenous to Canaan. The strong insistence in the patriarchal narratives that the ancestors of Israel were *not* Canaanites is a reflection of the process of ethnic boundary-marking by which the early Israelite community was defined and by which its identity was subsequently maintained. This kind of boundary-marking is well known to modern students of the social phenomenon of ethnicity.[47] In this case, it probably derives from the early conflict between the hill-dwelling people from whom Israel emerged and the population of the Canaanite cities of the plains and valleys controlled by Egypt in the Late Bronze Age.*[48] Through the tradition of Mesopotamian origin, as well as through the biblical genealogical materials, the Israelites acknowledge ethnic solidarity with the peoples of the East, the Transjordanians and the Arameans, but deny any link with the peoples of the Egypto-Canaanite West.**

The basic genealogical structure of the patriarchal tradition, therefore, emerged at the end of the Late Bronze Age, contemporary with the early formation of Israel. This conclusion, however, pertains only to the patriarchal tradition, not to the patriarchs themselves. We must now attempt to discover the extent to which the tradition was based on historical people and events.

This is a difficult task. As we have seen, the structure of the tradition came into existence at the same time as the community itself. A careful

*Avraham Faust, "How Did Israel Become a People," BAR, November/December 2009.
**For a similar argument concerning Israel's origins east of the Jordan River, see Anson Rainey, "Inside, Outside: Where Did the Early Israelites Come From?" BAR, November/December 2008.

investigation of this structure and its purposes might help us understand the circumstances under which the community first coalesced in central Canaan, but this structure cannot be expected to shed light on an earlier period.

If we accept the genealogical self-understanding of the stories as stemming from the period of Israel's emergence as a nation (c. 1200–1000 B.C.E.), then, following the principle enunciated by Gunkel, we may ask whether any features that are anomalous in their current setting might be more intelligible in an earlier cultural or historical context. This is the most reliable procedure for detecting traces of the preliterary history of the tradition.

Personal names and geographical references provide clues

In the patriarchal narratives, the personal names and geographical references provide the best clues for tracing historical memories. Two bodies of evidence provide the strongest indications for the roots of the tradition in pre- and early Israelite times, perhaps reaching back to the mid-second millennium B.C.E. These are (1) the divine elements in the patriarchal names and (2) the location of the patriarchal homeland in the Middle Euphrates region of Syro-Mesopotamia.*[49]

In his groundbreaking essay of 1929, "The God of the Fathers," Albrecht Alt observed that the name Yahweh does not appear as part of patriarchal and tribal names. This indicates that the origins of the patriarchal tradition lie in early or pre-Israelite traditions. Two of the literary sources of the Pentateuch, E (the Elohist source) and P (the Priestly Code), explicitly date the revelation of the name Yahweh to the time of Moses (E in Exodus 3, and P in Exodus 6). As Alt observed:

> The well-known restriction of the name of Yahweh to the period from Moses on, in the Elohist and Priestly treatment of the sagas, can hardly be explained as simply the result of later theories about Israel's prehistory without any basis in the tradition, although there is no doubt that it was quite consciously seized on by the authors of these narratives in order to mark off different eras in the past ... The names of the tribes and their forefathers do not give a single reliable indication of [Yahweh's] existence.[50]

By these arguments, Alt traces the origin of the pattern of divine names to early Israelite tradition, prior to the time of the Pentateuchal writers.

*Ronald S. Hendel, "Finding Historical Memories in the Patriarchal Narratives," *BAR*, July/ August 1995. Personal and tribal names often incorporated elements of divine names, called theophoric elements, as in *Yeho*-shua (which includes a divine element based on Yahweh) and Isra-*el*.

These arguments can be made even stronger, however. If we consider the position of the J source in this pattern, we find a systematic anomaly. After the creation story, J consistently refers to the Israelite deity as "Yahweh." (Alt plausibly explains the J [Yahwist] source's departure from this pattern as a function of J's universalistic theology reflected in the creation story.) But the personal names in the patriarchal narratives in J (as elsewhere) retain the divine element -el (as in the names Ishmael, Israel and Bethuel) rather than the divine element based on Yahweh. Not until the era of Moses do personal names contain the divine element derived from Yahweh (as in Joshua [Yehoshua] and Jochebed [Yochebed], Moses' mother). How then are we to explain the absence of Yahweh as a divine element and the presence instead of -el in the patriarchal names? As noted, E and P explicitly state that the name Yahweh was not known to the patriarchs. We would therefore not be surprised to find -el names in the patriarchal narratives in E and P. But these -el names also show up in J despite J's overt use of only the name Yahweh to designate the Israelite God from the beginning of his patriarchal narrative. This is a clear indication that on one level J is drawing on the same traditions as E and P, even though J is trying on another level to reject that tradition. Despite J's use of the name Yahweh to designate the Israelite God, the personal names in J nevertheless preserve a tradition that the patriarchal God was not Yahweh, but El. Although J would have it otherwise, the God of the (patriarchal) fathers is El, as revealed by the divine element in the names in J's patriarchal narratives. According to Gunkel's principle, "Such features betray to the investigator the existence of an earlier narrative." Here we detect a clear trace of the history of the tradition in which the patriarchs worshiped El.

Is there an earlier historical or cultural context within which this preservation of an El tradition is intelligible? Canaanite religious texts from ancient Ugarit, dated to about 1400 B.C.E., tell us that the high god of the Canaanite pantheon was indeed named El.[51] Moreover, Frank Moore Cross has demonstrated that several of the titles of the deity named El in the patriarchal narratives (such as El-Shaddai, God of the [Sacred] Mountain) have close parallels in the titles and descriptions of Canaanite El.[52] We may conclude that the use of divine names in the patriarchal narratives preserves an early tradition of the patriarchal worship of the god El. This tradition, understood by the biblical writers as describing pre-Mosaic times, finds its intelligible context in the culture of Canaan in the second millennium B.C.E. and in Israel (note the name El in Isra-el) of the premonarchic period.[53] In other words, the presence of El and the absence of Yahweh in the patriarchal names preserve memories of pre- and early Israelite times of the second millennium B.C.E.

A second body of evidence, the geographical references to the patriarchal homeland in the region of Haran, corroborates the evidence of personal names and points us to the mid-second millennium B.C.E. The Amorite hypothesis advanced by Albright and others has been justly criticized and generally abandoned (see above). But amid the wreckage of this hypothesis, some features remain that require us to consider an early date. The region of Haran in the Middle Euphrates region of Syro-Mesopotamia was the home of the Arameans, not the Amorites, from the 12th century B.C.E. onwards. If the region of Haran is where the patriarchs go to live with—and marry— their kin (Genesis 24 and 29), then for Iron Age Israelites this designates the patriarchs as Aramean. Hence the prayer in Deuteronomy 26:5: "My father was a wandering (or perishing) Aramean," referring to the patriarchal homeland. The problem with this tradition is that it clashes with the cultural context of the first millennium B.C.E.; from the time of David, the Arameans were enemies of Israel. No group would trace its ancestral homeland to the home of its enemies unless the tradition was so well established that it had no choice but to do so.

Following Gunkel's principle, we should look for a historical context within which this anomalous tradition is intelligible. For this we must look to the period prior to the 12th century B.C.E., back when the region of Haran was the homeland of a rural people we call the Amorites.[54] The Amorites of this period were pastoralists and agriculturalists living in a tribal society. They spoke an early Northwest Semitic dialect (or dialects). What we know of their lifestyle and religion is comparable to the picture of the patriarchs in Genesis.[55] The divine name El is found commonly in Amorite personal names, and in Akkadian texts this god is referred to as "El Amurru," El of the Amorites.[56] Thus the tradition of the patriarchal homeland in the region of Haran is intelligible in the context of Amorite culture in the Middle and Late Bronze Ages, but its Aramean context would be exceedingly strange in the Iron Age (the time when the narrative was written). The first-millennium identification of the patriarchs with the hated Arameans makes sense only as a revision (according to the then-current ethnic map) of a much older tradition.[57]

Neither of these arguments constitutes definitive proof that the patriarchal traditions stem from Canaanite or Amorite culture of the mid- to late second millennium B.C.E. But our application of Gunkel's principle suggests that this derivation is plausible. These traces of the history of the patriarchal traditions point to earlier oral narratives in Israel and pre-Israelite Canaan that told of the ancestors' migration from the Amorite homeland in Syro-Mesopotamia to Canaan, and their devotion to the ancestral god El.

This historical reconstruction has several intriguing implications. It indicates that some early Israelites indeed traced their ancestry to Syro-Mesopotamia and felt an ethnic kinship to that region. It also means that a strong substratum of El-worship merged with or transformed itself into the worship of Yahweh. El was worshiped in the Amorite region of Syro-Mesopotamia as well as in the Canaanite region farther west. The spread of El-worship was probably a contributing factor in the formation of a common Israelite identity among the diverse groups in the hill country during Iron Age I (1200–1000 B.C.E.). The equivalence between El and Yahweh was perhaps made by another group, the Moses-group who recounted their momentous escape from Egypt via Midian (see Chapter II, "Israel in Egypt: The Egyptian Sojourn and the Exodus"). The merging of El and Yahweh in the religion of Israel corresponds to the merging of different groups in early Israel—some with stories of Syro-Mesopotamian origins, and some with memories of slavery in Egypt and Yahweh's revelation at Mount Sinai. Somehow—and the details elude us—these different groups coalesced into a single ethnic identity, and the stories coalesced into the complex epic traditions that join together Syro-Mesopotamia, Egypt and Sinai, with all paths leading to the Promised Land.

Are the patriarchs genealogical fictions?

The invention of ancestors is a common way of establishing the kinship bonds that are necessary for the cohesion of a community. The practice is known among modern Bedouin, and it is well attested in antiquity. The "Amorite" dynasties of Hammurabi of Babylon and Shamshi-Adad I of Assyria shared a common tradition about their tribal origins, and many of the names of their early ancestors are also known as names of West Semitic tribes.[58]

Similar fictitious heroes are frequently encountered in biblical genealogies, and often their origins can be traced. Jerahmeel, for example, was the name of a non-Israelite tribe living somewhere in the Negev in the time of David (1 Samuel 27:10, 30:29). In the course of time, however, the Jerahmeelites were incorporated into Judah, and the new relationship was expressed genealogically by the identification of Jerahmeel as a great-grandson of Judah in a line collateral to that of David (1 Chronicles 2:9,25–27).

There is no question that the patriarchal genealogies contain the names of many individuals who originated as fictitious eponyms.* Moab and Ben-ammi, the sons of Lot and ancestors of the Moabites and Ammonites (Genesis 19:37–38), are obvious examples, as is Shechem son of Hamor, the prince of the city of Shechem (Genesis 34:2). Sometimes these figures play prominent roles in the story, as in the case of Ishmael, the ancestor of the Ishmaelites

---

*To repeat, an eponym is a person, real or imaginary, from whom the name of a later group is derived or is supposed to be derived.

(see Genesis 16:10–12, 17:20, 25:12–16). The Edomite genealogy recorded in Genesis 36 contains a mixture of personal and tribal or clan names. Esau's (Edom's) eldest son, for example, bears the name "Eliphaz," which has the form of a personal name. Eliphaz was probably a hero of the past rather than an eponym (see Job 2:11), but his sons' names (Genesis 36:11–12) include eponyms of well-known tribes or places, including Teman, the home of the Eliphaz of the Book of Job. This, then, is what we expect from the early genealogies: a few names of traditional heroes sprinkled among a preponderance of eponymic names derived from clans, tribes, places or regions.

Abraham

Abraham seems to belong in the former category. His name (in contrast to those of Isaac, Jacob, Israel and Joseph) appears only as a personal name in the Bible, never as a tribal or local designation. Thus it seems fairly certain that he was not an eponymous ancestor. He may have been a historical individual before he became a figure of tradition and legend. If so, however, it seems impossible to determine the period in which he lived. "Abram," at least in the form "Abiram," is a very common type of name, known in all periods. It is especially well attested in the Late Bronze Age (1550–1200 B.C.E.),[59] though this may be no more than a coincidence. The variants "Abram" and "Abraham" arose in different languages and dialects.[60]

Nor can we determine whether any of the biblical stories told about Abraham has a historical basis. The claim that Abraham came to Canaan from Mesopotamia is not historically implausible. Such a journey could have taken place in more than one historical period. As we have seen, however, the insistence that the Israelites were not Canaanite in origin was so pervasive that the belief that the first patriarch came from a foreign land could have arisen as part of the ethnic boundary-marking that characterized the development of the tradition. Still, the connections between the family of Abraham and the city of Haran in northern Mesopotamia (Eski Harran or "Old Haran" in modern Turkey) are very precise in our earliest narrative source (J, or the Yahwist). Terah, Nahor and Serug—Abraham's father, grandfather and great-grandfather (Genesis 11:22–26)—seem to be the eponymous ancestors of towns in the basin of the Balikh River, near Haran. All three names appear in Assyrian texts from the first half of the first millennium B.C.E. as the names of towns or ruined towns in the region of Haran, namely, Til-(sha)-Turakhi (the ruin of Turakh), Til-Nakhiri (the ruin of Nakhir) and Sarugi. Earlier, in the second millennium B.C.E., Til-Nakhiri had been an important administrative center, called Nakhuru. The patriarchal connection with this region may be rooted in historical memories of Amorite culture of the second millennium B.C.E.

Abraham is represented as the founder of religious sites in the regions of Shechem (Genesis 12:7), Bethel/Ai (Genesis 12:8, see also 13:4), Hebron (Genesis 13:18), Mount Moriah (Genesis 22:2) and Beersheba (Genesis 21:33). As Benjamin Mazar has noted, all these sites lie within the boundaries of early Israelite settlement in Iron Age I (1200–1000 B.C.E.).[61] These stories present Abraham as the founder of major cultic sites both in Manasseh-Ephraim and in Judah, the dominant tribes of the north and south. Here we see Abraham functioning as the founder of a common social and religious identity, uniting northern and southern tribes.*

The earliest reference to Abraham may be the name of a town in the Negev listed in a victory inscription of Pharaoh Shishak I (biblical Sheshonk). The campaign occurred in about 925 B.C.E. during the reign of Rehoboam (1 Kings 14:25–26; 2 Chronicles 12:2–12). A place-name in the Negev section of the inscription is *pa' ḥa-q-ru-'a 'i-bi-ra-ma*, which is best read "the fortification of Abram" or, more simply, "Fort Abram."[62] The location and chronological context of this site make it plausible that the Abram after whom the site was named was the Abram of biblical tradition. Although we cannot be certain of this identification, the place name probably indicates the presence and importance of the Abram/Abraham tradition in the tenth century B.C.E.

Isaac

The biblical Isaac has clear geographical associations with the northern Negev, and particularly the oases of Beersheba and Beer-lahai-roi (Genesis 24:62, 25:11, 26:32–33). The archaeological record indicates that this area was not settled before the end of the Late Bronze Age. Expansion into the Negev from the north began no earlier than the latter part of the 13th century B.C.E. Archaeological excavations at Beersheba have shown that a deep well associated with the sanctuary was dug at about this time.**[63] Apparently, this is the well mentioned in Genesis 21:25 and 26:25. The settlement of the Negev spread southward and was complete by the 11th century.[64] This shows that the attachment of the patriarchal tradition to the Beersheba region cannot have preceded the 12th century and, in fact, may have occurred later as a part of the southern development of the tradition

---

*Amos's references to Beersheba (in the south) as a pilgrimage shrine for northerners (Amos 5:5, 8:14) is consistent with the connection between Abraham and Beersheba in the E source, and must derive from some prior northern religious association with Beersheba. In the J source, Abraham's southerly home is Hebron, not Beersheba (which is founded by Isaac in J), an address that points to Hebron's importance in Judah in the Davidic period (2 Samuel 5:1–5, 15:7–10).

**Ze'ev Herzog, "Beer-sheba of the Patriarchs," *BAR*, November/December 1980.

in the time of David and Solomon.

As we have noted, "Isaac" is structurally suitable as a personal, tribal or geographical name. We might expect the meaning of the name to indicate which of these possibilities is most likely. Though it is unattested outside the Bible, we assume that "Isaac" is a shortened form of a name like "Isaac-El," which may mean "May [the god] El smile," that is, "May El look favorably upon."[65] If this is correct,* the name then seems equally acceptable as the designation of an individual, group or place. In referring to the northern kingdom in the eighth century, moreover, Amos twice uses the name Isaac as parallel to Israel (Amos 7:9, 16). This usage must reflect a recollection of the name Isaac as a designation for the northern tribal region.[66] In this light, it is intriguing to note that J depicts Isaac as the founder of the religious site at Beersheba (Genesis 26:23, 25), a southern shrine to which northerners made pilgrimage (Amos 5:5, 8:14).

Jacob

According to Genesis, the events of Jacob's birth and childhood take place at Beersheba, Isaac's home; but after returning from Haran, Jacob lives in the region of Shechem in the central hill country. He is the founder of the religious site of Bethel (Genesis 28:10–22, 35:1–15), and like Abraham he builds an altar at Shechem (Genesis 33:18–20). Both sites are in the north. It is not surprising that Jacob dwells in the central hill country, since at this point Jacob *is* Israel. The historical association of Israel with the central hills was strong, as its persistence during the time of David and beyond shows. In contrast to Abraham and Isaac, therefore, Jacob was never thought of in close association with the southern part of the country.

It is generally agreed that the biblical name "Jacob" is a shortened form of "Jacob-El" or something very similar. An early form of "Jacob," constructed with "El" or another divine name, was a common West Semitic personal name of the Middle Bronze Age and the Hyksos period, when Egypt was ruled by Asiatic princes (c. 1675–1552 B.C.E.).[67] It is also attested at Ugarit (in Syria) in the Late Bronze Age. But it does not appear again (outside of the biblical patriarchal narratives) until the Persian period. "Jacob-El," however, was also a Late Bronze Age place-name. It occurs in lists of enemies conquered by Tuthmosis III (c. 1479–1425 B.C.E.) and other kings of Egypt.[68] Most of the identifiable names in these documents refer to cities, though some designate districts and even tribal groups. Because of the loose organization of the lists, the precise location of Jacob-El cannot be determined. It is clear, however, that

---

*Our uncertainty about this meaning arises from the fact that the verbal element does not have quite this sense elsewhere; it ordinarily means "laugh, laugh at, sport, jest."

HERSHEL SHANKS

Beersheba well. *According to Genesis 26:18–25, "Isaac dug again the wells of water that had been dug in the days of his father Abraham; for the Philistines had stopped them up after the death of Abraham ... [Isaac] went up to Beersheba ... [and] Isaac's servants dug a well." Dated by the excavator to the 13th century B.C.E., this 100-foot-deep shaft at Beersheba may be the well the author of this passage had in mind.*

it was in central Canaan,[69] most probably in the general vicinity of Rehov and Beth-Shean, both of which lay north of Shechem.[70] In view of the proximity of both time and place, therefore, it does not seem reckless to conclude that the Jacob-El conquered by Tuthmosis had something to do with the biblical Jacob tradition.

We must ask, then, which had priority, the patriarch Jacob or the place Jacob-El. The name probably means "Let El protect,"* and this seems equally suitable as the name of a person or a place. It is possible that there was an early hero called Jacob-El who gave his name to the town or district mentioned in the Egyptian lists.[71]

Archaeologist Aharon Kempinski suggested, on the basis of a scarab of Jacob-Har found in a tomb at Shiqmona, Israel, dating to the 18th century B.C.E., that the later Hyksos king of Egypt named Jacob-Har may be the

---

*The verb is known with this meaning in Ethiopic and Old South Arabic but not in biblical Hebrew.

descendant of a local Palestinian king of the same name. This local ruler may be the Jacob for whom the place was named.[*72] Although this argument is speculative, it offers an intriguing possibility for the origin of the Jacob tradition in the central hills of Palestine in the second millennium B.C.E.

In the Bible, Jacob has two names. According to the earliest written account, Jacob was given the name Israel after wrestling with a divine being on the bank of the Jabbok River (Genesis 32:28–29).[**] In the latter part of Genesis, the two names Jacob and Israel are used more or less interchangeably. Modern biblical scholars have explained this in a variety of ways. Noth concluded that Israel, the collective name of the tribes, was assigned to the patriarch Jacob at a fairly late point in the development of the tradition.[73] On the other hand, the elaborate genealogical structure of the tradition was itself an early feature; the purpose of this structure was to give a social definition to Israel. Jacob, the eponym of the people or district of Jacob-El, was the key figure in the genealogical scheme. It is very likely, then, that he was identified as Israel, the eponym of the newly emerging community, when the kinship tradition was devised at the time of the formation of the tribal alliance.

This is not to suggest that the name "Israel" was invented at this time. Several scholars have attempted to identify a distinctive group of traditions around a patriarch Israel, whom they would distinguish from Jacob,[74] and it is possible that there was some kind of early tribal group in the central hills called Israel.[75] In fact, however, our sources give us no hint of the use of the name in Canaan before the time of Merneptah (c. 1207 B.C.E.), which, as we have seen, must have been very close to the time of the formation of the community itself. Since we know that the population of the hill country was growing steadily at this time,[76] we must also consider the possibility that the name "Israel" was brought into the region by one of the arriving peoples.

Finally, Jacob's relationship with Esau may predate the identification of the two brothers with Israel and Edom in the genealogical structure. As Gunkel noted, Esau's name and personality have little to do with Edom, which had a reputation for wisdom in biblical tradition.[77] Gunkel associated the conflict of the two brothers with a cultural memory of the ascent of herders over hunters in Palestinian history, which Noth localized to the history of Gilead.[78] It is doubtful, however, that a socioeconomic history of the region can be derived from the rivalry between the two brothers. The relationship is more adequately characterized as a conflict between civilization and nature. Note the consistent series of contrasts between Jacob and Esau in Genesis

*Aharon Kempinski, "Jacob in History," *BAR*, January/February 1988.
**According to the later account in Genesis 35:6–10, the renaming took place at Bethel.

25 and 27: man of the tents (civilized habitat) vs. man of the steppe (wild habitat); cooking (characteristic of human culture) vs. hunting (common to humans and predatory animals); cunning intelligence vs. stupidity; smooth skin vs. hairy skin; domestic animals (as meal and disguise) vs. wild game; and, finally, the culmination in blessing and political dominance vs. curse and subjection. (Compare the way Gilgamesh and Enkidu are contrasted in the Mesopotamian Gilgamesh epic.)[79] The fraternal relationship, therefore, falls into the category of ethnic boundary-making, as one's own ancestor is identified with civilization in contrast to another's ancestor, who is wild and uncivilized (compare the characterization of Ishmael, as opposed to Isaac, in Genesis 16:12 and 21:20, and the parentage of Ammon and Moab in Genesis 19). In other words, the relationship between Jacob and Esau is best comprehended as an expression of cultural and ethnic self-definition. This feature may predate the identification of the two with Israel and Edom, but it continues to function in this identification.

Joseph

Turning finally to the sons of Israel, we begin by recalling that the name "Joseph" belongs in the category of "Isaac," "Jacob" and "Israel," as noted earlier. We assume that it is a shorter form of "Joseph-El," which means "May El increase," and this too seems equally suitable as a personal, tribal or geographical designation.* Thus it is possible that Joseph was a hero of the past or the fictitious eponym of a group or district. The latter possibility is suggested by the use of "the house of Joseph" as a collective designation for the northern tribes in the literature of the early monarchy (2 Samuel 19:21) and elsewhere. A strong case can be made, however, that this expression was coined after the unification of Judah and Israel as a term parallel to "the house of Judah."[80] References to a tribe of Joseph, moreover, are rare and appear only in late materials (Numbers 13:11, 36:5). It thus seems more likely that "Joseph" was a personal name belonging to a local hero of the past.[81] During the period of the formation of the Israelite community, Joseph was identified as a son of Jacob and the father of the tribal eponyms Ephraim and Manasseh.

The special prominence of Joseph in the biblical narrative must be, at least in part, a reflection of the eminence of "the house of Joseph" at the end of the settlement period (about 1000 B.C.E.) and the continuing historical importance of the Manasseh-Ephraim region. Scholars believe that the long story about Joseph and his family in Genesis 37 and 39–47 originated

*That is, it might be a wish for another child (see Genesis 30:24) or for the increased fertility or prosperity of a tribe or town.

independently of the other patriarchal narratives. This story depicts Joseph as preeminent among his brothers and as the favorite of his father, Jacob (Israel). The story was probably passed down orally among the inhabitants of the region around Shechem and Dothan (see Genesis 37:12 and 37:17), in the heart of the traditional territory of Ephraim and Manasseh, the two "half-tribes" of Joseph's sons. In an early form, this story may have eulogized Joseph, the tribal patriarch, as a man who went to Egypt as a slave and rose to a position of authority in the Egyptian court.

Many scholars believe that the events described in the story of Joseph have an ultimate basis in historical fact. It has often been supposed, especially by those scholars who believe that Abraham, Isaac and Jacob lived in the Middle Bronze Age (about 2000–1550 B.C.E.), that Joseph lived during the so-called Hyksos period (c. 1675–1552), when Egypt was ruled by two dynasties of Asiatic princes. The scholars who hold this view argue that since Joseph was himself an Asiatic, he would have been most likely to find a favorable reception from an Asiatic king of Egypt. Moreover, the capital of Egypt during the Hyksos period was located in the eastern Delta, which is generally agreed to have been the site of the biblical "land of Goshen," where the family of Joseph settled (Genesis 45:10, 46:28–29, 47:1).[82]

But even if the general outline of the Joseph story is based on the life of a historical individual, it is unlikely that much of the information found in Genesis 37 and 39–47 is historically factual. The biblical Joseph story has more in common with a historical romance than a work of history. Its carefully planned story line is fashioned from narrative motifs that were widespread in the literature and folklore of the ancient Near East. The episode of Potiphar's wife, who accuses Joseph of attempted rape after she fails to seduce him (Genesis 39:6b–20), has numerous parallels in the literature of the ancient world,[83] including the popular "Tale of Two Brothers" of XIXth-Dynasty Egypt (13th century B.C.E.).[84] The motifs of dreams and dream interpretation are found in literature, folklore and myth throughout antiquity.[85] The convention of the seven lean years is known from Egyptian, Akkadian and Canaanite literature.[86]

Further, the author of the biblical Joseph story displays only a limited knowledge of the life and culture of Egypt.[87] Recalling the hot wind that blows across the Transjordanian plateau into Israel, he writes of the east wind scorching pharaoh's grain (Genesis 41:23,27), but in Egypt it is the south wind that blights crops.[88] The titles and offices the author assigns to various Egyptian officials have closer parallels in Syria and Canaan than in Egypt.[89]

There are a number of authentic Egyptian details in the Joseph story, but these details correspond to the Egyptian way of life in the author's own day, not in the Hyksos period. The king of Egypt is called "Pharaoh," an Egyptian phrase meaning "great house," which was not used as a title for the king before the reign of Tuthmosis III (c. 1479–1425 B.C.E.). In Genesis 47:11, the area in which the family of Joseph settles is called "the land of Rameses," a designation that could not have been used earlier than the reign of Ramesses II (c. 1279–1213 B.C.E.).*

Some of the personal names in the story are Egyptian. Joseph's wife is called Asenath (Genesis 41:45), which could correspond to one of several Egyptian names from the second and first millennia B.C.E.[90] The name of Asenath's father is Potiphera (Genesis 41:45), and this name has been found on an Egyptian stela dating to the XXIst Dynasty (c. 1069–945 B.C.E.) or later.[91] The name of Joseph's Egyptian master, Potiphar (Genesis 37:36), is probably a shorter form of the name Potiphera. Joseph's own Egyptian name, Zaphenath-paneah (Genesis 41:45), has no exact parallel in extant Egyptian records, but names with a similar structure are attested from the XXIst Dynasty and later.[92]

It is unlikely, therefore, that the Joseph story as we know it in the Bible was composed before the establishment of the United Kingdom (that is, before about 1000 B.C.E.). Many of the elements of the plot and most of the narrative details are fictional. It does not follow from this, however, that the tradition upon which the story is based is unhistorical. We cannot exclude the possibility that there was a historical Joseph who went to Egypt as a slave and rose to a position of power there.

Egyptian records from the Middle Kingdom to the Roman period cite numerous individuals of Syrian, Canaanite and nomadic origin who rose to high positions in the Egyptian government.[93] An especially interesting parallel to the story of Joseph is that of an Asiatic named Irsu, who seized power in Egypt during a period of hardship (probably famine) at the end of the XIXth Dynasty (c. 1200 B.C.E.).[94] Many Egyptologists believe that Irsu was another name for Bay, the powerful chancellor who ruled Egypt during the minority of the last king of the XIXth Dynasty and who may have come from Palestine.**[95]

Clearly, then, the biblical description of Joseph's career is historically plausible in its general outline. We might surmise that Joseph was the leader of a group of people from the vicinity of Shechem and Dothan who migrated

---

*It is possible, however, that "in the land of Rameses" in Genesis 47:11 is a scribe's gloss, intended to harmonize the account of the Israelites' entry into Egypt with the statement in Exodus 1:11 that locates the Israelites in "Pithom and Rameses."

**Another striking parallel may be the Semitic-named vizier Aper-El whose tomb was discovered at the ancient burial ground of Saqqara in Egypt.

to Egypt seeking pasturage during a time of drought in Canaan. Such groups are amply attested in Egyptian records. In a text from the reign of Merneptah (c. 1212–1202 B.C.E.), for example, a frontier official reports:

> [We] have finished letting the Bedouin tribes of Edom pass the Fortress [of] Mer-ne-Ptah ... which is (in) Tjeku* ... to the pools of Per-Atum** ... which are (in) Tjeku, to keep them alive and to keep their cattle alive.[96]

Alternatively, the people of the central hills may have preserved memories of Hyksos kings of local origin (perhaps even from the line of a local king named Jacob) and combined these memories with the tradition of the Exodus of slaves from Egypt. By this means the patriarchal stories may have been joined with those of the Exodus, yielding a coherent epic tradition, uniting all the tribes. Of course these are mere speculations about the history of the Joseph tradition. We have few clues from the narrative itself.

Jacob's other sons

The names of most of the other sons of Jacob (Israel) do not have the form of personal names. Several are geographical names. "Asher" was a name by which the Egyptians knew the coastal region north of Carmel in the Late Bronze Age.[97] "Judah," "Ephraim"[†] and "Naphtali" seem first to have been the names of ranges of hills (see Joshua 20:7); the people who inhabited the hill country of Judah were called běnê yěhûdâ, "the children of Judah," or "Judahites"; and so on.[98] The name "Benjamin" probably arose from the location of the tribe's territory; it lay to the south of the other (northern) tribes, so that the people were called běnê yāmîn "the children of the south," or "Benjaminites."[99]

On the other hand, the names of a few of the sons of Jacob (Israel) do take the form of personal names. "Simeon" and "Manasseh," for example, are most easily understood in this way,[100] and the corresponding tribes may have been named after tribal heroes or even patriarchs. In the genealogical structure, the 12 sons of Israel are eponyms of the 12 tribes of Israel, created in the course of the evolution of the Israelite tradition during the period of settlement. The process of community formation, which began in about 1200 B.C.E., at the end of the Late Bronze Age, presupposes the existence of the tribes with established names. The origin of the various tribal names—whether derived

---

*"Tjeku" is the Egyptian name for the land called Goshen in the Bible.
**Per-Atum is biblical Pithom (Exodus 1:11).
[†] Ephraim and Manasseh were sons of Joseph and grandsons of Jacob (Israel). According to Genesis 48:5, however, they were adopted by their grandfather.

from geographical associations, ancestral traditions or something else—was already in the remote past. When the tribes were joined together into the larger entity of Israel, their kinship was expressed in terms of brotherhood; and a group of 12 sons, the eponyms of the 12 tribes, was assigned to the patriarch Jacob (Israel).

It follows from all this that the setting of the prehistory of the Israelite community was the central hill country, between the valley of Aijalon and the Beth-Shean corridor, in the Late Bronze Age. This region was very sparsely populated before 1200 B.C.E.,[101] suggesting that the people among whom the Israelite tradition germinated were pastoralists, as the patriarchal stories would lead us to expect. They venerated a local hero called Abram or Abraham, who was probably already regarded as a patriarchal figure; that is, he was identified as the ancestor of one or more of the groups in the region. Jacob and Isaac may also have been revered as ancestors in local tribal lore.

These proto-Israelites were hill people and shepherds, and they must have seen themselves as distinct from the peoples of the cities, which, in this period, were situated on the coastal plain and in the major valleys.[102] This was the period of Egypt in Canaan, but the remoteness of the highlands from the population centers and the major trading routes sheltered Israel's forerunners from the full influence of Egypt. These circumstances were favorable to the creation of a national community larger than the city-states of the Bronze Age,[103] a development that needed only an increase in population to make it possible. This requirement was fulfilled at the end of the Late Bronze Age when new peoples penetrated into the forests of the Ephraimite plateau and the saddle of Benjamin to the south. At this time a larger tribal alliance was formed, and the old relationships were formalized genealogically. Abraham was identified as the father of Isaac and Isaac of Jacob. Jacob became the father of a large group of sons, eponyms of the various groups and districts that made up the new alliance. A core group of this alliance (to which the Merneptah Stele refers) bore the collective name "Israel." Thus the eponym Israel had an equal claim to the status of tribal father, and he was identified with Jacob.

TWO

Israel in Egypt
The Egyptian Sojourn and the Exodus

NAHUM M. SARNA AND HERSHEL SHANKS

ACCORDING TO THE BIBLE, A FAMINE OF UNUSUAL SEVERITY and duration in the land of Canaan brought the patriarch Jacob and his family to Egypt. They settled in the region of Goshen, in the Nile Delta, through the influence of Jacob's son Joseph, who was a high official in the Egyptian administration (Genesis 41:1–47:12). This Hebrew migration was intended to be temporary (Genesis 46:4, 50:24) but soon extended itself.

After the death of Joseph and his brothers, a change of fortunes occurred when a new pharaoh "who did not know Joseph" came to the throne (Exodus 1:8). The Israelites' proliferation and prosperity were perceived as a threat to Egyptian security. The new pharaoh introduced drastic measures to curb the Hebrews' population growth, and the Israelites were pressed into *corvée* service (Exodus 1:9–13). As the biblical text describes it: "They set taskmasters over them to oppress them with forced labor; and [the Israelites] built garrison cities for Pharaoh: Pithom and Rameses" (Exodus 1:11). The harsh labors to which they were subjected did not have the anticipated results: "The more they were oppressed, the more they increased and spread out, so that the [Egyptians] came to dread the Israelites" (Exodus 1:12). New repressive measures were instituted. In addition to intensifying the various

35

physical labors imposed on the Israelites, the king ordered midwives to kill the newborn males at birth. Motivated by compassion, however, the midwives resisted the infamous decree. Pharaoh then ordained that all male Hebrew babies were to be abandoned to the Nile (Exodus 1:15–22).

A married couple from the tribe of Levi attempted to thwart this royal edict by hiding their infant son, but after three months this was no longer possible, and the mother was forced to yield him to the river. Placing him in a waterproof basket, she set him among the Nile reeds and appointed his sister to keep watch over him. The basket was soon discovered by Pharaoh's daughter. At the suggestion of the baby's sister, the Egyptian princess hired the baby's Hebrew mother to nurse the child. Of course, the relationship was not disclosed. When the boy was sufficiently grown, he was taken to the palace and adopted by Pharaoh's daughter, who named him Moses (Exodus 2:10).[1]

The Bible relates practically nothing about Moses as a young man. The few recorded incidents testify to his hatred of injustice. On one occasion Moses struck down and killed an Egyptian whom he saw beating a Hebrew. Later, the deed became known and Moses was forced to flee from Egypt. He found refuge in the land of Midian, and there, by a well, he saw another injustice: Male shepherds were taking advantage of their female counterparts who were waiting their turn at the well. Moses saved the shepherdesses from maltreatment. The upshot was that he eventually married one of the women, thereby becoming the son-in-law of Jethro, priest of Midian, who employed Moses to tend his flocks (Exodus 2:11–21).*

One day, while grazing the sheep deep in the wilderness, Moses catches sight of a bush that is all aflame yet remains unaffected (Exodus 3:1–22).[2] Fascinated by the scene, he approaches the burning bush, only to hear himself addressed by a voice disclosing that he is standing on holy ground. Here Moses experiences his first encounter with God. Moses is informed that the divine promises that had been made to the patriarchs of Israel—Abraham, Isaac and Jacob—are now to be realized. God designates Moses to assume the leadership of Israel and to wage the struggle for liberation from Egyptian bondage. Moses' instinctive reaction is to shrink from the task. "Who am I," he asks, "that I should go to Pharaoh and free the Israelites from Egypt?" (Exodus 3:11). After considerable resistance, Moses finally agrees when his brother Aaron is appointed his spokesman.

Moses returns to Egypt to rally his people and to engage the obdurate monarch. His initial efforts are ineffective. Pharaoh is unyielding. Pharaoh

---

*Moses' father-in-law is also called Reuel (Exodus 2:18; Numbers 10:29) and, perhaps, Hobab (Judges 4:11; but see Numbers 10:29).

The Song of the Sea: Israel's Earliest Memory

Like the patriarchal stories of Genesis, the events of Israel's Exodus from Egypt are extremely difficult to locate in history. But as historian and biblical scholar Baruch Halpern argues in the pages of *BAR* ("Eyewitness Testimony," September/October 2003), close examination of the biblical text reveals that a small but extremely significant portion of the Exodus story—the defeat of Pharaoh's army in the waters of the Red Sea—may have actually been composed within living memory of the event itself.

Immediately following the long narrative account of the miraculous parting and crossing of the Red Sea (Exodus 14), the Bible reports that Moses leads the Israelites in a victory hymn celebrating Yahweh's crushing defeat of Pharaoh's army (Exodus 15:1–18). The hymn, often called "The Song of the Sea," is thought to be one of the oldest pieces of Hebrew poetry preserved in the Bible. As Halpern explains, such passages are marked by certain linguistic and grammatical features that clearly distinguish them from later Hebrew texts composed during the period of the Israelite monarchy or the Exilic period. In the case of the Song of the Sea, these textual considerations, and the historical and cultural context presented in the hymn, suggest that it was first composed between 1125 and 1000 B.C.E., perhaps only a generation or two after the miraculous defeat of the Egyptians had occurred. —*Ed.*

tells Moses: "Who is the Lord that I should heed him and let Israel go? I do not know the Lord, nor will I let Israel go" (Exodus 5:2). Pharaoh imposes even harsher measures on the Israelites, and their situation deteriorates further (Exodus 5:1–22).

A series of ten plagues are then visited upon the land and people of Egypt. Man and beast, the soil and the ecology, are all severely affected.[3] In the course of these plagues, Pharaoh repeatedly makes concessions, only to withdraw them at the last moment. Finally, his will is broken. He summons Moses and Aaron in the middle of the night and capitulates. The Israelites assembled at Raamses and marched to Succoth, the first stopping place on their route out of Egypt. From there they enter the wilderness, headed for the land of

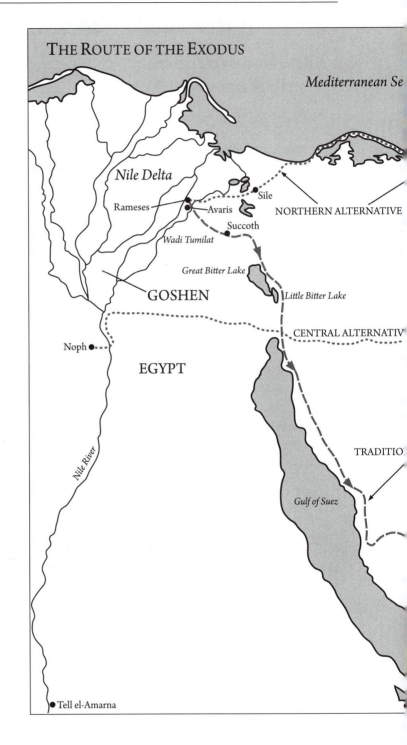

THE ROUTE OF THE EXODUS

Mediterranean Se

Nile Delta

Sile

Rameses

Avaris

NORTHERN ALTERNATIVE

Succoth

Wadi Tumilat

Great Bitter Lake

GOSHEN

Little Bitter Lake

CENTRAL ALTERNATIV

Noph

EGYPT

Nile River

TRADITIO

Gulf of Suez

Tell el-Amarna

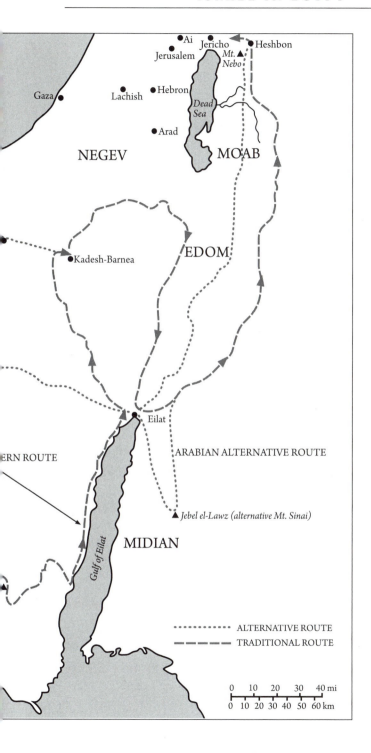

Ai
Jericho • Heshbon
Jerusalem *Mt.* ▲
Nebo

Gaza

Lachish • Hebron

*Dead
Sea*

• Arad

NEGEV

MOAB

Kadesh-Barnea

EDOM

Eilat

ARABIAN ALTERNATIVE ROUTE

ERN ROUTE

Jebel el-Lawz (alternative Mt. Sinai) ▲

Gulf of Eilat

MIDIAN

· · · · · · · ALTERNATIVE ROUTE
— — — TRADITIONAL ROUTE

0   10   20   30   40 mi
0 10 20 30 40 50 60 km

Canaan (Exodus 7:14–11:10, 12:29–37).

The shortest route would have taken them up the Mediterranean coastal road, but they deliberately avoided it, following instead a roundabout course that led far into the wilderness . The Egyptians interpreted this to mean that the fleeing Israelites were hopelessly lost. Pharaoh mustered his forces and went after them in hot pursuit. The Israelites suddenly found themselves hemmed in by the Sea of Reeds (Red Sea) on one side and the Egyptian army on the other. At that critical moment, they are told by God to advance into the sea. As they do so, the waters part, allowing the Israelites to cross over to the other shore. Just as the Egyptian forces are halfway across in pursuit, the waters return. The entire Egyptian infantry and chariotry are drowned, and Israel is free at last (Exodus 13:17–14:31). Then Moses and the Israelites sing the Song of the Sea in praise of God (see "The Song of the Sea: Israel's Earliest Memory," p. 37), and Miriam leads the women in a dance (Exodus 15:1–21).* Forever after, the event has been celebrated annually in the Passover festival (Exodus 12:1–28,43–50, 13:1–10).

Placing the Exodus account in historical context

It is extremely difficult to fit this narrative, set forth in the first 15 chapters of Exodus, into the framework of known history. On the other hand, rarely, if ever, can archaeology confirm the occurrence of individual events portrayed in narratives like this. Events of this sort are not "likely to have left marks in the archaeological record, or even in contemporaneous monuments."[4]

Moreover, the biblical writers were not concerned with the objective recording of details or even with the processes of historical change, as a modern historian would. The biblical writers were not consciously engaged in what we would consider history writing, or historiography. Their concern was with the didactic use of selected historical traditions for a theological purpose. Exclusive concentration on the criterion of literal historicity tends to obscure the purpose and message of the text, which, after all, are the enduring qualities of scripture. Finally, the miracles—divine intervention—are not the stuff of history, but of faith.

The Egyptian sojourn cannot be fictional

With all these limitations what can we say as historians? Actually, quite a lot. First, was there a sojourn and an enslavement in Egypt? The answer is almost surely yes. This answer does not depend so much on an analysis of the text or

---

*Many scholars now attribute the Song of the Sea to Miriam. See Phyllis Trible, "Bringing Miriam Out of the Shadows," BR, February 1989.

on archaeological finds, but on common sense. No nation would be likely to invent for itself, and faithfully transmit century after century and millennium after millennium, such an inglorious and inconvenient tradition unless it had an authentic historical core.[5] Many peoples have fashioned foundational narratives recounting how they came to be, some with more, some with less historical value. But none, so far as we are aware, has ever suggested that its origins were as slaves.[6]

Though archaeology cannot confirm the Israelite sojourn in Egypt, it can provide a context. In general, archaeology can sometimes contradict—or suggest problems with—a biblical narrative. But it cannot confirm it. If the biblical account had said that the Israelites were forced to cut stones to build the store-cities of Pithom and Rameses (see Exodus 1:11), we would question the authenticity of the account because we know that mudbricks were the standard construction material in the Nile Delta but stones were not (they had to be shipped in, usually by water). If, on the other hand, the account says, as it does, that the Israelites were forced to make mudbricks, this does not confirm the historicity of the account. It merely provides a plausible context. Indeed, a 15th-century B.C.E. tomb painting shows Semitic slaves making mudbricks at Thebes. A text complains of not enough straw, just as the Israelites complained. Especially significant is the fact that straw was not typically used to make mudbricks in Canaan.[7] The account seems even more plausible when we consider that stone was the building material of choice in Jerusalem hundreds of years later when the account was written down. Still, confirmation eludes us.

Finding a suitable context for the Exodus

Indeed, much of what we know about life in Egypt in the second millennium B.C.E. provides a plausible context for the Egyptian sojourn. For example, there is considerable evidence of Asiatic slaves serving in Egypt. One papyrus lists more than 40 female slaves with Semitic names.[8] One of these female slaves is named Shiphrah, the name of one of the midwives in the Exodus narrative whom Pharaoh called to account because they were not following orders to kill male Israelites as soon as they were born (Exodus 1:15–18). We certainly do not mean to suggest that the two Shiphrahs were the same. We are talking about plausibility, not confirmation.

Or take geography. The region of Israelite settlement in Egypt is consistently designated as Goshen (Genesis 45:10, 46:28,29,34, 47:1,4,6,27, 50:8; Exodus 8:22, 9:26). This territory surely lay in the eastern Nile Delta. In a text known as "The Instruction for Merikare" (c. 2040 B.C.E.), an Egyptian ruler speaks to his son:

Brick-making in Pharaoh's Egypt. *"The Egyptians became ruthless in imposing tasks on the Israelites," the Book of Exodus 1:13–14 recounts, "and made their lives bitter with hard service in mortar and brick." The Hebrews' labors for Pharaoh were no doubt similar to these realistic scenes painted on the walls of the tomb of Rekhmire, the Egyptian vizier (or prime minister) in the mid-15th century B.C.E. Two workmen with hoes (bottom left) knead clay moistened with water; a third, kneeling figure (lower right) tightens his hoe. Other workers pass buckets of wet clay to two brick makers (upper right), who use molds to form the bricks. At top left, a worker constructs a wall with the newly manufactured bricks. The accompanying inscription declares that the workers are "making bricks to build anew the workshops in Karnak."*

The east [the Nile Delta] abounds with foreigners ... Now speaking about these foreigners, as for the miserable Asiatic, wretched is the place where he is ... Food causes his feet to roam about ... But as I live and will be what I am, these foreigners were indeed a sealed wall, its gates were opened when I besieged it. I caused the Delta to attack it. I plundered their inhabitants, having captured their cattle. I slaughtered [the people] among them so that the Asiatics abhorred Egypt.[9]

Here, according to an Egyptian record, Asiatics have roamed into the eastern Delta (Goshen) to find food, just as the Israelites are said to have done hundreds of years later.

Another Egyptian ruler at about the same time is advised to deal with the Asiatic infiltrators by reinforcing Egypt's border defenses "to prevent Asiatics from going down into Egypt. They beg for water in the customary manner in order to let their flocks drink."[10] Apparently there was a drought where they lived. The famous "Admonitions of Ipuwer" describes Egyptian border defenses designed "to repulse the Asiatics, to trample the Bedouin."[11]

A text known as Papyrus Anastasi 5, which dates to the 13th century B.C.E., contains a report from an Egyptian officer on the eastern frontier who is trying to track down two runaway slaves who have escaped into the wilderness. A scout has seen them near Migdol (one of the sites mentioned in Numbers 33:7 on the route of the Exodus). The Egyptian report has a dramatic immediacy that rivals the Bible: "When my letter reaches you, write to me about all that has happened to [them]. Who found their tracks? Which watch found their tracks? What people are after them? Write to me about all that has happened to them and how many people you send out after them."[12] This surely does not confirm the Israelite Exodus. But it does provide a context for the Israelite escape, and perhaps even makes the story more plausible.

A famous painting on a tomb wall at Beni Hasan in Middle Egypt portrays Asiatic traders in a donkey caravan coming down to Egypt with their families and their wares in about 1890 B.C.E. A century later, Canaanite workers were employed by the Egyptians in the turquoise mines of Sinai at the desolate site of Serabit el-Khadem. It was here that Canaanite miners developed the first alphabetic script based on the pictorial forms of the Egyptian hieroglyphs they saw all around them.*

We have already mentioned mudbricks, which the Bible says the Israelites were forced to manufacture. A well-known painting in the tomb of Rekhmire (15th century B.C.E.) shows slaves making mudbricks. The Bible indicates that a brick-making quota was imposed on the Israelites. At one point, they were required to find their own straw, but the quota nevertheless remained the same (Exodus 5:6–18). There is evidence from Egypt that such quotas did exist; the Louvre Leather Roll (1274 B.C.E.) reports the shortfalls of the assigned quotas,[13] just as the Bible reports that the Israelite foremen were beaten because their charges failed to meet the quotas (Exodus 5:14). This same Egyptian text indicates that workers were granted time off for their religious holidays. Similarly, a text discovered in the workmen's village of Deir el-Medineh states that workers had gone "to offer to their god."[14] This of course is reminiscent of the Israelites' request to take off three days to go into the wilderness to worship their God (Exodus 3:18, 5:3).

If an Egyptian sojourn is so plausible, why then do some scholars deny it?

*Orly Goldwasser, "How the Alphabet Was Born from Hieroglyphs," BAR, March/April 2010; see also "Mining the History of the Alphabet at Serabit el-Khadem," sidebar to "Frank Moore Cross—An Interview, Part III: How the Alphabet Democratized Civilization," BR, December 1992.

Denying the Exodus

It must be admitted that there is no direct evidence of Israel in Egypt.* No existing Egyptian source even hints at Israel's presence there. This, combined with what has been called a "hermeneutic of suspicion,"[15] has produced extreme skepticism, if not denial of the value of the biblical text for reconstructing ancient Israel's history. This stance is often associated with a group of scholars known as biblical minimalists. The following statement by Thomas Thompson of the University of Copenhagen is typical: "Israel's own origin tradition is radically irrelevant to writing such a history."[16] Or consider this statement by Robert Coote of San Francisco Theological Seminary: "The writers of the Hebrew Scriptures knew little or nothing about the origin of Israel ... [The] period [of the Exodus] never existed."[17]

Some of the skepticism about Israel's sojourn in Egypt relates to the difficulty of dating it. No synchronism exists between any event recorded in the Book of Exodus and a dated occurrence documented in extrabiblical sources.[18] The Egyptian evidence for plausibility set forth above comes from a variety of periods. For the most part, this does not detract from the plausibility argument because it suggests the conditions existed over an extended period of time. Even if these conditions existed at a single period, however, this would not provide a date for the Egyptian sojourn, unless, as is almost never the case, these conditions were absent at other periods. And even if we could date the conditions to a particular period, this still would not confirm the biblical narrative, only make it somewhat more plausible.

Questions of chronology

The biblical chronology itself is problematic. The pentateuchal texts do not agree with one another as to how long the sojourn in Egypt lasted. Various biblically preserved traditions mention four generations (Genesis 15:16), 400 years (Genesis 15:13) and 430 years (Exodus 12:40–41). The first-century C.E. Jewish historian Flavius Josephus records a tradition of 215 years,[19] and an ancient rabbinic source gives 210 years.[20] The confusion is reflected in the case of Machir, grandson of Joseph. Machir's sons were born in the lifetime of Joseph, yet, according to the Bible, they participated in the conquest of Canaan and the settlement of the land (Genesis 50:23; Numbers 32:39–40; Joshua 13:31, 17:1). If this is true, then the Hebrew enslavement was limited to one generation. How, then, could it be that the Israelites in Egypt had, as

---

*A possible exception may be a rudimentary Israelite four-room house identified at the temple of Medinet Habu in Egypt. Egyptologist Manfred Bietak suggests the house could have been used by Israelite laborers tasked with dismantling a portion of the temple in the mid-12th century B.C.E. See Manfred Bietak, "Israelites Found in Egypt," *BAR*, September/October 2003.

the opening words of Exodus declare, "multiplied and increased very greatly, so that the land was filled with them" (Exodus 1:7)? Indeed, how could this occur in four generations?[21]

Calculating backward from a relatively secure date in biblical history produces no better results. The only biblical reference that provides a chronological hook is found in 1 Kings 1:6, which states that King Solomon began to build the Temple 480 years after the Israelites left Egypt. It is generally agreed that Solomon came to the throne in about 960 B.C.E., so that according to this reckoning the Exodus would have occurred in about 1440 B.C.E. (or 1436 B.C.E., since he started to build the Temple four years after he became king [1 Kings 6:1]). Most scholars question the accuracy of the number 480, however. It bears the marks of a symbolic rather than literal number. It equals 12 generations of 40 years each, a conventional figure in the Bible. The wilderness wanderings lasted 40 years (Numbers 14:33–34, 32:13; see also Deuteronomy 2:7, 8:2, 29:4; Joshua 5:6; Amos 2:10, 5:25; Psalm 95:10); 40 is used repeatedly in the period of the Judges (Judges 3:11, 5:31, 8:28, 13:1; see also Judges 3:30 [80 = twice 40]); and it also determines the incumbency of Eli the priest (1 Samuel 4:18) and the reigns of David (2 Samuel 5:4; 1 Kings 2:11; 1 Chronicles 29:27) and Solomon (1 Kings 11:42; 2 Chronicles 9:30). Exactly 480 years also elapsed from the commencement of the building of the Temple to the end of the Babylonian Exile, according to the data given in Kings.[22] All this suggests that we are dealing with a schematized chronology that dates the Temple from the Exodus (and we try to work backward). The biblical writer wanted to place the Temple at the center of biblical history.

Scholars have defended two principal possibilities for the date of the Exodus: (1) the 15th century B.C.E., as the Bible seems to indicate, and (2) the 13th century B.C.E.[23] The latter is far more likely and is widely accepted by scholars today.

Problems with a 15th-century Exodus

In the 15th century, Pharaoh Tuthmosis III (1479–1425 B.C.E.) and his son Amenhotep (Amenophis) II (1425–1401 B.C.E.) conducted extensive campaigns in Canaan. It would be very unlikely for the Exodus to have occurred during the reigns of these powerful kings. Egypt is not even mentioned in the biblical accounts of Joshua's conquest of Canaan. This would be most unlikely if the escape to Canaan took place when Egypt controlled Canaan in the 15th century.*

*Egyptian control over Canaan at this time is well attested in the Amarna Letters. See Nadav Na'aman, "The Trowel vs. the Text: How the Amarna Letters Challenge Archaeology," BAR, January/February 2009.

Another difficulty with a 15th-century Exodus is that it appears to conflict with the archaeological evidence. As is clear from the next chapter, Israel makes its first appearance in the archaeological record in the central hill country of Canaan in about 1200 B.C.E. This would place the Exodus in about 1240 B.C.E., assuming 40 years in the desert. If the Exodus occurred in the 15th century, we would expect to find much earlier evidence of the settlement in Canaan.[24]

A 13th-century Exodus?

The emergence of Israel in the hill country of central Canaan at the beginning of the 12th century is one of the reasons that most scholars have opted for a 13th-century Exodus. As we will see in more detail in the next chapter, far-reaching changes occurred in Canaan around 1200 B.C.E., with the close of the Late Bronze Age and the beginning of the Iron Age.* The landscape of the central highlands underwent a major transformation. New settlers appeared in sizable numbers. Villages were founded on the hilltops, and extensive deforestation took place. Large-scale terracing of the slopes was undertaken to create areas for agricultural cultivation so that the needs of the enlarged population could be met. Throughout the central highlands, cisterns were constructed, distinguished by waterproof linings of lime plaster that rendered them impermeable.**[25]

There is no direct evidence to prove that the new arrivals who were responsible for these changes were the tribes of Israel. But this is a thoroughly reasonable assumption. This is indeed where the Bible tells us the Israelites settled (Joshua 17:14–18, 20:7, 21:11,20).

The absence of any mention in the conquest narratives of Egyptian military might in Canaan is also understandable in the 13th century B.C.E., when Egyptian hegemony waned.

Ramesses II

The area of the Israelite settlement in Egypt is called the land of Rameses (Genesis 47:11). A city built by the Israelites is named Rameses (Exodus 1:11), and this was the rallying point for their departure from Egypt (Exodus 12:37; Numbers 33:3,5). This strongly suggests a connection with Pharaoh Ramesses II (1279–1213 B.C.E.), who shifted the administrative center of Egypt to the northeast Delta and named the capital that he had built there

---

*Adam Zertal, "Israel Enters Canaan—Following the Pottery Trail," *BAR*, September/October 1991; Israel Finkelstein, "Searching for Israelite Origins," *BAR*, September/October 1988.
**Lawrence E. Stager, "The Song of Deborah—Why Some Tribes Answered the Call and Others Did Not," *BAR*, January/February 1989.

after himself.[26] This long-lived pharaoh was famous for his extensive and massive building program, which he executed by conscripting large numbers of civilians, especially foreigners.

The city that Ramesses built is called Pi-Ramesses (meaning "House of Ramesses") in Egyptian records.[27] This is probably the site now called Tell ed-Daba. (During an earlier period, when an Asiatic people known as the Hyksos ruled Egypt, Tell ed-Daba was known as Avaris, the Hyksos capital.* More about the Hyksos later.)

Egyptian history suggests Ramesses II as the pharaoh of the oppression. Toward the end of Ramesses's long reign, Egyptian national power declined. Apart from a raid into Canaan by his successor, Merneptah, the Egyptian hold on Asian lands weakened appreciably. Around 1200 B.C.E., the XIXth Dynasty came to an end, amidst anarchy and chaos. The political situation at this time provides the most appropriate background for the events of the Israelite oppression and liberation.

The situation in Transjordan also figures in the equation. In Numbers 20:14–21 and 21:21–35, we are told that Moses was in contact with the kingdoms of Edom, Moab and Ammon. Archaeological surveys have shown that these settled kingdoms did not come into existence before the 13th century B.C.E., at the earliest.**[28] Assuming the biblical references are accurate, this would eliminate a 15th-century date for the Exodus.

The Bible is clear that Pharaoh† pursued the Israelites with chariots pulled by horses (Exodus 14:6–9, 15:1–4). Both horses and chariots were extremely rare in the 15th century B.C.E. They begin to appear in significant numbers only in the 13th century B.C.E.[29] If these are historical references, the Exodus most likely did not occur before the 13th century B.C.E. Another possibility is that the references to horses and chariots are anachronistic; that is, the biblical author, writing when horses and chariots were common, assumed, contrary to fact, that horses and chariots were used in pursuit of the Israelites.

The Merneptah Stele

The famous Merneptah Stele is also relevant, if inconclusive, at this point.[30] More about this in the next chapter. The Merneptah Stele, or Israel Stele as it is sometimes called, is a hieroglyphic account of Pharaoh Merneptah's

---

*Manfred Bietak, BAR, forthcoming.

**For new archaeological evidence for the establishment of an Edomite state, possibly as early as the 13th century B.C.E., see Thomas E. Levy and Mohammad Najjar, "Edom & Copper: The Emergence of Ancient Israel's Rival," BAR, July/August 2006.

†According to Exodus 2:23, the pharaoh of the oppression died, so the pharaoh of the Exodus is a successor.

military campaigns, including one in Canaan.* Merneptah (1212–1202 B.C.E.) boasts that he has destroyed several named cities as well as "Israel": "Israel is laid waste; his seed is not." An Egyptian sign called a determinative is attached to the name Israel. It tells the reader that Israel is a people. Different signs are used to indicate a city or a state. The campaign described in the stele can be confidently dated to 1207 B.C.E., give or take a year or two. About all this there is universal agreement. Some have used the Israel Stele as support for a 13th-century Exodus, in about 1250 or so. Those who deny that there was an Exodus argue that the Israel referred to in the Merneptah Stele is different from the Israel of the Bible.[31] (See next chapter.)

A centuries-long Exodus

Another suggestion from a leading Israeli historian, Abraham Malamat, is that we should not look for a specific date for the Exodus because it involved "a steady flow of Israelites from Egypt over hundreds of years. If the Exodus was a durative event, as seems likely, the search for a specific date for it is futile."**[32] Malamat argues that, based on historical circumstances in Egypt, the outflow probably peaked in the 12th century B.C.E. with the collapse and exhaustion of the Near East's two superpowers, the Hittite and Egyptian empires. (See next chapter.)

Although the Exodus cannot be fixed with certainty at any particular time, this does not necessarily mean there was no Exodus. It simply means we cannot date it precisely.

Settlement in Canaan

We have already noted the presence of what are apparently Israelites in the hill country of central Canaan beginning in about 1200 B.C.E., a subject that will be treated at length in the following chapter but that must also be considered in connection with the Exodus. Various historical models have been proposed to account for the hundreds of new settlements in central Canaan at this time. Initially, scholars asked whether these settlers came by way of conquest or by way of peaceful infiltration. More recently, it has been argued that these people who became Israelites were actually Canaanites fleeing from the declining cities to the central hill country at the end of the Late Bronze Age (1550–1200 B.C.E.). As this contention became more widely adopted, the debate centered largely on whether the

---

*See "The Mernpetah Stela: Israel Enters History," sidebar to "Face to Face: Biblical Minimalists Meet Their Challengers," BAR, July/August 1997.

**Abraham Malamat, "Let My People Go and Go and Go and Go and Go," BAR, January/February 1998.

Israelites came from outside Canaan or from inside. The best scholarship today suggests that the emergence of Israel involved all of these things: There must have been some military confrontations; surely some people infiltrated peacefully; and just as surely many Canaanites accreted to the emerging Israelites.[33] Recent linguistic evidence indicates at least some of these emerging Israelites came from Transjordan.*[34] Biblical support can, in fact, be found for all these theories. What seems increasingly clear, however, is that at least some Israelites came from Egypt. Otherwise, how can we account for the adoption of this epic as Israel's foundational narrative? Indeed, no other event figures as prominently in the Bible as Israel's liberation from Egyptian bondage. It is pervasive not only in the historical narratives, but even in the Prophets and the Psalms.

Had Israel really arisen in Canaan and never been enslaved in Egypt, a biblical writer would have had no reason to conceal that fact and could surely have devised an appropriate narrative to accommodate that reality. We are simply at a loss to explain the need to fabricate such an uncomfortable account of Israel's disreputable national origins. Nor can we explain how such a falsity could so pervade the national psyche as to eliminate all other traditions and historical memories, let alone become the dominant and controlling theme in the national religion.[35]

How large the Exodus was is another matter. Surely the biblical claim of six-hundred thousand able-bodied men (and their families, for a total of approximately two million) (Exodus 12:37–38) is a gross exaggeration (a few hundred is a better figure),[36] but the historical core of an Exodus of some sort seems highly likely. If they were slaves in Egypt, they must have gotten out somehow.

Evaluating the historicity of the biblical narrative

Another objection to a historical Exodus relates to the fact that the biblical version was written centuries after the events it purports to describe. According to this objection, what we can glean from the biblical text relates only to the time when the account was written, not to the time it describes.

The composition of the Pentateuch is admittedly a complicated process that extended over centuries. Not surprisingly, scholars disagree considerably about the details of this process. It is widely recognized, however, that embedded in the text are four authorial strands identified as J (for Yahwist or, in German, Jahwist), E (the Elohist), P (the Priestly Code) and D (the Deuteronomist). The

---

*Anson Rainey, "Inside, Outside—Where Did the Early Israelites Come From?" BAR, November/December 2008.

intertwining of these four sources was the work of an editor or editors referred to as R (the Redactor). This is a vastly simplified description of a nuanced and, in its broad outlines, convincing explanation of how the Pentateuch developed.* Scholars sometimes disagree as to what passages are to be ascribed to which source, as well as how the process occurred. Some posit an oral element in the text that developed side by side with its written composition.[37] But there is general agreement on the overall process.

Quite naturally, there are also disagreements as to when the various strands were composed. J is generally thought to be the earliest, E next, then J and E were combined to form JE, which was subsequently combined with P. D is a separate book, Deuteronomy. Exodus is a combination of JE and P. Some scholars date J as early as the tenth century B.C.E. A better date is probably a century or two later. The date of P is the most controversial. Some date it before the Babylonian Exile (sixth century B.C.E.); others date it during or after the Exile.

Scholars who deny any historicity to the Exodus account generally date the text late, some as late as the Hellenistic period (third to second century B.C.E.). Known as minimalists, they argue that the biblical account cannot be relied on to reveal *any* historical information because the text was composed so long after the events. This question must be addressed regardless of when the texts were composed. Even the earliest date proposed by scholars is still hundreds of years after the events described.

It is difficult to believe that these stories were simply concocted out of whole cloth. Whoever first wrote the accounts, regardless of when they lived, must have had sources. What these sources were is hard to determine. Some were probably written; the Bible itself refers to a number of books that have not survived. The Chronicles of the Kings of Judah is mentioned 15 times. The Chronicles of the Kings of Israel is mentioned 18 times. Collections of even earlier accounts may have been contained in such titles as the Book of Jashar (quoted in Joshua 10–12) and the Book of the Wars of Yahweh (Numbers 21:14).** Other sources may have been oral, a part of the developing tradition of the people Israel.†

---

*For a concise summary of the documentary hypothesis and the various authorial and editorial strands of the Pentateuch, see Richard Elliot Friedman, "Taking the Biblical Text Apart," BR, Fall 2005.

**Duane Christensen, "The Lost Books of the Bible," BR, October 1998.

†Alan R. Millard, "How Reliable is Exodus?" BAR, July/August 2000. See also Ronald S. Hendel, "Finding Historical Memories in the Patriarchal Narratives," BAR, July/August 1995.

Excavating the historical core of the Exodus account

For those minimalists who reject the Bible as a source for the history of Israel, the Exodus account is sheer fiction,[38] a myth[39] created to provide Israel with a past that never occurred. Even mainstream scholars recognize legendary elements in the story. But, in addition to the legendary additions and exaggerations, there is also a historical core that can be excavated, as it were, much as an archaeologist excavates the layers of a tell. So even though centuries separate the events described from the compositions, this in itself is no reason totally to reject the history they report. Sometimes we can even demonstrate that a late account is quite reliable.

An example: In the third century B.C.E., Manetho, an Egyptian priest, wrote a history of Egypt in Greek in which he described the Hyksos rule of Egypt in the mid-second millennium B.C.E. No copy of Manetho's history has survived. What we do have are extracts quoted by the first-century C.E. Jewish historian Josephus, who apparently did not know Manetho's work firsthand but only from other accounts.[40] Extracts from Manetho are also preserved in the writings of Eusebius (third to fourth century C.E.), but he too worked without a copy of Manetho's work, relying instead on the secondhand account of Julius Africanus.[41] As even a skeptical modern historian concedes, however, "Manetho is still an important source in the reconstruction of Egyptian history. Whatever the difficulties with using his work—whatever the lateness and textual corruption of the surviving manuscripts—Egyptologists would regard it as rather foolish to allow these to prevent the use of Manetho."[42] Historians must make use of what evidence is available. That a text was written long after the event it describes does not necessarily mean it is inaccurate. Nor is a contemporaneous account necessarily accurate. In both cases the text must be critically examined. For example, the Hyksos ruler Iannas identified by Manetho has turned up at the Hyksos capital, Avaris (=Yinassi). Another inscription bears the name of a Hyksos princess, Tany.[43]

The Hyksos period in Egypt described by Manetho has additional relevance: As noted, even late accounts of Hyksos rule—1,500 years after the event—have some reliability. The flip side of this is also worth noting: We would know almost nothing about the Hyksos period if we depended on contemporaneous Egyptian records. As the distinguished Egyptologist John Wilson long ago noted, "It was not in character for an ancient people to enlarge on defeat and subjection at the hands of others. Only the victorious elimination of peril would enter the literature."[44] Might this suggest why extant Egyptian documents, fragmentary though they are, contain no hint of an Israelite presence?

The Hyksos ruled Egypt between the 18th and 16th centuries B.C.E., an era Egyptologists call the Second Intermediate Period. A motley population of Asiatics, they infiltrated Egypt in increasing numbers, eventually taking control of Lower Egypt. The Asiatics came mainly from Canaan. The governing class of these Asiatics became known as Hyksos, which means "Rulers of Foreign Lands."[45] Hyksos rulers formed the XVth and XVIth Egyptian dynasties (c. 1675–1552 B.C.E.). The Hyksos were ultimately expelled from Egypt and chased back into Canaan—in about the middle of the 16th century B.C.E. Freed of Hyksos domination, the Egyptians established a new dynasty, the XVIIIth Dynasty,[46] with which the New Kingdom began.

The site of the Hyksos capital, Avaris, is currently being excavated by Manfred Bietak of the University of Vienna. The site in the eastern Nile Delta is now known as Tell ed-Daba. Bietak has excavated an Asiatic settlement in just the archaeological period (Middle Bronze IIA) when the Hyksos dominated Lower Egypt. The pottery is like that of southern Canaan. The vaulting of the tombs, unknown in Egypt, has parallels in Canaan. The grave goods in some of the tombs include bronze weapons; in front of the tombs are burials of pairs of donkeys, which have parallels in Canaanite burials.[47]

Whether the Hyksos experience in Egypt provided the inspiration for the Joseph cycle in the Bible (Genesis 37–50) can never be known. Some scholars think so. Two things are clear, however: (1) Asiatic domination of Egypt is not an impossibility; and (2) late texts can often provide reliable information about earlier periods.

The route of the Exodus

Other problems with the biblical account may affect our view of the historicity of the narrative—for example, the difficulties in tracing the route of the Exodus. When the Israelites left Egypt, they sensibly avoided the shortest and best route to Canaan—along the Mediterranean coast (Exodus 13:17–18). That route, unfortunately for the Israelites, was heavily defended with Egyptian forts. The 15th-century B.C.E. reliefs carved by Pharaoh Tuthmosis III on the outer wall of the hypostyle hall of the Temple to Amun at Karnak display a chain of forts, way stations and wells along this route. Excavations have uncovered ancient Egyptian citadels strung all the way from the Nile Delta to Gaza.*[48] Just what route the Israelites took out of Egypt is unclear.[49]

---

*James K. Hoffmeier, "Out of Egypt: The Archaeological Context of the Exodus," *BAR*, January/February 2007; Trude Dothan, "Cultural Crossroads: Deir el-Balah and the Cosmopolitan Culture of the Late Bronze Age," *BAR*, September/October 1998.

Numbers 33 contains an itinerary that includes a lengthy list of place-names tracing the route of the Exodus all the way from the Israelites' departure to their arrival in Canaan. While most of these sites cannot be identified, the locations of some have been confirmed.* Does this mean that they were made up centuries later, or does it mean that the names have simply been lost to the historical record?

Some sites east of the Jordan mentioned in Numbers 33 have been identified in the reliefs of Tuthmosis III at Karnak. In an extensive list of place-names, presumably in geographical order, four of the names on the Karnak list can be identified in the same order and in the same general location as the names in Numbers 33. Does this mean that the still unidentified sites in Numbers 33 are fictional or that they simply have not yet been found?

The Red—Or Reed—Sea

Other sites in the Exodus account are problematic, among them the so-called Red Sea. Even the name is a crux. The Hebrew name is "Yam Suf." *Yam* indeed means "sea." But the word for "red" is *adam*. For some unknown reason, Yam Suf was translated in the early Greek translation of the Bible known as the Septuagint (made for Greek-speaking Jews of Alexandria) as "Erythra Thalassa" (Red Sea); from there it got into the Latin Vulgate as "Mare Rubrum" and "Mare Erythraeum"; and from there into English translations as Red Sea. But "Yam Suf" really means "Sea of Reeds," and that is the more customary English translation today.

In some biblical passages, it is clear that the body of water referred to as the Yam Suf is the modern Red Sea or one of its two northern fingers, the Gulf of Suez or the Gulf of Eilat (or Aqaba) (see, for example, Numbers 21:4; 1 Kings 9:26; Jeremiah 49:21). Perhaps the Red Sea was known by that name even in ancient times; the Septuagint translators knew that the body of water referred to in some passages was the Red Sea, so they simply translated all the occurrences of the term as Red Sea.

Although Yam Suf does sometimes refer to the Red Sea, that cannot be the case for the body of water that the Israelites supposedly crossed dry-shod (Exodus 15:4). The Red Sea is a very large, wide body of water. Besides, there are no reeds there.

In Exodus 14:2 the location of the Yam Suf is given fairly precisely—in relation to Pi-hahiroth, Migdol and Baal-zephon. Unfortunately, none of these sites can be located with any certainty. Many bodies of water have

*Charles Krahmalkov, "Exodus Itinerary Confirmed by Egyptian Evidence," *BAR*, September/October 1994.

been suggested as the biblical Yam Suf, but no identification is much more convincing than any other. We simply cannot identify with any assurance the body of water referred to in the Bible.[50]

Among the suggested possibilities are Lake Bardwil (the Gulf of Serbonitis) and other gulfs in the northern Delta, Lake Menzaleh, Lake Timsah, the Bitter Lakes, the Gulf of Eilat (the Gulf of Aqaba) and the Gulf of Suez. The last two would seem to be ruled out by the absence of reeds or, more accurately, papyrus marshes.

Some scholars have argued that Yam Suf is a mythological body of water. In this scenario, Yam Suf should be read "Yam Sof." "Sof," which is spelled the same as "Suf" in consonantal biblical Hebrew, means "end"; the Yam Sof in this hypothesis would be the Sea of the End, or the sea at the end of the world, or the sea that lay beyond. The principal proponent of this view, Bernard Batto, contends that Yam Suf/Sof can sometimes refer to the Red Sea and sometimes to this mythical body of water at the end of the world.* As the Red Sea, it is simply the sea at the end of the world, as the ancients regarded it. As a mythological body of water, the Sea of the End is associated with the chaos existing before God formed the universe (see Genesis 1:1–2). The Exodus is thus a second creation, this time of the Israelite nation instead of the world. The Sea of the End is the chaos out of which the Israelites emerged; the Egyptians perished in this sea at the end of the world.[51]

Searching for Mount Sinai

Mount Sinai presents some of the same kind of difficulties as Yam Suf. It, too, cannot be located with any certainty. Many sites have been suggested—from the traditional Mount Sinai, Jebel Musa (a tradition that goes back only to the fourth century C.E.), to other mountains in southern Sinai to a mountain in northwestern Saudi Arabia, to a site near the present Egyptian-Israeli border.** Often the site is chosen to conform to a particular hypothetical route of the Exodus, which is equally uncertain.[52] In the case of the traditional Mount Sinai, this particular mountain in southern Sinai may have been so designated because it became associated with traditions of sanctity when early monasteries were established in the area. The monks, however, apparently settled here because of favorable environmental conditions, rather than out of any

---

*Bernard Batto, "Red Sea or Reed Sea?" BAR, July/August 1984.
**Emmanuel Anati, "Has Mt. Sinai Been Found?" BAR, July/August 1985; Allen Kerkeslager, "Mt. Sinai—in Arabia?" BR, April 2000. For a chart listing a dozen possibilities, see Itzhaq Beit-Arieh, "The Route Through Sinai: Why the Israelites Fleeing Egypt Went South," BAR, May/June 1988, pp. 36–37.

conviction that the site was Mount Sinai.*

A site in Saudi Arabia is propounded by one of the leading biblical scholars of our time, Harvard's Frank Moore Cross.[53] He notes that the Bible is somewhat schizophrenic about the Midianites. Moses marries the daughter of a Midianite priest, Jethro (Exodus 2:15–22). Moses' offspring were thus half Midianite. Israel's judiciary system was created by the Midianite priest Jethro (Exodus 18:14–27). Yet in later tradition, the Midianites are the Israelites' intractable archenemy who led Israel into gross sin (Numbers 25, 31). Unless there were some truth to the Midianite connection, it would have been suppressed by the authors of later biblical texts who recounted the Midianites as enemies.

Midian lies south of biblical Edom, in the mountainous regions of southern Jordan and northwestern Saudi Arabia. (The name Midian survives in the name of the Nabatean site of Mada'in Salah, the so-called Saudi Arabian Petra.) The area comprising ancient Midian is full of archaeological sites dating to the 13th–12th centuries B.C.E., in contrast to the Sinai, which was almost completely uninhabited during this period. An Exodus route through Midian is also supported by the fact that, in the Bible, the Israelites enter the Promised Land through the territory of Reuben in Transjordan (often called the "Plains of Moab," north of Edom).

Midian is filled with huge mountains. The tallest, which is most frequently mentioned as a candidate for biblical Mount Sinai, is Jebel el-Lawz (at 8,500 feet). Even though we cannot identify biblical Mount Sinai with any certainty, it does seem highly likely that the Israelites (or what emerged as the Israelites) had some kind of religious experience in connection with a mountain.** We have the biblical account of this experience. Yet it is difficult to say anything more from a historical viewpoint.

The case of Kadesh-Barnea

In some ways the case of Kadesh-Barnea is instructive. According to the biblical account, after the Israelites received the law at Mount Sinai, they camped for 38 years at Kadesh-Barnea. Most scholars accept the identification of the site as modern Ein el-Kudeirat. Its location, the impressive tell, the availability of water and other environmental conditions make it by far the best candidate—in some ways the only candidate—for Kadesh-Barnea. There is one problem, however. It has been extensively excavated and no remains have been found earlier than the tenth century B.C.E., several

---

*Avraham [incorrectly Aviram] Perevolotsky and Israel Finkelstein, "The Southern Sinai Exodus Route in Ecological Perspective," *BAR*, July/August 1985.
**In the Book of Deuteronomy, the mountain is called Horeb rather than Sinai.

hundred years after the Exodus.*[54] What are we to conclude? That the correct site has not been identified? That the area of the site with earlier remains has not yet been discovered? That the Israelites were there but left no remains? That this aspect of the biblical story was simply made up?

Before deciding, consider the case of Dibon. The Israelites encamped at Dibon-gad (Numbers 33:45), east of the Jordan, where presumably there was a settlement if not a city. The site is confidently identified as Tell Dhiban, which, like Kadesh-Barnea, has been extensively excavated. No settlement from the Late Bronze Age (1550–1200 B.C.E.), when the Israelites encamped at Dibon, has been found there. Since this is the invasion route of the Israelite tribes, one might expect to find a destroyed Late Bronze Age settlement of some sort. Yet from the archaeological viewpoint, Dibon did not exist then. That is not the end of this particular story, however. The 15th-century B.C.E. list of cities in this area carved by Tuthmosis III on the wall of the Temple of Amun in Karnak includes a site named Dibon![55] According to Tuthmosis, there *was* a city at this time even though it is not attested archaeologically! What does this tell us about the absence of early remains at Kadesh-Barnea?

To summarize: The biblical account is complex and contains many different kinds of assertions. At one end of the spectrum are facts we can be relatively certain of. At the other end are theological assertions that historians cannot deal with; by definition, miracles are outside the historians' ken.[56] They are matters of faith to be addressed by theologians, not historians.

What we can know about the Exodus

We can confidently assert, however, that a group of people who later became Israel went down to Egypt from Canaan, eventually settling there. At some point they were conscripted in a *corvée* and were oppressed as foreigners. Some of them later escaped and had a theophanous experience in the desert. Still later, they or their descendants entered Canaan, where, joined by other peoples, they became Israel.

Did they have a leader named Moses? This is not the kind of information that we can expect to cull from the archaeological record. It is certainly highly likely that they had a leader of some sort. And Moses is an Egyptian name.[57] In the biblical narrative, the name was chosen by Pharaoh's daughter (Exodus 2:10).[58] The name Moses derives from the Egyptian verb meaning "to give birth" and is a common element in Egyptian names such as Ramesses (which means "born of Ra"), Tuthmosis, Amenmosis, Ptahmosis and numerous others.[59] That Moses had an Egyptian name, however, does not mean that all

*Rudolph Cohen, "Did I Excavate Kadesh-Barnea?" *BAR*, May/June 1981.

the events of his life as described in the text are historically accurate. On the other hand, it does make his existence as an Israelite leader more plausible.

In short, the overall authentic Egyptian coloration of the story and its background certainly lends plausibility to the broad sweep of the account, especially because we would expect some major gaffes if the story were made up centuries later. But this authentic coloration does not confirm the biblical account.

Some traditions in the stories have the undeniable feel of folklore rather than history. In cuneiform texts dating to the seventh and sixth centuries B.C.E., but relating to King Sargon of Akkad who ruled in the mid-third millennium, the story is told that Sargon's mother, for reasons that are not entirely clear, tried to conceal her son's birth and placed him in a reed basket waterproofed with bitumen and set him adrift, not in the Nile, but in the Euphrates. The similarity to the story of Moses' birth (Exodus 2:3) is clear. Was this element in the story simply incorporated from the cuneiform account or, perhaps, from a common tradition?[60]

Ultimately, the Exodus tradition often deals with people and events that we cannot expect to find in the archaeological record or surviving contemporaneous records. And the supernatural, by its nature, cannot be affirmed or denied by the natural.

Nor was the biblical author concerned with history in the way a modern historian is. The theological perspective dominates. And in the end the narrative takes its meaning on a nonhistorical plane. It is not whether everything happened just as the Bible describes it that justifies the story, although it is a fascinating, important and relevant endeavor to ask whether it did; it is the power and inspiration of the tale as it comes down to us that gives the text its ultimate meaning.

THREE

The Settlement in Canaan
The Period of the Judges

JOSEPH A. CALLAWAY AND HERSHEL SHANKS

THE BIBLE PRESENTS TWO VERY DIFFERENT — ONE MIGHT almost say diametrically opposed — accounts of the Israelite settlement in Canaan — in two successive books, Joshua and Judges.

Joshua vs. Judges

In the Book of Joshua, Joshua and the Israelites enter the land from east of the Jordan River, capture Jericho with the aid of divine intervention and take the rest of Canaan in a series of lightning military campaigns. The various peoples of Canaan are defeated and, as in the case of the inhabitants at Jericho, are "utterly destroyed ... both men and women, young and old, oxen, sheep, and asses, with the edge of the sword" (Joshua 6:21). "So Joshua defeated the whole land, the hill country and the Negev and the lowland and the slopes, and all their kings; he left none remaining, but utterly destroyed all that breathed, as the Lord God of Israel commanded" (Joshua 10:40). "There was not a city that made peace with the people of Israel, except the Hivites, the inhabitants of Gibeon; they took all in battle" (Joshua 11:19).

The land is acquired by military conquest in less than five years of struggle (Joshua 14:7,10) and is divided among the nine and one-half tribes that did not receive territorial allotments east of the Jordan River (Joshua 13:8–19:51). The Israelites displaced the various peoples that occupied the towns and villages, and all Israel was involved in taking the land and in settling the portions then allotted to the various tribes. Joshua 21:43 summarizes this view: "Thus the Lord gave to Israel all the land which he swore to give to their fathers; and having taken possession of it, they settled there."

The Book of Judges presents a far different picture. It purportedly relates to the period "after the death of Joshua" (Judges 1:1). But the picture of Israel in Canaan is not at all what one would expect from reading the Book of Joshua. For instance, the sequence of "conquest followed by allotment of land" is reversed; in Judges, the land is allotted first, then conquered. Thus, Judah says to Simeon, his brother, "Come up with me into the territory allotted to me, that we may fight against the Canaanites; and I likewise will go with you into the territory allotted to you" (Judges 1:3).

In contrast to the sweeping statements in Joshua that Israel wiped out the inhabitants of the land, Judges 1 concludes with a list of 20 cities in which the people were not driven out by the newcomers (Judges 1:21,27–33). The list contains some of the most strategically located and influential cities in the later history of Israel: Jerusalem, Beth-Shean, Taanach, Dor, Ibleam, Megiddo, Gezer and Beth-Shemesh. By contrast, in the summary of Israel's victories in Joshua 12:7–24, it is expressly stated that Jerusalem, Gezer, Taanach, Megiddo and Dor were defeated by "Joshua and the people of Israel."

The Book of Judges preserves a tradition that the ancient Israelites gained possession of the land of Canaan over a long period of time, with individual tribes or groups of related tribes acting independently. Also, according to Judges, the land was acquired in various ways. Judah and Simeon, as noted above, conducted small military operations "against the Canaanites" for their allotments. The Kenites, on the other hand, who descended from Moses' father-in-law, "went up with the people of Judah from the city of palms into the wilderness of Judah, which lies in the Negev near Arad; and they went and settled with the people" (Judges 1:16), apparently peacefully. Still other tribal groups seem to have coexisted with Canaanite enclaves, such as the Jebusites, who are said to "have dwelt with the people of Benjamin in Jerusalem to this day" (Judges 1:21).

These two quite different scenarios by which the Israelites settled in the land of Canaan, roughly following Joshua on the one hand and Judges on the other, have been dubbed the Conquest Model and the Peaceful Infiltration Model.

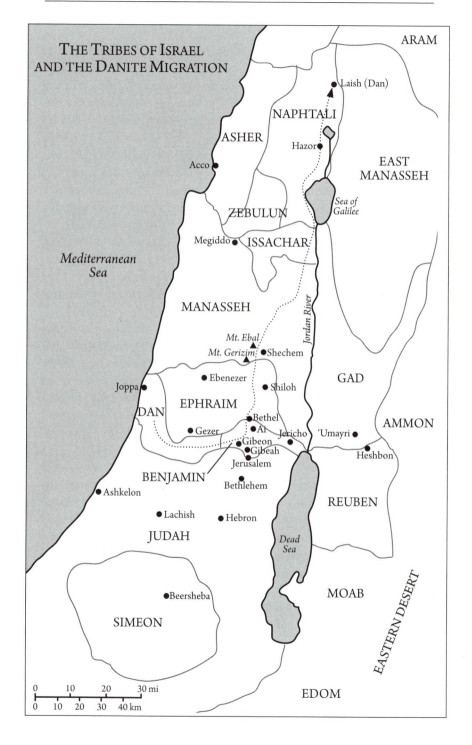

THE TRIBES OF ISRAEL
AND THE DANITE MIGRATION

ARAM

Laish (Dan)

NAPHTALI

ASHER

Hazor

EAST
MANASSEH

Acco

Sea of
Galilee

ZEBULUN

Megiddo

ISSACHAR

Mediterranean
Sea

MANASSEH

Jordan River

Mt. Ebal
Mt. Gerizim   Shechem

GAD

Ebenezer

Joppa

Shiloh

EPHRAIM

DAN

Bethel

AMMON

Gezer

Ai

Gibeon

Jericho

'Umayri

Gibeah

Heshbon

Jerusalem

BENJAMIN

Bethlehem

Ashkelon

REUBEN

Lachish

Hebron

Dead
Sea

JUDAH

MOAB

Beersheba

EASTERN DESERT

SIMEON

0   10   20   30 mi

0   10   20   30   40 km

EDOM

61

Archaeology and the Conquest Model

Today, as a result of modern archaeological excavations, few, if any, scholars would defend a pure version of the Conquest Model. Yet until the last third of the 20th century, some leading biblical archaeologists, like the American polymath William Foxwell Albright of The Johns Hopkins University and Israeli military hero Yigael Yadin of The Hebrew University, as well as the most distinguished biblical historians like Avraham Malamat of The Hebrew University, subscribed to this model with only minor qualifications.[1]

They, as almost all scholars today, place the Exodus from Egypt and subsequent settlement in Canaan at the end of the Late Bronze Age (1550–2000 B.C.E.). The close of that archaeological age, approximately the late 13th century B.C.E., was marked in Palestine by a pattern of city destructions, which Albright attributed to the invading Israelites. As late as 1982, Yadin argued that "excavation results from the last 50 years or so support in a most amazing way (except in some cases ...) the basic historicity of the biblical account [in Joshua]."[2] Malamat likewise wrote, "At the core, a military conquest remains."[3]

The most serious difficulty with the concept of a military conquest is in fact the negative archaeological evidence. Even when Albright first proposed a connection between the Israelite conquest and the Late Bronze Age (13th century B.C.E.) city destructions, scholars recognized that the theory had rough edges. As additional archaeological data became available, these problems became increasingly evident.[4] In more recent years, careful examination of the archaeological evidence has almost thoroughly destroyed the Conquest Model.

Take Jericho, for instance. Jericho is the first city encountered in the conquest account (Joshua 6:1–21). According to the Book of Joshua, the walls of Jericho "fell down flat" (Joshua 6:20). The kidney-shaped mound of ancient Jericho still has about 70 feet of occupation layers intact, dating from the earliest settlement at the site, in about 9000 B.C.E., beside a spring known today as Ain es-Sultan.

In the 1930s, British archaeologist John Garstang discovered collapsed mudbrick walls under the ruins of houses, which he identified as evidence of the destruction by the Israelites. The walls had fallen outward, down the slope of the mound. Up to 3 feet of ash from burned houses had accumulated on top of the mound.[5]

Garstang's conclusions were later undermined, however, by Kathleen Kenyon, who excavated the site extensively from 1952 to 1958.[6] Using improved techniques for controlling the removal of layers of ancient remains, she reconstructed the phases of occupation from the first crude shrine, built on bedrock, to the last fragmentary corner of a small 14th-century B.C.E. hut on top of the mound. The prehistoric phases (from 9000 to 3200 B.C.E.) were dated by radiocarbon (carbon-14) analyses of wood, grain and other organic remains, while the phases after 3200 B.C.E. were placed in their chronological context by comparative studies of pottery and other finds, as well as by radiocarbon dating.[7]

Kenyon concluded that Garstang's collapsed mudbrick wall, which he dated to about 1400 B.C.E., actually dated to about 2300 B.C.E., a thousand years before the close of the Late Bronze Age. In fact, Kenyon found evidence of many collapses of mudbrick walls at Jericho between 3200 and 2300 B.C.E., which she attributed mostly to frequent earthquakes in the area. (When the Bible says the Israelites conquered Jericho, there was no city there.) Jericho sits on top of the fault line along the west side of the Jordan Valley. Formed in geological ages past by parallel faults on each side of the valley, this fault line allowed the entire valley to settle down almost 3,000 feet below the level of the plateaus on either side.

The only serious archaeological defense of an Israelite conquest of Jericho has been proposed by American archaeologist Bryant Wood, who is committed to a more literal reading of the Bible. For this reason, he is sometimes given less credence by scholars not so committed. Wood places the Exodus from Egypt in the 15th century B.C.E., unlike almost all other scholars. After a review of the archaeological evidence from Kenyon's excavation, Wood finds a walled city at Jericho that the Israelites could have destroyed toward the end of the Late Bronze Age, in about 1400 B.C.E.* Both of these unlikely positions, however, only emphasize the difficulty Wood's position faces in the scholarly world.**

Yet Wood stresses some interesting facts: The mudbrick walls of Jericho did indeed collapse. Perhaps this was the result of an earthquake. But in Israelite memory it was an act of God. Wood also notes the heaps of grain that Kenyon found in her excavation, indicating that the city was destroyed in the spring—just when the Bible says the Israelites destroyed it. In short, the settings that the biblical historiographer paints for us can be uncannily accurate. But this does not answer the basic historic question: Did the Israelites destroy Jericho?

A somewhat similar situation occurs with respect to the second Canaanite

---

*Bryant G. Wood, "Did the Israelites Conquer Jericho?" *BAR*, March/April 1990.

**For a response to Bryant Wood's dating, see Piotr Bienkowski, "Jericho Was Destroyed in the Middle Bronze Age, Not the Late Bronze Age," *BAR*, September/October 1990. For Wood's rebuttal, see "Dating Jericho's Destruction: Bienkowski Is Wrong on All Counts," *BAR*, September/October 1990.

city on the biblical route of the Israelite conquest, Ai. At Ai (modern et-Tell), Judith Marquet-Krause led three seasons of excavation from 1933 to 1935. Marquet-Krause concluded that Ai was unoccupied from about 2400 B.C.E. until about 1200 B.C.E. when an unwalled village of about three acres was built on the acropolis of the mound.[8] Nine seasons of excavations at Ai led by Joseph Callaway, from 1964 to 1976, confirmed the results of Marquet-Krause's excavations.[9] There was no walled city at Ai after about 2400 B.C.E., and the only evidence of occupation afterward was a small unfortified village built over the earlier ruins on the acropolis. This village was constructed in about 1200 B.C.E. and was abandoned in about 1050 B.C.E.—prior to the emergence of the Israelite monarchy under David in about 1000 B.C.E.

Bryant Wood and others who defend the Conquest Model have argued that et-Tell is not biblical Ai. Biblical Ai, they say, is at Khirbet Nisya (very near et-Tell),* but this has not won much scholarly support.

The best candidates for confirmation of the biblical account of the conquest are (1) Lachish, southwest of Jerusalem, and (2) the largest city in Canaan, Hazor, in the north. Both suffered devastating destructions toward the end of the Late Bronze Age or early in Iron Age I (1200–1000 B.C.E.). But together they do not admit of a swift Israelite destruction as described in Joshua for they were destroyed about a century apart. If they were part of the Israelite military campaign, it was not a swift one. Moreover, as to Lachish, recent excavations under the leadership of Tel Aviv University's David Ussishkin have shown that the Late Bronze city that suffered a destruction (Stratum VII) was quickly rebuilt as an Egypto-Canaanite settlement (Stratum VI) that served as defense against Philistine expansion. In these circumstances, destruction of Stratum VII by the Israelites is highly unlikely.**

Hazor, however, is a different story. Both Yigael Yadin, who excavated Hazor from 1955 and 1958 (and again in 1968) and Amnon Ben-Tor of The Hebrew University, the current excavator who has been digging there since 1987, attribute the destruction of the city to the Israelites.[†] They are the best candidate and really the only reasonable agent of the destruction of

---

*"Khirbet Nisya—Is it Ai?" BAR, September/October 1987.

**David Ussishkin, "Lachish—Key to the Israelite Conquest of Canaan?" BAR, January/February 1987.

†Yigael Yadin, "Hazor and the Battle of Joshua," BAR, March 1976; Amnon Ben-Tor and Maria Teresa Rubiato, "Excavating Hazor, Part Two: Did the Israelites Destroy the Canaanite City?" BAR, May/June 1999. More recently, however, Sharon Zuckerman, codirector of the Hazor excavations, has proposed the Late Bronze Age city was destroyed not by invading Israelites but rather by the town's peasants and commoners. See Sharon Zuckerman, Archaeological Views, "Giving Voice to the Silent Majority of Ancient Generations," BAR, January/February 2008.

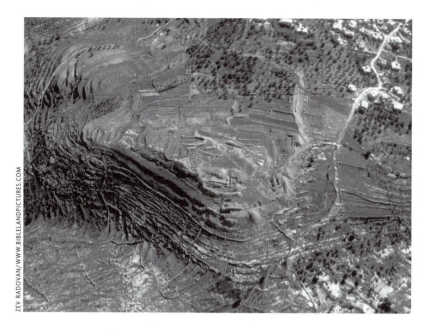

ZEV RADOVAN/WWW.BIBLELANDPICTURES.COM

Ai. *Stone ruins in the center of the photograph mark the excavations at modern et-Tell, which has been identified with biblical Ai. The Bible attributes the destruction of this city to invading Israelite forces: "Joshua burned Ai, and made it forever a heap of ruins" (Joshua 8:28). But archaeological excavations reveal that Ai was in ruins by 2400 B.C.E., long before the Israelites arrived on the scene.*

the Late Bronze Age city. A leading American excavator, Harvard's Lawrence Stager, agrees.[10] So does William Dever.[11] Hazor is the last major city featured in the Joshua account of the conquest. It was the head of an alliance that included Madon (possibly Merom), Shimron, Achshaph and some unnamed villages around southern Galilee and in the hills of northern Galilee (Joshua 11:1ff.). Hazor was "the head of all those kingdoms" (Joshua 11:10). Hazor itself lies on the west side of the fertile Huleh Valley and on the route that runs north-south on the western side of the Sea of Galilee. According to the biblical account, the Israelites "burned Hazor with fire" (Joshua 11:11). The fire that destroyed Hazor, Ben-Tor reports, was so intense that it vitrified the mudbricks.[12] Assuming Ben-Tor is right that it was the Israelites who burned and destroyed Hazor, the Israelite conquest of the land of Canaan, did indeed involve some military penetration, followed by settlement of a politically fragmented land. But the Israelite military settlement of the land was nevertheless quite limited.

Even Avraham Malamat, who had defended the Conquest Model, ended with doubts. His defense of the Conquest Model had relied not so much on archaeology as on the extraordinarily realistic military stratagems described in the Bible that were used by the Israelites in their various conquests, such as night marches with surprise attacks at dawn (Gibeon = modern el-Jib—Joshua 10:9–10). Joshua commanded the sun to "be silent," or not shine (stand still), according to Malamat, so that the darkness of the early morning would be extended while Israel followed up the surprise attack in hot pursuit of the fleeing enemy. Malamat observes that "utilization of the veil of darkness in achieving surprise was ingrained in Israelite tactical planning, from the days of the Conquest to the beginning of the Monarchy."[13]

Similarly with Ai, the biblical text reflects, as Malamat reminds us, that the biblical writer had "an intimate and authentic knowledge of the land, and a knowledge of its topography ... as they relate to military strategy."[14] But still the fact remains that Ai was an unwalled city at the time of the alleged Israelite conquest.

Malamat thus came to recognize the basic historical weakness of the Conquest Model: "The tradition of the conquest that the Bible records crystallized only after generations of complex reworking and, in certain respects, reflects the conceptions ... of later editors and redactors."[15] The resulting biblical historiography "explained historical events theologically," in a fashion that "accentuated the role of the Lord of Israel and submerged the human element."[16]

The Conquest tradition in the Book of Joshua is therefore better seen as a literary, theological account, rather than an historical one.

An alternative perspective: peaceful infiltration

In 1925 the German Bible scholar Albrecht Alt enunciated an alternative to the Conquest Model that became known as the Peaceful Infiltration Model. In a book entitled (in German) "The Settlement of the Israelites in Palestine," Alt set forth his view of the semi-nomadic Israelites' infiltration into the central highlands of Canaan.[17] Alt concluded that the central highlands were only sparsely settled at the time; when the power of the XIXth Dynasty of Egyptian pharaohs collapsed and with it suzerainty over Canaan, the semi-nomadic Israelites, following their flocks year after year from east of the Jordan River moved into the hills west of the river. Eventually these semi-nomads began to build villages and become sedentary. Thus, the settlement occurred relatively peacefully, rather than by military conquest

Military encounters, according to Alt, did occur, but only in a second stage of Israelite settlement, which Alt characterized as "territorial expansion." Late in the period of the Judges and the early monarchy, Israel expanded into the

The Merneptah Stele. *After defeating a coalition of Libyan tribesmen and Sea Peoples, in about 1207 B.C.E. Pharaoh Merneptah commissioned a victory ode to be carved on this 7.5-foot high, black granite stele from Thebes. At top, the stele depicts Merneptah receiving a scimitar from Amun, the god of Thebes.*

The hieroglyphic text recounts the pharaoh's earlier campaign in Canaan. In the earliest known reference to Israel, the inscription states, in the second line from the bottom (see detail, below), that "Israel is laid waste and his seed is not." This suggests that a people called Israel had emerged in Canaan by the end of the 13th century B.C.E. But scholars today are divided about whether the "Israel" in the inscription refers to the people of the Exodus or to a group whose roots were in Canaan long before the time of Merneptah.

plains and valleys that had long been occupied by groups of Canaanites, and in this stage there were some military conflicts, as in Jerusalem with the biblical Jebusites (2 Samuel 5:1–9). Presumably, the memory of these wars would account for what Malamat characterizes as "a basic element of Israelite consciousness ... that Canaan was 'inherited' by force."[18]

Alt's pupil, Martin Noth, developed this "gradual settlement" approach further, spelling out a more detailed scenario. Noth contended that tribes developed over time as

MARYL LEVINE

the various semi-nomadic elements settled down in different parts of the hill country. Eventually, some of these tribes formed an alliance; and the alliance was expanded in stages until there were 12 tribes. In this way, 12-tribe

Israel came into existence.[19]

In the 1950s, Yohanan Aharoni, a young Israeli archaeologist who was to become almost as famous as Yigael Yadin, his bitter rival, conducted a pioneering archaeological survey in the Upper Galilee that provided solid archaeological evidence for the Peaceful Infiltration Model of Alt and Noth. Aharoni found numerous small unwalled settlements in the early Iron Age (shortly after about 1200 B.C.E.) and an absence of sites from the end of the Late Bronze Age. This, combined with the lack of appropriate destruction levels at cities that the Book of Joshua said the incoming Israelites had destroyed, led Aharoni to support the Peaceful Infiltration Model.*

The Merneptah Stele and the evidence of archaeology

Despite the sometimes rancorous scholarly controversy reflected in the foregoing discussion, virtually all scholars agree upon two important facts, one inscriptional and the other archaeological.

The Merneptah Stele is a slab of black granite 7.5 feet high and 3 feet wide covered in Egyptian hieroglyphs and found by Sir William Flinders Petrie in 1896 in Pharaoh Merneptah's funerary temple at Thebes. The text commemorates the victories of Merneptah (1213–1203 B.C.E.) mostly in his Libyan wars. But it also devotes a small space to the pharaoh's earlier campaign in Canaan.

There is no question about the date of the inscription—even more precise than simply the reign of Merneptah. The stele is dated within one or two years of 1207 B.C.E., the end of the 13th century B.C.E.

And there is no question that the hieroglyphic text mentions "Israel." Indeed, it is the earliest extant mention of Israel in any ancient inscription. For that reason it is also known as the Israel Stele.

And there is no question about the translation of the passage in which Israel is mentioned. Merneptah's victory ode proclaims:

> The princes are prostrate, saying "Peace!"
> Not one is raising his head among the Nine Bows.
> Now that Tehenu [Libya] has come to ruin, Hatti is pacified;
> The Canaan has been plundered into every sort of woe:
> Ashkelon has been overcome;
> Gezer has been captured;
> Yano'am is made nonexistent.
> Israel is laid waste and his seed is not;
> Hurru is become a widow because of Egypt.

*Yohanan Aharoni, "The Israelite Occupation of Canaan," *BAR*, May/June 1982.

Pharaohs did not report their defeats, only their victories. The Merneptah Stele is no exception. The notice that "Israel is laid waste; his seed is not" is clearly a gross exaggeration. But there is much more of interest in this reference.

Unpronounced hieroglyphic signs called "determinatives" are attached to some words to indicate the lexical category to which they belong. Thus, the determinative for "foreign land" is attached to the place-names Canaan, Hatti and Hurru. To the words for Ashkelon, Gezer and Yano'am are attached the determinative for city-state.

The determinative attached to Israel is different. Attached to Israel is the hieroglyphic determinative indicating that Israel is "a people," comprised of a man, a woman and three strokes to indicate plural or collective.

A brilliant young Egyptologist, Frank Yurco, was able to identify a pictorial illustration, as it were, of this passage from the Merneptah Stele engraved on the western wall of the Cour de la Cachette of the Karnak Temple in Upper Egypt.* The identification had not been recognized before because the pharaoh whose name was thought to have appeared in the cartouches in the battle engravings was Ramesses II. These cartouches had been twice "usurped," that is, partially erased and recarved. But Yurco was remarkably able to identify the original cartouche as that, not of Ramesses II, but of Merneptah. Interestingly, a second fragmentary copy of the Merneptah Stele was found in the Cour de la Cachette near the battle reliefs described in the stele. The battle scenes illustrate the text of the stele. One of the battle scenes is even labeled "Ashkelon." Which of the other panels represents Israel is a matter of scholarly dispute.**

From the geographical context (the sequence of other geographical sites in Canaan) it appears that the people Israel is located in the highlands of Canaan, just where the Bible says the early Israelites settled. The military campaign in Canaan proceeds from the southwest to the northeast, from Ashkelon to Gezer, then north to Yanoam (somewhere near the Sea of Galilee), and finally to Israel. Even Gösta Ahlström of the University of Chicago, a critic of the stele's significance for biblical Israel recognizes that "the name Israel logically refers to the remaining sparsely populated hill country area [of Palestine] where few cities were located."[20]

*Frank Yurco, "3,200-Year-Old Picture of Israelites Found in Egypt," *BAR*, September/October 1990.

**Anson F. Rainey, "Anson F. Rainey's Challenge," *BAR*, November/December 1991. In the picture that Yurco identifies as Israelites, they are dressed as Canaanites. Rainey identifies another panel as the Israelites, who he says are dressed as Shasu Bedouin with whom the earliest Israelites may be identified.

Thus, Merneptah's inscription verifies the presence of a people known as Israel in the hill country of Palestine at the end of the 13th century B.C.E. Moreover, this people was apparently able to muster a military force sufficient to engage the Pharaoh—just like the city-states of Ashkelon, Gezer and Yano'am. Merneptah was clearly exaggerating when he declared that Israel's "seed is not"; but this also says something in the other direction: Israel was sufficiently important for the great Egyptian empire to brag about defeating.

Doesn't this pretty much settle the argument about whether the Israelite people existed at this time? Not quite. According to Ahlström, and others, the "Israel" referred to in the Merneptah Stele is not biblical Israel. Biblical Israel, the argument goes, had not been formed yet in the 13th century B.C.E. Indeed, if the Exodus is dated to about 1200 B.C.E., the Israelites had hardly left Egypt at the time Merneptah inscribed his stele. Nevertheless, the Merneptah Stele does seem to imply that Israel (whatever it was) was already capable of fielding a sizable fighting force against pharaoh's chariots.

Regardless of the relevance of the Merneptah Stele's reference to "Israel," another archaeological fact is also undeniable: At the end of the Late Bronze Age, beginning in about 1200 B.C.E., more than 250 small, almost tiny, settlements sprang up in the hitherto sparsely settled hill country of Canaan. Who were these people if not the Israelites—semi-nomads who were settling down as farmers and who were perhaps just beginning to define themselves as Israelites? William Dever, a leading American archaeologist, has characterized these early settlers as "proto-Israelites."

Another factor suggests these were early Israelites: There is a clear continuity of material culture from these early Iron Age hill-country settlements to the later centuries of the Iron Age, when this area was the center of an Israelite monarchy.

A third theory: the Peasant Revolt Model

In 1962, George Mendenhall of the University of Michigan published a path-breaking article that presented some entirely new ideas about where these hill-country settlers came from and how they got there: The Israelites—or at least the hill-country settlers who ultimately became Israel—were Canaanites! And they got there as a kind of "peasant's revolt." These hill-country settlers were simply peasants who revolted against their coastal Canaanite overlords during a moment of social disintegration and fled from the lowlands to the central highlands.[21]

This thesis was elaborated in a tome of 700 pages by Norman Gottwald of New York Theological Seminary.[22] Interestingly enough, Mendenhall vehemently denied paternity of Gottwald's vastly influential "Peasant Revolt" thesis.* The reason was that Mendenhall attributed the peasant revolt to an entirely different motivation from Gottwald. For Mendenhall, the revolutionaries were motivated by their religious beliefs—a commitment to Yahweh, the Israelite God. For Gottwald, a committed Marxist, the motivation was inevitable social forces—a breakdown of the Late Bronze Age urban Canaanite culture. His was a thorough-going anthropological analysis.

What was largely missing from the Mendenhall/Gottwald hypothesis, however, was archaeological support. This would later be supplied and summarized by William Dever in a 2003 volume titled *Who Were the Early Israelites and Where Did They Come From?*[23] After acknowledging this archaeological deficiency in Gottwald's argument, Dever goes on to characterize Gottwald's "insights" as having been "proven brilliantly correct, even if [they were] largely intuitive at the time. Gottwald was *right*: the early Israelites were mainly 'displaced Canaanites'—displaced both geographically and ideologically."[24] Dever then purports to supply the firm archaeological grounding for the theory, while at the same time modifying it: It was not a revolt but an "agrarian frontier reform." In Late Bronze Age Canaan the sovereign—that is, the pharaoh or his surrogates—owned all public land. When this social structure collapsed at the end of the Late Bronze Age, the family unit substituted for the state apparatus. This agrarian land reform accounted for the rush to the highlands, according to Dever.[25]

Much of Dever's archaeological support for Gottwald's model comes from pottery analysis in which he is expert. The pottery traditions of the hill-country settlements in Iron Age I are the same as those of the Canaanite areas of the coastal plains. The proto-Israelites settling in the hill-country brought with them their knowledge of Canaanite ceramics, says Dever, thus demonstrating their origin. In Dever's own words: "Early Israelites look ceramically just like Canaanites."[26]

Israel Finklestein, a well-known archaeologist from Tel Aviv University who is also well-versed in ceramic typology disagrees with Dever's assessment: "Although it is possible to point to a certain degree of continuity in a few types, the ceramic assemblage of the Israelite Settlement types, taken as a whole, stand in sharp contrast to the repertoire of the Canaanite centers."[27]

More to the point, however, even those pottery forms that do show some continuity with earlier Canaanite forms, Anson Rainey argues, have recently been found east of the Jordan as well, so the pottery cannot answer the question of the geographical origin of the Israelites in the hill country.

*Bernard W. Anderson, "Mendenhall Disavows Paternity," *BR*, Spring 1986.

ISRAEL FINKELSTEIN/TEL AVIV UNIVERSITY

Israelite four-room house. *This well-preserved four-room house was uncovered at the Iron Age I site of Izbet Sartah in the Judahite hill country. Such houses, characterized by rows of pillars and walls dividing the dwelling into three long rooms and an adjoining broad room, were common to hill-country settlements of Iron Age I. The plan was uniquely adapted to the simple agrarian life of these settlers and may, as archaeologist Avraham Faust has argued, be another reflection of the egalitarian ethos that distinguished the Israelites from their neighbors.*

Dever counters, however, that Rainey's Transjordanian ceramic parallels are all later than Iron Age I.*

The same kind of scholarly disagreement concerns the four-room house, the characteristic domestic architecture of the hill-country settlers. These four-room houses have also been found both east and west of the Iron Age I settlements in the highlands of Canaan. Those who, like Dever, reject the view of any Transjordanian origins of these hill-country settlements argue that the examples of Transjordanian four-room houses are later than Iron Age I.

There is yet another problem with the "Peasant Revolt" hypothesis: As Harvard's Lawrence Stager has observed, "Given the low aggregate of the Late Bronze Age population throughout Canaan, it appears unlikely that the peasantry, even if they had all 'revolted,' could have been large enough to account for the total Iron Age I village population, where in the central highlands alone, I would put their number at about 40,000."[28] Stager describes

*See Strata, "Verbal Fisticuffs over Early Israelite Origins," *BAR*, July/August 2010.

the increase in the population in the highlands on both sides of the Jordan (the Israelite tribes of Reuben, Gad [Gilead] and half of Manasseh originally settled east of the Jordan) as "extraordinary ... That cannot be explained only by natural population growth of the few Late Bronze Age city-states in the region."[29]

Still, another weakness in the Peasant Revolt Model lies in the similar villages that sprung up at this time east of the Jordan in areas that were clearly not Israel, in the territories of Ammon and Moab and even Edom. As Stager put it: If the Peasant Revolt Model is sound, "then how does one account for an almost equal number of 'egalitarian' villages outside the confines of premonarchic Israel?"[30]

These new hill-country settlements in Canaan had several archaeological characteristics in common.* They subsisted on a combination of herding and farming—a combination of pastoralism and agriculture. Grain, olives and grapes (for wine) were especially important. Their pottery repertoire featured a large storage vessel that scholars call a collar-rim jar. The architecture of their homes was similar: "pillared houses" consisting of three long rooms separated by pillars and a broad room across the long rooms—the four-room house. When there are only two long rooms with a broad room across the two, scholars call them three-room houses. Another typical feature of these hill-country settlements are agricultural terraces, held in place by stone retaining walls. Thus were slopes transformed into steps, or agricultural fields. The walled terraces also captured rain runoff; this was especially important because there are no rivers or even all-season streams in the hill country. Because the area must survive so much of the year (from May through September at least) without rain, bell-shaped cisterns were typically cut into the bedrock (and mostly lime-plastered), thus providing a continuous water supply for the homes.

While all this does not specifically identify the material culture as Israelite, another kind of evidence may be more significant in this respect. The animal bones found in these settlements include sheep, goat and cattle. But no pigs! By contrast, pig bones are common at the older Canaanite sites on the coastal plan, as well as at contemporaneous Philistine sites. Moreover, the highlands are quite suitable for raising pigs. If the new highland settlers had come from the Canaanite cities where pigs were domesticated, why didn't they bring this tradition with them?

*Volkmar Fritz, "Israelites and Canaanites: You *Can* Tell Them Apart," *BAR*, July/August 2002; Shlomo Bunimovitz and Avraham Faust, "Ideology in Stone: Understanding the Four-Room House," *BAR*, July/August 2002.

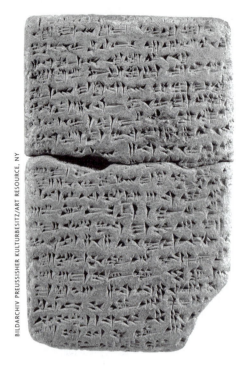

A letter from Amarna. *The cuneiform archive known as the Amarna Letters was discovered at the short-lived Egyptian capital city of Akhetaten (Tell el-Amarna). Consisting of Late Bronze Age correspondence between the pharaoh and his Canaanite vassals, Canaanite rulers repeatedly wrote to Pharaoh concerning the persistent threat of the Habiru or 'apiru.*

Because of the surface similarity of the words habiru and "Hebrew," many scholars assumed the Habiru were closely related, if not identical to, the earliest Israelite tribes. Upon closer examination, however, the similarity disappears. It is linguistically impossible to equate habiru and 'ivri (the Hebrew word for "Hebrew") and, in any case, the word habiru was not used to describe a single ethnic group but rather an array of disenfranchised groups on the margins of society.

Pigs were not raised, however, on the steppe land east of the Jordan. Since pigs do not have sweat glands, they suffer greatly in the heat; sheep and goats are best adapted to the steppe land. This may explain the absence of pigs in the diet of the hill-country settlers: They were not accustomed to raising pigs because they did not have them in their former habitat on the steppe lands east of the Jordan, where Israeli scholar Anson Rainey contends they came from. Rainey (based largely on recent research of Avraham Faust; see below) suggests that the cultural/religious ideology that seems to have accompanied the prohibitions on eating pork, preserved in Jewish kosher laws, probably derives from a rejection of the values of the sedentary Canaanite and Philistine religions on the coastal plains to the west of the hill country. In cultures around the eastern Mediterranean, pigs were sacred to the underworld deities and were sacrificed to them. That this was true for the Aegean suggests that it could also have been true of Philistia.

Looking to the East

Thus, while it seems pretty clear that the hill-country settlers were early Israelites—or at least proto-Israelites—the question remains: If they did not come from the lowland cities of Canaan as a result of a peasant revolt,

The Origins of the Israelites

Who were the ancient Israelites and where did they come from? Archaeologists and historians have long grappled with these problematic questions, but two scholars, writing in the pages of *BAR*, have pointed the way towards new understandings of these complex phenomena.

In his article "Inside, Outside" (November/December 2008), historian, linguist and biblical geographer Anson Rainey proposes that the early Israelites did not emerge out of Canaanite society, as is so often argued, but actually entered Canaan from the lands east of the Jordan River, exactly as the Bible claims. Not only do Israelite ceramic and architectural traditions—like the collared-rim *pithos* and the four-room house—conform to styles that appear in Transjordan as well, but the ancient Hebrew language itself seems to share a great deal more in common with eastern dialects like Moabite and Aramaic than with the Canaanite and Phoenician languages of the Levantine littoral.

But even if the Israelites did originate in the East, how do we explain their emergence as a single people, a people who saw themselves as unified and ethnically distinct from their Canaanite, Philistine and even Transjordanian neighbors? In his path-breaking article, "How Did Israel Become a People?" (November/December 2009), archaeologist Avraham Faust uses archaeological, historical and anthropological evidence to show that Israelite identity formed in opposition to the cultural, dietary and religious customs of neighboring groups, particularly the urban Canaanites and the pork-eating Philistines. Thus, by at least the time Israel is first mentioned in the Merneptah Stele in 1207 B.C.E., the Israelites, newly settled in their small farming communities in the hill country, had already developed an egalitarian ethos that set them apart culturally, economically and ethnically from the Canaanite populations around them. —*Ed.*

where did they come from?

Rainey's answer is clear: They came from just where the Bible says they came from—east of the Jordan (see "The Origins of the Israelites," previous page). According to the Bible, Abram (later Abraham), the first Hebrew, was born in Ur, far east of the Jordan; then the family "set out ... for the land of Canaan," while first sojourning in Haran, another site east of Canaan (Genesis 11:27–32).

Biblical traditions also stress the close affinity of the earliest Israelites with the Arameans who lived east of the Jordan, and not with the Canaanites. When Abraham's servants go out to find a wife for Isaac, as commanded by Abraham, they go east, back to Aram-Naharim, the city of Nahor, Abraham's grandfather (Genesis 24:10). Rebecca, the bride they find, is an Aramean (Genesis 25:20).

Jacob's wives, Rachel and Leah, are the daughters of "Laban [Abraham's nephew] the *Aramean*" (Genesis 31:20,24).

In the long speech of Moses that is Deuteronomy, he tells the people to recite before the Lord: "My father was a wandering Aramean" (Deuteronomy 26:5).

The Bible also describes the Israelites' ancestors as pastoralists, not refugees from cities. When Jacob and his sons go down to Egypt to escape the drought in Canaan, Joseph tells them that he will explain to Pharaoh that "My brothers and my father's household ... are shepherds. They have always been breeders of livestock, and they have brought with them their flocks and herds and all that is theirs" (Genesis 46:31–34; also Genesis 47:3–4). When the Israelites leave Egypt and come to the land of Edom, they assure the Edomites they will pay for any water the Israelite cattle drink (Numbers 20:19; also Numbers 32:1). The Bible's description of the early Israelites as pastoralists clearly conflicts with the Peasant Revolt Model.

Rainey not only disputes Dever's pottery evidence that supposedly supports the Peasant Revolt Model, but he also cites his own evidence in a field where his expertise is nonpareil: linguistics. Rainey maintains that Hebrew has more affinities with languages used east of the Jordan—like Aramean and Moabite—than with Canaanite or Phoenician. His arguments are quite technical,[31] but a few simple examples may suffice here.

Coastal Canaanite (including Phoenician) and Ugaritic (both farther north on the coast) have a different root for the verb "to be" than that found in Hebrew, Moabite and Aramaic.

The word for highly-prized gold in Hebrew is *zahab*. In Transjordanian Aramaic it is *dahab*. This is entirely different from the word for gold in coastal Canaanite/Phoenician (*harus*).[32]

The Hebrew and Moabite word for the relative pronoun "that" is

Shasu bedouin. *Many scholars believe that a social group known as the Shasu provides a more accurate depiction of early Israel than Habiru. The Shasu appear repeatedly in Egyptian texts of the Late Bronze Age as pastoral-nomads from the area of Transjordan and often show up in Egyptian art as bounded prisoners with bag-shaped headdresses, as in this colorful faience tile found at the temple of Medinet Habu, near Luxor.*

asher. This has no relationship to the Canaanite/Phoenician word that does the same linguistic service.

Several word sequences (called syntagmas) are shared by Hebrew, Moabite and Aramaic, but are not found in coastal Phoenician.

This is enough to make the point: This linguistic evidence, says Rainey, is strong evidence that the hill-country settlers came from east of the Jordan—like Moabites, Ammonites and Arameans—and not from the Canaanite cities on the coastal plain. Dever disagrees: "Since the birth of modern linguistics it has been clear that biblical Hebrew is a Canaanite dialect."[33]

An archaeological survey conducted by Adam Zertal of Haifa University tends to confirm the movement of incoming settlers from east to west. In his view, the settlements fan out from the northeast toward the southwest.*

Were these Hebrew from east of the Jordan the Habiru (or 'Apiru) widely referred to in ancient inscriptions? For

*Adam Zertal, "Israel Enters Canaan—Following the Pottery Trail," *BAR*, September/October 1991.

a long time, many scholars thought so. Some still do.[34] There would certainly appear to be a linguistic affinity between the words "Habiru" and "Hebrew." The question came to the fore in 1887 with the accidental discovery by some Egyptian peasants of a cuneiform archive at Tell el-Amarna, on the east bank of the Nile about halfway between Cairo and Luxor.* Amarna is the modern name of the site of an ancient Egyptian capital established by Akhenaten (Amenophis IV) in the 14th century B.C.E. The language of the tablets is Akkadian, the diplomatic *lingua franca* of the day. The tablets consist of diplomatic correspondence between Akhenaten (and his father) with numerous city-states under Egyptian suzerainty. Seven letters were sent to the pharaoh by Abdi-Heba, ruler of Jerusalem. Several of the letters refer to Abdi-Heba's neighbors as "Habiru" who are disloyal to the pharaoh. A frequent complaint is that "Habiru have plundered all the lands of the king." And again: "The Habiru have taken the very cities of the king." If Pharaoh does not send archers, "the land of the king will desert to the Habiru."

Abdi-Heba complains that the pharaoh is not sufficiently helpful to him: "I am treated like a Habiru."

It was not long before some scholars suggested a relationship between "Habiru" and "Hebrew."

Since then, hundreds of references to Habiru ('*apiru*) have been documented from Egypt, Nuzi (beyond the Tigris), Syria and Canaan. Most recently an 8.5-inch-high square cuneiform prism was recovered from Anatolia that lists 438 names of Habiru.[35] The references to Habiru extend over an 800-year period, from the 18th century B.C.E. to the seventh century B.C.E.

The Habiru appear to be uprooted, anti-state peasants who fled to the countryside, often living by banditry. The word is sometimes used as a synonym for mutineer or pauper. Sometimes Habiru are individuals and sometimes members of a group. Some were servants in a household or hired laborers. In other instances, individual Habiru were recruited as mercenaries into a militia. But the term is clearly pejorative.

Only a few scholars today would argue for the Habiru/Hebrew linguistic connection.[36] Anson Rainey regards the suggestion as "silly."[37] He notes that the Habiru are never pictured as pastoralists, like the Hebrews; and socially they do not live in tribes.[38] On the lack of connection between Habiru and Hebrew, Dever agrees with Rainey.[39] Habiru is ultimately derived from "freebooter," Hebrew from "cross over," two entirely different etymologies.[40]

But another vague term may indeed have something to do with early

*Nadav Na'aman, "The Trowel vs. the Text: How the Amarna Letters Challenge Archaeology," *BAR*, January/February 2009.

Israelites, not linguistically, but socially—namely the Shasu.* Whether the original meaning of the term was "pastoralist" or "plunderer" is uncertain. What is clear, however, is that the Shasu (unlike the Habiru) were pastoralists (nomads) who lived in symbiosis with sedentary populations. In times of distress, they were prone to violence. One group of these Shasu may have developed into early Israelites. An Egyptian papyrus from the 13th century B.C.E. describes some Shasu Bedouin who came to Egypt to water their flocks in the same area to which the Bible says the early Israelites went. As Carol Redmount of the University of California at Berkeley has observed, "A number of scholars think that elements of the Shasu were among the proto-Israelites who formed the core of the settlers in the hill country of Canaan in the late thirteenth and early twelfth centuries."[41]

Who were the Israelites?

How then can we put all of this together? As Harvard's Frank Moore Cross has observed, "I prefer a complex explanation of the origins of Israel in the land to any of the simple models now being offered."[42] It appears that each model has elements of truth. But each forms only part of the picture. Let's start with the Exodus from Egypt, as discussed in the previous chapter. Several escapees from Egyptian bondage, perhaps coming over a long period of time, surely formed part of the group that emerged as early Israel, although their number was "in hundreds rather than millions," as the biblical text describes it.[43] Their story became the national story. In the national lore, *all* Israelites came from Egypt and wandered in the desert. This is surely not the case. But some did. As an analogy, consider how all of those who immigrated from various parts of the world to what later became the United States, along with the Native Americans who were already here, may be lumped together as early Americans. And we all celebrate Thanksgiving as if we all came over on the Mayflower. My ancestors did not come over on the Mayflower, but the Mayflower story is my story. The Exodus account is, in the same way as Thanksgiving, the collective story of the Israelites.[44]

As we have seen, the best explanation for the 13th-century destruction of Hazor is that it occurred at the hands of incoming Israelites. William Dever (and excavator Larry Herr) also suggest that Israelites from the tribe of Reuben may have destroyed the site of `Umayri in modern Jordan.** As Cross has observed, "The biblical tradition of a systematic, all-encompassing

---

*Anson F. Rainey, "Shasu or Habiru," *BAR*, November/December 2008.
**For `Umayri, see Larry G. Herr and Douglas R. Clark, "Excavating the Tribe of Reuben," *BAR*, March/April 2001.

military conquest is, no doubt, much overdrawn ... But I do not believe that Israel moved in the land without any conflict. Tribal people are almost by definition warriors as well as keepers of small cattle (chiefly sheep and goats)."[45]

And Dever: "The newer archaeological evidence does not mean that there were *no* military conflicts that accompanied Israel's emergence in Canaan. And the fact that we now know that the biblical conquest stories are partly later literary inventions certainly does not mean that the *entire* story of ancient Israel was 'invented' by the biblical writers, as many revisionists maintain."[46]

The Song of Deborah (Judges 5), a poem that recounts an Israelite military confrontation with the kings of Canaan in the Settlement period, is, by almost all scholarly judgments one of the very oldest texts in the Bible. From its archaic language and references, scholars date it to the 12th century B.C.E., essentially contemporaneously with the event.* A later prose account of the conflict is given in Judges 4, where we learn that the Canaanite forces were led by Jabin, king of Hazor. In the poem, we learn that only six Israelite tribes answered the call to arms; four did not; two are not even mentioned. The poem comes from a time when the Israelite tribes were just coalescing into a nation. The tribe of Manasseh is still known by an earlier name, Machir; and Gad is still Gilead. Judah and Simeon are not mentioned at all. Whether or not the battle occurred in just the way it is described, some military confrontation must have occurred and the tribal background of the poem must have seemed plausible to a contemporary 12th-century B.C.E. audience.**[47] From it, we also get a picture of early tribal relationships before the tribes solidified into what was to become Israel.

The main influx of migrants to the central hill country, however, did not come as a result of a military conquest or from Egyptian slavery. Is anything left of the Peasant Revolt Model? Or did the early Israelite settlers come from the other side of the Jordan? The answer is probably both, although the majority probably came from outside rather than inside Canaan. As Lawrence Stager has observed: "It is unlikely that all these newly founded early Iron Age I settlements derived from a single source—whether of Late Bronze Age sheep-goat pastoralists settling down or from disintegrating city-state systems no longer able to control peasants bent on taking over lowland agricultural regimes for themselves or pioneering new 'free' lands in the highlands."[48] The implication is that at least *some* of the highland settlers did come from

*Richard Hess, "The Name Game: Dating the Book of Judges," *BAR*, November/December 2004.

**Lawrence E. Stager, "The Song of Deborah—Why Some Tribes Answered the Call and Others Did Not," *BAR*, January/February 1989.

these lowland regimes.

This is Cross's view too: "I think this [Peasant Revolt] theory is not without some merit, but I don't think this single explanation of Israelite origins in the land is the whole story. Israel also moved from the east into the hill country, a country largely uninhabited."[49]

The most sophisticated scholarship puts the Israelite settlement in an even broader context. At the end of the Late Bronze Age, the world seemed to be falling apart. Civilizations were in turmoil. Archaeologists sometimes describe it as a "dark age." By the time of the death of Ramesses III (1153 B.C.E.), Egypt had lost control of Canaan. But it was much broader than this. The Mycenaean empire in mainland Greece had collapsed with the Dorian invasion. The once great Hittite empire in Asia Minor (Anatolia) and Syria fell apart. The Sea Peoples, which included the Philistines, embarked from the Aegean for Cyprus, Egypt and then the coast of Canaan.

Canaan was not the only place to see an influx of outsiders. As Anson Rainey describes it: "The Libyans (with their constituent tribes or nations) invaded the Egyptian Delta. The Phrygians/Mushku invaded Anatolia. The Sea Peoples (including the Philistines, Sikels and others) destroyed Canaanite cities and settled in a long swath on the eastern Mediterranean coast. Hordes of Aramaeans stormed into North Syria and Mesopotamia. In each of these cases a new ethnic group, fully conscious of its ethnicity, found a new homeland."[50]

Closer to Canaan, in Transjordan, the Ammonites, Moabites and Edomites, each with their own god—Milkom, Chemosh and Qaus, respectively—emerged as a people. In the same way, the new immigrants into the hill-country areas of Galilee, Samaria and Judea brought with them a consciousness of their own ethnic identity as Israelites with their distinctive God Yahweh.

J. Maxwell Miller calls the situation out of which Israel emerged a "melting pot composed of diverse elements living under various 'ad hoc' political and religious circumstances."[51]

A recent study examined the process by which Israel became Israel, in short, how Israel became an ethnic group, a people—in scholarly terms, Israel's ethnogenesis (see "The Origins of the Israelites," p. 75). Ethnicity, says Israeli archaeologist Avraham Faust, must be identified in relation to other groups. It is the result of interaction and negotiations with "other" groups. And this can be observed in the archaeological record.[52]

According to Faust, the earliest Israelites became an ethnic group in the late 13th century B.C.E. when the Egyptians were losing their control of Canaan. The new highland settlers were able to "push" against the

Egyptian-dominated culture. In contrast to the highly stratified Canaanite society under Egyptian rule, the highland group defined itself as egalitarian, avoided imported or decorated pottery, for example, again in contrast to Canaan of the Late Bronze Age. The typical Israelite four-room house was composed of "equal" spaces in contrast to hierarchical spaces of Egyptian society, another aspect of Israel's egalitarian social structure. These Israelites, says Faust, are the "Israel" of the Merneptah Stele.

This situation prevailed for about 200 years, during what archaeologists call Iron Age I (1200–1000 B.C.E.). Toward the end of this period, this Israel was again threatened—this time by the movement of the Philistines as they pushed inland from their settlements on the Mediterranean coast into areas inhabited by the Israelites. At this time, the Israelites abandoned their small unfortified highland settlements and moved into major towns like Mizpah, Dan and Bethel. The old ethnic markers were stressed again—for example, simple undecorated pottery in contrast to the Philistine's highly decorated pottery. In addition, things like circumcision and avoidance of pork became symbols of Israelite ethnic identity. At some Philistine sites for which data are available, more than 20 percent of the diet consisted of pork—a pointed contrast to Israelite sites. And of course the Philistines were uncircumcised.

Ultimately, in Iron Age II, the Philistine pressure led to the creation of the Israelite monarchy. But that is the subject of the next chapter.

Early Israelite religion

We end this chapter with a few remarks about the religion of the emerging Israelite nation. The Book of Judges sometimes reflects a too-simple view of the religious picture: The Levites led the tribes in the worship of the Israelite God Yahweh, which contrasted sharply with the idolatry of the Canaanites. Once we get behind this editorial framework, however, we find a far more complex situation. For instance, when Gideon was called upon to deliver Israel from the Midianite oppression, an angel of Yahweh appeared before him at Ophrah and commanded him to "pull down the altar of Baal which your father has, and cut down the Asherah that is beside it; and build an altar to the Lord your God on top of the stronghold" (Judges 6:25–26). Apparently, the altar to Baal served as a village shrine. Gideon pulled down the altar by night to escape the notice of his family and the men of the town; he built the altar to Yahweh and offered a bull upon it. When the men of the town discovered what he had done, they went to the house of Gideon's father and demanded that he be brought out so they could execute him. Joash, Gideon's father, interceded and saved his son from the townspeople.

In another episode, Micah, an Ephraimite, steals 1,100 pieces of silver from his mother, for which she curses him (Judges 17:2ff.). Repentant, Micah restores the silver; his mother then gives him 200 pieces of silver, which he turns over "to the silversmith, who makes it into a graven image and a molten image; and it was in the house of Micah" (Judges 17:4).

This description of a household shrine finds an echo in Iron Age I houses excavated by Joseph Callaway at Khirbet Raddana, two of which had small platforms built up of stones beside the roof support pillars of the great room. In one house, two offering stands were recovered. The account of Micah's household shrine suggests, as does this excavation, that the religion of Yahweh that we meet later in the Bible went through a process of development. We cannot trace this development to an imageless Yahweh with any certainty.[53]

In the 1980s an Israeli kibbutznik accidentally discovered a bronze bull in the territory of Manasseh, at a site near Mount Gilboa. Archaeologist Amihai Mazar dates the bull by associated pottery to about 1200 B.C.E.* Also associated with an altar, the bull seems part of a "high place" that the Bible later condemns. Whether this bull was a representation of a deity, a votive offering, or simply a tribute to the Israelite God's power and strength remains a mystery. Indeed, although Mazar claims the site is Israelite, he cannot say whether Yahweh or Baal was worshiped there.

The period of the Judges, when "there was no king in Israel [and] every man did what was right in his own eyes" (Judges 21:25), lasted about 200 years—from around 1200 to 1000 B.C.E. Toward the end of this period there emerged as a leader an exemplary man of God who was recognized widely as a prophet and a judge. Faced with continued threats from the Philistines, the elders of Israel called on Samuel to appoint a king to rule over them. Samuel's position on this matter is unclear because 1 Samuel preserves conflicting traditions. In 1 Samuel 8:6–22, Samuel is instructed by Yahweh to oppose the appointment of a king; in 1 Samuel 9:15–24, Samuel is instructed to anoint Saul secretly as king. Perhaps Samuel was of two minds on the question. In any event, Samuel played a decisive role in the creation of the monarchy when he appointed Saul king over all Israel.

Thus the era of the settlement and Judges ended. Israel was embarked on the road to nationhood.

---

*Amihai Mazar, "Bronze Bull Found in Israelite 'High Place' From the Time of the Judges," *BAR*, September/October 1983.

FOUR

The United Monarchy
Saul, David and Solomon

ANDRÉ LEMAIRE

THE UNITED KINGDOM WAS THE MOMENT OF ISRAEL'S GLORY ON THE regional scene—a moment to be remembered and recalled for millennia. What led to the creation of the Israelite monarchy? In the words of William E. Evans, "The impetus ... [was] the Philistine threat."[1] As most historians recognize, this is certainly part of the truth. However, external pressure was not only from the Philistines: An Ammonite threat also played a role in bringing an end to the loose tribal confederacy—if indeed that is what it was—by which Israel had been led and protected. Moreover, internal (social, economic and demographic) pressures must also be taken into account.[2] Charismatic tribal leaders who arose as needed were no longer enough to lead the emerging nation. The United Kingdom of Israel lasted for about a century (c. 1030–931 B.C.E.). Three strong personalities occupied the throne: Saul, David and Solomon. Then the United Kingdom split in two, with Israel in the north and Judah in the south.

Under Saul, the Israelite monarchy controlled a small, petty territory. Under David and then Solomon, Israel was transformed into a larger, unified kingdom eventually with vassal states subject to it. As the monarchy assumed a regional role, other powers in the ancient Near East, mainly Phoenicia and Egypt, had to take it into account.

The historian looks very fortunate in this period: The biblical record is copious because this period was later conceived as a kind of "golden age." The Bible probably devotes more space to this century than to any other in ancient Israel's history. Accounts of this period appear in both of the Bible's parallel histories—1 Samuel 8 to 1 Kings 11 and from 1 Chronicles 3 to 2 Chronicles 9.

The principal difficulty in reconstructing the history of the period is that we are dependent almost exclusively on the Bible. The assurance that comes from a variety of sources is missing here, and the biblical account is often tendentious and includes traditions that are not reliable as history. It tends to idealize this period with legendary aspects. As underlined by J. Maxwell Miller: "The important question is not whether we should use the Hebrew Bible in our attempts to understand the origin and early history of Israel, but how we should use it. In my opinion, it should be approached critically, examined with the careful attention to its internal typology and stratigraphy that archaeologists give to their data, and then used very cautiously, alongside other kinds of evidence."[3] (For a summary of how scholars can date ancient Israel's kings, including David and Solomon, see "Why Do We Date David and Solomon to the Tenth Century?" opposite page.)

To understand this period of Israel's history, we must therefore consider questions of literary criticism, as well as differences in the various traditions preserved in the Bible. Finally, we must consider the light archaeology sheds (or fails to shed) on the monarchy—not an easy task, as exemplified by the contemporary controversy over the archaeology of the tenth century B.C.E.*[4] Two divergent views of this century have recently emerged, one known as the maximalist viewpoint, the other as the minimalist. The former group contends that the biblical account of the United Monarchy has a historical core, while the latter practically tends to deny that the biblical traditions of this period have any basis whatsoever in history.**[5] The ensuing debates remind us that the results of literary critcism and the interpretation of archaeological discoveries are seldom clear-cut. One must therefore be very careful to distinguish what the biblical record says from the historical interpretation of it based on archaeology. Each reign presents different aspects of the problem.

*For overviews and differing perspectives of this ongoing scholarly debate, see Hershel Shanks, "Where is the Tenth Century?" BAR, March/April 1998; Hershel Shanks, "A 'Centrist' at the Center of Controversy: BAR Interviews Israel Finkelstein," BAR, November/December 2002; Amihai Mazar, "Does Amihai Mazar Agree with Finkelstein's 'Low Chronology'?" BAR, March/April 2003, and, most recently; Hershel Shanks, "The Devil Is Not So Black as He Is Painted," BAR, May/June 2010.

**Hershel Shanks, "The Biblical Minimalists," BR, June 1997; see also Hershel Shanks, "Biblical Minimalists Meet their Challengers," BAR, July/August 1997.

Why Do We Date David and Solomon to the Tenth Century?

In the ongoing scholarly debate over the historicity of David and Solomon, most attention has focused on the tenth century B.C.E. But why do scholars think these two kings should be placed in the tenth century in the first place? After all, the biblical writers only tell us how long both kings reigned, not specifically when they reigned. In a masterful *BAR* article ("How We Know When Solomon Ruled," September/October 2001), Egyptologist and biblical historian Kenneth Kitchen explains that datable records and events from ancient Assyria and Egypt help establish specific calendar dates for the reigns of almost all of Israel's kings, including David and Solomon. Not only did these foreign powers keep extensive lists of the reigns of their own kings, but they often mention surrounding states and kings that they conquered or subdued, including Israel and Judah. In this way, the reigns of Israel's kings are linked with the known dates of Assyrian and Egyptian rulers and their foreign campaigns.

Dating the excavated material remains that come from the time of David and Solomon, however, is a somewhat different matter. While there is increasing hope that advanced scientific techniques like carbon-14 dating will ultimately be able to date a particular archaeological level to within a decade or two of its use, archaeologists are still largely dependent on tried and true "relative" dating techniques—like pottery analysis and stratigraphy—to understand the world that David and Solomon built (see Lily Singer-Avitz, Archaeological Views, "Carbon 14—The Solution to Dating David and Solomon?" *BAR*, May/June 2009). In the pages of *BAR* ("Pottery Talks: What Ceramics Tell Us About the Social World of Ancient Israel," March/April 2004), archaeologist Avraham Faust explored the social and political significance of a unique type of pottery that, according to the traditional chronology, was made and used primarily in the tenth century B.C.E., the time of the appearance of the first Israelite state under David and Solomon. This so-called "red-slipped burnished ware," says Faust, is not only a key chronological indicator, but also a material manifestation of Israel's emergence as a male-dominated state society under King David. —*Ed.*

Philistine warrior. *The Philistines and other Sea Peoples inhabited several cities on the eastern Mediterranean coast in the early 12th century B.C.E. A large-scale sea battle between the Sea Peoples and Egyptian forces is depicted in wall reliefs from Ramesses III's mortuary temple at Medinet Habu, in Thebes. This detail of a warrior's face from one relief showcases the Philistines' characteristic battle headdress, which included a headband and upright strips that may be feathers, reeds, leather strips, horsehair or an unusual hairdo. The military threat posed by the warlike Philistines was one of the factors leading to the creation of the United Kingdom of Israel.*

ERICH LESSING

SAUL (c. 1030?–1009 B.C.E.)

The Philistine threat

The Bible depicts Saul as a study in contrasts. Although he was Israel's first king, he was ultimately rejected (1 Samuel 15:10). His dark, fitful personality suffers by contrast with the two legendary figures between whom he seems wedged—Samuel, the prophet-priest, and David, Saul's hero-successor.[6] The Bible describes Saul rising to the throne in the face of the Philistine military threat. The Philistines are known both from the Bible and from extrabiblical sources.[7] Egyptian inscriptions mention them as one of the so-called Sea Peoples. Apparently, they originally came from the Aegean area or from southern Anatolia.* Other Sea Peoples include the Tjekkar, the Sheklesh, the Danuna and the Weshesh. The Sea Peoples destroyed a number of cities of the Syro-Phoenician coast at the beginning of the 12th century B.C.E. and even tried to invade Egypt. However, they were stopped in a large-scale battle, fought both on land and on sea, in the eighth year of the reign of Pharaoh Ramesses III (c. 1177 B.C.E.). Reliefs and hieroglyphic accounts

*For the migrations of the Sea Peoples, see the contrasting views of Tristan Barako and Assaf Yassar-Landau in "One if by Sea ... Two if by Land: How Did the Philistines Get to Canaan?" *BAR,* March/April 2003.

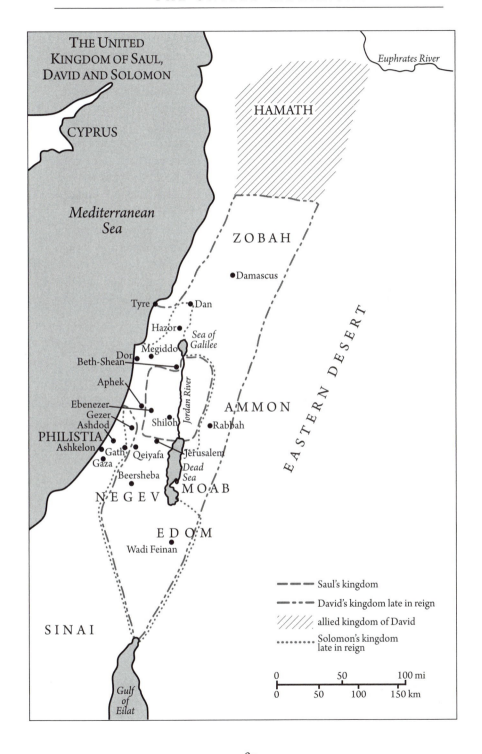

THE UNITED
KINGDOM OF SAUL,
DAVID AND SOLOMON

CYPRUS

Euphrates River

HAMATH

*Mediterranean
Sea*

ZOBAH

•Damascus

Tyre• •Dan

Hazor•

*Sea of
Galilee*

Megiddo•

Dor•

Beth-Shean

Aphek

EASTERN DESERT

Jordan River

Ebenezer
Gezer
Ashdod

Shiloh•

AMMON

•Rabbah

PHILISTIA
Ashkelon• •Gath
•Gaza

Qeiyafa•

Jerusalem•

*Dead
Sea*

Beersheba•

MOAB

N E G E V

E D O M

Wadi Feinan

— — — Saul's kingdom

— · — · David's kingdom late in reign

///// allied kingdom of David

········· Solomon's kingdom
late in reign

S I N A I

0		50		100 mi
0	50	100		150 km

*Gulf
of
Eilat*

of this battle appear on Ramesses III's temple at Medinet Habu in Thebes.[8] The Sea Peoples settled in various parts of the Egyptian province of Canaan, probably with Egypt's agreement: the Philistines occupied the coastal plain between Gaza and Jaffa; the Tjekkar occupied the Sharon plain around the city of Dor; the Cherethites (Cretans?), perhaps another Sea People, settled the so-called Negev of the Cherethites (1 Samuel 30:14).

In the coastal plain, the Philistines organized themselves into a pentapolis, a confederation of five cities: Gaza, Ashdod, Ashkelon, Gath and Ekron. Each city was ruled by a *sérèn*. (The only Philistine word that is known with certainty, *sérèn* [Joshua 13:3; Judges 16:5,8,23,27; 1 Samuel 5:8,11] may be related to the Greek word *tyrannos*.)[9]

Eventually, the Philistine military expansion near Aphek brought the Philistines close to the territory occupied by the Israelite confederation.[10] The Philistines were apparently skilled warriors who used the most advanced military equipment of their time. Their weapons were made of both bronze, the predominant metal until about 1200 B.C.E., and iron, which was becoming increasingly available.*

According to the biblical record, the Israelites mustered in the hill country near Ebenezer overlooking Aphek.** A two-stage battle between the Israelites and the Philistines ensued. In the first phase of the battle, "Israel was defeated by the Philistines, who slew about four thousand men on the field of battle" (1 Samuel 4:2). In desperation, the Israelites brought the Ark of the Covenant, which had been installed at Shiloh, to lead them in battle. In the second phase of the battle, the Israelites were again defeated, and the Ark was captured by the Philistines.† After the battle of Ebenezer (1 Samuel 4), the Philistines occupied at least part of the Ephraimite hill country. After their victory at Ebenezer, the Philistines installed garrisons (or governors) in the hill country of Ephraim and Benjamin, the most important of which was at Geba (1 Samuel 13:3–5).

Like the Habiru/'Apiru of the Late Bronze Age, hundreds of years earlier, and the Jews of the Maccabean revolt, hundreds of years later, some Israelites took to the hill country and hid in natural caves (1 Samuel 14:11,22).

*In the 12th to 11th century B.C.E., iron technology developed in the Aegean, in Cyprus and in Canaan; this development apparently had an Aegean origin. See James D. Muhly, "How Iron Technology Changed the Ancient World and Gave the Philistines a Military Edge," *BAR*, November/December 1982.

**The Iron Age I site of Izbet Sartah is generally identified with biblical Ebenezer. See Aaron Demsky and Moshe Kochavi, "An Israelite Village from the Days of the Judges," *BAR*, September/October 1978.

†According to the Bible, however, the Ark did the Philistines no good and was ultimately returned. See Aren M. Maeir, "Did Captured Ark Afflict Philistines with E.D.?" *BAR*, May/June 2008.

ZEV RADOVAN/WWW.BIBLELANDPICTURES.COM

Ammonite king. *This life-size limestone head, with plaited hair, curled beard, earrings and crown, is said to have been discovered near Amman, Jordan, a city whose name preserves its Ammonite origins. According to the Bible, the Ammonites, who lived east of the Jordan during the Israelite monarchy, were one of Israel's most important adversaries, second only to the Philistines.*

The choice of Saul

Facing these dire circumstances, the Israelite tribes determined that they must have a king. The story of the choice of Saul as king appears in three different traditions: In the first, Saul is looking for his father's lost she-asses; he meets Samuel who anoints him prince (*nasi*) over Israel (1 Samuel 9:3–10:16). In the second tradition, Saul is hiding among baggage at Mizpah when Samuel casts lots to choose the king (1 Samuel 10:17–27); in the third and most probably reliable tradition,[11] Saul, at the head of Israelite columns, has rescued Jabesh-Gilead from an Ammonite attack, and the people, with Samuel's agreement, proclaim their allegiance to Saul at Gilgal (1 Samuel 11–15). In each of these accounts, Saul is installed and anointed as king by Samuel, now an old man.[12]

Samuel was regarded as the last of the Judges (1 Samuel 7:6,15, 8:1–3), the charismatic leaders who emerged at times of crisis. Another tradition, probably a later one, regarded Samuel as a prophet (1 Samuel 3:20). He also officiated at the tabernacle at Shiloh, where the Ark was kept, which means he was a priest. But Samuel's leadership was regarded as insufficient. The tribal elders apparently felt that the appointment of a king was a historical necessity: "Now appoint for us a king to govern us like all the nations," they told Samuel (1 Samuel 8:5). Saul, a Benjaminite, seems to have been chosen because he was tall and strong and well qualified to wage war against Israel's enemies.

Like earlier charismatic leaders, Saul's principal task was to conduct a war of liberation. Saul's successful expedition against the Ammonites at Jabesh-Gilead (1 Samuel 11:1–11) was no doubt an important consideration in his selection.[13] Now he was called upon to lead the people against the Philistines, a people who were well organized, well equipped and motivated by an expansionist ideology that included plans to bring the whole country west of the Jordan under its control.

The first battle—at Michmash—was a victory for Israel (1 Samuel 13:5–14:46). The decision to appoint a king seemed to have been a wise one. But this was by no means the last battle of the war.

Saul the warrior

"There was hard fighting against the Philistines all the days of Saul; and when Saul saw any strong man, or any valiant man, he attached him to himself" (1 Samuel 14:52).

The Philistine war thus became a guerrilla war, characterized by ambushes and surprise attacks against enemy posts. Generally, it did not involve great numbers of fighters. Saul had only "about six hundred men with him" near Gibeah (1 Samuel 14:2). Unfortunately, the Bible gives only brief intimations of the details of the continuing wars with the Philistines. Saul probably succeeded in driving the Philistines out of the central part of Israel. But the Philistines did not give up. They apparently attacked from the south, threatening Judah in a confrontation in which a young Judahite named David distinguished himself (1 Samuel 17).

Saul seems to have been generally successful as long as he fought in the hills, but his troops could not win a battle in the open plain. Witness what happened near Mount Gilboa (1 Samuel 28–31). The Philistines attacked from the north through the Jezreel Valley. The Israelites should never have come down into the plain to fight.

> The Philistines fought against Israel; and the men of Israel fled before the Philistines, and fell slain on Mount Gilboa ... Thus Saul died, and his three sons, and his armor-bearer, and all his men, on the same day together. And when the men of Israel who were on the other side of the valley and those beyond the Jordan saw that the men of Israel had fled and that Saul and his sons were dead, they forsook their cities and fled; and the Philistines came and dwelt in them.
>
> (1 Samuel 31:1,6–7)

This sober presentation of an Israelite disaster has a ring of truth even though, beginning in David's time, there were divergent traditions concerning the details of Saul's death (compare 1 Samuel 31:3–5 with 2 Samuel 1:6–10).

Other than the Philistine war, which seems to have been the principal feature of Saul's reign, the biblical text mentions wars against the Moabites, the Ammonites, the Edomites, the king of Zobah and the Amalekites (1 Samuel 14:47–48).

The main battle of the war with the Amalekites is described in 1 Samuel 15. The Amalekites were the Israelites' special enemies because they were the first to confront Israel in the wilderness after the Israelites left Egypt. Without provocation, the Amalekites are said to have attacked Israel from the rear (Exodus 17:8–16).

Actually Samuel is said to have instructed Saul and his men to kill all the Amalekites and their animals, according to the tradition of *hérèm* (compare Joshua 6:18 and 7), which allotted the fruits of victory to the Lord alone. However, Saul spared the Amalekite king Agag and the best of the Amalekites' domestic animals. For this sin, Samuel denounced Saul and declared that the Lord had irrevocably rejected him. Samuel, the Bible tells us, "never saw Saul again ... And the Lord was sorry that he had made Saul king over Israel" (1 Samuel 15:35).

Tentative evaluation of Saul's reign

We do not know how long Saul ruled. According to the traditional Hebrew text (the Masoretic text), which unfortunately is badly preserved at this point, Saul became king when he was one year old (!) and his reign lasted only "two years" (1 Samuel 13:1).[14] Two years seems improbable, and several commentators correct it to "twenty-two years"; but this remains conjectural.

Although the length of Saul's reign is uncertain, two biblical passages offer some information about the general economic and political conditions under Saul:

> Now there was no smith to be found throughout all the land of Israel; for the Philistines said, "The Hebrews must not make swords or spears for themselves"; so all the Israelites went down to the Philistines to sharpen their plowshare, mattocks, axes, or sickles; and the charge was a *pim* [= two-thirds of a shekel] for the plowshares and for the mattocks, and a third of a shekel for sharpening the axes and for setting the goads. So on the day of the battle, neither sword nor spear was to be found in the possession of any of the people with Saul and Jonathan; but Saul and Jonathan his son had them.
>
> (1 Samuel 13:19–22)

This first passage reflects a nonspecialized society of peasants and shepherds in which even iron implements were rare.

The second passage describes Saul's family:

> Now the sons of Saul were Jonathan, Ishvi, and Malchishua; and the names of his two daughters were these; the name of the firstborn was Merab and the name of the younger Michal; and the name of Saul's wife was Ahinoam daughter of Ahimaaz. And the name of the commander of his army was Abner the son of Ner, Saul's uncle.
>
> (1 Samuel 14:49–50)

This passage demonstrates that Saul's kingship was essentially a family matter. The principal specialized responsibility, leadership of the army, was in the hands of Saul's cousin Abner.

It is difficult to give a balanced historical assessment of Saul's reign.[15] In the biblical tradition, he seems to be presented as the typical "bad" king,[16] in contrast to his adversary and successor David. This contrast is the central theme of the stories in 1 Samuel 16–27, the bulk of which seems to have been written by David's companion and priest Abiathar (cf. 1 Samuel 22:20) or someone close to him.[17] These chapters may contain some reliable information,[18] but it is presented in a one-sided and tendentious way. They describe, in sometimes divergent traditions, the stormy relationship between Saul and the young David. David had distinguished himself in the Philistine wars and had been given Saul's second daughter, Michal, in marriage. Saul became increasingly jealous of David, accusing his son-in-law of conspiring against him. On several occasions, Saul tried to kill David. David fled to Judah, but Saul pursued him. Finally David took refuge in Philistine territory. Written from David's viewpoint, the stories in 1 Samuel 16–27 tend to depict David as right in rebelling against Saul and seeking refuge in Philistine territory.[19] But they also reveal that people from Bethlehem in Judah joined Saul in battle when the Philistines tried to invade the central hill country from the southwest (1 Samuel 17:1). Saul obviously exerted some political influence south of Jerusalem in the northern mountains of Judah, preparing the way for the federation of Israel and Judah under David.[20]

The historicity of many of Saul's other wars, however, is doubtful. The wars against the Moabites, the Edomites, the king of Zobah and even the Amalekites (1 Samuel 14:47–48, 15) may simply be a transposition from David to Saul made by the Judahite historian because he had so little information about Saul. Such wars far from Saul's home base seem improbable, especially when the Philistine threat was so strong and Saul's army was so poorly organized.

Unfortunately, we are left with little solid information about Saul or his reign. All that can be said with confidence is that Saul seems to have been named king so that he would lead the Israelites in their wars against the Philistines, which he did.

Saul's "kingdom" was not very large. It probably included Mount Ephraim, Benjamin and Gilead.[21] He also exerted some influence in the northern mountains of Judah and beyond the Jezreel Valley. Instead of a capital or a palace, Saul maintained his tent "in the outskirts of Gibeah under the pomegranate tree which is at Migron" (1 Samuel 14:2) or in Gibeah, where he sat "under the tamarisk tree on the height with his spear in his hand, and all his servants [i.e. ministers] were standing about him" (1 Samuel 22:6).[22]

Saul's "kingship," as might be expected from the biblical record, left hardly a trace archaeologically speaking. Surveys and excavations in the hill country of Manasseh,[23] Ephraim[24] and Benjamin,[25] and at sites like Izbet Sartah,[26] have revealed farms, small villages and open-air cult places on hilltops. To the south, in northern Judah, settlement was even sparser.[27] The fortified site of Khirbet ed-Dawwara, northeast of Jerusalem, had perhaps a hundred inhabitants, and this was large for Saul's kingdom. However, this site could well have been built as an Israelite center to receive refugees during the struggle with the Philistines.[28] The principal Israelite site of the previous period, Shiloh,[29] seems to have been destroyed in the mid-11th century B.C.E.*[30] by an intense conflagration. This destruction is often attributed to the Philistines as a follow-up operation after their victory over the Israelites at Ebenezer (1 Samuel 4). Shiloh is mentioned only once in the stories of Saul and David (1 Samuel 14:3).

Archaeology seems to confirm that until about 1000 B.C.E., the end of Iron Age I, Israelite society was essentially a society of farmers and stock-breeders without any truly centralized organization and administration.[31] Recent population estimates set "a figure of about 50,000 settled Israelites west of the Jordan at the end of the eleventh century B.C."[32]

By contrast, Philistine urban civilization was flourishing in the 11th century B.C.E., as revealed by recent excavations at Ashdod,** Tel Gerisa, Tel Miqne (biblical Ekron),† Ashkelon‡[33] and lately Tell es-Safi (Gath).††[34]

Saul's reign apparently ended in total failure. After the rout on Mount Gilboa and the lamented death of Saul as a hero (2 Samuel 1:19–27),[35] the Israelite revolt against Philistine domination seemed hopeless. Under the leadership of Saul's adversary, David, however, the fight for independence from the Philistines—the *raison d'être* of Saul's kingship—was taken up once again.

DAVID (c. 1009/1001–969 B.C.E.)

With David's reign, we begin to see Israel emerge as a national entity. The loose confederation of tribes has been transformed into a strong chiefdom. Israel's political existence is confirmed by its king, its army, its royal cabinet, its extended territory and its relations with neighboring countries. Even historians, like Mario Liverani[36] and J. Alberto Soggin,[37] who hesitate to say anything about the early history of Israel, agree that from about 1000 B.C.E.,

---

*See Israel Finkelstein, "Shiloh Yields Some, But Not All, of Its Secrets," *BAR*, January/ February 1986; "Did the Philistines Destroy the Israelite Sanctuary at Shiloh? The Archaeological Evidence," *BAR*, June 1975.

**Trude Dothan, "What We Know About the Philistines," *BAR*, July/August 1982.

† Seymour Gitin, "Excavating Ekron," *BAR*, November/December 2005; Trude Dothan and Seymour Gitin, "Ekron of the Philistines," *BAR*, January/February 1990.

‡Lawrence E. Stager, "When Canaanites and Philistines Ruled Ashkelon," *BAR*, March/April 1991.

††See Carl S. Ehrlich and Aren M. Maeir, "Excavating Philistine Gath: Have We Found Goliath's Hometown?" *BAR*, November/December 2001.

"the History of Israel leaves the realm of pre-history, of cultic and popular traditions, and enters the arena of history proper."[38]

That does not mean, however, that everything is clear and that no historical questions remain. Indeed, a few scholars have recently gone so far as to deny that David really founded the kingdom of Jerusalem as a political power.[39] According to Ernst A. Knauf, "Archaeologically speaking there are no indications of statehood being achieved before the 9th century B.C.E. in Israel and the 8th century B.C.E. in Judah".[40] Although it may be true that Israel was more of a powerful chiefdom than a well-administered state or, still less, a centralized empire, there is no reason to deny the historicity of David's kingdom as *some* sort of political power. The methodological weakness of this extreme position is highlighted by two monumental ninth-century B.C.E. inscriptions written by enemies—Mesha of Moab[*41] and Hazael of Damascus[**42]—who designate the kingdom of Judah as *Be(y)t Dawid,* "the House of David," probably the official diplomatic name of this period.[43]

A model king

The Bible tells the story of David's reign in detail (1 Samuel 16 to 1 Kings 2:11), reflecting its importance, as well as its length. David "reigned over Israel for forty years, seven in Hebron and thirty-three in Jerusalem" (c. 1009/1001–969 B.C.E.). His long reign was later regarded as Israel's "golden age"; David himself was seen as the model king.

David's later glorification may seem paradoxical in light of the fact that he was a Bethlehemite, from the tribe of Judah, and not from any of the original, northern tribes (Ephraim, Manasseh and Benjamin). Furthermore, David was one of Saul's adversaries, who had been banned because he was considered the personal enemy of the first Israelite king. Moreover, at the time of Saul's death, David was serving as a mercenary in the army of the Philistines, Israel's bitter enemy.

According to 1 Samuel 16:1–13, David was the youngest son of Jesse. The prophet-priest Samuel "anointed him in the midst of his brothers; and the Spirit of the Lord came mightily upon David from that day forward."

The Bible offers two accounts of how David became part of Saul's household. In the first, Saul takes David into his service as his "armor-bearer" (1 Samuel 16:14–23). In the second version, David, having killed the Philistine champion Goliath in single combat (1 Samuel 17), is officially

---

*On Mesha, see André Lemaire, "'House of David' Restored in Moabite Inscription," *BAR,* May/June 1994.

**On Hazael and the Dan inscription, see "'David' Found at Dan," *BAR,* March/April 1994.

presented to Saul as a hero. The biblical account of David's rise to power may well represent an amalgation of different traditions concerning the early relationship between David and Saul.

In any event, with the support of his friend Jonathan (Saul's son), David was "made ... a commander of a thousand [in the army]; and he went out and came in before the people. And David had success in all his undertakings; for the Lord was with him" (1 Samuel 18:13–14).

This happy situation did not last. David was soon accused of conspiring against Saul (1 Samuel 22:8). David decided it would be prudent to flee to the hill country:

> David departed from there and escaped to the cave of Adullam; and when his brothers and all his father's house heard it, they went down there to him. And every one who was in distress, and every one who was in debt, and every one who was discontented gathered to him; and he became captain over them. And there were with him about four hundred men.
>
> (1 Samuel 22:1–2)

Among them were Abiathar (the son of Ahimelech the son of Ahitub the priest of Nob, descendant of Eli the chief priest at Shiloh) and the prophet Gad (1 Samuel 22:5,20). That these religious personalities joined David suggests the importance of Yahwism among David's partisans.

After some time hiding in various locations throughout Judah as Saul pursued him, David sought refuge in Philistine territory:

> So David ... and the six hundred men who were with him [escaped to the land of the Philistines] to Achish son of Maoch, king of Gath. And David dwelt with Achish in Gath, he and his men, every man with his household and David with his two wives.
>
> (1 Samuel 27:2–3)

After a while "Achish gave him [David] Ziklag" (1 Samuel 27:6).[44]

During this period, David attempted to maintain good relations with the leaders of the territory of Judah by fighting Judah's enemy, the Amalekites (1 Samuel 17:8, 30:1–31). His efforts proved fruitful. After Saul's death at the battle of Mount Gilboa,

> David went [to Hebron in the territory of Judah] and his two wives also, Ahinoam of Jezreel, and Abigail the widow of Nabal of Carmel. And David brought up his men who were with him, every one with his household; and they dwelt in the towns of Hebron.

And the men of Judah came, and there they anointed David king over the house of Judah.

(2 Samuel 2:2–4)

This does not seem to have provoked any Philistine reaction, who, at first, were apparently pleased that one of their vassals controlled the territory of Judah. The same was not true, however, of Saul's descendants:

Now Abner the son of Ner, commander of Saul's army, had taken Ishbosheth the son of Saul, and brought him over to Mahanaim;[45] and he made him king over Gilead and the Ashurites and Jezreel and Ephraim and Benjamin and all Israel. Ishbosheth, Saul's son, was forty years old when he began to reign over Israel; and he reigned two years.

(2 Samuel 2:8–10)[46]

King David

A "long war" ensued between the house of Saul and the house of David (2 Samuel 3:1). But in the meantime a disagreement soon split Abner and Ishbosheth (Eshbaal). Both of them were killed, apparently as a result of personal vengeance (2 Samuel 3–4).[47] The way was open for David to become the king of all Israel.

All the elders of Israel came to the king at Hebron; and King David made a covenant with them at Hebron before the Lord, and they anointed David king over Israel.

(2 Samuel 5:3)

The Philistines could no longer remain indifferent in face of the unification of their longtime enemy. They attacked twice in the central hill country, once near the Valley of Rephaim and probably once near Gibeon. But David defeated them both times (2 Samuel 5:17–25).[48] The Philistines then gave up their efforts at military expansion.

After driving off the Philistines, David was free to attack the Jebusites of Jerusalem and take the city, which until then had remained in Canaanite hands: "And David dwelt in the stronghold [of Jerusalem] and called it the City of David" (2 Samuel 5:9).

Jerusalem soon became not only the political capital of Judah and Israel, but also a religious center for all Israel. To accomplish this, David brought the Ark of the Covenant to the City of David (2 Samuel 6). This was the Ark that, according to tradition, had accompanied Israel in the Sinai, that had rested in the tabernacle of Shiloh before being captured by the Philistines and that had remained in storage at Kiriath Yearim after being returned by the Philistines. When David brought the Ark to Jerusalem, the religion of Yahweh became a unifying factor, strengthening the bond between Judah and Israel.

From the beginning of his career, David has shown himself to be a fervent Yahwist. His religious devotion is confirmed by the presence in his retinue of the priest Abiathar and the prophet Gad. David's devotion to Yahweh probably made it easier for the leaders of Israel to accept him as their king.

David cemented his relations with various political and national groups through marriage. His wives included Abigail of Carmel; Ahinoam of Jezreel; and Maacah, daughter of the Transjordanian king of Geshur (2 Samuel 3:2–5).[49]

Militarily, David had already developed a cadre of well-trained troops when he fled from Saul. These devoted soldiers were ready to follow him anywhere, and, in fact, had followed him from the wilderness of Judah to Gath, Ziklag, Hebron and, finally, Jerusalem. These troops became his personal guard and the core of his regular army.[50] His nephew Joab served as chief of the army (2 Samuel 8:16).

After checking the Philistine advances on Israel's western border, David was free to expand his kingdom to the east. There he defeated the Moabites, who then became a vassal state, paying tribute to David (2 Samuel 8:2). As discussed below, David also fought with the Ammonites, although the precise sequence of these wars is unclear. He also led a campaign to Edom, where he won a battle in the valley of Salt. David then appointed "garrisons (or governors) in Edom; throughout all Edom he put garrisons, and all the Edomites became David's servants" (2 Samuel 8:14).

In the biblical tradition, after the Philistines, the Ammonites were Israel's most important adversary. The Ammonite war began as a result of a diplomatic incident. Nahash, the king of the Ammonites, had been David's friend. When Nahash died, David sent condolences to his son and successor, Hanun. But Hanun treated David's messengers with contempt: He cut away half of their beards and half of their garments, accusing them of being David's spies (2 Samuel 10:1–5). Hanun probably thought he could get away with this because of an alliance he had made with the Aramean kingdoms of northern Transjordan and southern Syria (1 Samuel 10:6).[51]

In retaliation, David's general, Joab, led an attack near the Ammonite capital. An Ammonite ally—Hadadezer the Rehobite, king of Zobah[52]— summoned other Arameans from "beyond the Great Bend of the Euphrates" to join forces against David (2 Samuel 10:16). David met and defeated this Aramean army at Helam (2 Samuel 10:17–18). He "took from him [Hadadezer] a thousand and seven hundred horsemen, and twenty thousand foot soldiers; and David hamstrung all the chariot horses, but left enough for a hundred chariots" (2 Samuel 8:4). (Apparently, chariots were not used much in David's army; otherwise, he would not have crippled so many horses.)

As a result of this enormous victory, David was able to conquer Rabbah, the Ammonite capital. David then "took the crown of their king (or of Milkom, their god) from his head ... and it was placed on David's head" (2 Samuel 12:30). The Ammonites became David's subjects. In addition, the kingdom of Zobah, headed by Hadadezer, became David's vassal: "David put garrisons (or governors) in Aram of Damascus; the Syrians [Arameans] became servants to David and brought tribute" (2 Samuel 8:6). Finally, "All the kings who were servants of Hadadezer ... they made peace with Israel and became subject to them" (2 Samuel 10:19). Among them was Toi, the king of the important kingdom of Hamath (2 Samuel 8:9–10). David would have thereby extended his political influence from the Red Sea to the bend of the Euphrates.

By gaining control over international trade routes, the Israelite kingdom became an economic power. David became rich from the spoil and tribute brought to Jerusalem. Even the Phoenician king of Tyre, Hiram, started trading with him, especially after David made Jerusalem his capital (2 Samuel 5:11–12).

The inchoate nature of the early state

The expansion of David's kingdom altered the status of Jerusalem.[53] From a small declining Canaanite city-state with a territory of a few square miles, it became—probably with little physical change—the capital of the united Israelite and Judahite kingdoms. These kingdoms, after David's victories, extended far and wide. The borders of the United Kingdom stretched from Dan to Beersheba, but its vassal states extended far beyond. David's kingdom may have been a strong chiefdom, but it was not really an empire. His kingdom was still not yet well organized, nor did it have a strong central administration.

At least toward the end of David's reign, there was a kind of royal cabinet where David's general Joab played an important role[54]:

> Joab the son of Zeruiah was over the army; and Jehoshaphat the son of Ahilud was recorder, and Zadok the son of Ahitub and Ahimelech the son of Abiathar were priests; and Seraiah was secretary; and Benaiah the son of Jehoiada was over the Cherethite and the Pelethites; and David's sons were priests.
> (2 Samuel 8:15–18; cf. 2 Samuel 20:23–26)[55]

The spoils of war, the levies from the administered territories, the tributes of vassal kings—all flowed into David's royal treasury. Justice was administered at the local level by the elders of the cities, but an appeal could now be taken directly to the king (2 Samuel 14:15).

David planned to build a new temple at Jerusalem (2 Samuel 7) and organized a census, probably as a basis for future administration, taxation and circonscription (see 2 Samuel 24:1–9). Both the temple project and the census met internal opposition. Even the prophet Gad, one of David's oldest and most loyal companions, opposed the census; he did, however, support the construction of an altar on the threshing floor of Araunah the Jebusite, the site David purchased for the temple (2 Samuel 24:18).

The guiding principles of the United Kingdom were organization and centralization. But the process of centralization really only began toward the end of David's reign. It was later applied more broadly by his son and successor Solomon.

The problem of succession

Internally, the problem of David's legitimacy as successor to Saul, and then of David's own successor, loomed large. It was doubtless exacerbated by the unstable union of the houses of Israel and Judah. This problem is treated at great length in the Bible. Indeed, this is the principal subject from 2 Samuel 6 through 1 Kings 2, often called the "History of the Succession."[56]

Initially, David tried to gain the good will of Saul's house.[57] He even married Michal, Saul's daughter. David also welcomed to his table on a regular basis Meribbaal (Mephibosheth), a cripple who was Saul's heir. True, this seeming act of kindness permitted David to control Meribbaal's activity (2 Samuel 9). And in the end David more or less abandoned Michal, who "had no child to the day of her death" (2 Samuel 6:23).[58] When David allowed the Gibeonites to take vengeance on seven of Saul's descendants, reconciliation between the two houses was no longer possible (2 Samuel 21:1–14).[59]

David's own house was also beset with rivalries and jealousies among his sons. His eldest son, Amnon, was killed by order of David's third son Absalom (2 Samuel 13). Absalom himself was killed by Joab, the general of David's army, after leading an almost-sucessful revolt against his father (2 Samuel 15–19). Absalom's revolt was connected with the rivalry between Israel and Judah and with Benjaminite opposition to David (compare the roles played by Shimei and by Sheba son of Bichri, both Benjaminites [2 Samuel 19:16–23, 20:1–22]).

After Amnon and Absalom were killed, Adonijah became David's heir apparent. David's old retainers, including his general Joab and the priest Abiathar, were ready to support Adonijah (1 Kings 1:5–7). However, according to 1 Kings 1, the aged David promised Bathsheba that their son Solomon would become king. With the help of the prophet Nathan, the priest

Zadok and the chief of the guards Benaiah, Solomon was recognized as king while David was still living. David himself died peacefully some time afterward (1 Kings 2:10–12).[60]

Assessing the biblical text

In the absence of any text contemporary with the biblical tradition, a historical appreciation of David's reign is difficult. A literary analysis of the biblical tradition seems to indicate, however, that a good deal of it was written either in David's or Solomon's time, close enough to the events to be reliable witnesses,[61] although there are doubtless later additions and glosses reflecting the influence of the so-called Deuteronomistic historians of later centuries.[62]

Of course, even early traditions are tendentious, and it does seem that most of the account of David's reign was written to glorify and justify David and his son Solomon. This is particularly true of the stories concerning David's accession, which reflect the most attractive side of his personality and justify his claim to the kingship.[63] This is also true of the account of Solomon's accession, which explains how Solomon, although one of the younger sons of David, could be his legitimate heir. The aged David's promise to Bathsheba to make her son king sounds more like literary artifice than history. Or perhaps Bathsheba, with the help of the prophet Nathan[64] and the priest Zadok, succeeded in convincing an old and weakened David to support their conspiracy to elevate Solomon and thus to legitimate what was in effect a *coup d'état*.[65]

The account of David's external policies also bears the marks of tendentiousness; the biblical text emphasizes David's military victories more than his political control of the conquered territories. But even if David was victorious against the invading Philistines, he was nevertheless probably unable to control the Philistines' territory. The biblical statement that David "subdued" the Philistines (2 Samuel 8:1,11–12) is ambiguous. Further, 2 Samuel 5:25 tells us that David defeated the Philistines only as far as Gezer, which lay on the eastern border of Philistine territory. Gezer itself did not become part of Israel until Solomon's reign.

David's relations with Hiram king of Tyre must also be looked at critically. The Phoenicians were technologically superior to the Israelites, and David's relationship with them was essentially commercial; there was no vassal submission. Moreover, even this commercial relationship probably dated to the very end of David's reign, or even more likely, to the beginning of Solomon's reign.[66]

After the Ammonite war, if David indeed took for himself the Ammonite crown, he probably dismissed the ruling Ammonite king only to put in his place another son of Nahash: "Shobi the son of Nahash from Rabbah of

SKY VIEW

Khirbet Qeiyafa. *This small but impressively fortified site, known today as Khirbet Qeiyafa, sat on the border between Judah and the Philistine kingdom of Gath during the late 11th–early tenth century B.C.E. While many have suggested Qeiyafa was a military outpost established by King David, it is also possible that it was a Philistine fort built to protect nearby Gath and its territories.*

the Ammonites," who supported David during Absalom's revolt (2 Samuel 17:27–29). In the Aramean territories that David administered (Zobah and Damascus),[67] the governors were probably chosen from local leaders. In the vassal kingdoms (like Moab), their own kings continued to rule, although they paid tribute to David. Sometimes it is difficult to tell the difference between a vassal state and an allied kingdom, or even a good neighbor. For instance, Toi, king of Hamath, probably considered himself as a good neighbor rather than an allied king, and certainly not a vassal (see 2 Samuel 8:9–10).

Even if David's sphere of influence did extend from the central Negev and Edom to the southern border of the kingdom of Hamath, we must realize that there are varying degrees of political control.[68] For example, David's influence over the outlying areas was often through good personal relations with the neighboring kings or local chiefs; his suzerainty was sometimes only nominal, mainly dependent on the military threat of his soldiers. As stated earlier, David's political sphere should probably be characterized as a strong chiefdom rather than an "early state," and probably not as an "empire."[69] Only at the very end of his reign, did he begin seriously to organize and centralize his power. According to biblical tradition, David's reign was characterized by wars (see 2 Samuel 8, 10; 1 Kings 5, 17); the few buildings attributed to him (2 Samuel 5, 9–11) are more likely to be connected with Solomon.

As would be expected, the archaeology of David's reign seems very sparse, aside from the possible destructions of Canaanite cities.[70] In the 1970s, Yohanan Aharoni argued that Dan and Beersheba were rebuilt by David and that the Iron Age gates of these cities could be dated to the beginning of the tenth century B.C.E.,[71] but few archaeologists today support his conclusions. More recently, Eilat Mazar has proposed identifying monumental archaeological fragments found north of the Ophel (City of David), in Jerusalem, with King David's palace.* However her general stratigraphic interpretation is far from clear**[72] and a public building from Solomon's reign might eventually be a better candidate. Moreover, the date of the "Jebusite ramp," or Stepped-Stone Structure, built on the eastern slope of the City of David is still hotly debated. It appears therefore—from the texts and from the archaeological excavations— that Jebusite Jerusalem did not change much during David's reign.[73]

The best candidates for archaeological remains that may be dated during David's reign lie in Hebron and in the Judean Hills: Avi Ofer's excavations in Hebron and his survey of the hill country of Judah reveal a "breakthrough in the settlement history of the Judean Hills."[74] However, it is difficult to date any artifact or architecture to the *beginning* of the tenth century.† Most of the building activity in the tenth century probably occurred later, during King Solomon's reign. Yosef Garfinkel and Saar Ganor, however, recently proposed that the ruins of Khirbet Qeiyafa, south of Beth-Shemesh, are those of a Judahite town called Sha'araim (1 Samuel 17:52) that was fortified by David around 1000 B.C.E.‡[75] Nadav Na'aman, on the other hand, interprets this site as connected with the Philistine kingdom of Gath and identifies it as "Gob," mentioned two or three times as a place where David and his men battled the Philistines (2 Samuel 21:16–19). In fact, this fortified town appears to be on the border between the kingdom of Jerusalem and the kingdom of Gath. We may hesitate between the two interpretations, even though Qeiyafa, being only 6.5 miles from Tell el-Safi/Gath, seems more likely to be a Philistine fort of the kingdom of Gath.

*Eilat Mazar, "Excavate King David's Palace!" *BAR*, January/February 1997; "Did I Find King David's Palace?" *BAR*, January/February 2006.

**Hershel Shanks, "The Devil Is Not So Black as He Is Painted," *BAR*, May/June 2010.

†Jeffrey Chadwick, "Discovering Hebron," *BAR*, September/October 2005.

‡Hershel Shanks, "Newly Discovered: A Fortified City from King David's Time," *BAR*, January/February 2009.

Despite all these reservations, however, David's reign represents a glorious achievement. Seizing the opportunity occasioned by the weakness of Assyria and Egypt,[76] a strong and brilliant personality[77] joined the houses of Israel and Judah, made Jerusalem the capital of both and used this unification as the basis of his dominion. Within this favorable international situation, David created, for a short time, one of the most important powers in the southern Levant. He also laid the foundations of religious institutions that would support the worship of the Hebrew God Yahweh for centuries.[78] What is more, as is now known from the Tel Dan stela, the kingdom of Jerusalem was later designated by his name: "House of David."[79]

SOLOMON (c. 970/969–931 B.C.E.)

David was occupied chiefly with fighting wars and with expanding his kingdom by both military and political means. Solomon was concerned mainly with consolidating the lands acquired by David and organizing the administration of the kingdom. But before he could turn to this, Solomon had to strengthen his position as king.

Threats to Solomon's rule

During the early years of his reign, Solomon was confronted first with an internal and then an external threat. As long as Adonijah, David's oldest surviving son, lived, this apparent Davidic heir was a danger; there was always the possibility that he would present himself as the legitimate successor to David. Solomon seized an early opportunity to rid himself of this threat: Adonijah was executed as soon as he was suspected of scheming against Solomon. David's powerful general Joab, one of Adonijah's supporters, was also executed, and Abiathar the priest, another of Adonijah's chief supporters, was exiled to his own estate in Anathoth (1 Kings 2:13–35). Solomon also put to death Shimei, a supporter of the house of Saul (1 Kings 2:36–46). In this way, the Bible tells us, "the kingdom was established in the hand of Solomon" (1 Kings 2:46).

Outside of Israel, the Egyptian pharaoh, probably Siamun, tried to take advantage of the change in rulers to intervene.*[80] He organized a military expedition that seized and destroyed Gezer (1 Kings 9:16), a destruction that now seems confirmed by archaeological excavations.[81] Apparently Pharaoh did not go any farther, however, that is, he did not enter Solomon's territory.

---

*Abraham Malamat, "The First Peace Treaty Between Israel and Egypt," BAR, September/ October 1979.

On the contrary, he gave one of his daughters to Solomon as a wife with the city of Gezer as her dowry (1 Kings 3:1, 7:8, 11:1).

Apparently no significant change in external policy occurred except, perhaps, a greater development in commercial relations with Hiram, king of Tyre (1 Kings 5:1–18) and, later on, the transfer of the land of Cabul (see below).

Like David, Solomon entered diplomatic marriages to ensure the fidelity of the neighboring Transjordanian kingdoms. He probably married "Naamah the Ammonitess" whose son later became King Rehoboam (1 Kings 14:21).[82] According to 1 Kings 4:21, like his father, "Solomon ruled over all the kingdoms from the River [the Euphrates] to Philistia, as far as the Egyptian frontier; they were bringing gifts (or tribute) and were subject to him all his life." However this general and late (probably Persian period)[83] assertion needs to be qualified, especially for Philistia (see above) and for Damascus' kingdom (see below), as well as more generally for northern Syria and the Phoenician coast.

Solomon also reorganized the administration of his kingdom, a task to which he devoted considerable effort and for which biblical tradition accords him the title "wise" (hakam)—that is to say, he was both a clever politician and a good administrator. Various areas of administrative organization or re-organization can be distinguished.[84] First was the central government, in which a new royal cabinet was nominated:

> And these were his high officials: Azariah the son of Zadok was the priest; Elihoreph and Ahijah the sons of Shisha were secretaries; Jehoshaphat the son of Ahilud was recorder; Benaiah the son of Jehoiada was in command of the army; Zadok and Abiathar were priests;[85] Azariah the son of Nathan was over the officers; Zabud the son of Nathan was priest and king's friend; Ahishar was in charge of the palace; and Adoniram the son of Abda was in charge of the forced labor.
>
> (1 Kings 4:2–6)

In comparison with David's royal cabinet (2 Samuel 8:16), Solomon's appointments reflect a certain continuity, a son often inheriting his father's position. We can also detect Egyptian influence in the bureaucratic structure.[86] There are new officials such as the man over the officers/governors, the man in charge of the administration of the palace and the man in charge of the forced labor levy. In general, the bureaucracy becomes more complex and more pervasive.

Two sons of the prophet Nathan were made members of this cabinet, probably because of the prominent part their father played in the designation of Solomon as king (1 Kings 1:11–38).

Israelite territory now included a number of annexed Canaanite city-states, such as Dor, Megiddo and Beth-Shean. As it expanded, Israel was divided into 12 administrative districts or provinces.[87] Each province had at its head a prefect or governor appointed by the king. Administration was thus centralized. In 1 Kings 4:8–19 we find a list of the governors with their territories and principal cities, which presents a good parallel to other ancient Near Eastern administrative lists.[88] At least two governors married Solomon's daughters (1 Kings 4:11,15), another way of centralizing and controlling the government administration.

Each administrative district was required to provide for the king and his palace for one month a year (1 Kings 4:7,27–28). This was a heavier economic responsibility than it might at first seem. It included the expenses of maintaining the royal harem, of providing for a number of functionaries and of equipping the army with horses and chariots (1 Kings 4:28 = 1 Kings 5:8 [Hebrew Bible]). As in David's reign, the royal treasury also received income from royal properties. Although the royal treasury no longer received booty in Solomon's reign, the Jerusalem treasury was probably supplied with tribute from vassal lands in Transjordan.

Trade and construction during Solomon's reign

Solomon also developed an important new source of income from the international trade that became so important during his peaceful reign.[89] The government operated this trade, and the royal treasury profited from it in various ways: Trade with Phoenicia provided timber (cedar and pine) and technical aid (mainly for the construction of Solomon's official buildings). In exchange, Israel supplied agricultural producucts like wheat and olive oil (1 Kings 5:8–11 = 1 Kings 5:22–25 [Hebrew Bible]). In cooperation with the Tyrians, Solomon sent trading expeditions to Ophir[90] through the Red Sea.[91] These expeditions brought back gold, precious stones and tropical products (*almug* wood, apes and baboons) (1 Kings 9:26–28, 10:11,22). Caravans through the Arabian desert returned with spices (1 Kings 10:1–10).

Although Solomon's reign was comparatively peaceful (David had been almost continually at war), he nevertheless took care to modernize his army.[92] He equipped it with large numbers of chariots imported from Egypt, for which he imported horses from the kingdom of Que (Cilicia) (1 Kings 10:26–29).[93] Solomon also built special garrisons in various administrative districts for his chariots and their horses (1 Kings 4:26–28 = 1 Kings 5:6–8 [Hebrew Bible]; 9:19).

Solomon is also famous for his building activities. He constructed a wall around Jerusalem and built three fortified cities, Hazor, Megiddo and Gezer (1 Kings 9:15). These building activities can be related to military defense (see 1 Kings 9:17–18).[94] Solomon's public works in Jerusalem were major accomplishments. It took him seven years to build the Temple (1 Kings 6:37–38) and 13 years to build his royal palace (1 Kings 7:1, 9:10). He also built a structure in Jerusalem known as the *millo*. No one today is certain what the *millo* was. The most likely suggestion is that it was some kind of terracing, since the word seems to be related to the Hebrew term for "fill."[95]

To plan and construct these official buildings, Solomon needed the technical aid of the Phoenicians, who provided assistance not only with the basic architecture and construction, but also with the decoration of the buildings and the acquisition of the raw materials (wood, ivory, gold). These imports were expensive. Indeed, during the second part of his reign, "King Solomon gave to Hiram twenty cities in the land of Galilee" (1 Kings 9:11–13), that is "the Land of Cabul"[96] (Asher with the rich plain of Acco),[97] to balance the trade deficit between the two kings. To cast the many bronze objects decorating the Temple and the royal palace, Solomon used his metalworks in the Jordan valley "between Succoth and Zarethan." The casting seems to have been supervised by a Phoenician who specialized in bronze craftsmanship (1 Kings 7:13–47). The origin of the metal is not specified (but see below).

The Bible's detailed description of Solomon's public buildings, especially of the Temple (1 Kings 5–6),* reflects the importance of these monuments to the king's glory. At first the Temple seems to have been a kind of royal chapel attached to the royal palace that was used primarily by the king and his court. Later, after the eighth century B.C.E. reforms, these buildings served as a souce of pride for the people. Moreover, such buildings helped legitimize the new political organization.[98] However, in order to build and maintain these symbols of power, Solomon needed a reservoir of cheap manpower. His solution was the *corvée*, forced labor required not only of non-Israelite peoples (1 Kings 9:20–21), but of Israelites as well. The statement in 1 Kings 9:22 that "of the people of Israel Solomon made no slaves" seems contradicted by several statements in Kings (1 Kings 5:13–18 = 1 Kings 6:27–32 [Hebrew Bible]; 11:28, 12:4). The *corvée* and the conscription of Israelites into Solomon's army (1 Kings 9:22) were probably the two principal sources of popular dissatisfaction with Solomon's reign.[99]

As often happens during long reigns, internal dissatisfaction grew in the latter half of Solomon's rule; at the same time, serious external threats

---

*Victor Hurowitz, "Inside Solomon's Temple," *BR*, April 1994.

surfaced. The biblical tradition gives us a few hints of the dissension inside Israel (1 Kings 11).[100]

The text speaks of two foreign adversaries (*satan*) of Solomon: The first one is "Hadad the Edomite [Aramean]." A member of the royal house of Edom (Aram),[101] Hadad sought refuge in Egypt and even married a sister of the queen (Tahpenes) before trying to go back to his country (1 Kings 11:14–22). The second adversary of Solomon was "Rezon the son of Eliyada," who fled from his master Hadadezer, king of Zobah, and took to the hills as the chief of a small troop: "They went to Damascus, and dwelt there and made him king in Damascus" (1 Kings 11:23–24). (Actually, as we will discuss below, these two enemies might have been one and the same: "the Aramean Prince/*Rezon* Hadad son of Eliyada.")

In Israel itself, internal dissatisfaction led to a revolt spearheaded by Jeroboam, an Ephraimite who had the support of the prophet Ahijah from Shiloh: "Solomon sought therefore to kill Jeroboam; but Jeroboam arose and fled into Egypt, to Shishak king of Egypt and was in Egypt until the death of Solomon" (1 Kings 11:29–40).[102]

The dissatisfaction with Solomon's rule probably had many sources, but the biblical tradition insists principally on the people's objections, based on religious grounds, to Solomon's many foreign wives.

> For when Solomon was old his wives turned away his heart after other gods ... He went after Ashtoret, the goddess of the Sidonians, and after Milcom, the abomination of the Ammonites ... Then Solomon built a high place for Chemosh the abomination of Moab, and for Molech (Milcom)[103] the abomination of the Ammonites, on the mountain[104] east of Jerusalem.
>
> (1 Kings 11:4–7)

The biblical account of Solomon's reign closes by again mentioning the wisdom of Solomon (1 Kings 11:41; see previously 1 Kings 4:29–34 = 1 Kings 5:9–14 [Hebrew Bible] and 1 Kings 10:1–13) and by fixing the length of his reign at 40 years (1 Kings 11:42).

Biblical text vs. history

As with David, it is difficult to assess as history the biblical traditions concerning Solomon's reign: In the absence of contemporary Hebrew texts or references to Solomon in ancient Near Eastern texts, we are dependent almost exclusively on the Bible and on archaeology. Yet the biblical materials have a long and complex history of their own and the Solomon which they present is largely a legendary figure.[105]

The principal parts of 1 Kings 1–11 contain an early literary tradition that appears to have been taken from a now-lost account of Solomon's reign, referred to in the Bible as the Acts of Solomon (1 Kings 11:41), which was probably written not long after Solomon's death. The lost account presented Solomon as a typically wise king since it could not speak about his glory at war.[106] However, this early tradition is often mixed with later Deuteronomistic additions and with emendations by later editors.[107] For instance, two different literary traditions seem to have been combined in 1 Kings 9:26–10:13, which concerns the journey to Ophir and the visit of the queen of Sheba. Part of the early tradition preserved in the Book of Kings tries to justify and exalt Solomon. This is even truer of later traditions.[108] For example, 2 Chronicles 8:3–4 refers to Solomon's expedition to northern Syria: "And Solomon went to Hamath-Zobah and took it. He built Tadmor [Palmyra] in the wilderness and all the store-cities which he built in Hamath." However, the Hebrew text of 1 Kings 9:15–18 does not mention Hamath-Zobah or Tadmor and these names are probably a conforming alteration of 1 Kings 9:15–18 by the author of Chronicles.[109] In the same way, the Hebrew text of 1 Kings 9:19 mentions "Lebanon," in addition to Jerusalem, as a place where Solomon conducted building activities; however, "Lebanon" is missing in some manuscripts of the Greek translation known as the Septuagint and probably has no historical basis.

Nonetheless, if we put aside overstatements and later additions, and discount for the flattering style of most of the texts, the principal points of the early biblical tradition seem generally trustworthy. We can rely most heavily on passages that are close in style to contemporaneous annals and administrative texts.[110]

Our extrabiblical knowledge of the history of the region during this period provides information regarding several aspects of Solomon's reign, especially in connection with his relations with Egypt,[111] but also with Phoenicia and Sheba.[112] And archaeology helps us to understand Solomon's reputation as a builder, as well as the social transformation that took place during his reign.

Relations with Egypt

Although Egypt is hardly mentioned as a political power in the biblical accounts of David's reign, several pharaohs did play an important role during Solomon's day. At the beginning of Solomon's reign, a pharaoh attacked Gezer. This pharaoh, as earlier mentioned, was probably Siamun, one of the last pharaohs of the XXIst Dynasty.[113] Although Egyptian texts thus far discovered do not confirm the matrimonial alliance between Solomon and Pharaoh's daughter, the event is factually presented in the Bible and is probably to be understood in the context of a strong Egyptian political and cultural influence on Solomon's kingdom. By this marriage, Solomon agreed to be in the sphere of Egyptian influence.[114]

As evidence of this Egyptian influence, several studies have cited the design of the royal cabinet[115] and Solomon's organization of the country into 12 administrative districts.[116] Regarding the 12 administrative districts, however, some scholars contend that the influence went in the opposite direction,[117] although that does not seem very likely. It is also quite possible that the literary tradition of the 12 sons of Jacob and of the 12 tribes of Israel find its origin in this organization into 12 administrative districts, as Gösta W. Ahlström has suggested.[118] The notion of 12 tribes of Israel would be a retrojection from this period to the patriarchal age.

Another pharaoh mentioned in the biblical account of Solomon's reign (in connection with Jeroboam's revolt [1 Kings 11:26–42]) is called "Shishak." This is Pharaoh Sheshonk, the founder of the XXIInd Dynasty. Shishak was a strong personality who wanted to restore Egyptian power, especially in the ancient Egyptian province of Canaan. His accession to the throne (c. 945 B.C.E.) probably marks a turning point in Solomon's reign. Instead of being a kind of benevolent godfather, Shishak was hostile to the Israelite king and supportive of all his opponents. Finally, in the fifth year of the reign of Solomon's successor and son, Rehoboam, Shishak organized a military expedition against the kingdom of Judah (1 Kings 14:25–28) which marched through Israel as well.[119]

It is therefore not suprising to find Shishak supporting Jeroboam's revolt. This political and military threat—and the independence of Damascus—probably increased the financial strains on Solomon. He received less tribute and had to spend more money on defense.

Relations with Phoenicia

A literary tradition sheds some light on the relationship between Israel and Phoenicia at this time. Preserved in Phoenician annals, the tradition has been transmitted to us second- or third-hand through Menander of Ephesus, Alexander Dius Polyhistor and Josephus.[120] Although we must read these works with some caution, because they evolved indirectly via two or three Greek intermediaries, they are part of a serious literary tradition; they reflect the use of actual Tyrian archives or annals telling about the principal military expeditions and building activities of the Phoenician kings.[121] Some kind of Solomonic annals probably existed as a contemporanous parallel—and may well have been partly inspired by the Phoenician annals.[122] Thus, Josephus quotes Dius Polyhistor, probably from his history of Phoenicia:

The Khirbet Qeiyafa ostracon. *The text written in ink on this broken pottery sherd (called an ostracon) was recently found in the excavations of the tenth-century B.C.E. site of Khirbet Qeiyafa (see p. 104). It may be the earliest example of a Hebrew inscription, although it could equally be a rare example of an early Philistine or Canaanite writing. The scripts would be the same. Even if Hebrew, however, the text is too broken and poorly preserved to provide a continuous translation. Initial readings have isolated the words and phrases "Do not do," "serve," "judge" and "king," all of which seem to place the text in the realm of ethics and justice.*

> On the death of Abibalus [Abibaal], his son Hirom came to the throne. He leveled up the eastern part of the city with embankments, enlarged the town, united it by a causeway to the temple of Olympian Zeus, which was isolated on an island, and adorned it with offerings of gold; he also went up to Libanus and had timber cut down for the construction of temples.[123]

Menander of Ephesus, as quoted by Josephus, writes of a similar tradition.[124] Even if these texts present historical problems of their own and differ in detail, they were probably based on the same annals of Tyre and thus shed some light on the cultural and commercial relations between Hiram and Solomon. Furthermore, other late traditions as well as some Phoenician inscriptions confirm the important part played by the Phoenicians, mainly by the Tyrians, in the maritime trade of the Red Sea during the first millenium B.C.E.[125]

The Queen of Sheba

Although in the Bible the story of the Ophir expedition through the Red Sea is now intertwined with the expedition of the queen of Sheba (1 Kings 9:26–10:22), these two events should not be confused. The queen of Sheba did not come on Phoenician-Israelite ships plying the Red Sea but traveled instead on camels and brought with her primarily spices. These two features are characteristic of the Arabian peninsula. Although the story of the queen of Sheba contains various literary and legendary themes and was clearly written to glorify Solomon, Assyrian texts of the eighth and seventh centuries B.C.E. do mention a kingdom of Sheba in Arabia and several queens of northern Arabian kingdoms.[126] Other Assyrian texts, connected with Hindanu on the Middle Euphrates, show that the international South Arabian trade was already in place in about 890 B.C.E.[127] In light of these texts, we know that an official mission of Sheba could well have come from southern Arabia to Jerusalem in the second half of the tenth century B.C.E.*[128]

Independence of Damascus

The confused story of Hadad the "Edomite" and "Rezon the son of Eliyada" (1 Kings 11:14–22) probably represents a distorted image of a historical tradition from an old source[129] concerning the first king of Damascus: the Aramean Prince (*Rezon*) Hadad son of Eliyada,[130] whose revolt Solomon apparently did not dare to crush by a military expedition (probably because Hadad was patronized by Pharaoh), which means that Solomon probably did not control any Aramean territory.

Writing

Epigraphic discoveries from the period of the United Kingdom are still very rare.[131] An exception is the famous Gezer calendar, a small limestone tablet containing a list of the 12 months with the agricultural work performed in each month.** However, this inscription may well be Philistine as well as Hebrew.[132] We meet the same problem of interpretation with the Tel Zayit abecedary and the Khirbet Qeiyafa ostracon.[133] The latter is often presented

---

*A newly discovered South Arabian inscription dating to the sixth century B.C.E. confirms the trading parternship between Sheba and Judah. See André Lemaire, "Solomon & Sheba, Inc.," *BAR*, January/February 2010.

**Philip J. King and Lawrence E. Stager, "Of Fathers, Kings and the Deity," *BAR*, March/April 2002.

ZEV RADOVAN/WWW.BIBLELANDPICTURES.COM

The Stepped-Stone Structure. *Located on the eastern ridge of the City of David, this massive stone structure originally stood nearly 90 feet tall and 130 feet wide at top. It is preserved to a height of 50 feet, making it one of the most imposing structures to have survived from ancient Israel. The Stepped-Stone Structure may have been built to support a large public building, quite possibly King David's palace, as recently proposed by archaeologist Eilat Mazar. Although scholars agree that the structure incorporates several centuries of building, the dating of the various elements is contested. The most recent excavations date its core to pre-Davidic times, suggesting it may have been part of the fortress that defended Jebusite Jerusalem when David successfully assaulted the city, in about 1000 B.C.E.*

as a didactic Hebrew inscription from the beginning of the tenth century B.C.E.,* but an interpretation as an 11th century list of Canaanite or Philistine names cannot be excluded since Qeiyafa could have been a Philistine fort (see above). In any event, these inscriptions and a handful of shorter ones show, directly or indirectly, that alphabetic writing was known and used in the Judah and Israel as well as in Philistia around the tenth century B.C.E.

Despite this paucity, the period of David and Solomon was probably an important period of literary creation, much of it composed to support ideological and political goals of the government. Although a matter of considerable scholarly dispute, Israelite historiography probably began

---

*See "Prize Find: Oldest Hebrew Inscription Discovered," *BAR*, March/April 2010.

at this time.[134] It may have begun with a history of David's accession written by Abiathar the priest or by someone close to him.[135] David and, even more so, Solomon probably promoted the writing of a history that brought together the early Israelite traditions originally connected with different sanctuaries (Shechem, Hebron, Beersheba, Shiloh, etc.).[136] The original unification of these early traditions may have been the work of the famous and much discussed Yahwist.[137] The Yahwist (also called J) is the earliest strand of tradition in the Pentateuch, according to the so-called documentary hypothesis, which divides the Pentateuch into four different strands, the others being E (for Elohist), P (Priestly code and history) and D (Deuteronomist). J probably established the tradition of the 12 sons of Jacob and was the first to present Abraham, Isaac and Jacob as members of the same family.

Solomon's state administration required officials who could read and write. The development of national historical and legal traditions, as well as a new royal ideology, also required literate scribes. We may therefore assume that there were scribes and probably schools in Jerusalem[138] and in the capitals of the administrative districts[139] as well as in some of the ancient Canaanite city-states. The tradition of Solomon "the wise ... who declared 3,000 proverbs and 1,005 songs" is clearly an exaggeration (1 Kings 4:32); nevertheless, the Solomonic period, probably in part under Egyptian influence (note the use of hieratic ciphers in later Hebrew epigraphy*), no doubt saw the birth of an important stream of Hebrew literature connected with royal ideology.

Solomon and archaeology

Archaeology also sheds some light on the activities of Solomon as a builder and on the contemporaneous transformation of Israelite society. According to William G. Dever, the tenth-century B.C.E. architectural remains "are not only the earliest evidence we possess of monumental achitecture in ancient Israel but [the buildings] are among the most impressive."[140]

The Solomonic Temple**[141] was probably completely destroyed by the Babylonians in 587 B.C.E. After the Israelites returned from the Babylonian Exile, a second temple was built. This Temple was rebuilt by Herod the Great in the first century B.C.E., and subsequently burnt by the Romans in 70 C.E. According to Ernest-Marie Laperrousaz, however, part of the Solomonic retaining wall of the Temple Mount can still be seen on the eastern side of the

*Anson F. Rainey, "The Saga of Eliashib," BAR, March/April 1987.
**For a nearly identical temple dating to the same period, see John Monson, "The New Ain Dara Temple, Closest Solomonic Parallel," BAR, May/June 2000.

Plate 1. The Sinai peninsula. *This view of the "great and terrible wilderness" (Deuteronomy 8:15) traversed by the Israelites on their Exodus wanderings was taken by a NASA satellite miles out in space. (See Chapter II.)*

Plate 2. Tomb painting from Beni Hasan, Egypt. *Leaning over his ibex, a figure named Abisha and identified by the title Hyksos leads brightly garbed Semitic clansmen into Egypt to conduct trade. Dating to about 1890 B.C.E., the painting is preserved on the wall of a tomb carved into cliffs overlooking the Nile at Beni Hasan, about halfway between Cairo and Luxor.*

Foreign groups often sojourned in Egypt, especially in pursuit of trade. In the early second millennium B.C.E., numerous Asiatics infiltrated Egypt, some of whom eventually gained control over Lower Egypt for about a century and a half. The governing class of these people became known as the Hyksos, which means "Rulers of Foreign Lands." Knowledge of this period of Asiatic rule in Egypt may have affected the biblical account of Joseph's rise to power. (See Chapter II.)

Plate 3. Philistine pottery. *The fine craftsmanship of these pitchers and bowls challenges the traditional characterization of the Philistines as a boorish, warlike people devoid of an aesthetic sensibility. Known as bichrome ware because it was decorated with two colors—black and red—this pottery displays typical Philistine designs, including birds (visible on the wine decanter, at right), checkerboards, spirals and other geometric patterns. (See Chapter IV.)*

Plate 4. Canaanite cult stand from Taanach. *Four tiers of cryptic scenes ornament this tenth-century B.C.E. pottery stand from Taanach (about 5 miles southeast of Megiddo). A shallow basin—presumably for offerings or libations—crowns the 21-inch-high stand. The bottom register depicts, in high relief, a nude female figure, perhaps the mother-goddess Asherah, holding the ears of two lions. Winged sphinxes flank the opening in the second register. Lions appear again on the third register; between them, two goats nibble on a stylized tree—perhaps a "tree of life"—a motif associated with Asherah. Two columns frame the top scene, which depicts a horse or calf with a winged sun-disk above its back.*

Although the images are often identified as the Canaanite deities Baal (represented as a bull) and Asherah, it has recently been suggested that they actually represent the Israelite deity Yahweh (represented by the horse and by the empty space in the second register) with Asherah as his consort. (See Chapters III and IV.)

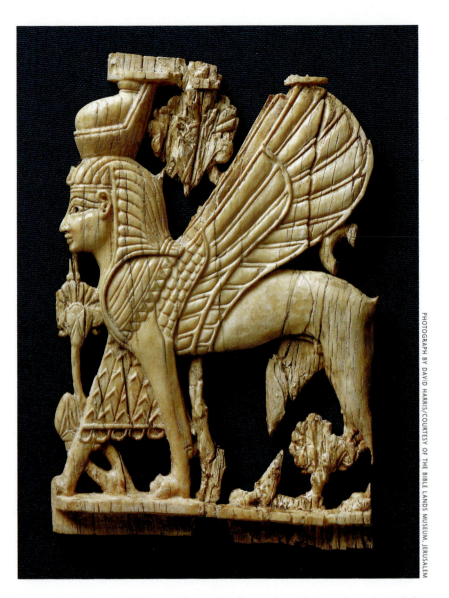

Plate 5. Ivory cherub. *Modeled in ivory, this 5-inch-tall ivory plaque, dating to the ninth or eighth century B.C.E., depicts a winged creature with an exquisite human face, the forequarters of a lion and what may be the hindquarters of a bull. Such composite creatures, like the Egyptian sphinx, were common in the ancient Near East, where they were often associated with divinity. This ivory, probably from Arslan Tash in northern Syria, recalls the cherub described by the prophet Ezekiel as combining characteristics of humans, lions, bulls and eagles (Ezekiel 1:10). Mentioned more than 90 times in the Hebrew Bible, cherubim guarded the gates of the Garden of Eden and stood over the Ark in the Holy of Holies in the Temple.*

Solomon's "great throne of ivory," described in 1 Kings 10:18, may have been decorated with such ivory plaques. Ornamenting thrones and beds with ivory was a well-known specialty of the Phoenicians, Solomon's trading partners. (See Chapter IV.)

Plate 6. Israelite bull figurine. *Dating to about 1200 B.C.E., this 4-inch-tall bronze statue was discovered at a cult site near biblical Dothan, in the heart of the hill country that was then being settled by the Israelites.*

Although the biblical writers consistently condemn the iconography of young bulls, archaeological finds such as this indicate that the bull was an early Israelite symbol of divinity. This figurine may resemble the bull statues erected by Jeroboam (c. 930–908 B.C.E.) at Bethel and Dan (1 Kings 12:26–33). (See Chapter V.)

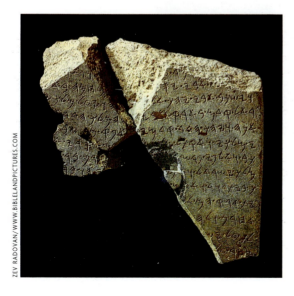

Plate 7. Tel Dan Stela. *An Aramean king—probably Hazael of Damascus—boasts of his victories over "[Jo]ram son of [Ahab], king of Israel," and "[Ahaz]iah son of [Jehoram, ki]ng of the House of David," in this Old Aramaic inscription from Dan. The dates of the reigns of the biblical kings Joram of Israel (c. 850–841 B.C.E.) and Ahaziah of Judah (c. 841 B.C.E.) provide a mid-ninth-century B.C.E. date for the inscription. The reference to "the House [or dynasty] of David" suggests that Judahite kings traced their descent back to an actual David who lived a century earlier. It is the earliest appearance of the name of David outside the Bible. (See Chapter V.)*

Plate 8. Ivory pomegranate from Solomon's Temple. *This exquisite carving was long thought to be the only surviving artifact from Solomon's Temple in Jerusalem. A small hole bored into the bottom of the ivory indicates that it probably served as the decorative head of a ceremonial scepter carried by Temple priests. Several such pomegranate scepters have survived, one of which is pictured here. The inscribed pomegranate reads around the neck "Holy to the priests, belonging to the H[ouse of Yahwe] h." Although most paleographers, including André Lemaire and the late Nahman Avigad, regard the inscription as unquestionably authentic, dating to the late eighth century B.C.E., some Israeli officials and archaeologists contend the inscription is the work of a modern forger. (See Chapter V.)*

122

Plate 9. Herodium. *To protect himself in case of insurrection, Herod the Great (37–4 B.C.E.) built a string of palace-fortresses—including this volcano-like structure that he named after himself—in the Judean wilderness. At Herodium, Herod started with a natural hill and then created an artificial mountain over it. Inside he fashioned a palace that included living rooms, a reception and dining hall, a colonnaded courtyard, cisterns and a bathhouse. Four massive towers and a double wall protected the intimate palace. At the foot of the mountain, a 135-foot by 21-foot basin (visible in the left foreground) served as a reservoir, a pool and a lake for small sailboats; picnickers may have enjoyed the circular pavilion at the center of this desert oasis. Herod was buried at Herodium, according to Josephus, and Israeli archaeologist Ehud Netzer has recently identified the tomb at the foot of the mound. (See Chapter VIII.)*

123

Plate 10. Masada. *This imposing citadel—built by Herod the Great (37–4 B.C.E.) on an isolated plateau at the edge of the Judean wilderness—is associated with a legendary act of defiance. According to the first-century C.E. Jewish historian Josephus, a band of Jewish fighters, unwilling to concede defeat during the First Jewish Revolt against Rome, held out at Masada for more than three years against a large imperial army after the fall of Jerusalem in 70 C.E. Masada fell in 73 or 74 C.E., when the Romans built a ramp on a spur on the western side of the plateau. (See Chapter VIII.)*

Gezer gate. *In 1 Kings 9:15, we read that Solomon fortified "Hazor, Megiddo and Gezer." In this view from inside Gezer, we see six chambers (three on each side) of a monumental gate dated to the tenth century B.C.E. Nearly identical gates have been discovered at Hazor and Megiddo, and for decades, archaeologists have believed that all three gates were evidence of Solomon's handiwork—mighty public works constructed by a powerful central authority. More recent excavators at Megiddo, however, using the so-called "Low Chronology," have redated the gate at their site to the ninth century B.C.E., nearly 100 years after Solomon. In renewed excavations at Hazor, the excavator confirms the tenth-century date of that gate.*

Temple Mount as it exists today.*[142] (This particular part of the wall begins north of the so-called straight joint that can be found on the eastern wall of the Temple Mount, 105.5 feet north of its southeast corner.)

The excavations in the City of David (a spur south of the present Temple Mount), led by Yigal Shiloh, have uncovered the huge Stepped-Stone Structure probably built to support an enlarged platform on top of the northern part of the City of David. The platform may have supported a

*Ernest-Marie Laperrousaz, "King Solomon's Wall Still Supports the Temple Mount," *BAR*, May/June 1987. More recently, archaeologist Eilat Mazar has discovered additional walls south of the Temple Mount that she believes date to the reign of Solomon. Eilat Mazar, *BAR*, forthcoming.

public building—perhaps a royal palace; or the Stepped-Stone Structure may also be the famous *millo* mentioned in 1 Kings 9:15. However this last interpretation is conjectural and the dating of this structure is disputed (13th/12th or tenth century B.C.E.),* as is the date of the monumental archaeological fragments (tenth or ninth century B.C.E.) found north of the Ophel which could be connected with Solomon's palace.[143]

Other remains from the City of David that have been dated to the tenth century B.C.E. include a few walls discovered by Yigal Shiloh and a wall fragment excavated by Kathleen Kenyon.[144] Further, Jane Cahill, who is preparing Shiloh's excavation for publication, has recently argued that the Stepped-Stone Structure (which she dates to the 13th/12th century B.C.E.) was partially dismantled in the tenth century to accommodate the construction of houses on top.**[145]

As noted, in 1 Kings 9:15–17 we are told that Solomon rebuilt three Canaanite cities which became part of his kingdom—Hazor, Megiddo and Gezer. Major excavations have been and are still conducted at each of these three cities and Yigael Yadin, followed by many others, tried to demonstrate that these three cities were probably rebuilt in about the middle of the tenth century B.C.E. (the time of Solomon).[146] Yadin and other archaeologists have based their conclusions on the presence of almost identical fortification plans at all three sites.† Each city is surrounded by a casemate wall‡ and has a gateway with three chambers on each side (that is, with four pairs of piers) of nearly the same dimensions. Furthermore the ashlar stones (hewn stones) of these three gateways are dressed the same way. All these similarities in design can best be explained as having been the work of the same architect or school of architects during Solomon's reign.[147] These dates and this interpretation have been corroborated by later excavations at Gezer by William Dever[148] and at Hazor by Amnon Ben-Tor.[149] The dating of the gate of Megiddo, however, is still a matter of dispute.[150]

The stratigraphy of Megiddo at the beginning of Iron Age II (beginning in

*Margreet Steiner, "David's Jerusalem: Fiction or Reality? It's Not There: Archaeology Proves a Negative," *BAR*, July/August 1998; Jane Cahill, "David's Jerusalem: Fiction or Reality? It Is There: The Archaeological Evidence Proves It," *BAR*, July/August 1998.
**Jane Cahill, "Jerusalem in David and Solomon's Time. It Really Was a Major City in the Tenth Century B.C.E.," *BAR*, November/December 2004.
†"Monarchy at Work? The Evidence of Three Gates," sidebar to "Face to Face," *BAR*, July/August 1997; Valerie M. Fargo, "Is the Solomonic City Gate at Megiddo Really Solomonic?" *BAR*, September/October 1983.
‡A casemate wall consists of two parallel walls crossed by short perpendicular walls that form internal rooms for storage, etc.

about 1000 B.C.E.) is not at all clear. So, for instance, the structures identified by early American excavators as Solomonic stables,[151] were redated by Yadin to be ninth century B.C.E.[152] Furthermore, their interpretation as "stables" is still a matter of dispute.*[153] However, Graham I. Davies has shown that a similar, earlier building at Megiddo might well have been the Solomonic stables.[154] Most archaeologists date level VA-IVB at Megiddo to the tenth century, corresponding to the Solomonic period.[155] This dating has been questioned by David Ussishkin, who argues that, at least for the "Solomonic" gate, this level must be dated to the ninth century;[156] moreover, G.J. Wightman[157] and Israel Finkelstein[158] propose a general shift in the dating, lowering what have been thought of as tenth-century B.C.E. remains to the ninth century. This proposal, however, is beset with major problems and has been rejected by many excavators at other sites.[159] One can only hope that the current excavations at Megiddo will clarify the dating of the relevant levels from that important site.

Another town mentioned in 1 Kings 9:18 is "Tamar in the wilderness," which has been identified with 'En Hazeva. Excavations led by Rudolph Cohen and Yigal Yisrael at this site have revealed a tenth-century B.C.E. level (Stratum VI), which seems to match with Solomonic building.[160]

More generally, many archaeological sites in ancient Israel seem to have been built or rebuilt about the middle of the tenth century.[161] These sites include new cities as well as fortresses. Indeed a network of early Iron Age fortresses in the Negev may be connected with Solomon's reign.**[162] Most of them were probably later destroyed by Pharaoh Shishak's military expedition to Palestine about 925 B.C.E.[163]

Excavations at Khirbet en-Nahas in the Wadi Feinan area of Jordan, south of the Dead Sea, revealed "the largest Iron Age copper-smelting site in the southern Levant."†[164] Even though the precise dates of this site are still debated,[165] it is clear that this important copper-smelting site was in use already in the tenth century B.C.E. This could well be the source of the copper used to cast the many bronze objects decorating Solomon's Temple (1 Kings 7:13–47).

From the point of view of archaeology, the general picture of ancient Israel in the mid-tenth century B.C.E seems to be that of a transitional society.

---

*Moshe Kochavi, "Divided Structures Divide Scholars," BAR, May/June 1999.

**Rudolph Cohen, "The Fortresses King Solomon Built to Protect His Southern Border," BAR, May/June 1985.

†Thomas E. Levy and Mohammad Najjar, "Edom & Copper—The Emergence of Ancient Israel's Rival," BAR, July/August 2006. See also Thomas E. Levy and Mohammad Najjar, BAR, forthcoming.

Israelite areas were inhabited not only by farmers and stockbreeders in villages but also, beginning in the tenth century, by some craftsmen, merchants and functionaries who served in the army and in the government administration and lived in royal fortified cities (many of these having been built upon ancient Canaanite cities). Archaeology attests to the beginning of a process of re-urbanization typical of an early state.[166] The beginning of this social change, from a tribal society to an early state under a central administration, probably accounts for the appearance of public buildings in the new fortified cities— governor's palaces, storehouses and administrative buildings.[167] At about this time, we also begin to find many small precious objects. As Yohanan Aharoni notes, "The change in material culture during the tenth century is discernable not only in luxury items but also especially in ceramics" which are of a higher quality (see "Why Do We Date David and Solomon to the Tenth Century?" p. 87).[168] The economic growth and development of new cities was probably connected with a population boom, natural in a period of peace and prosperity. In the area inhabited by Israel, the population could well have doubled in the century that extended from the beginning of Saul's reign to the end of Solomon's.[169] By this time, the sedentary population of the Judahite hills (not including the Shephelah and the Negev) made up probably only 3 percent of the total population of the country.[170]

Social and political tensions

The beginning of the transformation of Israelite society into an early state and the burden of the new state's administrative structures[171] were resisted by many levels of Israelite society.[172] This was especially so among the "house of Israel" (the northern tribes), who wanted to retain their own religious and political traditions. Social tensions were also produced by the mixing of the populations in Solomon's military conscription and the forced levy (the *corvée*). All this certainly served to sharpen the antagonisms between Israel and Judah.[173] No doubt, members of the House of Israel resented the Judahites, who probably held the better positions in the civil government and in the military. Solomon's death and the political errors of his successor soon revealed the unstable base on which he and David had set their achievements, and probably delayed the further evolution of Israelite and Judahite society into a well-organized national state. Moreover, that evolution would now occur in two separate states.

FIVE

The Divided Monarchy
The Kingdoms of Judah and Israel

SIEGFRIED H. HORN AND P. KYLE McCARTER, JR.

THE EARLY YEARS

The schism at the death of Solomon

WHEN SOLOMON DIED, HIS SON REHOBOAM (C. 930–913 B.C.E.) succeeded him as king of Judah, apparently without incident (1 Kings 11:43). Rehoboam then traveled north to Shechem to lay his claim to the throne of Israel as well. The account of the ensuing negotiations preserved in 1 Kings 12 suggests that the leaders of the northern tribes were prepared to accept Rehoboam's rule, as long as the new king mitigated the harsh labor policies of his father. Historians assume that part of their concern was the tax burden required to support Solomon's building projects and to maintain his palace, as detailed in the description of revenue collection in the administrative districts he established (1 Kings 4:7–28), but the only grievances expressed in the account of the Shechem parley are "the hard service of your father and the heavy yoke that he placed on us" (1 Kings 12:4). According to 1 Kings 9:15–23, Solomon imposed *corvée*, or conscript labor, only on the foreign, non-Israelite population, while the Israelites involved in his work projects served as overseers and officers (1 Kings 12:22–23). Nevertheless, the language of the northern leaders' complaint indicates that they felt enslaved by Solomon's labor policies, and it is noteworthy that when the secession movement found a leader, he was a dissident officer in Solomon's labor force and a fugitive from the king's justice.

As a young man from Zeredah (a town west of Shiloh in the Ephraimite highlands), Jeroboam son of Nebat had come to Solomon's attention because of his administrative skills and energy. Solomon placed him in charge of the *corvée* labor of the House of Joseph—that is, the conscript labor battalions of the territories of the half-tribes of Ephraim and Manasseh (1 Kings 11:26–28). Despite this high-ranking appointment, Jeroboam proved not to be a loyal member of Solomon's administration and, in circumstances not explained, he "lifted his hand against the king" (1 Kings 11:26), that is, he led some kind of insurrection. With Solomon's police seeking his life, Jeroboam fled to Egypt and found refuge with Pharaoh Sheshonk I (c. 945–924 B.C.E.), the biblical Shishak, in whose safekeeping he remained until Solomon's death.

Shishak, a Libyan nobleman, was the founder of the XXIInd Egyptian Dynasty, superseding the weak XXIst Dynasty, which, under Pharaoh Siamun (978–959 B.C.E.), seems to have made common cause with Israel and Judah against the Philistines. (See Chapter IV, "The United Monarchy: Saul, David and Solomon.") Shishak's hospitality to Jeroboam, however, may be an indication that Egypt, invigorated and ambitious after the rise of the XXIInd Dynasty, no longer felt the need for a policy of accommodation with Jerusalem. On the contrary, Shishak may have viewed the burgeoning power of Solomon's dual kingdom as a serious threat to Egyptian interests in Canaan.

After Solomon's death, Jeroboam returned to Israel. According to the account in 1 Kings 12, he exercised a leadership role in the parley at Shechem. As already noted, Rehoboam might have been able to win over the northern tribal leaders if he had dealt with them respectfully and assured them of less oppressive treatment. Indeed, his senior advisors recommended this course of action (1 Kings 12:7). But Rehoboam followed the advice of more junior advisors, his contemporaries, and replied to the petition of Jeroboam and his companions with hostility and even vulgarity: "My little finger is thicker than my father's loins" (1 Kings 12:10). Having been threatened by Rehoboam with policies even harsher than Solomon's, the northern leaders took up the slogan of Sheba's revolt—"What share do we have in David?" (compare 2 Samuel 20:1 with 1 Kings 12:16)—and withdrew from Shechem. When Rehoboam sent Adoram (or Adoniram; compare 1 Kings 4:6), his chief *corvée* officer, to raise a work levy, the Israelites stoned him to death (1 Kings 12:18), and the division of the kingdoms became an accomplished fact. Rehoboam was obliged to flee to Jerusalem for his own safety (1 Kings 12:18).

The Bubastite Portal. *In the fifth year of the reign of Rehoboam, "King Shishak of Egypt ... took the fortified cities of Judah and came as far as Jerusalem" (2 Chronicles 12:2–4). Scenes depicting the military exploits of Pharaoh Sheshonk I (c. 945–924 B.C.E.)—biblical Shishak—decorate a doorway in the forecourt of the Great Temple of Amun at Karnak, in Thebes.*

ERICH LESSING

What role, if any, was played by Egypt in these events is difficult to say. A strong Israelite state, unified and including Judah, would be a threat to Egypt's interest in freely accessing, if not controlling, the trade routes along the coastal highway—the Via Maris or, as the Egyptians called it, the Way of Horus—and through the corridor running from Jezreel to Beth-Shean. Jeroboam must have used the time he spent in Egypt to prepare for his role in the schism, and we may suspect that he did so with Shishak's encouragement if not his active tutelage. After the Israelites embraced Jeroboam as their king (1 Kings 12:20), however, there is no reason to think that he ruled as an Egyptian puppet or even with active Egyptian support. The earlier pharaoh Siamun may have been content to forge alliances with Israelite kings, but Shishak's ambition was greater.

Shishak's invasion

Not long after the separation of Israel and Judah, Shishak led a large Egyptian army across the Sinai peninsula into Canaan. Our knowledge of this campaign comes from brief accounts in 1 Kings 14:25–26 and 2 Chronicles 12:1–12, where it is dated to the fifth year of Rehoboam's reign (c. 926 B.C.E.), and from the hieroglyphic text that accompanies Shishak's triumphal relief on the so-called Bubastite Portal[1] on the south wall of the first forecourt of the Great Temple of Amun at Karnak in Thebes (modern Luxor). The biblical account gives the impression that the incursion was directed at Jerusalem (1 Kings 14:25) or at Jerusalem and the fortified cities of Judah (2 Chronicles 12:4), as if Shishak, who had given asylum to Jeroboam when he was a refugee, was now acting on his behalf in his ongoing conflict with Rehoboam of Judah (cf. 1 Kings 14:30; 2 Chronicles 12:15b). The list of conquered cities in the Karnak relief, however, shows that Shishak attacked cities throughout Canaan, north and south. In fact, many northern, or Israelite, cities appear on the list, but few Judahite cities. The Egyptian army marched through the heartland of the northern kingdom, subduing many of Jeroboam's own cities as well as the adjoining regions. Though the sequence of cities attacked is unclear in the Karnak list,[2] the itinerary included cities in the Plain of Sharon (Socoh, Yahma, Borim, Aruna), through the Jezreel corridor (Megiddo, Taanach, Shunem, Beth-Shean, Rehov) and east of the Jordan (Succoth, Penuel, Mahanaim, Adam). This shows that Shishak's campaign was not aimed at Judah in particular but was intended instead to reassert Egypt's ancient interests in Canaan and to reestablish some measure of influence, if not control, along the major trade routes. Both the organization of the campaign and the rhetoric of its memorialization at Karnak suggest that Shishak was nostalgically emulating the style of the great conqueror Ramesses II.[3]

Even if Shishak cannot be said to have been acting on behalf of Jeroboam, however, it seems probable that his initial target was Jerusalem. The hieroglyphic text on the Bubastite Portal asserts that the campaign was undertaken in response to attacks by Asiatics, who were threatening Egyptian frontier settlements,[4] and it is possible that Shishak viewed Solomon's construction of fortresses in the southern Negev[5] as a provocation. After leaving Egypt and Sinai and entering Canaan, Shishak marched north through Gaza and began the assault at Gezer; from there he turned east into the southern Ephraimite hills and made his way towards Jerusalem along the usual northern approach, via Aijalon, Beth-horon and Gibeon.[6] It was probably at this point, with the Egyptian army encamped in the hills north of Jerusalem, that Rehoboam paid Shishak the heavy tribute described in 1 Kings 14:26: "He took away the treasures of the house of the Lord and the treasures of the king's house; he took everything." Shishak, evidently satisfied with this payment, turned north, sparing the principal cities of Judah and Jerusalem itself. Later in the campaign, when the Egyptian army came south again, Shishak gave his attention to the region south of Judah; the Karnak list contains an extensive roster of places conquered in the Negev.

Shishak's invasion is especially important as a source of information for reconstructing the history of Israel. It provides our earliest clear connection between the history of Israel and the history of Egypt. The Egyptian materials in the Joseph story and the Exodus narrative, though rich and suggestive, are much more difficult to control as historical sources. In addition, Shishak's invasion gives us a conspicuous point of reference in the archaeological record. The techniques of siege warfare, which the neo-Assyrian conquerors would perfect a century later, were already well enough developed for Shishak to be able to capture and destroy cities throughout the region.[7] Excavators have found evidence of violent conflagrations in strata corresponding to the late tenth century at a number of sites along the itinerary recorded in the Bubastite Portal reliefs. Shishak's army has been posited as the agent of destruction at a large number of these sites, including some named in the extant portions of the itinerary and many others that are not.[8] The former group includes Arad, Gezer, Taanach and Megiddo,* where a fragment of a stela erected by Shishak was found.

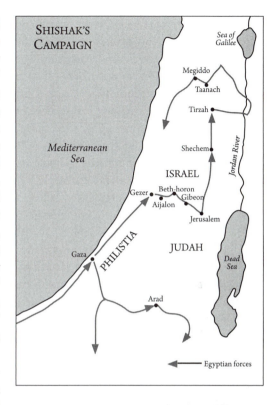

Two aspects of the archaeological record that emerge from an examination of the Shishak destructions are especially impressive and noteworthy.[9] One is the wide distribution and high quality of the tenth-century fortifications and other architecture, lending credence to the assumption that Solomon's later reputation as a great builder, as reflected in the biblical account of his reign (1 Kings 6–7, 9:15–23), is well deserved. The other noteworthy aspect of the archaeological record is the rapidity and thoroughness with which the destroyed cities were rebuilt, sometimes to an even higher standard.[10] This suggests that Shishak's incursion, as devastating as it was, had little lasting impact on the region.[11]

The religious policies of Jeroboam

Shechem, where Rehoboam had failed to win the allegiance of the northern tribes, became the site of Jeroboam's government, but he soon moved his base of operations to Penuel, a town in Gilead that he is said to have fortified (1 Kings 12:25). Although historians have speculated that Jeroboam withdrew

---

*Timothy P. Harrison, "The Battleground: Who Destroyed Megiddo? Was it David or Shishak?" *BAR*, November/December 2003.

to Transjordan to seek refuge at the time of Shishak's incursion, the biblical narrative provides no reasons for the move. Nor is there any explanation why he eventually returned west and established a capital at Tirzah, as is implied by 1 Kings 14:17. In any case, Tirzah (now usually identified with the extensive tenth-century ruins at Tell el-Far'ah [North], northeast of Shechem) was the capital during the reigns of his successors, Baasha (1 Kings 15:33; cf. 1 Kings 15:21), Elah (1 Kings 16:8) and Zimri (1 Kings 16:15), until the sixth year of Omri, when Samaria was founded (1 Kings 16:23; cf. 1 Kings 16:24).

The paucity of information about Jeroboam's political headquarters in the biblical account contrasts sharply with the extended report on the national religious centers he established at Dan and Bethel (1 Kings 12:26–33; see also 1 Kings 13:1–14:18). This contrast is an indication of the interests of the writers whose work is preserved in the Book of Kings, our principal biblical resource for the history of the monarchy. This literature was given its primary shape by a historian whom scholars describe as Deuteronomistic, because his perspective on the history of Israel is based on religious ideas preserved in the Book of Deuteronomy. Many scholars believe that the Deuteronomistic historian wrote during the reign of King Josiah of Judah (640–609 B.C.E.) in support of the king's program of religious reform and cultic centralization.[12] In any case, the historian placed special emphasis on Jerusalem as the divinely ordained central sanctuary for all Israel and the only place where sacrifice could legitimately be offered to the God of Israel. It was, in his view, "the place that the Lord your God will choose," foretold by Moses as the one acceptable place of sacrifice after the conquest of Canaan (Deuteronomy 12:13–14). From this perspective, Jeroboam's installation of national sanctuaries at Dan and Bethel was a fundamental breach of religious law and a flaunting of the divine will.

As the Deuteronomistic historian saw it (1 Kings 12:26–33), Jeroboam established these two cult centers because he feared that if his people continued to make regular pilgrimages to Jerusalem, they might eventually renew their allegiance to Rehoboam. He therefore established northern sanctuaries to replace Jerusalem in direct violation of Yahweh's instructions to Moses in Deuteronomy 12, and instituted a festival at Bethel beginning the fifteenth day of the eighth month—"a month that he alone had devised" (1 Kings 12:33), that is, without divine authorization—to rival the authorized festival of Sukkot, which was celebrated in Jerusalem one month earlier (Leviticus 23:34; cf. Deuteronomy 16:13–17). He compounded this crime by fashioning two golden calves to be worshiped at the two sanctuaries and installing nonlevitical priests to officiate.

It is unlikely, however, that the people whose allegiance Jeroboam was trying to win, his contemporary Israelites from the northern tribes, viewed his actions as arbitrary innovation. For them, Jerusalem held no special claim to religious authority. A Canaanite enclave conquered by David, Jerusalem was the city of the Judahite kings Solomon and Rehoboam, and as such it represented outside rule and oppression. By contrast, Bethel was an ancient Yahwistic sanctuary, strongly associated with Israel's patriarchs (Genesis 12:8, 28:10–22). Dan, too, was a long-established center of Yahwism.[13] Even the bulls were probably old and authentic Yahwistic symbols.* In any case, there is no suggestion, even in our hostile Deuteronomistic account, that Jeroboam introduced any kind of non-Yahwistic cult. Nevertheless, from the Deuteronomistic perspective that shapes the larger biblical narrative of the early Divided Monarchy, Jeroboam's installation of the golden calves at Dan and Bethel was a heinous crime ("This thing became a sin," 1 Kings 12:30), for which his kingship would be divinely rejected and his family condemned (1 Kings 14:9–11). In the Deuteronomistic interpretation of history, moreover, the disastrous consequences of Jeroboam's crime spread beyond his own reign. "The sin of Jeroboam," as the Deuteronomistic historian called it, was perpetuated by his successors (1 Kings 15:26,34, etc.), and it eventually led to the fall of the northern kingdom and the exile of its people (2 Kings 17:21–23).[14]

The wars of the early Divided Monarchy

The early years of the Divided Monarchy were characterized by almost constant warfare between Israel and Judah. When Rehoboam died after a reign of some 17 years (1 Kings 14:21), he was succeeded by his short-lived son, Abijam (c. 913–911 B.C.E.) or Abijah (as he is called in Chronicles), about whom little is said except that he was victorious over Jeroboam in a major battle fought on

---

*The iconography of the young bull is consistently condemned by the biblical writers, and it may never have had a place in the Jerusalem cult. Nevertheless, there is considerable evidence to suggest that it was an Israelite symbol of divinity with a venerable pedigree. A bronze bull figurine was found at a probable 12th-century B.C.E. cultic site, in the heart of the region that was then being settled by Israelites in the hill country of Samaria (Amihai Mazar, *Archaeology of the Land of the Bible 10,000–586 B.C.E.*, Anchor Bible Reference Library [New York: Doubleday, 1990], pp. 350–351; and "Bronze Bull Found in Israelite 'High Place' from the Time of the Judges," *BAR*, September/October 1983). The depiction of "Yahweh of Samaria" in bovine form on a pithos from Kuntillet 'Ajrud shows that bull iconography was still a viable form of religious expression at the beginning of the eighth century B.C.E. (P. Kyle McCarter, Jr., *Ancient Inscriptions: Voices from the Biblical World* [Washington, D.C.: Biblical Archaeology Society, 1996], pp. 106–108; Ze'ev Meshel, "Did Yahweh Have a Consort?" *BAR*, March/April 1979; and André Lemaire, "Who or What Was Yahweh's Asherah?" *BAR*, November/December 1984). Hosea's diatribes against "the calf of Samaria" (Hosea 8:5–6) and "the calf of Beth-aven" (Hosea 10:5, where *Beth-aven*, "House of Wickedness," is a pejorative distortion of Bethel, "House of God") show that it was still a part of the northern cult later in the eighth century B.C.E.

the southern boundary of Ephraim (2 Chronicles 13:3–20; cf. 1 Kings 15:7).

Jeroboam died a few years later, and his son, Nadab (c. 908–907 B.C.E.), after only a couple of years rule, was assassinated by Baasha son of Ahijah, a member of the tribe of Issachar and one of Nadab's senior officers (1 Kings 15:25–31). The coup took place during an Israelite siege of the Philistine-controlled fortress of Gibbethon. This may be taken as an indication of ongoing border disputes between Israel and Philistia in this period, especially in view of the fact that Gibbethon (usually identified with Tell el-Malat, just west of Gezer) was under Israelite siege again a generation later when Baasha's son was unseated in another military coup (1 Kings 16:8–10). Baasha, having quickly secured his position by a massacre of the remaining members of the family of Jeroboam (1 Kings 15:29), was able to stabilize the situation and establish himself in Tirzah as the new king of Israel. He ruled for a substantial number of years (c. 907–884 B.C.E.), though we are told in 1 Kings 15:16 that his reign was troubled by constant warfare with Judah, which was now ruled by the even more long-lived Asa (c. 911–870 B.C.E.), Rehoboam's grandson.

At some point in the long reigns of these two kings (Baasha in the north and Asa in the south)—the year is uncertain and disputed—a series of events drew Damascus into the hostilities between Israel and Judah (1 Kings 15:17–22 = 2 Chronicles 16:1–6). Baasha's forces had captured and fortified the border fortress of Ramah (modern er-Ram) and imposed an embargo on Jerusalem, a few miles to the south. Asa sought the help of Ben-hadad, the king of Damascus.[15]

Asa, appealing to a former or still-existing treaty between Jerusalem and Damascus, asked Ben-hadad to invade Israel. He enticed the Aramean king with a large gift of silver and gold collected from the Jerusalem Temple and his own royal palace. Although Ben-hadad seems also to have had a treaty with Baasha (see 1 Kings 15:19), he accepted Asa's invitation and sent an Aramean army south to ravage Israelite cities in the region north of the Sea of Galilee. Thus, Asa's strategy was successful, and Baasha was forced to withdraw from Ramah and lift the embargo. The Israelite withdrawal gave Asa the opportunity to strengthen the northern border of Judah. According to 1 Kings 15:22, the Judahites took the building materials with which the Israelites had fortified Ramah, transported them to Geba and Mizpah* and fortified those places, thus shoring up the Judahite frontier against Israel.

*A massive, 15-foot-thick wall constructed at this time has been found at Tell en-Nasbeh, ancient Mizpah. See Jeffrey R. Zorn, "Mizpah: Newly Discovered Stratum Reveal's Judah's Other Capital," BAR, September/October 1997. For an alternative proposal for the location of Mizpah, see Yitzhak Magen, "Nebi Samwil: Where Samuel Crowned Israel's First King," BAR, May/June 2008.

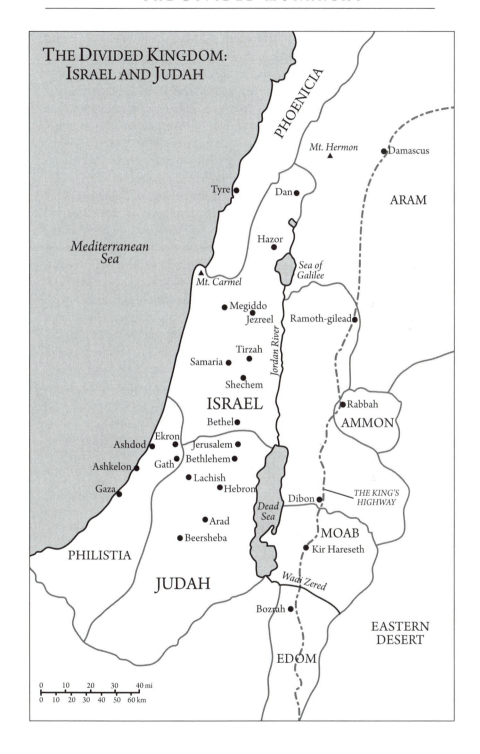

THE DIVIDED KINGDOM:
ISRAEL AND JUDAH

PHOENICIA

Mt. Hermon

Damascus

ARAM

Tyre

Dan

Mediterranean
Sea

Hazor

Sea of
Galilee

Mt. Carmel

Megiddo

Jezreel

Ramoth-gilead

Jordan River

Tirzah

Samaria

Shechem

ISRAEL

Rabbah

AMMON

Bethel

Ekron

Ashdod

Jerusalem

Bethlehem

Ashkelon

Gath

Lachish

Gaza

Hebron

Dibon

THE KING'S
HIGHWAY

Dead
Sea

Arad

Beersheba

MOAB

Kir Hareseth

PHILISTIA

JUDAH

Wadi Zered

EASTERN
DESERT

Bozrah

EDOM

0   10   20   30   40 mi

0   10   20   30   40   50   60 km

Although the silver and gold with which Asa is said to have bribed Ben-hadad might have been enough to entice him into action, it is also clear that the region he attacked had strategic importance to Damascus. The cities listed in 1 Kings 15:20 as having been conquered by Ben-hadad, "Ijon, Dan, Abel-beth-maacah," lie at the northern extreme of Israelite territory, on or beneath the western slope of Mount Hermon in the direction of the watershed of the Litani River. Control of this region provided Damascus with passage into the river valley and thus to the Phoenician port city of Tyre, situated only 6 miles south of the mouth of the Litani. Having access to Tyre without having to negotiate with Israelite intermediaries was a major advantage for the merchants of Damascus in the ongoing struggle for control of the important trade routes of northern Palestine.

Baasha's son and successor, Elah (c. 884–883 B.C.E.), succumbed to a coup early in his reign (1 Kings 16:8–20). He was assassinated in his palace at Tirzah while his army, commanded by Omri, was away from the capital besieging the Philistine city of Gibbethon. The assassin, a chariot officer named Zimri, quickly massacred the rest of Baasha's family, as Baasha himself had done to the family of Jeroboam.* When word reached Gibbethon, however, the Israelite army proclaimed Omri king and set out for Tirzah. Zimri, after only a week's rule, took his own life. There followed a brief struggle for the crown when Omri's followers were challenged by a group who favored a certain Tibni son of Ginath (1 Kings 16:21–22), but the Omri party prevailed and he became king of Israel in Tirzah.

---

*The repeated pattern of royal assassinations in the early history of the northern kingdom creates an impression of political turmoil in Israel that contrasts with the stability that the Davidic dynasty gave Judah. Neither Jeroboam nor Baasha was able to establish a dynasty, since in each case the son and successor was removed in a coup early in his reign.

Many historians have interpreted this as indicating that the northern kingdom had embraced a tradition of "charismatic" kingship, according to which leaders were expected to arise in times of crisis, receiving divine designation and popular acclamation. The paradigm for this kind of leadership is found in the stories of the premonarchical period, when Israel was ruled by "judges" who were divinely appointed to office in times of need. The transitional figure was Saul, who was appointed and subsequently rejected as king by the prophet Samuel, acting on behalf of Yahweh. This is the pattern in the biblical account of the early years of the northern kingdom, where kingship is repeatedly bestowed and removed by prophetic decrees. Thus Jeroboam is designated (1 Kings 11:29–39) and rejected as king by Ahijah the Shilonite (1 Kings 14:6–16; see also 1 Kings 15:29), and Baasha is designated (see 1 Kings 16:2) and rejected (1 Kings 16:1–4; 1 Kings 16:12) by Jehu son of Hanani. Omri does succeed in establishing his dynasty, but its rule is prophetically condemned and, during the reign of Ahab, formally rejected by Elijah (1 Kings 21:20–24). Scholars disagree whether this is only a literary phenomenon, with later interpretation of the events being expressed by prophetic speeches composed *ex post facto*, or an indication of a distinctly northern ideal of kingship that differed from the dynastic principle that became entrenched early in Judah.

ISRAEL'S KINGS

The United Monarchy

Saul	c. 1030?-1009 B.C.E.
David	c. 1009/1001–969 B.C.E.
Solomon	c. 970/969–931 B.C.E.

The Divided Monarchy

Kingdom of Judah c. 930–587/6 B.C.E.		Kingdom of Israel c. 930–722 B.C.E.	
Rehoboam	c. 930–913	Jeroboam I	c. 930–908
Abijam (Abijah)	c. 913–911	Nadab	c. 908–907
Asa	c. 911–870	Baasha	c. 907–884
		Elah	c. 884–883
		Zimri	c. 883
		Omri	c. 883–872
Jehoshaphat	c. 870–846	Ahab	c. 872–851
		Ahaziah	c. 851–850
Jehoram	c. 846–841	Joram	c. 850–841
Ahaziah	c. 841	Jehu	c. 841–818
Athaliah	c. 841–835		
Jehoash	c. 835–801	Jehoahaz	c. 818–802
Amaziah	c. 801–783	Joash	c. 802–787
Azariah (Uzziah)	c. 783–732	Jeroboam II	c. 787–748
		Zechariah	748–747
		Shallum	747
Jotham	750–735	Menahem	747–738
		Pekahiah	738–737
Ahaz	735–727	Pekah	737–732
		Hoshea	732–724
Hezekiah	727–697		
Manasseh	697–642		
Amon	642–640		
Josiah	640–609		
Jehoahaz	609		
Jehoiakim	609–598		
Jehoiachin	598–597		
Zedekiah	597–586		

THE DYNASTY OF OMRI
King Omri and the restoration of Israel as a trading power

The biblical account of Omri's reign is cryptic (1 Kings 16:23–28). The writers are more interested in his son Ahab, whom they hold up as an example of a bad ruler. Nevertheless, though Omri ruled only 12 years (c. 883–872 B.C.E.), he seems to have accomplished quite a bit, founding a dynasty and restoring Israel to its position as an important trading nation. In the records of the neo-Assyrian empire, Israel came to be known as *māt Bit-Ḥumri*, "the (land of) the House of Omri." Though this practice is only known—ironically and probably by accident of survival—in Assyrian texts from the period following Omri's dynasty, it indicates how Omri's achievement was assessed internationally. The biblical account mentions only one of his accomplishments, the founding of Samaria.

Tirzah's location permitted easy communication with the Jordan Valley via the Wadi Farʿah. (This may have been of paramount importance when Jeroboam moved the capital there from Transjordanian Penuel.) Otherwise, Tirzah was isolated, surrounded by hills that made access to the principal international trade routes difficult. After six years, Omri founded a new capital at Samaria, northwest of Shechem, a choice that favored communication and trade.* The site, a strategically located and easily defended summit in a fertile part of the Ephraimite highlands, overlooked one of the main roads into the hills from the coastal highway and the Mediterranean, about 25 miles to the west. Perhaps most important, the location permitted extensive contact with Phoenicia. In many respects, the most salient characteristic of the Omride dynasty was its close relationship with Tyre.

Omri entered into amicable relations with King Ittobaal of Tyre, the biblical Ethbaal, and secured the alliance by marrying his son Ahab to Ethbaal's daughter Jezebel.** This couple, reviled by the biblical writers for being corrupt leaders and for promoting the worship of a foreign god, became notorious in biblical tradition. Nevertheless their marriage cemented a diplomatic and commercial relationship with the prosperous mercantile cities of the Mediterranean coast that brought substantial wealth to the landlocked cities of Israel. What was at stake for Phoenicia was a

---

*Norma Franklin, "Lost Tombs of the Israelite Kings," *BAR*, July/August 2007. See also David Ussishkin, Another View, "The Disappearance of Two Royal Burials," *BAR*, November/ December 2007; Norma Franklin, Another View, "Don't Be So Quick to be Disappointed David Ussishkin," *BAR*, March/April 2008.

**Marjo C.A. Korpel, "Fit for a Queen: Jezebel's Royal Seal," *BAR*, March/April 2008. See also Queries and Comments, "Post-Postscript," *BAR*, May/June 2008; Queries and Comments, "Seal Scholar Defends Her Position," *BAR*, July/August 2008.

passage through the central hill country into Transjordan, where caravans arrived from the south transporting luxury items along "the King's Highway" (cf. Numbers 20:17, 21:22), the name given to the north-south road that ran along the edge of the entire Transjordanian plateau from the northern tip of the Gulf of Aqaba to Damascus. The caravans were a source of immense wealth, and it was in the interest of Tyre and the other Phoenician ports to divert them west before they reached Damascus. The topography of the region determined the best route for this. It diverged from the King's Highway somewhere near Ramoth-gilead (possibly Tell er-Ramith, near the modern border of Jordan and Syria), descended through the Wadi Yabis into the Jordan Valley, continued on the other side through the Beth-Shean and Jezreel Valleys, and came out on the Plain of Acco with Tyre and the other Phoenician ports dead ahead.[16]

Phoenician expansion eastward along this route in the tenth and ninth centuries B.C.E. is illustrated archaeologically by characteristically Phoenician pottery found at a series of sites extending from Horvat Rosh Zayit[17] on the Plain of Acco to Tel 'Amal, just west of Beth-Shean, to Tell el-Ḥamma in the Jordan Valley.[18] The presence of these sites does not imply direct Phoenician control of the region but rather political amity and commercial cooperation with Israel, within whose borders the route lay. The same pattern is in evidence at northern Israelite sites of the same period, which have yielded a substantial amount of imported Phoenician pottery as well as architectural remains showing the use of building materials imported from Phoenicia and Phoenician building techniques, including ashlar masonry,* Proto-Aeolic capitals** and especially ivory carving. Elegant ivories, Phoenician in style and probably in manufacture, have been found at a number of Israelite and Judahite sites of the tenth to eighth century. The royal palaces at Samaria yielded a hoard of some 500 pieces of carved ivory inlay, bringing to mind "the ivory house that [Ahab] built" in Samaria (1 Kings 22:39) and the "houses of ivory" and "beds of ivory" in Amos's oracles against Samaria (Amos 3:15, 6:4).

*Ashlars are square-cut stones smoothed on all sides and cut precisely enough to fit together tightly without mortar. To give additional strength, the long and short sides of the rectangular blocks are sometimes laid parallel to the face of the wall in an alternating pattern—a technique known as "header and stretcher." The use of ashlar masonry is characteristic of both Solomonic and Omride architecture and, for that matter, later periods in which Israel or Judah were actively engaged in international trade. The techniques of ashlar stoneworking are believed to have radiated out of Phoenicia.

**A characteristic feature of ashlar construction was ornamentation with a type of engaged pillar capital called "Proto-Aeolic" or "Proto-Ionic" because it anticipates in some respects the capitals of those orders of later Classical architecture. A typical Proto-Aeolic capital consists of a pair of palmette volutes (spiral ornaments) flanking a central triangle.

This commercial arrangement with Phoenicia brought Israel into conflict with its immediate neighbor to the north, the Aramean state of Damascus. Though we have no biblical or extrabiblical report of Omri's foreign wars, there are strong indirect indications that he successfully pursued the struggle against Damascus begun in the reign of Baasha, when much of the northern Galilee fell to the depredations of Ben-hadad son of Tabrimmon. Excavations at sites like Dan and Hazor, where archaeologists have found destruction levels they associate with Ben-hadad's raid, indicate that the cities were rebuilt quickly, often to a higher standard and exhibiting the Phoenician-influenced building techniques noted above.[19] This restoration probably corresponds to the rise of Omri, when the region was returned to Israelite control. Eventually, however, the conflict between Samaria and Damascus ended as the two states made common cause against the Assyrian threat, as explained below.

The reign of Ahab

Ahab succeeded Omri as king and ruled 22 years in Samaria (872–851 B.C.E.). Generally speaking, his reign seems to have been a prosperous period for the northern kingdom, although much of its history must be reconstructed from the archaeological record and extrabiblical texts. The biblical account of the Omride dynasty has been shaped by writers whose primary interest was to express a distinctive religious viewpoint that was suspicious of kingship as an institution. Most of the episodes narrated involve the public and private affairs of the royal family, especially their conflicts with opposition groups. The result is that, despite the extensive treatment of the period in the biblical text, relatively few of the events reported there can be associated with external history and evaluated by the historian. This is especially true of the account of Ahab's reign (1 Kings 16:29–22:40), which is similar in spirit to the stories of Saul's kingship in 1 Samuel, which are dominated by the figure of the prophet Samuel, and to stories of certain abuses of power by both David, in which the prophet Nathan is prominent, and by Solomon. The point of view of this type of literature may be called "prophetic," since it places emphasis on the authority of prophets who are shown to be divinely inspired.[20] Kings of Israel are depicted as abusive of the rights of their subjects and dangerous to the religious integrity of Israel since they are often involved in foreign alliances, leading to the worship of foreign gods in Israel.

Ahab in particular is presented as a paradigm of the bad king. He acquires the throne by inheriting it from his father, Omri, rather than by divine choice and prophetic selection. He is married to a foreign woman, Jezebel of Tyre, who aggressively promotes the worship of Baal in Israel. Together, Ahab and Jezebel abuse and exploit their Israelite subjects—the story of Naboth's vineyard (1 Kings 21) is the parade example. Ahab's adversary is the prophet Elijah. Their story is presented as an extended struggle between Yahweh, the God of Israel, for whom Elijah speaks, and Baal, the biblical term for any foreign god. We might understand this as reflecting a historical situation in which the God of Israel was being challenged by Jezebel's god—presumably Melqart, the god of Tyre—but this seems an unlikely scenario. There is little question that Yahweh was recognized in Samaria as the national God of Israel, even though his worship was conducted in ways that the biblical writers, from their perspective in later Jerusalem, found abhorrent. Ahab's allegiance to Yahweh is demonstrated by the fact that the three of his children whose names we know all had Yahwistic names—two sons, Joram and Ahaziah, both of whom eventually became king, and one daughter, Athaliah, who became queen of Judah. The religious conflict in Samaria was not between Yahwists and non-Yahwists, but rather between the adherents of exclusivistic Yahwism (the prophetic party) and the adherents of an inclusivistic religion (the Samaria aristocracy), which recognized the preeminence of Yahweh as the God of Israel but did not exclude the worship of foreign gods (the policy that Solomon is said to have adopted).

In any case, the literary character of the biblical account of the Omride dynasty makes it less useful than we would hope (in view of its length) for the reconstruction of ninth-century history. There are only a few allusions to Ahab's substantial building projects and little reliable information about his foreign relations. Most striking, there is no reference at all to his participation in the great anti-Assyrian coalition of 853 B.C.E. (see below), despite the major role he is known to have played, as shown by the Assyrian records. Nevertheless, it is possible to give a general description of his reign based on a critical reading of the biblical text and drawing heavily on extrabiblical documents and the archaeological record of the period.

As already noted, the first half of the ninth century is characterized archaeologically by extensive building projects throughout Israel. While these are likely to have begun during Omri's reign, it seems safe to assume that his son Ahab brought them to completion. This is true in particular of the Samaria acropolis, where excavations have shown the ninth-century royal palace to have been an architectural achievement of the highest order, with its finely dressed header-and-stretcher ashlar masonry, Proto-Aeolic capitals and ivories. This is the palace described in the summary of Ahab's reign in 1 Kings 22:39 as "the ivory house that he built." The same passage refers to "all the cities that he built" throughout Israel, and monumental structures have been found at sites like Dan,* Hazor,** Megiddo,† Jezreel (where the Omrides seemed to have maintained a royal estate, if not a subsidiary capital)‡ and many others.

Ahab also perpetuated the essentials of Omri's foreign policy. Since his queen was the Tyrian princess Jezebel, the alliance with Phoenicia remained strong, and Israel continued to benefit from the relationship. In the ongoing conflict with the Aramean kingdom of Damascus, including the contest for control of the east-west trade routes to the Mediterranean port cities, Israel probably maintained ascendancy during most of Ahab's reign. In his latter years, however, he found it expedient to enter into a defensive alliance with King Hadadezer of Damascus to counter the threat posed by Assyria, a situation reviewed in detail below.[21]

During the dynasty of Omri, Israel seems generally to have held sway over Judah. Jehoshaphat (870–846 B.C.E.), who had succeeded his father Asa as king of Judah early in Ahab's reign, is said in 1 Kings 22:44 to have "made peace with the king of Israel," and we learn in 2 Kings 8:26 that this peace was sealed by the marriage of Ahab's daughter Athaliah to Jehoshaphat's son Jehoram.

Omri and Ahab, like David and Solomon, exercised control east of the Jordan, at least in Gilead and as far south as the region north of the Arnon River, which was disputed with Moab. According to 2 Kings 3:4–5, King Mesha of Moab brought tribute (sheep) during the reigns of Omri and Ahab, then rebelled when Ahab died. A major inscription of Mesha, found at Dhiban (about 20 miles south of Amman), ancient Dibon, Mesha's capital,††[22] indicates that "the land of Medeba" (the region surrounding modern Madaba, about 18 miles southwest of Amman) was under Israelite sway "during [Omri's] days and half the days of his son," seeming to indicate that the revolt began earlier than the time of Ahab's death. A reasonable interpretation would be to assume that Ahab maintained firm control of central Transjordan until the latter part of his reign, when his participation with Damascus in the coalition against Assyria diverted his attention to the

---

*Avraham Biran, "Sacred Stones: Of Standing Stones, High Places and Cult Objects at Tel Dan," BAR, September/October 1998.

**Amnon Ben-Tor, "Excavating Hazor, Part One: Solomon's City Rises from the Ashes," BAR, March/April 1999.

† Israel Finkelstein and David Ussishkin, "Back to Megiddo," BAR, January/February 1994.

‡ David Ussishkin, "Jezreel—Where Jezebel Was Thrown to the Dogs," BAR, July/August 2010.

†† Siegfried H. Horn, "Why the Moabite Stone Was Blown to Pieces," BAR, May/June 1986. For more on the Moabites, see P.M. Michèle Daviau and Paul-Eugène Dion, "Moab Comes to Life," BAR, January/February 2002.

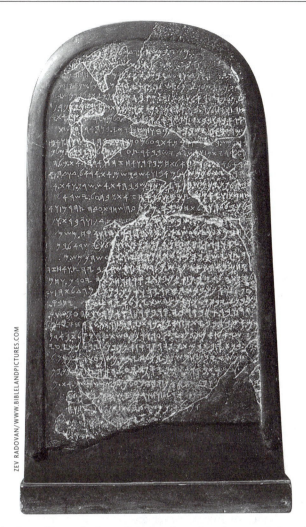

ZEV RADOVAN/WWW.BIBLELANDPICTURES.COM

Mesha Stela. *Erected by Mesha, king of Moab in the mid-ninth century B.C.E., this black basalt stela stands about 40 inches high and 24 inches wide. The inscription in Moabite, which is closely related to Hebrew, expresses Mesha's gratitude to his god Chemosh for delivering the Moabites from Israelite rule. Mesha claims he conquered Israelite territory east of the Jordan and humiliated the tribe of Gad. Among the towns mentioned is Dhiban (biblical Dibon), the site, about 20 miles south of Amman, where the stela was discovered. The Book of Kings also tells of a ninth-century Moabite rebellion; but the Bible and the stela may or may not refer to the same conflict. Each paints a different outcome from the other.*

André Lemaire and others have argued that the inscription, which is poorly preserved in places, contains one of the earliest extrabiblical references to "the House of David," that is, the dynasty of David. Another reference to "the House of David" has been identified in the nearly contemporaneous Tel Dan Stela (see Plate 7).

north.[23] As explained below, a final, unsuccessful attempt to reimpose Israelite control over Moab was made by a later Omride, Joram (c. 850–841 B.C.E.).

Shalmaneser III and the rise of imperial Assyria

After a long period of weakness at the beginning of the first millennium, the Upper Mesopotamian kingdom of Assyria, with its capitals on the east bank of the Tigris at Calah and Nineveh, arose to become a leading factor in the history of the Near East during the ninth to seventh century B.C.E. The Assyrian kings were motivated first by a desire to control the trade routes through northern Syria into the mineral-rich mountain country of Anatolia, but eventually their ambition spread south into the middle Orontes region, southern Syria and even Palestine. By the time Ahab ascended the throne in 872 B.C.E. it was already clear that the growing power of Assyria was a threat that would have to be reckoned with. Ahab must have quickly realized that he could not avoid becoming embroiled in the affairs of imperial Assyria.

A major factor in the resurgence of Assyria was the enormous wealth accumulated by the campaigning of Assurnasirpal II (884–859 B.C.E.), a contemporary of Omri and the early Ahab. A ruthless warrior and master tactician, he conquered Upper Mesopotamia, including numerous Aramean states; campaigned in the West through Syria and the mountains of Lebanon; and washed his weapons in the sea, receiving tribute from Byblos, Sidon, Tyre and several other coastal cities.[24] Despite his success in amassing plunder, however, Assurnasirpal was less talented than his successors at military strategy and diplomacy; he campaigned without a master plan and had little impact on the states of the southern Levant.

By contrast, Assurnasirpal's son and successor, Shalmaneser III (859–824 B.C.E.), was an accomplished strategist who campaigned with tenacity and purpose, if not always with success. He established a pattern, continued by his successors, of annual campaigns by the king or his representative. His repeated forays into Syria seem to have been driven by a master plan to subdue the West, either by outright annexation or, in the case of territories more distant from the Assyrian homeland, by the imposition of regular payments of tribute. That he was never entirely successful in achieving this goal was probably, at least in part, the ironic result of his father's successes. Rankled and impoverished by the strictures that Assurnasirpal's raids had put on the trade routes west of the Euphrates, a number of states in north Syria and the eastern Taurus (Bit Adini, Carchemish, Hattina, Sam'al) formed a coalition that opposed Shalmaneser almost immediately after his accession. In his first year he marched west to reassert Assyrian control of the major routes across northern Syria into the Amanus, the Cilician highlands and the

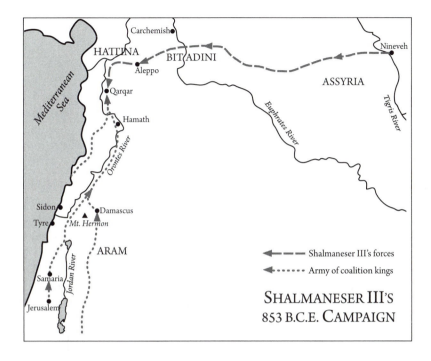

SHALMANESER III'S
853 B.C.E. CAMPAIGN

approaches to the mining areas of the Taurus. His advance was finally checked by the combined forces of the coalition in a battle at Lutibu, near Zinjirli in southeastern Turkey (ancient Sam'al).[25] Shalmaneser's response was to focus his attention on Bit Adini, which, lying between the Balikh River and the Euphrates, was the coalition state that lay nearest the Assyrian homeland. He marched west every year for three years (857–855 B.C.E.) until he had conquered Bit Adini and annexed it as an Assyrian province, refounding its riparian capital city, Til Barsib (modern Tell Ahmar), as Kar-Shulman-asharidu, "Shalmaneser's Landing."

After the subjugation of Bit Adini, most of the states of north Syria regularly paid tribute to Assyria. Quickly, however, a new anti-Assyrian coalition was formed by states farther to the south, who now felt threatened by Shalmaneser's relentless campaigns. The new alliance extended from Arvad, Byblos and other Mediterranean coastal cities as far south as Ammon in Transjordan and even Arabia.[26] The ringleader of the coalition—and the target of Shalmaneser's retaliation—was Irhulena of Hamath, a state situated in the rich agricultural lands of the middle Orontes region. Among the 12 kings allied with Irhulena, the most important, in terms of the size of the forces they committed to the cause, were Hadadezer of Damascus and Ahab of Israel. So began Samaria's conflict with the empire that would eventually destroy it.

The showdown began during Shalmaneser's sixth-year campaign (853 B.C.E.), when the Assyrian army marched into central Syria for the first time, subduing three of Irhulena's towns and capturing the fortress of Qarqar (probably Tell Qarqur in the northern Gab or Orontes Valley, northwest of the capital city of Hamath, modern Hama). After the fall of Qarqar, the Assyrian army was confronted by the full forces of the coalition. According to Shalmaneser's own records, the main contributors to the opposition force were Irhulena of Hamath (700 chariots, 700 horsemen and 10,000 footsoldiers), Hadadezer[27] of Damascus (1,200 chariots, 1,200 horsemen and 20,000 footsoldiers) and Ahab of Israel (2,000 chariots and 10,000 footsoldiers).[28]

After a brief respite when the Assyrian army was campaigning close to home from 852 to 850 B.C.E., Shalmaneser resumed his assault on the coalition in his tenth year (849 B.C.E.), marching west repeatedly in 848, 845 and 841 B.C.E. The persistence of Shalmaneser's attacks suggests that the alliance was effective, at least during the lifetime of Hadadezer of Damascus, who seems to have assumed the role of coalition leader after the 853 B.C.E. devastation of the domain of Irhulena of Hamath. Hadadezer died during the 845 B.C.E. campaign or shortly afterwards, and the throne of Damascus was seized by Hazael, a usurper.[29] The usurpation is described in detail in 2 Kings 8:7–15, a prophetic narrative in which Elisha foretells the later depradations of Israel by Hazael, who is depicted as personally assassinating his predecessor.[30]

The Assyrian records designate Hazael as the sole target of Shalmaneser's 841 B.C.E. campaign, suggesting that the supporting coalition had dissolved with Hadadezer's death. According to the Assyrian account, Hazael amassed his forces in "Mount Senir" (Mount Seir or Hermon, the highpoint of the Anti-Lebanon range) but was defeated and forced to retreat eastward into Damascus.[31] Shalmaneser besieged the city briefly, destroying its orchards and devastating the Hauran, the agriculturally rich plateau south of Damascus. He then marched west to a point on the Mediterranean coast where he received tribute from Tyre, Sidon and Israel. Israel's role in these events will be discussed below, but the point to be emphasized here is, once again, the isolation of Damascus—all of its former coalition members having chosen to capitulate rather than stand with Hazael against Assyria. Despite this isolation, however, and the devastation of his territory in 841 B.C.E., Hazael was not defeated. Shalmaneser marched against Damascus once more, in 838 B.C.E., and then spent the rest of his reign campaigning in northern Syria to secure Assyrian control of that region. Hazael survived to become an increasingly powerful force in southern Syria and northern Palestine and to expand his territory at the expense of his neighbors, especially Israel.

ISRAEL AND JUDAH UNDER THE
HEGEMONY OF DAMASCUS

Jehu's revolt

During most of the time that Shalmaneser was pressing his cause against Damascus, Israel was ruled by Ahab's son Joram (c. 850–841 B.C.E.). Ahab himself does not seem to have lived long after the battle of Qarqar (853 B.C.E.), although Jezebel survived and exercised considerable influence in her role as queen mother. Their older son, Ahaziah, succeeded Ahab as king, but after reigning for only a couple of years (c. 851–850 B.C.E.) he died of injuries sustained in an accident, having fallen through the railing of his balcony at Samaria (2 Kings 1:2–17), and was replaced by his brother Joram. Although the Assyrian records from Shalmaneser's 848 and 845 B.C.E. campaigns do not mention Israel by name, they do indicate that Hadadezer of Damascus was still supported by a 12-king coalition, and we assume that Joram was among the 12, as his father had been before him. The biblical account of Joram's decade-long reign (2 Kings 3) is silent on this issue, alluding to international events only in connection with his unsuccessful campaign against Moab.[32]

During much of his reign, Joram's counterpart in Judah was a king with the same name, Jehoram (846–841 B.C.E.).* As already noted, Jehoram's father, Jehoshaphat, had arranged for him to be married to Athaliah, daughter of Ahab and Jezebel, so that during Jehoram's reign Judah remained allied with Israel, apparently as a sort of junior partner. Our limited information suggests that Jehoram was no more successful in his military efforts than Joram; the account of his reign in 2 Kings 8:16–25 mentions revolts by Edom, which Jehoram tried but failed to suppress, and Libnah (possibly Tell Bornaḥ, north of Lachish), a city on Judah's western border with Philistia. When Jehoram died and was succeeded as king of Judah by his son Ahaziah, Joram was still on the throne in Samaria.

Not long after Ahaziah's accession, Jehu son of Jehoshaphat son of Nimshi, a high-ranking officer in the Israelite army, instigated a bloody purge that resulted in the deaths of the kings of both Israel and Judah. This was another in the series of military *coups d'état* that had brought both Baasha and Omri to the throne of Israel earlier. In this case, however, we have a better

---

*Jehoram and Joram are variants of the same name. In the ninth century B.C.E. this name was pronounced *Yāhū-rām* in Judah and *Yaw-rām* in Israel, both of which mean "Yahweh is exalted." The spellings of these names are not consistent in the Hebrew Bible, and the variations are preserved in most English translations, in which the king of Judah is most often called Jehoram, but frequently Joram, and the king of Israel is called Jehoram and Joram in roughly equal proportion. To minimize the confusion, and for convenience, the king of Judah is always called Jehoram in our discussion and the king of Israel is called Joram.

understanding of the factors that led to the revolt. From the viewpoint of the biblical writers, the uprising was the inevitable consequence of outrage (both divine and human) over the religious policies and social abuses of the Omrides, especially Ahab (cf. 1 Kings 21:17–26). A prophetic narrative in 2 Kings 9:1–13 depicts Jehu as having been anointed for his task by an anonymous prophet dispatched for the purpose by Elisha. Though many critics think this episode is merely a literary conceit, there is little doubt that the conflict between the prophetic party and the Omride aristocracy that animates the biblical account reflects real religious and political tensions in ninth-century Israel that arose from the reaction of conservative elements in Israelite society to the policies of the court at Samaria. Nevertheless, we can identify other factors, also important but not emphasized in the biblical account, that must have contributed to dissatisfaction with Omride rule. One of the most important of these was the economic setback represented by the successful revolts of Moab against Israel and Edom against Judah. As already noted, these losses greatly diminished the ability of both countries to benefit from the caravan trade that traveled the King's Highway. Another factor that must have undermined confidence in Joram was his conspicuous lack of success in military endeavors—both in his failed attempt to restore Israelite sovereignty over Moab and, more generally, in the ongoing struggle against Assyria. In fact, it was a serious wound that Joram received on the battlefield that created the circumstances in which the insurrection against Omride rule finally erupted. As the biblical account in 2 Kings 8–9 makes clear, however, the enemy on this occasion was not Moab or Assyria, but Israel's old anti-Assyrian ally, Damascus.

According to 2 Kings 8:28, the trouble began when Joram, accompanied by his ally, Ahaziah of Judah, marched into Transjordan "to wage war against King Hazael of Aram at Ramoth-gilead." We have already noted that after the death of Hadadezer in 845 B.C.E. and the seizure of the throne of Damascus by Hazael, the anti-Assyrian coalition seems to have dissolved, leaving Hazael to face Shalmaneser alone. The confrontation at Ramoth-gilead of the allied kings of Israel and Judah against the Damascene monarch Hazael suggests that Israel's Joram not only refused to support Hazael but became his open adversary.[33] Viewed from the perspective of the long-term relationship between Samaria and Damascus, this was less a reversal of policy than a return to normalcy—another flare-up of the smoldering rivalry between the two states like the one that occurred, for example, during the reigns of Baasha of Israel and Ben-hadad son of Tabrimmon of Damascus in the early ninth century B.C.E. As on that occasion, the principal cause of the hostilities between Joram and Hazael is likely to have been conflicting commercial interests involving the control of trade routes—a likelihood underscored by the location of the confrontation at the critical commercial junction of Ramoth-gilead.[34]

The violent sequence of events that the prophet Hosea would later refer to as "the blood of Jezreel" (Hosea 1:4) is described in detail in 2 Kings 8:28–10:28. Joram and Ahaziah led their armies to Ramoth-gilead, where they engaged the forces of Hazael. In the ensuing battle, Joram was wounded and retreated to recuperate in the town of Jezreel,[35] where he was soon joined by Ahaziah. Jehu may have been left in charge of the Israelite forces at Ramoth-gilead; in any case, he was one of the ranking officers who remained at the front. When Joram departed, the army turned to Jehu and proclaimed him king (2 Kings 9:13).[36] He then rode quickly to Jezreel, where he assassinated Joram, then pursued the fleeing Azariah and killed him too. The coup was secured in the usual way, by tracking down and massacring the surviving members of the fallen dynasty, the Omrides. Ahab's descendants ("seventy sons") were executed by the intimidated city leaders of Samaria and their heads were sent in baskets to Jehu in Jezreel (2 Kings 10:1–11). The once-powerful Israelite queen mother, Jezebel, was killed in Jezreel, where she was hurled from the window of her palace into the streets and her corpse was consumed by dogs (2 Kings 9:30–36).* The grim account of her death reflects the strong animosity towards this foreign queen on the part of the prophetic tradition and the biblical writers, who interpret her violent end as the fulfillment of Elijah's prediction in 1 Kings 21:23.

The carnage extended to the Judahite kin of Ahaziah (2 Kings 10:12–14), since as the son of Athaliah, daughter of Ahab and Jezebel, Ahaziah of Judah, too, was of Omride descent. Finally, Jehu instigated a wholesale slaughter of "the prophets of Baal, all his worshipers, and all his priests" (2 Kings 10:19), that is, all those Israelites who represented the religious practices inimical to the conservative Yahwism of the prophetic party. This part of Jehu's purge is stressed by the biblical writers (2 Kings 10:18–28), who, as already noted, regarded Ahab as a paradigm of the wicked king and viewed Jehu primarily as a religious revolutionary, who "wiped out Baal from Israel" (2 Kings 10:28). These events probably took place shortly before 841 B.C.E., when the Assyrian army returned to southern Syria after a few years respite. It has even been suggested that Jehu's revolt was timed to curry favor with Shalmaneser towards Israel by wiping out the anti-Assyrian faction—that is, the Omrides.[37] But new evidence—frustratingly incomplete and inconclusive—raises the possibility that in staging his coup Jehu was in league, not

---

*Ussishkin, "Jezreel—Where Jezebel Was Thrown to the Dogs," *BAR*, July/August 2010.

with Shalmaneser, but with Hazael. This evidence comes from the fragments of a basalt stela found at Tel Dan in 1993 and 1994.*[38]

Not enough remains of the broken monument to reconstruct a continuous translation of its elegantly carved Old Aramaic inscription, but the surviving portions of the text show that it was left at Dan by an Aramean ruler in commemoration of a victory over a large enemy force. Evidently the defeated enemy was Israel, as indicated not only by the erection of the victory stela at the Israelite city of Dan but also by the language of the first part of the surviving text, which seems to refer to earlier hostilities with a king of Israel. In the latter part of the inscription, describing the Aramean victory, two kings, one of Israel and the other of "the House of David"—that is, Judah—are mentioned by name. Though the text is too fragmentary for certainty, it seems likely that the two kings are said to have been killed. Despite the defective condition of the text at this point, only one reconstruction of these names seems possible: "[Jo]ram son of [Ahab], king of Israel," and "[Ahaz]iah son of [Jehoram, ki]ng of the House of David." It follows from this that the Aramean ruler who erected the monument is very likely to have been Hazael, who was the only king of Damascus contemporary with both Joram and the short-lived Ahaziah.[39] This in turn suggests that Hazael claimed responsibility for the deaths of Joram and Ahaziah, and that he may have regarded Jehu as, in some sense, his agent.[40]

The use of "House of David" as a designation for the kingdom of Judah in the Tel Dan stela deserves special attention. It is the earliest occurrence—or one of the two earliest occurrences**[41]—of the name of David outside the Bible, and it confirms the intimate association, already clear from the biblical writings, between the kingdom of Judah and the Davidic dynasty. "House of David" occurs 21 times in the Bible as a way of referring to the ruling family of Judah, either during David's lifetime or, more often, later (2 Samuel 7:26 = 1 Chronicles 17:24; Isaiah 7:2,13; etc.).[42]

Hazael's ascendancy

In political and territorial terms, Jehu's revolt was disastrous for Israel. "In those days," we are told in 2 Kings 10:32–33, "the Lord began to trim off parts of Israel." The passage goes on to describe Hazael's seizure of all of the Israelite territories east of the Jordan. If it is true that Jehu carried out his revolt with the encouragement or even support of Hazael, we may imagine that the two had an understanding that Jehu would receive Hazael's support in return for

---

*"'David' Found at Dan," BAR, March/April 1994.

**André Lemaire, "'House of David' Restored in Moabite Inscription," BAR, May/June 1994.

Black Obelisk. *The reliefs on this 7-foot tall, black stone monolith (left) depict the leaders of territories conquered by Shalmaneser III paying tribute to the Assyrian emperor. In the detail (above), a king of Israel (or perhaps his emissary) kneels before Shalmaneser, who appears to be admiring a vessel he has received. The annals of Shalmaneser III date the event to 841 B.C.E. The cuneiform inscription on the obelisk identifies the kneeling figure as "Yaw, son of Omri," leading scholars to identify the king as Omri's successor Jehu (c. 883–872).*

The obelisk was discovered among the ruins of Nimrud, the royal seat of King Shalmaneser III of Assyria, on the eastern bank of the Tigris.

ceding Transjordan to Damascus. It is also possible that Jehu fell out of favor with Hazael because he capitulated, shortly after the Jezreel revolt, to Hazael's arch-foe, Assyria. As already noted, Shalmaneser III returned to the West in 841 B.C.E. with Damascus as his principal target. After pursuing Hazael to Damascus and conducting a perfunctory siege of the city, Shalmaneser contented himself with marauding Aramean settlements in the Hauran, and then marched west to a headland on the Mediterranean coast called Ba'li-ra'si, probably Ras en-Naqura (Rosh ha-Niqra, about 12 miles north of the Acco spur), one of the peaks of the "Ladder of Tyre,"[43] where he received tribute from a number of regional states, including Israel. The so-called Black Obelisk of Shalmaneser III from Nimrud,[44] which celebrates this campaign, includes a panel in relief depicting an Israelite king identified as "Yaw, son of Omri" (presumably Jehu) prostrating himself in submission before the Assyrian monarch. Whatever the relationship between Hazael and Jehu might have been previously, this gesture would have made Jehu an enemy of Damascus.

Following a final visit in 838 B.C.E., also directed at Damascus,

Shalmaneser departed and never returned to the West, though he continued to rule for another decade. His successor, Shamshi-Adad V (824–811 B.C.E.), was greeted by a major rebellion in the Assyrian capital of Nineveh, and although he was eventually able to quell the Great Revolt (827–822 B.C.E.), as it was called, he was left in too weak a position to control territory farther west than Til Barsib on the Euphrates. In fact, Assyria would not return in force to southern Syria and Palestine until the final years of the ninth century (805 B.C.E.), as explained below. Thus in 838 B.C.E., Hazael, having survived the onslaughts of Shalmaneser III, emerged as the dominant figure in the region, free to exact revenge for what he may have regarded as Jehu's treachery and to realize his ambition to expand the hegemony of Damascus at the expense of Israel, Judah and his other neighbors.

When Ahaziah of Judah was assassinated, his mother Athaliah, daughter of Ahab and Jezebel and widow of Jehoram of Judah, seized power for herself (2 Kings 11:1–3). To consolidate her position, she attempted to eradicate the royal family of Judah. This part of her plan was foiled, however, by Ahaziah's sister Jehosheba, who hid her infant nephew, Jehoash* son of Ahaziah, from Athaliah's executioners and then took the young Davidide secretly to the Temple, where she entrusted him to the protection of the high priest, Jehoiada.[45] Jehoash remained in hiding in the Temple during the seven years that Athaliah ruled in Jerusalem (841–835 B.C.E.). The reference in 2 Kings 11:18 to the dismantling of a "house of Baal" after Athaliah's death suggests that she attempted to introduce the Tyrian religion of her mother into Jerusalem (cf. 2 Chronicles 24:7), but otherwise the biblical record provides no information about her reign. It represented an interruption in the continuity of Davidic rule in Judah, and the biblical writers' silence on the subject is probably a reflection of their contempt for Athaliah, which they make clear in their accounts of her ruthless acquisition of power and the disgraceful manner of her removal from office. The latter is described in detail in 2 Kings 11:4–20. When Jehoash was seven years old, Jehoiada, operating under heavy guard, publicly presented him in the Temple and proclaimed him rightful king of Judah. When Athaliah arrived with a cry of treason, she was led outside of the Temple precincts and summarily executed.

---

*Like the names Jehoram and Joram, Jehoash and Joash are variants of the same name, which in the ninth century was pronounced Yāhū-'āš in Judah and Yaw-'āš in Israel, both meaning "Yahweh has given." English Bibles use both names for Jehoash son of Ahaziah, king of Judah (c. 835–801 B.C.E.), and for his northern namesake, Joash or Jehoash of Israel (c. 802–787 B.C.E.). The variation arises from inconsistencies in the spelling of the names in the Hebrew Bible. To minimize the confusion, and for convenience, the king of Judah is always called Jehoash in our discussion and the king of Israel is called Joash.

Three shekels ostracon. *This Hebrew inscription appears to be a receipt for a donation of three silver shekels to the "the House of Yahweh," that is, the Jerusalem Temple. The inscription states that King Ashyahu has commanded that the money be given to one Zechariah. Although the Bible mentions no king of Judah named Ashyahu, this name may be a form of Joash or Jehoash. The inscription probably dates to the early years of King Jehoash (835–801 B.C.E.) of Judah, who, according to 2 Kings 12:4, proclaimed that all contributions to the Temple should be turned over to the priests for repairs. Zechariah was a prominent priest at the time (2 Chronicles 24:20). At least two Israeli scholars regard the ostracon with "suspicion," saying it may be a modern forgery. Other equally prominent scholars defend its authenticity.*

The biblical account of Jehoash's reign deals primarily with the relationship between the royal palace and the Temple. The version in Kings (2 Kings 11–12) presents Jehoash in a favorable light and implicates the priesthood in corruption. It gives the impression that during Jehoash's minority, Jehoiada ruled on his behalf, an arrangement that worked to the advantage of the Temple and the priesthood. A proclamation is said to have been issued in the king's name requiring that all contributions of silver brought to the Temple should be turned over to the priests, who were then to use the funds to repair the Temple. As Jehoash matured, however, he became disenchanted with this arrangement, noting that the silver received by the priests was not reaching its intended destination, so that the Temple remained in disrepair.* He insisted that arrangements be made for the funds to be channeled directly to the repairmen, thus eliminating the intermediary role of the priests. The Chronicler's version (2 Chronicles 24) exonerates the priests at the expense of the king. There we are told that the Temple restoration proceeded well until Jehoiada died, after which Jehoash fell under the influence of "the officials of Judah" (2 Chronicles 24:17), who persuaded him to abandon the project. When Jehoiada's own son, Zechariah, publicly objected, he was stoned to death.

An ostracon (an inscribed potsherd) dramatically illustrates the biblical account of Jehoash's Temple project.**[46] It refers to an order in the name of Jehoash (called Ashyahu here)† for a small amount of silver to be contributed to the Temple: "As Ashyahu the king commanded you to give into the hand of [Ze]chariah silver of Tarshish for the House of Yahweh: three shekels." Since Zechariah is the name of a prominent priest of the period—the son of the high priest Jehoiada—the expression "into the hand of Zechariah" suggests that the ostracon reflects the situation early in Jehoash's reign when contributions of silver were made to the Temple through a priestly intermediary.

Though the Chronicler blames "the officials of Judah" for Jehoash's abandonment of the Temple project, the decision may have been forced on him by external circumstances—specifically, by the threat to Judah posed by Hazael of Damascus. As explained above, Assyria ceased to be an active presence in the west after Shalmaneser's 838 B.C.E. campaign, and this left Hazael with a free hand to satisfy his territorial ambitions. We have already noted that he took control of all of Transjordan as far south as Wadi Arnon, the Moabite frontier, during the reign of Jehu (2 Kings 10:32–33). The biblical summary of the reign of Jehu's successor, Jehoahaz (818–802 B.C.E.), refers to a series of battles lost to the Arameans (2 Kings 13:3) and describes a drastic depletion of the Israelite military capability (2 Kings 13:5). Thus

---

*Jehoash's repairs to the Temple, as described in the biblical text (2 Kings 12), are also referred to in a recent inscription that surfaced on the antiquities market and is widely believed to be a forgery by some scholars. See Hershel Shanks, "Is It or Isn't It?" *BAR*, March/April 2003; "Assessing the Jehoash Inscription," *BAR*, May/June 2003.

**Hershel Shanks, "Three Shekels for the Lord," *BAR*, November/December 1997.

†The name appears as *šyhw*, that is, *'ašyāhû*, "Ashyahu," instead of yāhû'āš the ninth-century B.C.E. form of Jehoash. In other words, the divine name (*yāhû*, "Yahu, Yahweh") and verbal (*'āš* "has given") elements are reversed in relation to the biblical form. This phenomenon is well known in Hebrew personal names, including royal names, in both the biblical and epigraphic record. For example, the name of Jehoash's father, Ahaziah (*'āḥazyāhû* also appears in the Bible (2 Chronicles 21:17; 25:23) as Jehoahaz (*yĕhô'āḥāz*), and the northern King Joash, called *yô'āš* or *yôhô'āš* in the Bible, appears on a pithos from Kuntillet 'Ajrud as *šyw*, "Ashyaw." See Strata, "What's in a Name?" *BAR*, May/June 1998.

Jehoahaz was in no position to resist when Hazael marched past Israelite territory, pressed down the coastal plain and conquered Philistia south of the Israelite town of Aphek in the Plain of Sharon.[47] According to 2 Kings 12:17–18, Hazael, after conquering the Philistine city of Gath, turned east to threaten Jerusalem. Jehoash was able to save the city only by paying the Aramean king a heavy tribute amassed by emptying the treasuries of both the Temple and the royal palace of several generations' accumulation of gold.[48] However rich this extorted treasure may have been, however, it was not the primary economic benefit of Hazael's coastal campaign. His conquests in Philistia and Judah gave him jurisdiction over the Via Maris, the primary coastal highway, and since he already controlled the northern portion of the King's Highway, the principal trade route east of the Jordan, Hazael now had a virtual monopoly on commercial traffic passing through Palestine and direct access to both the Egyptian and the Arabian markets.

EIGHTH-CENTURY PROSPERITY
The resurgence of Israel and Judah

The ascendancy of Damascus over Israel and Judah extended from the 830s B.C.E. until the early eighth century B.C.E. Hazael must have died sometime before 805 B.C.E., when his son Ben-hadad (Aramaic Bir-hadad), also known as Mari', first begins to appear in Assyrian records. During Jehoahaz's reign, Ben-hadad II* seems to have been able to maintain the domination of Israel that Hazael had established (cf. 2 Kings 13:3), and there are other indications that Ben-hadad was a capable successor to his mighty father. He had the misfortune, however, to come to the throne at about the time that Assyria, its long period of weakness ending, began to reassert itself in Syria-Palestine. The revival of Assyrian power was the achievement of Adad-nirari III (811–783 B.C.E.), who, after a six-year period of minority, turned his attention to the West. Although we have no true annals for Adad-nirari's reign, and his surviving inscriptions do not provide full information about his two western campaigns in 805–802 B.C.E. and 796 B.C.E., there can be little doubt that one of his principal targets was Damascus,[49] which had now regained the dominant role in Syria that it had had under Hadadezer.[50] By the time Adad-nirari's second western campaign was over, however, Ben-hadad had been subdued. An inscription found in Iraq in 1967[51] indicates that at that time

---

*Since he had the same name as Ben-hadad son of Tabrimmon, the nemesis of Baasha of Israel in the early ninth century B.C.E., we will call him Ben-hadad II. If Hadadezer was succeeded briefly by a son named Ben-hadad, a possibility strongly supported by 2 Kings 8:7–15, then we should call Hazael's son Ben-hadad III.

ZE'EV MESHEL AND AVRAHAM HAI

Kuntillet 'Ajrud. *Travelers may have stopped for rest and refreshment at this desert way-station halfway between Beersheba and Elath. The ruins of two late-ninth- to early-eighth-century B.C.E. buildings are visible on the isolated hilltop, which overlooks three major routes across northeastern Sinai. Archaeologists have discovered abundant evidence here of early Israelite worship, predating the great religious reforms of Hezekiah and Josiah. (See photo and drawing, p. 160.)*

(796 B.C.E.) Adad-nirari received tribute from "Mari' of Damascus ... Joash of Samaria, the Tyrians and the Sidonians."

The return of Assyria brought an end to the aggressive policies of Damascus, since Ben-hadad and his successors were now obliged either to submit to Assyria and pay tribute on a regular basis or to defend themselves against the Assyrian army. For the kings of Israel, Judah and the other regional states that had suffered at the hand of Damascus, the arrival of Adad-nirari III was a welcome development. The tribute Joash of Israel (c. 802–787 B.C.E.) paid to Adad-nirari in 796 B.C.E. was probably given, at least in part, in a spirit of gratitude; it has even been suggested that Adad-nirari is the unidentified "savior" of Israel who helped the people escape from the Land of the Syrians (2 Kings 13:5). In any case, Joash was subsequently able to defeat Ben-hadad three times in battle and recover Israelite towns lost to Hazael (2 Kings 13:25). The Edomite campaign of Amaziah of Judah (c. 801–783 B.C.E.)—reported briefly in 2 Kings 14:7 with an expanded account in 2 Chronicles 25:5–16—may also have been inspired by the weakening position of Damascus and the consequent hope on Amaziah's part that he could recover the territory—and trade access— that had been lost to Edom in the days of his great-grandfather, Jehoram (cf. 2 Kings 8:20–22). In the flush of a victory at the Edomite stronghold of Sela (possibly el-Sela, southwest of Tafila, Jordan), however, Amaziah overreached himself and sent a defiant message to Joash (2 Kings 14:8–14 = 2 Chronicles 25:17–24), apparently believing that the Israelite army was either too weak or too preoccupied with Damascus to respond. This proved to be a catastrophic miscalculation. Joash marched to Beth-Shemesh in the Shephelah and routed the Judahite army, taking Amaziah prisoner. He then proceeded to Jerusalem, where he broke down the northern wall, looted the treasuries of the Temple and the royal palace, and returned to Samaria with hostages. Thus in 783 B.C.E., when Amaziah's son Azariah became king,[52] Judah was virtually a vassal state of Israel, a situation reminiscent of the heyday of the Omride dynasty.

In the 1970s two ruined buildings dating to the early eighth century B.C.E. were excavated at a remote site in the Sinai peninsula called Kuntillet 'Ajrud.*[53] The better preserved of the two buildings yielded an unusually large amount of written material, including Hebrew inscriptions written in ink on *pithoi* (large storage jars) and on plastered walls as well as inscribed on large stone bowls. Although its nature and function are not fully understood, the site is located at the junction of three of the principal roads across the northeastern Sinai, and it is tempting to associate it in some way with Amaziah's interest in controlling the trade routes south and east of Judah, as shown by his Edomite campaign. The corpus includes inscriptions written in both the northern (Israelite) and southern (Judahite) dialects of Hebrew, and this suggests that the site should also be understood in the context of Judah's subjugation by Joash, whose name actually appears on one of the *pithoi* as one who bestowed a blessing.[54]

A surprising feature of the Kuntillet 'Ajrud inscriptions is that their content is substantially religious. They shed invaluable light on the nature of Israelite religion at the dawn of the eighth century B.C.E., before the

---

*For an early report by the excavator, see Meshel, "Did Yahweh Have a Consort?" *BAR*, March/ April 1979.

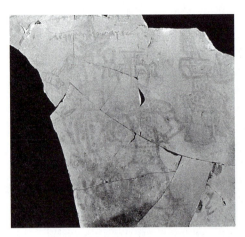

Yahweh and his asherah. *"I have blessed you by Yahweh of Samaria and his asherah"
declares the Hebrew inscription on this pithos, or storage jar, from Kuntillet 'Ajrud. The
accompanying painting depicts two grotesque figures standing side-by-side with arms
akimbo. The larger figure, at left, has a man's torso and posture, but a bovine face, horns
and a tail. The smaller figure has a human body with breasts and a bovine face and tail.
A seated musician appears at far right. Some scholars identify the two standing figures as
Yahweh and Asherah (although others have suggested that both depictions represent the
Egyptian deity Bes). A goddess by the name of Asherah is mentioned with contempt in
the Bible; this inscription suggests that in the late ninth or eighth century B.C.E., she was
conceived of as Yahweh's consort.*

destruction of Samaria and the incorporation of the northern kingdom
into the Assyrian empire—and, more significantly, long before the great
reforms of Hezekiah and Josiah, which transformed Yahwism, centralizing
it in Jerusalem and giving it many of the features familiar from the Bible.*
(For more on the popular religion of ancient Israel, see "Popular Religion
in Ancient Israel," p. 163.) Thus the Kuntillet 'Ajrud inscriptions provide
a window on an early form of Israelite religion and offer clues to some
characteristics that later disappeared. In view of the movement towards
cult centralization in later Judah, for example, it is important to note that
at 'Ajrud the name of the God of Israel is always qualified by a geographical
designation, so that it appears not simply as "Yahweh" but as "Yahweh
of Samaria" or "Yahweh of Teman."[55] Also, when Yahweh is addressed at

*Some of these features can already be seen in the blessings inscribed on two silver amulets
recovered from the late seventh-century B.C.E. tombs of Ketef Hinnom in Jerusalem. The
texts closely parallel the so-called priestly blessing recorded in Numbers 6:24–26. See Gabriel
Barkay, "The Riches of Ketef Hinnom," *BAR*, July/August/September/October 2009.

Fertility figurine. *Excavated in the Jewish Quarter of Jerusalem's Old City, this clay figurine may be a household fertility amulet representing the Canaanite goddess Asherah. The pillar-shaped body may represent a tree, a motif connected with Asherah.*

Kuntillet 'Ajrud, it is often in the accompaniment of "his asherah"; for example, the blessing of Joash mentioned above is invoked "by Yahweh of Samaria and his asherah." Goddesses known as Asherah are known from a number of ancient Near Eastern societies, and a goddess by that name is mentioned several times in the Bible—always with contempt (1 Kings 18:19, etc.). In the Bible, however, the word appears more often as the name of an object used in worship (an asherah; plural, asherim) than as the name of a goddess (Asherah). Though it is clear that an asherah was part of the conventional paraphernalia of a local shrine or "high place" and that, in form, it was a wooden object of some kind—perhaps a simple pole but also possibly a carved female image (cf. 2 Kings 21:7) or even a sacred tree—its exact function and appearance are never described by the biblical writers, who unanimously condemn its use. The Hebrew word *'ăšērâ* may originally have meant something like "track" or "trace," so that "the asherah of Yahweh" would have signified the presence of the God of Israel, and the cult object may have served as a concrete representation of the divine presence as it was available for worship. Clearly, though, it was also associated with a goddess, presumably the consort of Yahweh. Taken together, all this suggests that Yahweh's asherah, as she is invoked at Kuntillet 'Ajrud, was a concretization of the divine presence—the technical term is hypostasis—which was personified and worshiped, alongside Yahweh, as a goddess and the consort of the national god.[56] On one of the *pithoi* a blessing invoking "Yahweh of Samaria and his asherah" is inscribed immediately above a drawing of two figures standing side-by-side with arms akimbo. Both figures combine human and bovine features—human torsos and posture with bovine faces, horns (at least on the larger figure), tails and hoofed feet. The smaller figure, who has stylized female breasts, stands alongside and slightly behind the larger figure. They are certainly a divine couple—a god with the visage and headdress of a bull and a goddess with a cow's face—and are almost certainly "Yahweh and his asherah."[57] The depiction of Yahweh with the visage of a young bull brings to mind "the calf of Samaria," as Hosea called the statue that was the focus of the cult of Yahweh in the capital of the northern kingdom (Hosea 8:6; cf. Hosea 8:5, 13:2).

The reigns of Jeroboam II and Azariah

Joash's policies—and his success in the ongoing conflict with Damascus— were continued by his successor, Jeroboam II (787–748 B.C.E.). The long reigns of Jeroboam II in Israel and Azariah in Judah (783–732 B.C.E.) corresponded to a period of considerable prosperity in both kingdoms. This was possible not only because of the weakness of Damascus, which had dominated the southern Levant for several decades, but also because of the absence of Assyria, which would not again pose a serious threat to Israel until the first western campaign (743–738 B.C.E.) of Tiglath-pileser III. After Adad-nirari's 796 B.C.E. incursion into Syria, the Assyrian armies were generally engaged near home, as a succession of three weak Assyrian kings dealt with a series of local revolts and other domestic problems. For many of these years, the Assyrian Eponym Chronicle indicates, there was no foreign campaign, and, when there was, it was often directed "against Urartu." Urartu, the biblical Ararat, was the region around Lake Van, north of Assyria. The Urartians had been gradually expanding westward since the end of the reign of Shalmaneser III, who had held them in check, and by the beginning of the eighth century they had taken control of much of Anatolia and Syria north of Aleppo. Because of the distractions caused by domestic unrest and the conflict with Urartu, the Assyrian kings of this period seem to have paid little attention to southern Syria. Only five Syrian expeditions are listed in the Eponym Chronicle, and only one of these—a campaign in 773 B.C.E.—is designated as "against Damascus."[58] Nevertheless, the fortunes of Damascus remained in decline. The devastation inflicted by Adad-nirari III seems to have left the once-powerful state broken and vulnerable.

This turn of events worked very much to the advantage of Israel, whose resurgence, begun under Joash, peaked during the reign of his son, Jeroboam II. According to 2 Kings 14:25, Jeroboam "restored the border of Israel from Lebo-hamath as far as the Sea of Arabah"—that is, from the town of Lebo (modern Lebweh), at the southern boundary of the state of Hamath on the Orontes, to the Dead Sea.[59] One of the implications of this assertion is that Damascus was reduced to the status of an Israelite vassal

Popular Religion in Ancient Israel

Archaeology has dramatically altered our view of ancient Israelite religion. While the biblical writers and the priestly circles of Jerusalem stressed Israel's exclusive devotion to the single, all-powerful and unseen God Yahweh, some everyday Israelites often worshiped their national God according to religious traditions that were already hundreds and even thousands of years old.

Among the relics of this more traditional Israelite religion are small ceramic altars and house shrines that were used for private rituals in domestic and small-scale industrial contexts. While the deity (or deities) to whom these altars and shrines were dedicated remains uncertain, archaeologists Amihai Mazar and Nava Panitz-Cohen reported in *BAR* ("To What God?" July/August 2008) that several of these objects found at the Israelite site of Tel Rehov in the Jordan Valley reflect much earlier Canaanite cultic traditions and religious ideas. In a separate *BAR* article ("A Temple Built for Two," March/April 2008), the esteemed American archaeologist William G. Dever proposes that many of the house shrines found in Iron Age Israel were meant to be private "temples" for the Canaanite mother-goddess Asherah who was often recognized as the consort of Yahweh. He argues that while there was indeed a general reluctance among even everyday Israelites to depict the God Yahweh in physical form, many of the shrines are replete with explicit or symbolic depictions of his consort, Asherah.

Archaeologist Uzi Avner discusses with *BAR* readers ("Sacred Stones in the Desert," May/June 2001) an even older—but no less enigmatic—religious tradition adopted by the Israelites: standing stones, or masseboth. Avner's surveys of the Negev and Sinai deserts found hundreds of unhewn stone pillars, often deliberately arranged in pairs or triads, that date as far back as the tenth millennium B.C.E. Based on numerous biblical passages that mention such masseboth, as well as other historical and ethnographic evidence, Avnerg argues that these stones were thought to represent the physical presence or abode of the deity. Indeed, two such stones were found in the inner sanctum of the temple to Yahweh at the Israelite fortress at Arad in the Negev, perhaps representing the Israelite God and his Asherah. —***Ed.***

state, a claim that seems to be made explicit in 2 Kings 14:28: "He recovered for Israel Damascus."[60] Jeroboam also extended the southeastern border of Israel "as far as the Sea of Arabah" at the expense of both Damascus and Moab. Jeroboam was reasserting Israelite control over trade along the King's Highway, which had been lost in the time of Jehu and Hazael. It is safe to assume that the western coastal route from Philistia north into the Galilee, which Hazael had also commandeered, was now back under Israelite control as well.

Though Jeroboam II had the longest reign of any Israelite king and presided over one of the most prosperous periods in the history of the northern kingdom, the account of his reign in Kings is remarkably brief—only seven verses (2 Kings 14:23–29)—and its tone is hostile. This is because the summary notices of his achievements (2 Kings 14:25,28) have been set in a negative framework by the Deuteronomistic historian, who looked on Jeroboam's reign from the perspective of the fall of Samaria half a century later. Thus Jeroboam is condemned, in formulaic Deuteronomistic language, for having perpetuated "all the sins of Jeroboam son of Nebat"—that is, Jeroboam I—the crimes that, from the Deuteronomistic point of view, led eventually to the destruction of the northern kingdom by the Assyrians (cf. 2 Kings 17:22–23). With regard to the recovery of territory for Israel and the expansion of its borders, we are told that Jeroboam II was permitted these accomplishments despite his shortcomings because Yahweh had pity for the plight of the Israelites and there was no one else available to do the job (2 Kings 17:26).

Though the Kings account of Jeroboam's reign is, in its final form, the work of the Deuteronomistic historian of the late seventh century B.C.E., it expresses continuity with the hostility towards Jeroboam found in the oracles of his eighth-century contemporary, the prophet Amos,[61] who confirms the prosperity of the period while presenting it as a facade masking social and religious corruption. In Amos's view, the wealthy, the Samarian aristocracy, were very wealthy indeed (note the description of their extravagant and sybaritic lifestyle in Amos 6:4–6) but their wealth was gained at the expense of the poor. Thus his oracles are often addressed at an exploitative ruling class that oppresses the poor and governs corruptly; they are the idle but powerful rich, who "trample on the needy and bring ruin to the poor of the land ... buying the poor for silver and the needy for a pair of sandals" (Amos 8:4, 6; cf. 2:6–7, 4:1). In Amos's polemic, even the enlarged national boundaries achieved by Jeroboam (2 Kings 14:25) become the basis of a threat of national disaster: "I am raising up against you a nation ... and they shall oppress you from Lebo-hamath to the Wadi Arabah" (Amos 6:14).

The oracles of Amos, therefore, provide confirmation—however indirect and grudging—that Jeroboam II's expansion of Israel's boundaries and recovery of control of the principal trade routes of Palestine led to a substantial increase in material prosperity in Israel. In contrast to the insight he provides about social tensions in the kingdom, however, Amos gives few hints about the ways in which the newly gained resources were put to use. The stinted account of Jeroboam's reign in Kings is no help in this regard, since it lacks any reference to his domestic achievements, including building projects and improvements in living conditions. Faced with this scarcity of information in the biblical sources, therefore, we are primarily dependent on the archaeological record for assessing the state of material culture in eighth-century Israel.[62] Excavations conducted at Israelite sites show that the first half of the eighth century B.C.E. was a period of extensive construction, characterized not by the founding of new cities but by the renovation, refurbishment and expansion of existing cities, some with newly built fortifications and most with more evidence of city planning than is found in previous periods. Nationwide, there was a substantial population increase, as indicated by the results of archaeological surveys of small, nonurban sites as well as estimates based on evidence suggesting the enlargement of existing cities (expansions of walls or settlements spilling over city walls into the surrounding countryside).

A good indication that the trade advantage Jeroboam achieved did result in an accumulation of wealth is the discovery of luxury items in eighth-century archaeological strata. Most characteristic of these are the elaborately carved ivory inlays found at various sites in the northern kingdom but especially at Samaria.[63] Carved ivory was an art form of Phoenician and north Syrian inspiration, so that its presence in the archaeological record points to a renewal of Israelite contact and cooperation with Phoenicia, which, as we have seen, was essential to a robust trade economy.[64] An immense hoard known as the Samaria ivories,[65] found in the ruins of the royal palace, provides direct testimony to the wealth of the aristocracy and is suggestive of extreme social stratification.[66] It is not surprising, therefore, that references to ivory play a part in Amos's invective against the excesses of the aristocracy (Amos 3:15, 6:4).

The epigraphic record also sheds light on life in Samaria during the reign of Jeroboam II. The most impressive Hebrew seal dating from the early to mid-eighth century B.C.E. is surely the seal of "Shema', the servant of Jeroboam," who must have been a high official of the Samarian government stationed at Megiddo, where the seal was found in 1904.[67] The largest corpus of Hebrew inscriptions from the northern kingdom dating to this or any other period are the well-known Samaria ostraca,[68] which were found in 1910 in the ruins of an administrative structure on the acropolis immediately to the west of the royal palace. Dating formulae indicate that the ostraca come from the ninth through the seventeenth year of an unnamed king, almost certainly Jeroboam II, so that they fall between the years 779 and 771 B.C.E. They record regional shipments of agricultural goods, thus shedding light on the support given by large estates to the activities of the court in Samaria. An especially interesting feature of the Samaria ostraca is the number of personal names containing the theophoric or divine element Yahweh (in the form *Yaw*) as opposed to the element Baal (*Ba'l*). The ratio is roughly 11:7.[69] It is difficult to assess the significance of this statistic for the religion of Israel in the period. The Baal names might belong to foreigners (perhaps Phoenicians) who owned property in the vicinity of Samaria or to Israelites who worshiped a foreign god, but it is also possible that *Ba'l*, which means "Lord," might have been an acceptable epithet for Yahweh in this period (cf. Hosea 2:16).

Judah, too, was prosperous in this period, under the rule of Jeroboam's contemporary Azariah (also known as Uzziah) (783–732 B.C.E.).* Though Azariah reigned even longer than Jeroboam, the account of his reign in Kings (2 Kings 15:1–7) is, again, very brief, and there is no mention of victories in foreign wars or other international achievements. The Chronicler's account of his reign (2 Chronicles 26:1–23) is somewhat longer; it presents Azariah as an effective military leader who reorganized the Judahite army and greatly increased both its size and readiness (2 Chronicles 26:11–15). It also describes successful military campaigns that he conducted.[70] Keeping in mind that Judah, since Joash's defeat of Amaziah early in the century, had been in the service of Israel as a junior ally if not actually a vassal state, we can assume that Azariah's build-up of the Judahite army and his various military enterprises were probably encouraged and abetted by Israel as part of Jeroboam's overall plan to reclaim control of the major trade routes of Palestine.[71] It is in this light that we should probably interpret Azariah's goals in the wars he is said to have conducted (2 Chronicles 26:6–7) against the Philistines and two Arabian groups, the Arabs of Gurbaal (an otherwise unknown group) and the Meunites.[72] After his Philistine campaign, during which he breached the walls of Gath, Jabneh and Ashdod, Azariah is said to have built "cities" in Philistine territory. These are most likely to have been fortified garrisons

---

*Both names are used in the Bible. Generally speaking, Azariah is preferred in the account of his reign in Kings and Uzziah elsewhere, but the pattern is not entirely consistent. Scholars usually assume that one of the names was his personal name and the other a throne name, but this is only a guess.

positioned to guard trade routes that ran through disputed territory and connected with roads farther south, which he seems also to have secured with protective fortresses—note the reference in 2 Chronicles 26:10 to Azariah's erection of "the towers in the wilderness." These activities brought him in conflict with the Meunites, a northwestern Arabian tribe who seem at this time to have controlled access from the Philistine ports through the Beersheba depression and the Wadi Zered (the modern Wadi el-Ha sa) to the southern end of the King's Highway and the Hejaz route. After defeating the Meunites, Azariah evidently left them in place as guardians of this highly lucrative thoroughfare, but diverted its wealth to Judah by imposing tribute on them (2 Chronicles 26:8).[73] It was probably at this point, after he had gained control of the southern trade corridor, that Azariah was able to recover the seaport of Elath*[74] on the Gulf of Aqaba from Edom and rebuild it (2 Chronicles 26:2; cf. 2 Kings 14:22).[75]

Although Azariah's domestic accomplishments may have been considerable—the Chronicler's account credits him with assembling large herds of cattles and employing farmers and viticulturists in the fertile parts of Judah (2 Chronicles 26:10)—he is remembered principally for having been a "leper."[76] After his diagnosis it was necessary for him to live in quarantine, and his son Jotham ruled Judah as his coregent (2 Kings 15:5). Since "leprosy" was determined by an examination by priests, who prescribed whether quarantine was required and how long it would last (Leviticus 13–14), Azariah's exclusion from power may have been the result of a continuation of the struggle in Judah between the king and the priesthood that had created turmoil during the reign of Jehoash in the late ninth century B.C.E.[77] In any case, as a "leper," Azariah was apparently assigned a special burial place in the vicinity of—but apart from—the royal tombs (2 Chronicles 26:23; contrast 2 Kings 15:7). A plaque inscribed with his name found in Jerusalem suggests that he was reburied in the late Herodian period.[78]

Everyday life during the Divided Monarchy

The rise of the Israelite and Judahite states in the early centuries of the first millennium B.C.E., the emergence of strongly centralized governments based in the capital cities of Samaria and Jerusalem, and the growth of large regional centers, such as Hazor, Megiddo and Dan in the north and Lachish and Beersheba in the south, led to a highly stratified society in both kingdoms. The upper stratum consisted of the king, his family and

---

*Gary Pratico, "Where is Ezion-Geber?" *BAR*, September/October 1986.

an aristocratic nobility that maintained the royal estates and ruled the regional centers as governors. Of somewhat lesser stature were artisans and skilled laborers of various kinds. Most of the rest of the population—indeed, the vast majority—were agriculturalists. The lucrative international trade that flourished in those periods when Israel enjoyed good relations with Phoenicia and Judah with Philistia, and when the competition with Damascus was successful, was a source of substantial wealth for the king and his aristocratic servants. The everyday livelihood of most of the ordinary citizens of Israel and Judah throughout the history of the monarchy, however, consisted of family-based farming and horticulture, usually supplemented by the maintenance of small flocks of sheep and goats.[79] In the lowland areas the staple crops were grain—wheat, barley and millet—while in the higher elevations and the western slopes of the hill country cereal farming was mixed with arboriculture—the cultivation of figs, pomegranates, dates, sycamores and especially olives—and viticulture. In some areas olive oil or wine could be produced in sufficient quantities to accumulate surpluses that provided a valuable export commodity.

Archaeological evidence indicates that the basis of this production throughout the monarchical period was the extended family or, to use the biblical term, the "father's house" (*bêt 'āb*). This is shown by the widespread persistence throughout the period of the four-roomed house, which consisted of a central courtyard enclosed by rooms designed not only to house the family (usually on a second story) but also livestock, and to provide storage for agricultural produce. The stockpiling of crop surpluses in individual households, rather than communal storage facilities, indicates that agriculture was family-based, with the work being done by individual "father's houses," consisting of three or more generations of an extended family (along with servants or slaves) and comprising perhaps one to two dozen individuals.*[80]

The larger structure of social organization described in the Bible parallels that of other agricultural societies investigated in cross-cultural anthropological studies and corresponds to the pattern that has prevailed in the eastern Mediterranean region from antiquity to the modern period.[81] Several families or "father's houses" constituted a clan. The families of a clan typically lived in the same village or at least in relatively close proximity to each other. A group of clans formed a tribe. Justice was ordinarily dispensed at the clan level by a group of elders, the senior men of the clan or village. In periods

---

*Lawrence E. Stager, "The Song of Deborah—Why Some Tribes Answered the Call and Others Did Not," *BAR*, January/February 1989.

in which the central government at the state level was strong, however, the intervention of the king and his officers in matters of local justice, especially the allocation of property rights, was common, and the tension that resulted is reflected in the oracles of the biblical prophets, who often expressed the grievances of the citizenry against what they perceived as royal abuses of power (see, for example, Micah 2:2).[82]

The social organization of ancient Israel and Judah was strongly patriarchal, and women had minimal official involvement in public affairs.[83] Women had extensive and varied involvement in the activities of their families, however, and given the central position of the family in the economy and social organization of the two states, the influence of women on society as a whole is assumed to have been pervasive despite their invisibility in the public record.[84] Spinning, weaving and sewing were tasks especially associated with women, but they also took part in the basic economic endeavors of the family—farming and caring for livestock. Within the family structure a woman's ultimate role was that of mother. Childbearing conferred prestige and position on a woman because of the advantage of numerous children to the economic livelihood of her family in its agricultural activities and because of the necessity of offspring to perpetuate the lineage of her husband.

A woman's legal status was subordinated to that of men in the family, so that she was dependent for her legal rights and protection on her father or husband. When women were orphaned, widowed or divorced, they lost these rights and needed special protection—hence the frequency of injunctions in the Bible calling for special provisions for the welfare of orphans and widows (Exodus 21:22 [Old Testament] = 21:21 [Hebrew Bible]); Deuteronomy 27:19; etc.).[85] On the other hand, the inability of women to act on their own behalf in legal and economic matters is called into question by the discovery of a number of personal seals and seal impressions bearing the names of Judahite women.[86] These seals and sealings, which date to the seventh and early sixth centuries B.C.E., raise the possibility that, at least in this period, women were sometimes involved in legal and economic transactions under their own names.[87] Similarly, a woman's name ("Meshullemeth daughter of Elichen") appears in a list of the recipients—or, less likely, contributors—of specified commodities on a recently published ostracon from the early sixth century B.C.E.,[88] and this seems to be another example of a woman transacting business on her own behalf during the final days of the kingdom of Judah.

ISRAEL AND JUDAH UNDER
THE ASSYRIAN EMPIRE

Tiglath-pileser III

Following Adad-nirari III's 796 B.C.E. campaign to Syria, a long period of Assyrian weakness began, during which the empire extended no farther west than the province of Bit Adini on the Euphrates; the Assyrian kings were unable to gain the upper hand in their competition with Urartu for control of Anatolia and northern Syria. With the accession of Tiglath-pileser III (745–727 B.C.E.), however, the situation began to change rapidly. After moving quickly to reorganize the kingdom administratively, Tiglath-pileser embarked on his first western campaign in 743 B.C.E. He broke the power of Urartu almost immediately and laid siege to Arpad, which was the key to the control of northern Syria (as it had been in the time of Adad-nirari). The fall of Arpad in 740 B.C.E. led to a surrender of most of the other states of northern and central Syria, including Hamath, and to their annexation into the empire.[89] Not content with this victory, Tiglath-pileser continued his march westward and extended the boundary of the Assyrian empire to the Mediterranean coast. In 738 B.C.E., at the end of this first western campaign, he received tribute from, among others, Rezin (*Ra-ḫi-a-nu*) of Damascus and Queen Zabibe of Arabia (see below), as well as Menahem (*Me-ni-ḫi-im-me*) of Israel.[90]

Menahem had ascended to the throne after a series of royal assassinations that brought the dynasty of Jehu to an end (2 Kings 15:8–22). Jeroboam II had died about 748 B.C.E. His son Zechariah (c. 748–747 B.C.E.) succeeded him, but was publicly assassinated after a reign of only six months by a certain Shallum son of Jabesh (c. 747 B.C.E.). One month later Shallum himself was assassinated by Menahem son of Gadi, who had marched against Samaria from the old Israelite capital city of Tirzah. Menahem ruled for a decade (c. 747–738 B.C.E.), witnessed the arrival of Tiglath-pileser in the West, and kept his throne by paying tribute to Assyria. Two years after his death, however, his son and successor, Pekahiah (c. 738–737 B.C.E.), was unseated in an anti-Assyrian coup led by Pekah son of Remaliah and an army of Gileadites. Between them, Menahem and Pekahiah had ruled Israel for 12 relatively stable years in very dangerous times, but the price they paid for peace with Assyria was very high, as the account of Menahem's tax collecting in 2 Kings 15:20 suggests, and we can assume that anti-Assyrian sentiment in the kingdom was strong. Even so, it seems very likely that the revolt was stimulated and supported by Rezin of Damascus, who was organizing the resistance to Assyria from Damascus, following in the footsteps of his ninth-century predecessors, Hadadezer and Hazael.[91]

Bulla of King Ahaz. *"Belonging to Ahaz (son of) Jotham, King of Judah," reads the Hebrew inscription impressed onto this bulla (lump of clay), which was originally used to secure a papyrus scroll. Ancient bullae and seals are not uncommon, but this is one of the first that can be attributed to a Hebrew king: Ahaz, who ruled over Judah from 735 to 727 B.C.E.*

For most of his reign, Menahem's Judahite contemporary was Jotham (c. 750–735 B.C.E.), who was still ruling as coregent for his leprous father, Azariah. The account of Jotham's reign in Kings (2 Kings 15:32–38) provides little information about his achievements, except that "he built the upper gate of the house of the Lord" (2 Kings 15:35), but the Chronicler (2 Chronicles 27:3–4) gives him credit for other construction projects in Jerusalem, where he "did extensive building on the wall of the Ophel" and in the Judean countryside. Jotham's motivation for these building activities (which are reminiscent of Azariah's efforts to fortify Jerusalem [2 Chronicles 26:9])[92] was probably concern over the possibility of an invasion—not by Assyria, which did not yet pose a direct threat to Judah, but by Israel and Damascus. Nor was such a concern ill-founded or premature. At some point, probably late in Jotham's reign, Pekah and Rezin began making incursions into Judah (2 Kings 15:37), anticipating their full-scale assault on Jerusalem in the time of Ahaz. Though, as explained below, the initial motivation for the alliance of Samaria and Damascus may have been territorial expansion in support of their trade ambitions, many modern historians have interpreted their later attack on Ahaz as an attempt to force him to join the anti-Assyrian coalition that had formed in southern Syria and Palestine: If this is correct, the hostilities against Jotham should probably be seen as the beginning of this policy of diplomacy by intimidation. Despite the pressure his northern neighbors brought to bear, however, Jotham did not yield, and his determination to remain unaligned, if not pro-Assyrian, is understandable. To Judah, which had not been among the nations that paid tribute to Tiglath-pileser III in 738 B.C.E., the Assyrian threat must have still seemed remote, and no doubt Jotham thought it wise not to antagonize Tiglath-pileser if he could avoid doing so.

After a few years in which the Assyrian army was occupied north and east of Syria campaigning against the Urartians and Medes,[93] Tiglath-pileser set out on his second western campaign (734–732 B.C.E.), which ended triumphantly with the fall of Assyria's old nemesis in Syria, Damascus. The biblical account of this campaign (2 Kings 16:5–9) claims that it was launched in response to a petition to Tiglath-pileser from Ahaz (735–727 B.C.E.), who was now king of Judah.* Rezin and Pekah had joined forces again, as they had during the reign of Jotham, and this time they laid siege to Jerusalem. After a pioneering study in 1929 by Joachim Begrich, most historians came to agree that Damascus and Israel launched the Syro-Ephraimite war, as Begrich called it, to intimidate Ahaz, so that he would renounce his policy of neutrality and join the anti-Assyrian cause.[94] Nevertheless, there is now wide agreement that the initial motivation of Rezin and Pekah was probably more commercial than conspiratorial. That is, the Aramean-Israelite coalition was formed in the first place out of a mutual interest in territorial expansion, especially into Transjordan, and the driving incentive for this expansion was commercial ambition, not hostility to Assyria, which may not yet have been perceived as an immediate threat.[95] Similarly, Phoenician and Philistine participation in the alliance was probably also motivated by a primary interest in the control of trade routes,[96] and the same was true of the involvement of Arabian tribes under the rule of Queen Samsi (see p. 177). Nevertheless, Tiglath-pileser regarded the new trade alliances as anti-Assyrian, and it was suspicions of this kind that led to Assyrian military intervention. In any case, if it was the intention of Rezin and Pekah to pressure Ahaz to resist Tiglath-pileser, the plan backfired. According to the biblical sources, Ahaz was, in fact, intimidated,[97] but instead of joining the resistance to Assyria, he voluntarily entered into Assyrian vassalage. He sent a message of subservience to Tiglath-pileser together with a gift of silver and gold garnered from the Temple and palace treasuries. The biblical account concludes by indicating that the Assyrian

---

*A clay bulla, or impression, of the personal seal of Ahaz has been published. The inscription reads "Belonging to Ahaz [son of] Jotham, king of Judah." It is the first seal or sealing of a king of Israel or Judah from the biblical period to have been discovered. (See Robert Deutsch, *Messages from the Past: Hebrew Bullae from the Time of Isaiah Through the Destruction of the First Temple* [in Hebrew] [Tel Aviv: Archaeological Center Publications, 1997], pp. 49–51 and pl. XVI; and "First Impression: What We Learn from King Ahaz's Seal," *BAR*, May/June 1998. See also Strata, "We Have a Winner," *BAR*, March/April 1997.)

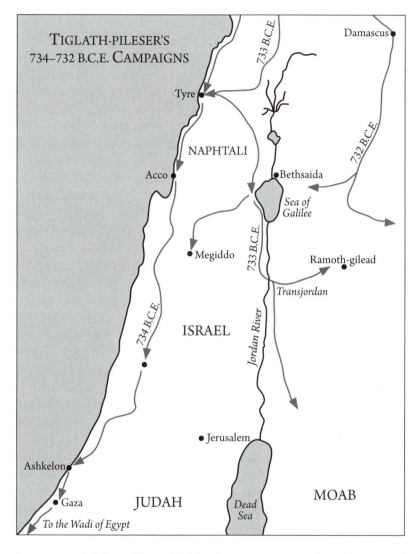

king responded favorably and led his forces into Syria, where he captured
Damascus, exiled its population and executed Rezin.

Despite the limited perspective of the biblical account of these events,
which naturally centers on the involvement of Judah, we know from
Assyrian sources that Rezin and Pekah were involved in a larger anti-
Assyrian movement in the West, which included Hiram of Tyre as well
as the kings of two Philistine cities, Mitinti of Ashkelon and Hanun (or
Hanno) of Gaza. Although the Damascene Rezin, as the ringleader of the
coalition, was clearly the primary target of the larger Assyrian campaign,

Tiglath-pileser's strategy seems to have been to subdue the other coalition members first, progressively isolating Damascus over the three years of the campaign. Thus in 734 B.C.E., which is designated "to Philistia" in the Assyrian Eponym Chronicle, he moved to subdue the western allies of Damascus and the northern kingdom of Israel. Although the annalistic fragments are too incomplete to permit more than an approximation of his itinerary, he seems to have begun by marching down the Phoenician coast, capturing Byblos and other cities until he came face-to-face with Hiram of Tyre (the namesake of the Hiram of Tyre who helped Solomon build the Temple), who capitulated and paid tribute. Tiglath-pileser then proceeded south to Ashkelon, where he accepted the Philistine Mitinti's surrender and an oath of loyalty that Mitinti would later break. When the Assyrian army reached Gaza, Hanun fled to Egypt, from which he would later return to accept vassalage and to rule over the port of Gaza as an Assyrian imperial entrepôt. The southernmost point reached on the 734 B.C.E. march was the "the Wadi of Egypt" (the Wadi el-'Arish, the traditional southern boundary of Palestine), where Tiglath-pileser was obliged to fight the Meunites, whom Azariah had subdued decades earlier after his own Philistine campaign. Having now subdued the entire coastal plain south of Phoenicia, Tiglath-pileser formally annexed the region from Dor and the Plain of Sharon south to Philistia as an Assyrian province with the name Du'ru (Dor), incorporated the Philistine states as vassaldoms and marked the southern boundary of the Assyrian empire with a stela erected at the Wadi of Egypt. At that time he accepted tribute not only from the kings of the states defeated on the march (Tyre, Ashkelon, Gaza) but also from Kaushmalaku of Edom, Salamanu of Moab, Sanipu of Bit-Ammon, as well as Ahaz (*Ia-u-ḫa-zi*)* of Judah.[98] Note that the three Transjordanian states, like Judah, seem to have bought their safety by offering tribute and by avoiding alliances with Rezin's coalition. They remained semi-independent—vassal states that were not formally annexed and incorporated into the empire.

Over the next two years (733–732 B.C.E.), both of which are designated "to Damascus" in the Eponym Chronicles, Tiglath-pileser turned his attention to Damascus and Israel. Again the fragmentary nature of the annals permits only an approximation of the sequence of events, but it seems clear that Damascus was placed under siege at the beginning of the 733 B.C.E. campaign. Then, leaving part of his army to carry out the siege, Tiglath-pileser marched

---

*The spelling in the Assyrian annals corresponds to the longer form of the king's name, "Jehoahaz," of which the biblical "Ahaz" is a hypocoristic (abbreviated) form.

ANDRÉ LEMAIRE

A record of Sheba's trade with Judah. *This fragmented but well-preserved South Arabian inscription mentions, among other things, a trading expedition from the kingdom of Sabaea (biblical Sheba) to "the towns of Judah." Believed to date to around 600 B.C.E., this inscription confirms Judah's role in the lucrative Arabian trade that was one of the primary economic drivers of Iron Age geopolitics from at least the time of King Solomon.*

through northern Israel, capturing all of Naphtali and the Upper Galilee, as well as northern Transjordan (2 Kings 15:29).* For the first time, Israelites went into exile under the Assyrian policy of deportations, as the captives—a total of 13,520 according to a recently published annals fragment[99]—were led off to Assyria. The rest of Israel was bypassed and spared when, sometime in 732 B.C.E., Hoshea son of Elah assassinated Pekah, took his place as king (2 Kings 15:30) and sent a message of fealty to Tiglath-pileser.[100] This

---

*Evidence of Tiglath-Pileser's destructive campaign through the Galilee region has been documented at the site of Bethsaida. See Rami Arav, Richard A. Freund and John F. Schroder, Jr., "Bethsaida: Lost and Rediscovered," *BAR*, January/February 2000.

ensured that Israel would be spared annexation and survive beyond the reign of Tiglath-pileser, if only as a tiny state in the Ephraimite highlands. Large tracts of former Israelite territory did not survive, however, and they were incorporated into three Assyrian provinces: Du'ru (Dor), which, as noted, had been annexed after the 734 B.C.E. campaign, Magidu (Megiddo), which included the entire Galilee as far south as Megiddo and the Jezreel Valley, and Gal'aza (Gilead), which consisted of Israelite Transjordan as far north as Ramoth-gilead.[101] By this time, Tiglath-pileser's troops had completed the siege of Damascus, which fell in 732 B.C.E. and was incorporated into the empire. Very little information about the fall of Damascus is preserved in Assyrian records,[102] except that Rezin was executed (cf. 2 Kings 16:9) and his hometown of Hadara was destroyed in reprisal.

It is important not to overlook the economic motivations and consequences of Tiglath-pileser's conquests in the West. By incorporating Syria, Phoenicia and the entire Mediterranean coast as far south as the Wadi el-'Arish into the empire, Assyria attained direct control of the major Syrian trade routes and the great coastal highway, the Via Maris, which was the land route to Egypt. Since the Transjordanian states remained semi-independent tributaries (states that paid tribute), Assyria did not directly control the King's Highway with its connection to the lucrative caravan route from the northern Hejaz and farther south. But this hardly mattered, since Assyria's sovereignty over Damascus and the Phoenician and Philistine port cities gave it control of all the regional outlets for this highly profitable traffic. It is thus no surprise that we find an Arabian queen listed as paying tribute after both of Tiglath-pileser's western campaigns: The last name in the 738 B.C.E. tribute list is "Zabibe, the queen of Arabia."[103] When Damascus, Israel and Tyre submitted to Tiglath-pileser of Assyria in 738 B.C.E., this threatened to disrupt the trade from South Arabia to Damascus and from there to Mediterranean ports; hence Zabibe's payment of tribute was probably an attempt to protect her interests and keep the routes open.[104] The 738 B.C.E. tribute list contains an abundance of luxury goods that were bartered in the South Arabian trade, including precious metals and ivory, exotic woods, and the hides of elephants and other exotic animals.

Near its southern end, the principal western bifurcation of the King's Highway ran south of the Dead Sea through the Wadi Hesa-Beersheba depression, then passed through Judahite territory and emerged at Ashkelon or another of the Philistine ports. In fact, a newly identified South Arabian inscription dating to the late seventh century B.C.E. records the movements of a South Arabian trading caravan through the southern territories of both

SHALMANESER V'S
AND SARGON II'S
CAMPAIGNS

Acco

Sea of
Galilee

Dor Megiddo

Jordan River

Samaria

Mediterranean
Sea

ISRAEL

Ashdod Ekron Jerusalem

Gath

JUDAH

Gaza PHILISTIA

Dead
Sea

Raphia

Wadi of Egypt

⬅——— Assyrian forces

◀┈┈┈┈ Egyptian forces

Gaza and "the towns of Judah."* This route was still free from Assyrian interference after 738 B.C.E., but Tiglath-pileser's 734 B.C.E. incursion into Philistia brought it under Assyrian control. The name of Samsi, who succeeded Zabibe as "queen of Arabia" at this time, has not survived in the damaged tribute list of 734 B.C.E.,[105] but it must have been there, because another fragment of the annals refers to her violation of an oath she swore to

*André Lemaire, "Solomon & Sheba, Inc.," *BAR*, January/February 2010.

Shamash, the Assyrian god of justice.[106] Mitinti of Ashkelon, who submitted to Tiglath-pileser in 734 B.C.E., later rebelled, and Tiglath-pileser's annals (though, as usual, they are too fragmentary for certainty) seem to associate Samsi's rebellion with Mitinti's.[107] Whether these two acts of defiance were jointly planned or simply simultaneous, they should probably be interpreted as desperate attempts to restore the independence of the spice and incense trade. Both rebellions were quickly suppressed—Mitinti's when he died and his son and successor submitted to Tiglath-pileser, and Samsi's when she surrendered, paid tribute and accepted an Assyrian-appointed overseer—but they serve as good illustrations of what was at stake economically in Tiglath-pileser's Philistine excursion.

The fall of Samaria

Israel enjoyed a brief period of stability after 732 B.C.E., while Hoshea (732–724 B.C.E.) was a loyal vassal of Tiglath-pileser. But in 727 B.C.E., when Tiglath-pileser died and was succeeded by Shalmaneser V (727–722 B.C.E.), Hoshea became embroiled in a revolt that broke out in the western part of the empire. We have no Assyrian historical records from Shalmaneser V's reign, but the general sequence of events can be reconstructed from the Eponym Chronicle, itself poorly preserved at this point, in combination with information that survives third-hand from the annals of Tyre.[108] Evidently Shalmaneser campaigned in Phoenicia in his first regnal year (727 B.C.E.), accepting tribute and then withdrawing. Subsequently, however, a group of Tyrian vassal cities revolted against Tyre and appealed to Assyria for help. In response Shalmaneser marched west again, probably in 725 B.C.E.,[109] and began a siege of Tyre that was lifted without success after five years—after Shalmaneser's reign had ended.

With this framework in mind, we can better understand the brief biblical account of Hoshea's reign and the fall of Samaria (2 Kings 17:1–6). The statement in 2 Kings 17:3 that Shalmaneser marched against Hoshea and accepted his tribute and fealty suggests that Shalmaneser visited Israel on his way to or from Phoenicia or even that Samaria was one of the "Phoenician" cities that, according to the Tyrian annals, paid tribute to the Assyrian king in that year. According to 2 Kings 17:4, however, Hoshea subsequently antagonized Shalmaneser by conspiring against him, communicating with Egypt[110]—presumably in search of support against Assyria—and withholding the annual tribute he had been paying. Shalmaneser responded by arresting Hoshea. Then, with Hoshea in Assyrian custody, Shalmaneser marched to Samaria and laid siege to the city (2 Kings 17:5). It is tempting to associate these developments with the events of 725 B.C.E. and Shalmaneser's attack on Tyre. If this reconstruction is correct, it suggests that Samaria and Tyre had probably formed an alliance against Shalmaneser, reminiscent of the anti-Assyrian coalitions of the past,[111] and that Egypt was encouraging if not actively supporting the alliance.[112] It further suggests that the sieges of Tyre and Samaria probably began at about the same time, in 725 or 724 B.C.E.

At that time, Hoshea's appeal to Egypt having evidently gone unheeded, Shalmaneser "invaded all the land"—that is, overran and devastated Israel as a whole—and put the capital, Samaria, under siege (2 Kings 17:5–6, 18:9–10). The siege lasted three years, concluding in 722 B.C.E.—evidently late in the summer—with the fall of Samaria, and thousands of Israelites were led into exile. The biblical account of these events is telescoped, giving the impression that the same king of Assyria was responsible for the fall of Samaria and the deportation of the Israelites, but this was not the case. Shalmaneser V died only a couple of months after the conclusion of the siege, in the winter of 722 B.C.E., so that the final disposition of Samaria and the exile of the Israelites was left to his successor, the usurper Sargon II (722–705 B.C.E.). In his annals and other inscriptions, Sargon boasts of having besieged and captured Samaria, but the Bible assigns responsibility for the successful siege to Shalmaneser, and this is corroborated by the Babylonian Chronicle (a record of annual events begun in the mid-eighth century B.C.E.).

Sargon was prevented from giving his immediate attention to Samaria by two major revolts in the empire that erupted when he seized the throne. One of these, which took place in Babylon, was an outburst of nationalistic fervor under the leadership of the Chaldean prince Marduk-apla-iddina II—the biblical Merodachbaladan (2 Kings 20:12 = Isaiah 39:1)—who proclaimed himself king of Babylon.[113] Sargon needed 12 years to dislodge him from the throne. The other revolt, which took place in the western provinces, was initiated by Ilu-bi'di of Hamath and Hanun of Gaza, who had also rebelled against Tiglath-pileser in 734 B.C.E. The revolt of Ilu-bi'di and Hanun quickly spread to several other cities including Damascus and Samaria.[114] It was this revolt that brought Sargon west in 720 B.C.E. and gave him the opportunity to complete the incorporation of Samaria into the empire and to initiate the deportation of its citizens. Sargon trapped and destroyed the forces of Hamath in the fortress of Qarqar, where Shalmaneser III had fought Hamath and its allies 133 years earlier. When the region had been pacified and Ilu-bi'di executed, the Assyrian army marched down the coast towards Gaza to deal with Hanun. Like Hoshea a few years earlier, Hanun had appealed to Egypt for help, and in his case the pharaoh[115] responded and sent his viceroy (*turtānu*) with a contingent of troops. Sargon met the combined forces of

Gaza and Egypt at "the city of the Wadi of Egypt," that is, Raphia (about 15 miles southwest of Gaza), where he won a decisive battle, capturing Hanun and driving away the Egyptian army. With the Assyrian victory, Egypt, for the first time, agreed to pay tribute to Assyria, as did South Arabian leaders[116] who, confronted with another show of Assyrian power in southern Palestine, were anxious to maintain good relations with Sargon in order to protect their trade interests in the region.

It was probably during the first, northern phase of the 720 B.C.E. campaign that Sargon began the deportation of Israelites—one summary inscription indicates that 27,290 people were involved.[117] Although the Assyrian practice of deporting captive peoples had already begun in the ninth century B.C.E., it was Sargon and his predecessor, Tiglath-pileser, who gave it its greatest notoriety, not only by employing it on a much vaster scale than their predecessors but also, in Sargon's case, by introducing the policy of two-way relocations. Conquered peoples from the western portions of the empire were resettled in Assyria and in the eastern provinces, while captives from the eastern and southern regions were resettled in the West. In clay prisms found at Nimrud[118] Sargon himself refers not only to his deportation of people *from* Samaria but also to deportations *to* Samaria. He does not indicate the places of origin of the peoples transported to Samaria, except that they came from countries he conquered. The biblical account, however, gives more detail. Thus we are told in 2 Kings 17:6 that Sargon transported captive Israelites to Assyria and in 2 Kings 17:24 that he repopulated the cities of Samaria with peoples from Babylonia and Elam (southwestern Iran).[119] More specifically, the Israelites were resettled in Halah (northeast of Nineveh), on the Habor (the Khabur River, a tributary that flows south into the Euphrates from the highlands of southeastern Turkey and northeastern Syria), and in the highlands[120] of the Medes (northwestern Iran).[121] Hoshea's former kingdom was reorganized as the Assyrian province of Samerina (Samaria), and the city of Samaria was rebuilt under Assyrian supervision to serve as the provincial capital. The once independent state of Israel, the northern kingdom, which had enjoyed periods of considerable regional power under the Omrides and the last kings of the Jehu dynasty, was no more. In its place were the four Assyrian provinces of Dor, Megiddo, Gilead and Samaria.

Sennacherib's invasion of Judah

King Ahaz of Judah died in about 727 B.C.E. He was succeeded by his son Hezekiah (727–697 B.C.E.), who presided over a critical period in the history of Judah, introducing cultic reforms that charted the course for the subsequent

ZEV RADOVAN/WWW.BIBLELANDPICTURES.COM

Beersheba horned altar. *Dating to the eighth century B.C.E., this is the first example discovered of an Israelite horned altar for animal sacrifice. Contrary to biblical law (Exodus 20:25), the 63-inch-tall altar was built of hewn stones. It also has a serpent motif incised on one of its blocks. Sacrifices had apparently been burnt on the altar, for the top stones were blackened. The Beersheba altar provides rare evidence of religious rituals carried out in a Judahite city other than Jerusalem.*

Although the altar had been disassembled and its blocks reused in a wall, archaeologists had no trouble distinguishing the calcareous sandstone of the altar blocks from the common limestone of the rest of the wall.

development of Israelite religion, and adopting a bold policy towards Assyria, based first on defiance and then on conciliation, that defined Judah's position in the international affairs of the seventh century B.C.E. Fortunately, Hezekiah's pivotal reign is one of the best documented of any king of Israel or Judah, both in biblical and extrabiblical texts. It is extensively reported in both Kings and Chronicles, and it is the setting of a substantial number of the oracles and narratives collected in Isaiah 1–33. The Assyrian annals provide a full account of Hezekiah's rebellion against Assyria and subsequent capitulation. A number of larger and smaller Hebrew inscriptions have survived from Hezekiah's reign, ranging from the famous Siloam tunnel inscription (discussed below) to the

Arad temple. *Limestone incense altars flank the steps leading into the Holy of Holies, or innermost chamber, of the temple to Yahweh at Arad, in the Negev; at the rear of the niche are two sacred standing stones. Built in the tenth century B.C.E., the Arad temple remained in use until it was destroyed during the religious reforms of either Hezekiah in the late eighth century B.C.E. or Josiah in the late seventh century. When the temple was abolished, the altars were reverently laid on their sides and covered with earth.*

extensive corpus of *lmlk* jar handles (also discussed below) to numerous personal seals and seal impressions belonging to the leading citizens of the day. These personal documents permit an especially intimate access to the time of Hezekiah, but none does so more dramatically than a clay impression that has recently come to light of the seal of King Hezekiah himself.[*][122] It reads "Belonging to Hezekiah (son) of Ahaz, king of Judah."

In the Deuteronomistic historian's summary of his reign (2 Kings 18:1–8,

*Frank Moore Cross, "King Hezekiah's Seal Bears Phoenician Imagery," *BAR*, March/April 1999.

Bullae of King Hezekiah. *When this damaged seal impression (upper right) was originally published, it was too fragmentary to allow scholars to reconstruct the inscription and thus to realize to whom the seal had originally belonged. Fortunately, a more complete impression (left) of the same seal later surfaced in a private London collection. The better-preserved inscription clearly reads: "Belonging to Hezekiah (son) of Ahaz, king of Judah." Above the inscription appears a winged scarab—a symbol found in hundreds of inscriptions dating to the reign of Hezekiah (727–697 B.C.E.).*

especially verse 4) we are told that Hezekiah "removed the high places" (the local shrines), "broke down the pillars" (standing stones that marked the sacredness of the shrines), "cut down the sacred pole" (the asherah, which seems to have signified the divine presence, sometimes personified as a goddess and consort of the God of Israel) and smashed Nehushtan, "the bronze serpent that Moses had made" (an otherwise unknown but obviously long-venerated cult object).* All of these except the last are often-mentioned Israelite cult objects that earlier kings were condemned for failing to abolish, and none of them is Assyrian. It would be a mistake, therefore, to associate Hezekiah's religious reforms with his revolt against Assyria in the closing years of the eighth century.[123] On the contrary, he is more likely to have initiated these reforms early in his reign, before Sennacherib threatened the country and before the elimination of local places of worship might have demoralized the citizenry who lived outside of

*Hershel Shanks, "The Mystery Nechushtan," *BAR*, March/April 2007.

Jerusalem.[124] The Chronicler states that Hezekiah began to purify the Temple immediately, in the first month of the first year of his reign (2 Chronicles 29:3). This claim seems intended to emphasize the piety of an ancient and revered king, but it may be only slightly exaggerated.[125] The grim example of Samaria gave credence to the voices of prophets like Hosea, who had warned that the gross religious improprieties in the northern kingdom would lead to disaster and exile, and Hezekiah may have hoped that religious reform would help Judah avoid the fate of Israel.

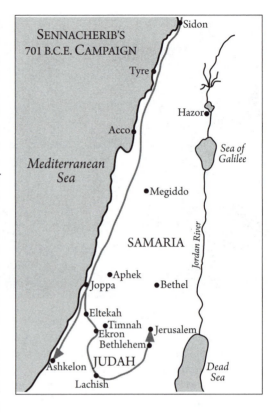

For the first two decades of his reign, Hezekiah seems to have remained a loyal vassal of Assyria. There is no Assyrian record of an attack on Judah by Shalmaneser V or Sargon II during this period.[126] When Ashdod rebelled against Assyria in 714 B.C.E., Hezekiah evidently refused to become involved, despite the seditious messages Ashdod is said in one of Sargon's inscriptions to have sent to Judah.[127] Ashdod had active support from Shabaka (716–706 B.C.E.), the Cushite ruler of Egypt, who had moved to assert the rule of the strong XXVth Dynasty over the entire Nile Valley after the death of the dynastic founder, his brother Piankhy. The "Oracle concerning Ethiopia [i.e., Cush]," in Isaiah 19, with its reference to "sending ambassadors by the Nile," is often taken as an indication that Shabaka contacted Hezekiah, urging him to join the revolt. If so, Hezekiah evidently refused, perhaps swayed by Isaiah's counsel (cf. Isaiah 20:6), and the decision proved to be the safe one, since by 712 B.C.E. Sargon had smashed the revolt in Ashdod* and had at least intimidated its Egyptian supporters—this is the

---

*After Sargon had suppressed the revolt, Ashdod was turned into an Assyrian city-state and provincial center. See Hershel Shanks, "Assyrian Palace Discovered in Ashdod," *BAR*, January/ February 2007.

background of the threats against Egypt and Ethiopia (Cush) in Isaiah 20.

Hezekiah's policy of compliance with Assyria ended dramatically with the death of Sargon II and the accession of his son Sennacherib (705–681 B.C.E.). Viewed in broad perspective, the reign of Sennacherib was a period of relative tranquility in the western provinces of the empire. This was partly because the Assyrian army was heavily committed to a long and difficult struggle with Babylon, but it was also because the conquest of the West was now complete. Although Sennacherib's successors would attempt to extend its boundaries to the Nile, the empire had reached its natural limits. Moreover, the imperial administration, to which Sennacherib made a number of improvements, was in place and working, and this brought an unaccustomed stability to Syria-Palestine—the so-called *Pax Assyriaca*. It is somewhat ironic, then, that just as this Assyrian Peace was taking hold in the West, Sennacherib sent an army across the Euphrates—his only western campaign—with Jerusalem as its principal target and final destination.

Sargon had been killed in battle in Asia Minor, and news of his death sparked hope throughout the empire that Assyrian power would diminish. Almost immediately a rebellion broke out in Babylon, led again by Merodach-baladan, who had also opposed Sargon at his accession (722 B.C.E.). He was supported by a coalition of Babylonian ethnic groups, including his fellow Chaldeans, as well as Arameans and Elamites. Merodachbaladan may also have tried to foment unrest in the West,[128] where, in any case, a major revolt was brewing. The ringleaders were, in the north, Luli, the king of Sidon, and, in the south, Sidqia (*Ṣid-qa-a-a*) of Ashkelon and Hezekiah of Judah. The people of Ekron also joined in, deposing Padi, their pro-Assyrian king, and consigning him to the custody of Hezekiah, who had "attacked the Philistines as far as Gaza and its territory, from watchtower to fortified city" (2 Kings 18:8), evidently attempting to force other Philistine states into the fold. Egypt, hoping to reassert control over the territories and trade routes lost to Tiglath-pileser and Sargon, supported the revolt.

Earlier, after Sargon's suppression of the 714–712 B.C.E. revolt in Ashdod, Pharaoh Shebitku (706–790 B.C.E.), the successor of Shabaka, had made friendly overtures to Assyria in order to stabilize the position of the XXVth Dynasty in Egypt by reducing the threat from Assyria. Now, however, Shebitku was ready to support rebellion against Assyria.

In 701 B.C.E., having ousted Merodachbaladan and brought things somewhat under control in Babylonia, Sennacherib marched against the western rebel states, beginning with Sidon.[129] When the Assyrian army arrived, the Phoenician cities surrendered without a fight. Luli fled to Cyprus (cf. Isaiah 23:12), where he later died, while Sennacherib installed

ERICH LESSING

Wall relief from Sennacherib's palace at Nineveh. *A family from the conquered Judahite city of Lachish walks barefoot into exile. According to the Assyrian annals, Sennacherib (705–681 B.C.E.) besieged and captured 46 of Hezekiah's fortified cities. Sennacherib's greatest success was against Lachish—then the second most important city in Judah—which guarded the southwestern entrance into the passes to Jerusalem. The Assyrian war camp at Lachish, which is depicted in the Nineveh reliefs, became the headquarters for the entire Judahite campaign.*

Sennacherib decorated the central ceremonial room of his Nineveh palace with reliefs like this depicting the conquest of Lachish. Other panels from the series show the Assyrians storming the city, executing the Judahites and carrying off booty.

Ittobaal (*Tuba'lu*) on the Sidonian throne. The Assyrian annals boast of the submission at this time of the rulers of a number of western states ("all the kings of Amurru"). Some or all of these—including the Transjordanian states of Ammon, Moab and Edom—may originally have supported the coalition, so that their surrender left Ashkelon, Ekron and Judah isolated. Sennacherib stormed down the coast and accepted the surrender of Ashkelon, deporting Sidqia to Assyria and replacing him with Sharruludari, who, despite his Assyrian name, is said to have been the son of a former king of Ashkelon who had been loyal to Assyria. At this point Sennacherib spent some time destroying and looting towns and cities, like Joppa, that had been dependent on Ashkelon. Before he was ready to march on Ekron, he was intercepted at Eltekeh (Tell esh-Shallaf, north of Jabneh) by a very large Egyptian expeditionary force that had responded to a request from Ekron for help.[130] Though the annals claim that Sennacherib defeated the Egyptians, he may have merely escaped them—or at best repulsed them—and their continuing presence in the region was probably a factor in his decision to withdraw permanently from Palestine before consummating his siege of Jerusalem. In any case, he moved on from Eltekeh to Ekron and captured the city, punishing the rebels but sparing those who had remained loyal to Assyria; he would eventually bring Padi back from Jerusalem and restore him to his throne.*[131]

After the capture of Ekron, the Assyrian army marched into Judah. For this stage of Sennacherib's campaign we have fairly extensive accounts not only in the Assyrian annals, on which we rely for almost all we know about the earlier stages, but also the Bible. The biblical account, which is found in 2 Kings 18:13–19:37 (= Isaiah 36–37), consists of two distinct sections that are widely recognized as deriving from different sources. The opening section (2 Kings 18:13–16) is a straightforward summary of the events, describing the devastation of the Judahite countryside by the Assyrian army and Hezekiah's payment of tribute to Sennacherib. The businesslike tone of this passage and the absence of ideological or even interpretive expansion suggest that it is a quotation from an early annalistic source. Although much more compact than the Assyrian account, it corresponds closely—sometimes remarkably so[132]—to the picture given there, so that these two annalistic sources, Judahite and Assyrian, tend to corroborate each other. The section that follows in the biblical account (2 Kings 18:17–19:34) is a long discursive narrative detailing demands for the surrender of Jerusalem made by Sennacherib's officers and placing special emphasis on the role of the prophet Isaiah in convincing Hezekiah not to surrender. This material probably originated in prophetic

---

*See Aaron Demsky, "Discovering a Goddess," *BAR*, September/October 1998.

Hezekiah's tunnel. *Anticipating an attack by Sennacherib of Assyria, the Judahite king Hezekiah (727–697 B.C.E.) built a 1,749-foot-long tunnel to bring the water of the Gihon Spring within the city walls of Jerusalem. This successful building project (with its fresh supply of water, Jerusalem managed to withstand the Assyrian siege) is referred to in 2 Kings 20:20 and 2 Chronicles 32:4.*

HERSHEL SHANKS

circles associated with Isaiah, and its language and ideology indicate it was transmitted in the Deuteronomistic tradition. For these reasons the historical value of this second section of the biblical account of the invasion is sometimes discounted, but a number of studies have demonstrated the presence, especially in the speeches of Sennacherib's ambassadors,[133] of stereotyped elements of style, ideology and language known from Assyrian royal inscriptions. This suggests that this section, too, is based on authentic events—or at least early accounts of events—and therefore has historical value despite its complex literary history[134] and its inclusion of numerous later expansions and interpolations.

According to the Assyrian annals, Sennacherib besieged and captured 46 of Hezekiah's fortified cities (cf. 2 Kings 18:13), turning many of them over to the Philistine states that had been loyal to Assyria. Most of these captured cities, we assume, were on Judah's western frontier, which, with Hezekiah's Philistine allies reduced to vassalage or worse, was vulnerable and unable to resist the Assyrian onslaught.* Sennacherib's principal success in this part of the campaign was against the fortress city of Lachish in the

---

*Extensive archaeological evidence of Sennacherib's Judahite campaign has recently been uncovered at Tel Halif south of Jerusalem. See Oded Borowski, "In the Path of Sennacherib," *BAR*, May/June 2005.

ERICH LESSING

Siloam inscription. *Discovered in 1880, this inscription celebrates the completion of Hezekiah's tunnel. Carved into the wall of the tunnel about 20 feet from its end at the Siloam Pool, the text describes how the workmen tunneled toward each other to build the channel: "While the stonecutters were still wielding the axe, each man towards his fellow, and while there were still three cubits to be cut through, they heard the sound of each man calling to his fellow, for there was a zdh [fissure?] in the rock to the right and the left. And on the day of the breakthrough the stonecutters struck each man towards his fellows, axe against axe, and the waters flowed from the source to the pool, for 1,200 cubits."*

Judahite Shephelah, which guarded the southwestern entrance into the passes to Jerusalem. Lachish is not specifically mentioned in Sennacherib's annals—it was presumably one of the 46 captured cities—and the siege is not reported in the Bible (though the presence of the Assyrian army at Lachish is mentioned several times in 2 Kings 18–19). Nevertheless, the siege is very well documented, both by the reliefs depicting the siege found in the ruins of Sennacherib's palace at Nineveh and by the excavation of Lachish.[135] The old annalistic summary at the beginning of the biblical account states that Hezekiah sent a message of contrition to Sennacherib while he was at Lachish, asking the Assyrian king to withdraw and promising that "whatever you impose on me I will bear" (2 Kings 18:14). This suggests that the Assyrian war camp at Lachish, which is depicted in the Nineveh reliefs, was the headquarters for the entire Judahite campaign including the siege of Jerusalem, which must have already been well advanced before Hezekiah dispatched his submissive message.

Despite the arrangement of the biblical materials, it must have been prior to Hezekiah's submission that Sennacherib sent a delegation of three officers to Jerusalem to demand the surrender of the city, as described in 2 Kings

18:17–19:7. The duties of these officers in the normal operations of the Assyrian bureaucracy are well known. Two of the officers, the Tartan (viceroy) and the Rabsaris (chief eunuch), had important military and diplomatic duties,[136] but the third, the Rabshakeh (chief cupbearer), who was the highest-ranking domestic attendant of the king, ordinarily did not. Yet it was the Rabshakeh who served as the Assyrian spokesman at Jerusalem, and this is best explained by the assumption that he spoke Hebrew.[137] The demand for surrender, though formally addressed to Hezekiah, was also a piece of military propaganda, designed to intimidate and demoralize the citizens of Jerusalem: Rabshakeh refused a request by Hezekiah's delegation that he speak Aramaic (the internationally accepted diplomatic language), and instead shouted a message "in the language of Judah" to the people listening on the city wall, denouncing Hezekiah and offering them favorable surrender terms.

Neither the Assyrian nor the biblical account indicates how long Jerusalem was under siege before Hezekiah submitted, but it was long enough for the Assyrian army to erect earthworks against the city gates and ravage the surrounding countryside while keeping Hezekiah confined, as Sennacherib boasted, "like a bird in a cage."[138] It may seem surprising, in fact, that the city wall was never breached,[139] but Jerusalem was not as vulnerable as the cities on Judah's western frontier. The four years (705–701 B.C.E.) it had taken Sennacherib to subdue Merodachbaladan had given Hezekiah time to make elaborate preparations, especially in the capital city itself. According to 2 Chronicles 32:5, he had rebuilt and strengthened the city wall of Jerusalem and the *millo*.* He also added "another wall" that was "outside" the first, part of which was uncovered in a Jerusalem excavation directed by Nahman Avigad.[140] Hezekiah's most remarkable achievement in this regard, though, was the construction of a tunnel to protect the city's water supply. The Gihon Spring, Jerusalem's principal source of water, was situated at a vulnerable location in the Kidron Valley outside the city wall. Hezekiah's workers sealed access to the Gihon and the other water sources outside the city (2 Chronicles 32:3–4) and excavated a tunnel, still extant, that diverted the water under the hill to a collecting pool in the western part of the city, within the walls (cf. 2 Kings 20:20; 2 Chronicles 32:30). This remarkable engineering feat—the excavation of a tunnel 1,749 feet long and in places 100 feet beneath the streets of the city—was described

*The enigmatic *millo* is first mentioned in connection with the rebuilding of the city after David's conquest (2 Samuel 5:9). It was evidently some kind of fortification, perhaps a filled-earth rampart.

and commemorated in an inscription found in 1880.*[141] It is also possible that a newly discovered fragment of a monumental inscription from the City of David mentions Hezekiah and the pool he may have had built to collect the diverted waters.**

Preceding his reference to Hezekiah's tunnel, the Chronicler indicates that Hezekiah maintained numerous storehouses for agricultural goods and places (cities) for quartering livestock (2 Chronicles 32:28–29), and these, too, should probably be seen as part of his preparations for the invasion. The possibility that he reorganized the kingdom fiscally, dividing it into four administrative districts for the distribution of supplies, arises from the study of a large group of stamps found on jar handles and whole vessels—more than 1,200 of them have been found at numerous sites—each of which bears the depiction of a winged scarab[142] and the legend *lmlk*, meaning "Belonging to the king," followed by the name of one of four towns, which may have been central distribution depots.†[143]

In the end, the siege of Jerusalem was lifted, and the Assyrian army departed. Although there may have been other factors,[144] Hezekiah's preparations probably made the completion of the siege seem more difficult than it was worth to Sennacherib, especially since he had already achieved his major goals. The revolt in the West had been completely quelled, and all the leading rebel states— Sidon, Ashkelon and Judah—had submitted and accepted vassalage status, the former two with new kings of Sennacherib's choosing. Hezekiah was still on the throne of Jerusalem, but Padi had been freed from his custody and returned to Ekron, and Hezekiah himself had accepted vassalage and paid an extremely high price to keep his throne.[145] To supply the precious metals required by Sennacherib, Hezekiah emptied both the palace and temple treasuries and stripped the gold ornamentation from the entryway of the Temple (2 Kings 18:15–16). True, the Egyptian army was probably still operating somewhere in the region, but, with the size of the force that ambushed him at Eltekeh still fresh in his mind, Sennacherib must have been content to go home and leave the Egypt problem for his successors.‡[146]

* For recent theories on how the tunnel was constructed, see Hershel Shanks, "Sound Proof: How Hezekiah's Tunnelers Met," *BAR*, September/October 2008; Dan Gill, "How They Met: Geology Solves Long-Standing Mystery of Hezekiah's Tunnelers," *BAR*, July/August 1994.
**Hershel Shanks, "A Tiny Piece of the Puzzle," *BAR*, March/April 2009.
† Gabriel Barkay has proposed that the site of Ramat Raḥel just south of Jerusalem may have been the store city of *mmšt* written on many of the *lmlk* impressions. See Gabriel Barkay, "Royal Palace, Royal Portrait: The Tantalizing Possibilities of Ramat Raḥel," *BAR*, September/ October 2006.
‡Mordechai Cogan, "Sennacherib's Siege of Jerusalem: Once or Twice?" *BAR*, January/ February 2001.

The reign of Manasseh and the Assyrian conquest of Egypt

Hezekiah died in 697 B.C.E. and was succeeded by his son Manasseh (697–642 B.C.E.). Judah was now a very small state, totally under the control of Assyria. Manasseh was a loyal vassal throughout most of his long reign. He is named several times in Assyrian records as one of the western kings required to transport materials to Nineveh or elsewhere for imperial building projects or to supply troops for the Assyrian assault on Egypt.[147] By complying with the demands of the Assyrian administration he managed to reign in peace, at least most of the time, for 55 years (2 Kings 21:1 = 2 Chronicles 33:1), and, to that extent, Judah can be said to have been a beneficiary of the *Pax Assyriaca* in Syria-Palestine. Nevertheless, Manasseh is judged extremely negatively in the Bible, especially in the account of his reign in 2 Kings 21:1–18, where he is condemned not for his loyalty to Assyria, but for his religious policies. The principal author of the account in Kings was an exilic historian of the Deuteronomistic school,[148] thus an advocate of the religious reforms of Hezekiah (Manasseh's father) and Josiah (Manasseh's grandson). The writer was trying to explain why Jerusalem fell despite these reforms, and he fixed on Manasseh because Manasseh was a counterreformer. In 2 Kings 21:10–15, the historian recites an oracle of Yahweh, attributed to unnamed prophets, that lays explicit blame on Manasseh for the fall of Jerusalem and the exile of its people.

It was once assumed that Manasseh's religious policies were the inevitable result of his Assyrian allegiance,[149] but this was not the case. As already noted in connection with Hezekiah's reforms, Assyria imposed no cultic restrictions on vassal states, permitting them to continue their indigenous religious customs.[150] The list of cultic practices for which Manasseh is condemned in 2 Kings 21:3–7 includes no reference to the worship of Assyrian gods. The cultic changes made by Manasseh were, instead, revivals of old Israelite and Judahite practices that had been accepted in the time of his grandfather, Ahaz, and earlier, but set aside by the reforms of his father, Hezekiah. In particular, "he rebuilt the high places," that is, the local places of sacrifice, "that his father Hezekiah had destroyed" (2 Kings 21:3), thus reversing the movement towards cultic centralization that lay at the core of Hezekiah's reform program. Manasseh's reversion to this and other abandoned practices was harshly condemned by reformers and biblical writers living in the time of Josiah and later.[151] But from another point of view, Manasseh's actions may be understood as a kind of reform in themselves—that is, as a counterreformation, involving a wholesale rejection of the innovative religious policies of Hezekiah, which, as Manasseh probably saw it, had not succeeded in protecting Judah from Assyria.

Manasseh was a vassal of three Assyrian kings. Sennacherib's last years were spent dealing with unrest in Babylon, which he finally destroyed in 689 B.C.E. Sennacherib was assassinated in 681 B.C.E. by his sons (cf. 2 Kings 19:37), leading to a power struggle that resulted in the accession of his youngest son Esarhaddon (681–669 B.C.E.), who had been Sennacherib's designated heir and not one of his assassins. Much of Esarhaddon's reign was spent in an effort to conquer Egypt, an enterprise that was completed by his own son Assurbanipal (668–627 B.C.E.). Throughout most of this period Egypt was ruled by Taharqa (690–664 B.C.E.), the biblical Tirhakah, whose reign was remarkable for both its achievements and its disasters. It was the highpoint of the Cushite Period (the XXVth Dynasty), marked by prosperity and building, especially in the dynasty's homeland of Nubia but also at Thebes; but, as we shall see, the XXVth Dynasty also suffered the first successful invasion of Egypt in a thousand years—that is, since the Hyksos period.

At the time of Esarhaddon's accession (681 B.C.E.) the Assyrian empire extended to the border of Egypt; thus, Esarhaddon inherited full control of the coastal trunk road, the King's Highway east of the Jordan, and all the northern outlets available to the South Arabian trade. With the consolidation of Egypt under Pharaoh Tirhakah, however, Assyria had a serious rival for control of commerce, by land and sea, in the eastern Mediterranean. A clash was inevitable. The pattern developed that Assyria became increasingly aggressive towards Egypt while Tirhakah acted covertly or openly to support anti-Assyrian uprisings in the western provinces of the empire.

Before he could turn his attention to the conquest of Egypt, however, Esarhaddon was obliged to spend a few years defending his northern borders against the Medes[152] and the incursions of Eurasian horse nomads, including both Cimmerians[153] and Scythians.[154] He then had to deal with a series of revolts in the West, which can be seen as the opening rounds in his fight with Egypt. Tyre and Sidon, which had been united in the days when Luli had rebelled against Sennacherib, were now rivals. King Baal of Tyre was, like Manasseh, one of Assyria's most submissive vassals, and as a reward Esarhaddon made a treaty with him giving him certain trade privileges such as free entry into all Mediterranean ports. Abdimilkutti of Sidon, provoked by what must have seemed to him unfair advantages for his rival, eventually decided to rebel, most probably with the encouragement and assurances of Pharaoh Tirhakah.[155] In response Esarhaddon marched west in 678 B.C.E. and besieged Sidon; within a year he had captured and beheaded Abdimilkutti and cast the city into the sea, reassigning portions of Sidonian territory to Tyre. Manasseh of Judah was one of several vassal kings required to help in the rebuilding of the ruined city as Kar-Ashur-ah-iddina, "Esarhaddon's Landing."[156]

According to the so-called Babylonian Chronicle, the first major battle between the Assyrian and Egyptian armies in Esarhaddon's reign occurred in his seventh year (674 B.C.E.), when "the army of Assyria was defeated in a bloody battle in Egypt."[157] Nothing more is known of this conflict, but it seems to have been a serious setback for Assyria, since Esarhaddon did not return west until his tenth year (671 B.C.E.). At that time, having accused his old ally Baal of Tyre of conspiring with Tirhakah, Esarhaddon marched past Phoenicia, leaving troops to enforce an embargo on food and water against Tyre, and proceeded south past the now-Egyptian fortress of Ashkelon to the Wadi of Egypt. From there the invasion of Egypt was launched in earnest. The Assyrian army crossed the Sinai, using camels and waterskins provided by "all the kings of Arabia."[158] After arriving in the Nile Delta, Esarhaddon reached Memphis after fighting three battles in 15 days. The city capitulated, and the queen and crown prince were captured, but Tirhakah himself fled south into Upper Egypt, where he still had control, and began to reorganize his forces.[159]

Esarhaddon, probably representing himself as the liberator of Egypt from Cushite rule,[160] accepted the surrender of local rulers of Lower Egypt and departed, leaving the Nile Delta in their hands. As soon as the Assyrian army had withdrawn, however, Tirhakah returned north and seized power again. This provoked Esarhaddon to launch another campaign against Egypt in 669 B.C.E., but the Assyrian emperor died at Haran, shortly after setting out,[161] and it remained for his son Assurbanipal (669–627 B.C.E.) to finish the war with Tirhakah. In 667 B.C.E. Assurbanipal sent an army to Egypt led by his viceroy (*turtānu*).[162] This expeditionary force was supported by ground troops that the Assyrian vassal kings, including Manasseh of Judah, supplied,[163] and it was reinforced by naval fleets launched from coastal vassal states. Again Tirhakah was defeated at Memphis, and again he fled south. This time, however, the Assyrian army pursued his troops up the Nile, establishing control as far south as Aswan. Tirhakah himself escaped to Nubia.

As the Assyrian army withdrew, it again entrusted Egypt to local rulers who had pledged loyalty, and again the local rulers betrayed the Assyrians and conspired with Tirhakah, who in 666 B.C.E. again returned to power. In reprisal, Assurbanipal sent soldiers to seize the disloyal rulers, executing many but bringing two, Necho of Sais and his son Psammetichus, to Nineveh. In 665 B.C.E. he established the former as Necho I (665–664 B.C.E.), the first king of the XXVIth (Saite) Dynasty. In 664 B.C.E. Tirhakah died, having first named his son Tantamani or Tanwetamani (664–656 B.C.E.) as his successor. When Tantamani attacked the Assyrian troops at Memphis and seized the city, Assurbanipal again sent the Assyrian army into Egypt, where it took back control of Memphis and marched on Thebes. Thebes was captured and sacked in 664/663 B.C.E. (cf. Nahum 3:8–11). Though Tantamani remained at least nominally in power as the Egyptian ruler controlling Upper Egypt from Nubia until his death in 656 B.C.E., Lower Egypt was now governed by Necho's son, Psammetichus I (664–610 B.C.E.), from Sais.

The Assyrian empire was now badly overextended, and Egypt soon became independent again. After the rebellion of 666–665 B.C.E., Assyria recognized Necho and then Psammetichus as sole king of Egypt on condition that neither would foment rebellion against Assyria. In 656 B.C.E. with the death of Tantamani and the end of the XXVth Dynasty, Psammetichus was able to extend the rule of the XXVIth Dynasty south to Thebes.[164] Meanwhile the Cimmerians, now well established in Asia Minor, continued to threaten Assyria's Syrian holdings. These factors destabilized the empire, but the first really critical blow came from Babylon, where a major revolt erupted in 652 B.C.E. at the instigation of Assurbanipal's own brother Shamash-shum-ukin, whom their father, Esarhaddon, had appointed as vice-regent in Babylon. This revolt soon spread.[165] In the East it was supported by Chaldean nationalists as well as Arameans and Elamites, the same groups who had backed Merodach-baladan earlier. In the West the primary supporters of the revolt seem to have been Arabs,[166] who probably perceived the vulnerability of Assyria as an opportunity to liberate the trade routes of the southern Levant. Though the Assyrian forces were able to contain the various Arab incursions associated with Shamash-shum-ukin's revolt, the victory was only temporary, since at this time much of Transjordan began to be overrun by Kedarites and other Arabian tribes who did not recognize Assyrian sovereignty. By 648 B.C.E. Assurbanipal had quelled the revolt in Babylon, but it was a foreboding of the fate of the empire.

We have no direct evidence of the way the news of the revolt in Babylon, and of Assyria's other troubles in the mid-seventh century B.C.E., was received in Judah. Apart from its polemic against Manasseh's religious policies, the Kings account of Manasseh's reign (2 Kings 21:1–18), with its Deuteronomistic orientation, provides little information about Manasseh's activities.[167] On the other hand, the Chronicler's account (2 Chronicles 33:1–20), though it draws heavily on that of Kings, supplies additional details suggesting that in the last decade of his reign, with Assyria substantially weakened, Manasseh may have begun to move Judah towards independence.

In particular, the Chronicler (2 Chronicles 31:14) credits Manasseh with building "an outer wall for the City of David, west of the Gihon, in the wadi" and assigning military officers to "all the fortified cities of Judah." The Chronicler does not indicate when in Manasseh's reign these things were done, but it seems probable that they began at the time of the revolt in Babylon (652–648 B.C.E.). The activities described are reminiscent on a smaller scale of Hezekiah's preparations for his revolt against Sennacherib, and they sound very much as if they were designed to strengthen Judah in preparation for a declaration of independence against Assyria. Manasseh's "outer wall" may have been identified archaeologically,*[168] and, more generally, excavations have found substantial evidence of refortification throughout Judah in the latter part of the seventh century. Most of this building should probably be associated with Josiah, but it may have begun during the last days of Manasseh.

THE FINAL YEARS OF
THE KINGDOM OF JUDAH
The reign of Josiah and the end of the Assyrian empire

Manasseh's son and successor, Amon (642–640 B.C.E.), died in a court assassination that historians have not been able to explain.[169] According to 2 Kings 21:23–24 (= 2 Chronicles 33:24–25), the assassins were executed by "the people of the land," who set Amon's eight-year-old son, Josiah, on the throne. Since Josiah came to the throne as a minor, Judah was probably ruled at first by a regent or group of regents—perhaps Josiah's mother or one of "the people of the land" who set him on the throne—but we are not told. In fact, the biblical writers, who are interested almost exclusively in Josiah's religious reform, report nothing about his reign before his 18th year (622 B.C.E.), when the reform began. By this time, Assurbanipal had died (627 B.C.E.). After a period of chaos, his son Sin-shar-ishkun (623–612 B.C.E.) succeeded him, but not before Assyria had descended into civil war and permanently lost control of Babylon, which was now ruled by the Chaldean Nabopolassar (625–605 B.C.E.). In short, the Assyrian empire was in its death throes. This meant that Judah was, in effect, an independent state again, and Josiah was free to institute administrative reforms and even to harbor territorial ambitions.

The overriding interest of the biblical writers, however, was Josiah's religious reform, which is reported in detail in 2 Kings 22:1–23:30. The chief characteristics of this reform, which revived the cultic innovations of Hezekiah and brought an end to the counter-reformation of Manasseh, were, first and foremost, the assertion of the centrality of the Jerusalem Temple and its priesthood. The reform included, as natural corollaries, the elimination

*See Eilat Mazar, "Royal Gateway to Ancient Jerusalem Uncovered," *BAR*, May/June 1989.

throughout the kingdom ("from Geba to Beersheba" (2 Kings 23:8) of the *bāmôt*, or "high places" (the local places of sacrifice and worship), and the exclusion of the regional priests from priestly service in Jerusalem. Other important measures included the prohibition of certain condemned cultic practices (2 Kings 23:4–7,10–12), such as child sacrifice, and the extirpation from Judah of cults of foreign gods (2 Kings 23:13–14).

According to 2 Kings 22:8 the reform was set in motion by the discovery of "the book of the law in the house of the Lord" by Hilkiah, the high priest. When this scroll was shown to King Josiah, he summoned the people of Judah to the Temple in Jerusalem, where he read them everything that was in the document and vowed to instigate religious reforms in conformity with the rules that were written there. When the Kings and Chronicles accounts of these events are compared, it is not clear whether the reform was initiated by the accidental "discovery" of a scroll as Kings suggests, or whether an already ongoing reform program received its crucial impetus when a scroll was brought forward by the priests. Although 2 Kings 22:3 dates the discovery to Josiah's eighteenth year, 2 Chronicles 34:3 states that he had begun to "seek the God of his ancestor David" in his eighth year, "while he was still a boy," and had begun instituting reforms by his twelfth. It is also true that, even in the account in Kings, Temple repairs were already underway before the finding of the scroll (2 Kings 21:3–7).

For nearly two centuries, most biblical scholars have accepted that Josiah's "book of the law" was the biblical Book of Deuteronomy in its penultimate form. This seems clear from the striking correspondences between the reform measures Josiah is said in 2 Kings 23 to have carried out and the laws of worship and religious devotion recorded in Deuteronomy. Thus, for example, Josiah's instructions to abolish various cultic practices conform to prohibitions in Deuteronomy; these condemned practices include the cult of Asherah and the "asherim," or sacred poles (compare 2 Kings 23:4,6,7,14 to Deuteronomy 7:5, 12:3, 16:21, 17:3); the *maṣṣēbôt*, or "pillars" (compare 2 Kings 23:14 to Deuteronomy 7:5, 12:3); the *bāmôt*, or "high places," of foreign gods (compare 2 Kings 23:13 to Deuteronomy 7:5, 12:2–3), and many others. Compare also Josiah's observance of the Passover in Jerusalem "as prescribed in this book of the covenant" (2 Kings 23:21–23) with the commandment to observe Passover "at the place that the Lord your God will choose" in Deuteronomy 16:1–8.[170]

There were certainly ideological and political dimensions, probably in motivation and certainly in result, to Josiah's religious reform. In terms of national ideals, the assertion of the centrality of Jerusalem served to unify the country and strengthen the central government, and the mandate to return to perceived ancestral customs and values promoted national pride and cultural nostalgia.[171] At the political level, the changes Josiah made represented a vindication for those in the country who still supported the principles of Hezekiah's reform and, by the same token, a repudiation of those who had defended Manasseh's policies. This was not a matter of throwing off the Assyrian yoke, however, since Judah was already free of Assyria when Hilkiah presented the "the book of the law" to the king. And in any case it was not Assyrian imperial policy to interfere with the religious practices of vassals or to require them to worship the Assyrian gods.[172]

On the other hand, the evaporation of Assyrian supervision in the region did permit one aspect of Josiah's reform that would not have been possible earlier, namely, its extension outside of Judah into the territory of the fallen kingdom of Israel. The Deuteronomistic historian gives special attention to the cancellation of the cult established by Jeroboam I at Bethel (2 Kings 23:15–20), and this would not have been possible if Josiah had not been able to expand his influence north into the territory of the former Assyrian province of Samerina (Samaria). While it seems certain that Josiah took advantage of the vacuum created by the Assyrian withdrawal, the existing sources do not provide a clear picture of the full extent of Josiah's territorial expansion.[173] It probably extended to most of Samaria, as 2 Kings 23:19 implies, and may well have penetrated into the Galilee, as suggested by the reference in 2 Chronicles 34:6–7 to his institution of cult reforms there. The possibility of western expansion into former Assyrian-controlled Philistine territory is less clear, especially since we know that this region was now dominated by Egypt, as explained below; but the 1960 discovery of a Hebrew ostracon dating to the end of the seventh century B.C.E. near Yavneh Yam (south of Tel Aviv)[174] provides strong circumstantial evidence that, at least in certain areas, Josiah's westward expansion reached the Mediterranean coast.

After the accession of Sin-shar-ishkun, the failing Assyrian empire lasted little more than a decade before the critical blow was struck. The agents were the Babylonians and the Medes. The Babylonian Nabopolassar organized the anti-Assyrian forces—Chaldeans, Arameans and Elamites—who had supported the Shamash-shum-ukin rebellion (652–648 B.C.E.) and the rebellions of Merodachbaladan still earlier. By 616 B.C.E. Nabopolassar was ready to begin his advance north and west against Assyria, but at first his results on the battlefield were at best mixed. At about the same time, however, the Medes began their own assault on Assyria from the north. They had found a strong leader in Cyaxares, who had established a major kingdom on the plateau north of Elam with its capital at Ecbatana (modern Hamadan in western Iran, southwest of Tehran). In 614 B.C.E. the Medes captured the ancient Assyrian capital of Ashu, and entered into an alliance with Nabopo-lassar. Then, in 612 B.C.E., Nineveh, which had been the imperial Assyrian capital since the time of Sennacherib, fell to the combined forces of the Babylonians and Medes. Sin-shar-ishkun seems to have died when the city fell, and Ashur-uballit II (612–609 B.C.E.) became the last Assyrian king, setting up a rump government in Haran, about 100 miles west of Nineveh. Though the Babylonians were not yet secure enough in central and northern Mesopotamia to attack Haran and finish the job, the fall of Nineveh signaled the end of Assyria. It was a major turning-point in the history of the ancient Near East and sent shock waves reverberating throughout the region. The biblical monument to this event is the Book of Nahum, which is entirely devoted to the prophet's "oracle concerning Nineveh" (Nahum 1:1).

Egypt played a prominent and somewhat surprising role in these events. As explained earlier, Egypt had been united since 656 B.C.E. under the XXVIth, or Saite, Dynasty. Psammetichus I (664–610 B.C.E.) had come to the throne as a protégé of Assyria. With the eclipse of Assyria, he became an independent and powerful ruler, not only presiding over the so-called Saite Renaissance at home, but also expanding north to take control of most of Philistia and coastal Palestine as far north as Phoenicia.[175] According to the testimony of Herodotus, Psammetichus took Ashdod by siege[176] and, on another occasion, negotiated the end of an incursion of Scythians into southern Palestine after they had plundered "the Temple of Aphrodite" in Ashkelon.[177] These reports lack direct substantiation in Near Eastern records, but they are plausible and seem to indicate Egyptian domination of Philistia in the latter part of the seventh century B.C.E.[178]

Despite his *de facto* departure from his old vows to Assurbanipal, however, the aging Psammetichus decided to come to the aid of Assyria in its hour of need. Egyptian troops fought alongside the Assyrians against Nabopolassar and his allies in 616 B.C.E., and under Psammetichus's successor, Necho II (610–595 B.C.E.), their support continued as long as there was anything left of Assyria to support—that is, until 609 B.C.E. Historians do not agree about what motivated the Egyptian kings to adopt this policy of attempting to help Assyria survive. Perhaps they envisioned joint Assyrian-Egyptian control of Syria-Palestine. Perhaps they were attempting to position themselves so that when Assyria fell, Egypt would be heir to its empire in the West. It seems likely, in any case, that they wanted to preserve the status quo, as Egypt was beginning to thrive again, and were apprehensive about what future perils a victory for the Chaldeans and the Medes might bring to Egypt.[179]

In 610 B.C.E. the army of the Medes entered Assyria and joined forces with the Babylonians, who already had Scythian support, and in October the Babylonian and Scythian armies advanced on Haran, the last capital of Assyria. Ashur-uballit abandoned the city and fled west to await the arrival of his Egyptian allies. In 609 B.C.E. Necho II set out with a huge expeditionary force and marched north. When the Egyptian army was crossing through the Megiddo pass, Josiah confronted it, and Necho captured and killed him. The circumstances under which this happened are not clear. It is usually assumed on the basis of 2 Chronicles 35:20–24, which describes a battle, that Josiah was trying to intercept the Egyptian army, and it is possible to think of a number of reasons why he might have wanted to do so. If he thought that his own resurgent kingdom was strong enough to wrest control

NEBUCHADNEZZAR'S
CAMPAIGNS

of western Palestine from Egypt, he might have viewed the accession of a new and inexperienced Egyptian king as an opportunity to assert himself. He might have felt an obligation to assist the Babylonians because he regarded Judah as a longtime ally of the Chaldeans, going back to the time of Merodachbaladan and Hezekiah (2 Kings 20:12–13). Or he might simply have wanted to do everything possible to prevent the recovery of Assyria, however unlikely, and the potential for a return to the conditions of subservient vassalage that had prevailed during the reign of his grandfather, Manasseh. On the other hand, the cryptic account of Josiah's death in Kings (2 Kings 23:29) says nothing about a battle. It indicates only that when Necho was on his way to join the king of Assyria, "King Josiah went to meet him; but when Pharaoh Necho met him at Megiddo, he killed him." This raises the possibility that Josiah did not go to Megiddo with a hostile encounter in mind. He might have been seeking an audience or attempting to enter into some kind of negotiation, but the interview became antagonistic and got out of control.

In any case, the Egyptian army proceeded north and, according to the Babylonian Chronicle, crossed the Euphrates in July of 609 B.C.E.; then, joining forces with the Assyrians, they marched against Haran. The results of a four-month siege seem to have been inconclusive—Ashur-uballit may never have reentered the city—but the time was sufficient for the Egyptian army to take control of Syria as far north as Carchemish (cf. 2 Chronicles 35:20), establishing its field headquarters at Riblah in the northern Beqa' (Tell Zerr'a on the Orontes, 21 miles south of Homs).[180] Necho summoned a group of Syro-Palestinian rulers to Riblah to require them to swear oaths of loyalty to Egypt. Among them was King Jehoahaz of Judah (2 Kings 23:33), Josiah's youngest son,[181] whom "the people of the land" had made king when his father was killed (2 Kings 23:30). Necho deposed Jehoahaz and replaced him with his brother Eliakim, changing his name to Jehoiakim (2 Kings 23:31–35), and imposed a heavy tribute on Judah. Judah's brief period of independence—between Assyrian and Egyptian control—was now over.

Egypt seems to have dominated Syria-Palestine, including northern Syria, for a few years, holding the Babylonians at bay until 605 B.C.E., when the Babylonian crown prince, Nabu-kudurri-usdur (the biblical Nebuchadnezzar or Nebuchadrezzar), was given charge of field operations in the West. The Babylonian Chronicle reports that under his leadership the Egyptian army was routed in a decisive battle fought at Carchemish. Necho fled south, but Nebuchadnezzar overtook him at Hamath and defeated him again. The Egyptian king then returned to the banks of the Nile, leaving Syria in Babylonian hands. By that time, though the fate of Ashur-uballit is unknown, the Assyrian empire was a thing of the past. Its former territories were divided between the Medes and the Babylonians. The Medes took the Assyrian heartland and northern territories, while the Babylonians took the rest of Mesopotamia and the western territories. This included rights to not only Syria but also Palestine, so that a further showdown between Babylonia and Egypt was inevitable.

The fall of Jerusalem

Nebuchadnezzar probably intended to follow up his victories at Carchemish and Hamath by continuing to march south into Palestine, but he was prevented from doing so by the death of his father, Nabopolassar, which required him to return to Babylon in August 605 B.C.E., and accept the crown as Nebuchadnezzar II (605–562 B.C.E.), the second king of the neo-Babylonian empire. Within a year, however, Nebuchadnezzar was back in the field, marching through Syria-Palestine and encountering minimal resistance since Necho

Lachish letter. *In 1935, while excavating a burned guardroom beneath a gate tower that had been destroyed by Nebuchadnezzar's army, archaeologists at Lachish found a small archive of wartime correspondence addressed to a certain Ya'ush, evidently the governor or commanding officer of Lachish, from a subordinate named Hawshi'yahu (both names contain forms of the name Yahweh). Written on inscribed potsherds called ostraca, the letters paint an intriguing picture of maneuvers taking place on the southwestern frontier of Judah. Most scholars believe that the ostraca were written on the eve of the destruction of Jerusalem in 586 B.C.E.*

The last four lines of this letter read, "And let [my lord] know that we are watching for the signals of Lachish, according to all the signs which my lord has given, for we do not see Azekah." This recalls Jeremiah's prophecies about a time when "the army of the king of Babylon was fighting against Jerusalem and the cities of Judah—against Lachish and Azekah, for these were the only fortified cities that remained of all the cities of Judah" (Jeremiah 34:7).

was now back in Egypt licking his wounds and rebuilding his forces.[182] In this western campaign of 604 B.C.E. Nebuchadnezzar concentrated on Philistia, especially Ashkelon, which he sacked in December 604, capturing its king, Aga.*[183] Judah was understandably intimidated by having the Babylonian army relatively nearby. A fast was proclaimed in Jerusalem (Jeremiah 36:9), and Jehoiakim, despite his pro-Egyptian leanings, submitted to Nebuchadnezzar and, according to 2 Kings 24:1, became his vassal for three years (604–602 B.C.E.).

*On the Babylonian destruction of Ashkelon, see Lawrence E. Stager, "The Fury of Babylon: Ashkelon and the Archaeology of Destruction," *BAR*, January/February 1996.

Nebuchadnezzar suffered one of his few setbacks in the winter of 601/600 B.C.E., when he attempted to invade Egypt[184] and was repulsed, probably at Migdol (Magdolos, according to Herodotus),[185] a fortress that guarded the entry into Egypt at a point not far south of Pelusium in the eastern Delta. Nebuchadnezzar was forced to withdraw to Babylon, where he remained for a full year, rebuilding his army. This gave Necho the opportunity to campaign along the southern coast of Palestine, capturing Gaza (cf. Jeremiah 47). Jehoiakim, sensing that the balance of power had shifted again, ceased to pay tribute to Babylon and tried to restore himself in the favor of Necho, who was attempting to build a coalition against Babylon.

Nebuchadnezzar returned to Palestine in 599 B.C.E. without much show of force, contenting himself with bivouacking at Riblah, as the Babylonian Chronicle seems to imply, and sending out razzias (raiding parties) to attack and plunder the camps of the Kedarites and other Arab tribes (cf. Jeremiah 49:28–33). On his next visit, however, he returned with his forces fully restored. Intent on reprisal against Jehoiakim for having withheld tribute, he marched on Jerusalem in the winter of 598/597 B.C.E. and put the city under siege in January. Not long before this, in 598 B.C.E., Jehoiakim had died, possibly by foul play,[186] and was replaced by his 18-year-old son Jehoiachin. Jerusalem capitulated with no great resistance on the second day of the Babylonian month of Adar in the seventh year of Nebuchadnezzar— that is, March 16, 597 B.C.E. Nebuchadnezzar, apparently content with the removal of Jehoiakim, followed a policy of relative leniency and ordered no general destruction of the city. He did, however, take Jehoiachin into exile, along with much of the royal family, many members of the court and other leading citizens and artisans. According to 2 Kings 24:14, this first deportation from Jerusalem involved 10,000 people; according to 2 Kings 24:16 the number was 8,000 (7,000 prominent people and 1,000 skilled craftsmen); and according to Jeremiah 52:28, it was 3,023, a number that may include only the male heads of households. Nebuchadnezzar made vassalage treaty with a third son of Josiah, Jehoiachin's uncle Mattaniah, whom he placed on the throne, changing his name to Zedekiah.

Over the immediately succeeding years, Nebuchadnezzar conducted repeated campaigns in Syria-Palestine, but with the memory of the Babylonian defeat of 601/600 B.C.E. still fresh, Judah and the other Palestinian states do not seem to have been entirely intimidated. Egypt remained ambitious and formidable under the successors of Necho—Psammetichus II (595–589 B.C.E.) and Apries, the biblical Hophra (589–570 B.C.E.). In these circumstances, anti-Babylonian plotting began almost immediately, and, in 594, probably emboldened by news of an uprising in Babylon in 595/594 B.C.E.,

Bulla of Jeremiah's scribe. *"Belonging to Berekhyahu, son of Neriyahu, the scribe,"
reads the inscription on this clay bulla, which appears to have been impressed with the
seal belonging to the prophet Jeremiah's scribe and faithful companion Baruch. The Bible
recounts that "Baruch son of Neriah ... wrote on a scroll at Jeremiah's dictation all the
words of the Lord that he had spoken to him" (Jeremiah 36:4). The biblical names appear
on the bulla with the suffix* yahu, *a form of Yahweh.*

*An even more arresting impression appears on the upper left edge of the late-seventh-
to early-sixth-century B.C.E. bulla: the whorls of a fingerprint, presumably left by the
biblical scribe himself.*

Zedekiah seems to have convened an international group of conspirators in
Jerusalem to plan a revolt, with representatives from Edom, Moab, Ammon,
Tyre and Sidon (cf. Jeremiah 27:3). This conspiracy collapsed quickly when
Nebuchadnezzar marched into Palestine in his 11th year (594/593 B.C.E.),
and Jehoiachin sent word to him assuring him of Judah's loyalty; but the
events foreshadowed what was to come.

In 592 B.C.E., Psammetichus II, flush with a victory in Nubia where he had
suppressed the remnant of the XXVth Dynasty, marched into Palestine and
conducted a peaceful show of force, encouraging anti-Babylonian sentiment
in Judah, Philistia and as far north as Phoenicia. Though a cause-and-effect
relationship is difficult to demonstrate, Zedekiah rebelled against Babylon
(2 Kings 24:20) soon after Psammetichus's "triumphal progress." Zedekiah's
revolt may have occurred as early as 591 B.C.E. and certainly by 589 B.C.E.,
when Hophra had come to the throne in Egypt and was encouraging anti-
Babylonian revolts even more aggressively than Psammetichus. Though
Nebuchadnezzar did not respond immediately, he eventually dispatched

a Babylonian army, which reached Jerusalem in January 587 B.C.E. There followed an 18-month siege, interrupted only briefly by the arrival of Egyptian aid (Jeremiah 37:5; cf. Jeremiah 37:11).[187]

The walls were breached in July 586 B.C.E. Zedekiah was captured while trying to escape under the cover of night and was led before Nebuchadnezzar, who put the Judahite king's sons to death before his eyes, then blinded the king and sent him into exile. The Babylonian leader commanded that the city and its Temple be razed, and the order was carried out in August 586 B.C.E. According to Jeremiah 52:29, there was an additional deportation of 832 people, a number that may include only male heads of households. There was no immediate plan to rebuild the city or repopulate it with foreign captives (which was not, in any case, Babylonian policy), and there was no plan for Jerusalem to become a provincial capital, probably because of its long history as a center of rebellion.

Nebuchadnezzar installed a cadre of pro-Babylonian Jews, led by a Judahite aristocrat named Gedaliah son of Ahikam, in a governance role at the town of Mizpah, 8 miles northwest of Jerusalem (2 Kings 25:23). The prophet Jeremiah, who had previously been incarcerated for his persistent warnings against resisting Babylon, was part of the new leadership (Jeremiah 40:1–6).

Not surprisingly, Gedaliah's regime was not popular. Many of the Jews who remained in the land regarded him and his colleagues as collaborators. Probably less than a year after his appointment as governor, Gedaliah was assassinated by a Davidide named Ishmael (2 Kings 25:25; cf. the much more detailed account in Jeremiah 41). Though Ishmael seems to have been supported by the Ammonite king Baalis (Jeremiah 40:14, 41:10), the assassination was hardly part of an anti-Babylonian conspiracy, which would have been completely futile; it was a terrorist act of revenge against a man perceived as a quisling. Members of Gedaliah's regime, fearing Babylonian reprisals, fled to Egypt (2 Kings 25:26), taking Jeremiah with them, while Ishmael and his followers fled to Ammon to escape the vengeance of Gedaliah's remaining supporters (Jeremiah 41:15).

EPILOGUE

The predicament of Judah in the final years before the destruction of Jerusalem was similar to that of Israel before the fall of Samaria. Both were small states swallowed up by great imperial powers, and both had attempted to avoid this fate and maintain some measure of independence by oscillating between policies of appeasement and defiance. In the northern kingdom of Israel this pattern began as soon as Assyria, under Shalmaneser III (859–824 B.C.E.), became a direct threat. Ahab and his Omride successors adopted the policy of defiance. They resisted Shalmaneser's incursions through military action in alliance with Damascus and other regional states. In 841 B.C.E., however, Jehu switched to a policy of appeasement, submitting to Shalmaneser and buying Israel's independence by payment of heavy tribute. The pattern was renewed a century later when Assyria threatened Israel once again under Tiglath-pileser III (745–727 B.C.E.) and his successors. Menahem of Israel chose the safe path of appeasement, paying tribute at the end of Tiglath-pileser's first western campaign (738 B.C.E.), but after the 737 B.C.E. coup of Pekah son of Remaliah, the policy shifted abruptly, and Israel once again took up a position of resistance, based as before on an alliance with Damascus and other local states. This was a dangerous step, and Israel was territorially decimated by Tiglath-pileser's second western campaign (734–732 B.C.E.), in which the anti-Assyrian coalition was crushed and Damascus was captured. Israel survived, however, because of a hasty resumption of the policy of appeasement following the 732 B.C.E. coup of Hoshea, who assassinated Pekah and quickly offered his fealty to Assyria.

The rapidly vacillating policies of Hoshea epitomize the predicament of the northern kingdom in its final years and foreshadow that of Judah a century and a half later. A loyal vassal of Assyria in 732 B.C.E., Hoshea defied Assyria when Tiglath-pileser died in 727 B.C.E. and once again joined neighboring states in revolt. When Shalmaneser V marched west in 727 B.C.E., however, Hoshea shifted positions again, buying a few more years for Israel by submitting and paying tribute. Then in about 725 B.C.E. Hoshea tried again to break free, rebelling against Assyria and seeking safety in yet another alliance of local states. But this time Hoshea had pushed his luck too far. His revolt brought the Assyrian siege engines to the walls of Samaria, and the city fell in 722 B.C.E.

Before the decline of the Assyrian empire, Judah's policy towards the Assyrian threat was essentially the same as that of Israel in its oscillation between defiance and appeasement. Hezekiah's revolt after the death of Sargon II in 705 B.C.E. followed the Israelite pattern of defiance, a policy of resistance to Assyria secured by an alliance with neighboring states, in this case Sidon and Ashkelon. But when Sennacherib invaded Judah in 701 B.C.E. and placed Jerusalem under siege, Hezekiah was forced to shift to a policy of appeasement, paying a heavy tribute to ensure the survival of his kingdom. This policy continued through most of the long reign of Manasseh (697–642 B.C.E.), whose loyalty to Sennacherib and his successors kept Judah secure.

The Assyrian empire collapsed in the last decades of the seventh century B.C.E., but the result was that Judah's position became more precarious rather than less. The vacuum left by Assyria's demise was now filled by not one but two great powers. The kings of the XXVIth Egyptian Dynasty, who had been allied with Assyria, asserted their power along the coast of Palestine. At the same time Babylon rose to preeminence under Nabopolassar and Nebuchadnezzar and began to take an interest of its own in the affairs of Palestine. These developments left Judah in the treacherous position of having to conduct its policies of resistance and appeasement in relation to two competing superpowers.*[188]

Assyria's demise seemed at first to present Judah with an opportunity to enlarge its territory, but Josiah's expansion of Judah to the north and west brought him into conflict with Egypt and may ultimately have led to his death at the hand of Pharaoh Necho II at Megiddo in 609 B.C.E. Josiah's succession by his like-minded son Jehoahaz signaled a policy in Judah of continued defiance of Egypt. Almost immediately, however, Necho replaced Jehoahaz with his pro-Egyptian brother Jehoiakim. Judah was now an Egyptian vassal state, and a policy of appeasement towards Egypt spared Judah the full measure of Necho's wrath. Soon after, however, Nebuchadnezzar asserted the power of Babylon in Palestine, capturing Ashkelon in 604 B.C.E. Despite his Egyptian leanings, Jehoiakim concluded that it was now Babylon that needed to be appeased, and he began paying tribute to Nebuchadnezzar. When Nebuchadnezzar was repulsed trying to invade Egypt in 601/600 B.C.E., however, Jehoiakim switched allegiances again, withholding tribute in defiance of Babylon. This proved to be a fatal error of judgment. When Nebuchadnezzar returned to Palestine in 598/597 B.C.E., Jehoiakim died— possibly by foul play—and was replaced by Jehoiachin, signaling a return in Judah to a policy of appeasement towards Babylon. Jerusalem capitulated to the Babylonian army, and Nebuchadnezzar followed a relatively lenient policy towards the captured city, exiling Jehoiachin and placing Zedekiah on the throne of Jerusalem.

Zedekiah, however, now faced the predicament that had doomed Jehoiakim, and he made the same mistake. Probably encouraged and pressured by Egypt, he revoked his vassalship to Nebuchadnezzar and rebelled, perhaps in 589 B.C.E. When Nebuchadnezzar returned to Jerusalem he was no longer in a lenient mood, and the Babylonian army besieged and destroyed the city in 587 to 586 B.C.E. In this way the kingdom of Judah suffered the same fate as the kingdom of Israel. Like Hoshea before them, Jehoiakim and Zedekiah were unable to find the right combination of resistance and appeasement that would permit their small kingdom to survive in an international arena dominated by two larger and more aggressive superpowers.

*Abraham Malamat, "Caught Between the Great Powers," *BAR*, July/August 1999.

SIX

Exile and Return
From the Babylonian Destruction to the Beginnings of Hellenism

ERIC M. MEYERS WITH THE ASSISTANCE OF SEAN BURT

THE NEO-BABYLONIAN PERIOD

THE INDEPENDENT KINGDOM OF JUDAH FINALLY CAME TO AN END when the neo-Babylonian ruler Nebuchadnezzar crushed Zedekiah's rebellion and destroyed Jerusalem in 586 B.C.E. The Book of Kings and Jeremiah arrestingly recount the series of humiliations Judah faced. The neo-Babylonians (as distinguished from the earlier Babylonian empire of the third millennium B.C.E.) executed Zedekiah's sons before his eyes, then blinded and imprisoned him; they burned the Temple and slaughtered the Temple officials, military commanders and noblemen; and they deported many of the survivors to Babylon (2 Kings 25:7–21; Jeremiah 39:1–10, 52:1–16). The rebellious Zedekiah was deposed and the grandson of Shaphan, Gedaliah, was appointed as governor' in his place. Thus ended Judah's Davidic monarchy (see 2 Kings 25; Jeremiah 39 and 52). Zedekiah, blinded and humbled was deported to Babylon along with many of Judah's elites. A new chapter in Israel's history had begun.

This period has traditionally been referred to as the Exile. The word "exile" and associated terms such as "exilic" and "postexilic," however, are not without problems. They give priority to the perspective of those who saw themselves as descendants of the "remnant" who survived in Babylon and then returned to Israel. As such, "Exile" excludes, or at least marginalizes, several important developments in the history of Judah and the Judeans in the sixth–fourth centuries B.C.E. For example, what about the reduced but still notable population that remained in the land of Israel? What about the emigrants to areas other than Babylon? What about those deportees who chose to remain in Babylon and elsewhere even after the Exile "ended"?[2]

The biblical accounts of life after the fall of Jerusalem are unfortunately fragmentary. The biblical writers seem to have regarded the events of the neo-Babylonian period as less interesting than what those events meant or what they produced. The Exile was interpreted as deserved divine punishment for breaking Israel's covenant obligations (see Jeremiah and the Deuteronomistic History) or for allowing impurities to defile the land (see Leviticus 18; Ezekiel; Chronicles). Once Jerusalem had fallen, the biblical writers turned their gaze toward Babylon and searched for new understandings of the meaning of history.

Life in the land after the fall of Jerusalem

Accordingly, the one-sided focus in biblical texts on the desolation of Jerusalem and Judah is somewhat distorted. Jeremiah 40:7 says that only "the poorest of the land" remained, a statement undermined, for example, by the presence of Judean administrative functionaries in Mizpah, north of Jerusalem. Even more extreme, 2 Chronicles 36:21 asserts that the Exile meant an effective emptying of the land, that it took place "to fulfill the word of the Lord by the mouth of Jeremiah, until the land had made up for its sabbaths. All the days that it lay desolate it kept sabbath, to fulfill seventy years."[3] These kinds of claims about the extent of the destruction have been vastly overstated in order to fit neat theological categories. On the contrary, life in fact continued in Judea much as before.[4]

True, recent analysis of settlement patterns and population size in the seventh–fifth centuries B.C.E. has shown that the destruction of Jerusalem and surrounding areas, particularly the western border of Judah, was indeed very real. In the sixth century B.C.E. urban life in Judah declined precipitously. From 150,000 persons in the seventh century, Jerusalem was reduced to a mere 3,000.[5] From Iron Age II (the biblical period) to the Persian period (after the neo-Babylonian period), the settled area in the environs of Jerusalem, as well as in the Shephelah, was decimated.[6] Life carried on, but Jerusalem was but a shadow of its former self. Deep poverty likely characterized life in the Holy City. The dire, visceral imagery of Lamentations (e.g., Lamentation 1:4: "The roads to Zion mourn, for no one comes to the festivals; all her gates are desolate, her priests groan; her young girls grieve, and her lot is bitter"), though undoubtedly shaped by literary conventions,[7] likely captures the flavor of life, such as it was, in Jerusalem.

The destruction in Jerusalem occasioned a region-wide economic depression, even collapse, particularly in the southern and the eastern parts of Judah.[*8] Judah may even have ceded territory to neighboring peoples; a few prophetic texts hint of significant losses at this time—to the Edomites (Obadiah 19; Ezekiel 36:5), Ammonites (Jeremiah 49:1; Ezekiel 25:10), as well as to the Philistines and Phoenicians (Obadiah 19; Ezekiel 25:15, 26).[9]

On the other hand, the entire land was by no means empty in the sixth century.[**] The Babylonian destruction of Judah was thorough and severe, but it was not wanton. The siege of Jerusalem was a part of a Babylonian strategy of escalating punishments for Judah's successive treaty violations. After wresting supremacy from the Egyptians—a feat solidified with their victory at Carchemish—the neo-Babylonians responded to Jehoiakim's rebellious alliance in 597 B.C.E. The neo-Babylonians invaded Judah and deported Jehoiakim's successor Jehoiachin along with others among Judah's elite, but allowed another member of Judah's Davidic dynasty, Jehoiachin's uncle Zedekiah (Mattaniah) to remain on the throne. From the Babylonian standpoint, Zedekiah's subsequent attempt to resist Babylonian authority was the final straw. Factions in Judah had repeatedly sought to assert its independence. Recognizing this in 587 B.C.E. Nebuchadnezzar's general[10] Nebuzadaran decided to end Jerusalem's political, as well as cultural, autonomy. The Babylonian campaign was carefully designed to eliminate key Israelite holdings like Jerusalem. Israeli archaeologist Oded Lipschits contends that the Babylonians barred the people from living in Jerusalem, and set up an alternative administrative center in Mizpah. They appointed Gedaliah, a non-Davidide, as governor, perhaps even before they destroyed the Holy City.

The material culture unearthed by archaeology in Benjamin and the northern hills of Judah indicates that, in the interest of maintaining an administrative outpost in the area, the Babylonians left Benjamin untouched. To a far greater extent than in Jerusalem and its environs, archaeologists find evidence of continuous occupation in Mizpah (Tell en-Nasbeh[†]), Gibeah, Tell el-Ful and elsewhere. More than 40 seal impressions likely dating to the sixth century B.C.E. (found on site but not in stratigraphically secure

---

*Ephraim Stern, "The Babylonian Gap," *BAR*, November/December 2000.

**See the two views of Joseph Blenkinsopp and Ephraim Stern in "The Babylonian Gap Revisited," *BAR*, May/June 2002.

†We reject the suggestion by Yitzhak Magen that Nebi Samuel is Mizpah. See Yitzhak Magen, "Nebi Samuel—Where Samuel Crowned Israel's First King," *BAR*, May/June 2008.

locations) reading the still undeciphered *MṢH/MWṢH*, appear in Benjamin from Sobah and Jericho to the west and east as well as in Mizpah and Ramat Raḥel to the north and south.[11] Though the word they contain has not yet been understood, they come from six stamp designs suggesting a standardized production of some commodity. Of the 43 examples of these seal impressions, 30 originate in Mizpah. This solidifies the identification of Mizpah as an active administrative city during the neo-Babylonian period.

If Mizpah served as the *de facto* capital of Judea after the destruction, it likely did so as an arm of the Babylonian bureaucratic structure. The extent of Babylon's administrative presence in the provinces is a matter of some controversy. Many scholars have assumed that the neo-Babylonians succeeded to the administrative network already put in place by the neo-Assyrians. Upon closer examination this suggestion does not seem to hold up, however. The neo-Assyrians replaced smaller, long-standing kingdoms and their political and religious institutions, and assimilated their populations. The neo-Babylonians, on the other hand, took over already-conquered areas with established administrative networks.[12] During the first decades of their empire, the neo-Babylonians either chose not to mobilize these bureaucratic resources or did not have the time or wherewithal to do so. The neo-Babylonian administration in the early years was mostly *ad hoc*. They made little attempt to build up trade networks or maintain fortresses. They simply filled their coffers by means of periodic campaigns through their empire.[13] It is unlikely that Babylon took over Assyria's institutions wholesale, though the evidence of the *MṢH/MWṢH* seal impressions suggests that a measure of administrative control was instituted some time in the early sixth century B.C.E.

Given Mizpah's prominence and Jerusalem's destruction and decimated population, the question arises as to whether the ancient Israelite cult site at Bethel, a few miles north of Mizpah, was revived as the principal place of sacrifice and worship. The evidence is scant, limited to a few hints in biblical passages such as Jeremiah 41:4–8, which speaks of meal offerings and frankincense to present at the House of the Lord.[14]

Mizpah and sites in Benjamin remained the population centers of Judah at least until the mid-fifth century B.C.E. The history of the area after the early sixth century, however, is little known. Judahite royalists, chief among them Ishmael son of Nethaniah, viewed the Babylonian-appointed Gedaliah as a collaborator and for this reason assassinated him shortly after he took power. Other pro-Davidic sympathizers fled to Egypt, among them the prophet Jeremiah (Jeremiah 43:7). Whether or not as a punishment for Gedaliah's murder, the neo-Babylonians also took a third wave of deportees back to Babylon in 582 B.C.E.[15]

Exilic seal impression. *Made by a sixth-century B.C.E. seal only three-fourths of an inch long, this impression reads "Belonging to Yehoyishma, daughter of Sawas-sar-usur." Yehoyishma, which includes the divine element* yeho, *a form of Yahweh, is a type of name that originated in Babylonia during the Exile. Sawas-sar-usur is a well-known neo-Babylonian name that means "Shamash [the Babylonian sun-god] protect the king!" Thus, the Jewish woman who owned this seal had a Yahwistic name, but her father had a neo-Babylonian pagan name.*

Israeli archaeologist Nahman Avigad suggested that one of the first exiles in Babylonia gave his son the local name Sawas-sar-usur. By the time this man had a daughter, there was a resurgence of national and religious feeling among the Jews in Exile. Perhaps seeking divine help to return to Jerusalem, Sawas-sar-usur gave his daughter a Jewish name that means "Yahweh will hear."

Settlement patterns in Benjamin and the northern hill country indicate that Mizpah remained the *de facto* capital of Judea until well into the Persian period.

Life in Babylon

Texts regarding living conditions in exile during the neo-Babylonian period (Daniel 1–6; 1 Esdras 4; Tobit; Esther) depict Israelites developing strategies for coping with and occasionally even thriving in the Diaspora.[16] However, these stories owe more to literary conventions than to historical events. How to live faithful Jewish lives in exile is of great interest, but hard information is scant.

According to Ezekiel (1:1–3, 3:15,23), Judeans lived in the vicinity of Nippur, at Tel Abib near "the river Chebar." A recently published set of trilingual texts comes from the Babylon-Borsippa region at a place named "al-Yahudu" (meaning something like "Judah-ville").[17] In some of these texts, "al-Yahudu" lacks the gentilic ending, suggesting that it was less an ethnic enclave than a place whose name recalls its original inhabitants.[18] The texts also include a number of Judean (Yahwistic) names of people active in commodity and property transactions as both creditors and debtors. The earliest of these texts dates to 572 B.C.E. (not long after the Babylonian destruction in 586 B.C.E.). In general they reflect the extent to which Judeans quickly integrated themselves into the Babylonian economy.

Other place names with Judean exiles are mentioned in Ezra—Tel-melah, Tel-harsha, Cherub, Addan, Immer (Ezra 2:59; Nehemiah 7:61) and Casipha (Ezra 8:17), but nothing about them is known.

Many deportees no doubt felt the loss of their homeland deeply. The classic statement is Psalm 137: "For there our captors asked us for song, and our tormentors asked for mirth, saying 'Sing us one of the songs of Zion!' ... If I forget you, O Jerusalem, let my right hand wither!"

The predictions of the prophet Hananiah (Jeremiah 28:2–4) hint at the hope for a quick return. Perhaps this was incited by a period of unrest that threatened Babylon's power in 595 B.C.E.

> Thus says the Lord of hosts, the God of Israel: I have broken the yoke of the king of Babylon. Within two years I will bring back to this place all the vessels of the Lord's house, which King Nebuchadnezzar of Babylon took away from this place and carried to Babylon. I will also bring back to this place King Jeconiah [Jehoiachin] son of Jehoiakim of Judah, and all the exiles from Judah who went to Babylon, says the Lord, for I will break the yoke of the king of Babylon.
>
> (Jeremiah 28:2–4)

Hananiah's prophecy failed to come to pass, however, and the exiles were left with little alternative but to adapt to their new home. Jeremiah's advice was to do so. In a letter to the Judeans he rejected oracles of hope (Jeremiah 29:8–9) and asked the exiles to "build houses and live in them; plant gardens and eat what they produce" (Jeremiah 29:5).

The exiles appear to have followed Jeremiah's advice. A set of Babylonian inscriptions known as the Weidner documents record the distribution of daily rations to Judah's former king Jehoiachin and his family.[19] These rations, which were 20 times the standard individual allotment,[20] indicate that Jehoiachin, referred to by the title "king of Judah" in these documents, was treated with some measure of respect.

What Happened to Israel and Judah in Exile?

The imperial conquests of Assyria and Babylon in the late eighth, seventh and early sixth centuries B.C.E. brought an end to the independent kingdoms of Israel and Judah. Not only were the royal houses of Omri and David dismantled, but much of their kingdoms' populations were taken into exile *en masse* to various corners of the Mesopotamian world.

But far from being lost to history, these deportees managed to survive and even thrive outside of their homelands. As explained by K. Lawson Younger, Jr. in his *BAR* article, "Israelites in Exile" (November/December 2003), both the Bible and various Assyrian documents indicate that many Israelites from the region of Samaria were resettled in towns like Halah and Gozan in the Assyrian heartland of northern Mesopotamia. Life for most of the thousands of Israelite deportees who were forced into hard labor or working in the fields was grueling and bleak, but documents also show that some managed to achieve positions of relative importance within Assyrian society, becoming soldiers, translators, bureaucrats and even priests. Eventually, many of these Israelites adopted Mesopotamian names and customs and fully assimilated into their new surroundings.

After the fall of Jerusalem in 586 B.C.E., populations of the kingdom of Judah were likewise carried off into exile and resettled in Mesopotamia where they lived and worked in their own communities, which they named after places from their native land, including their former capital and holy city. As André Lemaire has argued in *BAR* ("The Universal God: How the God of Israel Became a God for All," November/December 2005), these ethnically-distinct "Judahite" neighborhoods, together with the survival and continuation of Judah's priestly classes, allowed Judahite culture and religion to flourish even in exile. In fact, it was the physical separation from both the Promised Land and Jerusalem that allowed Israel to fully embrace, possibly for the first time, its monotheistic vision of a universal God for all peoples. —*Ed.*

Judeans, on the other hand, may have interpreted the situation differently: 2 Kings 25:27 notes that Jehoiachin was released from his "prison" by Nebuchadnezzar's successor Awel-Marduk (biblical Evil-Merodach).

The Murashu archive tablets provide further evidence that the Judeans integrated into Babylonian society and economy. Consisting of over 700 cuneiform tablets of administrative and economic content from Nippur, they document many West Semitic and Yahwistic names. Although less applicable to the neo-Babylonian period than the al-Yahuda tablets because they were composed in the mid-fifth century, the Murashu archive documents Judean participation in a variety of economic transactions. Moreover, there is little indication that the Judeans were slaves; rather they appear to have been agricultural producers living as semi-free tenants on royal lands.[21]

Thus, although the Babylonians forcibly removed peoples from their homelands, they did not greatly interfere with their cultural autonomy. Many Judeans, to be sure, felt their displacement as a devastating loss.[22] One can draw parallels to other displaced populations throughout history to understand the exiles' experience.[23] Perhaps because so much that the Israelites thought secure was lost—not just the city and its Temple, but also the foundational theological concept that God would reside in and protect Zion—the neo-Babylonian period became a crucible of creative reinterpretations of history both recent and distant. More particularly, the exile was interpreted not as a punishment (or not as a punishment alone) but as a new beginning (see "What Happened to Israel and Judah in Exile?" previous page). Jeremiah, consistent with his pro-Babylonian (or anti-rebellion) position during the last days of Judah, interpreted the exile as divinely willed. The prophet regards the exiles as the recipients of God's favor and those who were not forcibly relocated as rejected afterthoughts:

> The Lord showed me two baskets of figs placed before the Temple of the Lord ... One basket had very good figs, like first-ripe figs, but the other basket had very bad figs, so bad that they could not be eaten ... Then the word of the Lord came to me: Thus says the Lord, the God of Israel: Like these good figs, so I will regard as good the exiles from Judah, whom I have sent away from this place to the land of the Chaldeans. I will set my eyes upon them for good, and I will bring them back to this land. I will build them up, and not tear them down; I will plant them, and not pluck them up. I will give them a heart to know that I am the Lord; and they shall be my people and I will be their God, for they shall return to me with their whole heart. But thus says the Lord: Like the

HIP/SCALA/ART RESOURCE, NY

Cyrus Cylinder. *The inscription written in cuneiform on this 10-inch-long clay barrel tells how the great god Marduk chose Cyrus (559–529 B.C.E.) to supplant the impious tyrant who was then king of Persia, and of how Cyrus went on to conquer the equally odious king of Babylon, Nabonidus. It then proclaims, "I am Cyrus, king of the world, great king," and describes his new religious policy of toleration, which allowed subject peoples to return to their homelands and repair their ruined sanctuaries.*

The Bible records a similar decree of Cyrus that permitted the Jews to resettle Jerusalem and rebuild their Temple in about 539 B.C.E. (2 Chronicles 36:23 and Ezra 1:2–3).

> bad figs that are so bad they cannot be eaten, so will I treat King
> Zedekiah of Judah, his officials, the remnant of Jerusalem who
> remain in this land, and those who live in the land of Egypt. I
> will make them a horror, an evil thing, to all the kingdoms of the
> earth—a disgrace, a byword, a taunt and a curse in all the places
> where I shall drive them.
>
> (Jeremiah 24:1–2,4–9)

This theology foreshadows coming conflicts in the subsequent Persian period. Similar ideas also appear in Ezekiel (11:14–20), where the land left behind becomes a place of abomination that those renewed by God in exile must eradicate so that God may once again dwell in the land. In the eyes of these prophetic theologians, God had great things in store for Israel when its faithful remnant return from their sojourn.

Other theological and religious developments can also be traced to this fertile time. The radical otherness of Ezekiel's deity, coupled with the soaring polemics of Deutero-Isaiah (Isaiah 40–55), suggest that exclusive monotheism (as opposed to a local, national deity tied to the land) comes to full flower in the neo-Babylonian and Persian periods.[24] Precursors to apocalyptic literature, particularly Ezekiel 38–39, Deutero-Zechariah (Zechariah 9–14) and Joel, also emerge after the destruction of Jerusalem, perhaps reflecting the influence of Persian dualistic thought.[25]

Though evidence for actual ancient synagogues does not appear until the early centuries C.E., Ezra's reading of "the Book of the Torah of Moses" at the Water Gate in Nehemiah 8 may be a move in this direction. It may be seen as an extension of the Iron Age practice of using city gates for public and cultural purposes that now included the public reading of scripture.[26] Ezekiel's idea of a "diminished sanctuary" (*miqdash me'at*) in 11:16 may perhaps refer to the origin of the synagogue, with the displaced population learning to create in exile an alternative form of religious worship without the Temple.

THE PERSIAN PERIOD

The neo-Babylonians had only a short time to enjoy their newly won hegemony. By the early 540s, Persia to the east had defeated and subsumed its neighbor Media. Babylon itself was already embroiled in internal controversy. The Babylonian ruler Nabonidus was developing a royal ideology, portraying himself as a historically-minded archivist and builder who restored the traditions of the past. The Marduk priesthood, however, regarded Nabonidus as a dangerous innovator who angered Marduk with his devotion to the cult of the moon god Sin.[27] The resulting political instability weakened the Babylonian state, and in 539 B.C.E. the Persian king Cyrus captured Babylon. Some contemporary sources, including the "Nabonidus Chronicle" and the Persian "Cyrus Cylinder," suggest that Nabonidus was so unpopular that the Babylonians welcomed Cyrus and enabled him to obtain power in a virtually bloodless coup. While this version of events may owe more to the propagandistic aims of the texts than to historical reality,[28] Cyrus no doubt did find some support in Babylon for his campaign. Cyrus returned the favor by depicting himself as a supporter of Marduk: "Marduk, the great lord, caused the magnanimous people of Babylon [to ...] me, (and) I daily attended to his worship ... I sought the welfare of the city of Babylon and all its sacred centers."[29] The famous Cyrus Cylinder now in the British Museum depicts Cyrus as a patron of Babylon. However, his policies should be considered as Persia's response to Babylonian politics, not as an empire-wide policy of religious tolerance.[30] Nevertheless, the generosity of spirit reflected in the cuneiform Cyrus Cylinder is also found in the Bible's description (Ezra 1:2–4; 2 Chronicles 36:23). In the biblical version, Cyrus fulfills the quasi-messianic hopes of Deutero-Isaiah (see Isaiah 44:28 and 45:1) and heralds the end of the Exile. Coming on the heels of Cyrus's decree allowing exiles to return, the words of Ezra indicate widespread support for the reconstruction of the Jerusalem Temple:

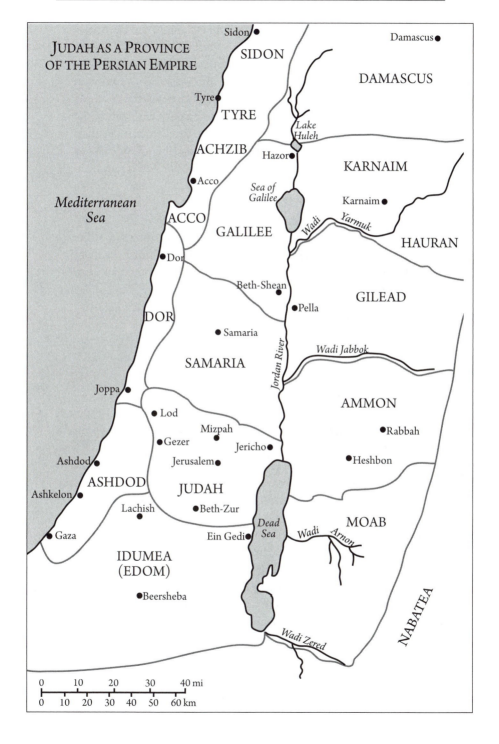

JUDAH AS A PROVINCE
OF THE PERSIAN EMPIRE

Sidon

Damascus

SIDON

DAMASCUS

Tyre

TYRE

Lake
Huleh

ACHZIB

Hazor

KARNAIM

Acco

Sea of
Galilee

Karnaim

Mediterranean
Sea

ACCO

GALILEE

Wadi

Yarmuk

HAURAN

Dor

DOR

Beth-Shean

GILEAD

Pella

Samaria

Jordan River

Wadi Jabbok

SAMARIA

Joppa

AMMON

Lod

Mizpah

Rabbah

Gezer

Jericho

Jerusalem

Heshbon

Ashdod

JUDAH

ASHDOD

Ashkelon

Lachish

Beth-Zur

Dead
Sea

MOAB

Gaza

Ein Gedi

Wadi

Arnon

IDUMEA
(EDOM)

NABATEA

Beersheba

Wadi Zered

```
0      10     20     30     40 mi
0  10  20  30  40  50  60 km
```

The heads of the families of Judah and Benjamin, and the priests and the Levites—everyone whose spirit God had stirred—got ready to go up and rebuild the house of the Lord in Jerusalem. All their neighbors aided them with silver vessels, with gold, with goods, with animals and with valuable gifts, besides all that was freely offered. King Cyrus himself brought out the vessels of the house of the Lord that Nebuchadnezzar had carried away from Jerusalem and placed in the house of his gods. King Cyrus of Persia had them released into the charge of Mithredath the treasurer, who counted them out to Sheshbazzar the prince of Judah. And this was the inventory: gold basins, thirty; silver basins, one thousand; knives, twenty-nine; gold bowls, thirty; other silver bowls, four hundred and ten; other vessels, one thousand; the total of the gold and silver vessels was five thousand four hundred. All these Sheshbazzar brought up, when the exiles were brought up from Babylonia to Jerusalem.

(Ezra 1:5–11)

With this magnanimous offer, gladly accepted by the exiles, a new chapter in Israel's history began.

Demography and the delayed restoration
If Cyrus's defeat of the hated Babylonians raised hopes and expectations of a speedy restoration, the early Persian period failed to live up to that promise. Sheshbazzar, denominated as "the prince of Judah,"[31] is credited with having laid the Temple's foundations (Ezra 5:6–17), but this is contradicted by Ezra 3.[32] Precisely who Sheshbazzar was and what he did, unfortunately, is lost to history, even to the tradents who composed Ezra-Nehemiah. The list of returnees in Ezra 2, because it comes on the heels of the description of the return of the vessels under Sheshbazzar, might be thought to imply a sizable return, but the list of names includes returnees like Zerubbabel from a second, later return (Ezra 2:1). The notion of a clean end to the Exile accompanied by a mass return in 539 B.C.E., as suggested by Ezra 1–3,[33] and assumed by many scholars, does not hold up under scrutiny. By the second half of the sixth century B.C.E., many of the exiles had successfully accommodated themselves to life in Babylonia. The same demographic situation that characterized the neo-Babylonian period in ancient Judah is also true for the early Persian period. Any return that may have taken place at the dawn of the Persian empire left no traces in the settlement patterns in "Yehud" as it is called as a Persian province.[34] The residents of Yehud lived in deep poverty

and had few complex social institutions.

The late-sixth-century prophets Haggai and Zechariah attest to Yehud's battered economy. Writing in about 520 B.C.E., a generation after Cyrus's conquest of Babylon, Haggai addresses the inhabitants of Yehud in vivid terms (Haggai 1:5–6):

> Thus says the Lord of hosts: Consider how you have fared. You have sown much, and harvested little; you eat, but you never have enough; you drink, but you never have your fill; you clothe yourselves, but no one is warm; and you that earn wages earn wages to put them into a bag with holes.

As a remedy for the people's economic ills, Haggai encouraged his fellow Judeans to regain the Lord's favor by rebuilding the Temple, to finish the task that was to have begun in the time of Cyrus. Indeed, the fact that Jerusalem lacked a temple years after Judah was no longer barred from rebuilding it created a problem even for the historian who wrote Ezra 1–6; he attributed the delay to outside interference, namely the machinations of non-Judean enemies. This strategy is also mirrored in Nehemiah's first person tale of the same events. However, to explain the delay in rebuilding the Temple required the historian to resort to creative chronology, jumbling events that took place over several time periods to create the illusion of unified opposition to the rebuilding of the Temple. The most jarring example of this technique can be found in Ezra 4:23–24:

> Then when the copy of King Artaxerxes' [465–424 B.C.E] letter was read before Rehum and the scribe Shimshai and their associates, they hurried to the Jews in Jerusalem and by force and power made them cease. At that time the work on the house of God in Jerusalem stopped and was discontinued until the second year of the reign of King Darius of Persia [520 B.C.E.].

Aside from the chronological disjunction—Artaxerxes I ruled nearly a century *after* Darius—the letter from Artaxerxes[35] cannot refer to the Temple project that was finished in 515 B.C.E. Rather, it would seem to relate to the construction of Jerusalem's wall in the mid-fifth century B.C.E., though, curiously, this letter makes no appearance in the primary narrative account of the wall project in Nehemiah 1–7, 13.

The people of Yehud did complete the Temple, however, during the reign of Darius I, most likely in 515 B.C.E. This date remains the scholarly consensus, notwithstanding Diana Edelman's recent attempt to attribute the Temple's construction to the mid-fifth century.[36]

The debate on the chronology of the Temple's rebuilding nevertheless points up a central problem with the Persian-era Second Temple: We have no concrete contemporary descriptions of the edifice, nor an account of its construction, biblical or otherwise, in striking contrast to the meticulously rendered descriptions of the tabernacle (Exodus 25–31, 35–40), Solomon's Temple (1 Kings 6–7) and Ezekiel's re-imagined temple (Ezekiel 40–44).[37] As Carol Meyers has observed, "It is perhaps ironic that the temple building that survived the longest—almost exactly five centuries—evoked the least descriptive material in the literary record."[38] Extrabiblical literary and iconographic descriptions of the Second Temple largely refer to Herod's rebuilding of the Second Temple, rather than the smaller earlier Temple.

The absence of any detailed description of this earlier Temple does not mean, however, that the biblical writers found it to be insignificant. The Temple is the centerpiece of the restoration theologies in the books of Haggai and Zechariah (particularly Zechariah 1–8) and Ezra-Nehemiah. In each of these biblical books, the religious significance of the Temple is inextricable from its political and social functions.

The rebuilding project was led by a Davidic heir, Zerubbabel son of Shealtiel, newly appointed governor of Yehud. Zerubbabel receives no title in Ezra, but Haggai and Zechariah invest great hopes in him. Haggai refers to Zerubbabel as "governor" and describes him in near-messianic terms, referring to him as the Lord's "signet ring" (Haggai 2:23). Though Haggai and Zechariah stop short of calling Zerubbabel a king, both prophets describe him with language that resonates with ancient Near Eastern kingship ideology. The imagery of divine sponsorship of public buildings, especially in Zechariah 4:6–10 is especially noteworthy.[39] Zechariah 1–8 envisions a diarchic government, with Zerubbabel paired with Joshua son of Jehozadak as high priest. This early Persian-period configuration may represent the first indications of the increasing power of the high priesthood moving into the Hellenistic period.[40] In any event, on the heels of the lofty praise by Haggai and Zechariah, Zerubbabel suddenly disappears from our sources and his fate is unclear.

Zerubbabel's brief governorship perhaps suggests that, in allowing an heir to the Davidic dynasty to govern, Persia did maintain a policy of allowing some measure of political and religious autonomy in their colonies. Persia's attitude toward their territorial possessions, however, should not be reckoned as one of systematized religious "tolerance." The Persian crown supported some local cults, but their policy was strategic and *ad hoc*—they provided support for temples when it served their purposes, whether for defense or for increasing revenue to the central government. In this regard,

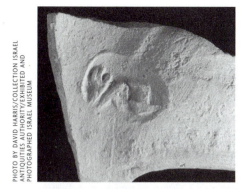

Yehud stamps and coin. *From Tell en-Nasbeh (biblical Mizpah) in the north to Beth Zur in the south, from Gezer in the west to Jericho in the east, archaeologists have discovered jar handals and coins stamped Yehud, the name for Judah in the Persian period (539–332 B.C.E.). The distribution of these stamps helps modern scholars to establish the borders of Judah at this time.*

A falcon with spread wings shares space with the Yehud stamp on the obverse of a small fourth-century B.C.E. silver coin discovered near Jericho. (A lily appears on the reverse.) The two pottery handles, found at Ramat Raḥel and also dating to the fourth century B.C.E., probably came from wine jars. The Yehud impression was literally an official stamp of approval.

the Cyrus Cylinder's allusions to particularly Babylonian concerns reveals Persia's pragmatic, not programmatic, aims. Although Persia projected itself as the source of peaceful order throughout the empire,[41] it could respond to perceived sources of rebellion swiftly and decisively, as shown in the accounts of the campaigns of Darius I recorded in the Behistun inscription. Darius's skillfully-executed and propagandized ascent to the Persian throne in 522 B.C.E. was followed by a thoroughgoing reorganization of the empire's administrative networks including the establishment of satrapies, roads and major building projects. Zerubbabel's appointment and/or the funding for the rebuilding of the Temple may have come as a small aspect of this reorganization. In fact, the inability of the people of Yehud to rebuild the Temple earlier under Sheshbazzar may have been due to a cause as prosaic as the lack of an economic or demographic base strong enough to support the project.

Thus Persia was not a tolerant, hands-off ruler. On the other hand, Yehud was not the focal point of its concerns in the West. Persia was surely concerned with the maximizing of tribute and "gift" revenues. It ran a meticulous bureaucracy[42] facilitated by a well-maintained road system; Yehud and Samaria played a significant part in this network. But the importance of Yehud to Persia's overall strategic goals has often been exaggerated. To quote Pierre Briant in this regard, "[T]he importance of Judah is only an 'optical illusion' created by the uneven distribution of evidence."[43] Perhaps it is best to think of Persia's policy toward its outlying provinces as attentive but somewhat aloof, even if punctuated with occasional targeted interventions, as in the case of Sheshbazzar, Zerubbabel, Nehemiah/Ezra and a possible administrative consolidation in the fourth century B.C.E.

Nehemiah and Ezra

In the sixth and early fifth centuries B.C.E. life in Yehud continued much as it did in the neo-Babylonian period, with the territory of Benjamin and the city of Mizpah maintaining their relative prominence and with Jerusalem (and the rest of Judah) remaining largely depopulated.

The Book of Ezra presents the early return of the exiles as the fulfillment of Jeremiah's prophecies (e.g. Jeremiah 25:12). As already noted, this time period is not described in any detail in the biblical texts, as if the ancient writers were themselves aware of the lackluster response to the end of the neo-Babylonian empire. Beginning in the mid-fifth century, in contrast, political events are detailed in the Bible and begin to manifest themselves in extrabiblical evidence as well. Archaeological surveys show that at this time, what we might call Persian II, Benjamin was becoming depopulated and at the same time, the population of the Shephelah (the low hills southwest of

Jerusalem) and Jerusalem increased.

Additionally, a series of stamp seals from this period inscribed *YHD* (Yehud) evidence a new bureaucratic system. The distributions of these *YHD* seals may be compared with the *MWṢH* seals of the neo-Babylonian period, now suggesting that the administrative center of government had shifted from Mizpah back to Jerusalem.[44]

Until this time, Persianized motifs on seals were mostly absent. Beginning in the late fifth century B.C.E., however, we begin to see much greater Persian influence in the local iconography.[45] In Anatolia and Egypt, Persian artistic influence can be seen much earlier, suggesting that Yehud was late to feel Persia's ruling hand.

Turning to the wider global context of the mid-fifth century, we see Persia struggling to fend off rebellions in the West and in Egypt, while at the same time challenging Greece militarily. All this may have encouraged Persia to shore up its frontier areas, including Yehud, by building networks of military fortresses and garrisons.[46] Although some scholars have questioned the date and the importance of these fortresses, the cumulative evidence indicates that the mid-fifth century marked a time of increased Persian interest in Yehud. The books of Ezra and Nehemiah, whose stories drop off after the completion of the Temple, pick up the thread in the mid-fifth century with the missions of Ezra and Nehemiah.

Nehemiah's journey from Susa, one of the Persian capitals, to Jerusalem reflects a significant sign of Persian intervention into an area that had otherwise seen little attention from Yehud's imperial masters. The poverty and underdeveloped infrastructure in Jerusalem through the sixth and early fifth centuries seems surprising nearly a century and a half after the fall of Jerusalem and 75 years after the completion of the Temple.[47] However, despite Nehemiah's characteristically exaggerated language, his description of Jerusalem, even with a rebuilt Temple, as poor and depopulated is eminently plausible.

Artaxerxes commissioned Nehemiah as the Yehud governor[48] and provided him with a military escort, official travel permissions and access to timber supplies (Nehemiah 2:7–9). This suggests an effort to reconfigure the Persian administration of Yehud and centralize it in Jerusalem. Nehemiah took full advantage of the Persian king's blessing, leading the effort to rebuild the wall around Jerusalem.* He likely also built a governor's residence and fortress near the city. Recent excavations in the City of David led by Israeli

*The size and extent of Jerusalem during this period are debated. See David Ussishkin, "Big City, Few People," *BAR*, July/August 2005; Hillel Geva, Another View, "Small City, Few People," *BAR*, May/June 2006.

archaeologist Eilat Mazar have found a small segment of wall, resting *atop* a sixth–fifth century (and therefore later) pottery assemblage, which may be a remnant of this construction project reported in the Book of Nehemiah,* although the identification of the segment as part of "Nehemiah's Wall" has been contested.[49]

Nehemiah describes the wall as an attempt to unify the people of Yehud. But the wall also created fierce opposition from neighboring peoples, such as Sanballat of Samaria, Tobiah of Transjordan and Geshem of Arabia. Nevertheless Nehemiah's enemies maintained significant ties with Yehud's elite, as may be inferred from Tobiah's connection with the high priest Eliashib (Nehemiah 13:4–9). Similarly, Sanballat and Tobiah were both likely worshipers of Yahweh and considered themselves part of the same people as those of Yehud—and were so considered by the people of Yehud.

That there were significant internal divisions in Nehemiah's Yehud becomes clear in the context of Nehemiah's other reforms, both religious and economic. Nehemiah relieved the debt of struggling small farmers (Nehemiah 5), regularized the distribution of Temple tithes to the Levites (Nehemiah 13:10–14,31), restricted mercantile activity on the Sabbath (Nehemiah 13:15–22) and condemned exogamous marriages (Nehemiah 13:23–29). These reforms can be understood as part of his effort to restore glory to the city, but they also reveal Nehemiah's sensitivity to Persian administrative goals. These reforms suggest that Nehemiah was commissioned by Persia for the purpose of maximizing tax and tribute revenues[50] and minimizing the potential threat of homegrown sources of power. Because the Temple maintained an economic function as well as a religious function,[51] the prohibition against non-Temple-related economic activity on the Sabbath day would have funneled worshipers' resources more efficiently through the religio-administrative system. The reorganization of Levitical portions worked in the same direction. One small example: Nehemiah's forcibly removed Tobiah from a chamber in the Temple "where they had previously put the grain offering, the frankincense, the vessels, and the tithes of grain, wine, and oil, which were given by commandment to the Levites, singers, and gatekeepers, and the contributions for the priests" (Nehemiah 13:5). Tobiah's offense was not solely his physical presence, though Nehemiah reports having the Temple cleansed as if contaminated by a foreign object, but Nehemiah also objected to Tobiah's influence over the flow of goods through the Temple.

Nehemiah's protracted complaints against Tobiah, as well as against Sanballat and Geshem, point to another area in which the newly-appointed

*Eilat Mazar, "The Wall that Nehemiah Built," *BAR*, March/April 2009.

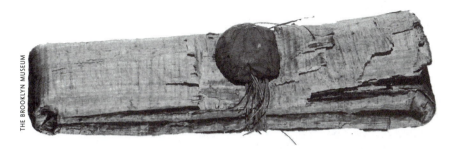

Elephantine papyrus. *Following the destruction of Jerusalem in 586 B.C.E., a Jewish community thrived on Elephantine Island, in the Upper Nile River. This well-preserved papyrus—folded several times, bound with a string, sealed with a bulla and endorsed— was discovered among a hoard of letters, deeds and other documents belonging to the community. According to the papyri, a Jewish temple, oriented toward Jerusalem, stood on Elephantine Island in the sixth and fifth centuries B.C.E.*

governor of Yehud was acting in Persia's and, consequently, in his own interests. Sanballat was part of a well-established family in Samaria, a family that had held control over the governorship for generations.[52] Geshem's history is more shrouded, but it is likely he was a ruler of Kedar. Tobiah could very well have been governor of Ammon,[53] but as the story of his presence in the Temple suggests, he was also a wealthy person, likely an early exemplar of the influential Tobiad family who held a still-impressive archaeologically-preserved compound at 'Iraq el-Amir in modern Jordan.[54] The cooperation of large landholders with the highest levels of the priesthood represented a potential threat to the control maintained by Persia through official channels. Perhaps to reverse this, Nehemiah reestablished the practice of allowing the Temple's goods to flow through lower-level Temple functionaries, such as the Levites. This was inevitably at the expense of people like Tobiah and Eliashib. The relief of debt granted to small land holders and tenant farmers (Nehemiah 5) would also have reduced the control of wealthy creditors.[55] None of this means that Nehemiah was following a laundry list of specific Persian directives.[56] Given Persia's inclination toward local autonomy, however (of course within established parameters), along with Yehud's small, though not insignificant, strategic importance, Nehemiah likely exercised considerable discretionary power to pursue his own interests. In many ways Nehemiah's situation was similar to Zerubbabel's, when an effective governor served the interests of both the empire and the newly established province of Yehud.

Ezra's part in the reconstruction of late-Persian-period Yehud is uncertain. The narrative of Ezra-Nehemiah places Ezra's mission—like Nehemiah's—as an official commission from the Persian king. But it is presented as prior to Nehemiah's. Compelling arguments have been made for Nehemiah's chronological priority, however.[57] The problem is far from solved.

Ezra's story is apparently patterned upon Nehemiah's—yet it is different. Ezra rejects the Persian military escort that Nehemiah accepts (Ezra 8:22; Nehemiah 2:9). Ezra arrives with an open letter from Artaxerxes and waits three days before declaring a public fast (Ezra 8:15–23); Nehemiah arrives with directives known only to himself and conducts a secret, nighttime inspection at the end of three days (Nehemiah 2:11–16). Ezra hears of exogamous marriages and tears his hair and clothes in ritual mourning (Ezra 9:3–4); Nehemiah reacts violently and tears the hair and clothes of the offending husbands (Nehemiah 13:23–27). In each case, the comparison portrays Ezra more positively than Nehemiah. Ezra also proclaims the Torah as the law of the land. Some scholars argue that this was the "Persian authorization of the Torah."[58] Proponents of this theory suggest that Ezra's public reading and oral translation of the "Book of the Law of Moses" (Nehemiah 8) was related to an empire-wide policy of ratifying local legal customs and giving them the official backing of the crown (see Ezra 7:26: "All who will not obey the law of your God and the law of the king, let judgment be strictly executed on them"). The actual content of the Pentateuch, however, does not quite fit the description of a law code.[59] Ezra's glorious commission from Artaxerxes in Ezra 7 could still plausibly relate to the Judean exiles alone, although Persian imperial "policy" was generally respectful of local legal traditions.[60] The authenticity of the commission to Ezra in Ezra 7 (along with the other Aramaic documents in Ezra 1–6) is uncertain. It is not clear why Artaxerxes would send a non-governmental official to establish the Persian law (Ezra 7:25–26) before, or at least independently of, sending a governor to establish a new administrative center in Jerusalem.

While the biblical text portrays Ezra as a formative figure in which the "reader" and "scribe" of the Torah is magnified into a full-blown "Second Moses,"[61] for the historian, this version of Ezra's story unfortunately raises more questions than it answers.

Temples at Elephantine and Gerizim

Contemporaneous with Nehemiah and Ezra, and shortly thereafter, the activities of a Jewish community on the Egyptian island of Elephantine appear on the historian's radar screen.

Judeans in Egypt are alluded to in several sources. The *Letter of Aristeas* records a legend that Judeans served as auxiliaries during a military campaign of Pharaoh Psammetichus II[62] in 591 B.C.E. Jeremiah alludes to Judean settlements in Migdol, Tapanhes, Memphis and Pathros (Jeremiah 44:1–14). An oracle in Deutero-Isaiah anticipates the return of Judeans from far-flung places, including "from the land of Syene" (Isaiah 49:12). Those Jews who designated themselves "Syenians"[63] (probably the residents of Elephantine) arrived in Egypt even before the Persian period.

The discovery of a Judean settlement with a cache of Aramaic documents on the Nile island of Elephantine (or "Yeb") revealed a treasure trove of information about the life and religious practices of a Diaspora community otherwise unknown. The island was the site of a former military colony. The Elephantine papyri, as they are known, include several collections of letters and administrative documents.* The most intriguing of these is the "Jedaniah archive," which contains eleven letters and other documents written for, addressed to or concerned with the late-fifth-century leader of the Jewish community. Included is the famous "Passover letter" from an otherwise unidentified leader named Hananiah that purports to instruct Jedaniah "and his colleagues of the Jewish Troop" in the proper observance of Passover.[64]

The military colony at Elephantine included Babylonians, Bactrians, Medes, Persians, Arameans and others who lived alongside the Judeans.[65] One group of texts in the Jedaniah archive gives us a snapshot of what appears to be friction between the Judeans and some of their neighbors. Two drafts of a letter by "Jedaniah and his colleagues the priests" addressed to the governor of Yehud, Bagavahya,[66] pleads for assistance in rebuilding their temple to the god "Yahu" (YHW, an alternate form of YHWH, the Israelite God). The Judeans complain that priests of the Egyptian goat deity Khnum, whose temple stood near Yahu's, had destroyed the Judean temple, with the permission of the loathed local authority Vidranga. This letter is dated to 410 B.C.E. The destruction may have been due to the Khnum priests' dislike of sheep and goat sacrifices at Yahu's temple; after all, the Khnum priests served a goat deity. Jedaniah and the priests mention that their temple, otherwise unknown to the modern world until the discovery of these papyri, had stood since before the Persian king Cambyses entered Egypt in 525 B.C.E. The letter notes that the Judeans responded to the destruction of their temple with a series of penitential practices characteristic of Persian period texts: wearing of sackcloth, fasting and prayer (see Jonah 3:5–9; Nehemiah 9:1–2). Whether the Elephantine community's appeal for help to the Jewish homeland was successful remains unknown, though one further document does describe a proposal on the part of the community to offer financial support and cease its animal offerings (perhaps in response to pressure from the Khnum priests) and may represent a compromise.

*Bezalel Porten, "Did the Ark Stop at Elephantine?" BAR, May/June 1995.

Another Elephantine archive—of Mibtahiah, the aunt of Jedaniah—deals with her life and estate. These documents provide valuable insights into the lives of Judean women—or at least one wealthy Judean woman. She appears to have been married twice, first to a Jezaniah and then to an Egyptian-named man, Eshor. Her marriage contracts indicate she had significant legal control over her marriage and property. She retained the right to initiate divorce proceedings, in marked contrast with later Jewish practice. She would also retain her own property in the event of the marriage's dissolution. Upon her first marriage, her father drew up a contract that granted his future son-in-law building rights on his daughter's land. Mibtahiah required her second husband Eshor swear that he had no other heirs outside of any future children with her; further, he would bequeath all his property to her in the event of his death before any heirs were born. Mibtahiah was also a party to litigation, in which she agreed to a settlement with one Peu son of Pahe regarding goods that she had entrusted to Peu.

In the lawsuit against Peu, Mibtahiah swore by the Egyptian goddess Seti, while another document notes that she swore by YHW. Other deities also appear in these documents. All this suggests that the Elephantine Jewish community practiced a syncretistic form of Yahwistic religion. On the other hand, no deity but YHW is mentioned in the context of the temple.

The prophet Jeremiah, a rigorous Yahwist, took a dim view of Judean settlements in Egypt, charging that they made offerings to the "Queen of Heaven" (Jeremiah 44:15). However, Jeremiah does not specifically speak of Elephantine.[67]

Elephantine contacts with officials of Yehud and Samaria suggest that the Jewish inhabitants of Elephantine understood themselves to be somehow connected to their homeland. Yet, because they migrated to Egypt on their own accord, they may not have understood their religion to be in crisis as many in Babylon surely did and thus felt no pressure to emphasize religious boundaries between Judeans and non-Judeans. Multiple deities and their iconographic traditions were always a part of life for some Israelites.[68] "Syncretistic" elements in the lives of the Jews of Elephantine are best understood as a continuation of this aspect of earlier Israelite religious culture, fostered by life in a multi-ethnic society.

Whether the temple to YHW on Elephantine was constructed as a rival to the Jerusalem Temple is unclear. Another temple, however, the Judean temple at Gerizim, may well have been such a competitor. Ultimately it became the temple of the Samaritans. Our understanding of the origins of this sanctuary, however, is spotty. Josephus's claim that it was constructed in the Hellenistic period has been undermined by the recent excavations on Mount Gerizim showing that the sanctuary at Gerizim dates back to the fifth century B.C.E.* These excavations have also uncovered hundreds of short votive inscriptions, many of which probably date to the Persian period.[69] The inscriptions are reminiscent of the refrain "remember me, O God, for good" in Nehemiah's valedictory (Nehemiah 13:31, and variations at 5:19, 6:14, 13:14,22,29)[70] and reflect the existence of a thriving cult site. (One man made an offering for himself, his wife and his sons "for good remembrance before God in this place.") These inscriptions resonate with Nehemiah's strident assertion that Sanballat, Tobiah and Geshem shall have no "historic right" (Nehemiah 2:20 NRSV; Hebrew Bible has *zikkaron*, or "remembrance") in Jerusalem.[71] Does this dispute hint at the beginning of the "Samaritan schism," or the break between Jews who worship at Jerusalem and those who worship at Gerizim? The Persian-period establishment of a temple at Gerizim suggests that the later tensions between Samaritans and Jews go back at least to the time of Nehemiah.[72] At this early stage, however, no clear religious differences between the two Yahwistic sanctuaries can be identified.

Literary activity in the neo-Babylonian and Persian periods

Religious diversity within Yahwism of the Persian period fits uneasily with the biblical description. The Bible's strict focus on the restored cult in Jerusalem is driven by an exilic and, to a lesser extent, Jerusalem-based perspective. The Babylonian exiles responded to the destruction of Jerusalem with great creativity, refining and defining matters of identity formation that were latent prior to the Exile, but only became explicit later. Much of the consolidation and editing—or even composition—of biblical narratives date to the neo-Babylonian and Persian periods.[73]

Some scholars point to the absence of any significant urban culture in impoverished Yehud as militating against the supposition of a sophisticated literary culture.[74] The loss of the complex social institutions required to support scribal activity may account at least in part for the dearth of Hebrew inscriptions. Instead, Aramaic seems to be the preferred language, perhaps due to Persia's use of Aramaic, the *lingua franca* in international dealings.[75]

If the inclination and wherewithal to produce Hebrew inscriptions was not present in Yehud, how then can we account for the robust literary activity mostly preserved in Hebrew? We have numerous biblical texts that are assumed to be written in the Persian period: Haggai, Zechariah, Malachi, Ezra-Nehemiah, Chronicles, some Psalms, Isaiah 55–65 (Trito-Isaiah), Jonah and Joel.[76] Haggai and Zechariah especially describe the impoverishment of

*Yitzhak Magen, *BAR*, forthcoming.

Yehud and their disappointment at the incomplete restoration of the Temple. They seem to provide a maximalist view of the Return in a minimalist social context. While small, the population of Yehud was nevertheless called upon to support a full Temple bureaucracy, which may have included Aaronide, Zadokite and Levitical priests (Ezra 8:15–36; Nehemiah 7:1,39,43); singers and gatekeepers (Nehemiah 7:1,23,45), Temple servants (Nehemiah 3:26,31, 7:46, 11:19) and a scribal class (Ezra 8:1,9), not to mention military officials, artisans and attendants of the governor. According to the latest scholarship, however, it takes only between 5 and 10 percent of elites or specialists in a society to produce a scribal oeuvre in pre-industrial societies.[77] By way of analogy, consider that the small community at Qumran was responsible for great literary productions (the Dead Sea Scrolls), some of which were written in what was then archaic Hebrew. In all likelihood, the literary production of the Babylonian Exile and of Persian Yehud included the promulgation and consolidation of the Pentateuch and the Former Prophets (Joshua, Judges, Samuel and Kings), known collectively as the Primary History, and the beginning of the process which led to the collection of the three major prophets (Isaiah, Jeremiah and Ezekiel) and of the Book of the Twelve Minor Prophets. Collectively this represents a creative response to the crisis of the Exile, a flowering of imagination and hope in the midst of a land that had not yet pulled itself out of its economic, political and social difficulties. It is an astonishing literary achievement.

The fourth century and the end of the Persian period

For the years following the time of Ezra and Nehemiah, narrative accounts of events are few and far between. Josephus (*Antiquities* 11.297–301) tells a story of the high priest Johanan (410–371 B.C.E.) who murdered his brother Jeshua in a dispute concerning control of the high priesthood.[78] Jeshua had been supported by the Persian functionary Bagoses. This story hints at Persian intervention in the affairs of the high priesthood (see Nehemiah's dispute with Eliashib [Nehemiah 13:4–9,28–29]) and foreshadows tales of bitter disagreements over and politicization of the high priesthood during the subsequent Seleucid and Hasmonean periods.

The first century B.C.E. Greek historian Diodorus Siculus mentions conflicts in the fourth century B.C.E. along the Persian western frontier (the "Revolt of the Satraps" and the "Tennes Rebellion" in Phoenicia) that supposedly rocked the entire region. These events were likely localized, however. There are no reports of Judea or Samaria being involved in them, although they may reflect tensions elsewhere in the empire.[79]

The archaeological evidence for the end of the Persian period is much richer than the narrative material and helps fill out the larger context of what was going on in Yehud. Israeli archaeologist Ephraim Stern has recently claimed that the Persian period witnessed an unprecedented reduction in the number of cultic figurines (so-called Judahite pillar figurines of the pre-Exilic period) and sanctuaries found in excavations in Samaria and Yehud.[80] Stern interprets this as evidence for the increased centrality of the Jerusalem and Gerizim temples in the religious life of the Judeans and Samarians, though the report of Nehemiah's religious reform may suggest otherwise; at any rate, no sources directly polemicize against the Iron Age Judahite pillar figurines or otherwise indicate that they were rejected by the Temple establishment.

On the political front, in addition to the western rebellions, Persia lost and then re-conquered Egypt. Instability in the empire appears to have induced Persia to solidify its administrative institutions in the Levant.

Oded Lipschits and David Vanderhooft point to a break in the paleography and orthography of the YHD stamp impressions from the sixth–fifth centuries and those of the fourth–third centuries, which display no governors' names, more use of paleo-Hebrew script and a change in the spelling of the name Yehud (from YHWD to YHD or the abbreviated YH).[81] This shift has two implications: First, it suggests the possibility that Persia, upon losing control over Egypt, tightened its control over Yehud and other territory along the border of Persia's newly reduced holdings in the Levant. Additionally, the fact that the typological break among the YHD stamp impressions lies between the sixth–fifth and fourth–third centuries means that the end of Persian rule appears not to have significantly disrupted the economic and political institutions in Yehud.

Similarly, a large number of unprovenanced Idumean Aramaic ostraca from the fourth century B.C.E. offers insight into the economic administration of this region, and suggests that the tax system after the arrival of Alexander the Great did not differ significantly from the policies under the Persians.*[82]

In short, the end of the Persian period did not mark a radical or immediate break. When the armies of Darius III were finally defeated by Alexander, the Achaemenid Persian empire fell. The empire did not self-destruct due to a lack of strong administrative oversight or economic or military weakness.[83] The success of Persia's royal ideology of peace and order, granting limited home rule and respecting local and ethnic religious practices, and indeed the success of its satrapal administrative system, meant that Alexander found much to emulate in Persian institutions.[84] Then again, Alexander's conquest was

*André Lemaire, "Another Temple to the Israelite God," BAR, July/August 2004.

followed almost immediately by severe political instability, which eventually opened the door for local Hasmonean independence.

Not only did aspects of the Persian period carry over into the Hellenistic period, but elements of Hellenism began to seep into Samaria and, to a lesser extent, Yehud, well before Alexander's conquest. The Wadi Daliyeh papyri and seal impressions provide a glimpse of the international, Greek- and Phoenician-influenced culture of the late fourth century B.C.E. These were discovered in 1962 by the Ta'amireh Bedouin who had discovered the Dead Sea Scrolls only 15 years earlier. In the central hill country halfway between Jericho and Samaria in a series of caves located at the heart of the Wadi Daliyeh, they uncovered a trove of papyri, many of which bore seal impressions depicting Persian and Greek figures. Months later the Bedouin sold the cache to the American Schools of Oriental Research in Jerusalem; director Paul Lapp then undertook systematic excavations of the caves the Bedouin had identified. The first papyrus unrolled revealed a date of 336/335 B.C.E., ultimately leading to Frank Moore Cross's theory that the papyri were taken to the caves by Samaritans fleeing from Alexander the Great's forces. The papyri and many small finds and coins of Wadi Daliyeh thus provide a rare glimpse of Palestine in the last days of Persian control.

Although the papyri are economic documents, and offer no narrative context, they enable scholars to reconstruct the names of the governors of Samaria and to document legal customs of the time. The appearance in the papyri of the name of one Sanballat, active and flourishing in Samaria in the first half of the fourth century, have led scholars to suggest that an eponymous great-grandson of Nehemiah's enemy Sanballat was governor of Samaria in 335 B.C.E. The seal impressions include numerous Greek images—Heracles, Hermes, Pericles and Dionysian satyr images. But they also include Near Eastern iconography such as sphinxes and what Mary Joan Winn Leith calls the "Persian-hero" motif, a variant on the Near Eastern "Master of Animals" motif showing the king holding animals aloft.[85] The iconography of these seals nevertheless strongly underscores the presence of Greek-influenced culture prior to Alexander. The Greek motifs may have been mediated through Phoenician styles. And the variety of styles suggests an already-internationalized culture and economy.

Numismatic evidence too indicates Greek influence in the late Persian Period. Although Persian coins appear with some regularity in the fourth century, only one Persian coin has been found in Israel from this later period, while dozens of Greek-Phoenician examples have surfaced displaying what appears to be standardized imagery, like the Athenian owl.[86] Additionally, Attic black-ware pottery from Greece turns up in fifth- and fourth-century

B.C.E. excavations in Palestine with great regularity, signaling closer ties with the Greek mainland, ironically in the Persian period. This black glazed pottery was a highly prized luxury item even in areas controlled by the Persians and is most frequently found at coastal sites.

Any full evaluation of the extent and nature of the penetration of Greek culture into Samaria and Yehud would require an investigation into the next phase of Jewish history (see next chapter). The evidence of the late-Persian-period material in general, suggests that later cultural Hellenism may have been preceded by a kind of economic Hellenism; that is, an international-ized mercantile economy based on money. The widespread appeal of Attic black-ware pottery throughout the Persian period, along with the other evidence from the fourth century, indicate that, notwithstanding the ongoing conflicts between Persia and Greece, Greek art and culture was very much part of the realia of Achaemenid Palestine long before Alexander.

SEVEN

The Age of Hellenism

From Alexander the Great through the Hasmonean Kingdom (332–63 B.C.E.)[1]

LEE I. LEVINE

IN 336 B.C.E. ALEXANDER THE GREAT BECAME KING OF MACEDONIA and the Greek city-states conquered by his father, Philip II, and within a decade he defeated the Persians, falling heir to their empire. Alexander's conquest of Judea in 332 B.C.E. would have profound and far-reaching effects on Jewish history. While foreign invasions were nothing new to the region, as Jews had been subject to imperial rule on many occasions in the past, this time the conqueror came from the West rather than the East (as had Assyria, Babylonia and Persia). However, two other, far more significant, factors made Alexander's conquest truly historic: The first was cultural, the second geographic.

The cultural dimension

Driven not only by military, political and economic gains, as were other conquerors, Alexander was also fully committed to disseminating the Greek way of life—its institutions, language, norms and ideas—into the world of the barbarians (referring to non-Greeks). His conquests thus exposed the eastern Mediterranean peoples and others farther east to an entirely new way of life, a process referred to as Hellenization,[2] often understood as the degree to which Greek religion and culture impacted upon the East.[3]

However, such an understanding should be calibrated by two additional factors. For one, other aspects of society, such as its economic, social, political and material components, must be considered as well, and, secondly, Hellenization should be measured not only by the degree to which the peoples and cultures of this region were drawn to Greek culture. Without denying the dominant role of Greek civilization in the East, the phenomenon of Hellenization was in reality far more complex than simply the West's influence in the East. The account of Alexander the Great and his soldiers marrying Persian women and adopting Persian customs is indicative of more complicated processes transpiring in the wake of Greece's conquest (Diodorus Siculus, *Bibliotheca Historica* 17.107.6; Plutarch, *Alexander* 70.2). In the encounter between West and East, it was the latter, be it of the Egyptian, Syrian, Iranian, Babylonian, Phoenician or Jewish variety, that also left its mark on the new reality of the Hellenistic era. Indeed, what took place had an element of mutuality. Finally, Hellenization for the peoples of the East involved a process of selection, adoption, adaptation and even rejection.[4] The resultant interactions—whether we refer to them as combining, amalgamating or synthesizing—are the very essence of what we refer to as Hellenization.

An effective means by which Hellenism was propagated in new regions was by the founding of new Greek cities (*poleis*) or by reconstituting an already existing city as a *polis*. Either step carried with it political, religious, social and cultural ramifications. The *polis* operated politically under a Greek constitution,* Greek deities were introduced into the city's pantheon, and Greek educational and entertainment institutions were established. Within a century of Alexander's conquest of Judea, Greek cities were founded along the Mediterranean coast, inland, in Beth-Shean and Samaria, and east of the Jordan River. These *poleis* served as centers of Greek life, supporting one another through joint commercial, cultural and athletic enterprises.[5] Thus, it is only partly surprising that a century and a half after Alexander, Jerusalem, too, was transformed into a Greek *polis* (see below).

---

*A *boule*, or legislative council, met regularly; *archei* ("heads") were chosen from this body to manage day-to-day affairs. A *demos* composed of ordinary citizens met from time to time.

Judea's key location

The second unique change under Greek rule that deeply affected the course of Israel's history was geographic. In previous conquests Israel had remained on the periphery of world empires, far from seats of power and authority, and its marginal location assured the Jews a measure of stability and insulation. However, with the death of Alexander in 323 B.C.E. and the division of his empire, Judea was thrown into the vortex of political and military activity. Flanked geographically by two powerful and rival kingdoms—the Seleucids based in Syria to the north and the Ptolemies in Egypt to the south—Judea became a battlefield on which these two dynasties confronted each other during the next one hundred years. No fewer than five major wars were waged in the course of the third century B.C.E., each lasting for several years. Garrison troops were posted throughout Judea (including Jerusalem), and large armies regularly traversed the country.

Either of the above factors—exposure to Hellenistic culture or geographic centrality—would have been unsettling under any circumstances. But for many Jews, having lived in relative isolation during the centuries immediately preceding Alexander's conquest, these factors were even more wrenching. The regnant policy under earlier Persian rule was one of actively supporting ethnic and religious groups, encouraging them to rebuild their institutions and develop their indigenous traditions, and Jewish leaders naturally embraced this policy with open arms. Only political loyalty and the payment of taxes were demanded. Thus, with the inundation of Judea in the third century by Ptolemaic government officials, merchants, soldiers and others, the Judean community was confronted by radically new circumstances and no longer able to remain insulated from the outside world.

Reactions to these new circumstances

Many of Jerusalem's inhabitants undoubtedly welcomed these changes; the opportunities and allure afforded by the Hellenistic world were not to be denied. The silver coins minted by the Jerusalem authorities between 300 and 250 B.C.E. provide a striking expression of the positive response of the city's Jewish political leadership to such contacts. These coins bear representations of Ptolemy I, his wife Berenike together with the image of an eagle, symbol of Ptolemaic hegemony. The presence of these motifs on Jewish coins clearly attests to the desire, at least by some, for successful integration into the new world order.[6]

Another example of the ties between Jerusalem's ruling elite and the wider Hellenistic world is documented in the correspondence between the Jewish High Priest Onias II and Areus, king of Sparta, around 270 B.C.E. According to 1 Maccabees (12:5–23) and Josephus (*Antiquities* 12.225–227), a bond was forged between the citizens of Jerusalem and the people of Sparta, who allegedly saw themselves as descendants of Abraham and thus sought to ally themselves with their brethren in Jerusalem. The following letter is reported in 1 Maccabees 12:20–23:

> Areus, King of Sparta, to Onias, the High Priest, greetings. A document has been discovered concerning the Spartans and Jews that they are brothers and that they are both of the seed of Abraham. And now, since these matters have become known to us, please write us concerning your welfare. We in turn write to you that your cattle and property are ours, and whatever belongs to us is yours. We have ordered that you be given a full report on these matters.[7]

The practical ramifications of this letter are unknown, but some 125 years later, Jonathan the Hasmonean renewed ties with Sparta (1 Maccabees 12:1–18). It is also noteworthy that between these two reports of correspondence, Jason, a former high priest, sought refuge in Sparta (2 Maccabees 5:9). While scholars may disagree as to the authenticity of the third-century B.C.E. epistle, there nevertheless seems to have been a connection between the two cities, and this, in turn, attests to a measure of political-diplomatic integration of Jerusalem into the wider Hellenistic world.

In the various excavations conducted in Jerusalem over the years, more than 1,000 jar handles bearing the official stamp of Rhodes have been discovered. Based on the names of Rhodian priests inscribed on them, these handles are to be dated to the Hellenistic era, with most deriving from the mid-third to the mid-second centuries B.C.E. These jars were used for wine from Rhodes that was shipped throughout the eastern Mediterranean.[8] The suggestion sometimes made, that the wine was intended for the small pagan garrison in the city, is most unlikely as the number of jar handles discovered clearly points to a more widespread consumption. Since only much later rabbinic laws banned gentile wine, it is unlikely that such prohibitions existed at this time, and therefore it seems safe to assume that many Jerusalemites availed themselves of this luxury commodity. Once again, archaeological remains point to the integration of Jerusalem into the wider Hellenistic world, this time with regard to international trade.

Other jar handles discovered in the city, however, point to a more conservative dimension of Jerusalem society. Several types of locally made jar handles—one with the inscription *Yehud* in ancient Hebrew script and another with a five-pointed star inscribed with the word "Jerusalem"—emphasize the

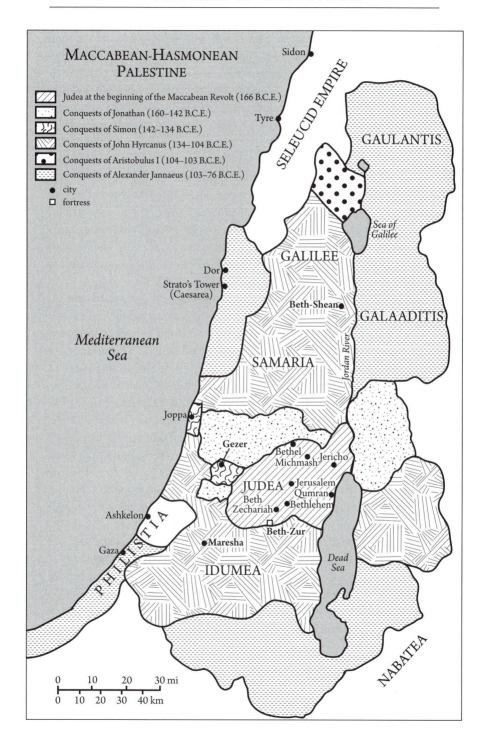

MACCABEAN-HASMONEAN PALESTINE

- Judea at the beginning of the Maccabean Revolt (166 B.C.E.)
- Conquests of Jonathan (160–142 B.C.E.)
- Conquests of Simon (142–134 B.C.E.)
- Conquests of John Hyrcanus (134–104 B.C.E.)
- Conquests of Aristobulus I (104–103 B.C.E.)
- Conquests of Alexander Jannaeus (103–76 B.C.E.)
- ● city
- □ fortress

Sidon

SELEUCID EMPIRE

Tyre

GAULANTIS

Sea of Galilee

GALILEE

Dor

Strato's Tower (Caesarea)

Beth-Shean

GALAADITIS

Mediterranean Sea

SAMARIA

Jordan River

Joppa

Gezer

Bethel
Michmash
Jericho

JUDEA   Jerusalem
Qumran
Beth Zechariah   Bethlehem

Ashkelon   PHILISTIA

Beth-Zur

Gaza   Maresha

Dead Sea

IDUMEA

NABATEA

```
0    10    20    30 mi
0   10  20  30   40 km
```

Jewish component in the city's culture and were probably used for taxation and administrative purposes. Alternatively, such inscriptions may simply indicate the place where the jar or its contents originated.[9]

Furthermore, much of the Jewish literature written or edited in the early Hellenistic period exhibits an awareness of ideas from the outside world. The biblical Book of Ecclesiastes (*Qohelet*) remains the most explicit and detailed statement on the impact of foreign influences on one's religious faith.[10] The book reflects a situation wherein faith and certainty had been lost, and in their stead, doubt, hesitancy and skepticism surfaced. Interestingly, around the turn of the second century B.C.E., Ben Sira composed a response to this type of thinking in a book called, in Latin, *Ecclesiasticus* ("the little Ecclesiastes"),* wherein he emphasizes the importance of loyalty to traditional values, ideas and institutions. The erotic love song that came to be called the Song of Songs was probably edited around this time and reflects themes well attested in Hellenistic poetry.[11]

The apocalyptic literature that first appeared around the third century B.C.E. (such as the early portions of Enoch) may further exhibit indications of outside influence. This literary genre is characterized, among other things, by descriptions of heavenly journeys, angelic revelations of cosmic secrets to man, visions of the end of days and the meting out of God's final judgment to the world. The second half of Daniel (7–12), written around 165 B.C.E., is the best-known example of this type of literature. Scholars are divided as to the source of this apocalyptic literature and worldview—whether it was the result of earlier prophetic literature from biblical times that underwent a series of transformations between the fifth and third centuries, or the result of new developments in Jewish society incurred by exposure to Hellenistic apocalyptic literature and thought. While certitude in this matter is elusive, the parallels with the non-Jewish world are significant enough to warrant some sort of connection with contemporary phenomena.[12]

Mention should also be made of the Letter of Aristeas, which tells of the translation of the Torah into Greek under the auspices of Ptolemy II Philadelphus (285–246 B.C.E.). The translation was reportedly carried out by 72 sages, each knowledgeable in the Torah and well-versed in Greek, who were brought from Jerusalem to Alexandria for this express purpose (which accounts for the name of this translation, the Septuagint, deriving from the Latin word for "seventy"). If there is any kernel of truth in this tradition, it would indeed testify to the penetration of Greek language and thought

---

Ecclesiasticus was included in the Greek translation of the Bible known as the Septuagint and remains a part of the Catholic Bible. For Jews and Protestants it is part of the Apocrypha.

into Jerusalem's scholarly circles by the third or, at the latest, second century B.C.E., when the Letter of Aristeas was composed.

Assessing the extent of Hellenism in Judea

It is difficult to assess how Jewish society as a whole responded to the challenges of the Hellenistic world. Did the isolated geographical circumstances of Jews (who lived primarily in the more remote hill country of Judea), combined with their ethnic and religious separation from their surroundings, create a partial buffer between them and the outside world? Or were Jews affected by these changes in much the same way as their pagan counterparts in the coastal cities, albeit at a somewhat slower pace? Unfortunately, our sources cannot answer these questions adequately. The fragmentary evidence that has been preserved offers but an inkling of the many and varied Jewish responses to the challenges of the new age. Generally speaking, one can safely assume that divisions within Jewish society deepened as a result of Hellenistic domination, such as the polarization of political allegiances into factions favoring either the north (Seleucids) or the south (Ptolemies), the exacerbation of economic and social gaps and challenges to traditional religious beliefs and practices, as noted above.[13]

Nevertheless, the degree of Hellenization among Jews during the Hellenistic period remains unclear. Scholars have staked out maximalist and minimalist positions; some view the impact of Hellenism as having been profound (Bickerman, Hengel) while others see it as having been more negligible and superficial (Tcherikover, Sandmel, Millar).[14] Both positions contain some truth, but the reality was undoubtedly much more complex than either extreme would suggest. Much depends on whom we are referring to (an urban aristocrat or village farmer), the specific time period involved (the late fourth or the second century B.C.E.) and the particular areas of society under scrutiny (material culture, religious beliefs or social institutions).

The difficulties in assessing the impact of the Hellenistic world on the Jews is reflected in Josephus's narrative of the Tobiad family, which represented Judean interests in the Ptolemaic court in Alexandria while playing a major role in internal Judean affairs as well. According to this account, the Tobiads had undergone a significant degree of acculturation over three generations, adopting Greek names, mannerisms and lifestyles (*Antiquities* 12.160–234).[15]

A striking instance of Tobiad Hellenization comes from the early second century B.C.E., when one member of this family, Hyrcanus, built a lavish complex of buildings and caves on his 150-acre estate in 'Iraq el-Amir, east of the Jordan River, between Jericho and Amman (*Antiquities* 12.230–233). Excavations revealed an enormous building erected on an artificial platform measuring 217 by 148 feet; the site, referred to as Qasr al-Abd, has been identified alternatively as a fortress, temple, villa, manor and palace. Animal reliefs, also noted by Josephus, once decorated the building on all sides. Lions and eagles were placed along the second story, while two felines sculpted in high relief were located on ground level and served as fountains. The overall lavishness of the estate, boasting an artificial lake possibly influenced by an Alexandrian model, a series of large caves and perhaps other buildings buried beneath the modern town of 'Iraq el-Amir, as well as animal decorations, is vivid testimony to the cosmopolitan proclivities within Judea's aristocratic class in the early second century B.C.E.*[16] The extent and intensity of these proclivities, however, remain unknown.

The same challenge in assessing the degree and scope of Hellenistic influences in Judea holds true with respect to two important sources that relate directly to Jerusalem society in the first quarter of the second century B.C.E. Each presents a very different picture of Jewish society, especially with regard to the balance between its traditional values and Hellenistic tendencies.

On the one hand, after the Seleucid ruler Antiochus III conquered Jerusalem (around 200 B.C.E.), he granted privileges to the Jews that appear to confirm the traditional status and leadership of the city; the elders, high priest, priests and other Temple personnel were recognized as leaders of the community and were accorded certain privileges. The concerns expressed in Antiochus's edict focus on the Temple and its cult, various religious precepts and the welfare of the city generally—issues that undoubtedly stood at the forefront of Jerusalem affairs for decades, if not centuries.[17]

On the other hand, we learn of a new and revolutionary situation that developed several decades later, as recorded in 2 Maccabees 4. In 175 B.C.E., Jason, a Jerusalemite of priestly lineage, offered the newly enthroned Seleucid monarch Antiochus IV (Epiphanes) a sum of money to appoint him as high priest in the Jerusalem Temple. The latter acquiesced since Seleucid kings were regularly in dire need of money to pay their annual tribute to Rome. Jason then added an additional sum for the right to convert Jerusalem into a Greek *polis*, which would make its inhabitants citizens of the *polis*, allow the city to be restructured politically and introduce Greek institutions such as the *gymnasium* and *ephebium*.**[18]

There is no question that such a transformation of Jerusalem was an extremely bold step, yet it is not clear what prompted such an innovation.

*Ehud Netzer, "Floating in the Desert: A Pleasure Palace in Jordan," *Archaeology Odyssey,* Winter 1999.

**These institutions were traditionally intended for the training of Greek citizens. The *gymnasium* was roughly equivalent to today's high school, with an emphasis on physical as well as academic subjects; the *ephebium* was a more advanced school specializing in military training.

Perhaps this move reflected the high degree of Hellenization that had penetrated Jewish society at this time, which then raises the question whether Jason had the backing, either active or passive, of a significant segment of the Jewish population or whether this initiative was but a superficial mimicry of Greek mannerisms by a small elite in Jerusalem society. In other words, was this small aristocratic coterie's sudden and dramatic step the result of little forethought or planning, or was it the culmination of a long and gradual process of Hellenization? These fundamental questions cannot be answered with any certainty and thus have resulted in very diverse scholarly assessments regarding Jason's initiative.[19]

Nevertheless, one brief incident mentioned in 2 Maccabees 4:22 seems to indicate that Jason's transformation of the city was not totally out of step with the city's inhabitants. When Antiochus IV visited Jerusalem a year or two later, perhaps on the occasion of the formal establishment of the *polis* "Antioch in Jerusalem," a not uncommon phenomenon in Hellenistic cities, "he was sumptuously greeted by Jason and the Jerusalemites, and was accompanied into the city with a torchlight parade and shouts of applause. Thereafter in the same manner (i.e., with the same enthusiasm—**L.L.**) he and his army marched off to Phoenicia." Given this warm reception, which, among other things, was apparently an expression of loyalty to the king, it seems safe to assume that the reaction of the Jerusalem populace to Jason's reforms, which were closely associated with the monarch, was far from hostile.

There is no indication whatsoever that any of the so-called "Hellenizers" had a religious, much less a pagan or syncretistic, agenda in mind.[20] No religious reforms were initiated in the city, as was to happen with a vengeance some eight years later. In fact, a Jerusalem delegation sent in 173 B.C.E. to participate in the athletic games in Tyre was careful to contribute its gifts to the Tyrian navy and not, as was customary, to the god of the city, Melqart-Hercules. Even Jason, who according to 2 Maccabees had intended the gifts to be offered as sacrifices to the god, probably considered such a tribute as no more than a mere entrance fee to the games (2 Maccabees 4:18–20).

Nevertheless, the following years witnessed a great deal of instability that was very marginally, if at all, linked to the issue of Hellenization. For the next decade and more, Jewish society was rocked by a series of events that shook it to its very foundations.

Turbulence in Jerusalem, the heavy hand of Antiochus IV and the Maccabean revolt

In 172 B.C.E., another Jerusalem priest, Menelaus, sought to follow Jason's precedent and successfully bribed the Seleucid king to appoint him high priest in place of Jason. To meet his financial commitment, Menelaus resorted to plundering the Temple treasury, an act that reportedly enraged the populace. Although the ensuing violence was quelled, tensions between the followers of Jason and Menelaus apparently remained high.

While matters seem to have quieted down thereafter, at least for several years, the city was again rocked by violence and destruction in the wake of Antiochus's disastrous Egyptian campaigns in 169 and 168 B.C.E.[21] In 169, a rumor of Antiochus's death reached the city and emboldened the former high priest Jason to regain his control of Jerusalem. Divided between the two contenders, the city was plunged into civil war, which ended only with the sudden return of Antiochus IV. The king proceeded to drive Jason and his followers out of the city and then plunder the Temple:

> While returning from his conquest of Egypt in the year 143 (= 169—**L.L.**), Antiochus marched against Jerusalem with a strong army ... Arrogantly entering the Temple, he took the golden altar and the candelabrum with all its furnishings and the table for the showbread and the libation jars and the bowls and the golden ladles and the curtain. He stripped off all the cornices and the ornamentation of gold from the front of the Temple and took the silver and the gold coins and the precious articles, whatever he found of the treasures on deposit. He took them all and carried them back to his own country. He massacred the people and spoke most arrogantly.
>
> (1 Maccabees 1:20–24)

In addition, 2 Maccabees notes that many in the city were massacred (5:12–14). Undoubtedly, the king's need to replenish his coffers—if not his self-confidence and public image following his unsuccessful Egyptian ventures—was a major motive for his aggressive actions and not merely the desire to punish the city for its insurrection.

A year later, in 168, Antiochus returned to Jerusalem, this time enraged by his humiliating retreat from Egypt caused by the Roman legate Popillius Laenas. It is impossible to know whether continued unrest in the city exacerbated his response; Tcherikover's theory that a full-fledged revolt was now in the making is unattested.[22] Whatever the explanation for Antiochus's anger and vindictiveness, the effects of his rage on Jerusalem were nothing short of devastating. Massacre, pillage and destruction were ubiquitous, and many were sold into slavery. The Temple was again plundered and buildings were destroyed along with the walls of the city. The Seleucid government now established a permanent presence in Jerusalem, accomplished in part by the appointment of an official named Philip who assumed responsibilities in the city along with Menelaus.[23] Of no less significance was the citadel (Akra) the king built to control Jerusalem and house both soldiers and Hellenizers who supported continued Seleucid rule (1 Maccabees 1:29–35; 2 Maccabees 5:1–21). The Akra, which stood in the city for 27 years,[24] was conquered and destroyed only in 141, after Simon the Hasmonean assumed the reigns of power in Jerusalem.

The precise location of the Akra is unknown since no physical remains have been conclusively identified. Literary sources such as 1 Maccabees and Josephus contradict one another, and at times themselves, with respect to important details. Josephus, for example, claims that the Akra was located in the Lower City (the City of David) to the south, yet was higher than the Temple Mount, a situation that defies explanation in light of the Mount's far higher elevation topographically (*Antiquities* 12.252). The Akra would have had to be a skyscraper by modern standards for it to have overlooked the Temple area. In contrast, 1 Maccabees (13:52) emphasizes the proximity of the Akra to the Temple, remarking that after its conquest the Akra was transformed into the Hasmoneans' palace which, according to Josephus, was situated on the hill (i.e., Mount Zion) west of the Temple Mount.

Other important details regarding the Akra are shrouded in mystery as well—its demographic composition, size, economic functions and political standing, as well as its relationship to the rest of Jerusalem.

Returning to the events in Jerusalem during 168–167, we come face to face with one of the most decisive episodes and intractable historiographical problems of the entire Second Temple period. We know nothing about what transpired in Jerusalem for the year following the building of the Akra (from fall 168 to fall 167), as our sources simply skip over this timeframe. Then, suddenly, in December (Kislev) 167, we learn that a religious persecution perpetrated by the king was decreed against the Jews in Jerusalem and Judea. They were forbidden to observe a wide range of commandments, from performing circumcisions, studying Torah, possessing a Torah scroll and observing the Sabbath and holidays, to offering sacrifices, meal offerings and libations at the Temple. No less severe was the attempt to force Jews to worship idols. They were compelled to build temples, shrines and altars to pagan deities, as well as offer sacrifices to them and eat forbidden foods, including those that had been offered as sacrifices to the gods (1 Maccabees 1:44–64; 2 Maccabees 6:1–17).

Why this happened, whose idea it was, what steps led to such an unusual and extreme decision, what kinds of contacts existed between Jewish leaders and the Seleucid monarch in the days, weeks and months preceding these decrees are some of the crucial questions simply not addressed in any extant source. No clear-cut rationale is offered for this persecution other than some very general remark regarding the need to unify all peoples (1 Maccabees 1:41); however, this was patently not Seleucid policy elsewhere in the realm. What is more, Antiochus IV's religious persecution only affected the Jews of Judea; elsewhere, as in Antioch, capital of the Seleucid kingdom, they apparently remained untouched. Most astonishing of all is the fact that there was a religious persecution at all. The pagan world was known for its religious tolerance, a characteristic that flowed, *inter alia*, from the recognition that there were many deities and temples in the world, and honor was due them all. In fact, no religious persecution is known before the events of 167. Since Antiochus IV himself had benefited from an enlightened Hellenistic education, to assume such a deviation from accepted norms would be most peculiar.

Because of these issues, and given the absence of any directly related source material, theories that try to explain the rationale behind Antiochus's decree abound. Most scholars, following the lead of 1 and 2 Maccabees and Josephus, have placed the blame at the feet of the king: Antiochus had some strange behavioral patterns that may have contributed to this irrational and unprecedented action, or he may have hoped to bring a greater coherency and unity to his kingdom politically and culturally, especially on its western frontier.[25] Other theories introduce different motives: (1) Antiochus witnessed a religious persecution first-hand while being held hostage in Rome, and introduced a similar policy in Jerusalem (Goldstein); (2) the profound anger and frustration of the king that led to this and other (irrational) steps stemmed from a deep sense of humiliation, which he suffered at the hands of the Romans in Egypt just a year or two before (Gruen); (3) the extreme Jewish Hellenizers under Menelaus were responsible for convincing the king to act in this manner (Bickerman, followed and amplified by Hengel); (4) the persecutions were, in reality, the Seleucid response to a religiously inspired revolt that had already broken out earlier, and Antiochus's response was therefore directed at the religious sphere of Jewish life as well (Tcherikover).[26]

Whatever the causes, these persecutions had enormous consequence for subsequent Jewish history. The immediate reaction was one of confusion. Some Jews passively acquiesced, a number fled to the nearby Judean wilderness and perhaps beyond the borders of Judea, while others despaired of worldly measures and took refuge in mystical-messianic aspirations of divine intervention and salvation (see, for example, Daniel 7–12).

In the year or so following the imposition of these decrees, armed conflict broke out in the town of Modi'in in northwestern Judea, which eventually led to a radical reshaping of Jewish society. The Modi'in uprising was organized and led by a priest named Mattathias and his five sons, Judah Maccabee,* Simon, Johanan, Eleazar and Jonathan. These sons would eventually reestablish, for the first time in 450 years, a sovereign state and a new dynasty of Jewish kings, the Hasmoneans.**

The road to an independent Jewish state

The Hasmoneans' rise to power was a long and arduous process, succeeding only after a 25-year struggle. This quarter-century can be divided into four periods:

1. 166–164 B.C.E.—These were years of continual guerrilla warfare. Under the command of Judah Maccabee, the Jews attacked the Seleucid armies as they attempted to reach Jerusalem and reinforce their garrison there. Seleucid forces approached the city from almost every direction—north, northwest, west and south—but each time they were defeated and their weapons confiscated to arm the expanding Hasmonean forces. The heroic and almost always victorious Hasmonean military efforts are vividly recorded in both 1 and 2 Maccabees.[27] The only inconclusive battle was fought at Beth Zur (south of Jerusalem) in the spring of 164 B.C.E., when a temporary armistice was declared as a result of the joint intervention of Jewish Hellenists and Roman envoys.[28] Six months later, however, Judah Maccabee and his troops surprised the Syrian garrison in Jerusalem, captured the city, purified the Temple and reinstituted the Jewish sacrificial rites. This occurred in the month of Kislev, 164 B.C.E., exactly three years after Antiochus IV's persecution had commenced. The recapture of Jerusalem, cleansing of the Temple and reinstitution of sacrificial rites are celebrated by Jews to this day with the festival of Hanukkah.[29]

2. 164–160 B.C.E.—These years were marked by a number of dramatic changes in the fortunes of the hitherto victorious Maccabees. Having purified the Temple, the Hasmoneans proceeded to avenge those gentiles who had taken advantage of the persecution and hostilities by attacking their Jewish neighbors. Troops were dispatched to Transjordan, the Galilee and the Mediterranean coastal region, resulting in the resettlement of many Jews in

*The additional name Maccabee was given to Judah and was later applied to the entire family. Thus far, no satisfactory meaning of this name has been suggested, although many have related it to the Hebrew word for "hammer," referring either to Judah "hammering" his enemies or perhaps to one of his distinct physical characteristics, "the hammer-headed"; see Sidney Tedesche (translation) and Solomon Zeitlin (commentary), *The First Book of Maccabees* (New York: Harper and Brothers, 1950), pp. 250–252.

**The name Hasmonean refers to an ancestor of Mattathias. It later became a family title of the Maccabees (*Antiquities* 12.265; *War* 1.36).

Jerusalem. The success of these campaigns won the Hasmoneans unprecedented popularity.

But in 162 B.C.E. the Hasmoneans' fortunes plummeted. Antiochus V sent his Seleucid army to crush the rebels, and at a battle near Beth Zechariah, south of Jerusalem, the Seleucids emerged victorious.[30] They were denied the full fruits of their victory, however, when word came of a major crisis in Antioch that required the immediate presence of the commander Lysias and his troops. A hasty but, from the Jewish viewpoint, favorable peace treaty was arranged, in which the decrees banning the practice of Judaism were officially revoked. The Jews, for their part, accepted as high priest one Alcimus, a moderate Jewish Hellenist. Most of the population appears to have been satisfied with this compromise, including the Hasidim, a pietist group that had joined the rebellion at its inception.[31] Only the Hasmoneans rejected this arrangement and were thus effectively isolated and forced to withdraw from Jerusalem.

In 161 B.C.E. Maccabean political and military fortunes changed once again, this time for the better. Judah Maccabee mustered a sizable army at Adasa, north of Jerusalem, and defeated the Greek general Nicanor in a major battle. His victory, though impressive, was short-lived. A year later a new Syrian army appeared in Judea, this time under the leadership of Bacchides. In a pitched battle, in which the Jews were badly outnumbered, Judah Maccabee was killed and any Hasmonean hope of regaining political power at this time was dashed.[32]

3. 160–152 B.C.E.—These were years of ebbing Hasmonean fortune. Few Hasmonean partisans remained in Jerusalem. At first members of the family fled to Teqoa in the Judean wilderness, southeast of Bethlehem. Driven from there, they resettled at Michmash, near Bethel in northeastern Judea, where they lived in semi-isolation, removed from the arena of power and bereft of any titles or privileges.

4. 152–141 B.C.E.—This was a period of Hasmonean ascendancy that culminated in the establishment of an independent sovereign Jewish state.

In 152 B.C.E. Alexander Balas and Demetrius, both pretenders to the Seleucid throne, sought to win the support of Jonathan, Judah Maccabee's brother and leader of the Hasmoneans, by outbidding one another in their attempts to win his loyalty and support. Jonathan finally threw his weight behind Demetrius, an act for which he was richly rewarded. He was made high priest, permitted to maintain troops and given extensive tax benefits. Thus, despite their quasi-exile during the previous eight years, the Hasmoneans had managed to remain the only potential leaders in the country capable of mustering a sizable force. With the benefits received from Demetrius,

Jonathan was soon in firm control of Jewish society and was recognized as the undisputed representative of the Seleucids in Judea.

It is ironic that, less than 15 years earlier, these same Seleucids had initiated a religious persecution against the Jews and that the two sides were engaged in hostilities against one another for the next seven years. Moreover, it should be remembered that a quarter of a century earlier Jason and Menelaus had acquired the high priesthood by bribing a Seleucid king. The Hasmoneans now followed suit, but instead of bribes the Hasmoneans paid with services to be rendered. As Seleucid officials, Jonathan and his brother Simon served the kingdom loyally, at one time even dispatching 3,000 troops at the Seleucid king's request in order to quell an uprising in Antioch. During the following decade the Hasmoneans were awarded additional territories to the north and northwest of Judea.

However, Jonathan soon fell victim to the intrigues and machinations of Seleucid politics. In 143 B.C.E. he was killed by forces opposed to his patron king, and Simon, the last of the Maccabean brothers, then assumed the high priesthood and political leadership. He drove out the remnants of the Syrian garrison and the Jewish Hellenizers from the Jerusalem Akra, and then, in an impressive public ceremony in 141 B.C.E., declared his independence from Seleucid rule.

Accounting for the Maccabees' success

Looking back over the 25 years since the appearance of the Hasmoneans in Judea, one might ask why this family succeeded as it did. Much of their success was undoubtedly due to the charisma of its leading figures. Their achievements in battle with the series of victories over the Seleucids, the recapture of Jerusalem, the purification of the Temple and their willingness to sacrifice their lives in defending the Temple and the city undoubtedly accorded them a strong claim to leadership. They were able to consolidate large elements of the Jewish population as evidenced by the elders, rural and urban leaders, priests, Levites and others who participated in Simon's coronation ceremony, vividly described in 1 Maccabees 14. In addition, the Hasmoneans' tenacity in pursuing their political goal of independence, despite all obstacles, put them in a position to take advantage of any opportunities that might, and indeed did, arise.

Finally, the Hasmoneans benefited from good fortune on the international front. The mid-second century B.C.E. witnessed the decline of the Ptolemies and the Seleucids. The political vacuum created in the region was soon filled by small ethnic kingdoms (e.g., Itureans, Nabateans) and independent city-states (e.g., Tyre, Sidon, Ascalon). It was precisely at this time that the Hasmoneans, too, strove for political independence, taking full advantage of these external circumstances to reach their goal. Only once before in the history of Israel had a similar international configuration occurred; in the tenth century B.C.E., David and Solomon carved out their kingdom (as did others—Ammon, Moab) in wake of the decline of a number of great powers (e.g., Egypt, Assyria).

Combining political and religious power

With the emergence of the Hasmonean state, the political circumstances of the Jews were radically altered. The power and trappings of a self-governing political entity were now introduced into Jewish society, and control of the various societal institutions involved enormous authority and influence. From the outset, the Hasmoneans established themselves as the supreme political and religious leaders of the people. Having already been awarded the high priesthood (Jonathan, as noted above, had been appointed high priest by Demetrius in 152 B.C.E.), they assumed two more titles in 141 B.C.E.—leader of the people (*ethnarch*)[33] and commander of the army (*strategos*). A generation later, in 104 B.C.E., Aristobulus adopted the title "king," and subsequently several generations of Hasmonean kings (and a queen) ruled Judea.

Combining the political authority of a sovereign state with the highest religious position (that is, high priest) was indeed an innovation in Jewish history. Earlier, in the First Temple period, the high priesthood was separate from the monarchy; priest and king functioned as two different sources of authority. Similarly, in the period following Hasmonean rule, Herod divided these two realms, reserving the political one for himself and relegating the religious one, over which he maintained control, to others. The combination of these two positions by the Hasmoneans proved to be explosive, in both a positive and a negative sense, as it provided a strong ideological component that motivated and justified ambitious political, social and military policies, yet at times also garnered severe opposition (see below).[34]

Expanding the Hasmonean state

One of the most remarkable achievements of the Hasmoneans was their radical redrawing of the map of Judea. Once a small and isolated subprovince in the Persian and early Hellenistic periods, Judea had become a major political entity by the end of the Hasmonean era, embracing all of modern-day Israel and the West Bank (except for the southernmost parts of the Negev and the northern coastal area), parts of southern Lebanon and western Jordan. It encompassed an area roughly the size of David and Solomon's kingdoms,[35] becoming a

HASMONEAN RULERS OF JUDEA, 142–37 B.C.E.

Simon	142–134
John Hyrcanus	134–104
Aristobulus	104–103
Alexander Jannaeus	103–76
Salome Alexandra	76–67
Aristobulus II	67–63
John Hyrcanus II	63–40
Mattathias Antigonus	40–37

significant regional power by the beginning of the first century B.C.E.

Jerusalem, of course, was the capital of the newly established Hasmonean state. While the city had already enjoyed this status for some 400 years in the First Temple period (c. 1000–586 B.C.E.), it had been reduced to a modest temple-city for the first 400 years of the Second Temple era (c. 536–141 B.C.E.), serving as the "capital" of a small and relatively isolated district. All this changed as Jerusalem assumed its role as the center of a sizable territory, and the city's dimensions and fortunes expanded accordingly. Jerusalem grew four- to fivefold, from a relatively small area centered in the City of David with some 5,000 inhabitants to a population of approximately 25,000–30,000 inhabitants now encompassing the western hill, later referred to as Mount Zion.[36]

Simon, who ruled the new state from 142 to 134 B.C.E., made a major military push to the northwest, toward the sea. He conquered Gezer, expelled its gentile inhabitants, purified the town and resettled it with observant Jews (1 Maccabees 13:43–48). After Gezer, Simon captured Joppa, which became the major seaport for the early Hasmonean state.

Simon's son and successor, John Hyrcanus, ruled for 30 years (134–104 B.C.E.). In 134 B.C.E., shortly after the latter's succession, Antiochus VII laid siege to Jerusalem. Although the relevant data are minimal, archaeological remains from this siege have been discovered in the excavations of the Tower of David near Jaffa Gate.[37] Hundreds of ballista stones and arrowheads were found at the foot of the Hasmonean wall. The Seleucid siege was ultimately lifted and Hasmonean hegemony was restored.

Hyrcanus expanded the borders of his realm dramatically. Broadening his hold along the coast and even establishing a presence east of the Jordan River, he devoted his major efforts to conquering various ethnic groups living in the hill country—the Idumeans in southern Judea and the northern Negev and the Samaritans to the north (*Antiquities* 13.254–283). Hyrcanus probably captured the Galilee as well, although the composition of its population at the time is difficult to determine.

Hyrcanus was succeeded by his son Aristobulus I, who, as noted, adopted the title "king." Although he ruled for only one year (104–103 B.C.E.), he successfully annexed Iturean territory in southern Lebanon and perhaps also the northern Galilee (*Antiquities* 13.318–319).

Aristobulus was succeeded by his brother Alexander Jannaeus (103–76 B.C.E.), the last and perhaps greatest military leader of the Hasmonean dynasty. Jannaeus annexed new territories in almost every direction. In the northwest he gained control of Strato's Tower (later Caesarea) and Dor, and in the southwest he took the coastal district, including Gaza, one of the major Hellenistic cities of the time, as well as parts of the Negev. In the northeast Jannaeus overran much of the Golan and Gilead (today's northwestern Jordan); and in the southeast he conquered large areas of Moab, east of the Dead Sea (*Antiquities* 13.320–397).[38]

Control of neighboring peoples, cities, important trade routes and major ports was clearly an objective that determined the course and extent of Hasmonean conquests. The religious-nationalist dimension, however, was no less significant a factor in Hasmonean policy. The Hasmoneans regarded themselves as the successors of past Jewish leaders, namely, the judges and kings of First Temple times. This is clearly, though subtly, reflected in 1 Maccabees, which was written under Hasmonean patronage toward the end of the second century B.C.E. Both the overall language and the specific terms it uses are reminiscent of the books of Judges and Kings, thus consciously drawing an analogy between the Hasmoneans, on the one hand, and the development and institutionalization of Jewish political leadership in biblical times, on the other.[39] The book culminates with Simon's coronation, described in 1 Maccabees 14, a carefully crafted account that often alludes to the glorious days of King Solomon.

In the same vein, Hasmonean coins bore the ancient Hebrew script that was commonly used in the First Temple period, rather than the square Aramaic script that had become the norm in the Second Temple era. This, too, was undoubtedly a conscious attempt by the Hasmoneans to identify their rule with that of the earlier Davidic monarchy.

Hasmonean religious ideology

Hasmonean identification with biblical precedents also entailed the adoption and implementation of certain biblical views, especially those spelled out in Deuteronomy that emphasize the religious dimension of political power (and vice versa). Deuteronomy's ban of idolatry and its hostility toward the indigenous gentile nations are strongly emphasized. On repeated occasions, Deuteronomy commands the conquering Israelites to destroy all sanctuaries and idols and to annihilate all traces of the heathens (7:1–6,16,25–26, 20:15–20).[40] Ezra interpreted the Deuteronomic injunction to ban intermarriage with the seven indigenous nations as referring to all non-Jews, and this seems to have constituted the religious underpinning for his sweeping prohibition. Thus, as a result of Deuteronomistic influence, the Hasmoneans not only annexed new areas but strove at the same time to purify them from the pollution of idolatry. On several occasions this zealousness found expression in the deportation of pagan populations and the destruction of their idols and shrines; on others, it included the purification and introduction of a religiously observant Jewish population into the conquered city (1 Maccabees 13:47–48). Both the Jerusalem Akra and the city of Gezer were subjected to such processes (1 Maccabees 13:49–53).[41]

Nevertheless, on occasion a more moderate policy was adopted. For instance, although John Hyrcanus destroyed the Samaritan temple on Mount Gerizim, he appears to have done little else to interfere with the Samaritan way of life, perhaps because it was so similar to that of the Jews (*Antiquities* 13.256). At other times, however, whole populations were converted to Judaism (willingly or coercively), as was the case with the Idumeans under John Hyrcanus and the Itureans under Aristobulus (*Antiquities* 13.257–258, 319).[42]

It is difficult to determine how smoothly this policy of assimilating other peoples was carried out. No mention of resistance is made in our sources, although undoubtedly some, either active or passive, must have occurred. It is hard to imagine, for example, that the ultimatum of conversion or death offered to the inhabitants of the Hellenistic city of Pella in Transjordan did not meet with outright hostility and opposition (*Antiquities* 13.397).

The ideological component that accompanied the Hasmonean successes was, as alluded to above, a double-edged sword. On the one hand, it provided a significant additional impetus and motivation for conquests and expansion, as well as a transcendent cause firmly rooted in a biblical faith that overshadowed ordinary political concerns. Understandably, a literary genre echoing this triumphalism surfaced at this time (e.g., Jubilees, Judith).

On the other hand, any sort of anti-pagan policy was bound to stir up animosity. Hasmonean zealousness might easily be interpreted as an onslaught against gentile values and the pagan way of life. Some of the earliest evidence of pagan anti-Semitism—such as the negative description of Jews and Judaism by Antiochus VII's advisors (as preserved by the Greek historian Diodorus) and the hostility of Posidonius of Syria (as noted by other early writers)—was in large part a reaction to Hasmonean anti-pagan drives. By the first century B.C.E. various anti-Jewish accusations were circulating: The Jews were misanthropes, Jewish religious precepts were engendering social animosity and moral perversion, Jewish worship in the Jerusalem Temple was primitive and barbaric, etc. Much of this anti-Jewish hostility seems to have been triggered by political and religious opposition to the Hasmoneans (*Apion* 2.71–142).[43] That many pagans and Jews viewed the Hasmonean conquests as part of a struggle for ultimate control of the country, in which each side claimed possession of the land, no doubt further exacerbated pagan sentiments.[44]

The Hasmonean combination of political power and religious ideology was equally problematic on the domestic front. Instead of being the art of the possible and characterized by compromise and inclusiveness, politics was fraught with the tensions and passions born from ideological inflexibility. Moreover, in response, such intolerance was likewise adopted by other elements in society, particularly in the religious realm. In contrast to the later Second Temple period, when the religious character of the various Jewish sects predominated, during the Hasmonean era the political involvement of such groups was very much in evidence. For example, at first the leaders of both major sects, the Pharisees and the Sadducees, held seats in the ruler's inner cabinet. However, toward the end of the second century B.C.E., the Sadducees worked hand in glove with John Hyrcanus and succeeded in forcing the Pharisees out of government.[45]

The Pharisees then quickly became an active opposition; in fact, much of the unrest during the reign of Alexander Jannaeus was probably supported, encouraged or at times even led by the Pharisees.[46] Open Pharisaic hostility, at times including insulting behavior toward Jannaeus,* finally led to severe countermeasures against members of this group—including exile, persecution and even crucifixion. The opposition, for its part, went to the extreme of inviting the Syrian king Demetrius VI to attack Jerusalem. When the battle was finally joined, the Seleucid side was bolstered by Jewish dissidents while the Hasmoneans were reinforced by gentile mercenaries!

Later, Jannaeus's wife and successor, Salome Alexandra (76–67 B.C.E.), reinstated the Pharisees, giving them complete control over the country's internal affairs. They lost little time in avenging themselves against the Sadducees and the wealthy aristocrats who earlier had persecuted them (*Antiquities* 13.408–415).[47]

The most extreme reaction to Hasmonean rule was taken by members

---

*According to Josephus (*Antiquities* 13.372), *etrogim* (small lemon-like fruits) were thrown at the high priest on the pilgrimage festival of Sukkot.

of another Jewish sect—the Essenes (or Dead Sea sect). In protest against the political and religious leadership of the Hasmoneans, the Essenes left Jerusalem and settled in the Judean wilderness,[48] where they awaited the removal of the Hasmonean leadership that they believed was part of the imminent messianic drama.

Hasmonean coin. *Hellenistic and Jewish iconography are blended in this bronze prutah minted by John Hyrcanus I (134–104 B.C.E.). The obverse depicts a double cornucopia, a pagan symbol, but one that was inoffensive to Jews.*

The reverse side of the coin, by contrast, demonstrates Jewish nationalism. The language of the inscription, including the name and title of the ruler, is Hebrew, not Greek: "Jehohanan the High Priest and the council of the Jews." Moreover, the coin is inscribed in an ancient Hebrew script used nearly a millennium earlier, at the time of the Davidic and Solomonic monarchies, as an expression of the Hasmoneans' identification with a glorious past, when Israel was first an independent nation.

Thus, the political involvement of religious sects in Hasmonean society was endemic. All groups—Sadducees, Pharisees and Essenes—were now organized politically as well, and such circumstances gave impetus to a passion and ideological rigidity that only aggravated tensions.

The integration of Hellenism and Judaism

In the cultural realm, the Hasmoneans established a pattern characterized by a synthesis of Jewish and Hellenistic elements, what Elias Bickerman has aptly described as a form of moderate Hellenism.[49] The Hasmoneans attempted to adapt a wide range of Hellenistic forms to Judaism rather than altering Judaism to conform to the dictates of Hellenism as, he claims, the extreme Hellenizers among the Jews had advocated earlier.

Three examples from the material culture of the Hasmonean era illustrate this type of synthesis. The earliest example is the Maccabean funerary monument in Modi'in built by Simon c. 142 B.C.E. following the murder of his brother Jonathan. The monument, built over an already existing family tomb, is described in 1 Maccabees 13:27–29 as follows:

> Simon built a monument of hewn stone on both the front and back over the tomb of his father and his brothers, and he made it high enough to be seen from afar. He erected seven pyramids, one

in front of the other, for his father, mother and four brothers. For the pyramids he devised an elaborate setting, surrounding them with massive columns on which he placed full suits of armor for a perpetual memorial. Besides the suits of armor were carved ships that could be seen by all who sailed the sea. This tomb, built in Modi'in, is there to this day.

Andrea Berlin and others have plausibly suggested that the Hasmonean structure was an imitation of similar types of Hellenistic funerary monuments found in Asia Minor,[50] and, indeed, the above description bears a resemblance to the earlier tombs of King Mausolus in Halicarnassus and the Belevi tomb in Ephesus. Each had a pyramidal top of polished stone and was surrounded by columns and other decorations. However, in striking contrast to the Hellenistic models, the Hasmonean tomb bore no figures of either animals or humans. Clearly, then, Simon built an impressive monument in memory of his family, following what seems to have become a well-known Hellenistic practice but in line with the new artistic policy that the Hasmoneans were now establishing (see below).*[51]

A further indication of the Hasmoneans' desire to integrate the two worlds is attested on their coins.** On these tiny bronze issues, intended as small change but used for propagandistic purposes as well, symbols and inscriptions convey a clear-cut message: The Jewish and Greek worlds are reconcilable. The language is either Greek or Hebrew; only a few issues are in Aramaic, the Semitic language in everyday use at the time. While the Greek inscription uses the Hellenistic title of the ruler (king) and his Greek name (Alexander [Jannaeus]), the Hebrew coins use his Jewish title (high priest) and his Hebrew name (Jonathan). Finally, the Hebrew appearing on these coins is not the later Aramaic "square" script, but an older style in vogue during First Temple times.[52]

The symbols on these coins are also an important indication of the balance that the Hasmoneans attempted to strike between Jewish needs and the givens of the surrounding culture. None of the symbols is uniquely Jewish. The palm branch, anchor, cornucopia, wheel/star, etc., all appear on Ptolemaic and Seleucid coins or on those minted by various cities of the region (such as Gaza, Tyre and Ascalon). The only exceptions to this rule are two issues minted by Alexander Jannaeus's grandson Mattathias

*Geoffrey B. Waywell and Andrea M. Berlin, "Monumental Tombs: From Maussollos to the Maccabees," *BAR*, May/June 2007.
**Sandy Brenner, "Spending Your Way through Jewish History: Ancient Judean Coins Tell Their Story," *BAR*, May/June 2003.

Antigonus (40–37 B.C.E.), the last of the Hasmonean rulers, on which we find the Temple menorah and showbread table. For the most part, however, Hasmonean coins display symbols drawn from the Hellenistic world, although they were carefully selected. Only neutral symbols devoid of blatantly pagan overtones were utilized. Thus, a policy of compromise was adopted; Hellenistic symbolism was accepted as long as it was not offensive to Jewish beliefs and practices.

Finally, the third example of this synthesis is attested in the magnificent Hasmonean winter palace complex excavated near Jericho.*[53] Some of the finest amenities of the Hellenistic world were found there—a large swimming pool, baths, a grand pavilion, frescoed walls with geometric designs, carefully hewn Doric columns and friezes. Between the pool and palace, however, were a number of Jewish ritual baths (*mikva'ot*). These were used, *inter alia,* by the Hasmoneans themselves, who in their role as priests were required to be ritually pure before partaking of the free-will (*terumah*) offerings from the Temple. *Mikva'ot* were unknown in earlier periods; no archaeological remains of such installations have been uncovered at pre-Hasmonean sites, nor are they ever mentioned in biblical sources. Thus, the Hasmoneans not only adopted Hellenistic architectural styles and associated social-recreational amenities, but they also included uniquely Jewish installations such as the ritual bath.

The above examples all appeared under Hasmonean auspices. However, this same proclivity to adopt and adapt Hellenistic patterns and practices is in evidence among the wealthy classes of Judean society as well, along with a significant degree of selectivity, which usually meant the rejection of overtly pagan forms.

For example, the funerary remains from the Jerusalem area, reflecting a significant degree of outside influence, invariably imitate well-known Hellenistic models. The tomb of Jason, a wealthy Jerusalem aristocrat from the first century B.C.E., had a pyramidal form; the tomb of the Hezir family (Bnei Hezir) in the Kidron Valley east of the Old City[54] followed another Egyptian tradition with a columned facade and adjacent funerary monument.**[55] The deceased were buried in *kokhim* (*loculi*), small cavities cut into the walls of a cave, measuring the length and width of a human body. This form of burial was derived from Hellenistic models originating in fourth-century Alexandria.[56] No less Hellenistic in origin were the tomb facades and series of outer courtyards (as at Jason's tomb). Columns, capitals, friezes and architraves of various Greek orders are

*Suzanne F. Singer, "The Winter Palaces of Jericho," *BAR*, June 1977.
**See Waywell and Berlin, "Monumental Tombs," *BAR*, May/June 2007.

regularly used in these tombs, and inscriptions are recorded in Greek, Hebrew and Aramaic. However, what is uniquely Jewish about these tombs (besides the appearance of *menorot* in Jason's tomb and a Hebrew inscription in the tomb of Bnei Hezir) is their artistic expression. Whereas figural representation is common on pagan tombs in Palestine (for example, at Maresha we find figures in a musical procession*) and throughout the Hellenistic world, it is virtually nonexistent in similar Jewish contexts.[57]

Yet another illustration of the synthesis of Jewish and Hellenistic cultures within Jerusalem society—but in this case with a heavy emphasis on Jewish particularism—is preserved in a small apocryphal work known as the Greek *Additions* to the biblical Book of Esther. These *Additions* attempt to give the book a more pious, Jewish-oriented, character. The biblical account as it stands raises some thorny issues: Why is God never mentioned? Why are no expressions of traditional Jewish piety, such as prayer, the Temple or Jerusalem, included? Why does a respectable Jewish girl like Esther marry a gentile king, sleep with him and eat at his table? This work deals with such issues by supplementing the biblical text with a series of additions promoting a decidedly religious emphasis and advocating a Jewish, anti-pagan, outlook. What is especially fascinating—and indeed ironic—is that the *Additions* were written in Hasmonean Jerusalem in a refined Greek literary style; moreover, they were written by a Jewish priest named Lysimachus and were brought to Alexandria by a Levite named Ptolemy. It would seem, therefore, that some highly educated and acculturated Jews (notice their names!) had made a clear bifurcation between their Hellenistic education and their strong Jewish loyalties.

Indeed, personal names often indicate cultural proclivities. Thus, in addition to the Hasmonean rulers who had Greek names (Hyrcanus, Aristobulus, Antigonus, Alexander), members of the leading political and diplomatic families of the Hasmonean kingdom also bore Greek names.[58]

Hellenistic influence also affected religious institutions and practices such as the introduction of the *ketubah*, the wedding document specifying the obligations of the groom to his bride (B *Ketubot* 82b). At first, a groom negotiated with the parents of the bride and was required to set aside a sum of money or property for the bride—a practice with roots in earlier Mesopotamia. In the fourth or third century B.C.E. another arrangement, first attested in Egypt, was introduced into marriage contracts; requiring an agreement between husband and wife, it stipulated that in the case of divorce the groom was to pay the settlement from his most valuable property; nothing

*David M. Jacobson, "Marisa Tomb Paintings," *BAR*, March/April 2004.

was set aside at the time of marriage. If this rabbinic tradition, though attested much later in time, is historically reliable, then Simeon ben Shataḥ, apparently inspired by Hellenistic models, introduced an Egyptian practice into the Jewish marriage ceremony some time in the early first century B.C.E.[59]

Another example of the impact of Hellenism on Pharisaic tradition may be found in its introduction of an institution of higher learning; the Pharisaic academy (*beth midrash*), although initially attested only in a first-century C.E. context, seems to have had something in common with Greek philosophical schools. The parallels are not so much in the material learned (although in the area of ethics, the overlap may have been quite recognizable),[60] but rather in the nature and organization of the institution. The *beth midrash* was a school of higher learning open to all, with rules governing its operation somewhat similar to those of the Greek philosophical schools. The relationship between master and pupil in the *beth midrash* and the principles of exegesis applied there also resembled those of its Greek counterpart.[61] Since no such institution existed in Palestine before Hellenistic times, and as influences from the Greek academy permeated Pharisaic-rabbinic tradition later on as well,[62] it is quite likely that the creation of such a Pharisaic study framework, which may have existed as early as Hasmonean times, was inspired by the Greek model.

Several other Pharisaic concepts, such as the belief in afterlife in the form of bodily resurrection and the concept of a dual law (written and oral), may also have been stimulated by outside influences. Neither has clear-cut biblical roots and both can be found, in one form or another, in non-Jewish (Greek and Babylonian) traditions.

Hellenistic influences appear among the Essenes as well, as reflected in the Dead Sea Scrolls. It has been noted that many aspects of the ideology and practices of this sect were quite different from biblical formulations and models yet remarkably similar to concepts of the surrounding, especially eastern, Hellenistic world.[63] Ideas such as dualism, predestination, astrology, angelology and demonology, the notion of wisdom and the spirit and the use of a solar calendar are all documented in the Hellenistic world. Other institutions at Qumran—the concept of "community" (*yaḥad*), communal living, initiation rites, the penal code, celibacy and asceticism—all new to a Jewish setting, also have striking parallels elsewhere.[64]

Explaining how such an array of outside influences reached a Jewish sect at Qumran is a formidable challenge. When one considers the fact that this community was the most self-consciously isolationist among the other Jewish groupings, having physically divorced itself from the rest of society, such a serious component of foreign influence becomes even more perplexing. Several explanations have been offered, each assuming that such influences were assimilated early on in the sect's history and that the community itself may well have been unaware of the non-Jewish origins of these traditions. One explanation, for example, posits that the sect emerged in the eastern Diaspora (Babylonia) and that by the time it reached Judea these concepts had already been internalized.[65] A second suggests that these foreign ideas were current in Judean society of the Hellenistic period and that the forerunners of Qumran adopted them as part of the accepted religious and cultural baggage of their time.[66] Whatever the explanation, the fact that such an extensive influence on a major Jewish sect of the period existed is indeed astounding.

In surveying Hasmonean society as a whole, therefore, it becomes evident that no realm of society or sector of the population remained unaffected by Hellenistic culture. The question is only a matter of degree—how much was assimilated into which parts of the population, in what areas and with what intensity?

The rise of the Hasmonean state has often been portrayed as a reaction against Hellenism, i.e., a reassertion of Jewish nationalist and religious will in the face of the demands, temptations and coercion of the larger world. This view, however, is only partially correct and, by itself, constitutes a distortion of reality. In a fuller and more profound sense, the Hasmonean state must be viewed, at least in part, as a product of Hellenism and no less as an affirmation of the surrounding culture than a rejection of it, an expression of national sovereignty nourished and shaped in many respects by its wider international context. Thus, the Hasmonean state embodied a new Jewish disposition that incorporated a resurgent Jewish identity and, at the same time, absorbed a range of Hellenistic components. Most Jews, it would seem, were prepared to adopt forms of Hellenism into their lifestyle, albeit in varying degrees and then only after certain adjustments and changes were introduced.

Jerusalem under Hasmonean rule

The creation of the Hasmonean kingdom had a revolutionary effect on Jerusalem. Since the beginning of the Second Temple period in the sixth century B.C.E., Jerusalem had occupied a small area that included only the original City of David and the area of the Temple Mount.* Altogether, the city encompassed some 30 acres and numbered only about 5,000 or 6,000 inhabitants. This situation prevailed for nearly 400 years (c. 536–141 B.C.E.), and then, in the short period of Hasmonean rule, Jerusalem expanded fivefold,

---

*In support of this view, see Hillel Geva, "Another View: Small City, Few People," *BAR*, May/June 2006. But for an alternative perspective on the size of Jerusalem at this time, see David Ussishkin, "Big City, Few People," *BAR*, July/August 2005.

stretching over more than 160 acres and numbering approximately 30,000 inhabitants.

The city now encompassed the entire western hill (Mount Zion) as far as today's Citadel of David (adjacent to the Jaffa Gate). Remains of the Hasmonean city wall have been discovered in the Jewish Quarter of the Old City, in the Citadel itself and on the slopes of Mount Zion. This wall followed the same course as the Israelite wall of the First Temple period; in fact, Hasmonean builders were not only aware of this earlier *enceinte*, but even utilized parts of it in their own fortifications.[67] Since there were several stages to the Hasmonean wall (as seen most clearly in the Citadel area), it would appear that it was first built in the second century B.C.E., probably under Jonathan or Simon, and then periodically repaired and reinforced.[68]

Jerusalem's population during this period was overwhelmingly, if not almost exclusively, Jewish. The Hasmonean intolerance of pagan worship and Jerusalem's exclusively monotheistic bent undoubtedly made the city a rather inhospitable place for non-Jews. There was no allowance for pagan cults and thus no temples to other deities were ever built there. The increasing emphasis on the centrality of the Temple and related practices would certainly have added to pagan discomfort. In fact, the only known non-Jewish presence in the city at this time was that of the military contingent that served the later Hasmonean rulers. These foreign mercenaries are first mentioned in connection with John Hyrcanus (*Antiquities* 13.249); later on, Alexander Jannaeus employed Pisidians and Cilicians (*Antiquities* 13.374); and Salome is reported to have recruited so many mercenaries that she, in fact, doubled the size of her army (*Antiquities* 13.409).[69]

Only two buildings are specifically noted in our sources with regard to Hasmonean Jerusalem. One is the royal palace which, according to 1 Maccabees 13:52, replaced the Akra.[70] Josephus, in describing the events preceding the outbreak of the Jewish revolt of 66 C.E., likewise takes note of a Hasmonean palace that was located west of the Temple Mount, on the eastern slope of the Upper City (*War* 2.344). Whether these two buildings are one and the same is uncertain, and in any case no material remains have been discovered to date. It is quite possible, however, that the first-century C.E. palace noted by Josephus was a continuation of the earlier one and that the Hasmoneans first took up residence in the newly incorporated area of Jerusalem, where the Akra once stood.

A second building is the Baris,[71] a fortress-palace built north of the Temple.[72] Three statements by Josephus are indicative of its location and function:

At an angle on the north side (of the Temple) there had been built a citadel, well fortified and of unusual strength. It was the kings and high priests of the Hasmonean family before Herod who had built it and called it Baris. Here they had deposited the priestly robe which the high priest put on only when he had to offer sacrifice.

(*Antiquities* 15.403)

One of the priests, Hyrcanus, the first of many by that name, had constructed a large house near the Temple and lived there most of the time. A custodian of the vestments, for to him alone was conceded the right to put them on, he kept them laid away there ... When Herod became king, he made lavish repairs to this building, which was conveniently situated, and, being a friend of Antony, he called it Antonia.

(*Antiquities* 18.91–92)

The tower of Antonia lay at the corner where two porticos, the western and the northern, of the first (i.e., outer) court of the Temple met.

(*War* 5.238)

From the above, it appears that the Baris filled a number of functions. It served on occasion as a Hasmonean palace; Hyrcanus used it regularly, and Aristobulus is said to have lay ill there (*Antiquities* 13.307). Its function as a citadel or fortress is attested by its very name, its solid construction and the fact that it continued to be so used during Herod's reign. It also served as a place for safekeeping the high priest's vestments, and in this regard Hasmonean practice was followed by Herod and the procurators.

The *communis opinio* is that the Baris was located at the site later occupied by Herod's Antonia.*[73] This certainly is the implication of the above-quoted excerpts. It is also possible that the Baris was located south of the Antonia, adjacent to the Hasmonean Temple precincts, which were much smaller than those built by Herod later on.[74] However, where precisely the Baris was is unknown, since traces of such a building or of the Hasmonean Temple Mount area have never been firmly established.[75]

The urban landscape of Jerusalem also included a necropolis located outside the city's walls. While many of the known burial caves were

*Ehud Netzer, "A New Reconstruction of Paul's Prison: Herod's Antonia Fortress," *BAR*, January/February 2009.

undoubtedly used during this earlier period, almost all the remains found therein date to the Herodian period. Two notable exceptions are the above-mentioned tombs of Jason and Bnei Hezir. As noted, the latter is located in the Kidron Valley just east of the city, while that of Jason (also probably of priestly lineage) is found to the west, in today's Rehavia neighborhood. Both tombs, as mentioned above, were built in typical Hellenistic style.[76]

The Temple in Hasmonean Jerusalem

There can be little question that, despite the expansion and growth of Jerusalem, the Temple remained its central focus. Before the Hasmoneans, the Temple's physical prominence was assured by its presence on the highest point of the eastern ridge where the city was then located. However, with the expansion of Jerusalem westward, the newly enclosed area was, in fact, on much higher ground. Nevertheless, even without topographical prominence, the Temple continued to command center stage. This prominence was further enhanced by the fact that the Hasmoneans themselves regularly officiated there and were able to mobilize the funds necessary for the ongoing mainte-nance, refurbishing, rebuilding and expansion of its facilities. Moreover, the Temple was revered as Judaism's single most holy site not only by an ever-growing population in Judea (partly by natural increment, partly by conver-sions), but also by the fact that it was the subject of much attention and debate among the newly established sects, each of which, in its own way, emphasized the importance of Jerusalem's sacred site. For all their differences, no group denied the inherent sanctity of the site, although the Essenes might have been extremely critical of those in charge and the way the Temple was being run (see below).

The centrality of the Temple found expression in a variety of ways.[77] One was through literary works, foremost among which was 2 Maccabees, a book that can be viewed in large part as Hasmonean propaganda for their city and Temple, and indirectly for themselves. The focus of the account is clearly the Temple, its sanctity having been preserved through the heroic efforts of Judah Maccabee and his family. The structure of 2 Maccabees is most revealing in this regard. The narrative begins and ends with incidents recounting how the Temple was saved from desecration, first by Heliodorus, a Seleucid official, and later by Nicanor, a Seleucid general. The first time required God's direct intervention, the second was accomplished in the battlefield through the agency of Judah Maccabee. However, the focal incident in the book was the purification and rededication of the Temple through Judah's valiant efforts, and thus can be understood as the basis for the legitimization of the family's right and authority to rule.

Jubilees, composed in all likelihood in the mid- to late second century B.C.E., is a second book emphasizing the centrality of the Jerusalem Temple.[78] Purportedly the words of an angel conveyed to Moses, *Jubilees* is, in effect, a midrash on Genesis and Exodus reflecting—as this genre invariably does—many of the concerns of its second-century priestly author.[79] One of its main purposes was to trace current Jewish practices to the earliest period in the history of the world and the people: counting years in a jubilee cycle (a 50-year period) began with Adam; the (solar) calendar was first revealed to Enoch; and the celebration of each of the holidays initiated by the patriarchs.

Jubilees pays special attention to many aspects of the Temple service. Adam offered sacrifices (3:26–27) and Enoch incense (4:25–26). Both Noah and Abraham are singled out for special mention in this regard (7:36, 21:7–10), the former for having made atonement for the land through a lavish sacrificial ritual (6:1–3), the latter for having offered tithes and celebrated the festivals of Shavu'ot and Sukkot (13:9,16,25–27, 14:9–12,19, 15:1–2, 16:20–31). Abraham not only provided Isaac with detailed instructions of sacrificial procedures before his death (21:7–16), but purportedly also offered his son as a sacrifice (per Genesis 22) on Passover (17:15–16). As might be expected, many observances connected with the Passover festival are associated with Moses (chapter 49). *Jubilees* concludes with a reemphasis of the Sabbath's sanctity: The only work allowed on that day related to the Temple; sacrifices, oblations and burning frankincense, all part of the required daily offerings, were permitted then since they ensure Israel's perpetual atonement before God. No greater significance could be attributed to the Temple's daily ritual.[80]

A third work, the *Letter of Aristeas*, devotes a long section to a description of the Jerusalem Temple (51–104). Although this book purportedly describes events that transpired in the third century B.C.E., and we have referred to it above with respect to certain aspects of Ptolemaic Jerusalem, there is general agreement today that the book itself is to be dated to the latter half of the second century. The particular section that purportedly describes Jerusalem seems to reflect the days of the Hasmoneans, after the city had begun expanding westward. For example, it describes the view of the city from the Temple's ramparts westward as resembling a theater's *cavea*, with streets crisscrossing at regular intervals. Moreover, the inhabitants' scrupulous behavior regarding purity seems more appropriate to Hasmonean than to Ptolemaic Jerusalem (105–106).

Aristeas's description of the Temple emphasizes its splendor and magnificence—as evidenced by the walls, sophisticated water supply system and reservoirs, inner furnishings, aspects of the sacrificial ritual and a description of the high priest in his elaborate garb (83–99). Wherever historical truth may lie in the particulars of this description,[81] the awe and pride reflected in this account of the Jerusalem Temple says a great deal about the standing that the institution commanded in the eyes of at least one Diaspora Jew.

Nevertheless, the Temple also had its detractors. For one, there were priests who left Jerusalem for Egypt or the Judean Desert in protest against Hasmonean hegemony. For them, the current Temple leadership (i.e., the Hasmoneans) and the halakhic regulations then in practice were misguided and thus profane. Onias IV built his own temple in Leontopolis, while the Essenes considered their sect, metaphorically, as a kind of substitute Temple. The sect's prayer was a substitute for sacrifices, and the community was led by the sons of Aaron, while all are acclaimed to be "men of holiness who walk in perfection" (1QS 9:4–9).

Another way members of the Qumran sect coped with what was considered the profaned Jerusalem Temple was by focusing on a heavenly one. Thus, the angelic liturgy, based on the vision of Isaiah (chapter 6), points to a preoccupation with the heavenly sphere. An elaborate description of this liturgy is offered in the Songs of the Sabbath Sacrifice.[82] The sect and those close to it developed an elaborate speculation of the future eschatological Temple as reflected in the Temple and New Jerusalem scrolls from Qumran.[83]

Some circles envisioned a future Jerusalem without a Temple. In the Animal Apocalypse of 1 Enoch (89, 73), it is stated that all the offerings of the Temple are impure. The Temple is represented by a tower, and in the new house (i.e., Jerusalem), to be built by God in the coming age, no mention is made of such a structure (90:28–29). John Collins has claimed that even the various calculations, or perhaps recalculations, in the Book of Daniel might indicate that the author refused to accept Judah Maccabee's restoration of the Jerusalem Temple as adequate and satisfactory.[84]

The priestly class

Without a doubt, the leading class within Judean society at this time was the priests. They not only were active in the most important institution within the city—the Temple—but were also an integral part of the local aristocracy. With the rise of the Hasmonean state, the priests played a central role in its political and diplomatic affairs. Note, for example, the names of emissaries sent by the Hasmoneans to Rome, Sparta and elsewhere, which seem to indicate that they were almost always of priestly stock.

- In the time of Judah Maccabee, in 161 B.C.E.—Eupolemus son of John, Jason son of Eleazar (1 Maccabees 8:17);

- In the time of Jonathan, c. 145 B.C.E.—Numenius son of Antiochus, Antipater son of Jason (1 Maccabees 12:16);
- In the time of Simon, c. 142 B.C.E.—Numenius son of Antiochus, Antipater son of Jason (1 Maccabees 14:22). Soon after these emissaries returned, Simon again dispatched Numenius and his entourage (1 Maccabees 14:24; 15:15);
- In the time of John Hyrcanus, there were no less than three missions to Rome:[85] (1) c. 134 B.C.E.—Alexander son of Jason, Numenius son of Antiochus, Alexander son of Dorotheus (*Antiquities* 14.146)[86]; (2) c. 125 B.C.E.—Simon son of Dositheus, Apollonius son of Alexander, Diodorus son of Jason (*Antiquities* 13.260)[87]; (3) 113–112 B.C.E.—Straton son of Theodotus, Apollonius son of Alexander, Aeneas son of Antipater, Aristobulus son of Amyntas, Sosipater son of Philip (*Antiquities* 14.248–249).[88]

From the above, it would seem that these diplomatic missions were entrusted to a small group of families, as many of the same names appear in various delegations.[89] Thus, it would seem that the foreign relations of the Hasmonean state were entrusted to specific families that bore this responsibility for generations.

A second conclusion is that most, if not all, of the above emissaries belonged to the priestly class. Yohanan, father of Eupolemus, is specifically mentioned as hailing from the priestly course of Hakkoz,[90] and Jason and Eleazar are well-known priestly names. Alexander and Aristobulus appear regularly as names within the priestly Hasmonean family itself, and Dositheus is likewise a common priestly name.[91]

Thirdly, these names clearly reflect a significant degree of Hellenization, and we even find blatantly pagan (Apollonius) and Seleucid (Antiochus) names among them. Simeon, the only Hebrew name listed, is very close to the Greek "Simon" and may possibly have been chosen for that very reason. It is no wonder that Jews with backgrounds in the Greek language (as their names seem to indicate), and presumably in Greek mores as well, were chosen for such tasks; it would have been essential that they be able to communicate easily with their hosts. Such Hellenized names bear certain cultural implications, allowing us to assume that, at the very least, some rhetorical training was available to these individuals, perhaps in Jerusalem itself.

The close ties between the priests, the upper classes and the phenomenon of Hellenization in Hasmonean Jerusalem are likewise reflected in several other types of evidence, already noted, from this period. As noted, the above Greek *Additions* to Esther informs us that this material, or at least part of it, was composed and translated (possibly together with the Book of Esther) by a Jerusalemite, Lysimachus, and were brought to Egypt by Dositheus and his son Ptolemy in 78–77 B.C.E.[92] Lysimachus is a priestly name[93] and Dositheus is identified specifically as a priest. Moreover, the Hellenistic component in their backgrounds is apparent not only from their Greek names but also from the fact that Lysimachus's translation reveals his superior command of Greek style and language.[94]

Priests and their Hellenization are further documented in archaeological remains. The two Jerusalem burial tombs noted above—the Bnei Hezir tomb to the east of the city and Jason's tomb to the west—reflect a significant appropriation of Hellenistic architectural forms by Jerusalem priestly families.

The prominence of priests as officials in the Hasmonean bureaucracy requires further comment. In addition to their diplomatic roles, there is also evidence that priests were among the military leaders of the Hasmonean armies.[95] The Hasmoneans themselves, being both priests and *strategoi*, served as models, and the distinctive role played by priests as military leaders in the first centuries C.E. is well documented; Josephus himself was a prime example.[96]

However, more direct evidence is also available. Toward the end of the Hasmonean period, when the Pharisees assumed a dominant role under the reign of Salome Alexandra, we read of the revenge they took on the priests who had persecuted them beforehand, in the days of Alexander Jannaeus. Those now on the defensive were referred to as "leading citizens" who had been granted the "greatest honors" by Jannaeus and were now close cohorts of Salome's son, Aristobulus II (*Antiquities* 13.411). They were clearly associated with the military, as they spoke of their suffering the perils of war and their potential value to surrounding rulers as mercenaries; they now requested of Salome that, at the very least, she station each of them in one of her garrisons, presumably as commanders (*Antiquities* 13.412–415).[97] These are most likely references to priestly (Sadducean?) commanders in the army who were now trying to cope with the dramatic shift in Hasmonean policy that accompanied Salome's ascension to the throne and allowed the Pharisees to threaten them at will.

Truth to tell, Josephus never explicitly reveals the identity of these military commanders, but the likelihood that they were priests is enhanced by the Qumran sect and its scrolls. This group was led in large part by priests and apparently had some sort of military orientation, as reflected in the Scroll of the War of the Sons of Light against the Sons of Darkness, a manual for their anticipated eschatological war. Of greater import, however, is the fact that Pesher Nahum (Columns 3–4) refers to contemporary Judean sects via biblical figures—Judah represents the Qumran sect itself, Ephraim the

Pharisees and Menasseh the Sadducean priests.[98] The scroll describes these priests not only as "nobles" and "respectable men," but also as "men of valor" and "warriors." This, then, appears to be a clear attestation of the military dimension of the Sadducean priesthood.

It should be remembered that priests were a diverse group—rich and poor, urban and village dwellers, more and less cosmopolitan. On the one hand, some were Hellenistic enthusiasts, such as the high priest Jason and others who reportedly flocked to the *gymnasium* in 175 B.C.E. On the other, Josephus recounts the heroic efforts of the Jerusalem priests during the siege of the city by the Roman general Pompey a century later, in 63 B.C.E. Despite near starvation, these priests faithfully continued to perform their cultic obligations. Some were even massacred by Romans troops while fulfilling their priestly duties (*Antiquities* 14.64–71). Finally, priests might have associated with different religious groups in Hasmonean society, not only with the Sadducees but also with the Pharisees, and were especially prominent among the Essenes or Qumran sect, as discussed below.

Religious sects

As already noted on several occasions, a notable development in Hasmonean times was the emergence of identifiable religious sects.[99] The term "sect" requires some clarification, as it usually is used with regard to Christian groups that periodically separated from the church for social and ideological reasons. In our period, only the Essenes or Qumran sect came close to fitting this definition as applied to Judaism. Other groups, such as the Pharisees, Sadducees, Hasidim of Maccabean days and later the Sicarii and early Christians, all operated in Jerusalem and the wider Judean society and were not opposed, in principle, to the Hasmonean religious establishment. The term "sect" is thus not the most appropriate for our historical context, but we have retained it out of convenience since it is universally used with reference to the above groups.

All evidence points to the crystallization of many of these Second Temple sects at the beginning of the Hasmonean period. Josephus first mentions the existence of religious groups in the mid-second century (*Antiquities* 13.171–173), and the Qumran scrolls likewise indicate that their sect had coalesced in the same period.[100] The first chapter of Mishnah *Avot* ("Ethics of the Fathers") attributes statements to the first generation of Pharisaic leaders (the *Zugot* or "Pairs") who lived in early Hasmonean times, and these sayings seem to reflect an early stage in the sect's formation.[101] The Pharisees quoted there speak of attaching oneself to a teacher, acquiring a colleague, opening one's home to sages and more. One rabbinic source, *Fathers According to Rabbi*

Nathan, though stemming in its final form from late antiquity or even the early Middle Ages, claims that the Pharisees and Sadducees emerged several generations after Antigonus of Socho, who himself seems to have lived in the early second century (see there, Version A, chapter 5).[102]

Religious sectarianism was indeed an unusual occurrence in ancient Judaism. Neither before the second century B.C.E. nor after 70 C.E. (prior to modern times) did a similar range of organized religious groups exist among Jews; thus, the religious configuration that crystallized under the Hasmoneans was quite unusual.[103] Indeed, the historical circumstances of the mid-second century B.C.E., a time of transition and upheaval, seem to have been conducive to spawning such groups.

Following the trauma of Antiochus's persecutions, the desecration of the Temple and its purification, the emergence of Hasmonean rule was undoubtedly viewed by many with exhilaration and pride and by others with disdain and as a source of profound disillusionment. Some may have been alienated by ever-increasing Hellenistic influences, by the Hasmonean usurpation of the high priesthood and its religiously problematic behavior (as perceived by some), by the overly ambitious military designs and increasingly centralized authority achieved by its synthesis of political and religious roles, by the emergence of a vigorous anti-gentile policy and by the unsettling circumstances of urban growth, especially in Jerusalem. All of the above may account, each in its own way, for the creation of alternative religious groups.[104] Since there were striking differences between the above sects, it is likely that different factors played a role in the formation of each.

Jerusalem was the focus of much of this sectarian activity. The Sadducees, by virtue of their being priests and involved in Temple affairs, were clearly based in the city, as were the Pharisees. A number of their traditions inform us that most of them functioned in Jerusalem, at times in connection with Temple and political (i.e., Hasmonean) affairs. In fact, the struggle between the Pharisees and Sadducees throughout this period would seem to indicate that each group was well represented in the city.

The various sects in Hasmonean Jerusalem shared a number of characteristics, yet differed from each other in significant ways. Common to the various groups was the fact that they were all voluntary frameworks. People searching for religious messages and inspiration may have tried several sects over the course of time and, as a consequence, were exposed to a series of religious figures and frameworks, as was Josephus in his own search for the most meaningful religious experience in the first century C.E. (*Life* 2.7–12).

None of these sects was cut from one cloth or large in number at this time.[105] Not all priests were Sadducees or Essenes, and not all Essenes were priests. Moreover, the early Pharisees do not appear to have had a common social identity. Nevertheless, most sect members, especially the leadership, seem to have hailed from the socially and economically established classes of Jerusalem society. The prominence of both the Sadducees and Pharisees in John Hyrcanus's court is a striking case in point (*Antiquities* 13.288–298).[106]

The small size of these groups is attested by the fact that even during Herod's rule in the latter first century B.C.E. the Pharisees numbered only some 6,000 members (*Antiquities* 17.42), and that in the first century C.E. there were approximately 4,000 Essenes (*Antiquities* 18.21; Philo, *Every Good Man is Free* 12.75).[107] The site of the Essene community at Qumran, specifically its dining area, is usually assumed to have been able to accommodate 200-or-so members; this figure is often regarded as indicative of the sect's size at any given time.[108] The Sadducees, for their part, were even fewer in number, if a comment by Josephus in this regard is to be believed.[109]

In choosing to belong to a particular sect, individuals declared their personal and then collective identity vis-à-vis others. Each sect meticulously erected boundaries to separate it from members of other groups, as well as ordinary Jews and non-Jews. This social separation was rigorously mandated, although articulated in a variety of ways; the Essenes residing in Qumran gave extreme expression to this tendency. The guidelines for entry into the sect, as well as the harsh punishment meted out to those who failed to keep the rules, indicate a determination to maintain communal standards at all costs. The Pharisees, or at least some of them, probably tended to separate themselves from the masses, at least according to the mishnaic laws dealing with the *ḥavurah*, with its stringent rules of both membership and separation from *'am ha-aretz* (the ordinary Jew).[110] For both the Qumran Essenes and many of the Pharisees, the strict observance of purity laws was one of the crucial means of maintaining this separation.[111] Part of the daily ritual of the Essenes in general, and at Qumran in particular, required immersion and its accompanying liturgy before the communal meal (*War* 2.130–132; 1QS 5–6).

With the publication of the scrolls, e.g., the Temple Scroll and MMT,[112] we have become more aware of the degree to which Jewish law (*halakhah*) was a pivotal factor in the self-definition of the sects, as later emphasized in rabbinic literature. This has helped to refocus attention on the importance of legal matters in defining and distinguishing these groups.[113]

Another common feature of the sects, at least regarding those for which we have information, is the centrality of Torah study. The Pharisaic emphasis on this activity is reflected in a statement found in Mishnah *Avot* (chapter 1) and ascribed to the early "Pairs," and in Josephus's repeated claim that this group excelled in its precise knowledge of the Law (e.g., *War* 1.110).[114] At Qumran, study was an ongoing activity throughout the day and evening.[115]

Besides some of the dimensions shared by these sects, there were also certain major differences between them. The latter are even more salient owing to the fact that our primary sources prioritize them. Rabbinic literature, as mentioned, emphasizes halakhic differences while the New Testament focuses on ideological ones, as well as ritual concerns that pitted the Pharisees against Jesus and vice versa.[116]

Josephus also comments on social-economic and halakhic differences, although he highlights certain theological distinctions. For example, he introduces the sects in his account of Jonathan, c. 150 B.C.E., as follows:

> Now at this time there were three schools of thought among the Jews, which held different opinions concerning human affairs; the first being that of the Pharisees, the second that of the Sadducees and the third that of the Essenes. As for the Pharisees, they say that certain events are the work of Fate, but not all; as to other events, it depends upon ourselves whether they shall take place or not. The sect of Essenes, however, declares that Fate is mistress of all things, and that nothing befalls men unless it be in accordance with her decree. But the Sadducees do away with Fate, holding that there is no such thing and that human actions are not achieved in accordance with her decree, but that all things lie within our own power, so that we ourselves are responsible for our well-being, while we suffer misfortune through our own thoughtlessness.
>
> (*Antiquities* 13.171–173)[117]

Truth to tell, however, we are at a distinct disadvantage in trying to define and understand these sects in the Hasmonean period through the prism of literary sources stemming from the first century C.E. or later. Josephus wrote in the second half of the first century C.E., the New Testament material comes from the late first and early second centuries C.E. and rabbinic literature dates from the third century C.E. on. Therefore, relating to the Hasmonean period in the second and first centuries B.C.E. on the basis of sources written centuries later is somewhat risky. The only sources contemporary with the Hasmonean period are those from Qumran. Despite this caveat, we will attempt to sketch in general terms what can be said with some degree of assurance specifically about the Sadducees and Pharisees at this time and then address the Dead Sea sect/Essenes.

The Sadducees[118]

With the usurpation of the high priesthood by Jason, Menelaus and then by the Hasmoneans, the traditional high priestly dynasty, the sons of Zadok split into three separate groups. Around 150 B.C.E., one branch of this family, under the leadership of Onias IV, erected a temple in Leontopolis in Egypt under Ptolemaic auspices, perhaps as a rival of sorts to the Jerusalem Temple then under Hasmonean control (*Antiquities* 13.62–73). Another branch of the family was instrumental in creating the Essene/Qumran sect, which eventually withdrew to the Judean wilderness (see below). A third priestly component remained in Jerusalem and became an integral part of that society for the next two centuries. These were the Sadducees,* who were largely, though perhaps not exclusively, a priestly aristocratic party commanding significant wealth and political prominence. Rabbinic literature and Josephus make this point abundantly clear (*Fathers According to Rabbi Nathan*, A, 4, and *Antiquities* 13.297, respectively).

One might have expected that the priestly descendants of Zadok would have regarded themselves as the sole legitimate bearers of the priestly tradition and therefore pitted themselves as implacable enemies of the Hasmoneans. Indeed, this happened with the other two branches of the family described above, those in Egypt and those who later took up residence in Qumran. However, with the third branch, i.e., the Sadducees, pragmatism proved decisive; by working closely with the Hasmonean rulers, they even succeeded, as noted, in ousting their Pharisaic rivals from positions of power toward the end of John Hyrcanus's reign (c. 110 B.C.E.). Sadducean political ascendancy remained in place throughout the reign of Alexander Jannaeus (103–76 B.C.E.), and only under Jannaeus's wife, Salome (76–67 B.C.E.), did the Pharisees regain power and remove their opponents from all positions of authority.

Undoubtedly, the basis for Sadducean power lay in this group's claim to priestly status. As such, they were recognized as the official religious authorities of the people, servants of the God of Israel in His holy sanctuary and guardians of the Torah tradition. Josephus claims that the Sadducees found their most loyal adherents among the wealthy, and not the populace (*Antiquities* 13.298). Moreover, as noted above, members of the priestly class, which certainly included Sadducees, served not only as diplomats but as military leaders (*Antiquities* 13.410–415).

---

*A number of explanations have been offered for the etymology of the Hebrew word "Sadducee," but it probably derives from "Zadok," the name of the high priest in the time of David whose heirs served in that role until Hasmonean times.

We are at a distinct disadvantage in our effort to understand the Sadducees more fully since they have left us no written documents. Moreover, whatever information we have not only derives from the first century C.E. and beyond, as noted, but originated in circles distinctly hostile to them. Rabbinic and New Testament sources preserve many traditions about the Sadducees; the Dead Sea Scrolls provide information and Josephus mentions this group on occasion. Each of these sources, however, is openly critical of Sadducean ideology and conduct (*War* 2.166). What the Sadducees might have said about themselves would have certainly been significantly different. Contrary to popular belief, no consistent halakhic or ideological pattern can be discerned in their disputes with the Pharisees, recorded for the most part in later rabbinic traditions.[119] At times the Sadducees are portrayed as being more lenient than the Pharisees; at others, more rigorous. Sometimes they reputedly adopt a strict constructionist approach toward the biblical text, sometimes they do not. In several disputes, they clearly took positions reflective of their wealthy, aristocratic background; in others, this dimension is not at all evident.

Josephus notes several doctrines associated with the Sadducees that may well have been espoused already in Hasmonean times. They denied the notion of immortality of the soul, rejected any concept of future reward and punishment and embraced a doctrine of unlimited free will (*War* 2.165). Perhaps the most significant tenet differentiating them from the Pharisees was their clear-cut distinction between the Torah of Moses, which they regarded as divine, and all other laws and regulations, which were not. They considered all other regulations as man-made and of an *ad hoc* nature, carrying no imperative for later generations. For the Sadducees, all such laws and regulations had the status of decrees, valid for specific times and places, and no more.

The Pharisees[120]

The Pharisees also crystallized in this period, playing a central role in Judean political and religious life, at times in alliance with the Hasmoneans and at times in opposition to them.

The name "Pharisee" appears to derive from Hebrew *parash*, meaning "to separate" or "to stand apart." However, we do not know to what the first Pharisees objected or from what they stood apart. Many suggestions have been offered: they opposed the dominant priestly class, the emerging Hasmonean dynasty and its political-military policies, those who were lax in the observance of purity and tithing laws or those overly enamored by Hellenistic influences—and perhaps in some combination of the above. Our primary sources indeed reflect this same vagueness or fluidity regarding the basic thrust of early Pharisaism. As noted, Josephus often describes the

Pharisees as an essentially philosophical sect while rabbinic sources and several Qumran scrolls emphasize a plethora of halakhic matters.

When all is said and done, however, we have very little solid evidence regarding the Pharisees of the Hasmonean era. Josephus treated the sects only peripherally in his historical accounts, not regarding them as primary forces in the political and military events with which he was preoccupied. Rabbinic literature, too, has preserved very little data relating to the Pharisaic sages who lived at the time; in contrast, we know a great deal more about the Pharisees under Roman rule (63 B.C.E.–70 C.E.) than we do about their predecessors. The overwhelming majority of sayings attributed to the pre-70 C.E. Pharisees come from two later sages, Hillel and Shammai, and their academies (Beth Hillel and Beth Shammai).

Moreover, we have no idea how many of the anonymous references to the Pharisees in rabbinic literature actually apply to the Hasmonean period. With but rare exception, it is impossible to date such material confidently. It is no less difficult to understand why so few traditions of these early sages were preserved by the later rabbis. The relatively large time gap between the Hasmonean period and the first redaction of rabbinic sources in the early third century C.E. may in part account for this phenomenon. Perhaps the later rabbis also harbored certain reservations about the political involvements and religious priorities of their distant forebearers and thus chose not to include much of their material in the rabbinic corpus. Whatever the reason, the insignificant quantity of reliable information about the early Pharisees is a serious obstacle to understanding their place in Hasmonean society. We will thus restrict ourselves to those aspects of early Pharisaism that are relatively well attested and thus perhaps more likely to be reliable.

As mentioned above, these early sages seem to have constituted a rather diverse group. On the one hand, they looked to the high priest Simon the Just of Zadokite stock as a link in their chain of tradition; on the other hand, an otherwise unknown Jewish savant, the Greek-named Antigonus of Socho, also found a place in this tradition. Some Pharisees dwelled in cities, others came from rural settings; they hailed from diverse places such as Jerusalem and Zeredah in Judea to Arbel in the Galilee. Much later, one Pharisee was recognized as a magician and miracle-worker (Joshua ben Peraḥiah); another, Simeon ben Shataḥ was reputed in a late Bavli tradition to have been a relative of the royal family and part of the court entourage. Moreover, the rather limited number of statements attributed to these Pharisaic sages are likewise diverse, some being of an ethical nature, others cultic or narrowly ritualistic. Rarely were opinions voiced on social or political issues, with the striking exception of those expressed by Simeon ben Shataḥ. According to Josephus, as noted, the

Pharisees under the Hasmoneans indeed appear to have been highly politicized.

Both Josephus and rabbinic literature claim that the Pharisees enjoyed a high degree of popularity among the people, although the historicity of this assertion has been questioned by scholars.[121] Their prestige as religious figures apparently won them political prominence. Little else seems to have been working in their favor. The Sadducees, by contrast, were prominent in diplomatic, military and aristocratic circles, not to speak of their central role in Temple affairs. It is difficult to pinpoint any particular Pharisaic base of power, either in the political, social or economic realm. Apart from Simeon ben Shataḥ, if the late talmudic tradition is to be believed, no specific Pharisee played a major role in affairs of state. Thus, we may conclude that the Pharisees' chief political asset was probably their prominence and acceptance as religious figures.

As noted, one of the basic Pharisaic doctrines distinguishing them from the Sadducees was that they considered their sect's Oral Law the authentic amplification of the Written Law of Moses. The crowning recognition of the Oral Law as legitimate and authentic was the Pharisaic claim that it, too, was given at Sinai; God gave the Israelites not only the Five Books of Moses but the Oral tradition as well (M *Avot* 1.1). Armed with this notion, the Pharisees presented themselves to the people as the sole legitimate bearers of Mosaic tradition, a claim held by the Essenes as well, though on different grounds.

The Essenes[122]

Oddly enough, and although he mentions them last when discussing the views of the various sects, Josephus describes the Essenes in far greater detail than either the Sadducees or Pharisees (*War* 2.119–166). The Essenes' role in Judean public affairs was not even remotely comparable to that of the Sadducees or Pharisees, and it is possible that Josephus presents them in such detail because he thought his readers would be fascinated by a group exhibiting such curious and unusual behavior.

Josephus was probably right about his readership, and the archaeological finds from Qumran have attracted widespread interest over these last 60 years. The descriptions of Josephus, Philo and Pliny, in addition to the more than 900 scrolls discovered in the Dead Sea caves, have revealed a sect so distinct in the annals of Judaism that it could not have been imagined beforehand.

Although scholars have debated the identity of the Qumran sectarians from the beginning, the consensus reached early in the history of research, and continuing until today, identifies them with the Essenes.[123] While the parallels between the Qumran scrolls and literary sources on the Essenes are extensive and striking, alternative suggestions take into consideration certain discrepancies discovered between them. For example, the scrolls speak of a war-oriented group whereas the literary sources speak of pacifists; the scrolls and archaeological finds offer evidence for the presence of women in the sect while the literary sources emphasize a group of celibate men. As a result of such discrepancies (and several more), as well as additional considerations, other groups among the Jews—the Pharisees, Zealots-Sicarii, Sadducees, Boethusians and early Christians—have been proffered as candidates for identification with the Dead Sea sect. However, there is no need to resort to alternative identifications; whatever differences exist between the literary descriptions of Josephus and Philo on the one hand, and the Dead Sea Scrolls on the other, can best be explained as referring to: (1) various subgroups within the Essene sect; (2) different periods in the sect's history; or (3) a product of the tendentious presentations by Josephus and Philo, each for his own apologetic purposes.

The Essenes flourished in the last centuries of the Second Temple period. Following their own chronology noted in the Damascus Document, the sect traced its beginnings to about 400 years after the destruction of the First Temple (i.e., 586 B.C.E.), while some 20 years later their founder, a priest referred to as the Teacher of Righteousness, first appeared to galvanize the sect. If this chronology is taken more or less at face value, admittedly an arguable assumption (see Ezekiel 4:5), it would place the first stages of this group some time in the mid-second century B.C.E., as discussed above, and the Teacher may have been killed by a Hasmonean leader referred to in the scrolls as the Wicked Priest, often identified as either Jonathan or Simon the Hasmonean.[124] Afterwards, members of this group seem to have withdrawn from society, eventually to take up residence in Qumran a generation or two later.[125] Qumran may have served as the group's headquarters from then until it was destroyed in 68 C.E. Groups of Essenes lived in other places as well, perhaps even in Jerusalem since Josephus makes mention of a Gate of the Essenes located in the southwestern quarter of the city (*War* 5.145).*

The Qumran sect was highly organized, with rigorous rules for acceptance and clearly defined penalties and punishments. According to The Community Rule (*Serekh ha-Yahad*), it was governed by a council of 12 headed by an "overseer" (*mevaker*); priestly influence, as noted, was considerable.[126]

The sect functioned as a commune; there was no private property, and everything was produced communally and shared equally. Community life focused on meals, scriptural readings, instruction and religious and spiritual observances highlighted by communal prayer. Although marriage was permitted in certain subgroups, members of the Qumran community were

---

*See Bargil V. Pixner, "Jerusalem's Essene Gateway: Where the Community Lived in Jesus' Time," *BAR*, May/June 1997.

generally celibate. It is assumed that the group sustained itself from generation to generation by attracting a continuous stream of newcomers from Jewish society at large.

One of the crucial and distinctive features of the Qumran sect was its calendar. In contrast to the rest of Jewish society, which was governed by a lunar calendar (with periodic correctives to realign with the solar calendar), the Essenes based their calendar on solar calculations alone. The year was divided into 12 months of 30 days each; every three months constituted a season, and seasons were separated from one another by a single day not counted in either season. The Essene year thus comprised 364 days. Holidays fell on the same day of the week every year. In addition to using a solar calendar, the sectarians also regarded the sun as sacred. Prayer was directed to the east, and members were enjoined never to expose the private parts of their bodies to the sun. It has been suggested by many scholars that the sect's calendar may have been the basic reason for its withdrawal from Jewish society. Believing that the lunar calculations were false and the holidays were thus not being celebrated at their "appointed times," as prescribed in the Bible, the Essenes chose to distance themselves from other Jews in order to follow the biblical prescriptions in what they believed to be the right way.[127]

There were other, no less distinctive, aspects of Essene Judaism.[128] For one, the sect firmly believed in a messianic-eschatological doctrine according to which the world was imminently coming to an end and they themselves would participate in this final denouement. To emphasize the high degree of their messianic expectations, the sect divided itself into battalions and even wrote a detailed scenario (the War Scroll) of the series of battles that would bring human history to its culmination. Perhaps the most distinctive type of literary genre found at Qumran was the *pesher*, a kind of scriptural interpretation that assumed that all future "messianic" references in the Bible, particularly from the Prophets, were to be fulfilled in the sect's own day.

Other components of Qumran ideology included dualism and predestination. The sect viewed the world as being governed by good and evil, each gaining the upper hand on various occasions. Only in the End of Days would the forces of good prevail. Even the heavens were divided into opposing camps of angels functioning in the service of these two forces. Just as the end of the present world had been carefully programmed in advance, so the life and fortunes of each individual were predestined. For the Essene, there was no room for individual free will.

Because many of the Essenes' ideas and customs were unique, they raise intriguing questions as to the nature of Judaism generally at the time. Might some of these beliefs have been common in Judean society as a whole or, as often assumed, were Essene practices and beliefs entirely *sui generis*. Given the striking parallels between the Dead Sea doctrines and communal organization on the one hand, and those of early Christianity on the other, these questions take on even greater import.[129] No firm answers have been forthcoming to date, but one can only hope that future studies will add to our understanding of Jewish life in the Hasmonean period and perhaps beyond.

Common Judaism under the Hasmoneans

Notwithstanding all that has been noted above about religious life under the Hasmoneans, it is important to bear in mind that dealing with competing sects and clashing ideologies is only part of the overall picture. It is indeed unfortunate that discussion of Judaism in the Hasmonean period often begins and ends with the sects, for, as we have noted above, only a small proportion of the population actually belonged to such groups. This does not mean that other Jews might not have been affected by these sects, but only a few actually joined their ranks and committed themselves to the full range of obligations and responsibilities that membership required. Most people in the late Second Temple period would probably have been identified with 'am ha-aretz, a term used in rabbinic literature referring to the people at large, those less punctilious in their observance.

What beliefs and practices characterized most Jews at the time?[130] There can be no question that the fundamental tenet was the belief in one God. In contrast to the pagan world, with its multiplicity of deities, the focus on one God who had but one Temple in one particular city was unique to the Jews. Judaism posited that God had chosen Israel as His people and had given them His Torah by which to guide their lives. This relationship with God was, in essence, a mutual agreement, a covenant between the two. God chose the people and promised them rewards and a glowing future; the people, in turn, took upon itself to fulfill God's commandments and obey His ways. Added to this was the belief in the sanctity of God's sacred word (the Torah), the Jerusalem Temple, and His designated holy city.

Religious observances of the masses centered around three areas: (1) biblical commandments such as the avoidance of certain foods and the observance of the Sabbath and holidays; (2) laws relating to agricultural produce (tithes, first fruits, etc.); and (3) Temple observances (sacrifices, pilgrimage, half-shekel contributions, etc.). Most of the commandments associated with the above categories are related in some fashion to the Temple. There was also the obligation to give a half-shekel and to be present in the holy city on each of the three pilgrimage festivals (Passover, Sukkot and Shavu'ot)—although the latter was often unobserved by those living at a distance. As the occasion arose, individual Jews would go to the Temple to offer sacrifices for personal reasons—a sin or guilt offering, a free-will offering, an offering in fulfillment of a vow or following childbirth. Thus, while the Temple's centrality held true for earlier periods, with the growth of Jerusalem and the increase in the Jewish population of Judea and throughout the Diaspora, the institution's importance, activities and status grew exponentially.

"Purity burst forth in Israel"

One of the most dramatic religious developments during this period, alluded to above, was the appearance of unprecedented purity concerns among a wide range of Jews.[131] The apocryphal books of Tobit (2:9) and Judith (12:6–10) already indicate such concerns with regard to corpse or gentile uncleanliness. The *Letter of Aristeas* (305–306) notes the Egyptian Jewish custom of washing hands before prayer, a practice also attested on several other occasions in the Diaspora (*Antiquities* 14.258; Acts 16:13), among the Essenes in general and at Qumran in particular (*War* 2.129, 150; 1QS 5:13; CD 10:11–13, 11:22 [bathing]).[132] A second document, issued by Antiochus III upon his conquest of Jerusalem in 198 B.C.E. also prescribes strict adherence to purity laws throughout the city: No foreigner was allowed to enter the Temple precincts; all Jews could enter only after purification; no flesh or skins of unclean animals were allowed in the city, nor could they be bred there (*Antiquities* 12.145–146). It is impossible to measure how effective such measures were; nor can we conclude whether these rules were reinforcing an established norm or attempting to create a new one.[133]

We have already noted the Hasmonean policy of purifying pagan settlements before resettling them with Jews. Cleansing the land from the impurity of idolatry appears to have been of major importance. Moreover, the Dead Sea Scrolls stress purity concerns for members of the sect. Admission into the sect involved a series of such requirements, meals had to be taken in a state of purity and immersion was required several times a day (many of the stepped cisterns at Qumran served as ritual baths).[134] For the sect, there seems to have been a direct correlation between degrees of purity and the religious and moral state of the individual.

Despite the fact that there is a dearth in rabbinic literature of Pharisaic halakhic traditions from Hasmonean times, a number of those preserved address purity issues.[135] Thus, the first "Pair" in *Avot* allegedly issued a decree declaring impure the "land of the gentiles" (all land outside the Land of Israel) as well as glass vessels; Joshua ben Peraḥiah ruled that wheat from Alexandria was impure (T *Makhshirim* 3.4, ed. Zuckermandel, p. 675).[136] From the later Hasmonean period, Judah ben Tabbai and Simeon ben Shataḥ declared metal vessels impure (Y *Shabbat* 1.4.3d and parallels).

The Mishnah speaks of the increased frequency of the Red Heifer ritual (Numbers 19) at this time, the purpose of which was to remove corpse impurity. This ceremony was performed on the Mount of Olives, east of the city, and according to M *Parah* 3.5 had been performed on only a few occasions throughout the entire biblical period. Yet, no less than four such ceremonies are recorded in the Hellenistic-Hasmonean period alone and another three during the ensuing Herodian era.

The most concrete expression of purity concerns comes from the material remains of *mikva'ot* at this time. The immersion ritual in the biblical period was geared primarily to priests and seems to have involved immersion in "live (= flowing) water" (Leviticus 14:1–32), i.e., streams, springs, rivers and the sea. Only in Hasmonean times do artificial water installations intended for purification appear. Both Qumran and the Hasmonean palace complex in Jericho provide us with a rich trove of such *mikva'ot*, and several have been identified at Gezer as well.[137]

Perhaps the most indicative evidence for the pervasiveness of purity requirements is the appearance of ritual baths alongside agricultural installations (olive and wine presses) throughout Judea. To date, more than 500 *mikva'ot* have been discovered throughout this region, the majority in agricultural contexts.[138] Whether this indicates self-motivated purity concerns characterizing a wide spectrum of Jews or Temple purity requirements which, in turn, influenced agricultural practices remains an open question, although the latter alternative seems more likely. Whatever the case, one important caveat must be borne in mind: Evidence for *mikva'ot* in Judea dates mainly from later Herodian times and it is therefore unclear to what extent this practice gained popular appeal under the Hasmoneans.[139]

Clearly, not all stepped and plastered cisterns were used as ritual baths, and a number of criteria have been suggested for identifying a cistern as a *mikveh*: a low partition(s) running down the middle of steps; two adjacent pools connected by a pipe or channel; a double entrance leading into such an installation.[140] As noted above, a definite Hasmonean date can be attributed to such pools at Gezer, Jericho and Qumran. One can probably assume that *mikva'ot* were in use in Jerusalem as well, although the remains found there date to the Herodian era.

Concern for ritual purity also found expression in the use of stone vessels. Excavations over the past several decades have produced a wealth of such vessels that were used by a broad segment of Jerusalem society.[141] These vessels include a wide variety of utensils: dishes, bowls, jars, drinking cups, measuring cups, etc. It is true that stone is readily accessible and is thus a relatively cheap commodity in the Jerusalem area, and this, in turn, may account for its use in the Hasmonean period. Nevertheless, it is difficult to disassociate the appearance of such vessels specifically at this time from the newly awakened concern for ritual purity among the priestly and non-priestly populations. If the later rabbinic tradition whereby stone vessels were not susceptible to impurity (M *Ohalot* 5.5) was indeed operative at this time, it would also account for their widespread presence.

We can only speculate as to why such purity concerns were so important in this period. Perhaps it was the desire to emulate priestly purity or respond to the growing influence of the Temple, with its punctilious observance of purity, perhaps it reflected the desire of increasing numbers of people to achieve holiness and sanctity—or a combination of the above.[142] Whatever the reason, this concern took hold, and the talmudic statement quoted at the beginning of this section, "Purity burst forth in Israel" (B *Shabbat* 13a), seems a most apt description of this phenomenon (T *Shabbat* 1.14, ed. Lieberman, pp. 3–4; Y *Shabbat* 1.3.3b).

The end of Jewish sovereignty

The Jews lost their political sovereignty when Pompey conquered Judea in 63 B.C.E. Was this conquest avoidable? Could the Hasmonean kingdom have avoided such a fate? Josephus answers in the affirmative, claiming that this loss was due to the internecine conflict between Hyrcanus II and Aristobulus II (*Antiquities* 14.34–79, esp. 77). These warring brothers, he claims, brought ruin to their kingdom through their failure to present a unified front against Rome. Josephus was certainly correct in his appraisal that Hasmonean disunity contributed heavily to the demise of their kingdom, and it is possible that had the brothers coordinated their efforts and jointly negotiated with Pompey, they might have been able to mitigate the results of the conquest. The Nabateans to the east of Judea succeeded in maintaining their kingdom for another century and a half, until 106 C.E., when it was finally incorporated into the Roman Empire.

Nevertheless, Josephus was certainly wrong in suggesting that a unified stand ultimately would have made a significant difference. Rome was destined to conquer the East irrespective of internal Hasmonean politics. The Hasmoneans could only have hoped to mitigate the conditions of conquest. By demonstrating a unified stand and a willingness to cooperate, their kingdom might have survived much longer and suffered less damage, as was the case with the Nabatean kingdom east of the Jordan River. Their behavior in this regard was a major political failure, one that cost them their hegemony over Jewish society and its independence.[143]

The Seleucus Stela. *This fragmented Greek inscription, dating to 178 B.C.E., gives King Seleucus IV a free hand to interfere in the affairs and treasuries of the sanctuaries of Syria and Palestine.*

While the upper portion of the inscription surfaced on the antiquities market, several pieces from its bottom were recently excavated by a volunteer at the site of Maresha in southwestern Israel, where the stela was presumably installed for public viewing.

The Roots of the Maccabean Revolt

An article in the November/December 2008 issue of *BAR* ("Inscription Reveals Roots of Maccabean Revolt") featured a newly discovered but fragmentary limestone stela from the reign of the Seleucid king Seleucus IV that provides fresh insight into the tumultuous events leading up to the Maccabean revolt of 165 B.C.E. The stela's Greek inscription, written as a series of correspondences between Seleucus, his chief advisor Heliodorus and two lower royal officials, publicly proclaimed the Seleucid king's right to interfere in the affairs and treasuries of religious sanctuaries throughout Syria-Palestine, including the Jerusalem Temple. Before breaking off, the last line of the preserved text mentions one Olympiodorus whom the king had appointed to administer temple affairs in the region.

Seleucus's brother and successor, Antiochus IV, took these exploitive policies even further. He continued to meddle in Judean affairs for financial gain but also set up an altar to Zeus in the Jerusalem Temple and imposed a series of harsh bans on traditional Jewish observance. By 165 B.C.E. the Jews had suffered enough at the hands of the Seleucids and, led by Mattathias and his son Judah Maccabee, arose in open revolt. The retaking of the Temple by Jewish forces and the miraculous relighting of the menorah for eight days with oil enough for only one are the basis for the Hanukkah festival (2 Maccabees 6–10).

Remarkably, three additional fragments from the lower portion of the same stela were recently excavated by a young volunteer at the site of Maresha in southwestern Israel (Dorothy D. Resig, "Volunteers Find Missing Pieces to Looted Inscription," *BAR*, May/June 2010). The new pieces not only secure the stela's authenticity and original provenance, but also list Olympiodorus's qualifications for administering the temple treasuries. —***Ed.***

EIGHT

Roman Domination
The Jewish Revolt and the Destruction of the Second Temple[1]

SHAYE J.D. COHEN

THE ROMANS ENTERED JUDEAN POLITICS, IRONICALLY, BY INVITATION of one Jewish faction that was in a power struggle with another. In 76 B.C.E. Alexander Jannaeus, the last great king of the Hasmonean line, died. He was succeeded by his widow Salome Alexandra, who herself died in 67 B.C.E.* The royal couple's two sons, Hyrcanus and Aristobulus, then fought each other for succession to the throne. Both Hyrcanus (usually called by scholars Hyrcanus II) and Aristobulus (usually called Aristobulus II) appeared before the Roman legate in Syria, each asking to be recognized as the ruler of Judea. Other Jews appeared as well, asking the Romans to reject the claims of both; by this time many Jews were thoroughly disillusioned with Hasmonean rule.

The Romans at first supported Aristobulus II, but when they realized he was a potential troublemaker, a suspicion amply confirmed by subsequent events, they transferred their support to Hyrcanus II. Aristobulus considered fighting the Romans, but, realizing the overwhelming might of Rome and the hopelessness of his situation, he surrendered in 63 B.C.E. to the Roman

*Kenneth Atkinson, "The Salome No One Knows," *BAR*, July/August 2008.

general Pompey. The supporters of Hyrcanus opened the city of Jerusalem to the Romans.

But that was not the end of the battle for Jerusalem. Although the city was in Roman hands, many of Aristobulus's supporters garrisoned themselves in the Temple and refused to surrender. After a three-month siege and some fearsome fighting, however, the Temple fell to Pompey's legions (63 B.C.E.).

To punish the Jews for refusing to yield peacefully to Roman dominion, Pompey greatly reduced the territory under Jewish jurisdiction. The empire the Hasmoneans had created through war and struggle (let us not be misled by the word empire—the Hasmonean state at its grandest was about the size of the state of Pennsylvania) was dismembered at a single stroke. The high priest of Jerusalem now ruled only those areas populated by a heavy concentration of Jews, primarily Judea (the district around Jerusalem) and Galilee. Although these Jewish areas were not legally incorporated into the Roman Empire, they were now *de facto* under Roman rule.[2]

Pompey takes Jerusalem

Pompey's conquest of Jerusalem closed one chapter in Roman-Jewish relations and opened another. A hundred years earlier, Judah the Maccabee had sought and obtained an alliance with the Romans, who were just then becoming the dominant power in the eastern Mediterranean. At that time, the Romans eagerly supported anyone who would help them weaken the power of the Seleucid kings of Syria. Judah's successors followed the same strategy of seeking Roman support in their struggles for independence from the Seleucids.

Gradually, Rome's power grew; her policy in the region, however, never wavered: Any power that might pose a threat to Roman interests was to be weakened. When the Jews were a useful ally against the Seleucids, they were embraced. When the Hasmonean state expanded, the Romans had no desire to see it become, in turn, a new threat to Roman interests. By the middle of the first century B.C.E., when the Romans at long last decided that the time had come to incorporate the eastern Mediterranean into their empire, the Jews were no longer allies but just another ethnic group that was to be brought into the inchoate imperial system.[3]

Although the struggle for succession between Hyrcanus II and Aristobulus II and their appeals for Roman support provided the occasion for the Roman takeover of the Hasmonean state, we may be sure that in one way or another the Romans would have found a satisfactory excuse to exercise hegemony over the Jewish state.

The three decades (63–31 B.C.E.) following Pompey's conquest of

Jerusalem were extremely turbulent, not only for the Jews of Judea but for the entire Roman world, especially in the East. This was the period of the decline of the Roman republic, of the struggle between Julius Caesar and Pompey, of Pompey's death and Caesar's ascension to sole power, of Caesar's assassination (on March 15, 44 B.C.E.), and of the struggle between the senate and Caesar's supporters and later between Octavian (Augustus) and Mark Antony. The dust did not settle until the sea battle of Actium in Greece (31 B.C.E.), where Octavian defeated Mark Antony and became the sole ruler of the Roman Empire. During the 20s B.C.E. Octavian consolidated his power and assumed the name "Augustus." He established a pattern of imperial administration that would endure for centuries.

As the Romans were changing their mode of government, so were the Jews. Under the Persian and the Hellenistic monarchies, the Jews had been led by high priests who wielded political as well as religious power. However, during the initial period of Roman rule after Pompey's conquest of Jerusalem, the high priesthood lost virtually all its temporal powers and a new royal dynasty emerged that was not of priestly stock. Its opponents claimed that it was not even wholly Jewish! The Romans, for their part, were delighted to install a dynasty that owed its very existence to Roman favor and therefore could be counted on to provide loyal support.

The rise of the Herodian dynasty

This new dynasty, usually called the Herodian dynasty after its most famous member, was founded by Herod's father, Antipater the Idumean. The Idumeans, who lived in the area south of Judea, had been incorporated into the Hasmonean empire and converted to Judaism by John Hyrcanus (Hyrcanus I). Antipater gradually insinuated himself into the circle of Hyrcanus II. When Julius Caesar came to Syria in 47 B.C.E., he conferred various benefits on the Jews. Hyrcanus II was appointed *ethnarch* (literally, "ruler of the nation"), and Antipater the Idumean was appointed *procurator* (literally, "caretaker").

A rival soon assassinated Antipater, and his mantle then fell to his son Herod. In 40 B.C.E. the Parthians invaded Syria, captured Hyrcanus II and installed the son of Aristobulus II as king and high priest of the Jews. Herod, now the Roman procurator, fled to Rome and persuaded the senate that only he could restore Roman rule in Judea. With Roman support Herod returned to Judea and, after some severe fighting, reconquered Jerusalem in 37 B.C.E. Herod remained the undisputed leader of the Jews for over 30 years (37–4 B.C.E.).

The reliability of Josephus

The vast bulk of what we know about this period derives from the testimony of an ancient Jewish historian, Flavius Josephus. Josephus was a complicated man, and his writings are not always easy to work with. As one scholar notes, "Sometimes the historian working with Flavius Josephus feels like a lawyer forced to build his case in court upon the testimony of a felon. While there may be some truth in what the witness says, the problem always is to separate it from self-serving obfuscation and outright lies."[4] Because so much rests on Josephus's testimony, it is worthwhile to review certain aspects of his life and his works.

Josephus was a Jewish leader in the First Jewish Revolt (66–70 C.E.) who, in the end, surrendered to the Romans. In 67 C.E. Josephus was the commander of the Jewish revolutionary forces in Galilee. When the Romans arrived, Josephus and his forces fled to the fortress of Jotapata. After a siege of 47 days, the fortress was taken, and Josephus and some of his men took refuge in a nearby cave. When the Romans discovered them, Josephus's companions argued that they should commit mutual suicide rather than be taken prisoners. But Josephus, remembering the "nightly dreams in which God had foretold to him the impending fate of the Jews and the destinies of the Roman sovereigns," realized that God was on the side of the Romans and that surrender to the Romans was the only legitimate course of action. Since his comrades insisted on suicide, Josephus reluctantly agreed to draw lots with the rest, but as luck would have it, he drew one of the last. After the others had killed themselves, Josephus was left with only one companion and had no trouble convincing him that surrender was a wiser course than death. Upon emerging from the cave Josephus was taken to Vespasian; he predicted that the general would become emperor of Rome, the master of land, sea and the entire human race—a prediction that subsequently proved accurate. Josephus's account of his surrender to the Romans is clearly a mixture of history, fantasy, apology and propaganda.[5]

After the Roman destruction of Jerusalem, Josephus was taken to Rome in the entourage of the Roman general Titus, Vespasian's son. With his newly acquired Roman patrons looking over his shoulder, Josephus wrote his account of the rebellion, *The Jewish War*, completing it in the early 80s C.E.

He wrote it originally in Aramaic, later translating the text into Greek; only the Greek version has survived. Josephus intended *The Jewish War* for an Aramaic-speaking audience, mostly Jews but also other Near Eastern peoples who were under—or on the verge of coming under—Roman domination. The book carries a dual message. To those who might contemplate revolt against Rome, *The Jewish War* advises "don't." Revolt against Rome is both impious and doomed to failure. To the Romans, the message is that the revolt was the work of various hotheads, fanatics and criminals within the Jewish community who in no way represented either Judaism or the Jews and who fomented rebellion for their own selfish and ignoble purposes. Josephus begins this book with the story of the Maccabean uprising (165 B.C.E.). The Maccabean victory established the Hasmonean dynasty, whose internal disputes led to Pompey's entry into Jerusalem, which, in turn, set in motion the chain of events that led to the revolt of 66 C.E. *The Jewish War* ends with a vivid account of the fall of the last Jewish rebels at Masada.

About a decade later, Josephus finished his second work, *Jewish Antiquities*. This is a much more ambitious project, written in Greek and intended to present the entire scope of Jewish history to a Roman audience. *Jewish Antiquities* begins with the biblical account of creation and ends on the eve of the Jewish revolt. Hence, it overlaps with much of the material from *The Jewish War*. Written at a time when the war was less immediate and political fortunes in both Rome and Judea had dramatically shifted, *Jewish Antiquities* is far more nuanced than *The Jewish War*. Shortly after publishing *Jewish Antiquities*, Josephus went on to write two more tracts: *Life*, an autobiography that responds to charges of betrayal (true or not, we do not know) by a rival Jewish historian, and *Against Apion*, an apologetic tract.

Political considerations, self-justification and apologetic tendencies are not the only factors that make Josephus difficult to use. Like most ancient historians, Josephus was a plagiarist. He freely appropriated the work of others, often without letting his readers know his sources. These sources themselves are often biased. His primary source for his discussion of Herod, for example, was the writing of Nicolaus of Damascus, Herod's "official," thus hardly unbiased, historian.

Bearing Josephus's limitations in mind, let us return to Herod.

Herod the Great

Herod is an enigmatic figure.[6] A tyrant, a madman, a murderer, a builder of great cities and fortresses, a wily politician, a successful king, a Jew, a half-Jew, a gentile—Herod was all these and more. He is perhaps best known to posterity as the murderer of several of his wives, children and other relations. The murders were prompted by Herod's suspicions (often justified) of anyone who had an equal or better claim to the throne than he. In the first years of his reign, Herod executed the surviving members of the Hasmonean aristocracy. Since he was married to Mariamme, the daughter of the Hasmonean king Hyrcanus II, Herod thus murdered his own wife's relatives—her brother, her aunt and her father. Finally, he murdered Mariamme too. At the end of his reign, he executed the two sons Mariamme had borne him.

Herod also executed various other wives, sons and close relations. The Christian tradition of Herod's "massacre of the innocents" (Matthew 2) is based on his unpleasant habit of killing anyone associated with the old aristocracy, including many teachers and religious leaders, but is otherwise of dubious historicity.

Herod created a new aristocracy that owed its status and prestige to him alone. He raised to the high priesthood men from families that had never previously supplied high priests, including families from the Diaspora (the Jewish communities outside the land of Israel).

Herod was also a great builder. Many of the most popular tourist sites in Israel today were Herod's projects—Masada, Herodium, Caesarea and many of the most conspicuous remains of ancient Jerusalem, including the so-called Tower of David, the Western Wall and much of the Temple Mount (see "Herod's Temple Mount Meets the Fury of Rome," opposite page). As a result of Herod's works, Jerusalem became "one of the most famous cities of the east"[7] and its Temple, which he rebuilt, was widely admired. In the new city of Caesarea, Herod created a magnificent harbor, using the latest technology in hydraulic cement and underwater construction. Herod also founded several other cities, notably Sebaste (on the site of ancient Samaria). He bestowed gifts and benefactions on cities and enterprises outside his own kingdom. Athens, Sparta, Rhodes and the Olympic games all enjoyed Herod's largesse.

Herod's building program had several purposes.[8] A network of fortresses (Masada, Herodium, Alexandrium, Hyrcania, Machaerus) was designed to provide refuge to Herod and his family in the event of insurrection. Herod rebuilt Jerusalem and the Temple so that his kingdom would have a capital city worthy of his dignity and grandeur and so that he would win the support of the Jews both in the land of Israel and in the Diaspora. Herod built Sebaste and other pagan cities (even Caesarea was a joint Jewish-pagan city) because he saw himself as the king not only of the Jews but also of the country's substantial pagan population. And last, but not least, the benefactions to the cities of the eastern Mediterranean were prompted by Herod's megalomania. Throughout his life Herod was hungry for power and prestige. He wanted desperately to be recognized as an important personage. He obtained that recognition through his lavish gifts. Even the city of Athens honored him with a public inscription.

Herod tried to win support and recognition from both Jews and pagans, both within his kingdom and outside of it. The support of these groups, however, would have meant nothing if Herod had not been supported by Rome. In 37 B.C.E., as we have seen, the Romans made Herod the leader of

Herod's Temple Mount Meets the Fury of Rome

Among the many architectural marvels that Herod built in Jerusalem was the magnificent Royal Stoa, an expansive colonnaded basilica that extended across the southern end of the Temple Mount. The basilica included four long rows of towering Corinthian columns that created three majestic halls, the central one with an especially high roof. On the Temple Mount side, the stoa was unwalled, providing a view of the Temple itself in the center of the mount. The structure's grandeur was apparently so awe-inspiring that the Jewish historian Josephus thought the Royal Stoa "more worthy of description than any other under the sun."

When the Romans burned Jerusalem's Temple Mount in 70 C.E., marble architectural fragments from Herod's Royal Stoa fell to the street below. As reported by archaeologist Orit-Peleg Barkat and geologist Aryeh Shimron in the pages of *BAR* ("New Evidence of the Royal Stoa and Roman Flames," March/April 2010), hundreds of limestone fragments from the stoa, many beautifully preserved and decorated with floral and geometric motifs, were uncovered by Professor Benjamin Mazar during his excavations along the southern wall of the Temple Mount. These elegantly crafted architectural elements, which include column bases and drums, Corinthian capitals, Doric friezes and modillion cornices, provide archaeological confirmation of the Royal Stoa's magnificence as described by Josephus.

But as Shimron explains, the recovered pieces from the Royal Stoa also help tell the story of Rome's destruction of the Temple Mount. Many of the marble fragments were covered with a fine white crust, originally thought to be a layer of decorative plaster. The crust, however, is not plaster, but rather the mineralogical residue left on the marble from an intense conflagration whose flames often exceeded a thousand degrees centigrade. —***Ed.***

Judea. In the struggle that developed soon thereafter between Antony and Octavian, Herod supported Mark Antony. This was perhaps because Antony was headquartered in the East. But, as noted above, at the battle of Actium in 31 B.C.E., Octavian defeated Antony, and the entire eastern Mediterranean, including Egypt, came into the hands of Octavian.

Herod had supported the losing side. He was obviously in deep trouble. But, ever the survivor, Herod managed to convince Octavian that everyone's best interests would be served if he remained king of Judea. He had been loyal to Antony, Herod argued, and now would be loyal to Octavian. Octavian accepted Herod's argument and never had cause to regret his decision. Herod was true to his word, and during the course of his long reign was rewarded several times by the emperor (now called Augustus) with grants of additional territory.

Like all other vassal kings subservient to the Romans, Herod was authorized to govern his subjects as he pleased as long as he maintained peace and stability, did not engage in any unauthorized activities outside his kingdom and actively supported Roman administrative and military activities in the area. Herod knew his place and followed these rules. At home he was the tyrant, but in his dealings with the Romans he was ever the dutiful subject. Before engaging in any major enterprise (killing his sons, for example), he consulted the Roman governor of Syria or even the emperor himself.

Herod's popularity during his own lifetime is hard to assess. Our major evidence, indeed virtually our only evidence, is provided by Josephus. His two books give somewhat varying appraisals. In the earlier work, *The Jewish War*, Josephus paints a portrait of Herod that is basically favorable: a brilliant and successful king who was plagued by personal disaster and calamity. Nevertheless, even here Josephus reports Herod's madness and the fact that he was widely hated. It is in *The Jewish War* that Josephus tells the (true?) story that Herod, fearing that his funeral would be an occasion for rejoicing among the Jews, planned to ensure general mourning by ordering that the distinguished men of the country be assembled and killed upon the news of his death. Nevertheless, as a rule, *The Jewish War* treats the king kindly and regards him as unfortunate rather than mad, and as powerful rather than unpopular. This is probably due both to the biases of Josephus's primary source, Nicolaus of Damascus. Here is the final verdict:

> In his life as a whole he was blessed, if ever man was, by fortune; a
> commoner, he mounted to a throne, retained it for all those years
> and bequeathed it to his own children; in his family life, on the
> contrary, no man was more unfortunate.[9]

Although *Jewish Antiquities*, completed in 93/94 C.E., repeats this verdict in almost identical words,[10] its perspective is somewhat different. *Jewish Antiquities* includes much more material unfavorable to Herod. *The Jewish War* either deemphasizes this unfavorable material or omits it altogether.

According to *Jewish Antiquities*, Herod maintained his rule through terror and brutality. His secret police were everywhere and reported to the king any murmurings of discontent. Many citizens were taken to Hyrcania, one of Herod's fortresses, never to be seen again. Herod is even supposed to have prohibited his subjects from assembling in public. These security measures were required because of the general dislike for Herod among the Jews.

Jewish Antiquities broadly recounts two major complaints the Jews had against Herod, aside from his violence and brutality. First was his violation of traditional Jewish laws. He built a theater (for plays) and an amphitheater (for gladiatorial games) in Jerusalem (neither has yet been discovered by archaeologists, although some stone bleachers and a ticket in the form of an inscribed bone disk are presumed to have come from the theater*) where he staged forms of entertainment that were foreign to Judaism and inimical to many Jews. He built pagan cities and temples, and seemed to favor the pagan and Samaritan elements in the population over the Jews. Furthermore, many of his judicial and administrative rulings were not in accordance with Jewish law. Certain elements in the population were offended at his introduction of Roman trophies into the Jerusalem Temple and his erection of a golden eagle over its entrance.

The second reason for the general dislike of Herod was his oppressive taxation. Someone had to pay for Herod's munificent benefactions to the cities of the East, generous gifts to the Romans and extravagant building projects at home. The Jewish citizens of Herod's kingdom had to foot the bill, and they objected.

But if *Jewish Antiquities* condemns Herod in these respects, it also reflects a certain ambivalence. It includes pro-Herodian material as well. Even if in his private life Herod did not follow the traditional Jewish observances (for example, Jewish law does not approve of the murder of one's wife and children), in his public life he often took care not to cause offense. He built no pagan temples or cities in the Jewish areas of the country, and he ordered that only priests were to work on the construction of the sacred precincts of the Temple in Jerusalem. Coins he intended for use in Jewish areas of the country were struck without images. Foreign princes who wished to marry

---

*Ronny Reich and Ya'akov Billig, "Triple Play: The Many Lives of Jerusalem's Building Blocks," *BAR*, September/October 2002.

a woman of the Herodian house had to be circumcised first. Moreover, it is in *Jewish Antiquities* that we find reports of several reductions in taxes. Here, too, Josephus notes that Herod was conspicuously generous in the distribution of food to the people during a famine.

Because of the bad press Herod has received, both in Josephus and in the New Testament, he is occasionally vilified by contemporary scholars as a "malevolent maniac" or worse, but he is too complex a figure to be dismissed so easily. As we have seen, even in *Jewish Antiquities*, which is the major source of anti-Herodian material, we find a more nuanced picture. Herod aimed to be both king of the Jews and king of Judea; he benefited the Jews both of the land of Israel and of the Diaspora. But he never forgot that his kingdom consisted of other groups as well.

Perhaps Herod's policy was dictated by the fact that he himself was the offspring of one of these groups, the Idumeans, who had been converted to Judaism only three generations earlier. Herod's court historian, Nicolaus of Damascus, claimed that Herod was a scion of one of Judea's noblest families, which had returned from Babylonia in the time of the Persians; but Herod's detractors called him a "half-Jew," or even a gentile, because of his Idumean extraction.[11] His marginal status in the native Jewish community perhaps explains his eagerness to solicit the support of the Samaritans and the gentiles of the country. Herod was also an astute politician who never forgot that the key to his success lay in the hands of the Romans. Above all else, he was resilient and resourceful. Protected by his paranoia, he succeeded in reigning 33 years in a period of tremendous upheaval and instability.

From Herod's death to the First Jewish Revolt

Herod's death in 4 B.C.E. released the accumulated passions and frustrations of the people which had been kept in check by his brutality. As Herod lay on his deathbed, two pious men and their followers removed the golden eagle that Herod had erected over the entrance to the Temple and hacked the bird to pieces. Immediately after Herod's death, riots and rebellions broke out in Jerusalem, Judea, Galilee and Transjordan (Peraea). The leaders of the riots had diverse goals. Some were simply venting their anger at a hated and feared regime; others were eager to profit from a period of chaos and disorder; still others dreamed of ridding themselves of Roman rule and proclaiming themselves king.

These riots illustrate the underside of Herodian rule. Herod's high taxes and extravagant spending caused, or at least accelerated, the impoverishment of broad sections of the population. A clear sign of social distress was the resurgence of brigands—landless men who marauded the countryside in groups and were either hailed by the peasants as heroes (like Robin Hood) or hunted as villains. Brigandage had surfaced earlier, decades after Pompey's conquest in 63 B.C.E. Although Pompey himself had respected the Temple and the property of the Jews, the governors he left behind (Gabinius and Crassus) did not. They engaged in robbery and pillage; Crassus even plundered the Temple. Perhaps as a result of these depredations Galilee was almost overrun by brigands. In 47/46 B.C.E. Herod routed and suppressed the brigands. Several years later, they resurfaced and Herod again suppressed them. Brigandage reemerged in the years after Herod's death, especially, as we shall see below, in the period from 44 C.E. to the outbreak of the Jewish rebellion against Rome in 66 C.E. The impoverishment of the country and its consequent social distress were an unfortunate legacy of Herod the Great.[12]

Roman-Jewish relations

During the first half of the first century C.E., the Romans used vassal kings to govern those areas of the eastern empire that, like Judea, were neither urbanized nor greatly "Hellenized" but were home to vigorous national cultures. Administration through a vassal king, a native aristocrat who could understand the peculiar ways of the population, was thought preferable to direct Roman rule. Thus, throughout the Roman East, native dynasts governed their territories in accordance with the wishes of the Romans. In accordance with this policy, after Herod's death, his kingdom was divided among three of his sons. Antipas received Galilee and Peraea; Philip, the Golan Heights and points east. Archelaus became ruler of the largest and most important part of Herod's kingdom—Judea. In 6 C.E., however, the Romans deposed Archelaus for misrule, and Judea, along with Idumaea, Samaria and much of the Mediterranean coast, was annexed to the province of Syria. Henceforth Judea was administered by functionaries in the Roman civil service known as *prefects* or (after 44 C.E.) *procurators*. The rest of the country remained in the hands of Antipas and Philip for another 30 years, but then became the domain of Herod's grandson Agrippa I. In 41 C.E. Agrippa I received from the emperor Claudius the kingship over Judea as well, thereby reigning over a kingdom almost as large as Herod's own. Agrippa I died, however, only three years later, in 44 C.E.

After Agrippa's death, all of the Jewish portions of the country were governed by Roman procurators. For a few years, from the middle of the century until the end of the First Jewish Revolt in 70 C.E., a small piece of Galilee was given to Agrippa's son, known as Agrippa II, but otherwise, an overall change in Roman policy and administration was unmistakable. At the beginning of the first century, the land of Israel was governed by vassal rulers—men like Herod and his sons; by the middle of the century it was governed by Roman procurators (with the exception of Agrippa II). This same shift can be found elsewhere in the Roman East.[13]

Judea, on the other hand, was governed by Roman prefects from 6 C.E. Of the six or seven Roman prefects who governed Judea following Archelaus's deposition, most are bare names to us. Even Josephus has little to say about them. The exception is the Roman prefect Pontius Pilate (c. 26 to 36 C.E.).[14] Pilate receives a negative assessment in the Gospels, in Philo, as well as in Josephus. According to the Gospels, Pilate massacred a group of Galileans (Luke 13:1) and brutally suppressed a rebellion (Mark 15:7), quite aside from crucifying Jesus. According to Philo, Pilate introduced into Herod's former palace in Jerusalem some golden shields inscribed with the name of the emperor Tiberius. The Jews objected strenuously, because they felt that any object associated with emperor worship, not to mention emperor worship itself, was idolatrous and an offense to Judaism. Previous Roman governors had respected Jewish sensitivities in this matter, but Pilate did not. After being petitioned by the Jews, the emperor ordered Pilate to remove the shields from Jerusalem and to deposit them in the temple of Augustus in Caesarea, a mixed Jewish-pagan city. Josephus narrates a similar incident (or perhaps a different version of the same incident) involving the importation of military standards (which of course contained images) into Jerusalem. The people protested loudly, saying they would rather die than see the ancestral law violated. Pilate relented and ordered the images to be removed. Ultimately, Pilate was removed from office when the Jews complained to his superiors.

When a procurator like Pilate was brutal or corrupt, the Jews could appeal to the governor of Syria or even to the emperor himself to remove the malefactor. But when the emperor was responsible for actions that were deleterious to the Jewish community, the Jews had nowhere to turn. This was the dilemma that confronted the Jews of both Alexandria and the land of Israel during the reign of the emperor Caligula (37–41 C.E.).

The Romans realized that Judaism was unlike the numerous other native religions of the empire; the Jews refused to worship any god but their own, refused to acknowledge the emperor's right to divine honors, refused to tolerate images in public places and buildings, and refused to perform any sort of work every seventh day. Aware of these peculiarities, the Romans, following the practice of the Seleucids, permitted Jewish citizens to refrain from participation in pagan ceremonies; allowed priests of the Jerusalem Temple to offer sacrifices on behalf of, rather than to, the emperor; minted coins in Judea without images (even if many of the coins that circulated in the country were minted elsewhere and bore images); and exempted the Jews from military service and ensured that they would not be called to court on the Sabbath or lose any official benefits as a result of their Sabbath observances. In many cities of the East, the Romans authorized the Jews to create *politeumata* (singular, *politeuma*), autonomous ethnic communities, that allowed the Jews to govern their own communal affairs.[15]

Riots in Alexandria

The mad emperor Caligula and his legate in Egypt withdrew, or attempted to withdraw, these rights and privileges. Riots erupted first in Alexandria—the "Greeks" (that is, the Greek-speaking population of the city, most of whom were not "Greek" at all) against the Jews. Exactly who or what started the riots is not clear. The root cause of the conflict, however, was the ambiguous status of the city's Jews. On the one hand, the Alexandrians resented the Jewish *politeuma* and regarded it as a diminution of the prestige and autonomy of their own city. On the other hand, the Jews thought that membership in their own *politeuma* should confer on them the same rights and privileges the citizens of the city had. The result of these conflicting claims was bloodshed and destruction. Aided by the Roman governor of Egypt, the Greeks attacked the Jews, pillaged Jewish property, desecrated or destroyed Jewish synagogues and herded the Jews into a "ghetto." The Jews were hardly passive during these events, and resisted both militarily and diplomatically. The most distinguished Jew of the city, the philosopher Philo, led a delegation to the emperor to argue the Jewish cause.

While in Rome, Philo learned of another, even more serious, assault on Judaism by the state. Angered by the Jews' refusal to accord him divine honors, Caligula ordered the governor of Syria to erect a colossal statue of the emperor in the Temple of Jerusalem. Whether something more than coincidence ties together the anti-Jewish riots in Alexandria with Caligula's assault on the Temple is not clear, especially because of some uncertainty in the relative chronology of the two sets of events.[16] In any case, the rights of the Jews of Alexandria and the sanctity of the Temple in Jerusalem were threatened simultaneously. The Roman governor of Syria, Publius Petronius, realizing that the execution of Caligula's order to erect his statue in the Temple could not be accomplished without riots and loss of life, procrastinated. In a letter to Caligula, Petronius explained that the matter should be delayed because otherwise it would interfere with the harvest; in a second letter, he asked the emperor to rescind his order outright. In the meantime, Agrippa II, who was a friend of Caligula's, convinced the emperor to rescind his demand. Caligula did so but was angered when he received Petronius's second letter, which indicated that Petronius had no intention of following the imperial order. In reply, Caligula ordered Petronius to commit suicide. Petronius received this ultimatum, however, only after he learned that Caligula had been assassinated. This brought to an end the potential troubles in the land of Israel. The troubles in Alexandria were settled by Claudius, Caligula's successor, who ordered both the Jews and the Greeks to return to the status quo: The Jews were to maintain their *politeuma,* but were not to ask for more rights than was their due.

Perhaps one of the most significant aspects of these events was the refusal of the Jews even to consider rebellion against the empire. In Alexandria, the Jews took up arms only in self-defense and only with reluctance—at least this is what Philo tells us. The Jews directed their fighting against their enemies, not against the emperor or the Roman Empire. In the land of Israel itself, when Caligula's edict to erect a statue of himself in the Temple became known, the Jews assembled before Petronius *en masse* and declared that he would have to kill every one of them before they would allow the Temple to be desecrated. But the Jews did not threaten rebellion. Instead, in anticipation of Mahatma Gandhi in India in the 20th century, they offered passive resistance. Because Petronius was an ethical man with a conscience, he was convinced by these mass demonstrations not to carry out his assignment. Even a governor with less moral fiber might have been persuaded by these tactics: Pontius Pilate removed the golden shields from Jerusalem after the Jews protested, declaring that they would rather be killed than allow the images to remain in the Temple. At no point in either story do "brigands" or revolutionaries make an appearance.

Agrippa I
Despite the success of this policy of passive resistance, the years after Caligula's reign saw the growth of violent resistance to Roman rule. Caligula's madness seems to have driven home the point that the beneficence of Roman rule was not secure, and that the only way to ensure the safety and sanctity of the Temple was to expel the Romans from the country and to remove those Jews who actively supported them.

This process might have been prevented had Agrippa I been blessed with as long a reign as his grandfather, Herod the Great. Had he lived as long as his grandfather, he would have reigned until approximately 63 C.E. Instead, Agrippa I ruled for only three years (41–44 C.E.).[17] Despite his short reign, he was a popular king; both Josephus and rabbinic literature have only nice things to say about him. In some respects he resembled his grandfather. He was a wily and able politician. He sponsored pagan games at Caesarea and

ZEV RADOVAN/WWW.BIBLELANDPICTURES.COM

Synagogue at Herodium. *During the First Jewish Revolt against Rome (66–70 C.E.), the reception and dining hall of Herod the Great's former palace-fortress Herodium was transformed into a synagogue. Benches were added around the walls and four columns supported a new roof.*

In Hellenistic times, worship at the Jerusalem Temple was complemented by regular prayer and the study of scripture in synagogues. Following the Roman destruction of the Temple in Jerusalem in 70 C.E., synagogues became the center of Jewish religious life.

bestowed magnificent gifts on Beirut, a pagan city. But, unlike Herod, he was not criticized for these donations, for in other respects he was Herod's superior. He lacked Herod's brutality. Whereas Herod refrained from flouting traditional Jewish laws in the Jewish areas of his domain, Agrippa was conspicuous for observing them. In the political sphere, he tried to attain a modest degree of independence from Rome. He even began the construction of a new wall on the northern side of Jerusalem; had it been completed, Josephus says, the city would have been impregnable during the Jewish revolt that erupted in 66 C.E.

Had Agrippa reigned a long time, perhaps the disaffected elements in Judea would have been reconciled again to foreign dominion. On Agrippa's death in 44 C.E., however, Judea once again became the domain of the Roman procurators. There was no longer a Jewish authority who, despite ultimate subservience to Rome, could satisfy Jewish nationalist aspirations.

Moreover, the procurators after 44 C.E. were incompetent and insensitive at best, corrupt and wicked at worst. A country that, even in the face of Caligula's assault on its religious sensitivities, had maintained peace was brought to rebellion after little more than 20 years of rule by the Roman procurators who followed Agrippa I. Josephus narrates a long string of minor incidents, disturbances, riots, assassinations and lootings, which, in retrospect, were forerunners of the Great Revolt against Rome. The participants in these incidents probably never realized that they were preparing the way for war. Nevertheless, various elements in the population were expressing their frustrations with the status quo, and the procurators were using the power of their office for fun and profit.

In the fall of 66 C.E., after Gessius Florus (who would be the last of the procurators) had stolen money from the Temple treasury (for overdue taxes, he claimed), a particularly violent riot led to the massacre of the Roman garrison in Jerusalem. The governor of Syria intervened, but even he failed to restore the peace. He was forced to withdraw from Jerusalem, suffering a major defeat. The Jews of Judea, it turns out, had rebelled against the Roman Empire.

Before recounting the story of this rebellion and its disastrous consequences, let us pause to look at the social and religious texture of Judea in the first century C.E.

Variegated Judaism

Judaism at the time was a remarkably variegated phenomenon.[18] Above all, Judaism was a belief in the God of Moses, who created the world, who chose the Jews to be his special people and who rewarded and punished his people in accordance with their loyalty to him. Judaism was also the practice of the laws and rituals that Moses had commanded in God's name, most conspicuously the rituals of circumcision, Sabbath and prohibited foods. The Jews vigorously debated among themselves the precise meaning and content of their beliefs and practices, but all, or almost all, were in agreement over the general outlines.

Judaism during this period was different from, or at least not identical to, the religion of pre-Exilic Israel.[19] Judaism in this period was a "book religion"; at its center was the recitation and study of a collection of sacred writings, the most important of which was the Torah ("Instruction") of Moses. By this time, many Jews had added two other categories of sacred literature to the Torah: the Prophets and the Writings. These three groups of writings together constitute the Bible, called the Old Testament by Christians and the Tanakh[20] by Jews. Pre-Exilic Israel, by contrast, did not have such a sacred book; to be sure, it preserved in written form many sacred traditions, but it was not a "book religion." Pre-Exilic Israelites communicated and communed with God through the sacrificial cult in the Jerusalem Temple and through the revelations of the prophets. By Hellenistic times, however, and certainly by the first century of our era, the institutional access to God through the Temple and the charismatic access to God through the prophets were being supplemented, and to some degree supplanted, by new forms of piety, especially regular prayer and study of scripture.

The institutional home of this new piety was the *synagogue* ("assembly" or "gathering") or *proseuche* ("prayer-house"), which is first attested in Egypt in the third century B.C.E. By the first century of our era, there were synagogues not only in many Diaspora communities but also in some towns and villages in the land of Israel. Archaeological remains of synagogues from this period have been discovered at Masada, Herodium, Gamla and various Diaspora sites.[21]

Pre-Exilic Israelite religion focused on the group, the community and the clan; first-century C.E. Judaism, by contrast, focused on the individual Jew. First-century Judaism enjoined the individual Jew to sanctify his (or her) life through the daily performance of numerous rituals. Sanctity was not restricted to the Temple; God's presence was everywhere, and the Jew was to be continually mindful of this fact. Every moment was an opportunity for the observance of the commandments, the sanctification of life and subservience to God. Not only were the people of Israel collectively responsible to God, but each individual Jew was as well. The cult of the Temple, therefore, was supplemented by a religious regimen that focused on the individual rather than the group.

Prophecy too no longer was what it had been. Many Jews believed that prophecy had ceased, or at least had so transformed itself that it no longer had the prestige and the authority it had commanded when the classical prophets like Isaiah and Jeremiah of the eighth and sixth centuries B.C.E. spoke. Those Jews who continued to see heavenly visions and hear heavenly voices no longer saw and heard them in the manner of their predecessors. The new literary genre, called by modern scholars *apocalypse* ("revelation"), assigned a much greater role to complex symbolic visions and angelic intermediaries than did biblical prophecy. Apocalyptic thinking was dominated by a sense that the world was in the throes of a final crisis that would be resolved by the immediate arrival of the end of time. Not only were the style and the atmosphere of apocalypse different from those of biblical prophecy, but much of its content was different as well. In pre-Exilic Israel, the Israelites believed that God rewarded the righteous and punished the wicked in this world, and did so by rewarding or punishing either the actor himself or his children. By the first century C.E., this doctrine had been rejected, and replaced by the idea that every individual received his or her just deserts from God either in this world or in the world to come. Elaborate theories were developed about the rewards and punishments that awaited people after death or at the end of time, or both. Then there would be a resurrection of the dead and a final judgment, and the nation of Israel, the plaything of gentile kingdoms in this world, would finally receive its due; God would send a redeemer, either a human being or an angel, who would restore Israel's sovereignty. The nations of the world would then recognize the Lord and accept the hegemony of the Jews. These new ideas were widely accepted in society, even though apocalyptic literature was so esoteric that it could be appreciated only by a few.

The new ideas, rituals and institutions that gradually emerged were adopted in their most extreme forms by various pietistic groups, but also had an impressive impact on broad reaches of the population. The evidence for "common Judaism,"[22] either in the land of Israel or the Diaspora, is far from complete, but the literary evidence of Josephus, Philo and the New Testament shows that "common Judaism" included the study of Scripture and the participation in synagogue services on the Sabbath; observance of the Sabbath, the dietary prohibitions and various other rituals; separation from pagans and anything connected with pagan religious ceremonies; and pilgrimages to the Temple in Jerusalem for the festivals. Many Jews of Jerusalem, rich and poor alike, believed in the ultimate resurrection of the dead. This is demonstrated by their practice of reburial. A year or so after depositing a corpse in a temporary grave, they would dig up the bones, carefully arrange them in a special box known as an ossuary and place the ossuary in a cave or some other safe location. Thus the dead would be ready for the resurrection; all the bones were united safely in one place, awaiting reassembly.[23] In the Diaspora, the most conspicuously observed rituals, to judge from the testimony of pagan writers, were circumcision, the Sabbath and the dietary prohibitions (notably the avoidance of pork).

Jewish society, at least in the land of Israel, also recognized the reality of the "magical" and the "miraculous." Magic brought divine activity into direct and immediate contact with humans. Teachers and holy men of all sorts roamed the countryside, preaching repentance and performing "miraculous" cures. Jesus spent much of his time exorcising demons and performing faith healings, but he was hardly unique in this respect. Holy men, who often modeled themselves to some extent on the prophet Elisha, answered the immediate needs of the populace, which was more concerned about good health and abundant harvests than about salvation and redemption.[24]

Temple Scroll. *One of the famed Dead Sea Scrolls, this text is named for its detailed plans for a temple—perhaps a visionary one—to be built in Jerusalem. Israeli archae-ologist Yigael Yadin, who published the scroll, believed that it was written by the Essenes, who considered it to be part of their Holy Scriptures, equal in authority to the Pentateuch.*

Pharisees, Sadducees and Essenes

Given the growing tensions and explosive mix of interests in first-century Judea, religious ferment is not particularly surprising. The major Jewish "schools"—the Pharisees, Sadducees and Essenes described by Josephus—continued through the Roman period. In addition to these groups, however, several new groups emerged in the first century C.E.: the Sicarii, various other revolutionary groups and, of course, the Christians. (At this early stage of its existence, however, the latter is perhaps more accurately called "the Jesus movement," as its adherents became known as "Christians" only in subsequent decades.) Josephus gives the impression that the countryside teemed with teachers and holy men. The diversity of religious movements within Judaism was a sign, and symptom, of the breakdown of social and religious order.

Apocalyptic expectations accompanied the increasing number of varieties of Judaism and the authority assumed by charismatic figures. Some of these new groups were revolutionary apocalypticists, who believed that their activities would usher in the new age. Josephus, for example, tells the story of an Egyptian "prophet" who convinced a large crowd to ascend the Mount of Olives, "for he asserted that he wished to demonstrate from there that at his command Jerusalem's walls would fall down, through which he promised to provide them an entrance into the city."[25] The Roman procurator correctly perceived this as a challenge to his authority, and promptly had the crowd imprisoned and/or slaughtered. A group that Josephus calls the "fourth philosophy," probably to be identified with the Sicarii, believed that God was Israel's only king; this served as justification for active opposition to Rome and those Jews who collaborated with Rome. These groups fused their apocalyptic beliefs to their political activities. By opposing Rome they were doing God's will, reforming Judaism in accordance with their view of the divine plan.

Other Jewish apocalyptic groups were isolationist. These groups believed no less than the active ones that the end of time was imminent. But they rejected the idea that human activity would bring it about. The Essenes and Therapeutae fall into this category. As described by classical authors, the Essenes organized themselves in a strict hierarchy and lived a life of purity and Torah study while they waited for the new age. Philo describes the Therapeutae—located in Egypt—in similar terms. Our sources do not tell us when or why these voluntary groups formed.[26]

The scrolls found at the settlement at Qumran (the Dead Sea Scrolls), whether or not they were written by the Essenes or any other group known to us from our sources, reveal both the growing apocalyptic mood and the tendency toward isolationism.[27] Although this group established itself before the Romans entered Judea, as time went on the group developed strikingly harsh and apocalyptic concepts. From its beginnings as a group concerned with the impurity of the Temple and the legitimacy of its priests, the Qumran community metamorphosed into the "sons of light" who eagerly anticipated—albeit in the utopian future—their ultimate bloody triumph over the "sons of darkness." For those at Qumran, the "sons of darkness" included not only the Romans but also, and perhaps primarily, those other Jews who did not adhere to the group's legal interpretations. In the meantime, they too organized themselves as a tightly knit, hierarchical community that waited in purity for the end of days in their isolated settlement on the western bank of the Dead Sea.[28]

At some point in the first century C.E., the Pharisees gained the upper hand over these various groups. Writing on the major Jewish "schools," Josephus says:

[The Pharisees are] extremely influential among the townsfolk; and all prayers and sacred rites of divine worship are performed according to their exposition. This is the great tribute that the inhabitants of the cities ... have paid to the excellence of the Pharisees.

There are but few men to whom this doctrine has been made known, but these [the Sadducees] are men of the highest standing. They accomplish practically nothing, however. For whenever they assume some office, though they submit unwillingly and perforce, yet submit they do to the formulas of the Pharisees, since otherwise the masses would not tolerate them.

[The Essenes] send votive offerings to the Temple, but perform their sacrifices employing a different ritual of purification. For this reason they are barred [alternative translation: they distance themselves] from those precincts of the Temple that are frequented by all the people and perform their rites by themselves ... The men who practice this way of life number more than four thousand.[29]

Thus, according to Josephus, the Pharisees had the support of the masses, especially the urban masses, while the Sadducees had the support of only the well-to-do. As a result, the Sadducees had to accept the dictates of the Pharisees and conduct all public rituals in accordance with Pharisaic rules. The Essenes, in contrast, distanced themselves from general society and from the Temple and were supported only by their own members, who numbered somewhat more than 4,000.

The characteristics and identity of the Pharisees have long exercised scholars. Were the Pharisees the leaders of Jewish society? Were all public rituals conducted in accordance with Pharisaic rulings? Was—or is—"Pharisaic Judaism" virtually synonymous with "Judaism"? The Gospel of Matthew (especially chapter 23) seems to indicate that they were the leaders of Jewish society and that public rituals were conducted in accordance with Pharisaic rulings. Josephus and rabbinic sources agree. Rabbinic sources, indeed, go further; according to them, the Pharisees provided the "norm" according to which other Jewish "deviations" were measured; in short, Pharisaic Judaism was, for the rabbis, synonymous with Judaism.

Matthew, Josephus and, to a lesser extent, the rabbis give the impression that the Pharisees were the "leading" Jewish group from at least the beginning of the first century C.E. But this impression might be misleading. Although Matthew, Josephus and rabbinic sources provide convergent testimony about the Pharisees, they were written after the destruction of the Temple and may reflect to some extent the conditions of that time—when the rabbis, the heirs of the Pharisees, were on the ascendant. Although in Matthew's field of vision the Pharisees loomed large, this may prove only that his Christian community in the 80s C.E. saw the Pharisees as their chief Jewish competitors; Matthew does not necessarily prove that Jesus and the disciples regarded the Pharisees as Matthew depicts them. Similarly, the testimony of Josephus proves only that in the 90s C.E., Josephus regarded the Pharisees as the most powerful Jewish group; Josephus's testimony does not necessarily prove that the Pharisees were powerful several generations earlier. (Of course, if it could be proven that Matthew and Josephus in their descriptions of the Pharisees were using sources that derived from the Second Temple period, their testimonies would have added weight.)[30]

Rabbinic literature, a third source, provides evidence consistent with Matthew and Josephus. However, the rabbis had a vested interest in presenting their ancestors as the group that controlled Jewish society, a position they themselves strived to attain in the centuries following the destruction of the Temple. Accordingly, we must view our sources on first-century Pharisaism with considerable caution, even skepticism.

Some modern scholars accept the primacy of the Pharisees as historical, but many others do not.[31] The main argument against the notion of Pharisaic primacy is the apparent absence of any strong central authority in ancient Judaism. Everywhere we look, once we get past the broad, commonly accepted beliefs and commonly practiced rituals which were outlined above, we see diversity. No one group and no one institution—neither the Pharisees, nor the high priests, nor the regular priests, nor the (mysterious) Sanhedrin, nor the (mysterious) scribes, nor the (mysterious) elders—seems to have been in charge. Not a single book of ancient Jewish literature can be attributed to a Pharisee, which is very odd if the Pharisees are everywhere and in charge. (However, it must be remembered that Paul and Josephus each claim to have lived their lives in obedience to the Law in the Pharisaic manner. But who is willing to consider Paul or Josephus as representative Pharisees?) When the war breaks out in 66 C.E., the Pharisees are barely to be found, and when they do make an appearance they are completely ineffectual in quieting the revolutionaries. In spite of the statements of Josephus, the Gospels and rabbinic literature, we have reason to question the reality of Pharisaic prominence.

Christians

Of all the Jewish groups that emerged in the first century C.E., the Christians are the most famous. Jesus, their leader, was a holy man and a teacher who, like many other such people, attracted admirers and disciples. Like many of his contemporaries, he apparently believed that the end time was imminent and that he was sent by God to prepare the way for its arrival. He therefore prophesied that the Jerusalem Temple would be removed because a new and more perfect temple would be erected by God as part of the new, perfect and permanent order of the end time. The high priests, however, regarded Jesus as a troublemaker and handed him over to the Romans for execution. In a paradoxical way, his death marked not the end but the beginning of Christianity (a development outside the purview of this book).

The earliest Christian community, as described by the Book of Acts, shares many features with the Jewish movements surveyed above. The group had a clear sense of its boundaries and a strong central organization. The apostles controlled the group, property was held in common, disbursements were made to the faithful from the common till, and disobedience to one's superiors was not tolerated (Acts 5:1–11). The group dined and prayed together. New members were "converted" through baptism and repentance (Acts 2:38–42). Like the Essenes, the Christians attempted to create a utopian community. A sense of alienation from the rest of society is apparent in the numerous calls for repentance and in the eschatological fervor of the group.

Although Christianity emerged in a Jewish context, as one among many first-century C.E. Jewish apocalyptic groups, by the end of the century it was clearly on its way to becoming a separate and distinctively unJewish society. Christianity's development of an independent identity was a process, however, not a single event. Several early Christian groups abolished circumcision and welcomed non-Jews. This change of ethnic composition alone was enough to make Christianity appear to its Jewish neighbors as something new. Religious innovations accompanied this "gentilization" of Christianity. Primary among these changes were the abrogation of food and Sabbath observances, and the elevation of Jesus to a theological position far higher and more significant than that of any angel or any other intermediary figure in Judaism. At this point, not only did the Jews see Christians as adherents of something distinct, but so did the Romans—and, as the Christian martyrs soon discovered, the Romans had a marked distaste for new religions. Curiously, while most Christians and Christian groups had ceased to identify themselves as Jews by the beginning of the second century C.E., several Christian groups continued to view themselves as Jewish over the next few hundred years. These groups would be rejected by Jews as "gentile" and by Christians as heretical.[32]

The Great Revolt

In 66 C.E. the Jews of Judea revolted against their Roman rulers. To this day, the reasons for the "Great Revolt," which ended in 70 C.E. with the destruction of the Second Temple, are not entirely clear. Josephus is, once again, our primary source. Despite his general unreliability, Josephus does provide enough information to piece together the array of causes that seem to have led to the revolt.

Chief among them were social ferment, Roman misadministration, revolutionary ardor and a leadership vacuum. As we have noted, brigandage, that unmistakable symptom of social distress, increased significantly in the countryside after Agrippa I's death in 44 C.E. Jerusalem too was racked by social turmoil. In the early 60s C.E., work on the Temple Mount, begun by Herod the Great many years earlier, was finally completed. Faced with the prospect of having 18,000 laborers added to the ranks of the unemployed, the priests suggested to Agrippa II that the porticoes be torn down so that they could be rebuilt! Agrippa II wisely remarked that it was easier to destroy than to build such edifices and suggested that the laborers devote their energies to repaving the streets. His suggestion was accepted. The laborers were paid for a full day of work even if they actually worked for only an hour. In short, the city of Jerusalem became, in effect, a welfare state, dependent on "make-work" projects for the maintenance of social peace.[33]

The wealthy, in contrast, lived their lives and buried their dead in opulence and splendor. Aristocrats in Jerusalem and throughout the country maintained bands of armed retainers to threaten their opponents and to work for their own interests. Within the priesthood there was strife, and sometimes violence, between the upper and the lower clergy. Peasants in Galilee in 66–67 C.E. wanted nothing more than to attack and loot Sepphoris, Tiberias and Gabara, the three largest settlements of the district. After the Great Revolt commenced in 66 C.E., many peasants of both Galilee and Judea fled to Jerusalem, where they turned on both the city aristocracy and the small, organized priestly elite. These tensions within Jewish society often surfaced violently during the Great Revolt. For many of the participants in the war, the primary enemies were not Roman but Jewish.[34]

According to Josephus, especially in *Jewish Antiquities*, the Roman procurators in the years leading up to the revolt went from bad to worse. Of all these corrupt and incompetent Roman administrators of Judea, none was worse than the last one, Gessius Florus. Albinus, himself an execrable procurator, is described by Josephus as a "paragon of virtue" when compared to Florus. Florus, according to Josephus, "ostentatiously paraded his outrages upon the nation, and, as though he had been sent as hangman of condemned criminals, abstained from no form of robbery or violence ... No man has ever poured greater contempt on truth; none invented more crafty methods of crime."³⁵ The Jews ultimately appealed to Florus's superior Celestius Gallus, the governor of Syria, for relief. Not only was the appeal unsuccessful, but it was soon followed by Florus's mishandling of ethnic tensions in Caesarea and then his plundering of the Temple treasury and slaughter of the Jews who sought to prevent him from desecrating holy ground.

The revolutionaries may also have believed that they were living at the threshold of the end time. Josephus narrates that "what more than all else incited them to the war was an ambiguous oracle, found in their sacred scriptures, to the effect that at that time one from their country would become ruler of the world."³⁶ In the years immediately preceding the revolt, many "eschatological prophets" were active, predicting the imminent approach of the end time or attempting, by means of a symbolic action (for example, splitting the Jordan River), to hasten or implement its arrival. Although Josephus states that the equivocal prophecy quoted above was the primary inducement for the Jews to go to war, in the body of his narrative he seldom alludes to the eschatological expectations of the revolutionaries. Perhaps some of the revolutionary leaders regarded themselves as messiahs, or were so regarded by their followers, but Josephus nowhere makes this point explicit. Accordingly, while few scholars would deny that eschatological expectations played a role in the motivation of the revolutionaries, the relative importance of this factor remains the subject of debate.³⁷

The Jewish aristocracy was just as unhappy with Roman rule as were the lower classes, and they took a leading role in the early stages of the revolt. Although established by the Romans as local leaders, the Jewish aristocrats were systematically deprived of the means to govern. Hence, they were left in the awkward position of being identified with the Romans, but of having no real power to respond to the needs of their compatriots. The way out of this predicament was to oppose the Roman procurator, a choice that put them on the fast track to war.

Yet it is clear that Josephus does not want his readership to conclude that the Jewish revolt was led and embraced by the Jewish aristocracy. Reading his *Jewish War*, one could easily conclude that it was the work of a few fanatics. In his desire to repair Roman-Jewish relations, however, Josephus protests too much. Aristocratic involvement in the revolt was far too prominent to conceal.

Josephus's apologetic for the Romans is also evident from his account of the war itself. Vespasian and Titus, the Roman generals, were perfect gentlemen who gave the Jews every opportunity to come to their senses and surrender. They even commiserated with the poor innocents who had to suffer the tyranny of the revolutionaries and the horrors of war. According to Josephus, Titus did his best to save the Temple (see below) and wept when he beheld the destruction of the city and of the house of God. Josephus is clearly saying that Titus and the Romans bore no responsibility for the destruction of the Temple, and that this unfortunate consequence of the war should not bar the resumption of normal relations between the Romans and their Jewish subjects.

In *Jewish Antiquities*, Josephus writes anew about the prehistory of the war. Here he is much less concerned about war guilt and much more prepared to admit that responsibility for the war should not be ascribed to the revolutionaries alone. In *The Jewish War* Josephus wanted to cover up any connection between the revolutionaries and the "official" representatives of Judaism; in *Jewish Antiquities* he no longer felt constrained to do so. For example, in *Jewish Antiquities*, one procurator even colludes with the assassins in order to remove an opponent; another empties the prisons of all those who were arrested for seditious activity. The emperor Nero, by favoring the pagan element of the city of Caesarea in its dispute with the Jewish citizenry, also bears some responsibility for the ensuing catastrophe.[38] Here the corruption and incompetence of the Roman procurators is far more evident.

Most modern scholars see the war as the result of a complex array of factors, both internal and external. The perspective of modern scholarship resembles that of *Jewish Antiquities* much more than that of *The Jewish War*. Moreover, unlike Josephus, many modern scholars admire the revolutionaries, or at least do not condemn them. For Josephus, even in *Jewish Antiquities*, they are villains and scoundrels, the dregs of society. For modern Israelis and for many others, they are heroes who were trying to reclaim what was rightly theirs.

The rabbis of the Talmud shared the perspective of Josephus in *The Jewish War*: The revolutionaries were crazed fanatics who did not listen to the sage counsel of the rabbis and persisted in their folly. They brought disaster upon the entire house of Israel. In the talmudic account, the hero of the war is Rabban Yohanan ben Zakkai, a man who fled from Jerusalem, went over to the Roman side and acknowledged the suzerainty of Vespasian, the Roman general and soon-to-be emperor. Isaiah's prophecy that "Lebanon shall fall to a mighty one" (Isaiah 10:34) was interpreted by Yohanan ben Zakkai to mean that the Temple (constructed from the cedars of Lebanon) would fall into the hands of Vespasian (a mighty one). The rabbinic hero thus hailed the Roman general as victor and emperor well before his actual victory and his elevation to the purple. From the perspective of the revolutionaries, this was treason; but from the perspective of the rabbis, viewed with acute hindsight, this was wisdom, a course of action that to their regret had not been followed.

Whether the historical Rabban Yohanan did anything even remotely approximating the deeds ascribed to him in the rabbinic account is, of course, unknown and unknowable. The story probably tells us much more about the political outlook of the rabbis of the third and fourth centuries than about the actions of Rabban Yohanan in the first.[39]

The social tensions and eschatological expectations that impelled Judea to war with Rome were not uniquely Jewish. In fact the war of 66–70 C.E. follows a pattern evident in other native rebellions against the Roman Empire. Tensions between rich and poor, and between city and country, were endemic to ancient society and often contributed to native rebellions. Like the uprising in Judea, other native rebellions were often led by aristocrats, although peasants, day laborers and the landless poor formed the bulk of the revolutionary army. As so often happens in revolutions ancient and modern, in its initial phases the struggle is led by aristocratic (or bourgeois) elements, which are later ousted, usually with great violence, by more extreme (or proletarian) groups. Like the Jews, other rebels in antiquity also dreamed of subjugating the universal Roman Empire. The revolt of the Gauls in 69 C.E. was prompted in part by a Druid prediction that Rome would be destroyed and that the rule of the empire would devolve on the tribes of Transalpine Gaul. The Jewish revolt was, therefore, hardly unique in the annals of Rome.[40] What makes it special is its intensity, its duration and, most important of all, the fact that an ancient historian saw fit to write its history in great detail. Because of Josephus's *The Jewish War*, we are better informed about this war than about any other native revolt against Rome.

The course of the First Jewish Revolt

With this background, let us turn to the course of the war itself. In the fall of 66 C.E., no one knew that a war between the Jews and the Romans was imminent. Some revolutionaries, perhaps, were dreaming of a final conflict, but even they had no way of knowing precisely when the conflict would erupt or what form it would take.

The spark was provided by the procurator Florus when he seized seventeen talents from the Temple treasury as compensation, he said, for uncollected back taxes. This act was not significantly worse than the depredations and misdeeds of previous procurators, and the riot it provoked was not significantly worse than the riots that had erupted during the tenures of previous procurators.

This riot, however, was the first act of a war, because it came at the end of a period of almost 20 years of unrelieved tension and lawlessness. When Florus brutally suppressed the riot, the people responded with even greater intensity, with the result that Florus had to flee the city.

At this point various revolutionary factions stepped forward. It is difficult to determine the interrelationship of all these groups. Some scholars argue that the anti-Roman forces formed a single "war party," which for purposes of convenience can be called "Zealots" after its most distinctive constituent group. Others argue that no single "war party" ever existed and that each of the groups and figures had a distinctive history. The diverse groups shared a common willingness to fight the Romans, but differed from each other in many other respects, which explains why they spent so much time fighting each other. The latter interpretation is much more plausible than the former.[41]

At the outbreak of the war, an aristocratic priestly revolutionary party, led initially by Eleazar, son of the high priest Ananias, seems to have controlled the proceedings. Eleazar suspended the daily sacrifice in the Temple that had been offered for the welfare of the emperor and the Roman Empire.[42] This act was tantamount to a declaration of war. As if to emphasize the point, Eleazar and his supporters turned on the Roman garrisons Florus had left in the city after his retreat and besieged them.

Whether the aristocratic priestly revolutionaries were truly committed to the revolution, or were merely playing for time in the hope of forestalling the emergence of more radical and more dangerous elements, is debated among scholars. Josephus seems to give contradictory answers: Although they probably began as revolutionaries who deeply resented the Roman diminution of their prestige and prerogatives, when they were faced with the opposition of other revolutionary groups whose primary targets were the Jewish aristocracy, it is likely the priestly revolutionaries began to hope for a peace agreement with the Romans.[43]

In any event, these priestly revolutionaries were soon eclipsed by another group, the Sicarii, led by one Menahem. In the fall of 66 C.E., the Sicarii entered Jerusalem. In addition to attacking the Roman forces that remained in the city, the Sicarii also attacked the Jewish aristocracy. They looted the homes of the well-to-do and massacred many of the nobility. The most prominent of their victims was Ananias the high priest, the father of Eleazar, who had led the priestly revolutionaries. The priestly group, headquartered in the Temple, fought back and killed the Sicarii leader, Menahem. Menahem's followers then fled to Masada, one of Herod's great fortresses in the Judean wilderness. There they remained for the rest of the war, doing nothing to help the struggle. Other bands of fighters, however, were already, or would soon become, active in Jerusalem.

Revolutionary ardor also spread outside Jerusalem. In Caesarea and in many other cities of Judea and Syria, Jews and pagans attacked one another.

The hostility toward pagans and paganism that motivated the revolutionaries in Jerusalem seems also to have motivated Jews throughout the country. The pagans, for their part, gave vent to the same kind of animosities that had exploded in the anti-Jewish riots in Alexandria 30 years earlier.

The Roman governor of Syria, Cestius, went to Judea to restore order, but after entering Jerusalem he decided that he was not strong enough to take the Temple from the revolutionaries. In the course of his withdrawal, his troops were set upon by the Jews and had to abandon much of their equipment.

After the defeat of Cestius, the revolutionaries, led by the priestly revolutionary party, assigned generals to each district in the country. Most of the commissioned generals were priests. Their task was to prepare the country for war, in anticipation of either negotiations or hostilities with the Romans. The general about whose activities we are best informed is, of course, Josephus. He was sent to Galilee, where he spent the next six months feuding with local leaders, trying to impose his rule on a fractious population that had little desire to fight the Romans. He fortified several key locations, raised and trained an army, brought local brigands into his employ, and intimidated the cities of the district (notably Sepphoris, which supported the Romans, and Tiberias, which was divided).

Josephus had had no military or administrative experience, and was not temperamentally suited to cooperative leadership; it is no surprise that he ultimately failed in his mission. With the appearance of the Roman army, led by the Roman general Vespasian, in the summer of 67 C.E., Josephus's army all but disappeared, and the Romans had little difficulty in subduing the district. Only one location gave them trouble, the fortress of Jotapata, a hilltop town fortified by Josephus, which became the refuge for the remnants of Josephus's army, such as it was. It held out for almost seven weeks before falling to the Roman assault. Josephus himself was captured and delivered his prophecy to Vespasian, as noted above. Galilee was now pacified.

The revolutionaries in the Golan congregated at Gamla, but after some fierce fighting, that fortress too was taken. The entire northern part of the country was once again brought under Roman rule.

After taking a winter break, Vespasian resumed operations in the spring of 68 C.E. and by early summer had pacified the entire countryside; Jerusalem alone (and some isolated fortresses, notably Masada) remained in the hands of the rebels.

A respite in the war is wasted

Everything seemed prepared for an immediate attack on Jerusalem, but during the summer of 68 C.E. Vespasian learned of the emperor Nero's assassination.

The death of the reigning emperor meant that Vespasian's commission as general had expired; accordingly, he discontinued his military activities but he was prudent enough not to release his army. In the summer of 69 C.E., Vespasian had himself proclaimed emperor by his troops. He left Judea and returned to Rome in order to establish his own imperial power. By the end of the year he had succeeded. Some months later, in the spring of 70 C.E., Vespasian once again turned his attention to Judea.

The two-year hiatus should have been a great boon to the revolutionaries in Jerusalem, allowing them time to organize their forces, fortify the city and lay away provisions. But the opposite was the case. As the refugees entered Jerusalem from the countryside, internecine strife intensified. The party of Zealots now emerged, consisting for the most part of Judean peasants. They turned against the aristocratic priests, who until that point had been in charge of the war, and appointed a new high priest by lot. The Zealots enlisted support from the Jews of Idumaea, country peasants like themselves who could be counted on to hate the city aristocracy.[44] At first, the Idumeans supported the Zealots in their attacks on the aristocracy, but after a while even they, says Josephus, were disgusted by the excesses of the Zealots and withdrew.

Thus 68 C.E. was spent in fighting between the aristocratic (or "moderate") revolutionary groups and the more radical proletarian ones. The latter triumphed. In 69 C.E. the radical revolutionaries themselves fell to attacking one another. John of Gischala, supported by his contingent of Galileans, turned on his former allies the Zealots and ultimately succeeded in ousting their leader and bringing them under his control. But a new revolutionary faction then emerged, led by Simon bar Giora, a native of Gerasa (a city in Transjordan). Like the Zealots, he had a radical social program and drew much of his support from freed slaves. The intense fighting among these various groups had disastrous consequences. Large stocks of grain and other provisions were destroyed. When the Roman siege began in earnest in 70 C.E., a famine soon ensued.

The Roman siege of Jerusalem

Vespasian had by then securely established himself as emperor and wanted a resounding success to legitimate his new dynasty. In his propaganda, Vespasian pictured himself as the savior of the empire, the man who, after a year and a half of political chaos, had restored order and stability. There was no better way to prove this point than to bring to a successful conclusion the protracted war in Judea. In order to emphasize the dynastic implications of the victory, Vespasian appointed his son Titus to command the Roman army

ERICH LESSING

Arch of Titus relief. *The golden menorah, a pair of trumpets, the golden table and other booty from the Jerusalem Temple are carried aloft in a Roman victory procession, depicted in this marble relief from the Arch of Titus. Erected in Rome in 80 C.E., the arch celebrates the Roman victory over the Jews and conquest of Jerusalem.*

in its assault on the holy city of the Jews. In the spring of 70 C.E., the Romans, under Titus, besieged the city and cut off all supplies and all means of escape.

The fighting for the city and the Temple was intense. The major rallying point of the revolutionaries, and consequently the major target of the Romans, was the Temple. The Temple was a veritable fortress, but it still was a temple. The priests maintained all the customary rituals, even with death and destruction all around them. Three weeks before the final catastrophe, the *Tamid*, the "continual sacrifice," which was offered every morning and evening, ceased because of a shortage of lambs. The severity of the famine is illustrated in many gruesome tales by Josephus; but despite their suffering, the Jews were still willing to sacrifice two lambs every day to God. Their only hope for success was through divine intervention, and only a properly maintained cult would convince God to aid the faithful.

Divine help, however, was not forthcoming. The Romans advanced methodically toward their goal. The Jews were weakened by famine and internecine strife and, although Titus made some serious tactical errors in prosecuting the siege, the Roman victory was only a matter of time. Each of the city's three protective walls was breached in turn, and the Romans finally found themselves, by mid-summer of 70 C.E., just outside the sacred precincts.

At this point, according to Josephus, Titus called a meeting of his general staff and asked for advice. What should he do with the Jewish Temple? Some of his adjutants argued that it should be destroyed, because as long as it was left standing it would serve as a focal point for anti-Roman agitation. According to the "rule of war" in antiquity, temples were not to be molested, but this Temple had become a fortress and therefore was a fair military target. No opprobrium would be attached to its destruction. Titus, however, argued that the Temple should be preserved as a monument to Roman magnanimity. Indeed, according to Josephus, during the siege Titus offered the revolutionaries numerous opportunities to surrender or, at least, to vacate the Temple and carry on the fighting elsewhere. Even at the end Titus was eager to preserve the Temple. But Titus's plan was thwarted. On the next day, a soldier, acting against orders, tossed a firebrand into the sanctuary, and the flames shot up, immediately out of control. Josephus insists that Titus did his best to douse the flames, but Josephus's apology for Titus is as unsuccessful as Titus's attempt to halt the conflagration.[45] It is very unlikely that this fantastic account of Roman magnanimity and self-restraint contains any historical truth. Scholars debate whether this portrait of moderate generals was concocted for a Jewish or a Roman audience, but most agree that it is as exaggerated as Josephus's other claim that the Jews were compelled by the revolutionaries to fight a war they did not want.

On the tenth of the month of Ab (in rabbinic chronology on the ninth), late August of 70 C.E., the Temple was destroyed. Titus and his troops spent the next month subduing the rest of the city and collecting loot as the reward for their victory.

Upon his return to Rome in 71 C.E., Titus celebrated a joint triumph with his father, the emperor Vespasian. In the procession were the enemy leaders Simon bar Giora and John of Gischala, and various objects from the Temple (notably the menorah, table and trumpets).* Simon was beheaded, John was probably enslaved and the sacred objects were deposited in the Temple of Peace in Rome.[46] Two triumphal arches were erected in the following years to celebrate the victory; one was destroyed in the 14th or 15th century, the other still stands, the Arch of Titus, with its famous depiction of the sacred objects from the Temple carried in the procession. The destroyed arch bore the following inscription:

> The senate and people of Rome (dedicate this arch) to the emperor
> Titus ... because with the guidance and plans of his father, and

*See Robert Deutsch, "Roman Coins Boast 'Judaea Capta,'" *BAR*, January/February 2010.

under his auspices, he subdued the Jewish people and destroyed the city of Jerusalem, which all generals, kings and peoples before him had either attacked without success or left entirely unassailed.[47]

To punish the Jews for the war, the Romans imposed the *fiscus Judaicus*, the "Jewish tax." The half-shekel that Jews throughout the empire had formerly contributed to the Temple in Jerusalem was now collected for the temple of Jupiter Capitolinus in Rome. The imposition of this tax, which was collected throughout the empire at least until the middle of the second century C.E.,* shows that the Romans regarded all the Jews of the empire as partly responsible for the war. Dio Cassius, a Roman historian of the third century C.E., records that the Judean revolutionaries were aided by their coreligionists throughout the Roman Empire.[48] Josephus implicitly denies this, but it is perhaps confirmed by the Jewish tax on Diaspora, as well as Judean, Jews.

The Romans did not, however, institute any other harsh measures against the Jews. They confiscated much Jewish land in Judea, distributing it to their soldiers and to Jewish collaborators (like Josephus), but this was a normal procedure after a war. They did not engage in religious persecution or strip the Jews of their rights. On the contrary, Josephus reports that the non-Jewish citizens of Antioch petitioned Titus to allow them to expel their Jewish population, but Titus adamantly refused; the Jews were still entitled to the protection of the state.

Masada

Titus's triumph in Rome in 71 C.E. marked the official end of the war. A few "mopping up" operations remained. Three strongholds, all originally fortified by Herod the Great, were still in rebel hands, but only one of them caused any real trouble for the Romans. This was Masada (which fell in either 73 or 74 C.E.). Archaeological excavations confirm Josephus's description of the magnificence of the site and the difficulty of the siege. The Romans built a ramp** against one side of the plateau and pushed a tower up against the wall of the fortress. We may assume that this activity was accompanied by a

---

*The half-shekel tax was at least partially repealed by the Roman emperor Nerva in 96 C.E. See Shlomo Moussaieff, "The 'New Cleopatra' and the Jewish Tax," *BAR*, January/February 2010; but see Manfred R. Lehmann, "Where the Temple Tax Was Buried," *BAR*, November/December 1993; and Hershel Shanks, Strata, "Adding Insult to Injury," *BAR*, May/June 2010.
**In building their siege ramp, the Romans took advantage of a natural spur that rises up Masada's western side. See Dan Gill, "It's a Natural: Masada Ramp Was Not a Roman Engineering Miracle," *BAR*, September/October 2001.

DAVID HARRIS

Lots cast by Masada's defenders? *The first-century C.E. Jewish historian Josephus tells us that three years after the Roman destruction of Jerusalem in 70 C.E., the remaining Jewish rebels, besieged at Masada, decided to commit suicide rather than succumb to the Roman army. With defeat just hours away, the Jewish commander Eleazar Ben Yair convinced his fighters to die with their families rather than become Roman slaves. By lot, the rebels selected ten men who would slay the rest of the community.*

The late Israeli archaeologist Yigael Yadin, who excavated Masada in the 1960s, speculated that these sherds, each inscribed with a different name, were the very lots used by the defenders. The sherd at lower left bears the name "Ben Yair." However, some scholars question whether Ben Yair ever made such a speech and even whether a mass suicide occurred.

constant hail of arrows and stones thrown by the rebels, although Josephus does not mention this. (Nor does he mention even a single Roman casualty!)

When the Masada rebels saw that the end was near, they had to decide whether to continue their struggle. At this point Josephus narrates a very dramatic tale. The leader of the Sicarii, Eleazar ben Yair, assembled the "manliest" of his comrades and convinced them that an honorable self-inflicted death was preferable to the disgrace of capture and enslavement. Acting upon his instructions, each man killed his own wife and family. Then ten men were chosen by lot to kill the rest. Finally, one was chosen to kill the remaining nine and then himself. All told, 960 men, women and children perished. When the Romans entered the fortress the next day, they expected a battle, but all they found was silence.

The historicity of this famous account is uncertain. The basic elements of the story are of course accurate and confirmed by the archaeological findings—the remains of the rebel presence at Masada, the Roman siege works, the Roman camps and the Roman ramp are in a remarkable state of preservation. Even the stones hurled by the Romans from their siege tower have been found. It is likely that *some* of the defenders slew their families, burned their possessions and set the public buildings on fire. It is likely that *some* of them killed themselves. That others tried to escape, however, is suggested by skeletons found at the site, which may have belonged to people who were found by the Romans and killed. Archaeological evidence also suggests that at least *some* of the defenders barricaded themselves in the northern palace and died fighting the Romans. In order to create a dramatic narrative, Josephus has taken the story of *some* of the defenders of Masada and turned it into the story of *all* the defenders of Masada.

Josephus probably invented or exaggerated the use of lots in the suicide process. True, Israeli archaeologist Yigael Yadin found 11 "lots" at Masada, but the first drawing required several hundred lots and the second only ten. Moreover, many of the details in Josephus's account are irreconcilable with the archaeological evidence. For example, Josephus says that all the possessions were gathered together in one large pile and set on fire, but archaeology shows there were many piles and many fires. Josephus writes that Eleazar ordered his men to destroy everything except the foodstuffs, but archaeology demonstrates that many storerooms that contained provisions were burned. Josephus implies that all the murders took place in the palace, but the northern palace is too small for an assembly of almost a thousand people. More important, the speeches Josephus puts into the mouth of the rebel leader Eleazar ben Yair are incongruous to say the least. Imagine a Jewish revolutionary leader justifying suicide by appealing to the example of the Brahmins of India! It is highly unlikely that there was time for such speeches or that the rebels acted with such unanimity.[49]

As we have seen, the Jewish revolt was not a reaction to an unmistakable threat or provocation by the state. In the fall of 66 C.E.—as the result of social tensions between rich and poor, between city and country, and between Jew and gentile; of the impoverishment of large sections of the economy; of religious speculations about the imminent arrival of the end time and the messianic redeemer; of nationalist stirrings against foreign rule; of the incompetent and insensitive administration of the procurators—the Jews of Judea went to war against the Roman Empire.

The war was characterized, as we have seen, by internecine fighting. The fighting was not only between revolutionary groups but also between the revolutionaries and large segments of the populace. Josephus is surely correct that many Jews opposed the war. Moreover, the number of people enrolled in the revolutionary parties was quite small. Many Jews had no desire to participate in the struggle. It was one thing to riot against the procurator, quite another to rebel against the Roman Empire. Wealthy and poor alike were afraid that war would mean the loss of everything they had, and since the Romans had not done anything intolerable, there was no compelling reason to go to war. This attitude was widespread. Aside from Jerusalem, only Gamla was the site of fierce fighting. Galilee, Peraea (in Transjordan), the coast, Idumaea—all these saw some anti-Roman activity, but all were pacified immediately upon the arrival of the Roman forces. Jerusalem was the seat of the rebellion—where it began, where it ended and where the vast majority of the combatants maintained their strongholds.

The causes for the failure of the war are not hard to see. The war began with little advance planning, the revolutionaries were badly divided and the timing was off. Had they rebelled a few years earlier while the Romans were fighting the Parthians, they might have been able to succeed at least to the point of exacting various concessions from the Romans in return for their surrender. Had they waited two years beyond 66 C.E.—after Nero's assassination in 68 C.E.—their odds would have been immeasurably better. At that time, the empire was in chaos; the succession was vigorously disputed; Gaul had risen in revolt. This would have been a perfect moment for revolt, but for the Jews it came too late.

A new beginning

The destruction of the Temple did not mean the end of Judaism, however.[50] The theological and religious crisis it caused seems to have been much less severe than that experienced in the aftermath of the Babylonian destruction of the First Temple in 586 B.C.E., perhaps because the Judaism of the Second Temple period had created new institutions and ideologies that prepared it for a time when the Temple and the sacrificial cult would no longer exist. By the time the Second Temple was destroyed, the Temple itself had been supplemented by synagogues, the priests had been supplemented by scholars, the sacrificial cult had been supplemented by prayer and Torah study, and the intermediation of the Temple priesthood had been supplemented by a piety that emphasized the observance of the commandments of the Torah by every Jew.

In short, the path to the future was already clearly marked. The sufferings of this world would be compensated by rewards in the hereafter. The disgrace of seeing Rome triumph over the God of Israel and destroy the Temple would be effaced by the glory of the new kingdom that God would establish for his people in the end time. The cessation of the sacrificial cult did not mean estrangement from God, since God could be worshiped through good deeds, prayer, the observance of the commandments and the study of the Torah. Synagogues could take the place of the Temple, and rabbis could take the place of the priests. Over the following centuries these were the responses of the Jews to the catastrophe of 70 C.E.

For all of the destruction caused by the events of 70 C.E., in many important respects the post-70 C.E. period does not mark a radical break with the past. But in other respects the post-70 C.E. period is discontinuous with the past. The period from the Maccabees to the destruction of the Temple was marked by religious and social ferment, but after 70 C.E. the ferment all but disappeared. Within a generation the Jews ceased to write (or at least ceased to preserve) apocalypses, and they desisted from making detailed speculations about God's control of human events in the present and the future. The Pharisees, Sadducees, Essenes, Sicarii and Zealots are no longer living realities in Jewish society. They are mentioned by sources of the second and third centuries only as figures of the Second Temple period. Instead of sectarian diversity, the post-70 C.E. period is characterized by a peculiar homogeneity. The only group to appear in our documentation is that of the rabbis, as a result of which the post-70 C.E. period is often called the rabbinic period.

The origins of the rabbinic group are most obscure. They were led by Rabban Gamaliel, a scion of a prominent Pharisaic family, a fact that implies that the heirs of the Pharisees of the Second Temple period were a dominant element in this new group. Various features shared by the Pharisees and the rabbis also imply some intimate link between them, but there is no indication that all Pharisees became rabbis or that all rabbis were the descendants of Pharisees.

The absence of other organized groups does not, of course, mean that all Jews everywhere instantly became pious followers of the rabbis. The contrary was the case. In Second Temple times, most Jews did not belong to any sect or group, but were content to serve God in the "traditional" way, that is, as they learned from their parents, grandparents and society at large. This pattern continued in the rabbinic period as well, as the rabbinic texts themselves make abundantly clear. But in the end, the masses recognized the rabbis as the leaders and shapers of Judaism. The rabbis were heirs to the legacy of Second Temple Judaism, but through their distinctive literature and patterns of religion they gave Judaism a new form of expression that would endure to our own day. The destruction of the Temple thus marked not only an end but also a beginning.

Notes

I. The Patriarchal Age

[1] The viewpoint is illustrated very well by the second chapter of William F. Albright's *Yahweh and the Gods of Canaan* (Garden City, NY: Doubleday, 1968), titled "The Patriarchal Background of Israel's Faith." Its fullest expression is perhaps the discussion in John Bright, *A History of Israel*, 3rd ed. (Philadelphia: Westminster Press, 1981), pp. 67–102.

[2] See especially Ephraim A. Speiser, *Genesis*, Anchor Bible 1 (Garden City, NY: Doubleday, 1964).

[3] William F. Albright, *From the Stone Age to Christianity*, 2nd ed. (Garden City, NY: Anchor/Doubleday, 1957), p. 241.

[4] William F. Albright, *The Biblical Period from Abraham to Ezra* (New York: Torchbooks/Harper & Row, 1963), p. 5.

[5] G. Ernest Wright, *Biblical Archaeology*, revised ed. (Philadelphia: Westminster Press, 1962), p. 40.

[6] Ibid., p. 50, n. 5.

[7] See William G. Dever, "Palestine in the Second Millennium BCE: The Archaeological Picture," in *Israelite and Judaean History*, eds. John M. Hayes and J. Maxwell Miller (Philadelphia: Westminster Press, 1977), pp. 70–120, especially pp. 99–101.

[8] The most forceful and complete statement of this position is probably that of Roland de Vaux (*The Early History of Israel*, trans. David Smith [Philadelphia: Westminster Press, 1978], pp. 161–287).

[9] See John Van Seters, *Abraham in History and Tradition* (New Haven, CT: Yale University Press, 1975), pp. 40–42, and Thomas L. Thompson, *The Historicity of the Patriarchal Narratives*, ZAW Supplement 133 (Berlin: de Gruyter, 1974), pp. 22–36.

[10] Speiser, *Genesis* (see endnote 2), passim; Cyrus H. Gordon, "Biblical Customs and the Nuzu Tablets," *Biblical Archaeologist Reader* 2, eds. E.F. Campbell and David Noel Freedman (Garden City, NY: Anchor/Doubleday, 1964), pp. 21–33.

[11] Speiser, *Genesis* (see endnote 2), pp. 120–121; Gordon, "Biblical Customs" (see endnote 10), pp. 22–23.

[12] Speiser, *Genesis* (see endnote 2), p. xi; for Speiser's full discussion, see "The Wife-Sister Motif in the Patriarchal Narratives," in *Biblical and Other Studies*, ed. A. Altmann (Cambridge, MA: Harvard University Press, 1963), pp. 15–28; also in *Oriental and Biblical Studies*, eds. Jacob J. Finkelstein and Moshe Greenberg (Philadelphia: University of Pennsylvania, 1967), pp. 62–82.

[13] See especially the studies of William G. Dever, "The Beginning of the Middle Bronze Age in Syria-Palestine," in *Magnalia Dei: The Mighty Acts of God—Essays on the Bible and Archaeology in*

Memory of G. Ernest Wright, ed. Frank M. Cross et al. (Garden City, NY: Doubleday, 1976), pp. 3–38; "The 'Middle Bronze I' Period in Syria and Palestine," in *Near Eastern Archaeology in the Twentieth Century: Essays in Honor of Nelson Glueck*, ed. J.A. Sanders (Garden City, NY: Doubleday, 1970), pp. 132–163; "New Vistas in the EB IV ('MB I') Horizon in Syria and Palestine," *BASOR* 237 (1980), pp. 35–64.

¹⁴ See the cautious conclusions of Dever in "Palestine in the Second Millennium" (see endnote 7), pp. 117–120.

¹⁵ This has been shown in several studies by M.B. Rowton, including the following: "Autonomy and Nomadism in Western Asia," *Orientalia* 42 (1973), pp. 247–258; "Urban Autonomy in a Nomadic Environment," *JNES* 32 (1973), pp. 201–215; "Dimorphic Structure and the Problem of the 'Apirû-'Ibrim," *JNES* 35 (1976), pp. 13–20.

¹⁶ See J.T. Luke, *Pastoralism and Politics in the Mari Period: A Re-Examination of the Character and Political Significance of the Major West Semitic Tribal Groups on the Middle Euphrates, c. 1828–1753 B.C.* (Ph.D. dissertation, University of Michigan [Ann Arbor, MI: University Microfilms, 1965]); V.H. Matthews, *Pastoral Nomadism in the Mari Kingdom ca. 1830–1760 B.C.*, ASOR Dissertation Series (Cambridge, MA: ASOR, 1978).

¹⁷ See the literature cited in Dever, "Palestine in the Second Millennium" (see endnote 7), pp. 102–111.

¹⁸ The two studies that were most effective in calling attention to the problems with the early-second-millennium hypothesis were Thompson, *The Historicity of the Patriarchal Narratives* (see endnote 9), and Van Seters, *Abraham in History* (see endnote 9). See also Nahum Sarna, "Abraham in History," *BAR*, December 1977, pp. 5–9.

¹⁹ See Barry L. Eichler, "Nuzi and the Bible: A Retrospective," in *DUMU-E₂-DUB-BA-A: Studies in Honor of Åke W. Sjöberg*, eds. H. Behrens, D. Loding and M. Roth (Philadelphia: University Museum, 1989), pp. 107–19.

²⁰ See Van Seters, *Abraham in History* (see endnote 9), pp. 40–42, and especially Thompson, *Historicity of the Patriarchal Narratives* (see endnote 9), pp. 22–36, for complete citation of the extrabiblical materials. In the Bible, "Abiram" is the name of a Reubenite who participated in the revolt against Moses in the wilderness (Numbers 16:1) and of the firstborn son of Hiel the Bethelite, who founded Israelite Jericho in the ninth century B.C.E. (1 Kings 16:34).

²¹ Compare the name "Ahiram" and its shortened form "Hiram." In the Bible it is mentioned as the name of a son of Benjamin, a clan of Benjaminites (Numbers 26:38); the Phoenician king contemporary with David and Solomon (2 Samuel 5:11; 1 Kings 5); and the craftsman who supervised the building of Solomon's Temple (1 Kings 7:13). It appears in Phoenician inscriptions as the name of a tenth-century B.C.E. king of Byblos and an eighth-century B.C.E. king of Tyre. See also Thompson, *Historicity of the Patriarchal Narratives* (see endnote 9), pp. 29–31, and Van Seters, *Abraham in History* (see endnote 9), p. 41.

²² See Herbert B. Huffmon, *Amorite Personal Names in the Mari Texts* (Baltimore, MD: Johns Hopkins Press, 1965), pp. 63–86.

²³ *Pace* Kenneth A. Kitchen in his review of *Ancient Israel*, ed. Hershel Shanks, *Themelios* 15:1 (October, 1989), p. 25. Kitchen's statistical analysis of name-types is dependent on random archaeological finds and cannot claim any kind of scientific consistency. See William G. Dever's criticisms of Kitchen's use of such archaeological data: "Is This Man a Biblical Archaeologist?" *BAR*, July/August 1996, p. 63. See Kitchen's (unchanged) position in his book, *On the Reliability of the Old Testament* (Grand Rapids, MI: Eerdmans, 2003), pp. 341–342.

²⁴ See Frauke Gröndahl, *Die Personennamen der Texte aus Ugarit*, Studia Pohl 1 (Rome: Pontifical Biblical Institute, 1967), pp. 41–42.

²⁵ For a sample of the inscriptional evidence, see Jeffrey H. Tigay, *You Shall Have No Other Gods: Israelite Religion in the Light of Hebrew Inscriptions*, Harvard Semitic Studies 31 (Atlanta: Scholars Press, 1986), pp. 52–56, 85. For biblical names, see Martin Noth, *Die israelitischen Personennamen im Rahmen der gemeinsemitischen Namengebung*, Beiträge zur Wissenschaft vom Alten und Neuen Testament, III/10 (Stuttgart: Kohlhammer, 1928; reprint Hildesheim: Olms, 1966), pp. 27–28.

²⁶ As a place name in Palestine, "Jacob-'el," to be discussed below, and as a personal name at Ugarit, *ia-qub-ba'l = ya'qub-ba'l*, "Jacob-Baal." See Gröndahl, *Personennamen* (see endnote 24), p. 41.

[27] Noth, *Die israelitischen Personennamen* (see endnote 25), pp. 45–46. See further, Thompson, *Historicity of the Patriarchal Narratives* (see endnote 9), pp. 43–50.

[28] Van Seters, *Abraham in History* (see endnote 9), pp. 68–71; See also Thompson, *Historicity of the Patriarchal Narratives* (see endnote 9), pp. 252–269.

[29] Van Seters, *Abraham in History* (see endnote 9), pp. 71–76.

[30] See Thompson, *Historicity of the Patriarchal Narratives* (see endnote 9), pp. 243–248.

[31] Martin Noth, *The History of Israel*, trans. P. R. Ackroyd (New York: Harper & Row, 1960), pp. 53–84.

[32] According to Hermann Gunkel, the critical time in the formation of the patriarchal traditions was the preliterary, oral stage, when the individual units of tradition were expressed in particular genres or forms (*Gattungen*). Thus the history of the traditions can best be studied through the identification of these units by reference to the forms in which they are preserved (form criticism) and the investigation of the manner in which these units were combined into larger narratives. See *The Legends of Genesis: The Biblical Saga and History* [1901], trans. W.R. Carruth (New York: Schocken, 1964).

[33] Martin Noth, *A History of Pentateuchal Traditions* [1948], trans. B.W. Anderson (Englewood Cliffs, NJ: Prentice-Hall, 1972).

[34] This is, of course, the biblical tradition, but there are many reasons to doubt it. In working through the materials for his commentaries for *I Samuel* and *II Samuel*, Anchor Bible 8–9 (Garden City, NY: Doubleday, 1980, 1984), P. Kyle McCarter, Jr. came to the conclusion previously reached by others that it was David who combined Judah with Israel for the first time. See, for example, James W. Flanagan, "Judah in All Israel," in *No Famine in the Land: Studies in Honor of John L. McKenzie*, eds. Flanagan and A.W. Robinson (Missoula, MT: Scholars Press, 1975), pp. 101–116.

[35] Noth, *History of Israel* (see endnote 31), p. 123. Other proponents of the history of traditions method have not been as negative as Noth. According to de Vaux (*Early History* [see endnote 8], p. 180), whose work represents the best attempt to exploit both tradition-historical and

archaeological methods, "It is true that the patriarchal tradition was only given its definitive form in the perspective of 'all Israel' after the conquest and settlement in the Promised Land ... However complicated this development may have been, and however obscure it may still be, we should not be justified in concluding that the traditions have no historical value at all, since without evidence it would be wrong to claim that the Israelites had no knowledge at all of their own origins."

[36] See the comments by Frank M. Cross in "The Epic Tradition of Early Israel: Epic Narrative and the Reconstruction of Early Israelite Institutions," in *The Poet and the Historian: Essays in Literary and Historical Biblical Criticism*, ed. Richard E. Friedman, Harvard Semitic Studies (Chico, CA: Scholars Press, 1983), pp. 13–40, especially pp. 24–25.

[37] On the importance of kinship relations in the stories, see Robert A. Oden, "Jacob as Father, Husband, and Nephew: Kinship Studies and the Patriarchal Narratives," *JBL* 102 (1983), pp. 189–205, with the valuable corrections of Naomi Steinberg, "Alliance or Descent? The Function of Marriage in Genesis," *JSOT* 51 (1991), pp. 45–55. On the functions of biblical genealogies generally, see Robert Wilson, *Genealogy and History in the Biblical World*, Yale Near Eastern Researches 7 (New Haven: Yale University Press, 1977).

[38] For more extensive criticisms of Martin Noth's history of traditions method, see Robert Polzin, "Martin Noth's *A History of Pentateuchal Traditions*," *BASOR* 221 (1976), pp. 113–120; on his form-critical presuppositions, see Rolf Knierim, "Old Testament Form Criticism Reconsidered," *Interpretation* 27 (1973), pp. 435–468; and Sean M. Warner, "Primitive Saga Men," *VT* 29 (1979), pp. 325–335.

[39] Hermann Gunkel, "The Influence of Babylonian Mythology upon the Biblical Creation Story," in *Creation in the Old Testament*, ed. B.W. Anderson (Philadelphia: Fortress Press, 1984; German original, *Schöpfung und Chaos*, 1895), p. 26.

[40] Also republished as Ronald S. Hendel, "When the Sons of God Cavorted with the Daughters of Men," in *Understanding the Dead Sea Scrolls*, ed. Hershel Shanks (New York: Random House, 1992), pp. 167–177.

[41] Some references in the J source indicate a historical context in the neo-Assyrian period.

These include the reference to Nineveh as a major Assyrian city (Genesis 10:11–12) and the boundary conflict between Israel (Jacob) and Aram (Laban) in Gilead (Genesis 31:51–53) which echoes the ninth-century Aramean wars in that region (1 Kings 20, 22; 2 Kings 8–13).

[42] See Terry J. Prewitt, "Kinship Structures and the Genesis Genealogies," *JNES* 40 (1981), pp. 97–98.

[43] This refers to a time before Machir had been replaced by Manasseh and reduced to the status of a Manassite clan (see de Vaux, *Early History* [see endnote 8], pp. 651–652) and before Gilead had been replaced by Gad south of the Jabbok and the name Gilead had been generalized to include all of Transjordan (pp. 571–572, 574–576).

[44] On the complex problems involved in the dating of the battle described in Judges 5, see Chapter III of this volume, "The Settlement in Canaan: The Period of the Judges," and de Vaux, *Early History* (see endnote 8), pp. 789–796.

[45] *ANET*, pp. 376–378.

[46] The emphasis in recent research on the sociological conditions out of which the community emerged has begun to lead to excellent results. It has created a tendency, however, to overlook the importance of the emergence of an ethnic identity. A valuable balance to this tendency is provided by Baruch Halpern in *The Emergence of Israel in Canaan*, SBL Monograph Series 29 (Chico, CA: Scholars Press, 1983), especially pp. 90, 100.

[47] For an overview of this subject, see the introduction to *Ethnic Groups and Boundaries*, ed. Frederick Barth (Boston: Little, Brown, 1969).

[48] For a recent comprehensive discussion of the formation of Israelite ethnic identity, see Avraham Faust, *Israel's Ethnogenesis: Settlement, Interaction, Expansion and Resistance* (London: Equinox, 2006).

[49] See also Ronald S. Hendel, *Remembering Abraham: Culture, Memory, and History in the Hebrew Bible* (New York: Oxford University Press, 2005), pp. 45–55.

[50] Albrecht Alt, "The God of the Fathers" [1929], *Essays on Old Testament History and Religion*, trans. R.A. Wilson (Garden City, NY: Doubleday, 1968), p. 7.

[51] See Frank Moore Cross, *Canaanite Myth and Hebrew Epic: Essays in the History of the Religion of*

Israel (Cambridge, MA: Harvard University Press, 1973), pp. 13–43.

[52] Ibid., pp. 44–75.

[53] According to the distribution of personal names in the Bible, El predominates as a divine element during the premonarchic period, with Yahweh becoming popular in the early monarchic period and thereafter. For the statistics and some implications, see Karel van der Toorn, *Family Religion in Babylonia, Syria and Israel: Continuity and Change in the Forms of Religious Life*, Studies in the History and Culture of the Ancient Near East 7 (Leiden: Brill, 1996), pp. 237–238.

[54] Giorgio Buccellati, "From Khana to Laqê: The End of Syro-Mesopotamia," in *De la Babylonie à la Syrie, en passant par Mari*, ed. Ö. Tunca (Liège: Université de Liège, 1990), pp. 229–253; and Daniel E. Fleming, *Democracy's Ancient Ancestors: Mari and Early Collective Governance* (Cambridge: Cambridge University Press, 2004), pp. 24–103.

[55] See the careful comments of Abraham Malamat, *Mari and the Early Israelite Experience* (Oxford: Oxford University Press, 1989), pp. 27–30; and the recent reassessment by Daniel E. Fleming, "Genesis in History and Tradition: The Syrian Background of Israel's Ancestors, Reprise," in *The Future of Biblical Archaeology: Reassessing Methodologies and Assumptions*, eds. James K. Hoffmeier and Alan Millard (Grand Rapids, MI: Eerdmans, 2004), pp. 193–232.

[56] Cross, *Canaanite Myth* (see endnote 51), p. 57.

[57] Arguments that the Aramaic connection stems from the mid-first millennium B.C.E. are exceedingly weak; see Van Seters (*Abraham in History* [see endnote 9], p. 34), who suggests that the Assyrian deportation of Israelites to the Middle Euphrates region after 722 B.C.E. and the resurgence of the trade route through Haran in the neo-Babylonian period may have been factors in the formation of an ethnic identification with Arameans in this period.

[58] Jacob J. Finkelstein, "The Genealogy of the Hammurapi Dynasty," *JCS* 20 (1966), pp. 95–118, especially pp. 97–98.

[59] See Van Seters, *Abraham in History* (see endnote 9), pp. 40–42, and Thompson, *Historicity of the Patriarchal Narratives* (see endnote 9), pp. 22–36.

[60] As pointed out first by Hugo Gressmann ("Sage und Geschichte in den Patriarchenerzählungen,"

ZAW 30 [1910], pp. 1–34, especially p. 2 and note 4), the best parallels to the longer form of the name "Abraham" occur in Aramaic. See also de Vaux (*Early History* [see endnote 8], pp. 197–198 and notes 73 and 74), who cites evidence for a similar phenomenon in Ugaritic and Phoenician; his examples, however, are not precisely parallel.

[61] Benjamin Mazar, "The Historical Background of the Book of Genesis," in *The Early Biblical Period*, eds. S. Ahituv and B.A. Levine (Jerusalem: Israel Exploration Society, 1986), p. 59; originally published in *JNES* 28 (1969), p. 81.

[62] The importance of this place-name was pointed out by James H. Breasted, "The Earliest Occurrence of the Name of Abram," *American Journal of Semitic Languages and Literature* 21 (1904), p. 36.

[63] Yohanan Aharoni, *The Archaeology of the Land of Israel*, trans. Anson F. Rainey (Philadelphia: Westminster Press, 1982), p. 168.

[64] Ibid., pp. 162–173.

[65] See Noth, *Die israelitischen Personennamen* (see endnote 27), p. 210.

[66] It is possible that the transferral of the Isaac tradition to Beersheba was partly the result of the historical movement of people from the northern hills into the Negev. Note, for example, the prominent role played by Simeon and Levi, the patriarchs of the tribes of southwestern Judah and the northern Negev, in the story of the rape of Dinah at Shechem (Genesis 34). See Noth, *History of Israel* (see endnote 31), pp. 71 and 76, note 1. Contrast de Vaux, *Early History* (see endnote 8), pp. 532–533.

[67] See Thompson, *Historicity of the Patriarchal Narratives* (see endnote 9), pp. 45–48

[68] For the citations, see Jan Simons, *Handbook for the Study of Egyptian Topographical Lists Relating to Western Asia* (Leiden: Brill, 1937), xxxiv, lists 1a and 1b/102 (Tuthmosis III), 23/9 (Ramesses II) and 27/104 (Ramesses III), and Shmuel Ahituv, *Canaanite Toponyms in Ancient Egyptian Documents* (Jerusalem: Magnes Press, 1984), p. 200. See *ANET*, p. 242.

[69] See Shmuel Yeivin ("The Short List of the Towns in Palestine and Syria Captured by Tuthmosis III During His First Campaign," *Eretz Israel* 3 [Jerusalem: Israel Exploration Society, 1954], pp.

32–38, especially p. 36), who proposes an identification with Tel Melat, west of Gezer, which is often associated with the biblical city of Gibbethon.

[70] Both of these cities are mentioned in the same part of the Tuthmosis list, as are a number of nearby places east of the Jordan in the Yarmuk region. See H. Wolfgang Helck, *Die Beziehungen Ägyptens zu Vorderasien im 3. und 2. Jahrtausen v. Chr*, Ägyptologische Abhandlungen 5 (Weisbaden: Otto Harrassowitz, 1962), p. 128.

[71] This was taken for granted by William F. Albright ("A Third Revision of the Early Chronology of Western Asia," *BASOR* 88 [1942], pp. 28–36, especially p. 36, n. 38).

[72] See also Aharon Kempinski, "Some Observations on the Hyksos (XVth) Dynasty and Its Canaanite Origins," in *Pharaonic Egypt: The Bible and Christianity*, ed. Sarah Israelit-Groll (Jerusalem: Magnes Press, 1985), pp. 129–137; See Baruch Halpern ("The Exodus from Egypt: Myth or Reality?" in *The Rise of Ancient Israel*, ed. Hershel Shanks [Washington, DC: Biblical Archaeology Society, 1992], p. 110, n. 20), who notes the possibility that the 18th-century Jacob-Har may have been a local ruler in pre-Hyksos Egypt, and that the Shiqmona seal was a sign of trade or other local relations with his dynasty.

[73] Noth, *History of Israel* (see endnote 31), p. 71, n. 2.

[74] See, for example, Victor Maag, "Der Hirte Israel," *Schweizerische Theologische Umschau* 28 (1958), pp. 2–28; Horst Seebass, *Der Erzvater Israel*, ZAW Supplement 98 (Berlin: A. Topelmann, 1966), pp. 1–5, 25–34.

[75] See Siegfried Herrmann, *A History of Israel in Old Testament Times*, trans. John Bowden (Philadelphia: Fortress Press, 1981), p. 51. Recent proponents of this idea in one form or another include Albert de Pury ("Genèse xxxiv et l'histoire," *RB* 76 [1969], pp. 5–49, especially pp. 39–48) and André Lemaire ("Asriel, šr'l Israel et l'origine de la confédération israelite," *VT* 23 [1973], pp. 239–243); and see P. Kyle McCarter, Jr., "The Origins of Israelite Religion," in *The Rise of Ancient Israel* (see endnote 72), pp. 132–136.

[76] See Israel Finkelstein, "Shiloh Yields Some, But Not All, of Its Secrets," *BAR*, January/February 1986, pp. 22–41, especially p. 35, and the demographic statistics cited by Lawrence

E. Stager, in "The Archaeology of the Family in Ancient Israel," *BASOR* 260 (1985), pp. 1–36, especially p. 3.

[77] Hermann Gunkel, *Legends of Genesis, the Biblical Saga and History* (New York: Schocken, 1964), pp. 23–24. See Jeremiah 49:7, Obadiah 1:8 and Job.

[78] Noth, *History of Pentateuchal Traditions* (see endnote 33), pp. 97–98.

[79] Ronald S. Hendel, *The Epic of the Patriarch: The Jacob Cycle and the Narrative Traditions of Canaan and Israel*, Harvard Semitic Monographs 42 (Atlanta: Scholars Press, 1987), pp. 111–131.

[80] See de Vaux, *Early History* (see endnote 8), pp. 642–643.

[81] Noth, *Die israelitischen Personennamen* (see endnote 25), p. 212; de Vaux, *Early History* (see endnote 8), p. 313.

[82] See Halpern, "Exodus from Egypt" (see endnote 72), pp. 92–99.

[83] Theodor H. Gaster, *Myth, Legend, and Custom in the Old Testament*, 2 vols. (New York: Torchbooks/Harper & Row, 1975), vol. 1, pp. 217–218; Thomas Thompson and Dorothy Irvin, "The Joseph and Moses Narratives," in Hayes and Miller, *Israelite and Judaean History* (see endnote 7), pp. 185–188.

[84] *ANET*, pp. 23–25.

[85] Thompson and Irvin, "The Joseph and Moses Narratives" (see endnote 83), pp. 188–190.

[86] Seven years of famine are described in an Egyptian text of the Ptolemaic period (perhaps the end of the second century B.C.E.), which claims to derive from King Djoser of the Third Dynasty (c. 2650 B.C.E.); see *ANET*, pp. 31–32. Tablet VI of the Akkadian Gilgamesh epic speaks of "seven years of husks"; see *ANET*, p. 85. The autobiographical inscription of Idrimi, king of the Syrian city of Alalakh in the 16th century B.C.E., refers to two unfavorable periods, each lasting seven years; see *ANET*, pp. 557–558. There is a prediction of seven to eight years of drought in the Ugaritic myth of Äqht; see *ANET*, p. 153.

[87] See Donald B. Redford, *A Study of the Biblical Story of Joseph*, VT Supplement 20 (Leiden: Brill, 1970).

[88] See *ANET*, p. 445 and n. 10.

[89] See de Vaux, *Early History* (see endnote 8), pp. 301–302.

[90] Herrman Ranke, *Die Ägyptischen Personnamen*, 3 vols. (Glückstadt, W. Ger.: J.J. Augustin, 1935), vol. 1, p. 14, names 13–17, and p. 15, name 3. See also Alan R. Schulman, "On the Egyptian Name of Joseph: A New Approach," *Studien zur altägyptischen Kultur* 2 (1975), pp. 238–239; Donald B. Redford, *Egypt, Canaan, and Israel in Ancient Times* (Princeton: Princeton University Press, 1992), p. 424; and Kenneth A. Kitchen, "Genesis 12–50 in the Near Eastern World," in *He Swore an Oath: Biblical Themes from Genesis 12–50*, eds. R.S. Hess, P.E. Satterthwaite and G.J. Wenham (Cambridge: Tyndale House, 1993), pp. 84–85.

[91] H. Hamada, "Stela of Putiphar," *Annales du Service des Antiquités de l'Égypte* 39 (1939), pp. 273–276 and plate 39.

[92] Ranke, *Die Ägyptischen Personennamen* (see endnote 90), pp. 409–412 and Schulman, "On the Egyptian Name" (see endnote 90), pp. 239–242; see also the imaginative proposal of Kitchen, "Genesis 12–50" (see endnote 90), pp. 80–84.

[93] Helck, *Die Beziehungen Ägyptens* (see endnote 70), pp. 77–81, 342–369; Jozef M.A. Janssen, "Fonctionnaires sémites au service de l'Égypte," *Chronique d'Égypte* 26 (1951), pp. 50–62; William F. Albright, "Northwest-Semitic Names in a List of Egyptian Slaves from the Eighteenth Century B.C.," *JAOS* 74 (1954), pp. 222–233; Georges Posener, "Les asiatiques en Égypte sous les XII and XIII dynasties," *Syria* 34 (1957), pp. 145–163.

[94] *ANET*, p. 260.

[95] See Alan H. Gardiner, *Egypt of the Pharaohs: An Introduction* (Oxford: Clarendon Press, 1961), p. 282.

[96] *ANET*, p. 259 (trans. John A. Wilson). The text is a model letter from a scribal school.

[97] See Alan H. Gardiner, *Ancient Egyptian Onomastica*, 3 vols. (London: Oxford University Press, 1947), pp. 191–193, no. 265. In the present state of our knowledge, we cannot be sure that the equation of the toponym in the Egyptian texts with the name of the Israelite tribe is linguistically valid. Albright associated the name of an Asiatic female slave in 18th-century B.C.E. Egypt with the tribal name ("Northwest Semitic Names", p. 229–231 and

note 51 [see endnote 93]). The sibilant of the slave name (š =*š) is different from that of the geographical term (ś=*t or *ś in the Egyptian texts. It seems to follow that the geographical term can have had nothing to do with the Israelite tribe (see Kenneth A. Kitchen, *Ancient Orient and the Old Testament* [Chicago: Inter-Varsity Press, 1966], pp. 70–71 and n. 53). But it is not certain that Albright's association of the slave and tribal names is correct. The sibilant in the tribal name "Asher" remains unidentified. Thus, despite Kitchen's objections, Shmuel Yeivin is justified in maintaining the possibility of a connection between the Egyptian toponym and the biblical tribal name ("The Israelite Settlement in Galilee and the Wars with Jabin of Hazor," in *Mélanges bibliques rédigés en l'honneur de André Robert*, Travaux de l'Institut Catholique de Paris 4 [Paris: Bloud and Gay, 1957], pp. 95–104, especially pp. 98–99).

98 See Martin Noth, *The Old Testament World*, trans. V.I. Gruhn (Philadelphia: Fortress Press, 1966), pp. 55–58. See Noth, *History of Israel* (see endnote 31), pp. 56, 60, 67 and n. 1, and the comments by de Vaux, *Early History* (see endnote 8), p. 665.

99 Noth, *Old Testament World*, p. 72; and in *History of Israel* (see endnote 31), pp. 62–63.

100 On "Manasseh," See Noth, *Die israelitischen Personennamen* (see endnote 25), p. 222.

101 This is confirmed by the survey of Ephraim (Israel Finkelstein, "Shiloh Yields Some, But Not All, of Its Secrets," *BAR*, January/February 1986, pp. 22–41, especially p. 35). See the demographic statistics cited by Stager, in "The Archaeology of the Family in Ancient Israel" (see endnote 76), pp. 1–36, especially p. 3.

102 The importance of the contrast between the mountains and the plains to the history of this period was first stressed by Albrecht Alt. See "The Settlement of the Israelites in Palestine," in *Essays on Old Testament History and Religion* (Garden City, NY: Anchor/Doubleday, 1968), pp. 173–221, especially pp. 188–204.

103 Giorgio Buccellati, *Cities and Nations of Ancient Syria*, Studi Semitici 26 (Rome: Ist. (Institute) di Studi del Vicino Oriente, 1967).

II. Israel in Egypt

1 On wet-nurses, see Brevard S. Childs, "The Birth of Moses," *JBL* 84 (1965), pp. 109–122. On the name "Moses," see Alan H. Gardiner, "The Egyptian Origin of Some English Personal Names," *JAOS* 56 (1936), pp. 192–194; J. Cerny, "The Greek Etymology of the Name of Moses," *Annales du Service des antiquités de l'Egypte* 51 (1951), pp. 349–354; and Jaroslav G. Griffiths, "The Egyptian Derivation of the Name Moses," *JNES* 12 (1953), pp. 225–231.

2 See Nahum M. Sarna, *Exploring Exodus* (New York: Schocken Books, 1986), pp. 39–42.

3 On the plagues, see Moshe Greenberg, "Plagues of Egypt," *Encyclopedia Judaica*, vol. 13, pp. 604–613; Ziony Zevit, "The Priestly Redaction and Interpretation of the Plagues Narrative in Exodus," *JQR* 66 (1976), pp. 193–211; Sarna, *Exploring Exodus* (see endnote 2), pp. 63–80.

4 Baruch Halpern, "The Exodus from Egypt: Myth or Reality?" in *The Rise of Ancient Israel*, ed. Hershel Shanks (Washington, DC: Biblical Archaeology Society, 1992), p. 87.

5 See Sir Alan Gardiner, perhaps the best-known and most highly respected Egyptologist of the 20th century, in "The Geography of the Exodus," in *Recueil d'études égyptologiques dediées à la mémoire de Jean-François Champollion* (Paris: Bibliothèque de l'école des hautes études, 1922), p. 205: "That Israel was in Egypt under one form or another no historian could possibly doubt; a legend of such tenacity representing the early fortunes of a peoples under so unfavorable an aspect could not have arisen save as a reflexion, however much distorted, of real occurrences."

6 This is an application of a more general principle: "Hints in the text which go contrary to its overall bias suggest some authentic information has survived the editorial process." Lester L. Grabbe, "Are Historians of Ancient Palestine Fellow Creatures—or Different Animals?" in *Can a 'History of Israel' Be Written?*, ed. Grabbe, JSOT Supplement Series 245 (Sheffield: Sheffield Academic Press, 1997), p. 30.

7 Halpern, "The Exodus from Egypt?" (see endnote 4), pp. 99–100.

8 William C. Hayes, *A Papyrus of the Late Middle Kingdom in the Brooklyn Museum* [Papyrus Brooklyn

35.1446] (New York: Brooklyn Museum, 1955). See also William F. Albright, "Northwest Semitic Names in a List of Egyptian Slaves from the Eighteenth Century B.C.," *JAOS* 74 (1954), pp. 222–223.

[9] The translation is that of James K. Hoffmeier, *Israel in Egypt* (Oxford: Oxford University Press, 1997), pp. 54–55.

[10] Ibid., p. 59.

[11] Ibid., p. 60.

[12] *ANET*, p. 259.

[13] Kenneth A. Kitchen, *Ramesside Inscriptions*, vol. 2 (Oxford: Blackwell, 1996), pp. 520–522.

[14] Kenneth A. Kitchen, "From the Brickfields of Egypt," *TB* 27 (1976), pp. 145–146.

[15] For a criticism of the hermeneutic of suspicion, see Jon D. Levenson, *The Hebrew Bible, the Old Testament and Historical Criticism* (Louisville: Westminster/John Knox Press, 1993), p. 116.

[16] Thomas L. Thompson, *The Origin Tradition of Ancient Israel*, vol. 1 (Sheffield: JSOT Press, 1987), p. 41.

[17] Robert B. Coote, *Early Israel* (Minneapolis: Fortress Press, 1990), pp. 2–3.

[18] For the problems and different approaches, see C. De Wit, *The Date and Route of the Exodus* (London: Tyndale, 1960); L.T. Wood, "The Date of the Exodus," in *New Perspectives on the Old Testament*, ed. J.B. Wane (Waco, TX: Word Books, 1970), pp. 66–87; B.K. Waltke, "Palestinian Artifactual Evidence Supporting the Early Date for the Exodus," *BS* 129 (1972), pp. 33–47; John J. Bimson, *Redating the Exodus and Conquest*, JSOT Supplement 5 (Leiden: Brill, 1978).

[19] Josephus, *Antiquities* 14.2

[20] *Seder Olam* 3:2

[21] For a summary of the chronological problems, see Roland K. Harrison, *Introduction to the Old Testament* (Grand Rapids, MI: Eerdmans, 1969), pp. 164–176, 308–325.

[22] See Charles F. Burney, *Notes on the Hebrew Text of the Book of Kings* (New York: KTAV, 1970), p. 60.

[23] In addition, a 16th-century-B.C.E. Exodus has often been proposed to coincide with the expulsion of the Hyksos dynasty from Egypt and the eruption

of the volcano at Thera. For a thorough refutation of this highly speculative theory, see Manfred Bietak, "The Volcano Explains Everything—Or Does It?" *BAR*, November/December 2006.

[24] In addition, if the Exodus occurred in the 15th century B.C.E., there would be a 400-year period before the institution of the monarchy at the end of the 11th century B.C.E. This is an unacceptably long time for the period of the Judges.

[25] Lawrence E. Stager, "The Archaeology of the Family in Ancient Israel," *BASOR* 260 (1985), pp. 1–35.

[26] Pierre Montet, *Everyday Life in Egypt in the Days of Ramesses the Great*, trans. A.R. Maxwell-Hyslop and Margaret S. Drower (London: E. Arnold, 1958); Raymond O. Faulkner, "Egypt from the Inception of the Nineteenth Dynasty to the Death of Ramesses II," in *CAH*, vol. 2, part 2, pp. 225–232.

[27] The scholarly debate as to whether the biblical city referred to as Rameses is the same as Pi-Ramesses in Egyptian records has been resolved to the satisfaction of most scholars. Manfred Bietak has shown that the "Pi-" drops off in various grammatical situations. See his "Comments on Exodus," in *Egypt, Israel, and Sinai*, ed. Anson F. Rainey (Tel Aviv: Tel Aviv University Press, 1987), pp. 163–171.

[28] H.J. Franken, "Palestine in the Time of the Nineteenth Dynasty: Archaeological Evidence," in *CAH*, vol. 2, part 2, pp. 331–337. Halpern, "The Exodus from Egypt" (see endnote 4), p. 101.

[29] Carol Redmount, "Bitter Lives: Israel in and out of Egypt," in *The Oxford History of the Biblical World*, ed. Michael Coogan (Oxford: Oxford University Press, 1998), p. 89.

[30] *ANET*, pp. 376–378.

[31] Gösta W. Ahlström, *Who Were the Israelites?* (Winona Lake, IN: Eisenbrauns, 1986).

[32] See also Abraham Malamat, "The Exodus: Egyptian Analogies," in *Exodus—The Egyptian Evidence*, eds. Ernest S. Frerichs and Leonard H. Lesko (Winona Lake, IN: Eisenbrauns, 1997).

[33] See William G. Dever, "Israelite Origins and the 'Nomadic Ideal,'" in *Mediterranean Peoples in Transition*, eds. Seymour Gitin, Amihai Mazar and Ephraim Stern (Jerusalem: Israel Exploration Society, 1998), esp. pp. 231–232.

³⁴ See also Anson Rainey, "Whence Came the Israelites and Their Language?" *IEJ* 57 (2007), pp. 41–64.

³⁵ It will not do, in refutation of this argument, to point to other peoples, such as the Romans, who also reproduced inglorious traditions about their own past. See, for example, J. Alberto Soggin, *A History of Ancient Israel* (Philadelphia: Westminster Press, 1984), pp. 110–111. On the contrary, such tales may well reflect historical reality, and in any case did not become a central and formative factor in shaping the religion and culture of their respective bearers over thousands of years.

³⁶ In several biblical passages, the word translated "thousands" (*alafim*) means not thousands but clans. It is sometimes suggested on this basis that the passage in Numbers 1:46 should be understood to refer to 600 families or clans, rather than 600,000 men. It is an ingenious theory, but it flounders. For example: The number of the Israelite firstborn sons who went on the Exodus as given in Numbers 3:43 is 22,273. Since the number is exact, the word *elef* cannot be translated as family or clan. Moreover, the context makes clear that the reference is to individuals (firstborn Israelites), not families or clans. If there were 22,273 firstborn Israelites, the total number of families had to be more than 600. See Sarna, *Exploring Exodus* (see endnote 2), pp. 98–100. Sarna writes, "The structures of thought within which the biblical writers operated permitted them to conceive of reality in ways quite different from our own ... [The account as a whole] is not meant to be history writing in the modern sense of that term, but a historiosophical understanding of a complex of events that happened in historical time" (p. 100).

³⁷ Susan Niditch, *Oral World and Written Word: Ancient Israelite Literature* (Louisville: Westminster/John Knox Press, 1996).

³⁸ See, for example, Niels Peter Lemche, *Early Israel: Anthropological and Historical Studies on the Israelite Society Before the Monarchy* (Leiden: Brill, 1985), p. 412.

³⁹ Myth, however, does not necessarily indicate a complete lack of historicity. Myth may have a historical core. See Bernard F. Batto, *Slaying the Dragon—Mythmaking in the Biblical Tradition* (Louisville: Westminster/John Knox Press, 1992), p. 103 and *passim*. Batto contends that "it was the biblical writers' intention to explode the exodus into an 'event' that transcends the particularities of space and time, making it the story of every Israelite in every generation" (p. 103). History has been "mythologized" (p. 109). For Batto, "myth is a sophisticated and abstract mode of thought" (p. 10). It "involves reflective thinking not through syllogistic reasoning or philosophical categories but through the medium of mythic narrative" (p. 40). "[Myth] attempts to express ultimate reality through symbol" (p. 11). "Whatever the historicity of the events that lie behind the biblical narrative, the exodus *as story* has been elevated to mythic proportions" (p. 103).

⁴⁰ *Encyclopaedia Judaica*, s.v. "Manetho."

⁴¹ Grabbe, "Are Historians of Ancient Palestine Fellow Creatures?" (see endnote 6), p. 23.

⁴² Ibid., pp. 23–24.

⁴³ Manfred Bietak, "Daba, Tell ed-," in *OEANE*, vol. 2, at p. 100. See, in general, James M. Weinstein, "Hyksos," in *ABD*, vol. 3, under "The Fifteenth Dynasty."

⁴⁴ *ANET*, p. 230b.

⁴⁵ On the Hyksos, see John Van Seters, *The Hyksos: A New Investigation* (New Haven, CT: Yale University Press, 1966); Donald B. Redford, "The Hyksos Invasion in History and Tradition," *Orientalia* 39 (1970), pp. 1–51; William C. Hayes, "Egypt from the Death of Ammenemes III to Seqenenre II," in *CAH*, vol. 2, part 1, pp. 54–64; T.G.H. James, "Egypt: From the Expulsion of the Hyksos to Amenophis I," in *CAH*, vol. 2, part 1, pp. 289–312; Yohanan Aharoni, *The Land of the Bible: A Historical Geography*, rev. and enlarged, trans. and ed. Anson F. Rainey (Philadelphia: Westminster Press, 1979), pp. 147–150.

⁴⁶ The XVIIth Dynasty is an obscure dynasty of Egyptian rulers who ruled part of Egypt from Thebes during the Hyksos era.

⁴⁷ Bietak, "Daba, Tell ed-," in *OEANE* (see endnote 43), at p. 100. See also Manfred Bietak, *Avaris, The Captial of the Hyksos* (London: Sackler Foundation, 1996).

⁴⁸ See also Trude Dothan, "Gaza Sands Yield Lost Outpost of the Egyptian Empire," *National Geographic* (December 1982), pp. 739–768.

⁴⁹ Hoffmeier, *Israel in Egypt* (see endnote 9), pp. 164–175.

[50] Ibid., pp. 199–222.

[51] See also Bernard Batto, "The Reed Sea: Requiescat in Pace," *JBL* 102 (1983), p. 27.

[52] There were four major routes through the Sinai in antiquity, the northern route along the Mediterranean coast, and three others through different wadi (or valley) systems. See Itzhaq Beit-Arieh, "The Route Through Sinai," *BAR*, May/June 1988; and Redmount, "Bitter Lives" (see endnote 29), pp. 91–94.

[53] Hershel Shanks, ed., *Frank Moore Cross: Conversations with a Bible Scholar* (Washington, DC: Biblical Archaeology Society, 1994), pp. 11–30.

[54] See also Lily Singer-Avitz, "The Earliest Settlement in Kadesh Barnea," *Tel Aviv* 35 (2008), p. 73.

[55] See Charles Krahmalkov, "Exodus Itinerary Confirmed by Egyptian Evidence," *BAR*, September/October 1994.

[56] As one commentator has observed, "We do the Exodus narrative a profound disservice by uncritically seeking natural interpretations for the clearly miraculous, and it is misguided to supply scientific explanations for such nonhistorical events as the ten plagues of Egypt, the burning bush that spoke to Moses, or the pillars of cloud and fire that accompanied the Israelites in the wilderness." See Redmount, "Bitter Lives" (see endnote 29), pp. 85–86.

[57] Donald B. Redford, *Egypt, Canaan and Israel in Ancient Times* (Princeton: Princeton University Press, 1992), p. 417.

[58] It is also possible to interpret the verse as stating that Moses' mother named him. But this seems less likely. The text explains the name on the basis of a traditional Hebrew etymology: "to draw out." Pharaoh's daughter explains the choice of name: "I drew him out of the water" (Exodus 2:10).

[59] See Hoffmeier, *Israel in Egypt* (see endnote 9), p. 140. The divine name seems to have been omitted in the case of Moses. This does sometimes occur in Egyptian records. Or the divine element may have been suppressed by the biblical writer, who would hardly want the name of such a central figure in the development of Israelite religion to suggest allegiance to a foreign god. See Redmount, "Bitter Lives" (see endnote 29), pp. 88–89.

[60] For an argument denying any relationship between the two texts, see Hoffmeier, *Israel in Egypt* (see endnote 9), pp. 136–137.

III. Settlement in Canaan

[1] For William F. Albright's pioneering work on the issue, see especially his "Archaeology and the Date of the Hebrew Conquest of Palestine," *BASOR* 58 (1935), pp. 10–18; "Further Light on the History of Israel from Lachish and Megiddo," *BASOR* 68 (1937), pp. 22–26; and "The Israelite Conquest of Canaan in the Light of Archaeology," *BASOR* 74 (1939), pp. 11–23. His views were developed and widely popularized by his students; see G. Ernest Wright and Floyd Filson, *The Westminster Historical Atlas of the Bible* (Philadelphia: Westminster Press, 1956); and John Bright, *A History of Israel* (Philadelphia: Westminster Press, 1959).

[2] Yigael Yadin, "Is the Biblical Account of the Israelite Conquest of Canaan Historically Reliable?" *BAR*, March/April 1982, p. 18.

[3] Abraham Malamat, "How Inferior Israelite Forces Conquered Fortified Canaanite Cities," *BAR*, March/April 1982, p. 27.

[4] Paul Lapp reviewed the archaeological picture in 1967 with the conclusion that, although the evidence admittedly was ambivalent, on the whole it supported the notion of a 13th-century Israelite military conquest. J. Maxwell Miller reviewed the archaeological evidence again ten years later and concluded that more archaeological evidence had to be "explained away" in order to accommodate the notion of a 13th-century military conquest than could be called upon to support such a notion. See Paul W. Lapp, "The Conquest of Palestine in the Light of Archaeology," *Concordia Theological Monthly* 38 (1967), pp. 283–300; and J. Maxwell Miller, "Archaeology and the Israelite Conquest of Canaan: Some Methodological Observations," *PEQ* 109 (1977), pp. 87–93.

[5] See Kathleen M. Kenyon and Thomas A. Holland, *Excavations at Jericho III* (Plates) (London: British School of Archaeology in Jerusalem, 1981), pl. 236. This master section of the north side of trench I shows dramatically the successive layers of mudbrick walls that collapsed down the slope of the mound.

[6] Kathleen M. Kenyon, *Archaeology in the Holy Land* (New York: Praeger, 1960), pp. 210–211.

[7] Paul W. Lapp, "The Importance of Dating," *BAR*, March 1977, pp. 13–32.

8 Albright, "The Israelite Conquest of Canaan" (see endnote 1), pp. 15–16; Louis-Hugues Vincent, "Les fouilles d'et-Tell 'Ai," *RB* 46 (1937), p. 256.

9 Joseph Callaway, "The 1964 'Ai (et-Tell) Excavations," *BASOR* 178 (1965), pp. 39–40.

10 Lawrence E. Stager, "Forging an Identity" in *The Oxford History of the Biblical World*, ed. Michael D. Coogan (Oxford: Oxford University Press, 1998), p. 97.

11 William G. Dever, *Who Were the Early Israelites and Where Did They Come From?* (Grand Rapids, MI: Eerdmans, 2003), p. 68.

12 Amnon Ben-Tor and Maria Teresa Rubiato, "Excavating Hazor, Part Two: Did the Israelites Destroy the Canaanite City," *BAR*, May/June 1999.

13 Malamat, "How Inferior Israelite Forces Conquered" (see endnote 3), p. 34.

14 Ibid., p. 27.

15 Ibid., p. 26.

16 Ibid.

17 Albrecht Alt, "The Settlement of the Israelites in Palestine," in *Essays on Old Testament History and Religion*, trans. R.A. Wilson (Garden City, NY: Doubleday, 1968), pp. 175–221; originally published in German in 1925.

18 Malamat, "How Inferior Israelite Forces Conquered" (see endnote 3), p. 34.

19 Martin Noth, *Das System der zwölf Stämme Israels*, Beiträge zur Wissenschaft vom Alten und Neuen Testament 4:1 (Stuttgart: W. Kohlhammer, 1930), and *A History of Israel*, 2nd ed., trans. Peter R. Ackroyd (New York: Harper and Row, 1958).

20 Gösta W. Ahlström, *Who Were the Israelites?* (Winona Lake, IN: Eisenbrauns, 1986), p. 40.

21 George E. Mendenhall, "The Hebrew Conquest of Palestine," *BA* 25 (1961), pp. 66–87.

22 Norman K. Gottwald, *The Tribes of Yahweh* (Maryknoll, NY: Orbis Books, 1979), pp. 210–219.

23 See endnote 1.

24 Dever, *Who Were the Early Israelites?* (see endnote 11), p. 54 (emphasis in original).

25 Ibid., p. 188.

26 Ibid., p. 121.

27 Israel Finkelstein, *The Archaeology of the Israelite Settlement* (Jerusalem: Israel Exploration Society, 1988), p. 274.

28 Lawrence E. Stager, "Response" in *Biblical Archaeology Today* (Jerusalem: Israel Exploration Society, 1985), p. 84.

29 Stager, "Forging an Identity" (see endnote 10), p. 100.

30 Ibid., p. 104.

31 Anson F. Rainey, "Redefining Hebrew—A Transjordanian Language," *Maarav* 14.2 (2007), p. 67.

32 "The few instances where the Phoenician vocable has penetrated the Hebrew Bible are restricted to poetic and wisdom passages where the Israelite/Judean kingdoms acquired an international literary tradition. The borrowing occurred a long time after the initial settlement in the Early Iron Age." See Ibid., p. 74. For a discussion of the Hebrew adoption of Northwest Semitic literary topoi, see also Anson F. Rainey, "The Northwest Semitic Literary Repertoire and Its Acquaintance by Judean Writers," *Maarav* 15.2 (2009).

33 Rainey, "The Northwest Semitic Literary Repertoire" (see endnote 32), p. 168.

34 See, for example, J. Maxwell Miller and John H. Hayes, *A History of Ancient Israel and Judah*, 2nd ed. (Louisville: Westminster/John Knox Press, 2006), pp. 37, 115.

35 See Strata, "A 3,500-year-old Inscription from a Syrian Kingdom May Tell Us Who the Habiru Were," *BAR*, November/December 2006, p. 22.

36 But see Frank M. Cross in Hershel Shanks, ed., *Frank Moore Cross: Conversations With a Bible Scholar* (Washington, DC: Biblical Archaeology Society, 1994), pp. 21–23.

37 Anson F. Rainey and R. Steven Notley, *The Sacred Bridge* (Jerusalem: Carta, 2006), p. 89.

38 Ibid.

39 Dever, *Who Were the Early Israelites?* (see endnote 11), p. 74.

40 Ibid.

41 Carol A. Redmount, "Bitter Lives: Israel in and out of Egypt," in *The Oxford History of the Biblical World* (see endnote 10), p. 74.

⁴² Shanks, ed., *Frank Moore Cross* (see endnote 36), p. 25.

⁴³ Ibid., p. 21.

⁴⁴ See Baruch Halpern, "The Exodus From Egypt: Myth or Reality?" in *The Rise of Ancient Israel* (Washington, DC: Biblical Archaeology Society, 1992): "The Exodus story was to the ancient Israelite what the stories of the Pilgrims and the Revolutionary War are to Americans ... The Exodus coded certain common values into the culture. All Israel shared the background of the ancestors— all Israel had been slaves in Egypt. Whatever one's biological ancestry, to be an Israelite meant that one's ancestors—spiritual or emotive or collective ancestors—had risen from Egypt," p. 88.

⁴⁵ Ibid., p. 23.

⁴⁶ Dever, *Who Were the Early Israelites?* (see endnote 11), p. 73.

⁴⁷ See also Lawrence E. Stager, "Archaeology, Ecology and Social History: Background Themes to the Song of Deborah," *VT* 40 (1988), p. 221.

⁴⁸ Stager, "Forging an Identity" (see endnote 10), p. 104.

⁴⁹ Shanks, ed., *Frank Moore Cross* (see endnote 36), p. 23.

⁵⁰ Anson F. Rainey, "Inside, Outside," *BAR*, November/December 2008, p. 50.

⁵¹ Miller and Hayes, *A History of Ancient Israel and Judah* (see endnote 34), p. 78.

⁵² Avraham Faust, *Israel's Ethnogenesis* (London: Equinox, 2006).

⁵³ See André Lemaire, *The Birth of Monotheism* (Washington, DC: Biblical Archaeology Society, 2007).

IV. The United Monarchy

¹ William E. Evans, "An Historical Reconstruction of the Emergence of Israelite Kingship and the Reign of Saul," in *Scripture in Context II*, ed. William W. Hallo et al. (Winona Lake, IN: Eisenbrauns, 1983), pp. 61–78, especially p. 77.

² Israel Finkelstein, "The Emergence of the Monarchy in Israel: The Environmental and Socio-Economic Aspects," *JSOT* 44 (1989), pp. 43–74.

³ J. Maxwell Miller, "Is It Possible to Write a History of Israel wihout Relying on the Hebrew Bible?" in

The Fabric of History, ed. Diana Vikander Edelman, JSOT Supplement 127 (Sheffield: Sheffield Academic Press, 1991), pp. 93–102, especially p. 101.

⁴ See, for example, Israel Finkelstein, "The Archaeology of the United Monarchy: An Alternative View," *Levant* 28 (1996), pp. 177–187; Amihai Mazar, "Iron Age Chronology: A Reply to I. Finkelstein," *Levant* 29 (1997), pp. 157–167; Lawrence E. Stager, "The Patrimonial Kingdom of Solomon," in *Symbiosis, Symbolism, and the Power of the Past: Canaan, Ancient Israel, and Their Neighbors from the Late Bronze Age Through Roman Palaestina*, eds. William G. Dever and Seymour Gitin (Winona Lake, IN: Eisenbrauns, 2003), pp. 63–73; Israel Finkelstein, "City-States to States: Polity Dynamics in the 10th–9th Centuries B.C.E.," ibid., pp. 76–83; Raz Kletter, "Chronology and United Monarchy: A Methodological Review," *ZDPV* 120 (2004), pp. 13–54; Steven M. Ortiz, "Deconstructing and Reconstructing the United Monarchy: House of David or Tent of David (Current Trends in Iron Age Chronology)," in *The Future of Biblical Archaeology*, eds. James K. Hoffmeier and Alan Millard (Grand Rapids, MI: Eerdmans, 2004), pp. 121–147; Amihai Mazar, "The Debate over the Chronology of the Iron Age in the Southern Levant: Its History, the Current Situation, and a Suggested Resolution," in *The Bible and Radiocarbon Dating: Archaeology, Text and Science*, eds. Thomas E. Levy and Thomas Higham (London: Equinox, 2005), pp. 15–30; Steven M. Ortiz, "Does the 'Low Chronology' Work? A Case Study of Tel Qasile X, Tel Gezer X, and Lachish V," in *"I Will Speak the Riddles of Ancient Times,"* Archaeological and Historical Studies in Honor of Amihai Mazar, eds. Aren M. Maeir and Pierre de Miroschedji (Winona Lake, IN: Eisenbrauns, 2006), pp. 587–611; Israel Finkelstein and Eliazer Piasetzky, "The Iron I-IIA in the Highlands and Beyond: 14C Anchors, Pottery Phases and the Shoshenq I Campaign," *Levant* 38 (2006), pp. 45–61; see also "Radiocarbon Dating and Philistine Chronology," *Ägypten und Levante* 17 (2007), pp. 73–82; Amihai Mazar, "The Spade and the Text: The Interaction between Archaeology and Israelite History Relating to the Tenth-Ninth Centuries BCE," in *Understanding the History of Ancient Israel*, ed. H.G.M. Williamson, Proceedings of the British Academy 143 (Oxford: Oxford University Press, 2007), pp. 143–171.

[5] See, for instance, Margaret M. Gelinas, "United Monarchy—Divided Monarchy. Fact or Fiction," in *The Pitcher is Broken, Memorial Essays for Gösta W. Ahlström*, JSOT Supplement 190 (Sheffield: Sheffield Academic Press, 1995), pp. 227–237; Israel Finkelstein and Neil Asher Silberman, *David and Solomon. In Search of the Bible's Sacred Kings and the Roots of Western Tradition* (New York: Free Press, 2006); and Brian B. Schmidt ed., *The Quest for Historical Israel: Debating Archaeology and the History of Israel*. SBL Archaeological and Biblical Studies 17 (Leiden/Boston: Brill, 2007).

[6] See Steven L. McKenzie, "Saul in the Deuteronomistic History," in *Saul in Story and Tradition*, eds. Carl S. Ehrlich and Marsha C. White, Forschungen zum Alten Testament 47 (Tübingen: Mohr Siebeck, 2006), pp. 59–70; Yairah Amit, "The Delicate Balance in the Image of Saul and its Place in the Deuteronomistic History," ibid., pp. 70–79; Gregory Mobley, "Glimpses of the Heroic Saul," ibid., pp. 80–87. See also Klaus-Peter Adam, *Saul und David in der judäischen Geschichtsschrebung*, Forschungen zum Alten Testament 51 (Tübingen: Mohr Siebeck, 2007).

[7] See Trude Dothan, "The Philistines Reconsidered," in *Biblical Archaeology Today 1984* (Jerusalem: Israel Exploration Society, 1985), pp. 165–176; see also "The Philistines and the Dothans: An Archaeological Romance, Part I," *BAR*, January/February 1990, pp. 26–36; Trude Dothan and Moshe Dothan, *People of the Sea. The Search for the Philistines* (New York: Macmillan, 1992); Ed Noort, *Die Seevölker in Palästina* (Kampen: Pharos, 1994).

[8] *ANET*, pp. 262–263.

[9] Franco Pintore, "Sèrèn, tarwanis, tyrannos," in *Studi orientalistici in ricordo di F. Pintore*, ed. Onofrio Carruba et al., Studia mediterranea 4 (Padua, Italy: GJES, 1983), pp. 285–322.

[10] Itamar Singer, "Egyptians, Canaanites, and Philistines in the Period of the Emergence of Israel," in *From Nomadism to Monarchy, Archaeological and Historical Aspects of Early Israel*, eds. Israel Finkelstein and Nadav Na'aman (Jerusalem: Israel Exploration Society, 1994), pp. 282–338.

[11] See A.D.H. Mayes, "The Period of Judges and the Rise of the Monarchy," in *Israelite and Judaean History*, eds. John H. Hayes and J. Maxwell Miller (Philadelphia: Westminster Press, 1977), pp. 285–331, especially p. 325; Nadav Na'aman, "The Pre-Deuteronomistic Story of King Saul and its Historical Significance," *CBQ* 54 (1992), pp. 638–658. Nahash's way of treating the Israelites (see Frank Moore Cross, "The Ammonite Oppression of the Tribes of Gad and Ruben," in *History, Historiography and Interpretation*, eds. Hayim Tadmor and Moshe Weinfeld [Jerusalem: Magnes Press, 1983], pp. 148–158) is attested in Assyria (see Albert Kirk Grayson, *Assyrian Royal Inscriptions I* [Wiesbaden: Harrassowitz, 1972], sec. 530 [especially n. 177]; vol. 2 [1976], sec. 549).

[12] See the essay of Volkmar Fritz, "Die Deutungen des Königtums Sauls in den Überlieferungen von seiner Enstehung, I Sam 9–11," *ZAW* 88 (1976), pp. 346–362.

[13] For a possible, but not probable, later date of this expedition, see Diana Edelman, "Saul's Rescue of Jabesh-Gilead (1 Samuel 11:1–11)," *ZAW* 96 (1984), pp. 195–209.

[14] This number seems to be accepted by J. Alberto Soggin (*A History of Ancient Israel* [Philadelphia: Westminster Press, 1984], pp. 49–50).

[15] See Joseph Blenkinsopp, "The Quest of the Historical Saul," in *No Famine in the Land, Studies in Honor of John L. McKenzie*, ed. J.W. Flanagan and A.W. Robinson (Missoula, MT: Scholars Press, 1975), pp. 75–79; Na'aman, "The Pre-Deuteronomistic Story of King Saul," (see endnote 11), pp. 638–658; V. Philips Long, "How Did Saul Become King? Literary Reading and Historical Reconstruction," in *Faith, Tradition, and History: Old Testament Historiography in its Near Eastern Context*, ed. Alan R. Millard (Winona Lake, IN: Eisenbrauns, 1994), pp. 271–284; Siegfried Kreuzer, "Saul—not always—at War. A New Perspective on the Rise of Kingship in Israel," in *Saul in Story and Tradition* (see endnote 6), pp. 39–58.

[16] See David M. Gunn, *The Fate of King Saul*, JSOT Supplement 14 (Sheffield: Sheffield Academic Press, 1980); Diana Vikander Edelman, *King Saul in the Historiography of Judah*, JSOT Supplement 121 (Sheffield: Sheffield Academic Press, 1991).

[17] See André Caquot and Philippe de Robert, *Les livres de Samuel* (Genève: Labor et fides, 1994), pp. 19–20; Robert P. Gordon, "In Search of

David: The David Tradition in Recent Study," in *Faith, Tradition, and History* (see endnote 15), pp. 285–298, especially p. 298.

[18] See W. Lee Humphreys, "The Rise and Fall of King Saul," *JSOT* 18 (1980), pp. 74–90; see also "From Tragic Hero to Villain: A Study of the Figure of Saul and the Development of 1 Samuel," *JSOT* 22 (1982), pp. 95–117.

[19] See P. Kyle McCarter, Jr., "The Apology of David," *JBL* 99 (1980), pp. 485–504. On this literary genre in Assyria, see Hayim Tadmor, "Autobiographical Apology in the Royal Assyrian Literature," in Tadmor and Weinfeld, *History, Historiography* (see endnote 11), pp. 36–57.

[20] André Lemaire, "La montagne de Juda (XIII–XIe siècle av. J.-C.)," in *La protohistoire d'Israël*, ed. Ernest-Marie Laperrousaz (Paris: Cerf, 1990), pp. 293–298.

[21] Walter Dietrich and Stefan Münger, "Die Herrschaft Sauls und der Norden Israel," in *Saxa Loquentur. Studien zur Archäologie Palästinas/Israels. Festschrift für Volkmar Fritz*, ed. Cornelis G. den Hertog et al., AOAT 302 (Münster, Germany: Ugarit Verlag, 2003), pp. 39–59.

[22] One may be sceptical of the idea that Saul was "initially ... a petty king of Gibeon," as proposed by Diana Vikander Edelman, "Saul Ben Kish in History and Tradition," in *The Origins of the Ancient Israelite States*, eds. Volkmar Fritz and Philip R. Davies, JSOT Supplement 228 (Sheffield: Sheffield Academic Press, 1996), pp. 142–159, especially p. 156. One may, however, compare Saul to Labayu, the Late Bronze Age king of Shechem. See Israel Finkelstein, "The Last Labayu: King Saul and the Expansion of the First North Israelite Territorial Entity," in *Essays on Ancient Israel in its Near Eastern Context: A Tribute to Nadav Na'aman*, ed. Yairah Amit et al. (Winona Lake, IN: Eisenbrauns, 2006), pp. 171–187.

[23] Adam Zertal, *The Manasseh Hill Country Survey I-II. Culture and History of the Ancient Near East* 21 (Leiden/Boston: Brill, 2004, 2008); see also "'To the Land of the Perizzites and the Giants': On the Israelite Settlement in the Hill Country of Manasseh," in *From Nomadism to Monarchy* (see endnote 10), pp. 47–69, especially pp. 57–60.

[24] See Israel Finkelstein, *The Archaeology of the Israelite Settlement* (Jerusalem: Israel Exploration Society, 1988), especially pp. 260–269.

[25] Israel Finkelstein and Yitzhak Magen, eds., *Archaeological Survey of the Hill Country of Benjamin* (Jerusalem: Israel Antiquities Authority, 1993); Amihai Mazar, "Jerusalem and its Vicinity in Iron Age I," in *From Nomadism to Monarchy* (see endnote 10), pp. 70–91, especially 70–78.

[26] See Moshe Kochavi, "An Ostracon of the Period of the Judges from 'Izbet Sartah," *Tel Aviv* 4 (1977), pp. 1–13; Israel Finkelstein, *'Izbet Sartah: An Early Iron Age Site near Rosh Ha'ayin, Israel*, British Archaeological Reports, International Series 299 (Oxford: Oxford University Press, 1986).

[27] A. Mazar, "Jerusalem and Its Vicinity," in *From Nomadism to Monarchy* (see endnote 10), p. 75.

[28] Israel Finkelstein, "Excavations at Khirbet ed-Dawwara: An Iron Age I Site Northeast of Jerusalem," *Tel Aviv* 17 (1990), pp. 163–208; Avraham Faust, "Settlement Patterns and State Formation in Southern Samaria and the Archaeology of (a) Saul," in *Saul in Story and Tradition* (see endnote 6), pp. 14–38, especially pp. 26–27.

[29] André Lemaire, "Aux origines d'Israël: la montagne d'Ephraïm et le territoire de Manassé," in *La protohistoire d'Israël* (see endote 20), pp. 183–292, especially pp. 251–255, 284–286.

[30] Israel Finkelstein and Zvi Lederman, "Shiloh 1983," *IEJ* 33 (1983), pp. 267–268; Finkelstein, *The Archaeology of the Israelite Settlement* (see endnote 24), pp. 225–226, 322–323. See also, on the destruction of Ai, Joseph A. Callaway, "A Visit with Ahilud," *BAR*, September/October 1983, pp. 42–53.

[31] Baruch Rosen, "Subsistence Economy in Iron Age I," in *From Nomadism to Monarchy* (see endnote 10), pp. 339–351.

[32] Israel Finkelstein, *The Archaeology of the Israelite Settlement* (see endnote 24), p. 82; comment in *Biblical Archaeology Today 1984* (see endnote 7); "The Emergence of the Monarchy in Israel: The Environmental and Socio-Economic Aspects," *JSOT* 44 (1989), pp. 43–74, especially p. 59.

[33] See "Philistine Temple Discovered Within Tel Aviv City Limits," *BAR*, June 1975, pp. 1, 6–9; Amihai Mazar, *Excavations at Tell Qasile I, The Philistine Sanctuary*, Qedem 12 (Jerusalem: Hebrew University Press, 1980); *Excavations at Tell Qasile II*, Qedem 20 (1985); Trude Dothan,

The Philistines and Their Material Culture (New Haven, CT: Yale University Press, 1982); Ze'ev Herzog, "Tel Gerisa," *IEJ* 33 (1983), pp. 121–123; see also "Tel Miqne/Ekron—The Rise and Fall of a Philistine City," *Qadmoniot* 27 (1994), pp. 2–28; Trude Dothan, "Tell Miqne Ekron: The Aegean Affinities of the 'Sea Peoples' ('Philistines') Settlement in Canaan in the Iron Age I," in *Recent Excavations in Israel: A View to the West. Reports on Kabri, Nami, Miqne-Ekron, Dor, and Ashkelon,* ed. Seymour Gitin (Dubuque, IA: Kendall/Hunt, 1995), pp. 41–59; Lawrence E. Stager, *Ashkelon. Seaport of the Canaanites and the Philistines,* Schweich Lectures on Biblical Archaeology (London, 2004); Moshe Dothan and David Ben-Shlomo, *Ashdod VI. Excavations of Areas H and K (1968–1969),* IAA Reports 24 (Jerusalem: Israel Antiquities Authority, 2005); Lawrence E. Stager, "New Discoveries in the Excavations of Ashkelon in the Bronze and Iron Ages," *Qadmoniot* 39 (131) (2006), pp. 2–19; "Ashkelon," *NEAEHL,* vol. 5 (2008), pp. 1577–1586.

[34] Aren M. Maeir, "Tell es-Safi/Gath, 1996–2002," *IEJ* 53 (2003), pp. 237–246; "Ten Years of Excavations at Biblical Gat Plishtim," *Qadmoniot* 40 (133) (2007), pp. 15–24.

[35] This *lament* could well not be from David himself but from saulide circles. See, for instance, Eben Scheffler, "Saving Saul from the Deuteronomist," in *Past, Present, Future,* eds. Johannes C. de Moor and Harry F. Van Rooy, Oudtestamentische Studiën 44 (Leiden/Boston/Köln: Brill, 2000), pp. 263–271, especially p. 266.

[36] Mario Liverani, "Le 'origini' d'Israele projetto irrealizzable di ricerca etnogenetica," *Rivista biblica* 28 (1980), pp. 9–31.

[37] J. Alberto Soggin, "The Davidic-Solomonic Kingdom," in Hayes and Miller, *Israelite and Judaean History* (see endnote 11), pp. 332–380; "The History of Israel—A Study in Some Questions of Method," *Eretz-Israel* 14 (Jerusalem: Israel Exploration Society, 1978), pp. 44–51; *History of Ancient Israel* (see endnote 14), pp. 19–40.

[38] Soggin, "Davidic-Solomonic Kingdom" (see endnote 37), p. 332.

[39] See Philip R. Davies, *In Search of 'Ancient Israel,'* JSOT Supplement 148 (Sheffield: Sheffield

Academic Press, 1992), pp. 68–69; see Giovanno Garbini, *History and Ideology in Ancient Israel* (New York: Crossroad, 1988), pp. 21–32; Ernst A. Knauf, "From History to Interpretation," in *The Fabric of History* (see endnote 3), pp. 26–64, especially p. 39. See also David W. Jamieson-Drake, *Scribes and Schools in Monarchic Judah, A Socio-Archaeological Approach,* JSOT Supplement 109 (Sheffield: Almond Press, 1991) and my critical review in *JAOS* 112 (1992), pp. 707–708.

[40] Knauf, "From History to Interpretation" (see endnote 39), pp. 26–64, especially p. 39.

[41] See also André Lemaire, "La dynastie davidique (*byt dwd*) dans deux inscriptions ouest-sémitiques du IXe s. av. J.-C.," *SEL* 11 (1994), pp. 17–19.

[42] See also André Lemaire, "Épigraphie palestinienne: nouveaux documents I. Fragments de stèle araméenne de Tell Dan (IXe s. av. J.-C.)," *Henoch* 16 (1994), pp. 87–93; Avraham Biran and Joseph Naveh, "The Tel Dan Inscription: A New Fragment," *IEJ* 45 (1995), pp. 1–18; William M. Schniedewind, "Tel Dan Stela: New Light on Aramaic and Jehu's Revolt," *BASOR* 302 (1996), pp. 75–90; André Lemaire, "The Tel Dan Stela as a Piece of Royal Historiography," *JSOT* 81 (1998), pp. 3–15; "'Maison de David,' 'maison de Mopsos', et les Hivvites," in *Sefer Moshe. The Moshe Weinfeld Jubilee Volume,* ed. Chaim Cohen et al. (Winona Lake, IN: Eisenbrauns, 2004), pp. 303–312; Hallvard Hagelia, *The Tel Dan Inscription.* Studia Semitica Upsaliensia 22 (Uppsala: Uppsala University Library, 2006), pp. 165–167.

[43] See, for instance, Gary N. Knoppers, "The Vanishing Solomon: The Disappearance of the United Monarchy from Recent Histories of Ancient Israel," *JBL* 116 (1997), pp. 19–44.

[44] Ziklag is generally located at Tell esh-Shari'a. See Eliezer D. Oren, "Ziklag—A Biblical City on the Edge of the Negev," *BA* 45 (1982), pp. 155–166, especially p. 163. However for a divergent identification at Tell es-Seba', see Volkmar Fritz, "Der Beitrag der Archäologie zur historischen Topographie Palästinas am Beispiel von Ziklag," *ZDPV* 106 (1990), pp. 78–85; see also "Where is David's Ziklag?" *BAR,* May/June 1993.

[45] For the location of Mahanaim at Tulul edh-Dhahab, see André Lemaire, "Galaad et Makir," *VT* 31 (1981), pp. 39–61, especially pp. 53–54.

[46] See Nadav Na'aman, "The Kingdom of Ishbaal," *BN* 54 (1990), pp. 33–37 (= *Ancient Israel's History and Historiography. The First Temple Period. Collected Essays: Volume 3* [Winona Lake, IN: Eisenbrauns, 2006], pp. 18–22).

[47] On the problem of David's possible responsibility, see James C. Vanderkam, "Davidic Complicity in the Deaths of Abner and Eshbaal: A Historical and Redactional Study," *JBL* 99 (1980), pp. 521–539; Jean-Claude Haelewyck, "La mort d'Abner: 2 Sam 3, 1–39," *RB* 102 (1995), pp. 161–192.

[48] N.L. Tidwell, "The Philistine Incursions into the Valley of Rephaim," in *Studies in the Historical Books of the O.T.*, ed. John A. Emerton, VT Supplement 30 (Leiden: Brill, 1980), pp. 190–212.

[49] Jon D. Levenson and Baruch Halpern, "The Political Import of David's Marriages," *JBL* 99 (1980), pp. 507–518.

[50] See Nadav Na'aman, "The List of David's Officers (*šālîšîm*)," *VT* 38 (1988), pp. 71–79 (= *Ancient Israel's History and Historiography* [see endnote 46], pp. 62–70).

[51] See Edward Lipiński, "Aram et Israel du Xe au VIIIe siècle av. n. è.," *Acta Antiqua* 27 (1979), pp. 49–102; P.E. Dion, *Les Araméens à l'âge du Fer: histoire politique et structures sociales*, Études bibliques NS 34 (Paris: Gabalda, 1997), pp. 79–84.

[52] On this kingdom, see Edward Lipiński, *The Aramaeans. Their Ancient History, Culture, Religion*, OLA 100 (Leuven: Peeters, 2000), pp. 331–341.

[53] Christa Schäfer-Lichtenberger describes this period as the "inchoate early state" ("Sociological and Biblical Views of the Early State," in *The Origins of the Ancient Israelite States* [see endnote 22], pp. 78–105, especially p. 92). For the social and political evolution, see also F.S. Frick, *The Formation of the State in Ancient Israel*, SWBAS 4 (Sheffield: Almond Press, 1985); Robert B. Coote and Keith W. Whitelam, *The Emergence of Early Israel in Historical Perspective of the Davidic State*, SWBAS 5 (Sheffield: Almond Press, 1987), pp. 139–166; Juval Portugali, "Theoretical Speculations on the Transition from Nomadism to Monarchy," in *From Nomadism to Monarchy* (see endnote 10), pp. 203–217, especially pp. 212–217.

[54] See Sophia Katharina Bietenhard, *Des Königs General. Die Heerführertraditionen in den vorstaatlichen und frühen staatlichen Zeit und die Joabgestalt in 2 Sam 2–20; 1 Kön 1–2*, OBO 163 (Freiburg/Göttingen: Universitätsverlag/Vandenhoeck und Ruprecht, 1998).

[55] However, Gordon J. Wenham ("Were David's Sons Priests," *ZAW* 87 [1975], pp. 79–82) proposed to read *sknym* instead of *khnym*.

[56] See Stefan Seiler, *Die Geschichte von der Thronfolge Davids (2 Sam 9–20; 1 Kön 1–2)*, BZAW 267 (Berlin: de Gruyter, 1998); John Barton, "Dating the 'Succession Narrative,'" in *In Search of Pre-Exilic Israel*, ed. John Day (London/New York: T & T Clark, 2004), pp. 95–106.

[57] For a literary analysis of these traditions, see François Langlamet, "David et la maison de Saül," *RB* 86 (1979), pp. 194–213, 385–436, 481–513.

[58] See Daniel Bodi, *The Michal Affair: From Zimri-Lim to the Rabbis* (Sheffield: Phoenix Press, 2005).

[59] Henri Cazelles, "David's Monarchy and the Gibeonite Claim," *PEQ* 87 (1955), pp. 165–175.

[60] Such is the presentation of 1 Kings 2. See J. Vermeylen, "David a-t-il été assassiné?" *RB* 107 (2000), pp. 481–494.

[61] Nadav Na'aman, "Sources and Composition in the History of David," in *The Origins of the Ancient Israelite States* (see endnote 22), pp. 170–186 (= *Ancient Israel's History and Historiography* [see endnote 46], pp. 23–37). His argumentation, however, in "In Search of Reality Behind the Account of David's Wars with Israel's Neighbors," *IEJ* 52 (2002), pp. 200–224 (= *Ancient Israel's History and Historiography* [see endnote 46], pp. 38–61) is not convincing.

[62] André Lemaire, "Vers l'histoire de la rédaction des livres des Rois," *ZAW* 98 (1986), pp. 221–236 (= "Toward a Redactional History of the Book of Kings," in *Reconsidering Israel and Judah. Recent Studies on the Deuteronomistic History*, eds. Gary N. Knoppers and J. Gordon McConville [Winona Lake, IN: Eisenbrauns, 2000], pp. 446–461); Caquot and de Robert, *Les livres de Samuel* (see endnote 17), pp. 19–20; see also Erik Eynikel, *The Reform of Kings Josiah and the Composition of the Deuteronomistic History*, OTS 33 (Leiden: Brill, 1996); Baruch Halpern, "The Construction of the Davidic State: An Exercise in Historiography,"

in *The Origins of the Ancient Israelite States* (see endnote 22), pp. 44–75.

[63] Niels P. Lemche, "David's Rise," *JSOT* 10 (1978), pp. 2–25. For a detailed historical interpretation, see Baruch Halpern, *David's Secret Demons. Messiah, Murderer, Traitor, King* (Grand Rapids, MI: Eerdmans, 2001), pp. 73–103.

[64] On Batsheba, see A. Wénin, "Bethsabée, épouse de David et mère de Salomon," in *Le roi Salomon: un héritage en question. Hommage à Jacques Vermeylen*, eds. Claude Lichtert and Dany Nocquet (Bruxelles: Lessius, 2008), pp. 207–228. On the problem of Nathan's personality, see Ilse von Loewenclau, "Der Prophet Nathan im Zwielicht von theologischer Deutung und Historie," in *Werden und Wirken des Alten Testaments, Festschrift C. Westermann*, ed. E. Albertz et al. (Neukirchen/Göttingen, Germany: Neukirchener Verlag/Vandenhoeck und Ruprecht, 1980), pp. 202–215.

[65] See Tomoo Ishida, "Solomon's Succession to the Throne of David—Political Analysis," in *Studies in the Period of David and Solomon*, ed. Ishida (Tokyo: Yamakawa-Shuppansha, 1982), pp. 175–187.

[66] See Herbert Donner, "The Interdependence of Internal Affairs and Foreign Policy During the Davidic-Solomonic Period (With Special Regard to the Phoenician Coast)," in *Studies in the Period* (see endnote 65), pp. 205–214.

[67] In 2 Samuel 8:13–14, there was probably a confusion between "Edom" and "Aram," which were written in the same way in the fifth through third centuries B.C.E. 2 Samuel 8:14a seems to be a doublet of 2 Samuel 8:6a.

[68] See Abraham Malamat, "A Political Look at the Kingdom of David and Solomon and Its Relations with Egypt," in *Studies in the Period* (see endnote 65), pp. 189–205; "The Monarchy of David and Solomon," in *Recent Archaeology in the Land of Israel*, ed. Hershel Shanks and Benjamin Mazar (Washington, DC/Jerusalem: Biblical Archaeology Society/Israel Exploration Society, 1984), pp. 161–172.

[69] See Ziony Zevit, "The Davidic-Solomonic Empire from the Perspective of Archaeological Biology," in *Birkat Shalom: Studies in the Bible, Ancient Near Eastern Literature, and Postbiblical Judaism Presented to Shalom M. Paul*, ed. Chaim

Cohen et al. (Winona Lake, IN: Eisenbrauns, 2008), pp. 201–224.

[70] These possibly include Megiddo (Stratum VIA), Beth-Shean (Stratum V) and Yoqneam. See Amihai Mazar, "The Excavations at Tel Beth-Shean in 1989–1990," in *Biblical Archaeology Today 1990*, eds. Avraham Biran and Joseph Aviram (Jerusalem: Israel Exploration Society, 1993), pp. 607–619, especially p. 617.

[71] Yohanan Aharoni, "The Building Activities of David and Solomon," *IEJ* 24 (1974), pp. 13–16; see also Hershel Shanks, "King David as Builder," *BAR*, March 1975, p. 13.

[72] See also Israel Finkelstein, Zeev Herzog and David Ussishkin, "Has King David's Palace in Jerusalem Been Found?" *Tel Aviv* 34 (2007), pp. 142–164; Ronny Reich and Eli Shukron, "The Date of City-Wall 501 in Jerusalem," *Tel Aviv* 35 (2008), pp. 114–122.

[73] That is part of the truth; see Margreet Steiner, "David's Jerusalem: Fiction or Reality? It's Not There: Archaeology Proves a Negative," *BAR*, July/August 1998, pp. 26–33, 62–63. However, such a small town may still have been the capital of a strong chiefdom: See Nadav Na'aman, "The Contribution of the Amarna Letters to the Debate on Jerusalem's Political Position in the Tenth Century B.C.E.," *BASOR* 304 (1996), pp. 17–27; "Cow Town or Royal Capital? Evidence for Iron Age Jerusalem," *BAR*, July/August 1997, pp. 43–47, 67; and "David's Jerusalem: Fiction or Reality? It Is There: Ancient Texts Prove It," *BAR*, July/August 1998, pp. 42–44. See also Jane Cahill, "David's Jerusalem: Fiction or Reality? It Is There: The Archaeological Evidence Proves It," *BAR*, July/August 1998, pp. 34–41, 63.

[74] Avi Ofer, "'All the Hill Country of Judah': From a Settlement Fringe to a Prosperous Monarchy," in *From Nomadism to Monarchy* (see endnote 10), pp. 92–121, especially pp. 104 and 119–121; "Hebron," in *NEAEHL*, pp. 606–609; "The Monarchic Period in the Judaean Highland: A Spatial Overview," in *Studies in the Archaeology of the Iron Age in Israel and Jordan*, ed. Amihai Mazar, JSOT Supplement 331 (Sheffield: Sheffield Academic Press, 2001), pp. 14–37.

[75] Yosef Garfinkel and Saar Ganor, *Khirbet Qeiyafa Vol. 1. Excavation Report 2007–2008* (Jerusalem: Israel Exploration Society, 2009), pp. vii, 3–18.

[76] Egypt was then practically divided between the kingdoms of Tanis and Thebes.

[77] Siegfried Herrmann, "King David's State," in *In the Shelter of Elyon, Essays on Ancient Palestinian Life and Literature in Honor of G.W. Ahlström,* ed. W. Boyd Barrick and John R. Spencer, JSOT Supplement 31 (Sheffield: Sheffield Academic Press, 1984), pp. 261–275.

[78] See André Lemaire, *The Birth of Monotheism. The Rise and Disappearance of Yahwism* (Washington, DC: Biblical Archaeology Society, 2007), pp. 36–41.

[79] See above endnote 42.

[80] Malamat, "A Political Look" (see endnote 68), especially pp. 197–201. Kenneth A. Kitchen, *The Third Intermediate Period in Egypt (1100–650 B.C.),* 2nd ed. (Warminster, UK: Aris and Phillips, 1986), pp. 280–283.

[81] William G. Dever, "Further Excavations at Gezer, 1967–1971," *BA* 34 (1971), p. 110; "Gezer", *NEAEHL,* pp. 496–506.

[82] See also 1 Kings 11:1,5,7. Since Rehoboam was 41 years old when he became king, the marriage of Solomon with Naamah must have taken place toward the end of David's reign. See Abraham Malamat, "Naamah, the Ammonite Princess, King Solomon's Wife," *RB* 106 (1999), pp. 35–40.

[83] See D. Noël, "Le surdimensionnement du royaume de Salomon en 1 R 5,1.4," *Transeuphratène* 29 (2005), pp. 155–170.

[84] E.W. Heaton, *Solomon's New Men, The Emergence of Ancient Israel as a National State* (London: Thames and Hudson, 1974).

[85] This mention of Zadok and Abiathar is probably a later addition taken from 2 Samuel 8:17.

[86] Trygve N.D. Mettinger, *Solomonic State Officials* (Lund, Sweden: Gleerup, 1971).

[87] Yohanan Aharoni, "The Solomonic Districts," *Tel Aviv* 3 (1976); Hartmut N. Rösel, "Zu den 'Gauen' Salomons," *ZDPV* 100 (1986), pp. 84–90; Volkmar Fritz, "Die Verwaltungsgebiete Salomos nach 1 Kön. 4,7–19," in *Meilenstein: Festgabe für Herbert Donner,* Ägypten und Altes Testament 30 (Wiesbaden: Harrasowitz, 1995), pp. 19–26. However there is some confusion about the Land of Hepher. André Lemaire, "Le 'pays de Hepher'

et les 'filles de Zelophehad' à la lumière des ostraca de Samarie," *Semitica* 22 (1972), pp. 13–20; *Inscriptions hébraïques I, Les ostraca* (Paris: Cerf, 1977), pp. 287–289. For a divergent historical appreciation, see Herrmann M. Niemann, *Herrschaft, Königtum und Staat,* Forschungen zum Alten Testament 6 (Tübingen: Mohr, 1993), pp. 17–41, 246–251; Paul S. Ash, "Solomon's? District? List," *JSOT* 67 (1995), pp. 67–86.

[88] See Richard S. Hess, "The Form and Structure of the Solomonic District List in 1 Kings 4:7–19," in *Crossing Boundaries and Linking Horizons, Studies in Honor of M.C. Astour,* ed. G.D. Young et al. (Bethesda, MD: CDL Press, 1997), pp. 279–292.

[89] Moshe Elat, "The Monarchy and the Development of Trade in Ancient Israel," in *State and Temple Economy in the Ancient Near East II,* ed. Edward Lipiński (Leuven: Dept Oriëntalistiek, 1979), pp. 527–546.

[90] On the problem of the identification of Ophir, see Vassilios Christidès, "L'énigme d'Ophir," *RB* 77 (1970), pp. 240–246; Lois Berkowitz, "Has the U.S. Geological Survey Found King Solomon's Gold Mines?" *BAR,* September 1977, pp. 1, 28–33; Manfred Görg, "Ofir und Punt," *BN* 82 (1996), pp. 5–8. By comparison with the ancient Egyptian texts, the most probable solution still seems Somalia-Ethiopia.

[91] See André Lemaire, "Les Phéniciens et le commerce entre la Mer Rouge et la Mer Méditerranée," in *Phoenicia and the East Mediterranean in the First Millenium B.C.,* ed. Edward Lipiński, Studia Phoenicia 5/OLA 22 (Leuven: Peeters, 1987), pp. 49–60; Avner Raban, "Phoenician Harbours in the Levant," *Michmanim* 11 (1997), pp. 7*–27*, especially 13*–15*; Maria E. Aubet, "Aspects of Tyrian Trade and Colonization in the Eastern Mediterranean," *Münstersche Beiträge zur antiken Handelsgeschichte* 19 (2000), pp. 70–120, especially pp. 84–90.

[92] On the change of defense strategy under Solomon, see Chris Hauer, "Economics of National Security in Solomonic Israel," *JSOT* 18 (1980), pp. 63–73.

[93] See Yukata Ikeda, "Solomon's Trade in Horses and Chariots in Its International Setting," in *Studies of the Period* (see endnote 65), pp. 215–238; André Lemaire, "Chars et cavaliers dans l'ancien Israël," *Transeuphratène* 15 (1998), pp. 165–182.

94 See Gösta W. Ahlström, *Royal Administration and National Religion* (Leiden: Brill, 1982). For this motive in Assyria, see Sylvie Lackenbacher, *Le roi bâtisseur, les récits de construction assyriens des origines à Téglatphalazar III* (Paris: Ed. Recherche sur les civilisations, A.D.P.F., 1982).

95 See Eilat Mazar, "Royal Gateway to Ancient Jerusalem Uncovered," *BAR*, May/June 1989; and "King David's Palace," *BAR*, January/February 1997.

96 Cabul is probably to be identified with Ras Abu Zeitun. See Zvi Gal, "Cabul, Jiphtah-El and the Boundary between Asher and Zebulun in the Light of Archaeological Evidence," *ZDPV* 101 (1985), pp. 114–127.

97 See André Lemaire, "Asher et le royaume de Tyr," in *Phoenicia and the Bible*, ed. Edward Lipiński, Studia Phoenicia 11 (Leuven: Peeters, 1991), pp. 135–152.

98 Keith W. Whitelam, "The Symbols of Power, Aspects of Royal Propaganda in the United Monarchy," *BA* 49 (1986), pp. 166–173.

99 See J. Alberto Soggin, "Compulsory Labor under David and Solomon," in *Studies in the Period* (see endnote 65), pp. 259–267.

100 Julio C. Trebolle Barrera, *Salomon y Jeroboan* (Valencia, Spain: Institucion San Jeronimo, 1980), especially pp. 364–366.

101 Actually "Hadad" sounds more like an Aramean name, and Hadad originally was probably an Aramean. In the Hebrew text of the Bible, there are several confusions between "Aram" and "Edom." The Edomites seem to have been independent, with their own king, only about the year 845 B.C. (see 2 Kings 8:20–22). So Solomon's political power over Aramean countries was very short, if it ever existed: See André Lemaire, "Hadad l'édomite ou Hadad l'araméen?" *BN* 43 (1987), pp. 14–18; "D'Édom à l'Idumée et à Rome," in *Des Sumériens aux Romains d'Orient, La perception géographique du monde*, ed. Arnaud Sérandour, Antiquités sémitiques 2 (Paris: Maisonneuve, 1997), pp. 81–103, especially p. 85; "Les premiers rois araméens dans la tradition biblique," in *The World of the Aramaeans I. Biblical Studies in Honour of Paul-Eugène Dion*, ed. P.M. Michèle Daviau et al., JSOT Supplement 324 (Sheffield: Sheffield Academic Press, 2001), pp. 113–143, especially

pp. 129–134. For a divergent view, see Nadav Na'aman, "Israel, Edom and Egypt in the 10th Century B.C.E.," *Tel Aviv* 19 (1992), pp. 71–93, especially p. 75.

102 For a literary criticism of these texts, see Helga Weippert, "Die Ätiologie des Nordreiches und seines Königshauses (1 Reg 11:29–40)," *ZAW* 95 (1983), pp. 344–375; A. Schenker, "Jéroboam et la division du royaume dans la Septante ancienne LXX 1 R 12,24 a-z, TM 11–12; 14 et l'histoire deutéronomiste," in *Israël construit son histoire, l'historiographie deutéronomiste à la lumière des recherches récentes*, eds. Albert de Pury, Thomas Römer and Jean-Daniel Macchi (Genève: Labor et fides, 1995), pp. 194–236.

103 The Masoretic text has "Molech," but the context indicates that we must read "Milcom."

104 Probably the Mount of Scandal or Mount of Perdition (*har hammashit*).

105 J. Maxwell Miller, "Separating the Solomon of History from the Solomon of Legend," in *The Age of Solomon. Scholarship at the Turn of the Millennium*, ed. Lowel K. Handy, Studies in the History and Culture of the Ancient Near East 11 (Leiden/New York/Köln: Brill, 1997), pp. 1–24, especially p. 24; J. Alberto Soggin, "King Solomon," in *Birkat Shalom* (see endnote 69), pp. 169–174; and Martin A. Sweeney, "Synchronic and Diachronic Considerations in the DtrH Portrayal of the Demise of Solomon's Kingdom," ibid., pp. 175–189.

106 André Lemaire, "Wisdom in Solomonic Historiography," in *Wisdom in Ancient Israel, Essays in Honour of J.A. Emerton*, eds. John Day, Robert P. Gordon and Hugh G.M. Williamson (Cambridge: Cambridge University Press, 1995), pp. 106–118; for a different view of "vor-Dtr Weisheitsquelle," see Pekka Särkiö, *Die Weisheit und Macht Salomos in der israelitischen Historiographie*, Schriften der Finnischen Exegetischen Gesellschaft 60 (Helsinki/Göttingen, 1994); "Die Struktur der Salomogeschichte (1 Kön 1–11) und die Stellung der Weisheit in ihr," *BN* 83 (1996), pp. 83–106; Nadav Na'aman, "Sources and Composition in the History of Solomon," in *The Age of Solomon* (see endnote 105), pp. 57–80 (= *Ancient Israel's History and Historiography* [see endnote 46], pp. 79–101); and Anne E. Gardner, "The Narratives of Solomon's Reign in the Light of the Historiography of Other Ancient Civilizations," *Australian Biblical Review* 56 (2008), pp. 1–18.

[107] For a general history of redaction of the books of Kings, see Lemaire, "Vers l'histoire de la redaction des livres des Rois" (see endnote 62), pp. 221–236.

[108] See Ronald S. Hendel, "The Archaeology of Memory: King Solomon Chronology, and Biblical Representation," in *Confronting the Past. Archaeological and Historical Essays on Ancient Israel in Honor of William G. Dever*, ed. Seymour Gitin et al. (Winona Lake, IN: Eisenbrauns, 2006), pp. 219–230.

[109] Hugh G.M. Williamson, *1 and 2 Chronicles*, New Century Bible Commentary (Grand Rapids, MI: Eerdmans, 1982), pp. 229–230.

[110] See, for instance, Alan R. Millard, "Texts and Archaeology: Weighing the Evidence: The Case for King Solomon," *PEQ* 123 (1991), pp. 19–27; "Solomon: Text and Archaeology," *PEQ* 123 (1991), pp. 117–118; J. Maxwell Miller, "Solomon: International Potentate or Local King?" *PEQ* 123 (1991), pp. 28–31; Alan R. Millard, "King Solomon's Shields," in *Scripture and Other Artifacts, Essays in Honor of Philip J. King*, eds. Michael D. Coogan, J. Cheryl Exum and Lawrence E. Stager (Louisville: Westminster John Knox Press, 1994), pp. 286–295; A. Millard, "King Solomon in His Ancient Context," in *The Age of Solomon* (see endnote 105), pp. 30–53.

[111] See Donald B. Redford, "The Relations Between Egypt and Israel from El-Amarna to the Babylonian Conquest," in *Biblical Archaeology Today 1984* (see endnote 7), pp. 192–205; Kenneth A. Kitchen, "Egypt and East Africa," in *The Age of Solomon* (see endnote 105), pp. 107–125; and Jacques Briend, "Les relations du roi Salomon avec les pays voisins," in *Le roi Salomon* (see endnote 64), pp. 27–35.

[112] Kenneth A. Kitchen, "Sheba and Arabia," in *The Age of Solomon* (endnote 105), pp. 126–153.

[113] See Albert R. Green, "Solomon and Siamun: A Synchronism Between Early Dynastic Israel and the Twenty-First Dynasty of Egypt," *JBL* 97 (1978), pp. 353–367; Kenneth A. Kitchen, *On the Reliability of the Old Testament* (Grand Rapids, MI: Eerdmans, 2003), pp. 107–112.

[114] See André Lemaire, "Salomon et la fille de Pharaon: un problème d'interprétation historique," in *"I Will Speak the Riddles of Ancient Times"* (see endnote 4), pp. 699–710. For a divergent interpretation, see Volkmar Fritz, "Solomon and

Gezer," in *Confronting the Past* (see endnote 108), pp. 303–307.

[115] Henri Cazelles, "Administration salomonienne et terminologie administrative égyptienne," *Comptes Rendus du GLECS* 17 (1973), pp. 23–25; Mettinger, *Solomonic State Officials* (see endnote 86).

[116] Donald B. Redford, "Studies in Relations Between Palestine and Egypt during the First Millenium B.C., I, The Taxation System of Solomon," in *Studies on the Ancient Palestinian World presented to F.V. Winnett*, eds. J.W. Wevers and Redford (Toronto: University of Toronto Press, 1972), pp. 141–156. Most of the commentators agree that this list is ancient: see above endnote 88, and Martin J. Mulder, *1 Kings 1–11. Historical Commentary on the Old Testament* (Leuven: Peeters, 1998), pp. 171–186; Jens Kamlah, "Die Liste der Regionalfürsten in 1 Kön 4,7–19 als historische Quelle für die Zeit Salomos," *BN* 106 (2001), pp. 57–78. The hypothesis of Nadav Na'aman ("Solomon's District List (1 Kings 4:7–19) and the Assyrian Province System in Palestine," *Ugarit-Forschungen* 33 [2001], pp. 419–435 = *Ancient Israel's History and Historiography* [see endnote 46], pp. 102–119) is not convincing.

[117] Albert R. Green, "Israelite Influence at Shishak's Court," *BASOR* 233 (1979), pp. 59–62.

[118] Ahlström, *Royal Administration* (see endnote 94), p. 33.

[119] For the Egyptian list of towns, see *ANET*, pp. 263–264; Benjamin Mazar, "The Campaign of Pharaoh Shishak to Palestine," in *Congrès de Strasbourg*, VT Supplement 4 (Leiden: Brill, 1957), pp. 57–66; Yohanan Aharoni, *The Land of the Bible: A Historical Geography*, rev. and enlarged, trans. and ed. Anson F. Rainey (Philadelphia: Westminster Press, 1979), pp. 323–330; Na'aman, "Israel, Edom and Egypt in the 10th Century B.C.E." (see endnote 101); David M. Rohl, "Some Chronological Conundrums of the 21st Dynasty," *Ägypten und Levante* 3 (1992), pp. 133–141, especially pp. 134–136; Gösta W. Ahlström, "Pharaoh Shoshenq's Campaign to Palestine," in *History and Traditions of Early Israel, Studies Presented to Eduard Nielsen*, eds. André Lemaire and Benedikt Otzen, VT Supplement 50 (Leiden: Brill, 1993), pp. 1–16; Israel Finkelstein, "The Campaign of Shoshenk I to Palestine. A Guide to the 10th Century BCE

Polity," *ZDPV* 118 (2002), pp. 109–135; Kevin A. Wilson, *The Campaign of Pharaoh Shoshenq I into Palestine*. Forschungen zum Alten Testament 2. Reihe 9 (Tübingen: Mohr Siebeck, 2005). This list of towns is generally interpreted as a list of towns *destroyed* by Sheshonk; however Jeroboam was patronized by Sheshonk and the Israelite towns could have welcomed the pharaoh.

[120] See Herbert Donner, "Israel und Tyrus im Zeitalter Davids und Salomos," *JNSL* 10 (1982), pp. 43–52; Albert R. Green, "David's Relations with Hiram: Biblical and Josephan Evidence for Tyrian Chronology," in *The Word of the Lord Shall Go Forth, Essays in Honor of D.N. Freedman* (Winona Lake, IN: Eisenbrauns, 1983), pp. 373–397; Kitchen, *Third Intermediate Period* (see endnote 80), pp. 432–447; Edward Lipiński, *On the Skirts of Canaan in the Iron Age*, OLA 153 (Leuven: Peeters, 2006), pp. 166–176.

[121] See Giovanno Garbini, "Gli 'Annali di Tiro' et la storiogafia fenicia," in *I Fenici, storia e religione* (Naples: Instituto Universitario Orientale, 1980), pp. 71–86; André Lemaire, "Les écrits phéniciens," in *Écrits de l'Orient ancien et sources Bibliques*, ed. A. Barucq et al., Petite Bibliothèque des Sciences Bibliques, Ancien Testament 2 (Paris: Desclée, 1986), pp. 213–239, especially pp. 217–219.

[122] For Phoenician royal tenth century B.C.E. inscriptions, see André Lemaire, "La datation des rois de Byblos Abibaal et Élibaal et les relations entre l'Égypte et le Levant au Xe s. av. n. è.," *Comptes rendus de l'Académie des Inscriptions et Belles-Lettres* (2006).

[123] *Apion* 1.113; See H.St.J. Thackeray, *Josephus I, The Life Against Apion*, Loeb Classical Library (London: Heinemann, 1966), p. 209.

[124] *Apion* 1.117–119; Thackeray, *Josephus I* (see endnote 123), p. 211.

[125] Lemaire, "Phéniciens et le commerce" (see endnote 91).

[126] See Israel Eph'al, *The Ancient Arabs* (Jerusalem: Magnes Press, 1984), pp. 28ff.; Giovanno Garbini, "I Sabei del Nord come problema storico," in *Studi in onore F. Gabrieli*, ed. R. Traini (Rome: Univ. di Roma, 1984), pp. 373–380.

[127] See Mario Liverani, "Early Caravan Trade Between South-Arabia and Mesopotamia," *Yemen* 1 (1992), pp. 111–115.

[128] See André Lemaire, "La reine de Saba à Jérusalem: la tradition ancienne reconsidérée," in *Kein Land für sich allein. Studien zum Kulturkontakt in Kanaan, Israel/Palästina und Ebirnâri für Manfred Weippert*, OBO 186 (Freiburg/Göttingen: Universitätsverlag/Vandenhoeck und Ruprecht, 2002), pp. 43–55.

[129] See, for instance, Nadav Na'aman, "Sources and Composition in the Biblical History of Edom," in *Sefer Moshe* (see endnote 42), pp. 313–320, especially 316.

[130] See Lemaire, "Les premiers rois araméens dans la tradition biblique" (see endnote 101), pp. 129–134.

[131] See, for instance, Amihai Mazar, "Three 10th–9th century BCE inscriptions from Tel Rehôv," in *Saxa Loquentur* (see endnote 21), pp. 171–184.

[132] See André Lemaire, "Phénicien et philistien: paléographie et dialectologie," in *Actas del IV Congreso Internacional de Estudios Fenicios y Punicos, Cadiz, 2–6 Octubre 1995*, eds. Maria E. Aubet and Manuela Barthélemy (Cadiz: Publicaciones, Universidad de Cadiz, 2000), pp. 243–249.

[133] For the Tel Zayit abecedary, see Ron E. Tappy et al., "An Abecedary of the Mid-Tenth Century B.C.E. from the Judaean Shephelah," *BASOR* 344 (2006), pp. 5–45. This inscription could be connected with the kingdom of Gath and date to around 900 B.C.E. See Christopher A. Rollston, "The Phoenician Script of the Tel Zayit Abecedary and Putative Evidence for Israelite Literacy," in *Literate Culture and Tenth-Century Canaan: The Tel Zayit Abecedary in Context*, eds. Tappy and P. Kyle McCarter (Winona Lake, IN: Eisenbrauns, 2008), p. 89. For the Khirbet Qeiyafa ostracon, see Garfinkel and Ganor, *Khirbet Qeiyafa Vol. 1* (see endnote 75), pp. 243–270. See also Émile Puech, "L'ostracon de Khirbet Qeiyafa et les débuts de la Royauté en Israël," *RB* 117 (2010), pp. 162–184, and Gershon Galil, *Ugarit-Forschungen* (in press).

[134] See Hannalis Schulte, *Die Entstehung der Geschichtsschreibung im Alten Israel*, BZAW 128 (Berlin: de Gruyter, 1972); Baruch Halpern, *The First Historians: The Hebrew Bible and History* (San Francisco: Harper and Row, 1988). According to John Van Seters ("Histories and Historians of the Ancient Near East," *Orientalia* 50 [1981], pp. 137–185, especially p. 185), "Dtr [Deuteronomist]

stands at the beginning of historiography," but this is probably too simplistic a view; see Lemaire, "Vers l'histoire de la rédaction," (see endnote 62).

[135] See Caquot and de Robert, *Les livres de Samuel* (see endnote 17), p. 20, "un Ebyataride … le premier historien de l'antiquité israélite."

[136] On Hebron, see André Lemaire, "Cycle primitif d'Abraham et contexte géographico-historique," in *History and Traditions of Early Israel* (see endnote 119), pp. 62–75.

[137] See Werner H. Schmidt, "A Theologian of the Solomonic Era? A Plea for the Yahwist," in *Studies in the Period* (see endnote 65), pp. 55–73; Richard E. Friedman, "Solomon and the Great Histories," in *Jerusalem in Bible and Archaeology. The First Temple Period*, eds. Andrew G. Vaughn and Ann E. Killebrew, SBL Symposium Series 18 (Atlanta: Society of Biblical Literature, 2003), pp. 171–180.

[138] Nili Fox, "Royal Officials and Court Families: A New Look at the *YLDYM* (*yelâdîm*) in 1 Kings 12," *BA* 59 (1996), pp. 225–232; Na'aman, "Cow Town or Royal Capital?" (see endnote 73).

[139] André Lemaire, *Les écoles et la formation de la Bible dans l'ancien Israël*, OBO 39 (Fribourg: Editions Universitaires/Göttingen, Ger.: Vandenhoeck und Ruprecht, 1981), especially pp. 46–50; Nili Shupak, *Where can Wisdom be Found? The Sage's Language in the Bible and in Ancient Egyptian Literature*, Orbis Biblicus et Orientalis 130 (Fribourg: Editions Universitaires, 1993), especially pp. 349–354. The contrary opinion of David W. Jamieson-Drake, *Scribes and Schools in Monarchic Judah* (see endnote 39) is ill-founded methodologically and has an incomplete archaeological basis. See André Lemaire, *JAOS* 112 (1992), pp. 707–708.

[140] William G. Dever, "Monumental Architecture in Ancient Israel in the Period of the United Monarchy," in *Studies in the Period* (see endnote 65), pp. 269–306; "Archaeology and the 'Age of Solomon': A Case-Study in Archaeology and Historiography," in *The Age of Solomon* (see endnote 105), pp. 217–251; see also Volkmar Fritz, "Salomo," *MDOG* 117 (1985), pp. 47–67. For provisory syntheses of Iron IIA (tenth century B.C.), see Larry G. Herr, "The Iron Age II Period: Emerging Nations," *BA* 60 (1997), pp. 114–183, especially pp. 120–129; William G. Dever, "Histories and Non-Histories of Ancient

Israel: The Question of the United Monarchy," in *In Search of Pre-Exilic Israel* (see endnote 56), pp. 65–94; Shlomo Bunimovitz and Zvi Lederman, "The Early Israelite Monarchy in the Sorek Valley: Tel Beth-Shemesh and Tel Batash (Timnah) in the 10th and 9th Centuries BCE," in *"I Will Speak the Riddles of Ancient Times"* (see endnote 4), pp. 407–427.

[141] For a general presentation, see Wolfgang Zwickel, *Der salomonische Tempel*. Kulturgeschichte der antiken Welt 83 (Mainz: Philipp von Zabern, 1999).

[142] Ernest-Marie Laperrousaz, "A-t-on dégagé l'angle sud-est du 'temple de Salomon'?" *Syria* 50 (1973), pp. 355–399; "Angle sud-est du 'temple de Salomon' ou vestiges de l'Accra des Séleucides'? Un faux problème," *Syria* 52 (1975), pp. 241–259; "Après le 'temple de Salomon,' la *bamah* de Tel Dan: l'utilisation de pierres à bossage phénicien dans la Palestine pré-exilique," *Syria* 59 (1982), pp. 223–237; "À propos des murs d'enceinte antiques de la colline occidentale et du temple de Jérusalem," *REJ* 141 (1982), pp. 443–458.

[143] See also Yigal Shiloh, *Excavations at the City of David I, 1978–1982*, Qedem 19 (Jerusalem: Hebrew University, 1984), especially p. 27: "Stratum 14"; "Jérusalem, la Ville de David (1978–1981)," *RB* 91 (1984), pp. 420–431, especially pp. 428–429; see also Margreet Steiner, "The Jebusite Ramp of Jerusalem: The Evidence from the Macalister, Kenyon and Shiloh Excavations," in *Biblical Archaeology Today 1990* (see endnote 70), pp. 585–588; "Re-dating the Terraces of Jerusalem," *IEJ* 44 (1994), pp. 13–20; "David's Jerusalem" (see endnote 73), pp. 26–33, 63; Eilat Mazar, "The Solomonic Wall in Jerusalem," in *"I Will Speak the Riddles of the Times"* (see endnote 4), pp. 775–786. For a date c. 1200, see Jane Cahill and David Tarler, "Respondents," in *Biblical Archaeology Today 1990* (see endnote 70), pp. 625–626; "Excavations Directed by Yigal Shiloh at the City of David, 1978–1985," in *Ancient Jerusalem Revealed*, ed. Hillel Geva (Jerusalem: Israel Exploration Society, 1994), pp. 30–45, especially pp. 34–35. See also Cahill, "David's Jerusalem" (see endnote 73), p. 50. For different tentative syntheses, see Jane Cahill, "Jerusalem at the Time of the United Monarchy: The Archaeological Evidence," in *Jerusalem in Bible and Archaeology* (see endnote 137), pp. 13–80; Israel Finkelstein, "The Rise of Jerusalem and Judah: The Missing Link," ibid.,

pp. 81–101; David Ussishkin, "Solomon's Jerusalem: The Text and the Facts on the Ground," ibid., pp. 103–115; Amihai Mazar, "Jerusalem in the 10th Century B.C.E.: The Glass Half Full," in *Essays on Ancient Israel in Its Near Eastern Context: A Tribute to Nadav Na'aman*, ed. Y. Amit et al. (Winona Lake, IN: Eisenbrauns, 2006), pp. 255–272.

[144] See also Eilat Mazar, "The Solomonic Wall in Jerusalem," in *"I Will Speak the Riddle of Ancient Times"* (see endnote 4), pp. 775–786.

[145] See David Tarler and Jane Cahill, "David, City of", *ABD*, vol. 2, pp. 52–67; Kathleen Kenyon, *Digging Up Jerusalem* (London: Benn, 1974), pp. 92, 114–115; G.J. Wightman, *The Walls of Jerusalem: From the Canaanites to the Mamelukes*, Mediterranean Archaeology Supplement 4 (Sydney: Meditarch, 1993), pp. 33–35; Na'aman, "Cow Town or Royal Capital?" (see endnote 73), p. 43; Cahill, "David's Jerusalem" (see endnote 73), p. 39. However, see also Steiner, "David's Jerusalem" (see endnote 73).

[146] Yigael Yadin, "Solomon's City Wall and Gate at Gezer," *IEJ* 8 (1958), pp. 82–86; "Yadin's Popular Book on Hazor Now Available," *BAR*, September 1975, pp. 14–17, 32; "A Rejoinder," *BASOR* 239 (1980), pp. 19–23.

[147] For a divergent view, see David Milson, "The Design of the Royal Gates at Megiddo, Hazor and Gezer," *ZDPV* 102 (1986), pp. 87–92.

[148] William G. Dever, "Late Bronze Age and Solomonic Defenses. New evidence," *BASOR* 262 (1986), pp. 9–34, especially 18–20; "Gezer," *NEAEHL*, vol. 2, pp. 504–505.

[149] Amnon Ben-Tor, "Tel Hazor," *IEJ* 45 (1995), pp. 66–68; Amnon Ben-Tor and Doron Ben-Ami, "Hazor and the Archaeology of the Tenth Century B.C.E.," *IEJ* 48 (1998), pp. 1–37. For a different view, see Israel Finkelstein, "Hazor and the North in the Iron Age: A Low Chronology Perspective," *BASOR* 314 (1999), pp. 55–66.

[150] See the following articles in *BASOR* 277/278 (1990): G.J. Wightman, "The Myth of Solomon"; John S. Holladay, Jr., "Red Slip, Burnish, and the Solomonic Gateway at Gezer"; David Ussishkin, "Notes on Megiddo, Gezer, Ashdod, and Tel Batash in the Tenth to Ninth Centuries B.C."; Israel Finkelstein, "On Archaeological Methods and Historical Considerations"; and William Dever,

"Of Myths and Methods." See also Hershel Shanks, "Where Is the Tenth Century?" *BAR*, March/April 1998, pp. 56–60; "San Francisco Tremors," *BAR*, March/April 1998, pp. 54–56, 60–61.

[151] P.L.O. Guy, *New Light from Armageddon*, Oriental Institute Communications 9 (Chicago: University of Chicago, 1931), pp. 37–47.

[152] Yigael Yadin, "The Megiddo Stables," in *Magnalia Dei, The Mighty Acts of God, in Memory of G.E. Wright*, ed. Frank Moore Cross et al. (Garden City, NY: Doubleday, 1976), pp. 249–252.

[153] See, for example, John S. Holladay, Jr., "The Stables of Ancient Israel: Functional Determinants of Stable Construction and the Interpretation of Pillared Building Remains of the Palestinian Iron Age," in *The Archaeology of Jordan and Other Studies Presented to S. Horn*, eds. Lawrence T. Geraty and Larry G. Herr (Berrien Springs, MI: Andrews University 1986), pp. 103–165; Ze'ev Herzog, "Administrative Structures in the Iron Age," in *The Architecture of Ancient Israel from the Prehistoric to the Persian Periods*, eds. Aharon Kempinski and Ronny Reich (Jerusalem: Israel Exploration Society, 1992), pp. 223–230; Deborah Cantrell, "Horse Troughs at Megiddo?" *Revelations from Megiddo* 5 (2000), pp. 1–2.

[154] Graham I. Davies, "Solomonic Stables at Megiddo After All?" *PEQ* 120 (1988), pp. 130–141.

[155] See for instance, Kempinski, *Megiddo: A City-State and Royal Centre in North Israel* (Munich: C.H. Beck, 1989), pp. 90–95; Baruch Halpern, "The Gate of Megiddo and the Debate on the 10th Century," in *Congress Volume, Oslo 1998*, eds. André Lemaire and Magne Saebo, VT Supplement 80 (Leiden: Brill, 2000), pp. 79–121.

[156] David Ussishkin, "Was the 'Solomonic' City Gate at Megiddo Built by King Solomon?" *BASOR* 239 (1980), pp. 1–18; "Fresh Examination of Old Excavations: Sanctuaries in the First Temple Period," in *Biblical Archaeology Today 1990* (see endnote 70), pp. 67–85; "Notes on Megiddo, Gezer, Ashdod, and Tel Batash" (see endnote 150), pp. 71–91; "Jezreel, Samaria and Megiddo: Royal Centres of Omri and Ahab," in *Congress Volume, Cambridge 1995*, ed. John A. Emerton, VT Supplement 66 (Leiden: Brill, 1997), pp. 351–364, especially pp. 359–361.

[157] Wightman, "The Myth of Solomon," (see endnote 150), pp. 5–22.

[158] See A. Mazar, "Iron Age Chronology" (see endote 4), pp. 157–167.

[159] Israel Finkelstein, "The Archaeology of the United Monarchy: an Alternative View," *Levant* 28 (1996), pp. 177–187; Israel Finkelstein and Neil Asher Silberman, *The Bible Unearthed* (New York: Free Press, 2001); *David and Solomon* (see endnote 5). See also Shanks, "Where is the Tenth Century?" (see endnote 150); "San Francisco Tremors," (see endnote 150).

[160] Rudolph Cohen and Yigal Yisrael, "The Iron Age Fortresses at 'En Haseva," *BA* 58 (1995), pp. 223–235; *On the Road to Edom, Discoveries from 'En Hazeva*, Israel Museum Catalogue 370 (Jerusalem: Israel Museum, 1995), especially p. 17. For a divergent dating, see Israel Finkelstein and Lily Singer-Avitz, "The Pottery of Edom: A Correction," *Antiguo Oriente* 6 (2008), pp. 13–24.

[161] For a provisory list, see Herr, "The Iron Age II Period" (see endnote 140), pp. 114–183, especially p. 121.

[162] Rudolph Cohen, "The Iron Age Fortresses in the Central Negev," *BASOR* 236 (1980), pp. 61–79; "Excavations at Kadesh-Barnea 1976–1978," *BA* 44 (1981), pp. 93–107; "Did I Excavate Kadesh-Barnea?" *BAR*, May/June 1981, pp. 20–33; Zeev Herzog et al., "The Israelite Fortress at Arad," *BASOR* 254 (1984), pp. 1–34, especially pp. 6–8. For a different dating and interpretation, see Israel Finkelstein, "The Iron Age 'Fortresses' of the Negev—Sedentarization of Desert Nomads," *Tel Aviv* 11 (1984), pp. 189–209; Alexander Fantalkin and Israel Finkelstein, "The Sheshonk I Campaign and the 8th-Century-BCE Earthquake—More on the Archaeology and History of the South in the Iron I–IIA," *Tel Aviv* 33 (2006), pp. 18–42; Rudolph Cohen and Rebecca Cohen-Amin, *Ancient Settlement of the Negev Highlands. The Iron Age and the Persian Period*, IAA Reports 20 (Jerusalem: Israel Antiquities Authority, 2004); Rudolph Cohen and Hannah Bernick-Greenberg, *Excavations at Kadesh Barnea (Tell el-Qudeirat) 1976–1982*, IAA Reports 34 (Jerusalem: Israel Antiquities Authority, 2007); and Lily Singer-Avitz, "The Earliest Settlement at Kadesh Barnea," *Tel Aviv* 35 (2008), pp. 73–81.

[163] See Zeev Herzog and Lily Singer-Avitz, "Redefining the Centre: The Emergence of State in Judah," *Tel Aviv* 31 (2004), pp. 209–244, especially 232–235.

[164] Thomas E. Levy et al., "Reassessing the Chronology of Biblical Edom: New excavations and 14C Dates from Khirbet en-Nahas (Jordan)," *Antiquity* 78 (2004), pp. 865–879, especially p. 867; G. Weisberger, "The Mineral Wealth of Ancient Arabia and its Use I: Copper Mining and Smelting at Feinan and Timna–Comparison and Evalutation of Techniques, Production and Strategies," *Arabian Archaeology and Epigraphy* 17 (2006), pp. 1–30; Andreas Hauptmann, *The Archaeometallurgy of Copper: Evidence from Faynan, Jordan* (Berlin: Springer-Verlag, 2007), p. 127.

[165] Thomas E. Levy and Mohammad Najjar, "Some Thoughts on Khirbet en-Nahas, Edom, Biblical History and Anthropolgy—A Response to Israel Finkelstein," *Tel Aviv* 33 (2006), pp. 3–17; Israel Finkelstein and Eli Piasetzky, "Radiocarbon and the History of Copper Production at Khirbet en-Nahas," *Tel Aviv* 35 (2008), pp. 82–96.

[166] See Volkmar Fritz, "Monarchy and Re-urbanization: A New Look at Solomon's Kingdom," in *The Origins of the Ancient Israelite States* (see endnote 22), pp. 187–195.

[167] See David Ussishkin, "King Solomon's Palaces," *Biblical Archaeologist Reader IV* (Sheffield: Almond Press, 1983), pp. 227–247; Yigal Shiloh, *The Proto-Aeolic Capital and Israelite Ashlar Masonry*, Qedem 11 (Jerusalem: Hebrew University Press, 1979); B. Gregori, "Considerazioni sui palazzi 'hilani' del periodo salomonico a Megiddo," *Vicino Oriente* 5 (1982), pp. 85–101.

[168] Yohanan Aharoni, *The Archaeology of the Land of Israel* (Philadelphia: Westminster Press, 1982), especially p. 239; see also John S. Holladay, Jr., "The Use of Pottery and the Other Diagnostic Criteria From the Solomonic Era to the Divided Kingdom," in *Biblical Archaeology Today, 1990* (see endnote 70), pp. 86–101, especially p. 95: "Red burnish is only introduced well into Solomon's reign, probably around 950 B.C.E. or so." See also "Red Slip, Burnish, and the Solomonic Gateway at Gezer," pp. 23–70 (see endnote 150).

[169] John Bright, *A History of Israel*, 3rd ed. (Philadelphia: Westminster Press, 1982), p. 217.

¹⁷⁰ Israel Finkelstein, "Environmental Archaeology and Social History: Demographic and Economic Aspects of the Monarchic Period," in *Biblical Archaeology Today 1990* (see endnote 70), pp. 56–66, especially pp. 62–63; see also Gunnar Lehmann, "The United Monarchy in the Countryside: Jerusalem, Judah, and the Shephelah during the Tenth Century B.C.E.," in *Jerusalem in Bible and Archaeology* (see endnote 137), pp. 117–162.

¹⁷¹ See Winfried Theil, "Soziale Wandlungen in der frühen Königszeit Alt-Israels," in *Gesellschaft und Kultur in alten Vorderasien*, ed. H. Klengel (Berlin: Akademie Verlag, 1982), pp. 235–246.

¹⁷² See Hayim Tadmor, "Traditional Institutions and the Monarchy: Social and Political Tensions in the Time of David and Solomon," in *Studies in the Period* (see endnote 65), pp. 239–257.

¹⁷³ On the distinction between Israel and Judah, see Edward Lipiński, "Judah et 'Tout Israël': Analogies et contrastes," in *The Land of Israel: Cross-Roads of Civilizations*, ed. Lipiński, OLA 19 (Leuven: Peeters, 1985), pp. 93–112.

V. The Divided Monarchy

¹ The name derives from the town of Bubastis in the Nile Delta, which was the capital of the kings of the XXIInd Dynasty, who constructed the first forecourt. For the reliefs and inscriptions, see George R. Hughes and Charles F. Nims, *The Bubastite Portal*, vol. 3 of *Reliefs and Inscriptions at Karnak*, Oriental Institute Publication Series No. 74 (Chicago: University of Chicago Press, 1954). See also P. Kyle McCarter, Jr., *Ancient Inscriptions: Voices from the Biblical World* (Washington, DC: Biblical Archaeology Society, 1996), pp. 56–57.

² For the details and a reconstruction of the route, see Benjamin Mazar, "Pharoah Shishak's Campaign to the Land of Israel," in *The Early Biblical Period*, eds. Shmuel Aḥituv and Baruch A. Levine (Jerusalem: Israel Exploration Society, 1986), pp. 139–150.

³ Donald B. Redford, *Egypt, Canaan, and Israel in Ancient Times* (Princeton: Princeton University Press, 1992), pp. 314–315.

⁴ Hughes and Nims, *Bubastite Portal* (see endnote 1), pl. 3, col. 7.

⁵ Rudolph Cohen, "The Fortresses King Solomon Built to Protect His Southern Border," *BAR*, May/June 1985, pp. 56–70. The date that the installations Cohen calls fortresses were established in the southern Negev (the highlands south of the Zered-Beersheba depression) is disputed, but many agree with him that they were built in the Davidic-Solomonic period (Iron Age IIA). Presumably their primary purpose was commercial—to control access from the northern Sinai and Philistia to the Gulf of Aqaba and the Hejaz trade route.

⁶ B. Mazar, "Pharaoh Shishak's Campaign" (see endnote 2), p. 145.

⁷ See the remarks in Redford, *Egypt, Canaan, and Israel* (see endnote 3), p. 313.

⁸ See the list at the end of Amihai Mazar's discussion of Shishak's campaign in *Archaeology of the Land of the Bible 10,000–586 B.C.E.*, Anchor Bible Reference Library (New York: Doubleday, 1990), pp. 397–398.

⁹ These conclusions hinge on the identification of the archaeological horizon associated with these destructions as late tenth century B.C.E. Archaeologists Israel Finkelstein and David Ussishkin of Tel Aviv University have proposed a redating of the strata in question to the ninth century B.C.E. This proposal seems improbable, and it has not received wide support among other leading archaeologists; but if it proves correct, it would eliminate the synchronism with Shishak's campaign. For an introduction to the archaeological issues at stake, see Hershel Shanks, "Where Is the Tenth Century?" *BAR*, March/April 1998, pp. 56–60. The Shishak stela fragment from Megiddo cannot settle the question since it was found in a nonstratified context.

¹⁰ John S. Holladay, Jr., "The Kingdoms of Israel and Judah: Political and Economic Centralization in the Iron IIA–B (ca. 1000–750 BCE)," in *The Archaeology of Society in the Holy Land*, ed. Thomas E. Levy (New York: Facts on File, 1995), pp. 372–375.

¹¹ Despite Shishak's ambition and aggressiveness, he and the succeeding Libyan rulers of the XXIInd Dynasty were unable to overcome internal divisions within Egypt and muster the resources to sustain a consistent Asiatic policy. For the details, see the discussions of Nicolas Grimal (*A History of Ancient Egypt* [Oxford: Blackwell, 1992],

pp. 319–331) and, succinctly, Redford (*Egypt, Canaan, and Israel* [see endnote 3], pp. 315–319), who calls Shishak's reign a "flash in the pan." The last, ill-fated attempt of the XXIInd Dynasty to assert its authority over Judah may have been the debacle described in 2 Chronicles 14:9–15 (Old Testament) = 2 Chronicles 14:8–14 (Hebrew Bible), in which a Cushite general named Zerah, presumably acting on behalf of Shishak's successor, Osorkon I, challenged and was routed by the army of King Asa (c. 911–870 B.C.E.).

[12] The principal formulation of this position is that of Frank Moore Cross, *Canaanite Myth and Hebrew Epic* (Cambridge, MA: Harvard University Press, 1973), pp. 274–289.

[13] The Israelite takeover of Dan, formerly the Canaanite city of Laish, is placed in the premonarchical period by the tradition of the migration of the Danites, preserved in an appendix to the Book of Judges (chapters 17–18).

[14] Cross, *Canaanite Myth and Hebrew Epic* (see endnote 12), pp. 279–283.

[15] Ben-hadad was the name of more than one king of Damascus. Here he is further identified as the son of Tabrimmon son of Hezion. Attempts have been made to identify his grandfather, Hezion, with Solomon's contemporary Rezon son of Eliyada. According to 1 Kings 11:23–24, Rezon was an officer of David's nemesis, Hadadezer of Aram-zobah, who fled from Zobah and gathered a band of soldiers around him. Sometime after David's conquest of Damascus, Rezon captured the city and declared himself king. (This was probably the time that Damascus supplanted Zobah as the dominant city in southern Syria, as it would remain until its demise in the late eighth century.) According to 1 Kings 11:25, Rezon caused problems for Israel throughout Solomon's reign and into that of Jeroboam.

The identification of Hezion with Rezon is unlikely on philological grounds, however, though Hezion might well have been Rezon's successor. For a full evaluation of the various arguments, see Wayne T. Pitard, *Ancient Damascus* (Winona Lake, IN: Eisenbrauns, 1987), pp. 101–104.

[16] Denis Baly, *The Geography of the Bible* (New York: Harper and Row, 1974), p. 99.

[17] See Zvi Gal, "Cabul: A Royal Gift Found," *BAR*, March/April 1993, pp. 38–44, 84.

[18] Zvi Gal, "The Diffusion of Phoenician Cultural Influence in Light of the Excavations at Hurvat Rosh Zayit," *Tel Aviv* 22 (1995), pp. 89–93.

[19] Holladay, "Kingdoms of Israel and Judah" (see endnote 10), pp. 372–373.

[20] The most successful comprehensive analysis of this material is the monograph of Antony F. Campbell, *Of Prophets and Kings: A Late Ninth-Century Document (1 Samuel 1–2 Kings 10)*, CBQ Monograph Series 17 (Washington, DC: Catholic Biblical Association of America, 1986).

[21] Two passages included in the biblical account of Ahab's reign seem to contradict both of these assumptions—that Israel was stronger than Damascus during Ahab's reign and that a mutual defense pact existed between Ahab and Hadadezer late in Ahab's reign. First Kings 20 describes a two-phase assault on Israel near the end of Ahab's reign by "King Ben-hadad of Aram." The first phase was a siege of Samaria that was broken when the much stronger Aramean force was defeated by Ahab's army after the intervention of an anonymous prophet; the second phase included an Aramean assault at Aphek the following spring, when the Arameans were again defeated and Ben-hadad sued for peace, agreeing to return "the towns that my father took from your father." First Kings 22 indicates that three years later Ahab marched with Jeshoshaphat of Judah to Ramoth-gilead to try to wrest its control from "the king of Aram." The Israelite army was defeated, however, and Ahab died in battle.

Serious problems arise if we accept these passages as accounts of historical events late in Ahab's reign. There is, in the first place, a series of discrepancies with information found in Assyrian inscriptions contemporary with the events. The Assyrian inscriptions represent Ahab as an ally of Damascus—at least in 853 B.C.E., at the end of his reign—while the biblical passages indicate that Samaria and Damascus had been at war for more than three years at the time of Ahab's death. Moreover, though the biblical account depicts Israel as militarily much inferior to Damascus, the Assyrian inscriptions describing the battle of Qarqar in 853 B.C.E. indicate that Ahab was very strong, especially in chariots—he is said to have sent 2,000 to Qarqar in comparison to 1,200 sent by Hadadezer. Also, the Assyrian inscriptions show that the king of Damascus in 853 B.C.E.

was Hadadezer, whereas the king of Damascus in 1 Kings 20 and 22 is called Ben-hadad. The references to the towns that Ben-hadad's father took from Ahab's father are also a problem, since, as already noted, we think Omri gained rather than lost territory to the Arameans. The final problem contains a hint of the solution: The name Ahab sits very loosely in the biblical text; most often "the king of Israel" is not named, and the places where he is named vary considerably in the ancient witnesses to the texts (Hebrew, Greek, etc.).

For all of these reasons, many historians, following suggestions by Alfred Jepsen and J. Maxwell Miller (for bibliography and an up-to-date discussion, see Pitard, *Ancient Damascus* [see endnote 15], pp. 114–125), believe that 1 Kings 20 and 22 derive from accounts of the Aramean campaigns of a later king of Israel, a member of the Jehu dynasty and most probably Joash, who is known to have had victories over Ben-hadad son of Hazael. If this is correct, 1 Kings 20 probably reflects the historical situation described in 2 Kings 13:22–25, and Ahab is not likely to have been killed by a randomly shot arrow at Ramoth-gilead, as indicated by 1 Kings 22:34–35, but to have died a natural death, as implied by the language of the notice in 1 Kings 22:40 that "Ahab slept with his ancestors."

[22] McCarter, *Ancient Inscriptions* (see endnote 1), pp. 90–92.

[23] For a full discussion of the issues, see Gösta W. Ahlström, *History of Ancient Palestine* (Minneapolis: Fortress Press, 1993), pp. 579–581.

[24] For an account of Assurnasirpal's campaign to "the Great Sea of the Amurru country," where he "cleaned [his] weapons in the deep sea," see *ANET*, pp. 275b–276b.

[25] See the annalistic account of Shalmaneser's first year in his Monolith Inscription from Kurkh: *ANET*, pp. 277a–278a; *COS*, vol. 2, pp. 261–262.

[26] See the sixth year of Shalmaneser's Kurkh Monolith: *ANET*, p. 278b–279a; *COS*, vol. 2, pp. 263–264. The participation of Que in Cilicia (southern Turkey), as suggested by A. Leo Oppenheim's translation in *ANET*, is surprising. Hayim Tadmor has shown that the apparent reading "Que" in the Monolith is likely to be a defective cuneiform spelling of Byblos (*qu-e-e*, "Que," is to be corrected to *gu-<bal>-e-e*, "Byblos").

[27] Called Adad-idri in the Assyrian text. The Aramean form of his name was Hadad-'iḏr and the Hebrew was Hadad-'ēzer—Hadadezer in English (see 2 Samuel 8:3)—though this Hadadezer, the contemporary of Ahab, is not mentioned in the Bible. Many historians have identified Hadadezer of Damascus with the Ben-hadad mentioned in 1 Kings 20 and 22, but this no longer seems likely; as explained above, the battles recounted in those chapters probably occurred much later than the reign of Ahab, whose name has been introduced secondarily into the text. For the reference to the Ben-hadad of 2 Kings 8:7–15, see below.

[28] *ANET*, pp. 278b–279a; *COS*, vol. 2, pp. 263–264.

[29] The last reference to Hadadezer in the Assyrian records is in 845 B.C.E., and the records from 841 B.C.E. identify the ruler of Damascus as Hazael. Hazael's status as a usurper is shown by the Assyrian inscription on an undated basalt statue from Qal'at Sherqat, ancient Ashur (*ANET*, p. 280b). The text on the front of this statue, which is now in Berlin, contains a summary of Shalmaneser's dealings with Damascus. After referring to a victory over Hadadezer and the coalition at the Orontes—evidently the 853 B.C.E. battle, since subsequent encounters took place farther south—and to the death of Hadadezer, which cannot have taken place before 845 B.C.E., it goes on to say that Hazael, "the son of a nobody," seized the throne, mustering an army and resuming the resistance before being defeated and driven back to Damascus—evidently a reference to the events of 841 B.C.E. The characterization of Hazael as "the son of nobody" shows that when he seized the throne, at some point between 845 and 841 B.C.E., he did so as a usurper, not as Hadadezer's legitimate successor. See further the translation and discussion of the Berlin statue by Pitard (*Ancient Damascus* [see endnote 15], pp. 132–138), who points out the telescoped and summary nature of the text.

[30] In the biblical account the name of the king from whom Hazael seizes the throne is Ben-hadad, not Hadadezer. It is possible that this is simply a mistake, since reports of Israelite encounters with the later Ben-hadad, Hazael's son (!), have intruded elsewhere into the story of Ahab (1 Kings 20 and 22). It is also possible, however, that Hadadezer died during or soon after the Assyrian campaign of 845 B.C.E. and was succeeded by a son named

Ben-hadad (Aramaic Bir Hadad), who reigned for a few years before being overthrown by Hazael.

[31] *ANET*, p. 280; *COS*, vol. 2, p. 267.

[32] As noted above, Moab had been subject to Israel under Omri and Ahab but had withheld tribute after Ahab's death. According to the account in 2 Kings 3:6–27, Joram attempted to retaliate. This was a time, as also noted earlier, that Israel and Judah were united in an alliance cemented by the marriage of Ahab's daughter Athaliah to Jehoshaphat's son Jehoram. In planning his Moabite campaign, therefore, Joram was able to summon the assistance of Jehoshaphat, who in turn called out forces from Edom, which was then a vassal state of Judah. Joram led these combined armies into Transjordan territory and invested the Moabite fortress of Kir-haresheth (el-Kerak, about 50 miles north of Petra), but the siege was lifted when the king of Moab sacrificed his firstborn son on the rampart wall. The language of the biblical text ("a great wrath came upon Israel," 2 Kings 3:27) suggests that the sacrifice succeeded in inducing the Moabite god to drive off the Israelite army. Such a concept would, of course, have been unacceptable to the final editors of the Book of Kings, but they may have preserved the report of the incident because they understood the language to mean that the Israelites were so appalled by the barbarity of the rite that they withdrew in disgust. See Baruch Margalit, "Why King Mesha of Moab Sacrificed His Oldest Son," *BAR*, November/December 1986, pp. 62–63, 76.

[33] This seems likely even if we assume, with many historians, that the prophetic narratives in 2 Kings 6 and 7 belong in a later historical context, so that Joram was not the unnamed "king of Israel" in the parts of those chapters that describe war with Damascus.

[34] As noted earlier, Ramoth-gilead was near the point at which goods transported through Transjordan along the King's Highway could be diverted west to the Phoenician ports via the Beth-Shean depression and the Jezreel Valley. For this reason there was a perennial and often bitterly contested rivalry for control of Ramoth-gilead between the Arameans, who wanted the caravans to continue north to Damascus without diversion, and the Israelites, who could exact tolls and other benefits if the traffic passed west through their territory.

[35] From its strategic position at the foot of Mount Gilboa, Jezreel held a commanding view of the Valley of Jezreel. It seems to have been a royal residence of the Omrides from the time of Ahab (see 1 Kings 18:45–46).

[36] In the biblical account, this is reported at the end of a prophetic narrative in which Jehu is anointed king by an anonymous prophet acting on Elisha's instructions (2 Kings 9:1–13). The reason given for Yahweh's rejection of Joram and selection of Jehu is vengeance against Ahab and Jezebel for their crimes, especially for "the blood of my servants the prophets and the blood of all the servants of the Lord."

[37] See Michael C. Astour, "841 BC: The First Assyrian Invasion of Israel," *JAOS* 91 (1971), pp. 383–398. This is unlikely, however, in view of the evidence already cited that the anti-Assyrian coalition that had opposed Shalmaneser from 853 to 845 B.C.E. had collapsed after the death of Hadadezer of Damascus, so that Damascus, now ruled by Hazael, was the only target of Shalmaneser's 841 B.C.E. campaign. Moreover, when Joram was wounded at Ramoth-gilead, setting off the sequence of events that eventually led to his assassination, he was at war with Hazael, Shalmaneser's enemy. Under these circumstances Jehu's actions can hardly be interpreted as appeasement towards Assyria. (Recognizing this problem, Ahlström [*History of Ancient Palestine* (see endnote 23), pp. 592–595], in an attempt to defend a position similar to Astour's, argued that, despite the biblical report to the contrary, Joram had gone to Ramoth-gilead to fight Shalmaneser rather than Hazael; but this is arbitrary and unconvincing.) It seems improbable, therefore, that Jehu was conspiring, either directly or indirectly, with Shalmaneser when he revolted against the Omrides.

[38] Avraham Biran and Joseph Naveh, "An Aramaic Stele Fragment from Tel Dan," *IEJ* 43 (1993), pp. 81–98; "The Tel Dan Inscription: A New Fragment," *IEJ* 45 (1995), pp. 1–18.

[39] This conclusion seems unavoidable, even though in the early part of the text of the Tel Dan stela the Aramean ruler claims to have succeeded his father as king. This is surprising in view of the fact that Hazael is depicted as a usurper both in the biblical account of his accession (2 Kings 8:7–15) and in the above-mentioned description of him

as "the son of nobody" in Assyrian records. One way to explain these contradictions is to assume that Hadadezer's legitimate successor was the invalid Ben-hadad of 2 Kings 8:7 and that Hazael was a younger, perhaps illegitimate son, who used the pretext of Ben-hadad's infirmity to seize the throne, contending that his kingship was divinely sanctioned—not in his view by the God of Israel acting through Elisha as presented in the Bible (1 Kings 19:15; see also 2 Kings 8:13) but by the god of Damascus, of whom he says in line 4 of the Tel Dan inscription, "Hadad caused me to become king."

[40] This was first suggested by Biran and Naveh, "Tel Dan Inscription" (see endnote 38), p. 18.

[41] André Lemaire has made a strong case for restoring *byt dwd*, "House of David," as a designation for Judah in the text of the stela of the Moabite king Mesha (see Chapter IV, "The United Monarchy: Saul, David and Solomon"). These two inscriptions—the Tel Dan stela and the Moabite stone—are roughly contemporary, mid-ninth century B.C.E. texts. Kenneth A. Kitchen has proposed an even earlier occurrence of the name of David in an Egyptian inscription (see "A Possible Mention of David in the Late Tenth Century BCE, and Deity *Dod as Dead as the Dodo?" *JSOT* 76 [1997], pp. 29–44, esp. pp. 39–41; and Hershel Shanks, "Has David Been Found in Egypt?" *BAR*, January/February 1999). Kitchen suggests the translation "the highland/heights of David" for a place-name in southern Judah or the Negev that appears in the list recorded on the so-called Bubastite Portal at Karnak of places conquered during Shishak's 925 B.C.E. invasion of Canaan (see above). Though there is nothing implausible about this suggestion, it is only a possibility, as Kitchen himself admits, and the equation of the hieroglyphic text, which is spelled d-w-t (!), with "David" is not straightforward.

[42] In the Tel Dan inscription "House of David" seems to be a synonym or substitution for "Judah," but in the Bible it is always clear that it refers to the ruling family or dynasty, not the kingdom as a whole. Why, then, is the southern kingdom called "House of David" in the Tel Dan inscription instead of simply "Judah," which, according to the biblical writers, was the official name of the kingdom from its founding and which is also used in the earliest extrabiblical references to the southern kingdom

(in the annals of the eighth-century B.C.E. Assyrian kings)? Parallels for the occasional use of dynastic names like "House of David" instead of national names like "Judah" are known from contemporary Syria-Palestine, but the phenomenon is not well understood and needs further study.

[43] The location is given in Shalmaneser's annalistic texts on monumental bulls from Calah (*ANET*, p. 280; *COS*, vol. 2, p. 267) and on a marble slab from Ashur (*COS*, vol. 2, p. 268). The Ashur text describes the spot as "opposite Tyre," and this better suits Ras en-Naqura than Mount Carmel, which is otherwise an attractive alternative. For bibliography, see Mordechai Cogan and Hayim Tadmor, *II Kings*, Anchor Bible 11 (Garden City, NY: Doubleday, 1988), p. 121, n. 11.

[44] McCarter, *Ancient Inscriptions* (see endnote 1), pp. 21–22.

[45] According to the slightly expanded version of the events in Chronicles, Jehosheba was Jehoiada's wife (2 Chronicles 22:11).

[46] The ostracon has been published by Pierre Bordreuil, Felix Israel and Dennis Pardee ("Deux ostraca paléo-hébraux de la collection Sh. Moussaïeff," *Semitica* 46 [1996], pp. 49–76; "King's Command and Widow's Plea: Two New Hebrew Ostraca of the Biblical Period," *Near Eastern Archaeology* 61 [1998], pp. 2–13), who assign it to the late seventh century B.C.E. But, despite one or two typologically advanced features, the script belongs to the Hebrew cursive tradition of the late ninth century B.C.E., the time of Jehoash of Judah. Since the ostracon, which is in the private collection of Mr. Shlomo Moussaieff of London, was not found in a controlled archaeological excavation, its authenticity has been questioned, especially in view of several unique or spectacular features in the text—a king of Judah is referred to by name for the first time in the corpus of Hebrew ostraca, the Temple ("the House of Yahweh") is mentioned, and there is a reference to "silver of Tarshish." Nevertheless, the ostracon and its ink have been subjected to a series of scientific tests in leading laboratories (see the sidebar by Christopher A. Rollston in "King's Command and Widow's Plea," pp. 8–9) and none of the results has cast doubt on its antiquity.

[47] We learn this from a notice following 2 Kings 13:22, which is preserved in the best manuscripts

of the Greek Bible. It reads, "And Hazael took Philistia from [Jehoahaz's] hand from the Western Sea as far as Aphek." This statement has been lost in the Masoretic text of the Hebrew Bible, and it is lacking in most English translations.

[48] Second Kings 12:20–21 indicates that Jehoash was murdered by members of his own government, a crime later avenged by his son and successor Amaziah (2 Kings 14:5). The Chronicler's account of the assassination plot (2 Chronicles 24:25–26) sets it in the immediate aftermath of Jehoash's capitulation to Hazael and attributes the motive of the conspirators to retribution for the death of Zechariah.

[49] The so-called Assyrian Eponym Chronicle, which identified each year by the name of an individual who served as its eponym official and listed a single significant event for the year, indicates that Adad-nirari's destination in 805 B.C.E. was the city of Arpad in northern Syria and that in 796 B.C.E. he marched to an unidentified place in central or southern Syria called Mansuate. There is no mention of Damascus, but Adad-nirari's few extant monuments make it clear that he regarded his victories over Damascus, in addition to the capture of Arpad, as his principal achievements.

[50] This is illustrated by a stela left by a king of Hamath named Zakkur, a successor of Irḫuleni, Ahab's ally in the 853 B.C.E. coalition against Shalmaneser III (*ANET*, pp. 655b–656a; *COS*, vol. 2, p. 155). The Aramaic inscription on the stela asserts Zakkur's claim to the small state of Hazrak (Hadrach in Zechariah 9:1 and Hatarikka in Assyrian inscriptions), which bordered Hamath on the north. Evidently Zakkur, who was probably a usurper (his father's name is not mentioned in the inscription), was an Assyrian vassal, since his annexation of Hazrak provoked a violent reaction among the Syrian states that were resistant to Assyrian domination. The leader of this group, according to the Zakkur stela, was "Bir-Hadad the son of Hazael," who assembled a coalition of ten kings. Some of the coalition states bordered Hazrak on the north, but others lay much farther north, beyond the Amanus and the eastern Taurus into northeastern Turkey. This shows that under Ben-hadad II, Damascus had once again assumed the leadership of anti-Assyrian resistance in southern and central Syria, allied at least in this case with like-minded states farther north.

[51] *COS*, vol. 2, pp. 275–276.

[52] Amaziah survived the debacle with Joash, but his subsequent death may have been an indirect result of the humiliation he had brought on his kingdom. Like his father Jehoash, he was the victim of a conspiracy in Jerusalem, which obliged him to flee to Lachish, where he was overtaken and killed (2 Kings 14:19 = 2 Chronicles 25:27).

[53] McCarter, *Ancient Inscriptions* (see endnote 1), pp. 105–110.

[54] The name appears in the form *'syw hmlk*, "Ashyaw the king," that is, "Yaw'ash" or Joash. The theophoric and verbal elements are transposed in the name, exactly as in the case of Jehoash of Judah in the ostracon described above.

[55] "Yahweh of Samaria" was the local form or manifestation of the God of Israel as he was worshiped in the capital of the northern kingdom. "Yahweh of Teman" was probably the local Yahweh of the region around 'Ajrud itself; biblical Teman, which means "Southland," was a region, not a city, and in modern times Kuntillet 'Ajrud has been given the Hebrew name Horvat Teman ("the Ruin of Teman"). For the advocates of cult centralization, these local cults posed a threat to the authority of the priesthood at the central sanctuary (see the later polemic against "high places"). For the advocates of incipient monotheism in the biblical form—those who stressed the oneness of Yahweh and insisted on the exclusiveness of his worship—the local cults posed another kind of threat, since, according to a widespread Near Eastern pattern, the local manifestations of a deity tended to attain quasi-independent status. See further, P. Kyle McCarter, Jr., "The Religious Reforms of Hezekiah and Josiah," in *Aspects of Monotheism: How God Is One*, eds. Hershel Shanks and Jack Meinhardt (Washington, DC: Biblical Archaeology Society, 1997), pp. 57–80.

[56] On this and other aspects of the religious characteristics of the Kuntillet 'Ajrud texts, see McCarter, "Aspects of the Religion of the Israelite Monarchy: Biblical and Epigraphic Data," pp. 137–155 in *Ancient Israelite Religion: Essays in Honor of Frank Moore Cross*, eds. Paul D. Hanson, S. Dean McBride and Patrick D. Miller, Jr. (Philadelphia: Fortress Press, 1987).

[57] Pirhiya Beck ("The Drawings from Horvat Teiman [Kuntillet 'Ajrud]," *Tel Aviv* 9 [1982],

pp. 3–68) interpreted the two figures as representations of the Egyptian dwarf-god Bes, whose traditional squat-legged posture is somewhat reminiscent of their bowlegged stance. Otherwise, however, the 'Ajrud figures are not at all like Bes. It is true that Bes is sometimes portrayed as ithyphallic, and Beck interpreted the appendages between the legs of the two 'Ajrud figures as phalli; but the appendages hang behind the abdomens, not in front—they are tails, not penises, and certainly are not erect. Moreover, Bes's head is leonine, not bovine, and his most characteristic feature is his protruding tongue, which is lacking in the 'Ajrud drawings.

58 The text of a stela found in 1982 at Pazarcik, Turkey (COS, vol. 2, pp. 283–284) shows that in that year the Assyrian king received tribute from a king of Damascus named Hadianu—possibly the same name as that of the grandfather of Ben-hadad I (1 Kings 15:18).

59 This approached the ideal limits of the Davidic-Solomonic empire; see 2 Samuel 8:1–14; 1 Kings 4:21 [Old Testament] = 1 Kings 5:1 [Hebrew Bible]; 1 Kings 8:65.

60 The verse goes on to say that Hamath was also "recovered," and it is, at best, improbable that Hamath became a vassal state of Israel, especially in view of the statement in 2 Kings 14:25 that the northern extent of the territory controlled by Jeroboam was at the southern border of Hamath. On the other hand, there is some evidence that Hamath had now become independent of Assyria (see Pitard, Ancient Damascus (see endnote 15), pp. 176–177), and it is possible that it had entered into an alliance with Israel, perhaps for the mutual containment of Damascus. In any case, the Hebrew text of 2 Kings 14:28 bristles with difficulties. A literal translation of the pertinent part of the verse reads "... and that he returned Damascus and Hamath to Judah in Israel ..." The expression "to Judah in Israel" makes no sense, and though scholars have made several ingenious attempts to emend the text, none carries conviction.

61 The superscription of the book that preserves his oracles (Amos 1:1) describes Amos as prophesying during the reigns of Jeroboam II of Israel and Uzziah (also called Azariah) of Judah. Most scholars think that his brief career as a prophet took place in the mid-eighth century B.C.E., sometime late in Jeroboam II's reign.

62 For a detailed survey, see Gabriel Barkay, "The Iron Age II–III," in The Archaeology of Ancient Israel, ed. Amnon Ben-Tor (New Haven and London: Yale University Press, 1992), pp. 302–373. The section on Iron IIB, Barkay's designation for the eighth century B.C.E., is found on pp. 327–334.

63 See Barkay, "The Iron Age II–III" (see endnote 62), pp. 320–323; and William G. Dever, "Social Structure in Palestine in the Iron II Period on the Eve of Destruction," in Archaeology of Society (see endnote 10), pp. 416–431.

64 Another indicator of the renewal of contact with Phoenicia is the presence of imported Phoenician pottery at Israelite sites. Careful examination of the ceramic repertoire at one well-stratified Israelite city (Hazor) shows that Phoenician imports constituted as much as 8.5 percent of the pottery in strata associated with the dynasty of Omri, when the Israelite-Phoenician alliance was strong. During the reign of Jehu they dropped to an all-time low (5 percent), as we might expect, but by the early eighth century B.C.E. they had returned to Omride levels or even higher (over 8.5 percent). See the discussion of Holladay ("Kingdoms of Israel and Judah" [see endnote 10], p. 381), who cites a study of Hazor-Sarepta parallels included in W.P. Anderson, Sarepta I: The Late Bronze and Iron Age Strata of Area II,Y, Publications de l'Université Libanaise, Section des Études Archéologiques 2 (Beirut: Département des Publications de l'Université Libanaise, 1988), pp. 139–313.

65 The ivories were found in the debris of the 722/721 B.C.E. Assyrian destruction of Samaria, so that they are technically eighth-century B.C.E. artifacts, and many must have come from the time of Jeroboam II; but dating ivories stratigraphically is somewhat precarious, since we assume they were preserved and reused from generation to generation (the heirloom factor). Thus it is possible—and usually assumed—that some number of the Samaria ivories were of ninth-century B.C.E. manufacture.

66 Dever, in his wide-ranging analysis of Israelite and Judahite society during the Divided Monarchy ("Social Structure in Palestine" [see endnote 63]), discusses the special significance of the Samaria ivories in this regard, explaining that they "constitute an especially eloquent witness to social stratification in ancient Israel: first, they are relatively rare in any context, i.e., true luxury items;

second, they were found not only at the capital, but in the ruins of the royal palace; and third, they provide clear evidence of both a sophisticated taste for 'exotic' furnishings of foreign derivation, and the means for acquiring such costly items" (p. 425).

[67] Unfortunately, this magnificent seal, which features an elegantly engraved roaring lion, disappeared soon after its discovery, and we have only a bronze cast; see McCarter, *Ancient Inscriptions* (see endnote 1), pp. 144-145.

[68] See McCarter, *Ancient Inscriptions* (see endnote 1), pp. 103-104.

[69] William F. Albright, *Archaeology and the Religion of Israel*, Anchor Books (Garden City, NY: Doubleday, 1969), p. 155.

[70] For the older theory, no longer tenable, that Azariah of Judah was a leader of the resistance to Tiglath-pileser III's first western campaign (743-738 B.C.E.), see discussions in Pitard, *Ancient Damascus* (see endnote 15), pp. 180-181, n. 90, and Cogan and Tadmor, *II Kings* (see endnote 43), pp. 165-166.

[71] On the other hand, Azariah is said to have greatly strengthened the defensive position of Jerusalem, erecting fortification towers at strategic points (2 Chronicles 26:9) and installing ingenious anti-siege devices on the walls (2 Chronicles 26:15). This could be seen as an attempt to render the city invulnerable to another incursion by Israel like that of Joash in the previous generation. Indeed, one of the gates Azariah fortified, the Corner Gate at the city's northwestern angle, was located in the area where Joash had breeched the wall (2 Kings 14:13). This may suggest that Azariah had begun to think of Judah as independent again, and although there is no record of hostility with Israel in his reign, the notice in 2 Kings 15:37 indicates that Israel, now in league with Damascus, began incursions into Judah in the reign of Jotham, Azariah's son and coregent.

[72] The original homeland of the Meunites was evidently in the vicinity of Ma'an, about 12 miles southeast of Petra. They are first mentioned in the Bible as participants in a raid into Judah conducted by the Moabites and Ammonites in the time of Jehoshaphat (2 Chronicles 20:1, where the second occurrence of "Ammonites" in the Hebrew text should be corrected to "Meunites" following the Greek).

[73] Reading "Meunites" with the Greek text of 26:8 in preference to the Hebrew "Ammonites." The Meunites not only remained in southern Judah but eventually became kin, having been incorporated into the Judahite genealogy (see Ezra 2:50; Nehemiah 7:52).

[74] Ancient Elath is sometimes identified with modern Aqaba, which, however, lacks evidence of occupation at this period or at any other time in the Iron Age. Tell el-Kheleifeh, between Aqaba and modern Elath, is usually said to have been biblical Ezion-Geber, though this, too, is disputed, and many scholars think that Ezion-Geber and Elath were two names (perhaps Israelite and Edomite?) for the same site.

[75] If Elath was another name for Ezion-Geber, it had been controlled by Judah since the time of Solomon (1 Kings 9:26, 22:48). It was probably lost in the Edomite revolt against Jehoram in the mid-ninth century B.C.E. (2 Kings 8:20-22). Azariah "restored it to Judah" (2 Kings 14:22), but only temporarily. It was lost again to Edom in the time of Ahaz, when Jerusalem was threatened by the alliance of Samaria and Damascus (2 Kings 16:6).

[76] The biblical term ṣāra'at, conventionally translated "leprosy," refers to a variety of skin ailments and conditions, ranging from the benign to the virulent. It does not necessarily connote true leprosy or Hansen's disease. See Kenneth V. Mull and Carolyn Sandquist Mull, "Biblical Leprosy—Is It Really?" *BR*, April 1992, pp. 32-39, 62.

[77] This likelihood is enhanced by the description in 2 Chronicles 26:16-21 of a conflict between Azariah and the priesthood. As the Chronicler presents it, the high priest, whose name was also Azariah—the king is called Uzziah in this account—and 80 of his colleagues accused the king of usurping priestly prerogatives by making offerings on the altar of incense in the Temple. When the king became angry, his forehead broke out with "leprosy," which the priests immediately diagnosed. They then rushed him into quarantine.

[78] The original location of the plaque and the circumstances of its discovery are unknown, but it was deposited and preserved in the Russian Orthodox Convent on the Mount of Olives. It bears an Aramaic inscription of late Herodian date

that reads "To this place have been brought the bones of Uzziah, the king of Judah—do not open!" See McCarter, *Ancient Inscriptions* (see endnote 1), pp. 132–133.

[79] See David C. Hopkins, *The Highlands of Canaan: Agricultural Life in the Early Iron Age*, SWBA 3 (Sheffield: Almond Press, 1985); and Oded Borowski, *Agriculture in Iron Age Israel* (Winona Lake, IN: Eisenbrauns, 1987).

[80] Lawrence E. Stager, "The Archaeology of the Family in Ancient Israel," *BASOR* 260 (1985), pp. 1–35; Hopkins, *Highlands of Canaan* (see endnote 79), pp. 251–261; Holladay, "Kingdoms of Israel and Judah" (see endnote 10), p. 392.

[81] Roland de Vaux, *Ancient Israel*, vol. 1: Social Institutions (New York: McGraw-Hill, 1965), pp. 4–8.

[82] See Raymond Westbrook, "The Abuse of Power," in *Studies in Biblical and Cuneiform Law*, Cahiers de la Revue Biblique (Paris: J. Gabalda, 1988), pp. 9–38.

[83] The principal wife of the kings probably exercised considerable power in her role as queen and, after her husband's death, queen mother. This is suggested, for example, by the activities that 1 Kings 16–21, despite its overall hostile tone, attributes to Jezebel. One queen mother, Athaliah, even ruled Judah as its principal sovereign for several years (c. 841–835 B.C.E.). But these cases are exceptional; women ordinarily had very limited roles outside their immediate families.

[84] On the roles and status of women in the biblical period generally, see Carol L. Meyers, *Discovering Eve: Ancient Israelite Women in Context* (New York: Oxford University Press, 1988). Phyllis A. Bird gives a concise summary of the evidence and issues in "Women (OT)," *ABD*, vol. 6, pp. 951–957.

[85] In ancient Near Eastern law and literature, the protection of the orphan and the widow is traditionally the responsibility of the king, and in the Bible this responsibility is usually assumed by Yahweh as the divine king. See F.C. Fensham, "Widow, Orphan and the Poor in Ancient Near Eastern Legal and Wisdom Literature," *JNES* 21 (1962), pp. 129–139, especially pp. 136–137.

[86] Nahman Avigad and Benjamin Sass, *Corpus of West Semitic Stamp Seals* (Jerusalem: Israel Academy of Sciences and Humanities, 1997), pp. 60–65; Robert Deutsch, *Messages from the Past:* *Hebrew Bullae from the Time of Isaiah Through the Destruction of the First Temple* (Tel Aviv: Archaeological Center Publications, 1997), pp. 65–69.

[87] The possibility is far from certain. In most cases the seals identify their owners as the wives of their husbands or the daughters of their fathers. In the former case, when the women are identified as wives, it seems unlikely that the seals were used by women acting with full independence. But in the latter case, when the women are identified as daughters, it is possible that the seals were used by women acting independently. This would be especially likely if the women were married but used seals identifying themselves as daughters of their fathers, just as men's seals usually identify their owners as sons of their fathers. On the other hand, the seals that identify their owners as daughters of their fathers might have belonged to unmarried women, so that the degree of independence implied is uncertain.

[88] Robert Deutsch and Michael Heltzer, *New Epigraphic Evidence from the Biblical Period* (Tel Aviv: Archaeological Center Publications, 1995), pp. 83–88.

[89] Tiglath-pileser's annals refer to an enemy named Azariah (*Az-ri-ia-a-ú*) who seized control of a large portion of central and coastal Syria in the years prior to 739–738 B.C.E., when the territory was reclaimed by Tiglath-pileser. For the pertinent section of the annals (lines 103–133), see *ANET*, pp. 282b–283a; *COS*, vol. 2, pp. 284–286. The opening lines of this section, where Azariah's name is not fully preserved, indicate that his country was *Iá-u-da-a-a*, which many scholars understood as Judah, thus leading to the hypothesis that Azariah of Judah played a major role in the effort to resist the first onslaught of Tiglath-pileser in the West. Research by Hayim Tadmor and Nadav Na'aman, however, has shown that the fragment containing the opening lines (103–119) does not belong to Tiglath-pileser's annals but derives instead from the records of a later Assyrian king. Thus the name of this Azariah's country is not preserved, and it seems very unlikely that he was the king of Judah. One intriguing fact remains unexplained, however. As Cogan and Tadmor point out, the name *Az-ri-ia-a-ú*, is Hebrew, not Aramaic, raising the possibility that he was an expatriot Israelite or Judahite who had gone to central Syria as a soldier of fortune and gained power there—a possibility

raised long ago by the historian Eduard Meyer. For bibliography and a fuller discussion of this episode, see Pitard, *Ancient Damascus* (see endnote 15), pp. 180–181, n. 90, and Cogan and Tadmor, *II Kings* (see endnote 43), pp. 165–166.

[90] For the names of Menahem and the other tributaries of Tiglath-pileser's first western campaign as listed in the final edition of his annals, see *ANET*, p. 283a; *COS*, vol. 2, pp. 285–286. Menahem's payment consisted of 1,000 talents of silver according to 2 Kings 15:19, where Tiglath-pileser is called "Pul." This shortened form of his name is often said to have been Tiglath-pileser's throne name as king of Babylon, a position he claimed in his first regnal year. This name has not been found in contemporary sources, however, though Tiglath-pileser was referred to as Pulu in much later cuneiform sources. See Cogan and Tadmor, *II Kings* (see endnote 43), pp. 171–172.

[91] This likelihood is increased by the fact that the revolt came out of Gilead, Transjordanian Israel, where the influence of Damascus would be strongest. Cogan and Tadmor (*II Kings* [see endnote 43], p. 178) have raised the possibility that Pekah, whose Transjordanian roots are clear because his army consisted of "fifty of the Gileadites" (2 Kings 15:25), may not have been the only Gileadite to stage a successful coup in Israel in this period. Shallum, the assassin of Jeroboam's son, is called "son of Jabesh," but "Jabesh" is not otherwise known as a personal name, and the meaning may be that he was from the town of Jabesh-gilead (Judges 21:8; 1 Samuel 11:1). Shallum's assassin, Menahem, is said to have marched out "from Tirzah," but Tirzah lies on a natural access route into the Samarian hills via the Jabbok Valley and the Wadi Far'ah, and Menahem's designation "son of Gadi" might mean that he was a member of the tribe of Gad, the northern boundary of which was the Jabbok. If, in fact, all three of these usurpers were Gileadites, it raises the possibility that much of the instability in Israel following the death of Jeroboam II was a result of interference by Damascus.

[92] Azariah is said to have greatly strengthened the defensive position of Jerusalem, erecting fortification towers at strategic points (2 Chronicles 26:9) and installing ingenious anti-siege devices on the walls (2 Chronicles 26:15). This could be seen as an attempt to render the city invulnerable

to another incursion by Israel like that of Joash in the previous generation. Indeed, one of the gates Azariah fortified, the Corner Gate at the city's northwestern angle, was located in the area where Joash had breached the wall (2 Kings 14:13). This may suggest that Azariah had begun to think of Judah as independent again, and although there is no record of hostility with Israel in his reign, the notice in 2 Kings 15:37 indicates that Israel, now in league with Damascus, began incursions into Judah in the reign of Jotham, Azariah's son and coregent.

[93] The Medes were an Indo-Iranian people who lived on a plateau corresponding to the northwestern part of modern Iran. Traditional enemies of Assyria, they would eventually become the principal ally of the Babylonians in the overthrow of the Assyrian Empire.

[94] Joachim Begrich, "Der syrisch-ephraimitische Krieg und seine weltpolitischen Zusammenhänge," *Zeitschrift der deutschen morgenländischen Gesellschaft* 83 (1929), pp. 213–237.

[95] The change in historical interpretation was stimulated especially by the influential study of Bustenay Oded, "The Historical Background of the Syro-Ephraimite War Reconsidered," *CBQ* 34 (1972), pp. 153–65.

[96] See Carl S. Ehrlich, *The Philistines in Transition. A History from ca. 1000–730 B.C.E.* Studies in the History and Culture of the Ancient Near East 10 (Leiden/New York: Brill, 1996), pp. 85–94.

[97] See Isaiah 7:1–2. In response to Ahaz's anxiety, the prophet does two things in Yahweh's name. First, he assures Ahaz that Rezin and "the son of Remaliah," as he calls Pekah, will never conquer Jerusalem, and, second, he gives a sign to certify the doom of the two nations that have attacked Jerusalem. This is the well-known Immanuel sign, according to which a child by that name will be born and "before the child knows how to refuse the evil and choose the good"—that is, before the child grows up—"the land before whose two kings you are in dread will be deserted" (Isaiah 7:16).

[98] For the names of Ahaz and the other tributaries of Tiglath-pileser's second western campaign as listed in his annals, see *ANET*, p. 282a; *COS*, vol. 2, p. 289.

[99] Hayim Tadmor, *The Inscriptions of Tiglath-Pileser III* (Jerusalem: Israel Academy of Sciences and

Humanities, 1994), annals 24:1'–9'. See also *COS*, vol. 2, p. 286.

[100] According to Tiglath-pileser's annals (*ANET*, p. 284a; *COS*, vol. 2, p. 288, see also pp. 291 and 292), the Israelites "overthrew their king Pekah (*Pa-qa-ha*) Tiglath-pileser] placed Hoshea (*A-ú-si-'*) as king over them." For other references to the installation of Hoshea in the Assyrian annals, see Cogan and Tadmor, *II Kings* (see endnote 43), p. 175.

[101] The region north of Ramoth-gilead, long disputed between Samaria and Damascus, became the Assyrian province of Qarnini (Karnaim).

[102] Pitard, *Ancient Damascus* (see endnote 15), pp. 187–188. See also *COS*, vol. 2, p. 286.

[103] *ANET*, p. 283a; *COS*, vol. 2, pp. 285–286.

[104] Israel Eph'al, *The Ancient Arabs: Nomads on the Borders of the Fertile Crescent 9th–5th Centuries B.C.* (Jerusalem/Leiden: Hebrew University/Brill, 1982), p. 83; Holladay, "Kingdoms of Israel and Judah" (see endnote 10), p. 386.

[105] *ANET*, p. 282; *COS*, vol. 2, p. 289.

[106] *ANET*, p. 283b. The section dealing with the rebellions of Samsi and Mitinti (lines 210–240) begins at the top of the second column (on p. 283b). For the other extant account of the suppression of Samsi's rebellion, see *ANET*, p. 284a; *COS*, vol. 2, p. 288; see also pp. 290–291, 291–292.

[107] See Eph'al, *The Ancient Arabs* (endnote 104), p. 84. The section dealing with the rebellions of Samsi and Mitinti (lines 210–240) begins at the top of the second column (on p. 238b).

[108] Nothing of the Tyrian annals survives in the original Phoenician, but they were translated into Greek by an obscure Hellenistic author known as Menander of Ephesus or Pergamon. Menander's work has also been lost, but portions of his translation of the annals of Tyre are cited in the writings of the Jewish historian Flavius Josephus. For the background to the fall of Samaria, the relevant passage in Josephus is *Antiquities* 9.283–287.

[109] For this date and a comprehensive evaluation of the sources, see Cogan and Tadmor, *II Kings* (see endnote 43), pp. 198–199.

[110] Who was the Egyptian king to whom Hoshea appealed? The Hebrew text of 2 Kings 17:4 identifies him as "So (*sô'*), the king of Egypt," but no king by that name is known. When Shalmaneser V came to the throne of Assyria, Egypt was emerging from a period of weakness under the last kings of the XXIInd and XXIIIrd Dynasties. Although Piankhy, the founder of the strong XXVth Dynasty had already conquered Egypt, at least formally, he was not yet ready to assert full control and had withdrawn for the time being to his native Nubia. This left the Egyptian Delta under the effective rule of Tefnacht, the very capable king of Sais in the western Delta, which was the dominant city of Egypt in the last half of the eighth century B.C.E. Osorkon IV, the last king of the XXIInd Dynasty, still ruled Tanis and Bubastis in the eastern Delta, and some historians argue that he was the biblical "So, the king of Egypt," pointing out that an Asiatic ruler like Hoshea would be more likely to be in contact with an Egyptian ruler whose realm was in the eastern Delta and that biblical references in Psalms and the prophetic works are common while Sais is never mentioned. This is the view, for example, of Ahlström (*History of Ancient Palestine* [see endnote 23], pp. 672–674), and Kenneth A. Kitchen (*The Third Intermediate Period in Egypt [1100–650 B.C]* [Warminster: Aris & Phillips, 1973], pp. 374–375), who speculates that "So" might be an abbreviation of "Osorkon" (though such abbreviations are unknown). Osorkon, however, seems to have accepted the suzerainty of Tefnacht, who founded the XXIVth Dynasty in 727 B.C.E. and was the *de facto* ruler of Egypt at the time of Hoshea's petition. Tefnacht, therefore, is the most likely candidate for "the king of Egypt" of 2 Kings 17:4, and Hans Goedicke's 1963 solution to the crux of "So, the king of Egypt" is still the best. He interpreted *sô'* as the Hebrew rendering of "Sais" (Egyptian S3w) and suggested that the original sense of the slightly corrupt biblical description of Hoshea's action was that "he sent messengers to Sais, to the king of Egypt"; see Goedicke, "The End of 'So, the King of Egypt,'" *BASOR* 171 (1963), pp. 64–66; see also Redford, *Egypt, Canaan, and Israel* (see endnote 3), p. 346.

[111] There is strong indirect evidence that the alliance included other states, from Philistia and perhaps elsewhere; see J. Maxwell Miller and John H. Hayes, *A History of Ancient Israel and Judah* (Philadelphia: Westminster Press, 1986), pp. 334–335.

¹¹² See Cogan and Tadmor, *II Kings* (see endnote 43), p. 199.

¹¹³ Merodachbaladan was from Bit-Yakin, the most southerly of the three Chaldean tribes in Babylonia. The Chaldeans, who were closely related to the Arameans, begin to appear in extant cuneiform sources in the ninth century B.C.E., and by the eighth they were vying for leadership in Babylonia. Eventually their name became synonymous with Babylonians (see Genesis 11:28). The nationalistic movement that Merodachbaladan led for more than 20 years during the reigns of Sargon and Sennacherib was fired in part by resentment of the Assyrian kings' practice (beginning with Tiglath-pileser III) of claiming the Babylonian throne for themselves.

¹¹⁴ Ilu-bi'di's revolt is well documented in Sargon II's records, including the annals (see *ANET*, p. 285; *COS*, vol. 2, p. 293) and other inscriptions (see *ANET*, p. 285b; *COS*, vol. 2, pp. 295, 296).

¹¹⁵ Probably Tefnacht again (see endnote 110).

¹¹⁶ These included Queen Samsi of Arabia, who had also paid tribute to Tiglath-pileser, and It'amar the Sabaean, chieftain of the powerful trading people of southwestern Arabia from whom the fabled Queen of Sheba of Solomonic lore also came. Their tribute came in the form of gold dust, horses and camels. When Sargon returned west in his seventh year (715 B.C.E.) to resettle captive peoples in the provinces, Samsi and It'amar brought tribute again. For both lists, see *ANET*, pp. 284b–285a, 286a.

¹¹⁷ *ANET*, pp. 284b–285a; *COS*, vol. 2, p. 296 (see also pp. 279, 280, 295).

¹¹⁸ *COS*, vol. 2, pp. 295–296.

¹¹⁹ The list in 2 Kings 17:24 is part of the peroration on the fall of Samaria by the exilic Deuteronomist (see below). It may contain the names of peoples transported to former Israelite territories at different times, thus collapsing several resettlements into a single statement. From Sargon's own records, we know only that he brought captives from a number of Arabian tribes and settled them in Samaria in 715 B.C.E. (*ANET*, pp. 285b–286a). He may well have resettled additional peoples in Samaria in 711 B.C.E., when he made his final visit to Palestine to suppress a revolt in Ashdod, and there were probably still other resettlements of which we have no record.

¹²⁰ Reading "mountain country" or "highlands" with the Greek of 2 Kings 17:6 in preference to the Hebrew reading "cities."

¹²¹ On the resettlement of Israelites (and Judahites) in Mesopotamia generally, see Bustenay Oded, "The Settlement of the Israelites and the Judean Exiles in Mesopotamia in the 8th and 6th Centuries B.C.E.," in *Studies in Historical Geography and Biblical Historiography Presented to Zecharia Kallai*, ed. Gershon Galil and Moshe Weinfeld. VT Supplement 81 (Leiden: Brill, 2000), pp. 91–103.

¹²² An impression of this seal published by Nahman Avigad (*Hebrew Bullae from the Time of Jeremiah* [Jerusalem: Israel Exploration Society, 1986], p. 110, no. 199) was not well enough preserved to be recognized, but a second, legible impression is in the collection of Shlomo Moussaieff of London. It has been published by Frank Moore Cross in *Realia Dei: Essays in Archaeology and Biblical Interpretation*, ed. Prescott H. Williams, Jr. and Theodore Hiebert (Edward F. Campbell Volume) (Atlanta: Scholars Press, 1999), pp. 62–67. Other royal bullae have now come to light, though the authenticity of all of them is strongly debated. See, for example, the extraordinary specimens in *Biblical Period Hebrew Bullae: The Josef Chaim Kaufman Collection*, ed. Robert Deutsch (Tel Aviv: Archaeological Center Publication, 2003), pp. 13–18.

¹²³ Many historians of Israel have assumed that the reforms were undertaken as an integral component of the revolt against Sennacherib, involving a repudiation of the Assyrian gods (John Bright, *History of Israel*, 3rd ed. [Philadelphia: Westminster Press, 1981], p. 282) and expulsion of Assyrian religious practices from the Temple in Jerusalem (Martin Noth, *History of Israel*, 2nd ed. [New York: Harper & Row, 1960], p. 266). Studies of the religious policies of the empire, however, have shown that, in contrast to the rules for annexed territories where worship of the Assyrian gods was required, it was not Assyrian policy to interfere with the religious practices of vassal states like Judah; see John W. McKay, *Religion in Judah Under the Assyrians*, Studies in Biblical Theology Second Series 26 (London: SCM, 1973); Mordechai Cogan, *Imperialism and Religion: Assyria, Judah and Israel in the Eighth and Seventh Centuries B.C.*, SBL Monograph 19 (Missoula, MT: Scholars Press, 1974).

[124] In fact, this very point was part of the rhetoric of Sennacherib's spokesman, the Rabshakeh, in his attempt to intimidate Hezekiah's delegation at the beginning of the siege of Jerusalem (2 Kings 18:22).

[125] The Chronicler's account of Hezekiah's reforms, which constitutes the bulk of three chapters (2 Chronicles 29-31), is much more extensive than the three verses assigned to the subject in the Kings account (2 Kings 18:4-6). This is explainable in part as the Chronicler's expansion of subjects in which he had a particular interest (note, for example, the emphasis on role of the Levites in the purification of the Temple in chapter 30). But we must also allow for a tendency on the part of the Deuteronomistic historian, who was responsible for the Kings account, to diminish the extent of Hezekiah's reform. To be sure, the historian admired Hezekiah and praised him highly, asserting that in his trust in Yahweh "... there was no one like him among all the kings of Judah after him, or among those who were before him" (2 Kings 18:5). But if, as many scholars believe, the historian was working in the time of Josiah—indeed, under the patronage of Josiah—it is not surprising that he would minimize Hezekiah's role in the reform movement in order to reserve the primary credit for Josiah.

[126] Sargon's boastful self-designation in his Nimrud Inscription (COS, vol. 2, pp. 298-99) as "the subduer of Judah [?] which lies far away" remains enigmatic; see K. Lawson Younger, Jr., "Assyrian Involvement in the Southern Levant at the End of the Eighth Century B.C.E.," Jerusalem in Bible and Archaeology: The First Temple Period, eds. Andrew G. Vaughn and Ann E. Killebrew (Atlanta: Society of Biblical Literature, 2003), pp. 235-63, esp. 237-240.

[127] Azuri's revolt is mentioned in Sargon II's annals (ANET, p. 286a; COS 2, p. 294) and other inscriptions (ANET, pp. 286; COS, vol. 2, p. 296), and in one broken prism (ANET, pp. 286b-287a) Judah is named explicitly as one of those states Ashdod tried to recruit.

[128] Second Kings 20:12-13 (see also Isaiah 39:1-2; 2 Chronicles 32:31) describes a visit of Merodachbaladan's envoys to Jerusalem, where Hezekiah showed them the Temple treasury. In the current arrangement of the biblical materials about Hezekiah's reign, this visit is placed after

Sennacherib's invasion, but it must have occurred earlier, since in 701 B.C.E. Merodachbaladan was no longer in power. It fits nicely into the events of 704-703 B.C.E., when it would have been very much in Merodachbaladan's interest to cultivate alliances with other Assyrian vassal states and encourage them to rebel. See Noth, History of Israel (see endnote 123), p. 267; Bright, History of Israel (see endnote 123), pp. 284-285 and n. 44; Ahlström, History of Ancient Palestine (see endnote 23), p. 695. Cogan and Tadmor (II Kings [see endnote 43], pp. 260-261) place the visit earlier, during Merodachbaladan's first term as king of Babylon (722-710 B.C.E.).

[129] This was the third of the eight campaigns of Sennacherib recorded in the final edition of his annals, preserved in the Taylor and Oriental Institute prisms (see McCarter, Ancient Inscriptions [see endnote 1], pp. 24-25), both of which are dependent, for this campaign, on the slightly fuller account in the so-called Rassam cylinder, which was composed shortly after the campaign itself (COS, vol. 2, pp. 302-303). When the Assyrian records are complemented and supplemented with information concerning the Judean part of the campaign found in the Bible (2 Kings 18:13-19:8; Isaiah 36:1-37:8; 2 Chronicles 32:1-22), and the ample archaeological testimony to the campaign and Hezekiah's preparations for it at sites like Lachish and Jerusalem, the story of the campaign that emerges is one of the most complete in the history of the Assyrian Empire. See David Ussishkin, "News from the Field: Defensive Judean Counter-Ramp Found at Lachish in 1983 Season," BAR, March/April 1984, pp. 66-73.

[130] Presumably this huge force ("an army beyond counting," ANET, p. 287b; "a countless army," COS, vol. 2, p. 303) had been dispatched by Shebitku (706-690 B.C.E.), king of Egypt. The biblical reference in 2 Kings 19:9 (= Isaiah 37:9) to "King Tirhakah of Ethiopia" is evidently a mistake, since in 701 B.C.E. Taharqa (690-664 B.C.E.), the biblical Tirhakah, was still a child living in Nubia and would not come to the throne of Egypt for another decade; see Redford, Egypt, Canaan, and Israel (see endnote 3), p. 353, n. 163. This lapse on the part of the Israelite historian has helped give rise to the hypothesis of a second, later campaign by Sennacherib against Judah. For arguments in favor of the two-campaign theory, see William F. Albright, "New Light from Egypt on

the Chronology and History of Israel and Judah," *BASOR* 130 (1953), pp. 8–11; Siegfried Horn, "Did Sennacherib Campaign Once or Twice Against Hezekiah?" *AUSS* 4 (1966), pp. 1–28; Bright, *History of Israel* (see endnote 123), pp. 296–398; and William H. Shea, "Sennacherib's Second Palestinian Campaign," *JBL* 104 (1985), pp. 401–418. For a thorough critique, see Cogan and Tadmor, *II Kings* (see endnote 43), pp. 248–251.

[131] Padi's name appears in a five-line inscription found in 1996 in the ruins of a temple at Tel Miqne, ancient Ekron (*COS*, vol. 2, p. 164). The inscription records the dedication of the temple to a goddess by "Ikayush (*'kyš*) son of Padi." Ikayush appears as one who paid tribute to Assyria in inscriptions of Sennacherib's successor Esarhaddon (681–669 B.C.E.), where he is called Ikausu (*ANET*, pp. 291a, 294a).

[132] At certain points the correspondences are remarkably close. At the beginning of the account of the advance against Hezekiah in the Assyrian annals, Sennacherib says, "I laid siege to 46 of his strong cities, walled forts ... and conquered them ... " (*ANET*, p. 288a; *COS*, vol. 2, p. 303), while the biblical account opens with the statement that "King Sennacherib of Assyria came up against all the fortified cities of Judah and captured them" (2 Kings 18:13). In the Assyrian account the amount of precious metal in the tribute Hezekiah paid is given as "30 talents of gold, 800 talents of silver" (*ANET*, p. 288a; *COS*, vol. 2, p. 303), while the biblical account specifies the amount as "three hundred talents of silver and thirty talents of gold" (2 Kings 18:14).

[133] H.W.F. Saggs, "The Nimrud Letters, 1952: I," *Iraq* 17 (1955), pp. 23–26; Chaim Cohen, "Neo-Assyrian Elements in the First Speech of the Biblical Rab-sûaqê," *Israel Oriental Studies* 9 (1979), pp. 32–48; Peter Machinist, "Assyria and Its Image in First Isaiah," *JAOS* 103 (1983), pp. 719–737; Cogan and Tadmor, *II Kings* (see endnote 43), pp. 242–243.

[134] The second section describes two visits to Jerusalem by Sennacherib's officer Rabshakeh—one from Lachish and one from Libnah (possibly Tell Bornat, about 5 miles north of Lachish). The prevailing view among biblical scholars is that this second section is a composite of two versions of one round of negotiations. The first version (2 Kings 18:17–19:7) seems to be older, with less

elaboration in the prophetic and Deuteronomistic traditions; it reports the Rabshakeh's attempt to intimidate Jerusalem, Hezekiah's reaction and Isaiah's reassurance. The second version (2 Kings 19:8–34) is probably later; it tells the same basic story, but with much more literary elaboration deriving, in the first place, from prophetic tradition—a poetic oracle of Isaiah reviling Sennacherib in 2 Kings 19:20–28, followed by a prophetic sign of reassurance in 2 Kings 19:29–31 and a prose oracle proclaiming the salvation of the city in 2 Kings 19:32–34—and, in the second place, from a Deuteronomistic compiler, whose hand is most evident in the language of Hezekiah's prayer (2 Kings 19:14–19). It is noteworthy, in this regard, that the historically problematic reference to "King Tirhakah of Ethiopia" (2 Kings 19:9) appears in the late version.

[135] See David Ussishkin, *The Conquest of Lachish by Sennacherib*, Publications of the Institute of Archaeology 6 (Tel Aviv: Tel Aviv University, 1982), reviewed by Hershel Shanks in Books in Brief, *BAR*, March/April 1984, pp. 48–65, and updated by Ussishkin, "News from the Field" (see endnote 129).

[136] According to Isaiah 20:1, for example, it was Sargon's Tartan (Hebrew *tartān* from Akkadian *turtānu*) who conducted the 714–712 B.C.E. campaign against Ashdod. A Babylonian Rabsaris is among the officers listed in connection with the fall of Jerusalem in Jeremiah 39:3,13.

[137] It has been speculated that the Rabshakeh was an exiled Israelite who had found a career in the Assyrian court; see Cogan and Tadmor, *II Kings* (see endnote 43), p. 230, and Ahlström, *History of Ancient Palestine* (see endnote 23), pp. 683–684.

[138] *ANET*, p. 288a; *COS*, vol. 2, p. 303.

[139] David Ussishkin has made a plausible case "that Sennacherib, given the choice, did not intend to conquer Jerusalem by force," preferring instead to reduce Hezekiah to Assyrian vassalage by a strategy of attrition and intimidation, holding up the fate of Lachish as a terrifying example; see "Sennacherib's Campaign to Philistia and Judah: Ekron, Lachish, and Jerusalem," in *Essays on Ancient Israel in Its Near Eastern Context. A Tribute to Nadav Na'aman*, ed. Yairah Amrite et al. (Winona Lake, IN: Eisenbrauns, 2006), pp. 339–57 and esp. 353–354.

[140] The well-constructed, 20-foot thick wall was discovered in the 1970 Jewish Quarter excavation. See Nahman Avigad, *Discovering Jerusalem* (Nashville: Abingdon, 1980), pp. 46–57. Magen Broshi and others have suggested that the region surrounding Jerusalem, and especially the western hill, became a camp for refugees after the fall of Samaria and during Sennacherib's depredations in the surrounding countryside, especially with the Assyrian reassignment of Judahite cities to the Philistines; see Magen Broshi, "The Expansion of Jerusalem in the Reigns of Hezekiah and Manasseh," *IEJ* 24 (1974), pp. 21–26. If this is correct, it is likely that Hezekiah's "outside" wall was built in order to incorporate the western hill into the city, with the result that the population of the city may have expanded, according to Broshi's estimate, three- or fourfold in the last quarter of the eighth century B.C.E. As noted earlier (pp. 176–177), however, Hezekiah seems to have remained compliant towards Assyria as long as Sargon II was alive, and in light of this policy Nadav Na'aman has recently pointed out that Jerusalem could hardly have accepted thousands of refugees from Samaria in 720 without provoking Sargon ("When and How Did Jerusalem Become a Great City? The Rise of Jerusalem as Judah's Premier City in the Eighth–Seventh Centuries B.C.E.," *BASOR* 347 (2007), pp. 21–56, esp. pp. 35–38). Pointing out (pp. 24–27) that some of the pottery types thought to be diagnostic of the time of Hezekiah were already in use in the early eighth century, Na'aman prefers to think of the Jerusalem population crest of the end of the eighth century as the result of a gradual increase that began in the early eighth century or earlier and culminated with the arrival of refugees from the events of 701. For a critique of this view by Israel Finkelstein, who strongly doubts an expansion of Jerusalem before the late eighth century, see "Concerning Disappearing Potsherds and Invented Population Growth: A Reply to Nadav Na'aman Regarding Jerusalem's Growth in the 8th Century B.C.E. [Hebrew]," *Zion* 72 (2007), pp. 325–337.

[141] Hezekiah's tunnel is commonly known as the Siloam Tunnel, a name derived from the Shiloah or Siloam Channel, an aqueduct that transported the waters of the Gihon along the southeastern slope of the Ophel to agricultural terraces in the Kidron basin; see further, on both the tunnel and the inscription, McCarter, *Ancient Inscriptions* (see endnote 1), pp. 113–115.

[142] Some of the scarabs have two wings, and some have four—a fact that was formerly interpreted as evidence of chronological development. It has now been shown, however, that all of the *lmlk* stamps belong to the time of Hezekiah, and this fact, combined with the vast numbers in which they appear in excavations (more than 1,200 have been found), strengthens the assumption that they had a function in Hezekiah's administration of the kingdom before the invasion; see Nadav Na'aman, "Sennacherib's Campaign to Judah and the Date of the *lmlk* Stamps," *VT* 29 (1979), pp. 61–86. It is interesting to note in this context that King Hezekiah's personal seal, an impression of which has come to light, also bore a two-winged scarab.

[143] Further evidence that the *lmlk* stamps were part of a centralized administrative program comes from the determination that they were all manufactured in a single site in the Judean Shephelah, as revealed by analysis of the clay from which they were manufactured. See further McCarter, *Ancient Inscriptions* (see endnote 1), pp. 142–143.

[144] The overall structure of the biblical narrative is designed to show that the survival of the city was the result of divine deliverance in fulfillment of the oracles of Isaiah, especially the oracle in 2 Kings 19:32–34 announcing that Yahweh would defend the city. The night after this prophecy was uttered, we are told (2 Kings 19:35), "The angel of the Lord ... struck down one hundred eighty-five thousand in the camp of the Assyrians ..." This is the biblical language of plague, as correctly interpreted in Ben Sira 48:21, and it might preserve a historical memory of one of the factors leading to the Assyrian withdrawal, namely, the spread of disease among the siege troops. Herodotus (*History* 2.141) relates the story of a similar deliverance of Egypt from "Sennacherib, king of the Arabs [!] and Assyrians," when mice gnawed the weapons of the Assyrians while they were encamped at Pelusium in the eastern Nile Delta. This story has been associated with Sennacherib's siege of Jerusalem by some historians, who regard the reference to mice as an indirect confirmation of an outbreak of plague in the Assyrian camp. But the Herodotus story is not historical in anything like its present form—Sennacherib never invaded Egypt—and, in any case,

it makes no mention of Judah or Jerusalem. At best it might be regarded as a distorted recollection of an event in the reign of Esarhaddon, Sennacherib's successor, who did invade Egypt and was assisted in doing so by Arab guides.

145 The list of Hezekiah's tribute, which is quite substantial in the Oriental Institute prism (*ANET*, p. 288a) and the Taylor prism, is even more so in the older Rassam cylinder (*COS*, vol. 2, p. 303)—indeed, it is the longest tribute list in any of Sennacherib's extant inscriptions. For the two prisms and the Rassam cylinder, see endnote 129.

146 Some historians argue that Sennacherib conducted a second campaign against Judah sometime after the accession of Tirhakah in 690 B.C.E. The two-campaign hypothesis is an attempt to solve the problems created by the reference to "King Tirhakah of Ethiopia" in 2 Kings 19:9 and especially the contradiction regarding the outcome of the siege between the Assyrian account, which says that Hezekiah capitulated and accepted vassal status, and the biblical account, which concludes with Sennacherib's army retreating from Judah after having been severely punished by the hand of Yahweh. According to the two-campaign theory, Sennacherib's surviving inscriptions refer to the 701 B.C.E. campaign, which ended in the reduction of Judah to vassalage, while the biblical references to the failure and withdrawal of the Assyrian army and to the involvement of Tirhakah refer to a campaign not mentioned in extant Assyrian sources. The occasion for this second campaign would have been a rebellion in the West, led by Hezekiah and supported by Tirhakah, that broke out after the Assyrian army was defeated by the Babylonians and Elamites in 691 B.C.E., and Sennacherib would have launched it after his capture of Babylon in 689 B.C.E. Though ingenious, the two-campaign theory does not inspire confidence, since the problems being addressed arise only in the final part of the biblical account of the siege, which, as noted earlier, is widely regarded as late in origin, while the opening summary of the biblical account (2 Kings 18:13–16), which is unanimously regarded as early, is in close agreement with the Assyrian account. For arguments in favor of the two-campaign theory, see endnote 130. For a thorough critique, see Cogan and Tadmor, *II Kings* (see endnote 43), pp. 248–251.

147 *ANET*, pp. 291a, 294a.

148 On the exilic Deuteronomist and his treatment of Manasseh, see Cross, *Canaanite Myth and Hebrew Epic* (see endnote 12), pp. 285–287. For the Chronicler's account of Manasseh's reign, which contains substantially different material, see the discussion below.

149 Noth, *History of Israel* (see endnote 123), p. 269; Bright, *History of Israel* (see endnote 123), p. 312.

150 See McKay, *Religion in Judah Under the Assyrians* (see endnote 123); Cogan, *Imperialism and Religion* (see endnote 123).

151 The rest of the list of practices for which he is condemned in 1 Kings 21:3–6 corresponds very closely to the cultic sins listed in 2 Kings 17:16–17, amid the long Deuteronomistic sermon on the fall of Samaria in 2 Kings 17:7–23. Thus, he erected altars to a foreign god (Baal; 1 Kings 21:3) and "the host of heaven," astral deities whose rooftop worship was condemned by prophets like Zephaniah (1:5) and Jeremiah (19:13); he reinstituted the "sacred pole" or asherah (1 Kings 21:3); and he made "his son pass through fire" and practiced soothsaying and augury (1 Kings 21:3). In 2 Kings 17:16–17 these are the very sins that, in the view of the Deuteronomist historian who composed the sermon (see Cross, *Canaanite Myth and Hebrew Epic* [see endnote 12], p. 281), led to the downfall of the northern kingdom, and it seems clear that the purpose of the exilic Deuteronomist in composing the present list was to accuse Manasseh of bringing similar judgment on Judah (Cross, *Canaanite Myth and Hebrew Epic* [see endnote 12], p. 285). This is surely the point of the comparison of Manasseh to "King Ahab of Israel" in 2 Kings 21:3.

152 The Medes were Indo-Iranian people living on the plateau corresponding to the northwestern part of modern Iran. Traditional enemies of Assyria, they eventually became the principal ally of Babylonia in the overthrow of the Assyrian Empire, as we shall see.

153 The Cimmerians—called *Kimmerioi* by the Greeks, *Gimirrai* by the Assyrians and *gōmer*, "Gomer," in the Bible (Ezekiel 38:6; see also Genesis 10:2–3)—were Indo-Aryan nomads, originally from southern Russia. In the eighth century B.C.E., they had been driven south across

the Caucasus under pressure from the Scythians and Assyrians into Asia Minor. Sargon II was fighting the Cimmerians in Asia Minor when he was killed in 705 B.C.E.

[154] The Scythians—called *Skythai* by the Greeks, *Ašûguzai, Išûguzai* by the Assyrians and *'ašûkênaz,* "Ashkenaz," in the Bible (Jeremiah 51:27; see also Genesis 10:3)—were a nomadic people who spoke an Indo-Iranian language. In the eighth century B.C.E. they had moved from their homeland in southern Russia (north and northeast of Black Sea) through the Caucasus into the Near East. Originally enemies of Assyria, they became allies briefly, then enemies again.

[155] Anthony Spalinger, "Esarhaddon and Egypt: An Analysis of the First Invasion of Egypt," *Orientalia* 43 (1974), p. 299.

[156] See, for the treaty between Esarhaddon and Baal, *ANET*, pp. 533b–534a; for Abdimilkutti's rebellion, *ANET*, pp. 290b–291a; and for the rebuilding project, *ANET*, p. 290.

[157] *ANET*, p. 302b.

[158] *ANET*, p. 292b. Earlier (c. 677 B.C.E.) Esarhaddon had pacified Arab tribes in the vicinity of the Wadi of Egypt (*ANET*, p. 291b–292a), guaranteeing their neutrality and learning from them the value of the camel and waterskin.

[159] This is according to the Babylonian Chronicle (*ANET*, p. 302b–303a); for the narrative account in the so-called Zinjirli stela from southeastern Turkey (ancient Sam'al), see *ANET*, p. 293a.

[160] In a stela carved on the rock wall of the Dog River near Beirut, he boasts, "I entered Memphis ... amidst (general) jubilation and rejoicing" (*ANET*, p. 292a).

[161] Again, according to the Babylonian Chronicle, *ANET*, p. 303b.

[162] According to the so-called Rassam cylinder from Kuyunjik, ancient Nineveh (*ANET*, pp. 294–296a), Assurbanipal led this expedition himself, but other inscriptions indicate that he stayed home and entrusted the task to his second-in-command, the *turtānu.*

[163] *ANET*, p. 294a.

[164] This was the period of the Saite Renaissance in Egypt, so-called because of the revival of the ancient Memphite traditions of Lower Egypt, which was now ruled from Sais in the north rather than from Thebes in Upper Egypt. The period was characterized by a revival of art and culture, a thorough reorganization of the government and an increasing openness to foreign contacts, including commerce with Greece. All this was possible because of the escalating collapse of Assyria and the corresponding increase in the autonomy of Egypt. It must be kept in mind, however, that Saite kings of Egypt maintained an official posture of allegiance to Assyria; see Anthony Spalinger, "The Concept of Monarchy During the Saite Epoch: An Essay of Synthesis, *Orientalia* 47 (1978), pp. 12–36.

[165] The enigmatic biblical tradition of Manasseh's arrest by the Assyrians (2 Chronicles 33:11) is sometimes thought to belong in the context of the Shamash-shum-ukin revolt. Manasseh is said to have been dragged in chains to Babylon (!), then released and restored to power. Apart from the defection just noted of some of Assyria's Arabian allies, we have only scant evidence to indicate that the revolt spread into the western provinces, but if there was more unrest there than our surviving records indicate, it would not be surprising to find that Manasseh had become involved, especially in view of the biblical and archaeological evidence cited below, which suggests he was moving towards independence later in his reign. Certainly there is nothing implausible about the story of his arrest and restoration to power, since it would parallel the experiences of others in the hands of Assurbanipal. In their overextended empire, Assurbanipal and Esarhaddon before him had little choice other than to try, with the help of intimidation and promises, to find native rulers who would be loyal to Assyria. The experience of Manasseh, as described in 2 Chronicles 33:11, for example, parallels that of Necho in Egypt and the Arab leader Uate' in Trans-jordan, both of whom rebelled, were captured and brought before the Assyrian king, then sent home to rule again.

[166] For Esarhaddon's campaign against the Arabs, which is also described on the so-called Rassam cylinder, see *ANET*, pp. 297b–301a.

[167] In 2 Kings 21:16 Manasseh is accused of "shedding innocent blood." The basis of this charge is unknown, although one was supplied in postbiblical tradition. According to a variety of Jewish and Christian sources, Manasseh, again like

Ahab (2 Kings 21:3), persecuted the prophets and even had Isaiah sawed in two (Josephus, *Antiquities* 10.38; BT Sanhedrin 103b; Ascension of Isaiah 5:1–7; Justin, *Dialogue with Trypho* 120; Jerome, *Comment on Isaiah* 57:2; see also Hebrews 11:37).

[168] For the principal suggestions, see Dan Bahat, "The Wall of Manasseh in Jerusalem," *IEJ* 31 (1981), pp. 235–236. Bahat calls special attention to a wall "of substantial appearance" found by Kathleen Kenyon, who dated it to the eighth-seventh century B.C.E., on the eastern slope of the City of David; see her *Digging Up Jerusalem* (London: Benn, 1974), p. 83 (Wall NA). The location fits with the biblical designation "west of the Gihon, in the wadi," and Bahat has suggested that it might be Manasseh's "outer wall." On the difficulties in the archaeological interpretation of the walls of Jerusalem during the last part of the Judean monarchy, see Avigad, *Discovering Jerusalem* (see endnote 140), pp. 46–60.

[169] If our assumption is correct that Manasseh was distancing himself from Assyria at the end of his reign, the assassination is unlikely to have been part of an anti-Assyrian coup, especially since there is no known external event with which it might be associated (the last Assyrian incursion into the West was a punitive attack on Acco and Ushu [island of Tyre], probably to be dated to 644 B.C.E.). Redford (*Egypt, Canaan, and Israel* [see endnote 3], pp. 440–441) has made an interesting suggestion that would connect the coup with the Scythian invasion of Palestine mentioned in Herodotus (*History* 1.103–106).

[170] For a convenient delineation of these and other major correspondences between Josiah's reform measures and the cultic laws laid down in Deuteronomy, see the table provided in Ernest W. Nicholson, *Deuteronomy and Tradition* (Philadelphia: Fortress Press, 1967), p. 3. The hypothesis that Josiah's "book of the law" was an early form of the Book of Deuteronomy was first articulated in W.M.L. De Wette's 1805 Berlin doctoral thesis, *Dissertatio Critica*.

[171] In this regard, it is important to understand that the Judahite reform movement of the late eighth and seventh centuries B.C.E. arose during a period of international neoclassicism in the ancient Near East, a time when classical forms and ideas were being revived or reconstructed in Egypt and Mesopotamia, as well as Judah.

In Egypt both the Cushite rulers of the XXVth Dynasty and the Saite kings of the XXVIth Dynasty promoted the return to traditional Egyptian values and revived long-forgotten practices and beliefs, sometimes on the basis of the discovery of ancient documents, such as the so-called Shabaka Stone, which was claimed to have been copied from an ancient papyrus, "a work of the ancestors, but worm-eaten, so that it could not be comprehended from beginning to end"; see McCarter, *Ancient Inscriptions* (see endnote 1), pp. 58–59; and for the text, *ANET*, pp. 4a–6a. In Assyria, Assurbanipal (668–627 B.C.E.) promoted his own form of Mesopotamian neoclassicism, instructing his officials to scour the countryside of Assyria and Babylonia, poring through the local temple archives for ancient documents that could be copied and added to the royal collection. The result was an extraordinary library, which, since its discovery in the mid-19th century in the mound of ancient Nineveh at Kuyunjik in northern Iraq, has remained our most important source for the "canonical" literature of ancient Mesopotamia.

[172] To be sure, foreign cults were outlawed by Josiah, but the deities whose cult places are listed in 2 Kings 23:13–14 as having been defiled were the gods and goddesses of Judah's West Semitic neighbors—Ashtart of Sidon, Chemosh of Moab, Milcom of Ammon—not those of Assyria.

[173] For a detailed statement of the difficulties and the various positions, see Nadav Na'aman, "The Kingdom of Judah Under Josiah," *Tel Aviv* 18 (1991), pp. 41–51. In Na'aman's own view, Josiah was probably able to expand into the Samarian hills, but not into Transjordan, the Jordan Valley, or the Galilee, as some have proposed, and no farther west than the northern Judean Shephelah, since the coastal plain was controlled by Egypt.

[174] See McCarter, *Ancient Inscriptions* (see endnote 1), p. 116.

[175] An inscription of Psammetichus, dated 612 B.C.E., boasts of Egyptian control of Phoenicia and its timber trade; see K.S. Freedy and Donald Redford, "The Dates in Ezekiel in Relation to Biblical, Babylonian and Egyptian Sources," *JAOS* 90 (1970), pp. 462–485.

[176] Herodotus, *History* 2.157.

[177] Herodotus, *History* 1.105.

[178] To what extent this created friction with Josiah, who, as noted above, may also have taken control of parts of Philistia, is unknown, but the potential conflict may have been a factor in Josiah's fatal encounter with Psammetichus's successor at Megiddo in 609 B.C.E.

[179] This is essentially the explanation of Redford (*Egypt, Canaan, and Israel* [see endnote 3], p. 446), who describes the Egyptian policy as "at once unexpected yet farsighted."

[180] Riblah had been an Assyrian administrative and military center earlier, and shortly after this it became a Babylonian military center.

[181] See 1 Chronicles 3:15: "The sons of Josiah: Johanan the firstborn, the second Jehoiakim, the third Zedekiah, the fourth Shallum." That Jehoahaz was Shallum is shown by Jeremiah 22:11–12. The reason "the people of the land" chose the youngest of Josiah's sons is not given. The firstborn, Johanan, is not mentioned earlier and may have died before his father. Jehoiakim, with whom Necho supplanted Jehoahaz, may have been passed over by "the people of his land" because of his pro-Egyptian leanings.

[182] In the words of 2 Kings 24:7, "The king of Egypt did not come again out of his land, for the king of Babylon had taken over all that belonged to the king of Egypt from the Wadi of Egypt to the River Euphrates."

[183] The mood in Philistia at this time is illustrated by a fragmentary papyrus found at Saqqara containing the Aramaic text of a letter from a certain Adon, ruler of a Philistine state (probably Ekron), requesting help from the pharaoh against the Babylonian army, which, he says, had already captured Aphek. See Bezalel Porten, "The Identity of King Adon," *BA* 44 (1981), pp. 36–52.

[184] Edward Lipiński, "The Egyptian-Babylonian War of the Winter 601–600," *Annali dell'istituto orientale di Napoli* 22 (1972), pp. 235–241.

[185] Herodotus, *History* 2.159.

[186] Bright, *History of Israel* (see endnote 123), p. 327. The final comment on Jehoiakim by his old nemesis, Jeremiah, shows that the king received no more sympathy in death than he had in life from the prophet, who constantly advised compliance with Babylon and deplored Jehoiakim's pro-Egyptian stance. See Jeremiah 22:18–19.

[187] Conditions in the Judahite countryside during this grim period are vividly illustrated by a group of ostraca found in the ruins of the fortress of Lachish, which, because of its position guarding the main access road into the Judahite Hills from the coastal plain, was attacked by Nebuchadnezzar just as it had been by Sennacherib in 701 B.C.E. The 22 Lachish ostraca constitute a small archive of wartime correspondence between the governor or commanding officer of Lachish and a subordinate. One of the ostraca (no. 3) refers to a general named Coniah son of Elnathan, who was passing by Lachish on a mission to Egypt; he may well have been carrying the invitation that brought Hophra's troops briefly to Jerusalem as described in Jeremiah 37:5; see McCarter, *Ancient Inscriptions* (see endnote 1), pp. 116–118. Another Lachish ostracon (no. 4) speaks of the disappearance of the signal fires of the nearby fortress of Azekah, a statement that poignantly brings to mind the reference in Jeremiah 34:7 to the time "when the army of the king of Babylon was fighting against Jerusalem and against all the cities of Judah that were left, Lachish and Azekah; for these were the only fortified cities of Judah that remained"; see *Ancient Inscriptions* (see endnote 1), pp. 118–119.

[188] See Abraham Malamat, "The Kingdom of Judah Between Egypt and Babylon: A Small State Within a Great Power Confrontation," *Studia Theologica* 44 (1960), pp. 65–77.

VI. Exile and Return

[1] For an argument that Gedaliah was installed as a king, see J. Maxwell Miller and John H. Hayes, *A History of Ancient Israel and Judah*, 2nd ed. (Louisville: Westminster/John Knox Press, 2006), pp. 482–485.

[2] See Jill Middlemas, *The Templeless Age: An Introduction to the History, Literature, and Theology of the "Exile"* (Louisville: Westminster/John Knox Press, 2007); Robert P. Carroll, "Exile! What Exile? Deportation and the Discourses of Diaspora" in *Leading Captivity Captive: The Exile as History and Ideology*, ed. Lester L. Grabbe, JSOT Supplement 278 (Sheffield: Sheffield Academic Press, 1998).

[3] All quotations of biblical texts come from the NRSV.

[4] See Hans Barstad, *The Myth of the Empty Land: A Study in the History and Archaeology of Judah during*

the "Exilic" Period (Oslo: Scandinavian University Press, 1996). Robert P. Carroll, "The Myth of the Empty Land," *Semeia* 59 (1993), pp. 79–93. For an up-to-date review of the archaeological material and one that is critical of Barstad and Carroll, see William G. Dever, "Archaeology and the Fall of Judah," in *Eretz Israel* 29, volume in honor of Ephraim Stern (2009), pp. 29–35.

⁵ From Oded Lipschits, *The Fall and Rise of Jerusalem* (Winona Lake, IN: Eisenbrauns, 2005). Lipschits's figures represent an upward revision of the numbers found in Charles Carter, *The Emergence of Yehud in the Persian Period*, JSOT Supplement 294 (Sheffield: Sheffield Academic Press, 1999).

⁶ Lipschits (*Fall and Rise* [see endnote 5], p. 262 [table 4.1]) notes an 89 percent decrease in settled dunams for Jerusalem environs and 83 percent for the Shephelah.

⁷ See, for example, F.W. Dobbs-Alsopp, *Weep, O Daughter of Zion: A Study of the City-Lament Genre in the Hebrew Bible* (Rome: Editrice Pontificio Istituto Biblico, 1993).

⁸ David Jamieson-Drake, *Scribes and Schools in Monarchic Judah: A Socio-Archeological Approach* (Sheffield: Almond Press, 1991).

⁹ See Rainer Albertz, *Israel in Exile: The History and Literature of the Sixth Century B.C.E.* (Atlanta: Society of Biblical Literature, 2003), p. 96.

¹⁰ Literally, "chief cook."

¹¹ Jeffrey R. Zorn, "Tell en-Naṣbeh and the Problem of the Material Culture of the Sixth Century," in *Judah and the Judeans in the Neo-Babylonian Period*, eds. Oded Lipschits and Joseph Blenkinsopp (Winona Lake, IN: Eisenbrauns, 2003), p. 437. Though decimated, Jerusalem was not uninhabited. See Gabriel Barkay's discovery of tombs in use in the sixth century at Ketef Hinnom. Barkay, "The Riches of Ketef Hinnom," *BAR*, July/August/September/October 2009; Barkay, "The Priestly Benediction on Silver Plaques from Ketef Hinnom in Jerusalem," *Tel Aviv* 19 (1992), pp. 139–192. See also Lipschits, *Fall and Rise* (see endnote 5), pp. 210–213. The silver amulet texts have been republished using high-quality imaging techniques in Gabriel Barkay, Andrew G. Vaughn, Marilyn J. Lundberg and Bruce Zuckerman, "The Amulets from Ketef Hinnom: A New Edition and Evaluation," *BASOR* 334 (2004), pp. 41–71.

¹² Lipschits, *Fall and Rise* (see endnote 5), p. 187.

¹³ David Vanderhooft, *The Neo-Babylonian Empire and Babylon in the Latter Prophets* (Atlanta: Scholars Press, 1999).

¹⁴ See Middlemas, *Templeless Age* (see endnote 2); Joseph Blenkinsopp, "Bethel in the Neo-Babylonian Period" in *Judah and the Judeans* (see endnote 11). There, Blenkinsopp (p. 100) adduces Zechariah 7:2 as further evidence of this idea, but his reading of this difficult text ("Sar-eser, Regemmelech, and his men had sent to Bethel to placate YHVH") is unlikely, because "Bethel" reads much more naturally as the subject of the sentence. See Carol L. Meyers and Eric M. Meyers, *Haggai, Zechariah 1–8*, Anchor Bible (Garden City, NY: Doubleday, 1987), p. 382.

¹⁵ Albertz, (*Israel in Exile* [see endnote 9], pp. 94–95) connects the 582 B.C.E. deportation to Gedaliah's assassination, an interpretation that Oded Lipschits (*Fall and Rise* [see endnote 5]) rejects.

¹⁶ On this literature, see Erich S. Gruen, *Diaspora: Jews amidst Greeks and Romans* (Cambridge, MA: Harvard University Press, 2002); W. Lee Humphreys, "A Life-Style for Diaspora: A Study of the Tales of Esther and Daniel," *JBL* 92 (1973), pp. 211–223; Lawrence Wills, *The Jew in the Court of the Foreign King* (Minneapolis: Fortress Press, 1990).

¹⁷ See Laurie Pearce, "New Evidence for Judeans in Babylonia," in *Judah and the Judeans in the Persian Period*, eds. Oded Lipschits and Manfred Oeming (Winona Lake, IN: Eisenbrauns, 2006), pp. 399–412. Naming a settlement for the place of origin of the inhabitants was common in Babylon.

¹⁸ Ibid.

¹⁹ *ANET*, p. 308

²⁰ Albertz, *Israel in Exile* (see endnote 9), p. 99.

²¹ Ibid., p. 101.

²² Ibid., p. 102. Albertz proposes that some of the dislike of exile was due to the social humiliation of former political and religious elites being reduced to having to farm.

²³ For this approach, see Daniel Smith-Christopher, *A Biblical Theology of Exile* (Minneapolis: Fortress Press, 2002).

²⁴ See Mark S. Smith, *The Origins of Biblical Monotheism: Israel's Polytheistic Background and the Ugaritic Texts* (New York: Oxford University

Press, 2001); André Lemaire, *The Birth of Monotheism: The Rise and Disappearance of Yahwism* (Washington, DC: Biblical Archaeology Society, 2007).

[25] C. Meyers and E. Meyers, *Zechariah 9–14*, Anchor Bible (New York: Doubleday, 1993); see also Stephen L. Cook, *Prophecy and Apocalypticism: The Postexilic Social Setting* (Minneapolis: Fortress Press, 1995).

[26] See Lee I. Levine, "The Nature and Origin of the Palestinian Synagogue Reconsidered," *JBL* 115.3 (1996), pp. 425–448.

[27] Paul-Alain Beaulieu, "King Nabonidus and the Neo-Babylonian Empire," in *Civilizations of the Ancient Near East*, ed. Jack Sasson (Peabody, MA: Hendrickson, 2000), pp. 969–979.

[28] Pierre Briant, *From Cyrus to Alexander: A History of the Persian Empire*, trans. Peter T. Daniels (Winona Lake, IN: Eisenbrauns, 2002), pp. 40–43.

[29] *COS*, vol. 2, p. 124.

[30] Amelie Kuhrt, "The Cyrus Cylinder and Achaemenid Imperial Policy," *JSOT* 25 (1983), pp. 83–97.

[31] Miller and Hayes (*History of Ancient Israel and Judah* [see endnote 1], p. 510) suggest two possibilities: That it indicates Sheshbazzar's royal status or that it is a Judean translation or reuse of a Babylonian title.

[32] Isaiah 52:11–12 may also be a reference to the Sheshbazzar, or at least to a return of the Temple vessels at the outset of the Persian period.

[33] The notice that many chose to send material support rather than, one would assume, return themselves might indicate that even the author of Ezra 1–6 knew of a tradition of a small initial return.

[34] Lipschits, *Fall and Rise* (see endnote 5), pp. 267–271.

[35] Based on analyses of comparable Aramaic letters, serious doubts have been raised about the authenticity of the documents in the Book of Ezra. See the discussion in Lester L. Grabbe, *A History of the Jews and Judaism in the Second Temple Period, vol. 1* (London: T & T Clark, 2004), pp. 76–77.

[36] Diana Edelman, *The Origins of the "Second" Temple: Persian Imperial Policy and the Rebuilding of Jerusalem* (London: Equinox, 2005). See also the critique

by Ralph Klein, "Were Joshua, Zerubbabel, and Nehemiah Contemporaries? A Response to Diana Edelman's Proposed Late Date for the Second Temple," *JBL* 127 (2008), pp. 697–701.

[37] See Robert P. Carroll, "So What Do We *Know* about the Temple? The Temple in the Prophets," in *Second Temple Studies 2. Temple Community in the Persian Period* (Sheffield: JSOT Press, 1994), pp. 34–51.

[38] Carol L. Meyers, s.v. "Temple, Jerusalem," in *ABD*, vol. 6, p. 363.

[39] Meyers and Meyers, *Zechariah 9–14* (see endnote 25); Antti Laato, "Zechariah 4:6b–10a and the Akkadian Royal Building Inscriptions," *ZAW* 106 (1994), pp. 53–69. On building inscriptions in general, see Victor Hurowitz, *"I Have Built You an Exalted House": Temple Building in the Bible in the Light of Mesopotamian and North-West Semitic Writings* (Sheffield: Sheffield Academic Press, 1991).

[40] See, however, the skepticism regarding the status of the high priesthood as a clearly defined role in the early Persian period, in Benjamin Scolnic, *Chronology and Papponymy: A List of the Judean High Priests of the Persian Period* (Atlanta: Scholars Press, 1999).

[41] See Maria Brosius, *The Persians: An Introduction* (London: Routledge, 2006), esp. pp. 72–76.

[42] See the evidence of the Persepolis Fortification Tablets. On this topic, however, note the cautions of Briant, *History of the Persian Empire* (see endnote 28), pp. 447–448.

[43] Ibid., p. 586.

[44] Lipschits, *Fall and Rise* (see endnote 5), pp. 179–181.

[45] Christoph Uehlinger, "'Powerful Persianisms' in Glyptic Iconography of Persian Period Palestine," in *The Crisis of Israelite Religion: Transformation of Religious Tradition in Exilic and Post-Exilic Times*, eds. Bob Becking and Marjo C.A. Korpel (Leiden/Boston: Brill, 1999), pp. 134–182.

[46] See Kenneth Hoglund, *Achaemenid Imperial Administration in Syria-Palestine and the Missions of Ezra and Nehemiah* (Atlanta: Scholars Press, 1992).

[47] Grabbe, *A History of the Jews and Judaism* (see endnote 35), pp. 292–294.

[48] Some scholars of Ezra-Nehemiah have expressed doubts over the idea that Nehemiah was originally a governor, suggesting that the notices that refer to him as governor (Nehemiah 5:14,18, 12:26) are part of later additions to the narrative. See H.G.M. Williamson, *Ezra, Nehemiah* (Waco, TX: Word Books, 1985); Jacob L. Wright, *Rebuilding Identity: The Nehemiah-Memoir and its Earliest Readers*, BZAW 348 (Berlin/New York: Walther de Gruyter, 2004).

[49] See John R. Bartlett, "Editorial," *PEQ* 140 (2008), pp. 77-78.

[50] Briant, *History of the Persian Empire* (see endnote 28), pp. 584-586.

[51] Joachim Schaper, "The Jerusalem Temple as an Instrument of the Achaemenid Fiscal Administration," *VT* 45 (1995), pp. 528-539.

[52] One document from Elephantine from the mid-fifth century mentions Shelemiah and Delaiah as the "sons of Sanballat governor of Samaria," and in another, that same Delaiah works in tandem with the governor of Yehud. Also, one of the Wadi Daliyeh seal impressions from the fourth century refers to another "son of Sanballat, governor of Samaria."

[53] Gary Knoppers, "Nehemiah and Sanballat: The Enemy Without or Within?" in *Judah and the Judeans in the Fourth Century B.C.E.*, eds. Oded Lipschits, Gary Knoppers and Rainer Albertz (Winona Lake, IN: Eisenbrauns, 2007), pp. 305-331.

[54] See Fawzi Zayadine, "'Iraq el-Amir," in *OEANE*, vol. 3, pp. 177-181.

[55] Lisbeth Fried, *The Priest and the Great King: Temple-Palace Relations in the Persian Empire* (Winona Lake, IN: Eisenbrauns, 2004).

[56] Conceding Lester L. Grabbe's point in *A History of the Jews and Judaism* (see endnote 35).

[57] Most recently, see Miller and Hayes, *History of Ancient Israel and Judah* (see endnote 1), pp. 528-530.

[58] See the essays in James W. Watts, ed., *Persia and Torah: The Theory of Imperial Authorization of the Pentateuch* (Atlanta: Society of Biblical Literature, 2001).

[59] Jean Louis Ska, *Introduction to Reading the Pentateuch* (Winona Lake, IN: Eisenbrauns, 2007).

[60] Briant, *History of the Persian Empire* (see endnote 28), pp. 510-511.

[61] See Joseph Blenkinsopp, *Ezra-Nehemiah: A Commentary*. Old Testament Library (Philadelphia: Westminster Press, 1988), esp. pp. 57-59.

[62] Bezalel Porten believes that the Letter of Aristeas refers to an earlier pharaoh, Psammetichus I. See "Settlement of the Jews at Elephantine and the Arameans at Syene," in *Judah and the Judeans in the Neo-Babylonian Period* (see endnote 11), pp. 451-470.

[63] *Textbook of Aramaic Documents from Ancient Egypt*, trans. Bezalel Porten and Ada Yardeni (Winona Lake, IN: Eisenbrauns, 1986), A4.10.

[64] Ibid., A4.1.

[65] Bezalel Porten, *The Elephantine Papyri in English: Three Millennia of Cross-Cultural Continuity and Change* (Leiden/New York: Brill, 1996), p. 18.

[66] Notes that copies were also sent to Shelemiah and Delaiah, sons of the Samarian governor Sanballat.

[67] A non-Jewish source, Hermopolis (letter 4:1), mentions a temple to the Queen of Heaven in Syene. See C. Houtman, "Queen of Heaven," in *Dictionary of Deities and Demons in the Bible*, 2nd ed. (Leiden/Boston: Brill, 1999), p. 1281.

[68] See especially Ziony Zevit, *The Religions of Ancient Israel: A Parallactic Synthesis* (New York: Continuum, 2001).

[69] Contrary to Josephus (*Antiquities* 11.302-312), who states that it was built in the Hellenistic period.

[70] Izchak Magen, Haggai Misgav and Levana Tsfania, *Mount Gerizim Excavations, volume 1: The Aramaic, Hebrew, and Samaritan Inscriptions* (Jerusalem: Israel Antiquities Authority, 2004).

[71] Zechariah 1-8 dates to an earlier period, but the assertion in Zechariah 6:14 that a person named Tobiah has a "memorial" (*zikkaron*) in the temple of Yahweh is also intriguing in this light.

[72] Parts of the Nehemiah Memorial may very well be speaking to tensions in later periods. See Diana Edelman, "Seeing Double: Tobiah the Ammonite as an Encrypted Character," *RB* 113 (2006), pp. 570-584; Jacob Wright, *Rebuilding Identity: The*

Nehemiah-Memoir and its Earliest Readers (Berlin/New York: Walter de Gruyter, 2004).

[73] On the Persian-period origins of the final shape of the Pentateuch, see Joseph Blenkinsopp, *The Pentateuch* (London: Sheed and Ward, 1971); Ska, *Introduction to Reading the Pentateuch* (see endnote 59); Rainer Albertz, *A History of Israelite Religion in the Old Testament Period* (Louisville: Westminster/John Knox Press, 1994).

[74] See, for example, Sara Japhet, "Can the Persian Period Bear the Burden? Reflections on the Origins of Biblical History," in *From the Rivers of Babylon to the Highlands of Judah: Collected Studies on the Restoration Period.* (Winona Lake, IN: Eisenbrauns, 2006).

[75] William Schniedewind, *How the Bible Became a Book* (New York: Cambridge University Press, 2004).

[76] Several of these are written in Standard Biblical Hebrew (SBH) and not, as one might expect, in Late Biblical Hebrew (LBH). For the issues and problems surrounding the chronological distinction between SBH and LBH, see the essays in Ian Young, ed., *Biblical Hebrew: Studies in Chronology and Typology* (London/New York: T & T Clark, 2003).

[77] Carter, *The Emergence of Yehud* (see endnote 5), pp. 287–288.

[78] See Grabbe, *A History of the Jews and Judaism* (see endnote 35), pp. 319–321.

[79] Briant, *History of the Persian Empire* (see endnote 28), pp. 674–675.

[80] Ephraim Stern, "The Religious Revolution in Persian-Period Judah," in *Judah and the Judeans in the Persian Period* (see endnote 17), pp. 199–206.

[81] Oded Lipschits and David Vanderhooft, "Yehud Stamp Impressions in the Fourth Century B.C.E.: A Time of Administrative Consolidation?" in *Judah and the Judeans in the Fourth Century B.C.E.* (see endnote 53), pp. 75–94, esp. pp. 89–90.

[82] André Lemaire, "Administration of Fourth-Century B.C.E. Judah in Light of Epigraphy and Numismatics," in *Judah and the Judeans in the Fourth Century B.C.E.* (see endnote 53), pp. 53–74. See also Bezalel Porten and Ada Yardeni, "Social, Economic, and Onomastic Issues in the Aramaic Ostraca of the Fourth Century B.C.E.," in *Judah and the Judeans in the Persian Period* (see endnote 17), pp. 457–490.

[83] Josef Wiesehofer, "The Achaemenid Empire in the Fourth Century B.C.E.: A Period of Decline?" in *Judah and the Judeans in the Fourth Century B.C.E.* (see endnote 53), pp. 11–32; see especially p. 28.

[84] Pierre Briant in fact calls Alexander "the last Achaemenid." Quoted in Wiesehofer (ibid.), p. 28.

[85] Mary Joan Winn Leith, *Wadi Daliyeh I: The Wadi Daliyeh Seal Impressions. Discoveries in the Judaean Desert* 24 (Oxford: Clarendon Press, 1997), pp. 39–94, 107–134, 209–228, 231–241.

[86] Einat Ambar-Armon and Amos Kloner, "Archaeological Evidence of Links between the Aegean World and the Land of Israel in the Persian Period," in *A Time of Change: Judah and its Neighbours in the Persian and Early Hellenistic Periods,* ed. Yigal Levin (London/New York: T & T Clark, 2007), pp. 1–22, at pp. 4–5.

VII. The Age of Hellenism

[1] For a fuller account of the period covered in this chapter, see Lee I. Levine, *Jerusalem: Portrait of the City in the Second Temple Period (538 B.C.E.–70 C.E.)* (Philadelphia: Jewish Publication Society, 2002), pp. 45–148.

[2] See, for example, William W. Tarn, *Hellenistic Civilization* (London: Arnold, 1952); Arthur D. Nock, *Conversion* (Oxford: Clarendon Press, 1933); Arnaldo Momigliano, *Alien Wisdom* (Cambridge: Cambridge University Press, 1975); Félix-M. Abel, "Hellénisme et orientalisme en Palestine au déclin de la periode séleucide," *RB* 53 (1946), pp. 385–402.

[3] Pierre Grimal, "The Hellenistic East in the Third Century," in *Hellenism and the Rise of Rome,* eds. Pierre Grimal, Hermann Bengtson and Werner Caskel (New York: Delacorte Press, 1968), pp. 124–206; Helmut Koester, *History, Culture, and Religion of the Hellenistic Age,* 2nd ed. (New York: de Gruyter, 1995), pp. 97–196.

[4] See Lee I. Levine, *Judaism and Hellenism in Antiquity: Conflict or Confluence?* (Seattle: University of Washington Press, 1998), pp. 16–32.

[5] Arnold H. M. Jones, *The Cities of the Eastern Roman Provinces* (Oxford: Clarendon Press,

1971), pp. 226–294; Victor Tcherikover, *Hellenistic Civilization and the Jews* (Philadelphia: Jewish Publication Society, 1959), pp. 90–116; Shimon Applebaum, "Hellenistic Cities of Palestine—New Dimensions," in *The Second Period in Palestine*, ed. Bezalel Bar Kochva (Tel Aviv: Hakibbutz Hameuchad, 1980), pp. 277–288 (in Hebrew).

[6] Ya'akov Meshorer, *Ancient Jewish Coinage* 1 (Dix Hills, NY: Amphora Books, 1982), pp. 13–34; Uriel Rappaport, "The Coins of Jerusalem at the End of Persian Rule and the Beginning of the Hellenistic Period," in *Studies in the History of Jerusalem in the Second Temple Period: Schalit Memorial Volume*, ed. Aaron Oppenheimer et al. (Jerusalem: Yad Izhak Ben Zvi, 1981), pp. 11–21 (in Hebrew).

[7] This letter is appended to the correspondence of Jonathan the Hasmonean with Sparta (c. 145 B.C.E.). Its authenticity has been the source of much scholarly discussion. Emil Schürer (*The History of the Jewish People in the Age of Jesus Christ [175 B.C.–A.D. 135]*, rev. ed., 3 vols. [Edinburgh: T & T Clark, 1973–1987] vol. 1, pp. 184–185, n. 33) and Jonathan Goldstein (*I Maccabees*, Anchor Bible 41 [Garden City, NY: Doubleday, 1976], pp. 455–462) assume that the letter is historical, as do Paul Cartledge and Antony Spawforth, *Hellenistic and Roman Sparta: A Tale of Two Cities* (London: Routledge, 1989), pp. 36–37; and Menahem Stern, *Hasmonean Judaea in the Hellenistic World: Chapters in Political History* (Jerusalem: Shazar Center, 1995), pp. 63–70 (in Hebrew). However, its authenticity has been questioned by Elias Bickerman, *The Jews in the Greek Age* (Cambridge, MA: Harvard University Press, 1988), pp. 184–185; Martin Hengel, *Judaism and Hellenism: Studies in Their Encounter in Palestine during the Early Hellenistic Period*, 2 vols. (Philadelphia: Fortress Press, 1974) vol. 1, p. 26; and, more recently, Erich S. Gruen, "The Purported Jewish-Spartan Affiliation," in *Transitions to Empire: Essays in Greco-Roman History, 360–146 B.C.*, eds. Robert W. Wallace and Edward M. Harris (Norman: University of Oklahoma Press, 1996), pp. 254–269, and Doron Mendels, *Identity, Religion and Historiography: Studies in Hellenistic History* (Sheffield: Sheffield Academic Press, 1998), pp. 28–30.

[8] Donald T. Ariel, *Excavations at the City of David 1978–1985*, Qedem 30 (Jerusalem: Institute of Archaeology, Hebrew University, 1990), pp. 13–25.

[9] Nahman Avigad, *Bullae and Seals from a Post-Exilic Judean Archive*, Qedem 4 (Jerusalem: Institute of Archaeology, Hebrew University, 1976), p. 25; Donald T. Ariel and Yair Shoham, "Locally Stamped Handles and Associated Body Fragments of the Persian and Hellenistic Periods," in *Excavations at the City of David 1978–1985 Directed by Yigal Shiloh*, vol. 6: *Inscriptions*, Qedem 41 (Jerusalem: Institute of Archaeology, Hebrew University, 2000), pp. 137–194.

[10] Robert Gordis, *The Wisdom of Koheleth* (London: East and West, 1950), pp. xii–xvii, and *Koheleth—The Man and His World* (New York: Jewish Theological Seminary, 1951), pp. 8–57; Hengel, *Judaism and Hellenism* (see endnote 7), pp. 115–130.

[11] Hengel, *Judaism and Hellenism* 1 (see endnote 7), pp. 131–153; Gerson D. Cohen, "The Song of Songs and the Jewish Religious Mentality," in *The Samuel Friedland Lectures 1960–1966* (New York: Jewish Theological Seminary, 1966), pp. 1–22; Mark Rozlar, "The Song of Songs Against the Background of Greek-Hellenistic Eastern Poetry," *Eshkolot* 1 (1954), pp. 33–48 (in Hebrew). However, see also Marvin Pope, *Song of Songs*, Anchor Bible 7C (Garden City, NY: Doubleday, 1977), pp. 22–33. For the Hellenistic background to the maxim of Simeon the Righteous at the beginning of the Ethics of the Fathers, see Judah Goldin, "The Three Pillars of Simeon the Righteous," *PAAJR* 27 (1958), pp. 43–58.

[12] See Paul Hanson, "Jewish Apocalyptic Against Its Near Eastern Environment," *RB* 78 (1971), pp. 31–58; John J. Collins, "Jewish Apocalyptic Against Its Hellenistic Near Eastern Environment," *BASOR* 220 (1975), pp. 27–36.

[13] Tcherikover, *Hellenistic Civilization* (see endnote 5), pp. 117–151; Eugene Taeubler, "Jerusalem 201 to 199 B.C.," *JQR* 37 (1946–1947), pp. 1–30, 125–137, 249–263.

[14] Elias Bickerman, *From Ezra to the Last of the Maccabees* (New York: Schocken Books, 1962), and *The God of the Maccabees* (Leiden: Brill, 1979); Hengel, *Judaism and Hellenism* (see endnote 7); Tcherikover, *Hellenistic Civilization* (see endnote 5), pp. 152–174; Samuel Sandmel, "Hellenism and Judaism," in *Great Confrontations in Jewish History*, eds. Stanley Wagner and Allen Breck (Denver: Center for Jewish Studies, University

of Denver, 1977), pp. 21–38; Fergus Millar, "The Background to the Maccabean Revolution: Reflections on Martin Hengel's 'Judaism and Hellenism,'" *JJS* 29 (1978), pp. 1–21.

[15] Tcherikover, *Hellenistic Civilization* (see endnote 5), pp. 126–142; Benjamin Mazar, *Canaan and Israel—Historical Studies* (Jerusalem: Mosad Bialik, 1980), pp. 270–290 (in Hebrew); Menahem Stern, "Notes on the Story of Joseph Son of Tobias," *Tarbiz* 32 (1963), pp. 35–47 (in Hebrew).

[16] On archaeological excavations at the site and suggested reconstructions, see Paul W. Lapp, "Soundings at 'Araq el-Emir," *BASOR* 165 (1962), pp. 16–34; Jean-Marie Dentzer, François Villeneuve and François Larché, "The Monumental Gateway and the Princely Estate of Araq el-Emir," in *The Excavations at Araq el-Emir*, eds. Nancy L. Lapp, AASOR 47 (Cambridge, MA: American Schools of Oriental Research, 1983), pp. 133–148; Ernest Will and François Larché, *'Iraq al-Amir: le château du tobiade Hyrcan* 1, Bibliothèque archéologique et historique 132 (Paris: P. Geuthner, 1991); Paul W. Lapp and Nancy L. Lapp, "'Iraq el-Emir," *NEAEHL* 2, pp. 646–649; Andrea M. Berlin, "Between Large Forces: Palestine in the Hellenistic Period," *BA* 60 (1997), pp. 11–12; Chan-ho C. Ji, "A New Look at the Tobiads," *LA* 48 (1998), pp. 417–440; Ehud Netzer, "Tyros, the Floating Palace," in *Text and Artifact in the Religions of Mediterranean Antiquity: Essays in Honour of Peter Richardson*, ed. Stephen G. Wilson and Michel Desjardins, Studies in Christianity and Judaism 9 (Waterloo, Ontario: Wilfrid Laurier University Press, 2000), pp. 340–353; and most comprehensively Stephen G. Rosenberg, *Airaq al-Amir: The Architecture of the Tobiads*, British Archaeological Reports International Series 1544 (Oxford: John and Erica Hedges/Hadrian Books, 2006).

[17] Elias Bickerman, "La charte séleucide de Jerusalem," *REJ* 100 (1935), pp. 4–35, and "Une proclamation séleucide relative au temple de Jerusalem," *Syria* 25 (1946–1948), pp. 67–85; Albrecht Alt, "Zu Antiochos' III Erlass für Jerusalem," *ZAW* 57 (1939), pp. 282–285; Hengel, *Judaism and Hellenism* 1 (see endnote 7), pp. 271–272.

[18] Tcherikover, *Hellenistic Civilization* (see endnote 5), pp. 160–169; Lester L. Grabbe, "The Hellenistic City of Jerusalem," in *Jews in the Hellenistic*

and Roman Cities, ed. John R. Bartlett (New York: Routledge, 2002), pp. 6–21.

[19] See endnote 18.

[20] On the accusation that some Jews underwent an operation to hide their circumcision (1 Maccabees 1:15), see Goldstein, *I Maccabees* (see endnote 7), p. 200; Grabbe, "Hellenistic City" (see endnote 18), pp. 12–13.

[21] The chronology of Antiochus's two Egyptian campaigns and his punishment of Jerusalem have been a subject of much debate and discussion. We have assumed that these campaigns took place in 169 and 168 B.C.E., respectively (contra 1 Maccabees 1:20 and 29; *Antiquities* 12.248), that after each one the king had occasion to wreak havoc on the city, and that the confrontation with Jason was in 169 (contra 2 Maccabees 5:1–7). For a review of the issues involved in the conflicting chronologies of the various sources, see Schürer, *History* 1 (see endnote 7), pp. 151–154; *GLAJJ* 1, pp. 115–116; Ralph Marcus's remarks in *Josephus, Antiquities* 9 (XVI–XVII), LCL 410 (Cambridge, MA: Harvard University Press, 1963), pp. 126–127, n. *e*; Tcherikover, *Hellenistic Civilization* (see endnote 5), pp. 186–191; Peter Schäfer, "The Hellenistic and Maccabean Periods," in *Israelite and Judaean History*, eds. John H. Hayes and James M. Miller (Philadelphia: Westminster Press, 1977), pp. 564–566, 582–585; Jonathan A. Goldstein, *II Maccabees*, Anchor Bible 41A (Garden City, NY: Doubleday, 1984), p. 246; Klaus Bringman, *Hellenistische Reform und Religionsverfolgung in Judäa: eine Untersuchung zur jüdisch-hellenistischen Geschichte (175–163 v. Chr.)* (Göttingen: Vandenhoeck & Ruprecht, 1983), pp. 36–40; Magen Broshi and Esther Eshel, "The Greek King is Antiochus IV (4QHistorical Text = 4Q248)," *JJS* 48 (1997), p. 128; Dov Gera, *Judaea and Mediterranean Politics: 219–161 B.C.E.* (Leiden: Brill, 1998), pp. 153–157; and, most recently, Daniel R. Schwartz, "Antiochus IV Epiphanes in Jerusalem," in *Historical Perspectives: From the Hasmoneans to Bar Kokhba in Light of the Dead Sea Scrolls*, ed. David Goodblatt et al. (Leiden: Brill, 2001), pp. 45–56.

[22] Tcherikover, *Hellenistic Civilization* (see endnote 5), pp. 192–193.

[23] Interestingly, this step was directed not only against Jerusalem, but one Andronikos was

appointed to take charge of the Samaritan temple on Mount Gerizim.

24 Bezalel Bar Kochva, "The Status and Origin of the Akra Garrison Before Antiochus' Decrees," *Zion* 36 (1972), pp. 32–47 (in Hebrew); Goldstein, *I Maccabees* (see endnote 7), pp. 213–219; Willis A. Shotwell, "The Problem of the Syrian Akra," *BASOR* 176 (1964), pp. 10–19; Bickerman, *God of the Maccabees* (see endnote 14), pp. 42–53.

25 Millar, who lays the blame squarely at the feet of the king, is unable to pinpoint the specific reason: "... there seems no way of reaching an understanding of how Antiochus came to take a step so profoundly at variance with the normal assumptions of government in his time" (Millar, "Background to the Maccabean Revolution" [see endnote 14], pp. 16–17).

26 Reviews of the various theories regarding the persecution are legion; see, for example, Goldstein, *I Maccabees* (see endnote 7), pp. 104–160; Erich S. Gruen, "Hellenism and Persecution: Antiochus IV and the Jews," in *Hellenistic History and Culture*, ed. Peter Green (Berkeley: University of California Press, 1993), pp. 238–274; Bickerman, *God of the Maccabees* (see endnote 14), pp. 76–92; *From Ezra* (see endnote 14), pp. 93–111; Hengel, *Judaism and Hellenism* 1 (see endnote 7), pp. 208–303; Tcherikover, *Hellenistic Civilization* (see endnote 5), pp. 175–203. See also Lester L. Grabbe, *Judaism from Cyrus to Hadrian*, 2 vols. (Minneapolis: Fortress Press, 1992), vol. 1, pp. 247–256; JoAnn Scurlock, "167 BCE: Hellenism or Reform?" *JSJ* 31 (2000), pp. 125–161; Steven Weitzman, "Plotting Antiochus' Persecution," *JBL* 123 (2004), pp. 219–234.

For an extensive treatment of a newly discovered inscription that may shed some light on this situation in Judea, see Hannah M. Cotton and Michael Wörrle, "Seleukos IV to Heliodoros: A New Dossier of Royal Correspondence from Israel," *ZPE* 159 (2007), pp. 191–205. On several proposed references in the Dead Sea Scrolls to the events (170–168 B.C.E.) behind the persecution, see Hanan Eshel, *The Dead Sea Scrolls and the Hasmonean State* (Grand Rapids, MI/Jerusalem: Eerdmans/Yad Izhak Ben-Zvi, 2008), pp. 13–27, and D. R. Schwartz, "Antiochus IV Epiphanes in Jerusalem" (see endnote 21), pp. 45–56.

27 For a detailed description of these battles, see Bezalel Bar Kochva, *The Battles of the Hasmoneans:*

The Times of Judas Maccabaeus (Jerusalem: Yad Izhak Ben-Zvi, 1980) (in Hebrew).

28 Tcherikover, *Hellenistic Civilization* (see endnote 5), pp. 211–220.

29 The festival of Hanukkah is unusual in the Jewish calendar. It is the only holiday not anchored in a biblical event and its duration for eight days is unprecedented (the dedication of the Wilderness Tabernacle and Solomon's Temple lasted only seven days [Leviticus 9:1; 1 Kings 8:65]). For a discussion of the various reasons offered for the length and character of the holiday, see Levine, *Jerusalem: Portrait* (see endnote 1), pp. 82–84.

30 Bar Kochva, *Battles of the Hasmoneans* (see endnote 27), pp. 225–263.

31 The attempts to shed light on this elusive group have been many and varied; see, for example, Tcherikover, *Hellenistic Civilization* (see endnote 5), pp. 187ff.; Hengel, *Judaism and Hellenism* 1 (see endnote 7), pp. 175–180; Otto Plöger, *Theocracy and Eschatology* (Oxford: Blackwell, 1968), pp. 44–52.

32 Bar Kochva, *Battles of the Hasmoneans* (see endnote 27), pp. 265–307.

33 See, however, Goldstein, *I Maccabees* (see endnote 7), pp. 501–502.

34 On reactions to this synthesis of the political and religious realms, see Martin Hengel, "The Polemical Character of 'On Kingship' in the Temple Scroll: An Attempt at Dating 11Q Temple," *JJS* 37 (1986), pp. 28–38.

35 Compare the relevant maps in Yohanan Aharoni and Michael Avi-Yonah, *Macmillan Bible Atlas* (New York: Macmillan, 1968), nos. 104, 113, 213. See also Schürer, *History of the Jewish People* (see endnote 7), pp. 200–215.

36 Hillel Geva, "The 'First Wall' of Jerusalem during the Second Temple Period: An Architectural-Chronological Note," *Eretz-Israel: Archaeological, Historical and Geographical Studies* 18 (1985), pp. 21–39 (in Hebrew). In a short note, Benjamin Mazar and Hanan Eshel ("Who Built the First Wall of Jerusalem?" *IEJ* 48 [1998], pp. 265–269) somewhat speculatively suggest that it had already been erected by the Seleucid king Antiochus III at the beginning of the second century B.C.E.

[37] Renee Sivan and Giora Solar, "Excavations in the Jerusalem Citadel, 1980–1988," in *Ancient Jerusalem Revealed*, ed. Hillel Geva, expanded edition (Jerusalem: Israel Exploration Society, 2000), pp. 168–176.

[38] Menaham Stern, "Judaea and Her Neighbors in the Days of Alexander Jannaeus," in *Jerusalem Cathedra* 1, ed. Lee I. Levine (Jerusalem: Yad Izhak Ben-Zvi, 1981), pp. 22–46.

[39] Goldstein, *I Maccabees* (see endnote 7), pp. 4–26.

[40] Other echoes of Deuteronomy in 1 Maccabees can be found in 3:55–60; 4:8–11 (see Deuteronomy 20:2–9); 5:46–51 (see Deuteronomy 20:10–15); 14:7 (see Deuteronomy 7:24 and 11:25); and elsewhere.

[41] On the conquest and Judaization of Gezer, see Ronny Reich, "Archaeological Evidence of the Jewish Population at Hasmonean Gezer," *IEJ* 31 (1981), pp. 48–52.

[42] This is the first time we read of large-scale conversions to Judaism, and the only time in antiquity when it resulted from coercion. According to Josephus, they were given the option to convert or be expelled. Strabo, however, offers a different picture, wherein the Idumeans accepted Judaism of their own free will (*Geographica* 16.2.34 [*GLAJJ* 1, p. 299]). According to Ptolemy, whose identity is not clear, the Idumeans were forcibly converted; see *GLAJJ* 1, no. 146. Strabo's view has been adopted by Aryeh Kasher (*Jews, Idumaeans, and Ancient Arabs* [Tübingen: Mohr, 1988], pp. 46–77); most scholars, however, prefer either Josephus's or Ptolemy's account (often not distinguishing between the two). A more nuanced view of this process, one which allows for elements of coercion, persuasion and local interests, has been advocated by Morton Smith ("The Gentiles in Judaism, 125 BCE–CE 66," in *CHJ* 3, pp. 198–213), followed by Seth Schwartz, "Israel and the Nations Roundabout: I Maccabees and the Hasmonean Expansion," *JJS* 42 (1991), pp. 17–21; and Shaye J. D. Cohen, *The Beginnings of Jewishness: Boundaries, Varieties, Uncertainties* (Berkeley: University of California Press, 1999), pp. 110–119 (and generally, pp. 109–139). However, see also Steven Weitzman, "Forced Circumcision and the Shifting Role of Gentiles in Hasmonean Ideology," *HTR* 92 (1999)," pp. 37–59.

[43] Leon Poliakov, *The History of Antisemitism* (London: Vanguard Press, 1965), pp. 3–16.

[44] Yochanan Lewy, *Studies in Jewish Hellenism* (Jerusalem: Mosad Bialik, 1960), pp. 60–78 (in Hebrew).

[45] Lee I. Levine, "The Political Struggle between Pharisees and Sadducees in the Hasmonean Period" in *Studies in the History of Jerusalem* (see endnote 6), pp. 61–83 (in Hebrew).

[46] Almost all scholars have assumed Pharisaic opposition; see, for example, Yigael Yadin, "Pesher Nahum (4Q Pnahum) Reconsidered," *IEJ* 21 (1971), pp. 1–12. Against this commonly held assumption, see Chaim Rabin, "Alexander Jannai and the Pharisees," *JJS* 7 (1956), pp. 3–11.

[47] Rabbinic sources confirm this sequence of events, focusing on the political activity of Simeon ben Shataḥ in the first third of the first century B.C.E. See Levine, "Political Struggle" (see endnote 45), pp. 61–83; Israel Ephron, "Simeon Ben Shataḥ and King Yannai," in *Gedaliah Alon Memorial Volume*, ed. Menahem Dorman et al. (Tel Aviv: Hakibbutz Hameuchad, 1970), pp. 69–132 (in Hebrew).

[48] The resettlement of the site and enlargement of its facilities is often associated with the reign of John Hyrcanus; this dating has been confirmed of late by Stephen Pfann, Jr. "The Second Temple Period Multimedia Educational Suite, with an Appendix (by Stephen J. Pfann) on the Ceramic and Numismatic Evidence for Qumran's Period Ia," in *The Dead Sea Scrolls and Contemporary Culture. Proceedings of the International Conference held at the Israel Museum, Jerusalem (July 6–8, 2008)*, eds. Adolfo Roitman, Lawrence H. Schiffman and Shani Tzoref (Leiden: Brill, in press). See, however, Jodi Magness (*The Archaeology of Qumran and the Dead Sea Scrolls* [Grand Rapids, MI: Eerdmans, 2002], pp. 47–69), who dates this occupation to the early first century B.C.E.

[49] Elias Bickerman, *The Maccabees: An Account of Their History from the Beginnings to the Fall of the House of the Hasmoneans* (New York: Schocken Books, 1947), pp. 85–97.

[50] Andrea Berlin, "Power and Its Afterlife: Tombs in Hellenistic Palestine," *NEA* 65 (2002), pp. 143–147; and "Between Large Forces" (see endnote 16), pp. 32–33; Steven Fine, *Art and Judaism in the Greco-Roman World: Toward a*

New Jewish Archaeology (Cambridge/New York: Cambridge University Press, 2005), pp. 60–65; Jodi Magness, "Ossuaries and the Burials of Jesus and James," *JBL* 124 (2005), pp. 124–125.

[51] See especially Geoffrey B. Waywell, "The Mausoleum at Halicarnassus," in *The Seven Wonders of the Ancient World*, eds. Peter A. Clayton and Martin J. Price (London/New York: Routledge, 1988), pp. 100–123. See, however, Oren Tal, "Hellenism in Transition from Empire to Kingdom: Changes in the Material Culture of Hellenistic Palestine," in *Jewish Identities in Antiquity: Studies in Memory of Menahem Stern*, eds. Lee I. Levine and Daniel R. Schwartz (Tübingen: Mohr Siebeck, 2009), pp. 69–70 and n. 54. Closer to the Hasmonean state, similar funerary monuments were found in southern Syrian (the tomb of Hamrath in Suweida) and Lebanon (Hermel and Kalat Fakra); see Janos Fedak, *Monumental Tombs of the Hellenistic Age: A Study of Selected Tombs from the Pre-Classical to the Early Imperial Era*, Phoenix Supplementary Volume 27 (Toronto: University of Toronto Press, 1990), pp. 148–50. On the ban promulgated by the Hasmoneans, to be discussed below, see Lee I. Levine, "Figural Art in Ancient Judaism," *Ars Judaica* 1 (2005), pp. 11–16; and most recently Lee I. Levine, *Visual Judaism in Late Antiquity: Historical Contexts of Jewish Art* (New Haven: Yale University Press, forthcoming), chapter 3.

[52] Ya'akov Meshorer, *Jewish Coins of the Second Temple Period* (Jerusalem: 'Am Hassefer, 1967); *Ancient Jewish Coinage* (see endnote 6), pp. 35–47. On Hasmonean coinage, see also Uriel Rappaport, "The Emergence of Hasmonean Coinage," *AJS* 1 (1976), pp. 171–186.

[53] Ehud Netzer, "The Hasmonean and Herodian Winter Palaces at Jericho," *IEJ* 25 (1975), pp. 89–100; "The Winter Palaces of the Judaean Kings at Jericho at the End of the Second Temple Period," *BASOR* 228 (1977), pp. 1–13; "Ancient Ritual Baths (Miqvaot) in Jericho," in *Jerusalem Cathedra* 2, ed. Lee I. Levine (Jerusalem: Yad Izhak Ben-Zvi, 1982), pp. 106–119.

[54] The other major adjacent tombs in the Kidron Valley date to the Herodian period.

[55] See, however, Dan Barag, "The 2000–2001 Exploration of the Tombs of Benei Hezir and Zecharia," *IEJ* 53 (2003), pp. 78–110.

[56] See, however, Tal, "Hellenism in Transition" (see endnote 51), p. 64, n. 30.

[57] Nahman Avigad, *Ancient Monuments in the Kidron Valley* (Jerusalem: Mosad Bialik, 1954), pp. 37–38 (in Hebrew); Levi Y. Rahmani, "Jason's Tomb," *IEJ* 17 (1967), pp. 61–100; Hillel Geva, "Jerusalem, Tombs," in *NEAEHL* 3, pp. 747–756; John P. Peters and Hermann Thiersch, *Painted Tombs in the Necropolis of Marissa* (London: Palestine Exploration Fund, 1905); see also Levine, *Visual Judaism* (see endnote 51), chapter 3.

[58] So, for example, the following: Eupolemus, Numenius, Antiochus, Jason, Antipater, Apollonius, Alexander, Dositheus, Diodorus, Lysimachus, Pausanias, Josephus, Mennaeus, Theodorus, Sopatrus, Straton, Theodotus, Aeneas, Aristobulus, Amyntas, Sosipater, Philip (1 Maccabees 8:17, 12:16, 14:22; *Antiquities* 13.260; 14.241, 247–248, 306–307).

[59] Markham Geller, "New Sources for the Origin of the Rabbinic Ketubah," *HUCA* 49 (1978), pp. 227–245. On the Jewish proclivity to adopt non-Jewish marital practices, as noted by the fourth-third century ethnographer Hectaeus of Abdera, see *GLAJJ* 1, p. 29.

[60] Judah Goldin, "A Philosophical Session in a Tannaitic Academy," *Traditio* 21 (1965), pp. 1–21.

[61] Elias Bickerman, "La chaîne de la tradition pharisienne," *RB* 49 (1952), pp. 44–54; David Daube, "Rabbinic Methods of Interpretation and Hellenistic Rhetoric," *HUCA* 22 (1949), pp. 239–264. See also Saul Lieberman, *Hellenism in Jewish Palestine*, 2nd ed. (New York: Jewish Theological Seminary, 1962), pp. 47–68; Bickerman, *From Ezra* (see endnote 14), pp. 148–165; Morton Smith, "Palestinian Judaism in the First Century," in *Israel: Its Role in Civilization*, ed. Moshe Davis (New York: Jewish Theological Seminary, 1956), pp. 67–81.

[62] Shaye J. D. Cohen, "Patriarchs and Scholarchs," *PAAJR* 48 (1981), pp. 57–85.

[63] David Winston, "The Iranian Component in the Bible, Apocrypha and Qumran," *History of Religions* 5 (1966), pp. 183–216. Shaul Shaked, "Qumran and Iran," *Israel Oriental Studies* 202 (1972), pp. 433–446, "Iranian Influence on Judaism: First Century B.C.E. to Second Century C.E.," in *CHJ* 1, pp. 308–325.

[64] Bruno W. Dombrowski, "היחד in 1QS and τὸ κοινόν: An Instance of Early Greek and Jewish Synthesis," *HTR* 59 (1966), pp. 293–307; Hans Bardthe, "Die Rechtsstellung der Qumran-Gemeinde," *Die Theologische Literaturzeitung* 86 (1961), pp. 93–104.

[65] Jerome Murphy-O'Connor, "The Essenes and Their History," *RB* 81 (1974), pp. 215–244.

[66] Hengel, *Judaism and Hellenism* 1 (see endnote 7), pp. 228–247.

[67] Nahman Avigad, *Discovering Jerusalem* (Nashville: Thomas Nelson, 1983), pp. 64–81; Ruth Amiran and Avraham Eitan, "Excavations in the Courtyard of the Citadel, Jerusalem, 1968–1969 (Preliminary Report)," *IEJ* 20 (1970), pp. 9–17. See also Kathleen Kenyon, *Digging Up Jerusalem* (New York: Praeger, 1974), pp. 188–204.

[68] Jan Simons, *Jerusalem in the Old Testament* (Leiden: Brill, 1952), pp. 226–281.

[69] According to *War* 1.112, Salome doubled the size of her army and added a large number of foreign troops. However, other than mercenaries, we have no solid information about other gentiles who may have lived in the city. Several scholars (Smith, "Gentiles in Judaism" [see endnote 42], pp. 196–213; Schwartz, "Israel and the Nations Roundabout" [see endnote 42], pp. 16–38) have opined that the Hasmoneans, beginning with John Hyrcanus, had forged a series of alliances with neighboring peoples (e.g., the Idumeans and Itureans), perhaps without the need to convert them. Whether this situation might have led some of these people to take up residence in the city is unknown.

[70] On the contradiction between 1 Maccabees and Josephus on the fate of the Akra, see above.

[71] On the term "Baris," see Ernest Will, "Qu'est-ce qu'une *Baris*?" *Syria* 64 (1987), pp. 253–259; G.J. Wightman, "Temple Fortresses in Jerusalem. Part II: The Hasmonean *Baris* and Herodian Antonia," *Bulletin of the Anglo-Israel Archaeological Society* 10 (1990–1991), pp. 7–10.

[72] Wightman, "Temple Fortresses" (see endnote 71), pp. 10–11.

[73] See G.J. Wightman, *The Walls of Jerusalem: From the Canaanites to the Mamluks* (Sydney: Meditarch, 1993), p. 187; Zvi U. Ma'oz, "More on the Town-Plan of Jerusalem in the Hasmonean Period," *Eretz-Israel: Archaeological, Historical, and Geographical Studies* 19 (1987), pp. 326–328 (in Hebrew).

[74] Jerome Murphy-O'Connor ("G. J. Wightman, *The Walls of Jerusalem*" [Review], *RB* 102 [1995], pp. 433–437) opines that the Second Wall was actually built twice, once by a Hasmonean ruler and ending at the Baris, which was continuous with the Hasmonean Temple, and later by Herod to connect it with his newly constructed Antonia (as noted specifically by Josephus) north of the Baris.

[75] One of the intriguing questions relating to Hasmonean Jerusalem is the location, plan and size of the Temple Mount in this era. For an interesting though somewhat speculative attempt to deal with this issue, see Leen Ritmeyer, "Locating the Original Temple Mount," *BAR*, March/April 1992, pp. 24–25, 64–65.

[76] Rahmani, "Jason's Tomb" (see endnote 57), pp. 61–100; Nahman Avigad, *Ancient Monuments in the Kidron Valley* (see endnote 57), pp. 37–78; *NEAEHL* 2, pp. 750–51. See also Erwin R. Goodenough, *Jewish Symbols in the Greco-Roman Period*, 13 vols. (New York: Pantheon, 1953–1968) vol. 1, pp. 79–84.

[77] For other second-century descriptions of the Jerusalem Temple, past and present, see Doron Mendels, *The Rise and Fall of Jewish Nationalism* (New York: Doubleday, 1992), pp. 143–147.

[78] James C. VanderKam, "Jubilees, Book of," in *ABD* 3, pp. 1030–1032.

[79] Ibid., pp. 1030–1031; Doron Mendels, *The Land of Israel as a Political Concept in Hasmonean Literature* (Tübingen: Mohr, 1987), pp. 57–88. Another concern of Jubilees that presumably reflects a priestly agenda is the emphasis on the renewal of the covenant associated with Shavu'ot (6:10–11,17).

[80] Jubilees 50:6–13. See generally, Charles T. R. Hayward, "The Jewish Temple at Leontopolis: A Reconsideration," *JJS* 33 (1982), pp. 85–107; as well as Martha Himmelfarb, "A Kingdom of Priests': The Democratization of the Priesthood in the Literature of Second Temple Judaism," *Journal of Jewish Thought and Philosophy* 6 (1997), pp. 89–98. For an earlier expression of this idea, see Psalm 20.

81 See Moses Hadas. ed., *Aristeas to Philocrates (Letter of Aristeas)* (New York: Harper, 1951), pp. 40–53, on the Hellenistic literary models and utopian descriptions that permeate the book. The New Jerusalem text from Qumran also seems to have been influenced by Hellenistic city-plan models; see Michael Chyutin, "The New Jerusalem: Ideal City," *DSD* 1 (1994), pp. 71–97.

82 Carol A. Newsom, *Songs of the Sabbath Sacrifice: A Critical Edition* (Atlanta: Scholars Press, 1985).

83 See John J. Collins, "Jerusalem and the Temple in Jewish Apocalyptic Literature of the Second Temple Period," *Ingeborg Rennert Center for Jerusalem Studies: International Rennert Guest Lecture Series* 1 (1998), pp. 12–24.

84 Ibid., pp. 9–11.

85 Menahem Stern, *The Documents on the History of the Hasmonean Revolt* (Tel Aviv: Hakibbutz Hameuchad, 1965), pp. 143–165 (in Hebrew). Josephus or his source mistakenly attributed this document to Hyrcanus II instead of Hyrcanus I; see Menahem Stern, *Studies in Jewish History: The Second Temple Period*, eds. Moshe Amit, Moshe D. Herr, and Isaiah Gafni (Jerusalem: Ben-Zvi, 1991), pp. 79–82 (in Hebrew).

86 Referred to as "worthy men and allies."

87 The document adds: "worthy and excellent men."

88 Here, too, referred to as "worthy and excellent men." This document has also been mistakenly attributed to Hyrcanus II; see Stern, *Studies in Jewish History* (see endnote 85), pp. 88–95.

89 Alexander (134 B.C.E.) and Diodorus (125 B.C.E.) were apparently brothers, sons of Jason. Apollonius served in two delegations (125 and 113 B.C.E.) and may have been the son of one Alexander, who is mentioned in connection with the delegation of 134 B.C.E. In the days of Jonathan and Simon, Numenius son of Antiochus fulfilled a similar function together with Antipater son of Jason (145 and 142 B.C.E.). The latter may have been the brother of Alexander and Diodorus. Numenius and Antipater were sent to Rome and Sparta c. 145 B.C.E., and Numenius went to Rome under Simon. Antipater may have been the father of Aeneas (113 B.C.E.). Jason, the father of three ambassadors, also served as such in 161 B.C.E. together with Apollonius son of Yohanan. Yohanan himself had also been sent on a diplomatic mission to Antiochus III and much earlier is credited with having gained the status of *ethnos* for the Jews (2 Maccabees 4:11). On the different meanings of the term *ethnos*, see Goldstein, *I Maccabees* (see endnote 7), pp. 194–196; David Goodblatt, *Elements of Ancient Jewish Nationalism* (Cambridge: Cambridge University Press, 2006), pp. 146–147.

90 See Ezra 2:61 (= Nehemiah 7:63); 1 Chronicles 24:10.

91 See, for example, the colophon of the Greek *Additions* to Esther; Josephus, *Apion* 2.49; and Tal Ilan, "The Greek Names of the Hasmoneans," *JQR* 78 (1987), pp. 1–20.

92 See Elias Bickerman, "The Colophon of the Greek Book of Esther," *JBL* 63 (1944), pp. 339–362; Carey A. Moore, *Daniel, Esther and Jeremiah: The Additions*, Anchor Bible 44 (Garden City, NY: Doubleday, 1977), pp. 153–252.

93 See 2 Maccabees 4:29, and possibly *Antiquities* 14.222.

94 However, on the stridently Jewish dimension of the *Additions*, see below.

95 See Shimon Applebaum, "The Fighting Priest," in *Nation and History: Studies in the History of the Jewish People*, ed. Menahem Stern (Jerusalem: Shazar Center, 1983), pp. 35–38 (in Hebrew); Martin Hengel, *The Zealots: Investigations into the Jewish Freedom Movement in the Period from Herod I until 70 A.D.* (Edinburgh: T & T Clark, 1989), pp. 271–290.

96 See David Goodblatt, "Priestly Ideologies of the Judean Resistance," *JSQ* 3 (1996), pp. 225–249.

97 One of them, Diogenes, was reputed to have advised Alexander Jannaeus to crucify 800 people. He was executed by the Pharisees when they assumed power (*War* 1.114; *Antiquities* 13.411).

98 Joseph D. Amoussine, "Ephraim et Manassé dans le Péshèr de Nahum," *RQ* 4 (1963), pp. 389–396; David Flusser, "Pharisees, Sadducees, and Essenes in Pesher Nahum," in *Essays in Jewish History and Philology: In Memory of Gedaliahu Alon*, eds. Menahem Dorman, Shmuel Safrai and Menahem Stern (Tel Aviv: Hakibbutz Hameuchad, 1970), pp. 133–168 (in Hebrew).

99 Grabbe, *Judaism* 2 (see endnote 26), pp. 463–554; *Judaic Religion in the Second Temple Period: Belief and Practice from the Exile to Yavneh*

(London: Routledge, 2000), pp. 183–209; Günter Stemberger, "The Sadducees—Their History and Doctrines," in *CHJ* 3, pp. 429–435.

100 See endnotes 105, 112 and 124.

101 See Albert I. Baumgarten, *The Flourishing of Jewish Sects in the Maccabean Era: An Interpretation* (Leiden: Brill, 1997), pp. 147–149.

102 See Günter Stemberger, *Jewish Contemporaries of Jesus: Pharisees, Sadducees, Essenes* (Minneapolis: Fortress Press, 1995), pp. 64–66.

103 See Baumgarten, *Flourishing of Jewish Sects* (see endnote 101), pp. 15–18.

104 For several general treatments of the phenomenon, see Anthony Saldarini, *Pharisees, Scribes and Sadducees in Palestinian Society: A Sociological Approach* (Wilmington: Glazier, 1988), pp. 239–308; Ed Parish Sanders, *Judaism: Practice and Belief 63 B.C.E.–66 C.E.* (London: SCM, 1992), pp. 13–29; Shaye J. D. Cohen, *From the Maccabees to the Mishnah* (Philadelphia: Westminster Press, 1987), pp. 160–162; and Baumgarten, *Flourishing of Jewish Sects* (see endnote 101), pp. 28–41, 88, 112–113; "City Lights: Urbanization and Sectarianism in Hasmonean Jerusalem," in *The Centrality of Jerusalem: Historical Perspectives*, eds. Marcel Poorthuis and Chana Safrai (Kampen: Kok Pharos, 1996), pp. 50–64.

105 See Albert I. Baumgarten, "Qumran and Jewish Sectarianism during the Second Temple Period," in *The Scrolls of the Judaean Desert: Forty Years of Research*, ed. Magen Broshi et al. (Jerusalem: Mosad Bialik and Israel Exploration Society, 1992), pp. 139–148 (in Hebrew).

106 Baumgarten, *Flourishing of Jewish Sects* (see endnote 101), pp. 47–48.

107 This assumes that these figures represent the total number of sectarians (and not just adult males) throughout the entire country.

108 Magen Broshi, "The Archaeology of Qumran—A Reconsideration," in *The Dead Sea Scrolls: Forty Years of Research*, eds. Devorah Dimant and Uriel Rappaport (Leiden: Brill, 1992), pp. 113–114. This is the generally accepted estimate, although figures as low as one to three score have also been suggested; for an overview of these opinions, see James VanderKam and Peter Flint, *The Meaning of the Dead Sea Scrolls: Their Significance for Understanding the Bible, Judaism, Jesus,*

and Christianity (New York: HarperSanFrancisco, 2002), pp. 51–54; and Hartmut Stegemann, *The Library of Qumran: On the Essenes, Qumran, John the Baptist, and Jesus* (Grand Rapids, MI: Eerdmans, 1998), pp. 45–51.

109 See *Antiquities* 18.17: "There are but few men to whom this doctrine has been made known, but there are men of the highest standing."

110 See T *Demai* 2.2, ed. Lieberman, p. 68; as well as Aharon Oppenheimer, *The 'Am Ha-Aretz: A Study in the Social History of the Jewish People in the Hellenistic-Roman Period* (Leiden: Brill, 1977), *passim*; Saldarini, *Pharisees, Scribes and Sadducees* (see endnote 104), pp. 216–220.

111 See Lawrence Schiffman, *Sectarian Law in the Dead Sea Sect: Courts, Testimony and the Penal Code* (Chico, CA: Scholars Press, 1983), pp. 161–168.

112 The *Miqṣat Ma'aśe ha-Torah* scroll ("Some of the Rulings Pertaining to the Torah") contains a statement by the leader of the breakaway sect discussing the major issues that separated his group from the Jerusalem authorities. See Lawrence Schiffman, *Reclaiming the Dead Sea Scrolls* (Philadelphia: Jewish Publication Society, 1994), pp. 83–95.

113 Schiffman, *Reclaiming the Dead Sea Scrolls* (see endnote 112), pp. 273–312. See, however, Baumgarten, *Flourishing of Jewish Sects* (see endnote 101), *passim*.

114 Albert I. Baumgarten, "The Name of the Pharisees," *JBL* 102 (1983), pp. 411–428. On the significance of the calendar controversy between Pharisees and Sadducees (here termed "Boethusians"), see Shlomo Naeh, "Did the Tannaim Interpret the Script of the Torah Differently from the Authorized Reading?" *Tarbiz* 61 (1992), pp. 424–439 (in Hebrew).

115 Steven D. Fraade, "Interpretive Authority in the Studying Community at Qumran," *JJS* 44 (1993), pp. 46–69.

116 Alexander Guttmann, *Rabbinic Judaism in the Making: A Chapter in the History of the Halakhah from Ezra to Judah I* (Detroit: Wayne State University Press, 1970), pp. 124–161; Saldarini, *Pharisees, Scribes and Sadducees* (see endnote 104), pp. 144–237; Steven N. Mason, "Chief Priests, Sadducees, Pharisees and Sanhedrin in Acts," in *The Book of Acts in Its First Century Setting 4: The*

Book of Acts in Its Palestinian Setting, ed. Richard Bauckham (Grand Rapids, MI: Eerdmans, 1995), pp. 115–177.

[117] A fuller account of the differences between the sects, with an especially long section devoted to the Essenes, is found in Josephus's *War* 2.119–166.

[118] On the Sadducees, see Abraham Geiger, *The Bible and Its Translations* (Jerusalem: Mosad Bialik, 1949), pp. 69–102 (in Hebrew); Louis Finkelstein, *The Pharisees*, 3 vols., 3rd ed. (Philadelphia: Jewish Publication Society, 1962), vol. 2, pp. 637–753; Jacob Lauterbach, *Rabbinic Essays* (Cincinnati: Hebrew Union College, 1951), pp. 23–83; and most comprehensively Rudolf Leszynsky, *Die Sadduzäer* (Berlin: Mayer & Müller, 1912); Jean Le Moyne, *Les sadducéens* (Paris: Lecoffre, 1972). See also Guttmann, *Rabbinic Judaism* (see endnote 116), pp. 136–176, where the major controversies between the sects are explicated.

[119] Ellis Rivkin, "Pharisaism and the Crisis of the Individual in the Greco-Roman World," *JQR* 61 (1970), pp. 27–53; Levine, "Political Struggle" (see endnote 45), pp. 61ff.

[120] See Jacob Neusner, *The Rabbinic Traditions about the Pharisees*, 3 vols. (Leiden: Brill, 1971), vol. 1, pp. 24–183; Yitzhak Fritz Baer, *Israel among the Nations* (Jerusalem: Mosad Bialik, 1955) (in Hebrew); Guttmann, *Rabbinic Judaism* (see endnote 116), pp. 33–56, 124–175; Grabbe, *Judaism* 2 (see endnote 26), pp. 463–499.

[121] For a maximalist position, see Gedaliah Alon, *Jews, Judaism, and the Classical World* (Jerusalem: Magnes Press, 1977), p. 22 and n. 11; Neil J. McEleney, "Orthodoxy in Judaism of the First Christian Century," *JSJ* 4 (1973), pp. 19–42. For a minimalist position, see Smith, "Palestinian Judaism," (see endnote 61), pp. 67–81; David Aune, "Orthodoxy in First Century Judaism? A Response to N. J. McEleney," *JSJ* 7 (1976), pp. 1–10.

[122] Publications on the Dead Sea sect and scrolls are legion. A classic introductory work in this field remains that of Frank Moore Cross, *The Ancient Library of Qumran and Modern Biblical Studies* (Garden City, NY: Doubleday, 1958); James VanderKam, *The Dead Sea Scrolls Today* (Grand Rapids, MI: Eerdmans, 1994); Schiffman, *Reclaiming the Dead Sea Scrolls* (see endnote 112);

VanderKam and Flint, *Meaning of the Dead Sea Scrolls* (see endnote 108). On the archaeology of Qumran, see Roland de Vaux, *Archaeology and the Dead Sea Scrolls* (Oxford: Clarendon Press, 1973); Stegemann, *Library of Qumran* (see endnote 108), pp. 34–57; and Magness, *Archaeology of Qumran* (see endnote 48); see also Hershel Shanks, *Mystery and Meaning of the Dead Sea Scrolls* (New York: Random House, 1998).

[123] VanderKam, *Dead Sea Scrolls Today* (see endnote 122), pp. 71–98; VanderKam and Flint, *Meaning of the Dead Sea Scrolls* (see endnote 108), pp. 239–254.

[124] Eshel, *Dead Sea Scrolls* (see endnote 26), pp. 29–61. On the Teacher of Righteousness in the interim period, 160–152 B.C.E., see Phillip R. Callaway, *The History of the Qumran Community: An Investigation* (Sheffield: JSOT Press, 1988), pp. 15–19, 212, n. 5.

[125] See endnote 124.

[126] The Damascus Document offers a somewhat different picture of the internal workings of the sect (including the presence of women and children) and may reflect either an early stage in its history or a competing model within the overall group. See Geza Vermes, *The Story of the Scrolls: The Miraculous Discovery and True Significance of the Dead Sea Scrolls* (London: Penguin Books, 2010), pp. 118–142.

[127] Shemaryahu Talmon, "The Calendar-Reckoning of the Sect from the Judaean Desert," *Scripta Hierosolymitana* 4 (1958), pp. 162–199.

[128] On the striking influence of Hellenistic culture on the Essenes, see endnotes 63–66.

[129] See, for example, VanderKam, *Dead Sea Scrolls Today* (see endnote 122), pp. 159–185; VanderKam and Flint, *Meaning of the Dead Sea Scrolls* (see endnote 108), pp. 311–378; Justin Taylor, "The Community of Goods among the First Christians and among the Essenes," in *Historical Perspectives* (see endnote 21), pp. 147–164.

[130] See the extensive discussion on this topic, albeit for the later, Herodian, period, by Sanders, *Judaism* (see endnote 104), pp. 45–314.

[131] See Alon, *Jews, Judaism* (see endnote 121), pp. 146–234; Ed Parish Sanders, *Jewish Law from Jesus to the Mishnah: Five Studies* (London: SCM,

1990), pp. 131–254; Eyal Regev, "Pure Individualism: The Idea of Non-Priestly Purity in Ancient Judaism," *JSJ* 31 (2000), pp. 176–202.

[132] See also the Sibylline Oracles 3.591–593, 4.162–169.

[133] Another expression of purity concerns was via a strict ban on intermarriage as spelled out in Jubilees and 4QMMT; see Cana Werman, "Jubilees 30: Building a Paradigm for the Ban on Intermarriage," *HTR* 90 (1997), pp. 1–22; Christine E. Hayes, "Intermarriage and Impurity in Ancient Jewish Sources," *HTR* 92 (1999), pp. 15–35.

[134] See Joseph M. Baumgarten, "The Pharisaic-Sadducean Controversies about Purity and the Qumran Texts," *JJS* 31 (1980), pp. 157–170; "Purification Rituals in DJD 7," in *Dead Sea Scrolls* (see endnote 108), pp. 199–209.

[135] For a later dispute between Hillel and Shammai on handwashing, see M *Berakhot* 8.2.

[136] It is unclear if the dissenting sages were his contemporaries or later, second-century, rabbis.

[137] Robert North, "The Qumran Reservoirs," in *The Bible in Current Catholic Thought*, ed. John L. McKenzie (New York: Herder & Herder, 1962), pp. 100–132; August Strobel, "Die Wasseranlagen der Hirbet Qumrān," *ZDPV* 88 (1972), pp. 55–86; Bryant G. Wood, "To Dip or to Sprinkle? The Qumran Cisterns in Perspective," *BASOR* 256 (1984), pp. 45–60; Ronny Reich, "Miqva'ot," in *Encyclopedia of the Dead Sea Scrolls* 1, eds. Lawrence Schiffman and James VanderKam (Oxford: Oxford University Press, 2000), pp. 560–563; as well as Netzer, "Ancient Ritual Baths" (see endnote 53), pp. 106–119; Reich, "Archaeological Evidence" (see endnote 41), pp. 48–52, and generally "Ritual Baths from the Second Temple Era," Ph.D. diss. (Hebrew University, Jerusalem, 1996) (in Hebrew).

[138] Whereas Reich offers a number between 300 and 350, Amit estimates that, as of 2001, some 500 *mikva'ot* have been discovered, 90 percent of which date to the pre-70 C.E. period (personal communication).

[139] A connection between the appearance of *mikva'ot* in Jewish society in the later second century B.C.E. and the use of public baths in the Hellenistic and Roman worlds at the time is an intriguing notion that deserves further attention.

[140] Reich, "Miqva'ot" (see endnote 137), pp. 560–563. See also the reservations regarding the identification of *mikva'ot* in Benjamin G. Wright III, "Jewish Ritual Baths: Interpreting the Digs and the Texts: Some Issues in the Social History of Second Temple Judaism," in *The Archaeology of Israel: Constructing the Past, Interpreting the Present*, eds. Neil A. Silberman and David Small (Sheffield: Sheffield Academic Press, 1997), pp. 190–214.

[141] See Ofra Rimon, ed., *'Purity broke out in Israel' (Tractate Shabbat 13a): Stone Vessels in the Late Second Temple Period* (Haifa: Hecht Museum, 1994), pp. 7–27; and especially Roland Deines, *Jüdische Steingefässe und pharisäische Frömmigkeit* (Tübingen: Mohr, 1993), pp. 71–115.

[142] See Hannah K. Harrington, "Did the Pharisees Eat Ordinary Food in a State of Ritual Purity?" *JSJ* 26 (1995), pp. 42–54.

[143] This point is meticulously documented in the magisterial work of Abraham Schalit, *King Herod: Portrait of a Ruler* (Jerusalem: Mosad Bialik, 1960) (in Hebrew); see also Lee I. Levine, "Roman Rule in Judea from 63 B.C.E. to 70 C.E.," in *The History of Eretz Israel*, vol. 4, ed. Menahem Stern (Jerusalem: Keter, 1984), pp. 11–25 (in Hebrew).

VIII. Roman Domination

[1] Bibliographical note: The most detailed and most heavily annotated history of the latter part of the Second Temple period remains Emil Schürer, *The History of the Jewish People in the Age of Jesus Christ*, rev. ed., ed. Geza Vermes et al., 4 vols. (Edinburgh: T & T Clark, 1973–1986). A shorter and more manageable survey is Lester L. Grabbe, *Judaism from Cyrus to Hadrian*, 2 vols. (Minneapolis: Fortress Press, 1992). Another valuable survey is E. Mary Smallwood, *The Jews Under Roman Rule* (Leiden: Brill, 1976, reprinted 1981). In this chapter, I provide only minimal bibliographical annotation, with a strong preference for works in English.

Quotations from Josephus are taken from the Loeb Classical Library edition, 9 vols., edited by H. St. J. Thackeray, Ralph Marcus, Allen Wikgren and Louis H. Feldman (London/Cambridge, MA: Heinemann/Harvard University Press, 1926–1965, frequently reprinted). An immensely useful new edition of Josephus (English translation and commentary) is now in the process of being published by Brill under the editorship of Steve Mason.

[2] The precise legal status of Judea in this period is obscure.

[3] See Menahem Stern, "The Relations Between Judaea and Rome During the Reign of John Hyrcanus," *Zion* 26 (1961), pp. 1–22 (in Hebrew); A.N. Sherwin-White, *Roman Foreign Policy in the East, 168 B.C. to A.D. 1* (Norman, OK: University of Oklahoma, 1984); Erich S. Gruen, *The Hellenistic World and the Coming of Rome*, 2 vols. (Berkeley: University of California, 1984); Dov Gera, *Judaea and Mediterranean Politics 219–161 BCE* (Leiden: Brill, 1998).

[4] Michael Wise, *Thunder in Gemini* (Sheffield: JSOT Press, 1994), p. 51.

[5] Josephus tells his story in *The Jewish War* 3.340–408.

[6] Peter Richardson, *Herod: King of the Jews and Friend of the Romans* (Columbia: University of South Carolina Press, 1996); Aryeh Kasher and Eliezer Witztum, *King Herod: A Persecuted Persecutor*, trans. Karen Gold (New York: de Gruyter, 2007).

[7] The phrase is from Pliny the Elder, *Natural History* 5.70; see Menaham Stern, *Greek and Latin Authors on Jews and Judaism*, 3 vols. (Jerusalem: Israel Academy of Humanities and Sciences, 1974–1984), vol. 1, p. 471, no. 204. For discussion of pagan statements about the glory of Jerusalem, see the article by Menahem Stern in *Jerusalem in the Second Temple Period: Abraham Schalit Memorial Volume*, ed. A. Oppenheimer et al. (Jerusalem: Ben Zvi Institute, 1981), pp. 257–270 (in Hebrew).

[8] See the symposium on "Herod's Building Projects," in *The Jerusalem Cathedra* 1 (with contributions by Ehud Netzer, Lee I. Levine, Magen Broshi and Yoram Tsafrir) (Jerusalem: Ben Zvi Institute, 1981), pp. 48–80; Duane Roller, *The Building Program of Herod the Great* (Berkeley: University of California Press, 1998).

[9] *War* 1.665.

[10] *Antiquities* 17.191–192.

[11] On Herod's genealogy, see *Antiquities* 14.8–10; 14.121 and 14.403; see also Eusebius, *History of the Church* 1.7.11–14. Jews who disliked Herod fastened upon his less-than-perfect pedigree to justify their dislike; Jews who liked Herod were quite willing to overlook his origins; see Mishnah *Sotah* 7:8 regarding Agrippa. See Shaye J.D. Cohen, *The Beginnings of Jewishness* (Berkeley: University of California Press, 1999), chapter 1 ("Was Herod the Great Jewish?").

[12] Richard A. Horsley and John S. Hanson, *Bandits, Prophets, and Messiahs: Popular Movements in the Time of Jesus* (New York: Winston-Seabury, 1985).

[13] D.C. Braund, *Rome and the Friendly King: The Character of Client Kingship* (London: Croom Helm, 1984).

[14] Helen K. Bond, *Pontius Pilate in History and Interpretation* (Cambridge: Cambridge University Press, 1998).

[15] In Books 14 and 16 of the *Antiquities*, Josephus quotes a series of edicts, laws and letters that bestow special privileges upon the Jews in order to allow them to practice their religion. Marina Pucci Ben Zeev, *Jewish Rights in the Roman World: the Greek and Roman Documents Quoted by Josephus Flavius* (Tübingen: Mohr Siebeck, 1998). On *politeumata*, see Aryeh Kasher, *The Jews in Hellenistic and Roman Egypt* (Tübingen: Mohr-Siebeck, 1985).

[16] Full discussion in Smallwood, *Jews Under Roman Rule* (see endnote 1).

[17] Daniel R. Schwartz, *Agrippa I: The Last King of Judaea* (Tübingen: Mohr-Siebeck, 1990).

[18] The word "Jew" derives from the Greek *Ioudaios* and the Latin *Judaeus*, which originally meant "an inhabitant or a native of the district of Judea; a member of the tribe of Judah." The English equivalent is "Judean." However, by the Hellenistic period the term began to have another meaning as well, one that approximates the English term "Jew." The Jews' distinctive manner of life was called *Ioudaismos*, "Judaism." For the sake of convenience I use the term "Jew" throughout this chapter. For a discussion of the word *Ioudaios*, see Cohen, *Beginnings of Jewishness* (see endnote 11), chapters 3 and 4.

[19] The argument of the following paragraphs is developed at much greater length in Shaye J.D. Cohen, *From the Maccabees to the Mishnah* (Philadelphia: Westminster Press, 1987; 2nd ed. 2006).

[20] Tanakh is an acronym for *Torah* (the Five Books of Moses), *Neviim* (the Prophets) and *Ketuvim* (the Writings).

[21] Lee I. Levine, ed., *Ancient Synagogues Revealed* (Jerusalem: Israel Exploration Society, 1981); Hershel Shanks, *Judaism in Stone: The Archaeology of Ancient Synagogues* (Washington, DC: Biblical Archaeology Society, 1978); Lee I. Levine, *The Ancient Synagogue: The First Thousand Years*, 2nd ed. (New Haven: Yale University Press, 2005).

[22] Following the work of E.P. Sanders (especially *Judaism: Practice and Belief 63 BCE–66 CE* [Philadelphia: Trinity Press International, 1992]), I use the phrase "common Judaism" to denote the aggregate of the beliefs that were generally believed and the practices that were generally practiced in Jewish communities of antiquity. "Common Judaism" is the Judaism as lived by large numbers of people who saw themselves, and were seen by others, as *Ioudaioi*. See *Common Judaism: Explorations in Second Temple Judaism*, ed. Wayne O. McCready and Adele Reinhartz (Minneapolis: Fortress Press, 2008); Shaye J.D. Cohen, "Common Judaism in Greek and Roman Authors, in *Redefining First Century Jewish and Christian Identities: Essays in Honor of Ed Parish Sanders*, ed. Fabian Udoh (Notre Dame, IN: University of Notre Dame Press, 2008).

[23] Eric M. Meyers, *Jewish Ossuaries: Reburial and Rebirth* (Rome: Biblical Institute, 1971); Pau Figueras, *Decorated Jewish Ossuaries* (Leiden: Brill, 1983); Craig Evans, *Jesus and the Ossuaries* (Waco, TX: Baylor University Press, 2003).

[24] Full discussion in Morton Smith, *Jesus the Magician* (San Francisco: Harper & Row, 1978).

[25] *Antiquities* 20.171.

[26] For an interpretation of early Jewish sectarianism, see A.I. Baumgarten, *The Flourishing of Jewish Sects in the Maccabean Era* (Leiden: Brill, 1997).

[27] On the disputed identity of the authors of the Dead Sea Scrolls, see Lawrence Schiffman, *Reclaiming the Dead Sea Scrolls* (Philadelphia: Jewish Publication Society, 1994), pp. 83–157; see also Hershel Shanks, *The Mystery and the Meaning of the Dead Sea Scrolls* (New York: Random House, 1998).

[28] See John J. Collins, *The Scepter and the Star* (New York: Doubleday, 1995).

[29] *Antiquities* 18.15, 17, 19–20.

[30] The classic statement of such an argument is Daniel R. Schwartz, "Josephus and Nicolaus on the Pharisees," *Journal for the Study of Judaism in the Persian, Hellenistic and Roman Periods* 14 (1983), pp. 157–171.

[31] The classic modern defense of the primacy of the Pharisees is Martin Hengel and Roland Deines, "E.P. Sanders' 'Common Judaism,' Jesus, and the Pharisees," *Journal of Theological Studies* 46 (1995), pp. 1–70.

[32] This discussion of early Christianity has been abridged from Cohen, *From the Maccabees to the Mishnah* (see endnote 19), pp. 159–162.

[33] *Antiquities* 20.219–222. This is the first securely attested instance of a government "make-work" project in antiquity. See Gabriella Giglioni, *Lavori pubblici e occupazione nell'antichità classica* (Bologna, Italy: Patron, 1974), pp. 171ff., with the comments of Lionel Casson in the *Bulletin of the American Society of Papyrologists* 15 (1978), pp. 50–51.

[34] On these social tensions, see Shaye J.D. Cohen, *Josephus in Galilee and Rome* (Leiden: Brill, 1979), pp. 206–221; Sean Freyne, *Galilee from Alexander the Great to Hadrian*, part II (Notre Dame, IN: University of Notre Dame Press, 1980); Peter A. Brunt, "Josephus on Social Conflicts in Roman Judaea," *Klio* 59 (1977), pp. 149–153; Horsley and Hanson, *Bandits, Prophets, and Messiahs* (see endnote 12).

[35] *War* 2.277–278.

[36] *War* 6.312. The Roman historian Tacitus reports the same information; see Stern, *Greek and Latin Authors*, vol. 1 (see endnote 7), p. 31, no. 281.

[37] See especially H. Kreissig, *Die sozialen Zusammenhänge des judäischen Krieges* (Berlin: Akademie-Verlag, 1970); Tessa Rajak, *Josephus: The Historian and His Society* (London: Duckworth, 1983), chapter 5; Martin Goodman, *The Ruling Class of Judaea: The Origins of the Jewish Revolt Against Rome* (Cambridge: Cambridge University Press, 1987).

[38] Cohen, *Josephus in Galilee* (see endnote 34), pp. 152–160.

[39] The Rabban Yohanan ben Zakkai tale appears in four different versions; they are conveniently

available in Jacob Neusner, *Development of a Legend* (Leiden: Brill, 1970). The bibliography on these stories is immense: See Horst Moehring, "Joseph ben Matthia and Flavius Josephus," in *Aufstieg und Niedergang der römischen Welt* 2.21.2, ed. W. Haase (Berlin: de Gruyter, 1984), pp. 864–944, especially pp. 917–944; and Shaye J.D. Cohen, "Josephus, Jeremiah, and Polybius," *History and Theory* 21 (1982), pp. 366–381.

[40] Tacitus, *Histories* 4.54.2. On native revolts, see Stephen L. Dyson, "Native Revolts in the Roman Empire," *Historia* 20 (1971), pp. 239–274, and "Native Revolt Patterns in the Roman Empire," in *Aufstieg und Niedergang der römischen Welt* 2.3, ed. H. Temporini (Berlin: de Gruyter, 1975), pp. 138–175. On the patterns of social revolutions, see Crane Brinton, *The Anatomy of Revolution* (New York: Prentice-Hall, 1952); compare the French and Russian revolutions.

[41] See especially Morton Smith, "Zealots and Sicarii: Their Origins and Relation," *HTR* 64 (1971), pp. 1–19, reprinted in his *Studies in the Cult of Yahweh* (New York: Brill, 1996), vol. 1.

[42] Ever since the Persian period, the priests of the Temple regularly prayed, and/or offered sacrifice, for the welfare of the reigning monarch; see Ezra 6:10. In addition, upon his accession to office the high priest took an oath of loyalty to the state; see *Antiquities* 11.318.

[43] For a defense of this view, see Cohen, *Josephus in Galilee* (see endnote 34), pp. 181–206; for another interpretation, see Rajak, *Josephus* (see endnote 37), pp. 65–103.

[44] That the Idumaeans were invited to participate in the war, and that they willingly accepted the invitation, shows that the regarded themselves as "Jews," and were so regarded by the Jews of Judea. The Idumaean Herod was a "half-Jew" only because he was disliked. See above endnote 11.

[45] The question of Titus's motives and actions has been much debated. See the discussion in Stern, *Greek and Latin Authors*, vol. 2 (see endnote 7), pp. 64–67, no. 282. See also Zvi Yavetz, "Reflections on Titus and Josephus," *Greek, Roman and Byzantine Studies* 16 (1975), pp. 411–432.

[46] Josephus does not explicitly state John's fate. On the subsequent history of the sacred vessels, see

Hans Lewy, "The Fate of the Sacred Vessels After the Destruction of the Second Temple," in *Studies in Jewish Hellenism* (Jerusalem: Bialik, 1960), pp. 255–258 (in Hebrew). See also Joan Taylor, "The Nea Church: Were the Temple Treasures Hidden Here?" *BAR*, January/February 2008. Despite the Jewish urban legend to the contrary, the Temple menorah is not in the Vatican; and despite the Indiana Jones movie to the contrary, the Temple ark is lost without a trace (the Second Temple had no Ark of the Covenant; the Holy of Holies was an empty room).

[47] The translation is from Naphtali Lewis and Meyer Reinhold, *Roman Civilization Sourcebook II: The Empire* (New York: Harper & Row, 1966), p. 92.

[48] Stern, *Greek and Latin Authors*, vol. 2 (see endnote 7), p. 373, no. 430. The standard discussion of the *fiscus Judaicus* is by Victor Tcherikover, *Corpus Papyrorum Judaicarum*, 3 vols. (Cambridge, MA: Harvard University Press, 1957–1964), vol. 2, pp. 110–116.

[49] For correctives to the Josephan account, which is followed whole by Yigael Yadin in *Masada* (New York: Random House, 1966), see: D.J. Ladouceur, "Masada: A Consideration of the Literary Evidence," *Greek, Roman and Byzantine Studies* 21 (1980), pp. 245–260; Menahem Stern, "The Suicide of Eleazar ben Yair and His Men at Masada," *Zion* 47 (1982), pp. 367–397 (in Hebrew); Shaye J.D. Cohen, "Masada: Literary Tradition, Archaeological Remains, and the Credibility of Josephus," *JJS* 33 (1982), pp. 385–405; Hillel Geva, The Siege Ramp Laid by the Romans to Conquer the Northern Palace at Masada," *Eretz Israel: Archaeological Historical and Geographical Studies* 25: Joseph Aviram Volume (Jerusalem: Israel Exploration Society, 1996), pp. 297–306 (Hebrew; Eng abstract on p. 100); Nachman Ben-Yehuda, *Sacrificing Truth: Archaeology and the Myth of Masada* (Amherst, NY: Humanity Books, 2002).

[50] The following paragraphs summarize the argument in Cohen, *From the Maccabees to the Mishnah* (see endnote 19), chapter 7.

Index

Note: Page numbers in italics refer to illustrations, maps and charts.

385

Aramaic, 231

Arameans: battles, 100–101, *121*, 327–28n.41, 350n.21; patriarchs as, 23, 76, 328n.57

Arav, Rami, 175n.

Arch of Titus, *317, 318*

Archelaus, 297

Areus, king of Sparta, 239–40

Ariel, Donald T., 372n.n8–9

Aristeas, Letter of *see* Letter of Aristeas

Aristobulus I, Hasmonean king, *241,* 252, *253,* 254, 255, 265

Aristobulus II, Hasmonean king, *253,* 269, 283, 287–88, 289

Aristobulus son of Amyntas, 268

Ark of the Covenant, 90, 90n., 99–100

Arpad, 170

Arslan Tash, Syria, *120*

Artaxerxes I, king of Persia, 221, 228

Asa, king of Judah, 136, 138, *139,* 349–50n.11

Ashdod, 96, 184, 199

Asher (son of Jacob), 33, 330n.97

Asher, tribe of, 330–31n.97

Asherah (goddess), *119, 160,* 161, *161*

asherah (object used in worship), 161

Ashkelon: Babylonian capture of, 202, 207; Philistines in, 96; revolt against Assyria, 185, 187; Scythian plunder of, 199

ashlars, 141n.

Ashur-uballit II, king of Assyria, 199, 200, 201

Ashyahu, king *see* Jehoash, king of Judah

Assurbanipal, king of Assyria, 193, 194–95, 365n.162, 365n.165, 366n.171

Assurnasirpal II, king of Assyria, 146

Assyria: aid from Egypt, 199, 200–201; bureaucratic officers, 190, 362n.136; campaign against Medes, 172; campaign in Damascus, 148, 153, 157–59, 162, 172, 174, 176, 354n.49; campaign in Egypt, 179–80, 192–96; campaign in Syria, 162, 354n.49; campaign in Syria-Palestine, 157; campaign in Urartu, 143, 172; claim of Babylonian throne, 360n.113; coalitions against, 143, 144, 146, 147–48, 151, 170, 171–72, 173, 179, 198–99, 352n.37, 354n.50; control of Israel, 170–85, 187–96, 205–6; control of Judah, 170–85, 187–96; control of trade routes, 176–78; deportation policy, 175,

180; end of empire, 196–201; imperialism, 146–48; neoclassicism, 366n.171; provinces, 176; rebellions against, 179–80, 185, 187, 195, 196; tributes to, 355n.58

Assyrian Eponym Chronicle, 162, 178, 354n.49

Astour, Michael C., 352n.37

Athaliah, queen of Judah: marriage, 144, 149; reign, *139,* 154, 357n.83; Yahwistic name form, 143

Atkinson, Kenneth, 287n.

Attic black-ware pottery, 234–35

Aubet, Maria E., 342n.91

Augustus (Octavian), 289, 294

Aune, David, 380n.121

Avaris (Hyksos capital), 51, 52

Avi-Yonah, Michael, 374n.35

Avigad, Nahman, 357n.86, 376n.57, 377n.67, 377n.76; on Exilic period, 213; on Hezekiah's seal, 360n.122; on ivory pomegranate inscription, *122;* Jerusalem excavations, 190, 366n.168

Avner, Uzi, 163

Awel-Marduk, 216

Azariah (Uzziah), king of Judah: accomplishments, 166, 167; ascension to throne, 159; conflict with priesthood, 356n.77; military campaigns, 166–67; name forms, 166n., 357n.89; reign, *139,* 162, 166–67; restoration of Elath to Judah, 356n.75; strengthening Jerusalem's defenses, 356n.71, 358n.92; tomb, 356n.78

Azariah son of Nathan, 107, 151

Azariah son of Zadok, 107

Azekah, 367n.187

Baal (god), 82, *119,* 143, 151, 166

Baal, King of Tyre, 193, 194

Baasha, king of Israel, 134, 136, 138n., *139*

Babylon: assault on Assyria, 199–200; assault on Egypt, 203; assault on Philistia, 202, 367n.183; Assyrian claims to throne, 360n.113; control of Jerusalem, 205; deportations, 209; destruction by Assyria, 193; division of Assyrian empire, 201; fall to Persia, 218; freedom from Assyria, 196; in Palestine, 207; revolts against Assyria, 179, 185, 195; *see also* neo-Babylonian period

Babylonian Chronicle, 194, 201, 365n.159

Bacchides (Syrian army leader), 250

Baer, Yitzhak Fritz, 380n.120

Bagavahya, 229

Bahat, Dan, 366n.168

Baly, Denis, 350n.16

Bar Kochva, Bezalel, 374n.24, 374n.27, 374n.30, 374n.32

Barag, Dan, 376n.55

Barako, Tristan, 88n.

Bardthe, Hans, 377n.64

Baris (fortress-palace), 263–65, 377n.74

Barkat, Orit-Peleg, 293

Barkay, Gabriel, 160n., 191n., 355n.n62–63, 368n.11

Barstad, Hans, 367n.4

Bartlett, John R., 370n.49

Barton, John, 340n.56

BAS On-Line Archive, xxvii

Bathsheba, 102, 103

Batto, Bernard F., 54, 333n.39, 334n.51

Baumgarten, Albert I., 379n.101, 379n.n103–6, 379n.n113–14, 381n.134, 383n.26

Bay, chancellor of Egypt, 32

B.C.E. (Before the Common Era), definition of, 4

Beaulieu, Paul-Alain, 369n.27

Beck, Pirhiya, 354n.57

Beer-lahai-roi, 15, 26

Beersheba: association with Abraham, 26n.; association with Isaac, 15, 26, 26n., 329n.66; horned altar, 181; well, 28

Begrich, Joachim, 172

Behistun inscription, 224

Beit-Arieh, Itzhaq, 54n., 334n.52

Ben-Ami, Doron, 347n.149

Ben-ammi, 6

Ben-hadad: distinguishing kings of same name, 157n., 350n.21, 351n.27, 351n.30

Ben-hadad I, king of Damascus, 136, 138, 142, 350n.15, 352–53n.39

Ben-hadad II, king of Damascus, 157n., 157–59, 350–51n.21, 354n.50

Ben-Shlomo, David, 338–39n.33

Ben Sira, 242

Ben-Tor, Amnon, 64, 65, 126, 144n.

Ben Yair, Eleazar, 320

Ben-Yehuda, Nachman, 384n.49

Ben Zeev, Marina Pucci, 382n.15

Benaiah (chief of guards), 103, 107

Beni Hasan, Egypt, 118

Benjamin, territory of, 95, 211–13, 224

Benjamin, tribe of, 33, 102

Berenike, 239

Berkowitz, Lois, 342n.90

Berlin, Andrea M., 258, 258n., 259n., 373n.16

Bernick-Greenberg, Hannah, 348n.162

Bes (Egyptian dwarf-god), 354–55n.57

Beth Hillel, 276

beth midrash, 261

Beth Shammai, 276

Beth Zechariah, 250

Beth Zur, 249

Bethel, 15, 121, 134–35, 212

Bethsaida (site), 175n.

Bible: components, 302; lost books of, 50

biblical maximalists, 86

biblical minimalists, 44, 86

biblical narrative: archaeology and, 41; Deuteronomistic writers, 134, 164; prophetic, 142, 150; purpose of, 40, 57, 66, 142, 333n.36; time of writing of, 231–32

Bickerman, Elias, 373n.17, 374n.24, 376n.61, 378n.92; on Antiochus IV's religious persecution of Jews, 248; on correspondence between High Priest Onias II and Areus, king of Sparta, 372n.7; on Hellenism, 243, 257

Bienkowski, Piotr, 63n.

Bietak, Manfred, 44n., 47n., 52, 332n.23, 332n.27, 333n.43

Bietenhard, Sophia Katharine, 340n.54

Billig, Ya'akov, 295n.

Bimson, John J., 332n.18

Biran, Avraham, 144n., 339n.42, 352n.38, 353n.40

Bird, Phyllis A., 357n.84

Bit Adini, 147

Black Obelisk, 153, 153

Blenkinsopp, Joseph, 211n., 337n.15, 368n.14, 370n.61, 371n.73

Bnei Hezir, 259, 260, 265, 269

Bodi, Daniel, 340n.58

Bond, Helen K., 382n.14

Bordreuil, Pierre, 353n.46

Borowski, Oded, 188n., 357n.79

Braund, D.C., 382n.13

Hebron, 19, 26n., 105

Hectaeus of Abdera, 376n.59

Hejaz route, 167

Helck, H. Wolfgang, 329n.70, 330n.93

Heliodorus (Seleucid official), 265, 285

Hellenism, age of, 237–85; Antiochus IV, 245–48, 249; common Judaism, 280–81; cultural dimension, 237–38; end of Jewish sovereignty, 285–86; Essenes, 277–80; Greek institutions, 244, 244n.; Hasmonean period, 249–57, 262–73, 280–81; integration with Judaism, 257–62; Jerusalem, 245–48, 249, 262–65; Jerusalem Temple, 265–67; Judea, 239, 243–45; Maccabean revolt, 245–49, 285; Pharisees, 275–77; priesthood, 222, 267–70; purity concerns, 281–83; reactions to, 239–40, 242–43; religious persecution of Jews, 247–48; religious sects, 270–80; Sadducees, 274–75

Heltzer, Michael, 357n.88

Hendel, Ronald S., 18n., 21n., 50n., 327n.40, 328n.49, 330n.79, 344n.108

Hengel, Martin, 372n.11, 373n.17, 377n.66, 378n.95; on Antiochus IV's religious persecution of Jews, 248; on authenticity of correspondence of Jonathan the Hasmonean with Sparta, 372n.7; on Hasidim, 374n.31; on impact of Hellenism, 243; on primacy of Pharisees, 383n.31; on syntheses of political and religious realms under Hasmoneans, 374n.34

hermeneutic of suspicion, 44

Hermopolis, 370n.67

Herod the Great, 291–96; Antonia, 266, 377n.74; brigandage, 296–97; brutality, 295; building projects, 292, 293, 310; compared to Agrippa I, 300–301; death and aftermath, 296–97; executions, 291–92; governance, 294, 295; as "half-Jew," 384n.44; high priests, 292; and Judaism, 295–96; official historian, 291; popularity, 294–95, 382n.11, 384n.44; relationship with Rome, 292, 294; rise to power, 289; Royal Stoa, Jerusalem, 293; taxation, 295

Herodian dynasty, rise of, 289

Herodium, 301

Herodotus, 199, 203, 363n.144

Herr, Larry G., 79, 346n.140, 348n.161

Herrmann, Siegfried, 329n.75, 342n.77

Herzog, Ze'ev/Zeev, 338–39n.33, 341n.72, 347n.153, 348n.n162–63

Hess, Richard S., 80n., 342n.88

Hezekiah, king of Judah: Assyrian invasions, 180–85, 187–91, 206, 362n.132, 362n.134, 363n.140, 364n.145; and Babylon, 361n.128; death, 192; reign, 139; religious reforms, 160n., 180–81, 182–84, 192, 360n.123; revolts against Assyria, 185, 206, 364n.146; seal of, 182, 183; successor, 192; tunnel, 188, 189, 190–91, 363n.141

Hezion, 350n.15

Hezir family see Bnei Hezir

hieroglyphs, 43

high priesthood see priesthood

Hilkiah (high priest), 197

Hillel (sage), 276, 381n.135

Himmelfarb, Martha, 377n.80

Hiram, king of Tyre (Davidic-Solomonic era), 103, 107, 109, 326n.21

Hiram of Tyre (eighth-century B.C.E.), 173, 174, 326n.21

history of traditions, 14–16, 18, 327n.32

Hobab see Jethro

Hoffmeier, James K., 52n., 332n.n9–11, 333n.49, 334n.50, 334n.n59–60

Hoglund, Kenneth, 369n.46

Holladay, John S., Jr., 347n.150, 347n.153, 348n.168, 349n.10, 350n.19, 355n.64, 357n.80, 359n.104

Holland, Thomas A., 334n.5

Hophra, king of Egypt, 204, 367n.187

Hopkins, David C., 357n.79, 357n.80

Horn, Siegfried H., 144n., 361–62n.130

horned altar, 181

Horsley, Richard A., 382n.12, 383n.34

Horvat Teman see Kuntillet 'Ajrud

Hosea (prophet), 184

Hoshea, king of Israel: appeal to Egypt, 359n.110; ascension to throne, 175, 359n.100; reign, 139; vacillating policy towards Assyria, 178, 206

House of David: as designation for kingdom of Judah, 152; on Mesha Stela, 145; as official diplomatic name of kingdom of Judah, 97; on Tel Dan stela, 152, 353n.42

Houtman, C., 370n.67

Huffmon, Herbert B., 326n.22

Hughes, George R., 349n.1, 349n.4

Hummarabi, 9

Lehmann, Manfred R., 319n.

Leith, Mary Joan Winn, 234

Lemaire, André, 336n.53, 338n.20, 338n.29, 339n.n41–42, 340n.62, 342n.78, 342n.91, 342n.93, 343n.97, 343n.106, 344n.114, 345n.121, 345n.125, 345n.128, 345n.130, 345n.132, 346n.139, 368–69n.24, 371n.82; on bull iconography, 135n.; on early Israelites, 329n.75; on Exile, 215; on Hadad the Edomite, 343n.101; on Hebron, 346n.136; on House of David, 152n., 353n.41; on Israelite historiography, 345–46n.134; on ivory pomegranate inscription, 122; on location of Mahanaim, 339n.45; on Mesha of Moab, 97n.; on Mesha Stela inscription, 145; on Persian period, 233n.; on Phoenician inscriptions, 345n.122; on redaction of the books of Kings, 344n.107; on Solomonic districts, 342n.87; on trade during Solomon's reign, 114n.; on trade routes, 177n.

Lemche, Niels Peter, 333n.38, 341n.63

Leontopolis temple, 267, 274

leprosy, 167, 356n.76, 356n.77

Leszynsky, Rudolf, 380n.118

Letter of Aristeas, 228–29, 242–43, 266–67, 281, 370n.62

Levenson, Jon D., 332n.15, 340n.49

Levi (Jacob's son), 4, 329n.66

Levine, Lee I., 369n.26, 371n.4, 375n.45, 376n.57, 380n.119, 383n.21; on age of Hellenism, 371n.1; on Hannukah, 374n.29; on Hasmonean period, 375n.47, 376n.51; on Herod's building projects, 382n.8; on Roman rule in Judea, 381n.143

Levy, Thomas E., 47n., 127n., 348n.n164–65

Lewis, Naphtali, 384n.47

Lewy, Hans, 384n.46

Lewy, Yochanan, 375n.44

Lieberman, Saul, 376n.61

Lipiński, Edward, 340n.n51–52, 345n.120, 349n.173

Lipschits, Oded, 369n.34, 369n.44; on Babylonian conquest of Jerusalem, 211; on Exilic period, 368n.n11–12, 368n.15; on population in the Exilic period, 368n.n5–6; on YHD stamp impressions, 233

Liverani, Mario, 96–97, 339n.36, 345n.127

lmlk stamps, 191, 191n., 363n.142, 363n.143

Long, V. Philips, 337n.15

Lot, 6

Luke, J.T., 326n.16

Luli, king of Sidon, 185

Lundberg, Marilyn J., 368n.11

Lysias (Seleucid commander), 250

Lysimachus (priest), 260, 269

Maacah daughter of Geshur, 100

Maag, Victor, 329n.74

Maccabean revolt, 245–48, 249, 285

Maccabees, 249n., 285; see also Hasmonean dynasty

Macchi, Jean-Daniel, 343n.102

Machinist, Peter, 362n.133

Machir, tribe of, 19, 80, 328n.43

Machir grandson of Joseph, 44

Maeir, Aren M., 90n., 96n., 339n.34

Magen, Yitzhak/Izchak, 136n., 211n., 231, 338n.25, 370n.70

Magidu see Megiddo

Magness, Jodi, 375n.48, 375–76n.n50, 380n.122

Maidman, Maynard, 5

Malamat, Abraham, 106n., 207n., 341n.68, 342n.80, 367n.188; on Amorites, 328n.55; and Conquest Model, 62, 65–66, 67; on dating the Exodus, 48; on Naamah, the Ammonite Princess, 342n.82

Malat, Tell el-, 136

Manasseh (region), 95

Manasseh, king of Judah, 192–96; accomplishments, 195–96; arrest by Assyrians, 365n.165; as Assyrian vassal, 192, 193, 206; blame for fall of Jerusalem, 192; building projects, 195–96; reign, 139; religious policies, 193, 364n.151, 365n.167

Manasseh, tribe of, 19, 30, 80, 328n.43

Manasseh son of Jacob, 33, 33n.

Manetho, 51

Ma'oz, Zvi U., 377n.73

maps: Abraham's journey, 2–3; ancient Israel and environs, ix; Canaan, settlement of, 61; Danite migration, 61; Exodus route, 38–39; Fertile Crescent and Egypt, viii; Maccabean-Hasmonean Palestine, 241; Nebuchadnezzar's campaigns, 200; Sargon II's campaign, 177; Sennacherib's campaign, 184; Shalmaneser III's campaign, 147; Shalmaneser V's campaign, 177; Shishak's campaign, 133; Tiglath-pileser's campaigns, 173; tribes of Israel, 61; United Monarchy, 89

Rösel, Hartmut N., 342n.87

Rosen, Baruch, 338n.31

Rosenberg, Stephen G., 373n.16

Rowton, M.B., 326n.15

Royal Stoa, 293

Rozlar, Mark, 372n.11

Rubiato, Maria Teresa, 64n., 335n.12

sacrifices, *181*, 317, 384n.42

Sadducees, 274–75; first century C.E., 305, 307; compared to Pharisees, 275; emergence, 271; etymology of word, 274n.; in Hasmonean government, 256, 274; Jerusalem base, 271–72; as military leaders, 270; number of, 272; priestly status, 274; as sect, 270; theology, 273, 275

Safi, Tell es- (Gath), 96

Saggs, H.W.F., 362n.133

Salamanu of Moab, 174

Saldarini, Anthony, 379n.104, 379n.110, 379n.116

Salome Alexandra, Hasmonean queen: death, 287; and Pharisees, 256, 269; reign, *253*; and Sadducees, 274; use of foreign mercenaries, 265, 377n.69

Samaria/Samaritans: acropolis, 143; anti-Assyrian alliance, 179; under Assyrian control, 180; as capital of Omride dynasty, 140; conquest by Hasmoneans, 255; control by Judah, 198; fall of, 178–80; Hellenism in, 234; ivories, 165, 355n.65, 355n.66; under Jeroboam II, 165–66; location, 140; ostraca, 166; relationship with Damascus, 150–51, 171; religious conflict in, 143; resettlement of captive Israelites, 360n.119; rulers, 142; schism, 231; siege, 179, 350n.21; Syrian annexation of, 297; tensions with Jews, 231

Samsi, queen of Arabia, 172, 177–78, 360n.116

Samuel, 83, 92, 93, 97

Sanballat of Samaria, 226, 227, 231, 234

Sanders, Ed Parish, 379n.104, 380n.n130–31, 383n.22

Sandmel, Samuel, 243

Sanipu of Bit-Ammon, 174

Saqqara, 32n., 367n.183

Sarai, 11, 14

Sargon, king of Akkad, 57

Sargon II, king of Assyria: campaign map, *177*; conquests, 179–80; death, 185, 364–65n.153; resettlement of captive Israelites, 360n.119; revolts against, 179–80, 184

Särkiö, Pekka, 343n.106

Sarna, Nahum M., 326n.18, 331n.n2–3, 333n.36

Sass, Benjamin, 357n.86

Saul, king of Israel, 88, 90, 92–96; appointment as king, 83, 92, 138n.; compared to David, 94–95; death, 93; family, 94; map of kingdom, 89; reign, 94–96; relationship with David, 95, 97–98; as warrior, 92–93, 95

Sawas-sar-usur, 213

Schäfer, Peter, 373n.21

Schäfer-Lichtenberger, Christa, 340n.53

Schalit, Abraham, 381n.143

Schaper, Joachim, 370n.51

Scheffler, Eben, 339n.35

Schenker, A., 343n.102

Schiffman, Lawrence, 379n.n111–13, 380n.122, 383n.27

Schmidt, Werner H., 346n.137

Schniedewind, William M., 339n.42, 371n.75

schools, Hellenistic influences on, 261

Schroder, John F., 175n.

Schulman, Alan R., 330n.90, 330n.92

Schulte, Hannalis, 345n.134

Schürer, Emil, 372n.7, 373n.21, 374n.35, 381n.1

Schwartz, Daniel R., 373n.21, 374n.26, 382n.17, 383n.30

Schwartz, Seth, 375n.42

Scolnic, Benjamin, 369n.40

Scroll of the War of the Sons of Light against the Sons of Darkness, 269

Scurlock, JoAnn, 374n.26

Scythians, 193, 199–200, 365n.154

Sea Peoples, 88, 90; *see also* Philistia/Philistines

Seba', Tell es-, 339n.44

Sebaste, 292

Second Temple *see* Jerusalem Temple

sect, definition of, 270

Seebass, Horst, 329n.74

Seiler, Stefan, 340n.56

Seleucids, 247–48, 249–50, 251, 253, 284, 285

Seleucus IV, Seleucid king, 284, 285

Seleucus Stela, *284*

Sennacherib, king of Assyria: assassination, 193; delegation to Jerusalem, 189–90, 362n.134; destruction of Babylon, 193; Judahite campaign,